Multinational Enterprises and the Law

Multinational Enterprises and the Law

Peter Muchlinski

BLACKWELL
Oxford UK & Cambridge USA

First published 1995
Reprinted 1996, 1997
Updated edition first published in paperback 1999

Blackwell Publishers Ltd
108 Cowley Road
Oxford OX4 1JF, UK

Blackwell Publishers Inc
350 Main Street
Malden, Massachusetts 02148, USA

British Library Cataloguing in Publication Data
A CIP catalogue record for this book is available from the British Library

Library of Congress Cataloging in Publication Data
Muchlinski, Peter
Multinational enterprises and the law / Peter Muchlinski
p. cm.   Includes index.
ISBN: 0–631–17311–0 (acid-free paper)
ISBN: 0–631–21676–6 (pbk: acid-free paper)
1. International business enterprises—Law and legislation.
2. International business enterprises. I. Title.
K1322.M83   1995   94–45856
341.7'53—dc20   CIP

Typeset in 10.5 on 12pt Plantin
by Best-set Typesetter Ltd, Hong Kong
Printed and bound in Great Britain
by MPG Books Ltd, Bodmin, Cornwall

This book is printed on acid-free paper

Contents

List of Cases   **xv**
List of Statutes   **xxviii**
List of Treaties   **xlii**
List of Publications of Governments and
International Organizations   **xlvi**
Preface and Acknowledgements   **lv**
List of Abbreviations   **lviii**

Part I   The Conceptual Framework   *1*

1 Concern over Multinational Enterprises   **3**

1 The Origins of Post-war Political Concern
over MNEs   3
1.1 The Attitudes of Countries and Regions   3
1.2 Sensational Abuses of Corporate Power by
MNEs   6
1.3 Moves towards an Economic Theory of the
MNE   7
1.4 The Ideological Dimension   8
1.5 Summary   8
2 The Contemporary Position   9
3 Problems of Definition   12
4 Concluding Remarks   15

2 The Evolution of Modern Multinational Enterprises   **19**

1 The Principal Phases of MNE Growth   19
1.1 The First Period: 1850–1914   20
1.2 The Second Period: 1918–1939   22
1.3 The Third Period: 1945 to the Present   25
1.3.1 The period of American dominance:
1945–1960   26

	1.3.2	The period of renewed international competition: 1960 to the present	28
	1.3.3	Possible future developments	32

2   Explanations for the Growth of MNEs and the Role of Legal Factors Therein ... 33
  2.1   Theories of MNE Growth ... 33
  2.2   The Role of Legal Factors ... 38
    2.2.1   Ownership- or firm-specific factors ... 38
    2.2.2   Locational factors ... 42
    2.2.3   Internalization factors ... 45
3   Concluding Remarks ... 47

3   Business and Legal Forms of Multinational Enterprise: towards a Theory of Control ... 57

1   MNEs as Transnational Business Organizations ... 57
2   Legal Forms of Multinational Enterprise ... 61
  2.1   Contractual Forms ... 62
    2.1.1   Distribution agreements ... 63
    2.1.2   Production agreements ... 63
  2.2   Equity Based Corporate Groups ... 65
    2.2.1   The Anglo-American 'pyramid' group ... 65
    2.2.2   European transnational mergers ... 66
    2.2.3   The Japanese *keiretsu* ... 69
    2.2.4   Changes in business organization and effects on equity based structures ... 71
  2.3   Joint Ventures ... 72
  2.4   Informal Alliances between MNEs ... 73
  2.5   Publicly Owned MNEs ... 75
  2.6   Supranational Forms of International Business ... 76
    2.6.1   Forms adopted by the European Community ... 77
    2.6.2   The Andean Multinational Enterprise adopted by the Andean Common Market (ANCOM) ... 78
    2.6.3   Public international corporations ... 79
3   Concluding Remarks: Business and Legal Forms and the Control of MNE Activities ... 80

4   Relations between MNEs and States: towards a Theory of Regulation ... 90

1   Developing a Regulatory Agenda: Interactions between MNEs and Home and Host States ... 90
  1.1   The Neo-classical Perspective ... 93
  1.2   The Orthodox Post-war Economic Perspective ... 93

1.3 The Marxist Perspective 95
1.4 The Influence of Nationalism 97
1.5 The Environmental Perspective 99
1.6 'Global Consumerism' 100
1.7 Synthesis: Framework for a Regulatory Agenda 101
2 Jurisdictional Levels and Methods of MNE Regulation 102
2.1 The Regulatory Priorities of Home and Host States 103
2.2 Bargaining between Host States and MNEs 104
2.3 Jurisdictional Levels of Regulation 107
2.3.1 National regulation 107
2.3.2 Regional regulation 111
2.3.3 International regulation 112
3 Concluding Remarks 114

Part II   Regulation by Home and Host States 121

5 **The Jurisdictional Limits of Regulation through National or Regional Law** 123

1 The Legal Bases for the Extraterritorial Regulation of MNEs 123
1.1 Nationality 124
1.2 Protective Jurisdiction 124
1.3 Objective Territorial Jurisdiction 125
2 The Extraterritorial Regulation of MNEs in State Practice 126
2.1 Jurisdiction to Prescribe 126
2.1.1 Nationality links 127
2.1.2 The 'effects' doctrine 129
2.1.3 Links of ownership and control 133
2.2 Personal Jurisdiction 134
2.2.1 Establishing a sufficient connection between the forum and the non-resident unit of the MNE 134
2.2.2 The doctrine of *forum non conveniens* as applied to non-resident units of MNEs 141
2.3 Jurisdiction to Enforce 144
2.4 The Disclosure of Evidence in Proceedings Involving a MNE 145
2.4.1 Disclosure of evidence in US antitrust proceedings 146
2.4.2 US disclosure orders and foreign secrecy laws 148

2.4.3   The reduction of conflicts over demands
for disclosure of evidence located in a
foreign jurisdiction   151
3   Concluding Remarks: the Limitation of
Extraterritoriality Conflicts   156

6   The Control of Inward Investment by Host States   172

1   The Scope of Host State Discretion   172
2   Techniques For Restricting Entry and Establishment   173
2.1   Total Exclusion and Sectoral Exclusion of
Foreign Investors   174
2.1.1   Total exclusion   174
2.1.2   Sectoral exclusion   175
2.2   Laws Restricting Foreign Shareholdings in
National Companies   177
2.2.1   Indigenization laws   177
2.2.2   Restrictions on foreign ownership in
privatized companies   181
2.2.3   Concluding remarks   184
2.3   Laws Regulating Equity Joint Ventures between
Foreign and Local Enterprises   184
2.3.1   The post-socialist states of Eastern
Europe   187
2.3.2   The People's Republic of China   188
2.3.3   The Soviet Union and its successor
states   192
2.3.4   Concluding remarks   193
2.4   'Screening Laws'   194
2.4.1   Screening laws in LDCs   195
2.4.2   Screening laws in economically
advanced countries   197
2.4.3   Concluding remarks   203
3   Concluding Remarks: the Movement towards
Liberalization of Controls over Foreign Investors   203

**7   Measures for the Encouragement of Inward
Direct Investment   222**

1   The Encouragement of Inward Direct Investment
by Host States   222
1.1   Host States without Specialized Controls on
Inward Direct Investment   223
1.2   Investment Incentives   225
1.3   Export Processing Zones (EPZs) and Related
'Policy Enclaves' within the Host State   228

		1.3.1	The evolution of EPZs	228
1.3.2	The principal legal and administrative features of EPZs in developing host states	230
1.3.3	The performance of EPZs	233
1.3.4	The Chinese 'special economic zone' policy	234

2 Bilateral and Multilateral Measures for the Encouragement of Direct Investment 238

  2.1 Regional Arrangements Dismantling Barriers to Inward Investment 238

    2.1.1 The North American Free Trade Area 239

    2.1.2 The Single European Market 245

  2.2 Multilateral Arrangements Dismantling Barriers to Inward Investment 247

    2.2.1 The OECD Codes of Liberalization 248

    2.2.2 The Uruguay Round and direct investment issues 250

3 Concluding Remarks 260

8 Taxation Problems Associated with MNEs 277

1 International Double Taxation and MNEs 277

2 Location of Investments and Tax Considerations 280

3 Tax Avoidance and MNEs 282

  3.1 The 'Transfer Pricing' Problem 282

    3.1.1 Establishing transfer prices in MNE networks 283

    3.1.2 Incentives, disincentives and empirical evidence for transfer price manipulations 286

    3.1.3 The regulation of transfer price manipulations: arm's length and comparable profit interval (CPI) 288

    3.1.4 Formula apportionment 299

  3.2 The Use of 'Tax Havens' by MNEs 303

4 Concluding Remarks 307

9 Group Liability and Directors' Duties 322

1 The Regulation of MNE Group Liability under Existing Legal Principles 323

  1.1 Equity Based MNE Groups 323

    1.1.1 Direct liability of the parent company 323

    1.1.2 Lifting the corporate veil 325

  1.2 Liability of Transnational Network Enterprises 327

2 New Approaches to MNE Group Liability 328

2.1   The 'Enterprise Entity' Theory and Its
      Limitations   328
2.2   Towards a New Law of MNE Group Liability?   330
3   Protection of Minority Shareholders in the Subsidiary
    of a MNE   333
4   Protection of Creditors upon the Insolvency of the
    Subsidiary of a MNE   336
5   Concluding Remarks   339

10   Accountability and Disclosure   346

1   Principal Motives and Interests behind Enhanced
    MNE Accountability and Disclosure   346
2   Reforming the Internal Structures of MNEs to
    Ensure Accountability   349
2.1   The Use of Non-executive Directors on the
      Managerial Boards of MNEs   349
2.2   European Initiatives for the Enhancement of
      MNE Accountability   350
3   Disclosure by MNEs in Annual Accounts and
    Other Statements   354
3.1   Consolidated Financial Statements   355
3.2   Segmental Disclosure   361
3.3   Social Disclosure   366
      3.3.1   Employee disclosure   366
      3.3.2   Value-added statements   367
      3.3.3   Environmental disclosure   368
3.4   Foreign Currency Translation   371
4   Concluding Remarks   372

11   Regulation through Antitrust Law   384

1   The Use of Antitrust Laws in the Regulation of the
    Anti-competitive Activities of MNEs   384
1.1   The Nature and Aims of Antitrust Regulation   384
1.2   The Incidence of Anti-competitive Conduct on
      the Part of MNEs and Regulatory Responses   386
      1.2.1   Anti-competitive agreements and
              concerted practices   387
      1.2.2   'Abuse of a dominant position' or
              'monopolization'   393
      1.2.3   Mergers and acquisitions   395
2   International Developments in the Regulation of
    Restrictive Business Practices Undertaken by MNEs   403
3   Concluding Remarks   411

12 Technology Transfer 425

1 The Nature of Technology Transfer 425
  1.1 'Technology' and 'Technology Transfer' 425
  1.2 The Generation and Use of Technology:
    the Interests of Technology-exporting and
    Technology-importing States Compared 427
2 Technology Transfer by MNEs and Its Legal Effects 431
3 Restrictive Terms in Technology Transfer
  Transactions 433
  3.1 Restrictions on the Commercial Policy of the
    Technology Recipient 433
  3.2 Restrictions on the Use of Technology on the
    Part of the Recipient 435
4 The Two Principal Models of Technology Transfer
  Regulation 436
  4.1 The Developed Country Model 437
  4.2 The LDC Model 438
    4.2.1 Reserved approach to the protection
      of intellectual property rights 438
    4.2.2 Specialized technology transfer laws 442
5 The Draft UNCTAD Code of Conduct on the
  Transfer of Technology 444
6 Concluding Remarks: the Demise of the LDC
  Challenge to the International System of Technology
  Transfer? 446

13 Labour Relations 457

1 The Evolution of the ILO and OECD Codes 458
2 General Policies of the Codes and Their Relationship
  to National Laws 459
3 Employment Issues 461
  3.1 Employment Promotion 462
  3.2 Equality of Opportunity and Treatment 462
  3.3 Security of Employment 464
4 Training of Workers 466
5 Conditions of Work and Life 467
  5.1 Wages, Benefits and Conditions of Work 467
  5.2 Safety and Health 469
6 Industrial Relations 470
  6.1 Freedom of Association and the Right to
    Organize 470
  6.2 Collective Bargaining and Consultation 476

6.3 Examination of Grievances and Settlement of
      Industrial Disputes   480
7 Concluding Remarks   480

Part III   The Emerging System of
International Regulation   491

14 Renegotiation and Expropriation   493

1 The Restriction of State Sovereignty in the Field
   of Contractual Relations with Foreign Investors   493
   1.1 The 'Internationalization' of International
         Investment Agreements   494
   1.2 Sanctity of Contract and Stabilization
         Clauses   496
2 Renegotiation of International Investment
   Agreements   497
3 Expropriation of Foreign Corporate Assets   501
   3.1 What Constitutes Expropriation?   501
   3.2 The Legality of Expropriatory Measures under
         the Law of the Host State   502
   3.3 The Legality of Expropriation at International
         Law   503
         3.3.1 The conflict of norms in this area   503
         3.3.2 The elements of lawful expropriation   504
   3.4 The Issue of Compensation   506
         3.4.1 The valuation of expropriated property   506
         3.4.2 The measure of compensation   511
         3.4.3 The settlement of claims through lump
                 sum agreements   513
4 Investment Guarantee Schemes   514
5 Concluding Remarks   519

15 The Settlement of International Investment
Disputes   534

1 The Limitations of Traditional International
   Dispute Settlement Mechanisms in MNE–Host
   State Relations   534
2 Alternatives to Diplomatic Protection: International
   Dispute Settlement Mechanisms Involving the MNE
   and Host State *Inter Se*   537
   2.1 *Ad Hoc* Arbitration and Conciliation   538
   2.2 Institutional Systems for International
         Dispute Settlement   538
   2.3 The Contribution of UNCITRAL   539

3   The International Centre for the Settlement of
    Investment Disputes   540
    3.1   The Aims of ICSID   541
    3.2   The Washington Convention and Its Effect
          on State Sovereignty over Investment
          Disputes   542
          3.2.1   The Contracting State's ability to control
                  jurisdiction   542
          3.2.2   Subject matter jurisdiction   546
          3.2.3   The delocalized character of ICSID
                  arbitration   547
          3.2.4   The extent to which an unfavourable
                  decision of an ICSID tribunal can be
                  challenged by the losing party   551
          3.2.5   Enforcement of ICSID awards   553
          3.2.6   Procedure and costs   553
    3.3   The Use of the Convention   555
          3.3.1   The membership   555
          3.3.2   The caseload   556
          3.3.3   The use of references to ICSID
                  arbitration in investment agreements
                  and national laws   557
    3.4   Conclusion   559

16 **The Codification of International Standards for
    the Treatment of Foreign Investors**   573

    1   The Andean Common Market (ANCOM)   575
    2   The OECD Guidelines on Multinational Enterprises   578
        2.1   The Policy of the Guidelines   579
        2.2   The Legal Nature of the Guidelines   580
        2.3   The Role of International Minimum Standards   580
        2.4   The Scope of Application   581
        2.5   National Treatment   583
        2.6   Dispute Settlement   587
        2.7   Substantive Provisions   588
        2.8   International Investment Incentives and
              Disincentives   591
        2.9   Concluding Remarks   592
    3   The Draft UN Code of Conduct on Transnational
        Corporations   592
    4   The Contribution of the World Bank: the 1992
        Guidelines on the Treatment of Foreign Direct
        Investment and Standard Setting by MIGA   597

4.1	The 1992 World Bank Guidelines	598
4.2	The Standard Setting Provisions of MIGA	602
5	Concluding Remarks	604

17   Bilateral Investment Treaties — 617

1	The Origins of BITs	617
2	The Principal Provisions Common to BITs	619
2.1	Preamble	619
2.2	Provisions Defining the Scope of Application of the Treaty	620
2.2.1	Application *ratione materiae*	620
2.2.2	Application *ratione personae*	622
2.2.3	Application *ratione territoriae*	624
2.2.4	Application *ratione temporis*	624
2.3	Standards of Treatment	625
2.3.1	General standards of treatment	625
2.3.2	Specific standards of treatment	628
2.4	Dispute Settlement Clauses	632
2.4.1	Disputes between the contracting parties	632
2.4.2	Disputes between the host state and the foreign investor	633
3	The Effect of BITs within the National Legal Systems of the Contracting States	634
4	The Use of BITs	637
5	Concluding Remarks: the Effect of BITs on the Content of International Law	638

Index   649

Cases

Decisions of National Courts and Tribunals

Argentina
Deltec Banking Corp v. Compania Italo-Argentina de Electricidad SA 171 NYLJ 18 col. 1, April 3 1974   332, 343
Deltec Case 6 Lawyer of the Americas 320 (1974)   332,343

Canada
Attorney-General of Canada v. Fallbridge Holdings Ltd 63 NR 17 (FCA 1985)   220
Dow Jones & Co. Inc. v. Attorney-General of Canada (1980) 113 DLR (3d) 395 aff'd 122 DLR (3d) 731 (FCA 1981)   220
Gulf Oil Corporation v. Gulf Canada Ltd (1980) 111 DLR (3d) 74 (Sup. Ct Can)   167
Re Westinghouse Electric and Duquesne Light Co. (1977) 78 DLR (3d) (Ont. HC)   167

France
Société Européene d'Etudes et d'Entreprises v. Yugoslavia (Cour de Cassation 18 November 1986) 26 ILM 377 (1987)   562
Société Fruehauf Corp. v. Massardy: 5 ILM 476 (1966)   127, 159, 344

Germany
Autokran 95 BGHZ 330 (1985)   345
Bundesgerichthof BGH 1 ZR 76/78 Judgment 9 May 1980   475
Krupp Maschinenbau GmbH v. Deutsche Bank AG 22 ILM 740 (1983)   468
Re Expatriation of a German Company (Case 3Z BR 14/92, Bayerisches Oberstes Landesgeright) [1993] 2 CMLR 801   271
Tiefbau BGH ZIP 1989, 440z, NJW 1800 (1989)   345

India
Life Insurance Corporation of India v. Escorts Ltd AIR 1986 SC 1370   340
Mehta v. Union of India AIR 1987 SC 965, 1086   326
Tata Engineering and Locomotive Co. Ltd v. State of Bihar AIR 1965 SC 40   341
Union of India v. Union Carbide Corporation (Gas Claim Case No. 113 of 1986) Order 17 December 1987; upheld in part: Civil Revision No. 26 of 1988 4 April 1988   340

Union of India v. Union Carbide Corporation: Submissions of the Union of India Before the Indian Supreme Court 340

Israel
Attorney-General of the Government of Israel v. Eichmann 36 ILR 5 (1961, Dist. Ct Jerusalem) 158

Netherlands
Compagnie Européene de Petroles v. Sensor Nederland BV 22 ILM 320 (1983) 160
The Saudi Independence (Hoge Rad 1983) 16 Jo. Mart. L. & Comm. 423 (1985) 488

Switzerland
Judicial Assistance in The Santa Fe Case (First Opinion Swiss Sup. Ct) 22 ILM 785 (1983) 152–3
Judicial Assistance in The Santa Fe Case (Second Opinion Swiss Sup. Ct) 24 ILM 745 (1985) 153

United Kingdom
A and others v. B Bank, Bank of England Intervening [1992] 1 All ER 778 (QBD) 168
Abidin Daver (The)[1984] AC 398 (HL) 165
Adams v. Cape Industries [1990] Ch. 433; [1991] 1 All ER 929 (CA) 145, 164, 340, 341
Amalgamated Investment & Property Co. v. Texas Commercial Bank [1982] QB 84 (CA) 340
Amin Rasheed Shipping Corporation v. Kuwait Insurance Company [1984] AC 50; [1983] 2 All ER 884; [1983] 3 WLR 241 (HL) 520
Anglo-Iranian Oil Co. v. Jaffrate: The Rose Mary [1953] 1 WLR 246 525
Arkwright Mutual Insurance Co. v. Bryanston Insurance Co. Ltd [1990] 2 QB 649; [1990] 2 All ER 335 (Com. Ct) 166
Attorney-General for Canada v. Attorney-General for Ontario [1937] AC 326 647
Barton v. Armstrong [1975] 2 WLR 1050 (PC) 523
Bell v. Lever Bros [1932] AC 161 (HL) 343
Berisford (S & W) plc v. New Hampshire Insurance Co. [1990] 2 QB 631; [1990] 2 All ER 321 (Com. Ct) 166
British Airways Board v. Laker Airways Ltd [1985] AC 58; [1984] 3 All ER 39; [1984] 3 WLR 413 (HL) 146–7
British Nylon Spinners v. Imperial Chemical Industries [1953] Ch. 19 (CA) and [1955] 1 Ch. 37 160, 166
Camelia Tanker SA v. ITF [1976] ICR 274 (CA) 487
Charterbridge Corporation Ltd v. Lloyds Bank Ltd [1970] Ch. 62 334, 343
Deutsche Schachtbau-und-Tiefbohrgesellschaft GmbH v. R'As Al Khaimah National Oil Company [1987] 2 All ER 769 (CA) reversed on other grounds [1990] 1 AC 295; [1988] 2 All ER 833 (HL) 521
DHN Ltd v. Tower Hamlets [1976] 1 WLR 852 (CA) 341
Dimskal Shipping Co. SA v. ITF 'The Evia Luck' [1991] 4 All ER 871, [1992] Lloyds Rep. 115 (HL) 487

DPP v. Joyce [1946] AC 347   158

Dunlop Pneumatic Tyre Co. Ltd v. AG fur Motor und Motorfahrzeugbau vorm Cudell & Co. [1902] KB 342 (CA)   164

Du Pont de Nemours & Co. and Endo Laboratories Inc. v. I. C. Agnew, K. W. Kerr et al. [1987] 2 Lloyds Rep. 585 (CA)   165

Equal Opportunities Commission v. Secretary of State for Employment [1994] 1 All ER 910 (HL)   483

Ex-Rajah of Coorg v. East India Co. (1860) 29 Beav. 300   47

In Re Westinghouse Electric Corp. [1978] AC 547; [1978] 2 WLR 91 (HL); also reported sub nom. Rio Tinto Zinc v. Westinghouse [1978] 1 All ER 434 (HL)   154, 167

Kleinwort Benson v. Malaysian Mining Corporation [1988] 1 All ER 714 (QBD), reversed [1989] 1 All ER 785 (CA)   340

Libyan Arab Foreign Bank v. Bankers Trust Co. [1988] 1 Lloyds Rep. 259   159

Libyan Arab Foreign Bank v. Manufacturers Hannover [1988] 2 Lloyds Rep. 494; [1989] 1 Lloyds Rep. 608   159

Lindgren v. L&P Estates Ltd [1968] Ch. 572   343

Litster and others v. Forth Dry Dock & Engineering Co. Ltd [1989] ICR 341; [1989] IRLR 161 (HL)   485

Lively Ltd v. City of Munich [1976] 1 WLR 1004   647

Lonrho v. Shell Petroleum [1980] 2 WLR 367 aff'd [1980] 1 WLR 627 (HL) 120, 167, 344

Luther v. Sagor [1921] 3 KB 532   525

MacKinnon v. Donaldson Lufkin and Jenrette Securities Corpn [1986] Ch. 482; [1986] 1 All ER 653; [1986] 2 WLR 453   150, 171

MacShannon v. Rockware Glass [1978] AC 795 (HL)   165

Maskell v. Horner [1915] KB 106   523

Mercur Island Shipping Co. v. Laughton [1983] 2 All ER 189 (HL)   487

Midland Bank v. Laker Airways [1986] QB 689; [1986] 1 All ER 526; [1986] 2 WLR 707 (CA)   148

Molvan v. A-G for Palestine [1948] AC 351 (PC)   158

Multinational Gas & Petrochemical Services Co. v. Multinational Gas and Petrochemical Services Ltd [1983] 2 All ER 563; [1983] 3 WLR 492 (CA) 120, 136, 344

Nabob of the Carnatic v. East India Co. (1791) 1 Ves. Jr. 371   47

National Dock Labour Board v. Pinn & Wheeler Ltd [1989] BCLC 647   341

North Ocean Shipping Co. Ltd v. Hyundai Construction Co. Ltd [1979] QB 705 522

NWL v. Woods [1979] ICR 867 (HL)   487

Oppenheimer v. Cattermole [1976] AC 249 (HL)   525

Panayiotou v. Sony Music Entertainment [1994] 1 All ER 755 (ChD)   170

Pao On v. Lau Yiu Long [1980] AC 614 (PC)   522

Parlement Belge (The) [1880] 5 PD 197   647

Philippson v. Imperial Airways [1939] AC 332   647

Prudential Assurance v. Newman Industries (No. 2) [1982] 1 ALL ER 354 343

R v. British Coal Corporation and Secretary of State for Trade and Industry ex parte Vardy and others [1993] 1 CMLR 721 (DC)   484

R v. Casement [1971] KB 98   158
R v. Grossman (1981) 73 Cr. App. R. 302 (CA)   168
Re Asbestos Insurance Coverage Cases [1985] 1 WLR 331   170
Re Augustus Barnett & Co. [1986] BCLC 170   340
Re Harrods (Buenos Aires) Ltd [1992] Ch. 72; [1991] 4 All ER 334 (CA)   144
Re Horsley & Weight Ltd [1982] Ch. 442   136
Re Oriel [1985] 3 All ER 216 (CA)   162
Re State of Norway's Application (Nos 1 and 2) [1990] 1 AC 723; [1989] 1 All
    ER 745; [1989] 2 WLR 458 (HL)   170
Re Technion Investments Ltd [1985] BCLC 434 (CA)   167
Rio Tinto Zinc v. Westinghouse: see In Re Westinghouse Electric Corp. above
Rome v. Punjab National Bank [1989] 1 WLR 1211   162
Ronleigh Ltd v. MII Exports Inc. [1989] 1 WLR 619 (CA)   165
Salomon v. Salomon [1897] AC 22   136
Scottish Co-operative Wholesale Society Ltd v. Meyer [1959] AC 324   334,
    343
Settebello Ltd v. Banco Totta e Acores [1985] 2 All ER 1025; [1985] 1 WLR
    1050 (CA)   525
Shipping Co. Uniform Inc. v. ITF Allen Ross & Davies (The Uniform Star)
    [1985] 1 Lloyds Rep. 173 (QBD)   487
Sirdar Gurdyal Singh v. Rajah of Faridkote [1894] AC 670 (HL)   162
Smith Kline & French Laboratories Ltd v. Bloch [1983] 2 All ER 72; [1983] 1
    WLR 730 (CA)   166
Société Nationale Industrielle Aerospatiale v. Lee Kui Jak [1987] AC 871;
    [1987] 3 All ER 510; [1987] 3 WLR 59 (PC)   166
South India Shipping Corp. v. Export Import Bank of Korea [1985] 1 WLR 585;
    [1985] 2 All ER 219 (CA)   162
Spiliada Maritime Corporation v. Cansulex Ltd 'The Spiliada' [1986] 3 WLR
    972 [1986] 3 All ER 843 (HL)   165
Universe Tankships of Monrovia v. ITF (The Universe Sentinel) [1983] 1 AC
    366; [1982] 2 All ER 67 (HL)   487
Williams and Humbert Ltd v. W and H Trade Marks (Jersey) Ltd [1986] AC
    368; [1985] 2 All ER 208; [1985] 2 All ER 619 (CA); [1986] 1 All ER 129
    (HL)   525
Woolfson v. Strathclyde Regional Council (1978) 38 P&CR 521 (HL)   341
XAG and others v. A bank [1983] 2 All ER 464 (QBD)   168

MONOPOLIES AND MERGERS COMMISSION REPORTS
British Aerospace plc/Thomson-CSF SA: Cm 1416 (1991)   421
Chlordiazepoxide and Diazepam: a Report on the Supply of Chlordiazepoxide
    and Diazepam (London, HMSO, 1973)   287, 310
Consolidated Gold Fields/Minorco: Cm 587 (1989)   396
Credit Lyonnais SA/Woodchester Investments plc: Cm 1404 (1991)   421
Elders IXL/Allied Lyons plc: Cmnd 9892 (1986)   401
Enersch/Davey International: Cmnd 8360 (1981)   420
GEC plc and Siemens AG/Plessey plc: Cm 676 (1989)   402
Hong Kong and Shanghai Bank/Royal Bank of Scotland: Cmnd 8472 (1982)
    401, 421

Kemira Oy/ICI: Cm 1406 (1991)   421
Kuwait/British Petroleum plc: Cm 477 (1988)   402
Silgos SA/Signet Ltd: Cm 1450 (1991)   421
Société Nationale Elf Aquitaine/Amoco Corporation: Cm 1521 (1991)   421
Weidmann/Whiteley: Cmnd 6208 (1975)   420

United States of America
Akzona v. Du Pont 607 F. Supp. 227 (DC Del 1984)   163, 164
Alcan Aluminum Ltd v. Franchise Tax Board of California 558 F. Supp. 624
    (SDNY) aff'd 742 F. 2d 1430 (2nd cir 1983) cert. den. 464 US 1041
    (1984)   318, 319
American Banana Company v. United Fruit Co. 213 US 347 (1909)   160
American International Group Inc. v. Islamic Republic of Iran 493 F. Supp. 522
    (DDC,1980)   636
Amoco Cadiz (The) [1984] 2 Lloyds Rep. 304   324, 328
Amusement Equipment v. Mordelt 779 F. 2d 264 (5th cir 1985)   164
Anaconda Corp v. Franchise Tax Board of California 103 S. Ct 3563 (1983)
    318
Anschuetz GmbH v. Mississippi River Bridge Authority 754 F. 2d 602 (5th cir
    1985)   155, 170
Asahi Metal Industry Co. v. Superior Court of California 26 ILM 702 (1987);
    74 L. Ed. 2d 92 (1987)   141
ASARCO Inc. v. Idaho State Tax Commission 458 US 307 (1982)   318
Banco Nacional De Cuba v. Chase Manhattan Bank 658 F. 2d 875 (2d cir 1981)
    525, 527
Banco Nacional De Cuba v. Farr 383 F. 2d 166 (2d cir 1967) cert. den. 390 US
    956 (1968)   525
Banco Nacional De Cuba v. Sabbatino 376 US 398 (1964)   525, 648
Barclays Bank v. Franchise Tax Board of California California Supreme Court
    11 May 1992 (Case S019064). Upheld by US Supreme Court 20 June 1994
    302
Bernstein v. NV Nederlandsche-Amerikaansche Stoomvart Maatschappij 173 F.
    2d 71 (2d cir 1949); 210 F. 2d 375 (2d cir 1954)   523
Bethlehem Motors v. Flynt 256 US 412 (1921)   262
Bhopal Case: see In Re Union Carbide Gas Plant Disaster At Bhopal India
    Opinion and Order below
Brock v. Alaska International Industries Inc. 645 P 2d 188 (Alaska SC 1982)
    340
Bryant v. Finnish National Airlines 15 NY 2d 426, 260 NYS 2d 625, 208 NE 2d
    439 (1965)   163
Burger King Corp v. Rudzewicz 471 US 462 (1985)   141
Burnham v. Superior Court of California 110 S. Ct 2105 (1990)   164
Cannon Manufacturing Co. v. Cudhay Packing Co. 267 US 333 (1925)   163
CCA Inc. v. CIR 64 TC 137 (US Tax. Ct 1975)   321
Charles Town Inc. v. CIR 372 F. 2d 415 (CA Md 1967)   313
Chicago Bridge and Iron Co. v. Caterpillar Tractor Co. 103 S. Ct 3562 (1983)
    318
Ciba-Geigy Corp v. Commissioner 85 TC 172 (1985)   314

CIR v. First Security Bank of Utah 405 US 394 (1972)   313

Commonwealth v. Beneficial Finance Co. 275 NE 2d 33 (SC Mass 1971) cert. den. 407 US 914 (1972)   162

Consolidated Gold Fields plc v. Minorco 871 F. 2d 252 (2d cir) cert. dismissed. 110 S. Ct 29 (1989)   418

Container Corporation of America v. Franchise Tax Board of California 463 US 159 (1983); Slip Opinion: 22 ILM 855 (1983)   299, 300, 301, 303, 318, 319

Continental Ore Co. v. Union Carbide and Carbon Corp 370 US 690 (1962)   161

Continental TV Inc. v. GTE Sylvania 433 US 376 (1977)   412, 413

Copperweld Corporation v. Independence Tube Corp. 467 US 752 (1984)   413

Dave Fischbein Manufacturing Company v. CIR 59 TC 338 (US Tax. Ct 1972)   321

Delagi v. Volkswagenwerk AG 328 NYS 2d 653; 278 NE 2d 895 (1972)   163, 340

Donahue v. Rodd Electrotype Co. 328 NE 2d 505 (Mass. 1975)   344

Dr Miles Medical Co. v. John D. Park and Sons Co. 220 US 373 (1911)   413

Dresser Industries Inc v. Buldridge 549 F. Supp. 108 (1982)   159

Eastman Kodak Co. v. Image Technical Services Inc. 112 S. Ct 2072 (1992); 62 ATRR 780 (1992)   417

EEOC/Boureslan v. ARAMCO 113 S. Ct 274 (1991)   483

Eickhoff Machinenfabrik v. Starcher 328 SE 2d 492 (1985)   170

E.I.Du Pont de Nemours & Co. v. US 608 F. 2d 445 (Ct Cl. 1979)   311

Eli Lilley & Co. v. Commissioner 856 F. 2d 855 (7th cir 1988)   291, 313, 314

EMI v. Bennett 738 F. 2d 994, 997 (9th cir) cert. den. 469 US 1073 (1984)   319

Exxon Corp v. Commissioner (TCM 1993–616)   313

Exxon Corporation v. Wisconsin Department of Revenue 447 US 207 (1980)   318

Federal Trade Commission v. Compagnie de Saint Gobain Pont a Mousson 636 F. 2d 1300 (DC cir. 1980); 20 ILM 597 (1981)   135

First National City Bank v. Banco Nacional de Cuba 406 US 759 (1972)   525

First National City Bank v. Banco Para El Commercia Exterior de Cuba 462 US 611 (1983); 22 ILM 840 (1983)   525

First National City Bank v. IRS 271 F. 2d 616 (2nd cir 1959)   168

Forman & Co. Inc. v. CIR 453 F. 2d 1144 (2nd cir 1972)   313

Franchise Tax Board of California v. Alcan Aluminum et al. 107 L. Ed. 2d 696 (1990)   301

Frummer v. Hilton Hotels Int'l 19 NY 2d 533; 227 NE 2d 851 (1967)   163, 340

F.W.Woolworth & Co. v. Taxation and Revenue Department of New Mexico 458 US 354 (1982)   318

Galle v. Allstate Insurance Co. 451 SO 2d 72 (Lo 4th cir 1984)   165

Garlock v. CIR 489 F. 2d 197 (1973)   321

Garpeg Ltd v. US 583 F. Supp. 789 (SDNY 1984)   168

G.D.Searle & Co. v. Commissioner 88 TC 252 (1987)   314

Grywczynski v. Shasta Beverages Inc. 606 F. Supp. 61 (Cal. 1984)   340

Gulf Oil v. Gilbert 330 US 501 (1947)   165
Hanson v. Denkla 357 US 235 (1958)   162
Hargrave v. Fireboard Corp 710 F. 2d 1154 (5th cir 1983)   163
Hartford Fire Insurance Co. v. California (US Sup. Ct 28 June 1993) 13 S. Ct 2891 (1993)   133
Head Money Cases: Edye v. Robertson 112 US 580 (1884)   648
Helicopteros Nacionales de Colombia v. Hall 466 US 408 (1984)   165
Hoffman Motors Corp. v. Alfa Romeo 244 F Supp. 70 (1965)   164
Hospital Corporation of America v. CIR 81 TC 520 (US Tax. Ct 1983)   314, 316
In Re Application of Chase Manhattan Bank 297 F. 2d 611 (1960)   168
In Re Grand Jury Subpoena Duces Tecum 72 F. Supp. 1013 (1947)   167
In Re Investigation of World Arrangements with Relation to . . . Petroleum 13 FRD 280 (1952)   167
In Re Union Carbide Gas Plant Disaster At Bhopal India Opinion and Order 12 May 1986 D. Ct SDNY (Keenan J) 634 F. Supp. 842 (1986), 25 ILM 771 (1986); USCA decision: aff'd as modified 809 F. 2d 195 (USCA 2d Cir); 26 ILM 1008 (1987); cert. den. 108 S. Ct 199 (1987)   110, 120, 142–3, 165, 340, 341, 342
In Re Westinghouse Electric Corp Uranium 563 F. 2d 992 (1977)   154, 167
Insurance Antitrust Litigation 723 F. Supp. 464 (ND Ca 1989); 938 F. 2d 919 (9th cir 1991) upheld on appeal sub. nom. Hartford Fire Insurance Co. v. California, supra   171
Interamerican Refining Corp v. Texaco Maracaibo Inc. 307 F. Supp. 291 (D. Del 1970)   161
International Association of Machinists v. OPEC 649 F. 2d 1354 (9th cir. 1981)   132
International Shoe Co. v. Washington 326 US 310 (1945)   141
Japan Line Ltd v. County of Los Angeles 441 US 434 (1979)   318
Jefferson Parish Hospital District No. 2 v. Hyde 466 US 2 (1984)   450
J M Sachlein Music Co. Inc. v. Nippon Gakki Co. Ltd 197 Cal. App. 3d 539 (1987)   163
Kalamazoo Spice Extraction Co. v. Provisional Military Government of Socialist Ethiopia 729 F 2d 422 (6 cir. 1984); 23 ILM 393 (1984); 78 AJIL 902 (1984)   262, 635
Kalamazoo Spice Extraction Co. v. Provisional Military Government of Socialist Ethiopia: (WD Mich, Southern Div) 24 ILM 1277 (1985)   513, 525, 530
Koering Company v. US 583 F. 2d 313 (7th cir 1978)   321
Kraus v. CIR 490 F. 2d 898 (2nd cir 1974)   321
Laker Airways v. Sabena 731 F. 2d 909 (DC Cir 1984)   156, 167, 171
Liberty Financial Management Corp. v. Beneficial Data Processing Corp. 670 SW 2d 40 (Missouri CA 1984)   340
Mannington Mills v. Congoleum Corp. 595 F. 2d 1287 (1979)   131
Marc Rich & Co. v. US 707 F. 2d 663 (2nd Cir 1983)   168, 316
Matsushita Electric Industrial Co. v. Zenith Radio Corp. 475 US 574 (1986)   161, 395
Messerschmitt Bolkow Blohm v. Walker 757 F. 2d 729 (5th cir 1985); 25 ILM 803 (1986) (submissions to the US Supreme Court)   155

Mobil Oil v. Commissioner of Taxes for Vermont 445 US 425 (1980)   318
Moffatt v. Goodyear Tyre Co. 652 SW 2d 609 (1983) (Texas CA)   340
Peck v. CIR 752 F. 2d 469 (9th cir 1985)   313
Pennoyer v. Neff 95 US 714 (1878)   162
Perkins v. Benguet Consolidated Mining Co. 342 US 437 (1952)   165
Piper Aircraft v. Reyno 454 US 235 (1981)   165
Procter & Gamble Co. v. Commissioner 95 TC 323 (1990) aff'd 961 F. 2d 1255
   (6th cir 1992)   313
Product Promotions Inc. v. Cousteau 495 F. 2d 483 (5th cir 1974)   163
Re International Labor Rights Fund 752 F. Supp. 495 (DDC 1990) aff'd No.
   90–00728 (DC cir 31 January 1992)   489
Rollins Burdick Hunter Inc. v. Alexander & Alexander Services Inc. 206 Cal.
   App. 3d 1 (1988)   163
Seagate Technology Inc. v. Commissioner 102 TC No. 9 (1994)   311, 314
SEC v. Banca Della Suizzera Italiana 92 FRD 111 (SDNY 1981)   168
Sei Fujii v. California 242 P. 2d 617 (1952)   648
Shell Petroleum NV v. Graves 709 F. 2d 593, 595 (9th cir) cert. den. 464 US
   1012 (1983)   319
Sinclair Oil Corporation v. Levien (1971) 280 A. 2d 717   344
Société Internationale v. Rogers (Interhandel Case) 357 US 197 (1958)   148
Société Nationale Industrielle Aerospatiale v. US District Court for the Southern
   District of Iowa 782 F. 2d 120 (8th cir 1986); 107 S. Ct 2542 (1987); 26 ILM
   1021 (1987)   155, 170
Sumitomo Stroji America Inc. v. Avagliano 638 F. 2d 552 (2d cir 1981) vacated
   457 US 176 (1982); 21 ILM 790 (1982)   262, 483
Taca International Airlines v. Rolls Royce 204 NE 2d 329 (1965)   163
Talking Pictures Corp v. Western Electric Co. 305 US 124 (1938)   451
Theatre Enterprises Inc. v. Paramount Film Distributing Corp 346 US 537
   (1954)   413
Timberlane Lumberco v. Bank of America 549 F 2d 597 (1976); 749 F 2d 1378
   (9th Cir. 1984) cert. den. 105 S. Ct 3514 (1985)   131
Timken Roller Bearing Co. v. US 83 F. Supp. 284 (1949), 341 US 593 (1951)
   16
Union Carbide Gas Plant Disaster: see In Re Union Carbide Gas Plant Disaster
   At Bhopal India Opinion and Order above
US v. Alcoa 148 F. 2d 416 (2d Cir. 1945)   164
US v. Aluminum Company of America 20 F. Supp. 13 (1937)   129
US v. Bank of Nova Scotia I 691 F. 2d 1384 (11th cir 1982) cert. den. 103 S.
   Ct 3086 (1983)   168
US v. Bank of Nova Scotia II 740 F. 2d 817 (11 cir 1984) cert. den. 469 US
   1106 (1985)   168
US v. Chase Manhattan Bank 590 F. Supp. 1160 (SDNY, 1984)   150
US v. First National Bank of Chicago 699 F. 2d 341 (7th cir 1983)   150
US v. First National City Bank 396 F. 2d 897 (2nd cir 1968)   168
US v. General Electric Co. 82 F. Supp. 753 (1949), 115 F. Supp. (1953)   160
US v. ICI 100 F. Supp. 504 (SDNY 1951), 105 F. Supp. 215 (SDNY 1952)
   160, 414
US v. Jerrold Electronics Corp 187 F. Supp. 545 (ED Pa 1960) aff'd 365 US

567 (1961)   450

US v. Minnesota Mining and Manufacturing Co. 92 F. Supp. 947 (D. Mass 1950) mod. 96 F. Supp. 356 (D. Mass 1951)   414

US v. National Lead Co. 63 F. Supp. 513 (SDNY 1945), 332 US 319 (1947) 160

US v. Penn Ohlin Chemical Co. 378 US 158 (1964)   414

US v. Scophony Corporation of America 333 US 795 (1948)   163

US v. Sisal Sales Corporation 274 US 268 (1927)   160

US v. Toyota Corp 569 F. Supp. 1158 (1983)   149, 168, 316

US v. United States Alkali Export Association Inc. 86 F. Supp. 59 (1949)   50, 160

US v. Vetco Inc. 644 F. 2d 1324 (9th cir 1981) cert. den. 454 US 1098 (1981) 168, 316

US v. Watchmakers of Switzerland Information Center Inc. 1963 Trade Cases CCH para. 70600, 1965 Trade Cases CCH para. 71352   130, 160, 166

Vanguard International Manufacturing Inc. v. US 588 F. Supp. 1229 (SDNY 1984)   168

Volkswagenwerk AG v. Schlunk 468 US 694 (1988); 27 ILM 1092 (1988) 163

Walker v. Newgent 583 F. 2d 163 (5th cir 1978)   163

Waters v. Deutz 460 A 2d 1332 (1983)   164

Wells Fargo & Co. v. Wells Fargo Express Co. 556 F. 2d 406 (9th cir 1977) 163

Westinghouse Case: see In Re Westinghouse Electric Corp Uranium above.

World-Wide Volkswagen v. Woodson 444 US 286 (1980)   141, 164

Yamaha Motor Co. v. FTC 657 F. 2d 971 (8th cir 1981) cert. den. 50 USLW 3799 (US Apr. 4 1982)   414

Zahn v. Transamerica Corporation (1947) 162 F. 2d 36   344

Zenith Radio Corp. v. Hazeltine Research Inc. 395 US 100 (1969)   131, 166

Zwack v. Kraus Bros & Co. 237 F. 2d 255 (2d cir 1956)   523

Decisions of the European Court and Commission

The European Court of Justice and the Court of First Instance

Ahlström (A) Oy v. EC Commission (Wood Pulp) [1993] 4 CMLR 407 (Merits) 412, 413

AKZO Chemie BV v. Commission [1993] 5 CMLR 215   416

BAT & Reynolds v. EC Commission [1987] ECR 4487; [1988] 4 CMLR 24 419

Béguelin Import v. GL Import Export [1971] ECR 949; [1972] CMLR 81   413

Centrafarm v. Sterling [1974] ECR 1147; [1974] 2 CMLR 480   414

Centrafarm v. Winthrop [1974] ECR 1183; [1974] 2 CMLR 480   414

Commercial Solvents v. EC Commission [1974] ECR 223; [1974] 1 CMLR 309 164, 416

Commission v. French Republic (Case 270/83) [1986] ECR 273; [1987] 1 CMLR 401   271

Commission v. UK (Cases C-382 and 383/92)   484

Compagnie Royale Asturienne des Mines SA and Rheinzink GmbH v. EC

Commission [1984] ECR 1679; [1985] 1 CMLR 688   413

Consten and Grundig v. Commission [1966] ECR 299; [1966] CMLR 418
414, 423

Continental Can v. EC Commission [1973] ECR 215; [1973] CMLR 199
164, 418, 419

Corrine Bodson v. Pompes Funèbres des Regions Libérées SA [1989] 4 CMLR
984   413, 422

France v. EC Commission (Case C-327/91)   169

Francovich v. Italian Republic [1993] 2 CMLR 66; [1992] IRLR 84   484

Guest Keen and Nettlefolds Limited, Sachs AG and the Brothers Sachs v.
Bundeskartellamt [1978] 1 CMLR 66   418

Hilti AG v. EC Commission [1992] 4 CMLR 16 (CFI) appeal dismissed Case
C-53/92 Hilti v. Commission [1994] 4 CMLR 614   416

Hoffman La Roche v. EC Commission [1979] ECR 461; [1979] 3 CMLR 211
416, 417

ICI et al. v. EC Commission (The Dyestuffs Case) [1972] ECR 619; [1972]
CMLR 557   164, 413

Katsikas v. Konstantinidis [1993] 1 CMLR 845   485

LTM v. Machinenbau Ulm [1966] ECR 235; [1966] CMLR 357   414

Nederlandsche Banden-Industrie Michelin NV v. EC Commission [1983] ECR
3461; [1985] 1 CMLR 282   416

Nungesser v. Commission (Maize Seeds) [1982] ECR 2015; [1983] 1 CMLR
278   414

R v. HM Treasury ex parte Daily Mail and General Trust plc [1989] 1 All ER
328 (ECJ)   246, 271

R v. Inland Reveue Commissioners ex parte. Commerzbank AG [1993] 3
CMLR 457; [1993] 4 All ER 37 (ECJ)   271

Re Polypropylene Cartel: SA Hercules NV v. EC Commission [1992] 4 CMLR
84 (CFI)   413

SA CNL-Sucal NV v. Hag GF AG (Hag No. 2) [1990] 3 CMLR 571   423

Segers [1986] ECR 2375   271

Stergios Delimitis v. Henninger Brau AG [1992] 5 CMLR 210   413

Suiker Unie v. EC Commission (Sugar Cartel) [1975] ECR 1663; [1976] 1
CMLR 295   413

United Brands v. EC Commission [1978] ECR 207; [1978] 1 CMLR 429
394, 416

Windsurfing International v. EC Commission [1986] ECR 611; [1986] 3
CMLR 489   451

EC Commission Decisions

Aerospatiale and Alenia/De Havilland OJ [1991] L 334/2; [1992] 4 CMLR M2
399, 403, 419

Aluminium Imports from Eastern Europe OJ [1985] L 92/1; [1987] 2 CMLR
813   137

BBC Brown Boveri/NGK [1989] 4 CMLR 610   415

ECS/Akzo OJ [1985] L 374/1; [1986] 3 CMLR 273   416

Eirepage OJ [1992] L 306/22; [1993] 4 CMLR 64   415

Hong Kong and Shanghai Bank/Midland Bank: (Case No. IV/M.213) OJ [1992]

C 113/11 and OJ [1992] C 157/8   397, 419
Mitchell Cotts/Sofiltra OJ [1987] L 41/31; [1988] 4 CMLR 111   414
Nestlé/Perrier OJ [1992] L 356/1; [1993] 4 CMLR M17   419
Olivetti/Cannon OJ [1988] L 52/51; [1990] 4 CMLR 832   83
Re Cartel in Aniline Dyestuffs [1969] CMLR D.23   164
Re ECR 900 [1992] 4 CMLR 54   414, 450
Re Enichem and ICI [1989] 4 CMLR 54   415
Re ODIN [1991] 4 CMLR 832   414
Re Optical Fibres OJ [1986] L 236/30   414
Re Vacuum Interrupters (No. 1) OJ [1977] L 48/32; [1977] 1 CMLR D67
    414
Re Vacuum Interrupters (No. 2) [1982] 2 CMLR 271   414
Re Wood Pulp OJ [1985] L 85/1; [1985] 3 CMLR 474   137, 164, 388, 412,
    413
Re Zinc Producer Group [1985] 2 CMLR 108   137, 138, 164, 413
Siemens/Fanuc [1988] 4 CMLR 945   415
Steetly plc/Tarmac [1992] 2 ECLR R-54   419
The Community v. International Business Machines [1984] 3 CMLR 147   416

Decisions of International Courts and Tribunals

European Court and Commission of Human Rights

Case of Lithgow and Others (ECtHR) Judgment of 8 July 1986   524
Case of Scott's Greenock (Est'd 1711) Ltd and Lithgows Limited Commission
    Report of 17 December 1987   524
Case of Sporrong and Lonnroth (ECtHR) Judgment of 23 September 1982,
    Series A No. 52   523

International Arbitrations

Aminoil v. Kuwait 21 ILM 976 (1982); 66 ILR 518   495, 496–7, 498, 507,
    522, 525, 527, 530, 531, 560
Aramco Case 27 ILR 117 (1963)   520
BP v. Libya 53 ILR 297 (1974)   496, 512, 526, 530
ITT, Sud America v. OPIC 13 ILM 1307 (1974)   531
Lena Goldfields Arbitration *Cornell Law Quarterly* (1950) p. 42; Annual Digest
    5 (1929–30) pp. 3, 426   520
Liamco v. Libya 20 ILM 1 (1981); 62 ILR 140   494–5, 512, 521, 530, 560, 562
Revere Copper Inc. v. OPIC 17 ILM 1321 (1978); 56 ILR 258   494
Sapphire International Petroleum Ltd v. National Iranian Oil Company 35 ILR
    136 (1963)   520
Sheikh of Abu Dhabi v. Petroleum Development (Trucial Coast) Ltd 1 ICLQ
    247 (1952); 18 ILR 144 (1951)   520
Texaco v. Libya 17 ILM 1 (1978); 53 ILR 389   494, 496, 512, 520, 521, 562,
    568

International Centre for the Settlement of Investment Disputes

DECISIONS AND AWARDS OF ICSID TRIBUNALS

AGIP Company v. Popular Republic of Congo 21 ILM 726 (1982)   509, 528
Alcoa Minerals of Jamaica v. The Government of Jamaica 4 YB Com. Arb. 206

(1979)(excerpts)   566, 567

Amco Asia Corp. v. Republic of Indonesia 23 ILM 351 (1984) (jurisdiction); 24 ILM 365 1022 (1985) (merits); resubmitted case 27 ILM 1281 (1988); 89 ILR (1992) p. 55; resubmitted merits: 89 ILR (1992) p. 580, rectification ibid. at p. 568   510, 528, 529, 546, 550, 551, 552, 559, 565, 566, 568

American Manufacturing & Trading Corp v. Zaire (Case ARB/93/1)   570

Asian Agricultural Products Ltd v. Sri Lanka 30 ILM 577 (1991)   550, 627, 644, 645, 647

Benvenuti & Bonfant v. Peoples Republic of the Congo 21 ILM 740 (1982)   510, 528

Company X v. State A News From ICSID Vol2.No. 2 Summer 1985 pp. 3–6   566

Holiday Inns v. Morocco: noted by Lalive 51 BYIL 123 (1980)   546, 565, 566

Klöckner v. Cameroon 1 J. Int. Arb. 145, 331 (1984); 3 J. Int. Arb. 93 (1986)   521, 551, 567, 568

LETCO v. Liberia 26 ILM 647 (1987)   526, 550, 566, 567, 569

Maritime International Nominées Establishment v. Guinea (Ad Hoc Committee Decision) 5 ICSID Rev-FILJ 95 (1990)   552

Scimitar Exploration Limited v. Bangladesh and Bangladesh Oil, Gas and Mineral Corp (Case ARB/92/2)   570

Southern Pacific Properties (Middle East) Limited v. Egypt 32 ILM 933 (1993)   510, 523, 528, 551, 562, 566, 571

Vacuum Salt Products Ltd v. Ghana (Case ARB/92/1) 9 ICSID Rev-FILJ 71 (1994)   566, 570

DECISIONS OF NATIONAL COURTS CONCERNING ICSID

Guinea v. Maritime International Nominées Establishment: 24 ILM 1639 (1985) (Belgium, Court of First Instance, Antwerp)   548, 567

505 F. Supp. 141 (1981), 20 ILM 666 (1981); 692 F. 2d 1094 (USCA DC Cir 1982), 21 ILM 1355 (1982) and 22 ILM 86 (1983)   548

26 ILM 382 (1987) (Swiss Surveillance Authority)   548, 567

LETCO v. Government of Liberia 650 F. Supp. 73 (SDNY 1986); 26 ILM 695 (1987) aff'd memo No. 86–9047 (2d cir, May 19, 1987)   570

SOABI (SEUTIN) v. Senegal (France, Cour de Cassation, 11 June 1991) 30 ILM 1167 (1991)   569

SOGUIPECHE v. Atlantic Triton Co. 24 ILM 340 (1985) (France, Court of Appeal Rennes, 24 October 1984); 26 ILM 373 (1987) (France, Cour de Cassation, 18 November 1986)   548, 567

International Court of Justice

Anglo-Norwegian Fisheries Case ICJ Reports (1951) p. 116   158

Barcelona Traction Light and Power Company Case ICJ Rep. (1970) p. 3   128, 159, 489, 536, 545, 561, 573, 604, 624, 642

Case Concerning Elettronica Sicula SpA (ELSI) ICJ Rep. (1989) p. 15   639

Nottebohm Case ICJ Rep. (1955) p. 4   158

Permanent Court of International Justice

Lotus Case (1927) PCIJ Reports, Series A, No. 10   125

Mavromatis Palestine Concessions Case (Jurisdiction) (1924 PCIJ Reports, Series A, No. 2   560

Oscar Chinn Case (1934) PCIJ Reports, Series A/B No. 63   526
Panevezys-Saldutsikis Case (1939) PCIJ Reports, Series A/B, No. 76   560
Serbian and Brazilian Loans Cases (1929) PCIJ Reports, Series A, Nos 20/21
   520

Iran–US Claims Tribunal
American Bell International Inc. v. Iran 6 Iran-US CTR 74 (1984)   523
American International Group v. Iran 4 Iran-US CTR 96 (1983)   528
Amoco International Finance Corporation v. Iran 15 Iran-US CTR 189 (1987
   II); 27 ILM 1314 (1988)   508, 511, 525, 526, 527
CBS Inc. v. Iran Award No. 486–197–2 28 June 1990   528
INA Corp v. Iran 8 Iran-US CTR 373 (1985)   529
Otis Elevator Co. v. Iran and Bank Mellat 14 Iran-US CTR 283 (1987)   523
Phelps Dodge Corp. & Overseas Private Investment Corp. v. Iran 10 Iran-US
   CTR 121 (1986 I); 25 ILM 619 (1986)   528
Sea Land Services Inc. v. Ports and Shipping Organization of the Islamic
   Republic of Iran 6 Iran-US CTR 149 (1984)   523
Sedco Inc. v. National Iranian Oil Co. & Iran 10 Iran-US CTR 180 (1986); 25
   ILM 629 (1986)   528, 529, 531
Sola Tiles Inc. v. Iran 14 Iran-US CTR 223 (1987)   523, 528
Starrett Housing Corp v. Iran (Interlocutory Award) 4 Iran-US CTR 122
   (1984); 23 ILM 1090 (1984)   523
Thomas Earle Payne v. Iran 12 Iran-US CTR 3 (1986)   528
William Pereira Associates, Iran v. Iran 5 Iran-US CTR 198 (1984)   523

Statutes

Andean Common Market (ANCOM)
Andean Commission Decision 24 'Andean Foreign Investment Code': 16 ILM
    138 (1977)   117, 442, 575–6
    Arts 1–7, 12–16, 18–44   606
    Art. 20   447
    Art. 21   454
    Arts 50, 51   576, 606
Andean Commission Decision 220: 27 ILM 974 (1988)   575, 576–7
    Arts 33, 34   607
Andean Commission Decision 291 March 21 1991: 30 ILM 1283 (1991)   447,
    575, 577
    Arts 2, 10   577
    Art. 15   454
Andean Commission Decision on Andean Multinational Enterprises (16–18
    March 1982): 21 ILM 542 (1982); revised decision 292 (1991): 30 ILM 1295
    (1991)   78–9

Argentina
1981   Law 22, 426 of 1981 Arts 2, 5   454
1985   Draft Code of Private International Law: 24 ILM 269 (1985)
       Art. 10   138, 342

Australia
1975   Foreign Acquisitions and Takeovers Act (as amended at 30 November
       1991 PRA 26/91)   197, 218
1976   Foreign Proceedings (Prohibition of Certain Evidence) Act   167
1979   Foreign Antitrust Judgments (Restriction of Enforcement) Act, s. 3   166
1984   Foreign Proceedings (Excess of Jurisdiction) Act(Austl. Acts No. 3)
       167

Brazil
1975   Normative Act 15 of 11 September 1975   452, 454
1984   Law No. 7232 of 29 October 1984 (Informatics Law)   448
1990   Decree No. 99541 of 21 September 1990   448
1991   Law No. 8238 of 23 October 1991   448

Law No. 8383 of 30 December 1991   456
1993   INPI Ruling 120 of 17 December 1993   448

Bulgaria
1980   Edict No. 535 of 25 March 1980: 19 ILM 992 (1980)   211

Canada
1973   Foreign Investment Review Act (c. 46 1973–74 Stat. Can. amended
       c. 52 1976–77 Stat. Can. 1274)   197–9, 219, 259
           ss 2, 10, 11   219
1974/5   Combines Investigation Act (c. 76)
           s. 12   166
           s. 31.5   166
           s. 31.6   166
1984   Foreign Extraterritorial Measures Act (c. 49)   167
1985   Investment Canada Act (c. 20 1985 Stat. Can.)   199–202, 240
           s. 2   199
           s. 3   219, 220
           s. 5(1)   221
           ss 6–9   220
           s. 10(1)   199
           s. 13 (1)(b)(ii)   220
           (3)   199
           s. 14   200
           s. 15   220
           ss 20–24   220
           s. 26   220
           s. 28(1)   200
           (3)   220
           s. 29   220
           s. 36   221
           ss 39–41   220
           s. 40   202

Cuba
1982   Legislative Decree No. 50 of 15 February 1982: 21 ILM 1106 (1982)
       212

Czech Republic/Czechoslovakia
1990   Foreign Investment Law (Act No. 173 of 1988 as amended by Act No.
       112 of 19 April 1990)   188, 213
1991   Commercial Code (Act No. 513 of 5 November 1991)

Egypt
1989   Foreign Investment Law Law No. 230 of 20 July 1989: 4 ICSID Rev-
       FILJ pp. 376–395 (1989)   264
           Art. 32   232

Ethiopia
1983   Joint Venture Establishment Proclamation No. 235/1983   212

France
1958   French Constitution Art. 55   635
1966   Law No. 66-537 of 24 July 1966   344
       Law No. 66-1008 of 28 December 1966 [1966] JO 11621   197
1967   Decree No. 67-78 of 1967 JO [1967] 1073 and 1074   197
       Law Concerning Economic Interest Groupings (Groupement D'Interêt
       Economique) Ordonnance No. 67-821 23 Septembre 1967   64, 84
1971   Decrees Nos. 71-143 and 71-144   218
1980   Law No. 80-538 of July 16 1980 [1980] JO 1799, English translation 75
       AJIL 382 (1981)   167
       Decrees Nos. 80-617 and 80-618 of 4 August 1980   218
1986   Law Concerning the Privatisation of Nationalised Enterprises Law No.
       86-912 of 6 August 1986: 26 ILM 1388 (1987)   183
       Code Général des Impôts (Tax Code)
           Art. 57   311
           Art. 209B   320
       Code du Travail (Labour Code)
           Art. L. 432–1, 432–4   367, 382

Germany
1957   Act Against Restraints of Competition (1957 BGB.I 1081 as amended
       1980)
           s. 1   412
           s. 22(1)   412
           ss 23, 24   412
           s. 24(2)   419
1959   Budget Law s. 18   531
1965   Joint Stock Corporations Act (Aktiengesetz)   328, 331, 335, 337
           ss 17, 18, 291–323   342, 344
           ss 319–322   342
           ss 303–322   345
       Act Against Unfair Competition ss. 1–3   475

Ghana
1971   Manufacturing Industries Act   197
1981   Investment Code (Law No. 437 of 11 August 1981)   196, 208
1985   Investment Code (Law No. 116 of 13 July 1985)   196, 208
           ss 12–15, 18–20   217
           ss 16, 21–26   217
1992   Technology Transfer Regulations (LI 1547 9 Sept 1992)   454

Hungary
1972   Decree of the Minister of Finance No. 28/1972 as amended by Decree
       No. 7/1977 of May 6 1977: 17 ILM 1451 (1978)   186, 211

1990   Act No. XCVIII   188, 213
       Act LXXIV on Privatization of State Owned Enterprises   213

India
1973   Foreign Exchange Regulation Act (Act 46 of 1973 AIR 1973 Acts), s. 29
       179
1993   Foreign Exchange Regulation Act 1973 as amended by Act 29 of 1993,
       s. 29   180

Indonesia
1967   Law on Foreign Capital Investment (No. 1 of 1967)   185, 210

Ireland
1958   Industrial Development (Encouragement of External Investment) Act
       262
1989   Finance Act s. 18 (as amended by Finance Act 1991)   263
1990   Finance Act   263

Japan
1947   Law on the Prohibition of Private Monopoly and Ensuring of Fair Trade
       (Anti-Monopoly Law) No. 54 of 1947   69
            Art. 2(6)   412
            Art. 3   412
            Arts 9, 11   70
            Arts 9, 10(1)   419
            Art. 15   412
1949   Foreign Exchange and Foreign Trade Control Law (Law No. 228,
       December 1, 1949 as amended) Chapter V. Arts 26–30   176, 197, 206,
       402
1950   Export Insurance Law as amended in April 1956 and May 1957   531
1980   Cabinet Order Concerning Direct Domestic Investments 11 October
       1980 Chapter III Conclusion etc of Agreements for Importation of
       Technology Arts 4–6   454
       Cabinet Decision Concerning Policy Applications on Inward Direct
       Investments (Decision of Cabinet Meeting of 26th Day of December
       1980)   176, 206

Madagascar
1985   Law No. 85-001 of June 18 1985 Arts 30–31   571

Mauritius
1970   Export Processing Zone Act (No. 51) (as amended by Acts Nos 50 of
       1975 and 13 of 1980)   264

Mexico
1973   Act on Foreign Investment   195
1976   Law on Inventions and Trademarks   440

1993   Act on Foreign Investment of 27 December 1993, English translation: 33
       ILM 207 (1994)   195–6
              Arts 5, 6   217
              Art. 7   196
              Art. 8   195
              Art. 26(II), 29, 30   217

New Zealand
1973   Overseas Investment Act (No. 14, 1973) (as reprinted 1 August 1989,
       Statutes Vol. 24, p. 617)   197, 218
1980   Companies Amendment Act s. 30   337
1985   Overseas Investment Regulations (1985/256, Statutory Regulations Vol.
       3, p. 1287)   218
       Overseas Investment Exemption Notice 1985 (1985/272)   218

Nigeria
1972   Nigerian Enterprises Promotion Act (No. 4 of 1972)   177, 178, 207
1977   Nigerian Enterprises Promotion Act (No. 3 of 1977)   177, 178, 207
1979   National Office of Industrial Property Act (Decree No. 70, 24 September
       1979)   447, 454
1988   Industrial Development Co-ordination Act (No. 36 of 1988)   217
              s. 4   207
1989   Nigerian Enterprises Promotion Act (No. 54 of 1989) CAP 303 Laws of
       the Federation of Nigeria Vol 23 (rev. edn, 1990)   177, 178, 207
              s. 1(1), (2)   208
              s. 3(2)   208
1991   Nigeria Export Processing Zones Decree (No. 34 of 13 June 1991)
       264
1992   Nigeria Export Processing Zones Decree (No. 63 of 19 November 1992)
       Official Gazette No. 62, Vol. 79 of 1992 (repealing and replacing the
       1991 Decree)   264

North Korea
1985   Joint Venture Law: 24 ILM 806 (1985)   212

Pakistan
1972   Generic Names Drug Act   440

People's Republic of China
1979   The Law on Joint Ventures 1 July 1979: 18 ILM 1163 (1979); as
       amended 4 April 1990: Beijing Review, 7–13 May 1990, pp. 27–8   186,
       189–91
              Art. 1   189
              Art. 2   214
              Art. 2(3)   191
              Art. 3   214
              Art. 4   214
              Arts 5–10   214
              Art. 14   190

1980 Regulations on Special Economic Zones in Guangdong Provice of 26 August 1980 (East Asian Executive reports Vol. 2, No. 10 (15 October 1980))   235, 266
        Art. 2   235
        Arts 4, 10, 13–15   266
        Arts 5, 9, 16–18, 19, 25   267
1983 Regulations for Implementation of Law on Joint Ventures 20 September 1983: 22 ILM 1033 (1983)   190
        Art. 5   214
        Arts 8–10   214
1985 Interim Regulations on the Transfer of Technology: 24 ILM 292 (1985) 454
        Regulations Controlling Technology Import Contracts: 24 ILM 801 (1985)   454
1986 Law on Enterprises Operated Exclusively with Foreign Capital 12 April 1986, Beijing Review No. 18, 5 May 1986, p. 16   175, 189, 191, 214, 236
        Provisions of the State Council Encouraging Foreign Investment 11 October 1986, Beijing Review, No. 43, 27 October 1986, p. 26   214
1987 Law of Technology Contracts, 23 June 1987   454
1988 Law on Chinese-Foreign Contractual Joint Ventures 13 April 1988: Beijing Review, 20–26 June 1988, p. 29   188–9
        Art. 3   214
        Arts 5, 6   214
        Rules for Implementation of the Regulations on the Administration of Technology Import Contracts adopted 20 January 1988, Vol. 2, 3 China Law and Practice, 28 March 1988, p. 38   454
1991 Income Tax Law for Enterprises with Foreign Investment and Foreign Enterprises 1 July 1991: Beijing Review, 24–30 June 1991, p. 23, Arts 5, 7   266
1992 Notice on Implementation Measures for the Administration of Transactions Between Affiliated Enterprises under the 1991 Income Tax Law (Guo Shui Fa 237 of 29 October 1992)   311

Poland
1988 Law No. 325 of 23 December 1988, which came into force on 1 January 1989, Dziennik Ustaw Polskiej Rzeczypospolitej Ludowej [1988] No 41 of 28 December 1988, English translation in 28 ILM 1518 (1989) 187
1990 Act on the Privatization of State-owned Enterprises of 13 July 1990 213
1991 Foreign Investment Act, Act of 14 June 1991: Dziennik Ustaw Rzeczypospolitej Polskiej [1991] No. 60, 4 July 1991, item 253, English translation 30 ILM 871 (1991)   187
        Arts 4(1), 2(2), 6(1)(3)(4), 22, 23, 25, 26   212

Romania
1972 Decree No. 424 of 2 November 1972   211

Russian Federation/USSR
1987   Decree on Joint Enterprises with Western and Developing Countries: 26
       ILM 749 (1987)   187, 192
1991   Foreign Investment Law of 4 July 1991: 31 ILM 397 (1992)   192, 216,
       234
1992   Law on Privatization of State and Municipal Enterprises of 5 June 1992
       216

South Africa
1974   Second General Law Amendment Act 94 of 1974   167

Spain
1986   Royal Decree 1265/1986 of 27 June 1986 (as amended 1991)   218
       Royal Decree 2077/1986 of 25 September 1986: 26 ILM 727 (1987)
       218

Sri Lanka
Constitution Art. 157   635

Switzerland
Banking Law, Art. 3   153
Criminal Code
       Art. 161   169
       Art. 162   152

Tanzania
1990   National Investment (Promotion and Protection) Act (Act No. 10 of
       1990): 6 ICSID Rev-FILJ 292 (1991)   217
              s. 29(2)   571

Togo
1985   Law No. 85-03 of January 29 1985 Art. 4   571

Uganda
1991   Investment Code (Statute No. 1, 1991)   217
              s. 30(2)(a), 40(6)(c)   571

United Kingdom
1947   Exchange Control Act   118, 223
1948   Companies Act, s. 210   334
1964   Shipping Contracts and Commercial Documents Act   167
1967   Companies Act   381
1973   Fair Trading Act Part V. Mergers   223, 412
              s. 84   420
1974   Trade Union and Labour Relations Act   472
1975   Evidence (Proceedings in Other Jurisdictions) Act s. 2(4)   154
       Industry Act   182, 223
              ss 11–20   210

1978   Inner Urban Areas Act   227
1980   Employment Act s. 17   487
       Local Government Planning and Land Act s. 179, Sched. 2   263
       Protection of Trading Interests Act   146
           s. 1(3)   160
           ss 5, 6   166
1982   Civil Jurisdiction and Judgments Act   162–3
           s. 49   143
       Derelict Land Act   227
       Industrial Development Act   227
1984   Finance Act ss 82–91   320
1985   Companies Act
           ss 227–232   377
           s. 228 (inserted by s. 5(3) Companies Act 1989)   379
           s. 229(1), (3) (inserted by s. 5(3) Companies Act 1989)   379
           s. 248 (as introduced by s. 13(3) Companies Act 1989)   360, 380
           s. 249(3) (inserted by s. 13(3) Companies Act 1989)   380
           s. 258 (inserted by s. 21(1) Companies Act 1989)   378
           s. 309   344
           s. 425   344
           s. 459   334
           ss 691 (as amended by s. 145 Companies Act 1989), 695   135, 162
           Part XIIIA   344
           Schedule 4   364
           paras 55–56   381
           Schedule 4A   377
           para. 1   381
           Schedule 5   377
       Finance Act s. 54   301, 302, 319
1986   Financial Services Act
           Part IV   363
           s. 144(2), 146(1)   381
       Insolvency Act
           s. 214   337
               (3)   344
               (7)   344
           s. 251   344
1987   Banking Act, s. 39(3)(a)   151
1988   Income and Corporation Taxes Act
           s. 240   308
           ss 402–403   308
           s. 770   289, 312
           s. 772   316
           s. 772(2)   297
           s. 772(3)   316
           ss 773(2), 840   316
       Multilateral Investment Guarantee Agency Act (c. 8)   532
       Regional Development Grants (Termination) Act (amending the Indus-

trial Development Act 1982)   227
1989 Local Government and Housing Act Part III   226
1991 Export and Investment Guarantees Act (c. 67)
   s. 1   531
   s. 2   515
1992 Trade Union and Labour Relations (Consolidation) Act
   s. 188   484
   ss 224, 226–234   487
1993 Trade Union Reform and Employment Rights Act, s. 20(4)   485

United States of America
Constitution Art. VI   635, 636
1890 Sherman Antitrust Act 1890, 26 Stat. 209 (1890), 15 USCA ss 1–7
   129, 130, 388
   s. 1   129, 412
   s. 2   129, 412
   s. 7   163
1914 Clayton Act, 38 Stat. 730 (1914), 15 USCA ss 12–27
   ss 2–4   412
   s. 7   412
   s. 12   163
1918 Webb–Pomerene Act   24, 50
1933 Securities Act, 15 USCA ss 77a ff   377
1934 Securities Exchange Act, 15 USCA ss 78a ff   377
1948 Economic Cooperation Act, 62 Stat 144 (1948)   514
1954 Mutual Security Act s. 413, 68 Stat 846 (1954) as amended 22 USC s.
   1933 (Supp. III, 1962)   531
1958 Federal Aviation Act, 49 US App. Ch. 20 s. 1301 (16)   205
1961 Foreign Assistance Act, 75 Stat 424 (1961)   514
1964 Civil Rights Act Title VII   463
1969 Foreign Assistance Act, 22 USC
   s. 2191 (1970)   514, 531
   s. 2197(i)   531
1972 Burke–Hartke Bill S. 2592, 92d Cong, 1st Sess. (1971)   5, 16, 281
1974 OPIC Amendments Act PL 93–390   531
   Trade Act s. 301, 88 Stat. 1978, 19 USC s. 2411 as amended by the
   Omnibus Trade and Competitiveness Act 1988 PL No. 100-418 102
   Stat. 1107 s. 1301   259, 276, 475
1976 Hart–Scott–Rodino Antitrust Improvements Act, 15 USC s. 18a   418
   International Investment and Trade in Services Survey Act, PL No. 94-
   472 90 Stat. 2509, Title 22 USC Cap. 46 ss 3101–3108   225
   Sovereign Immunity Act s. 1605(3)   525
1977 Foreign Corrupt Business Practices Act PL No. 95–213   7, 127
1978 Agricultural Foreign Investment Disclosure Act, Title 7 USC Cap. 66 ss
   3501–3508   225
   OPIC Amendments Act PL 95–268   531
1981 OPIC Amendment Act 95 Stat 1021 (1981)   531
1982 Foreign Trade Antitrust Improvements Act   132
1984 Trade and Tariff Act s. 301 as amended by the Omnibus Trade and

Competitiveness Act 1988   274
National Cooperation Research Act, 15 USC ss 4301-4305   437, 451
1988   Generalized System of Preferences, 19 USC s. 2462(a)(4)   474, 489
Insider Trading and Securities Fraud Enforcement Act: PL No. 100-704
102 Stat. 4677(1988)   153
Omnibus Trade and Competitiveness Act Public Law 100–418 August
23 1988 102 Stat. 1107; 28 ILM 460 (1989)
        s. 1301   489
        s. 1303   441, 453
        s. 5021 (the original 'Exon–Florio Amendment')   205
1991   Civil Rights Act   463
Reinstated 'Exon Florio Amendment': Defense Production Act Extension Amendments PL 102–99, 105 Stat. 487, 17 August 1991   176,
205, 224
US Treasury Regulations Implementing Exon–Florio Amendment 21
November 1991: 31 ILM 424 (1992)   176, 205
1994   International Antitrust Enforcement Assistance Act (S2297 and
HR4781, 103rd Cong., 2nd Sess., 1994)   169

Internal Revenue Code
        s. 482 (26 USCA s. 482, as amended by the Tax Reform Act 1986)
        289, 291
        s. 951ff   305–6, 320–1
Treasury Regulations under s. 482
    1968 Regulations (26 CFR s. 1.482-1 (1971))   289–90, 313
    1992 Proposed Regulations (s. 1.482 57 Fed. Reg. 3571 (1992)   293–4,
    315
    1993 Temporary Regulations (Treas. Reg. 1.482–1T to 1.482–6T: TD 8470,
    Notices of Proposed Rule Making IL 21–91 and IL 401–88)   295, 315
National Labor Relations Act   472
Third Restatement of the Foreign Relations Law of the United States
(American Law Institute, 1987)
        s. 401   158
        s. 402   159
        s. 403(1)   132
            (2)   133, 162
            (3)   133
        s. 414   159, 162
        s. 416   159
        s. 421   162
        s. 431   166
        s. 442(1)   145
            (1)(a)   145–6, 167
            (1)(b)   146, 167
            (1)(c)   145, 149, 167
            (2)   148
        s. 444, 455(3)   525
        s. 712   524, 527, 530
        s. 713   561

California
Wests Annotated California Codes 1989 Cumulative Pocket Part Ch. 17 ss
  25101–25141   318
Senate Bill 85 of 1986 entered force 1 January 1988   319
Senate Bill 671 enacted 6 September 1993   302, 319

Venezuela
1986   Decree No. 1200 of 16 July 1986: 26 ILM 760 (1987)   576

Vietnam
1990   Law on Foreign Investment as amended 30 June 1990: 30 ILM 930
       (1991)   186, 212
1991   Decree Regulation in Detail the Implementation of the Law on Foreign
       Investment 6 February 1991: 30 ILM 942 (1991)   212

Yugoslavia
1976   Associated Labour Act of 25 November 1976   211
1978   Law on Investment of Resources of Foreign Persons in Domestic
       (Yugoslav) Organisations of Associated Labour of 7 April 1978   211
1989   Law on Foreign Investments of 8 January 1989: 28 ILM 1543 (1989)
       211

Zambia
1991   Investment Act (No. 19 of 1991)   217

EEC/EC Materials

Treaties
1957   EEC Treaty
               Art. 48(3)   246
               Art. 52   246
               Art. 55   183, 209
               Art. 56   183, 209, 246
               Art. 58   245, 246
               Art. 66   245, 246
               Art. 85   137
                   (1)   392, 412, 437
                   (3)   412
               Art. 86   137, 412
               Art. 92   228
               Art. 119   483
               Art. 221   182
               Art. 223   183, 209
1968   Brussels Convention on Jurisdiction and the Enforcement of Civil and
       Commercial Judgments   143
1990   Convention on the Elimination of Double Taxation in Connection with
       the Adjustment of Profits of Associated Enterprises (90/463/EEC) OJ
       [1990] L 225/10   298

      Arts 6–11   317
1992   Maastricht Treaty 7 February 1992: 31 ILM 247 (1992)   376

Secondary Legislation
1968   Regulation 802/68/EEC OJ [1968] L 1148/1   258, 276
1977   Directive 77/187/EEC (Transfer of Undertakings) OJ [1977] L 61/26
      466
1978   Fourth Company Law Directive OJ [1978] L 222/11   354, 356, 362,
      364
      Art. 27   360
      Art. 52   379
1979   Council Directive 79/729 OJ [1979] L 66/21   381
1980   Council Directive 80/390 OJ [1980] L 100/1   381
1982   Council Directive 82/121 OJ [1982] L 48/26   381
1983   Commission Regulation (Exclusive Distribution Block Exemption)
      1983/83 OJ [1983] L 173/1   413
      Commission Regulation (Exclusive Purchasing Block Exemption)1984/
      83 OJ [1983] L 173/5   413
      The Seventh Directive on Company Accounts: 83/349/EEC OJ [1983] L
      193   354, 355–61, 362, 378
      Art. 1   357–8
      Art. 2(1)   378
      Art. 3   379
      Art. 5   360
      Arts 7, 8, 9, 10   379
      Art. 11   359, 379
      Art. 12   358, 360
      Arts 13, 14   379
      Arts 16, 17, 29   378
      Arts 18–38   356–7
      Art. 34   380
      Art. 47   379
1984   Commission Regulation (Patent Licensing Block Exemption) 2349/84
      OJ [1984] L 219/15 (as amended by reg. 151/93 OJ [1993] L 21/8)
      392, 415, 437, 451
1985   Commission Regulation (Specialisation Agreements Block Exemption)
      417/85 OJ [1985] L 53/1 (as amended by Reg. 151/93 OJ [1993] L 21/
      8)   392, 415
      Commission Regulation (Co-operative R&D Block Exemption) 418/85
      OJ [1985] L 53/5 (as amended by Reg. 151/93 OJ [1993] L 21/8)
      392, 415, 437
      Regulation Establishing the European Economic Interest Grouping:
      Council Reg. 2137/85 of 25 July 1985 OJ [1985] L 199/1   77–8, 88
1986   Directive on Annual and Consolidated Accounts of Credit Institutions
      86/635/EEC OJ [1986] L 372   361
1989   Commission Regulation (Know How Licensing Block Exemption) 556/
      89 OJ [1989] L 61/1 (as amended by Reg. 151/93 OJ [1993] L 21/8)
      392, 415, 437, 451
      Second Banking Directive 89/646/EEC OJ [1989] L 386/1

Art. 9   247

1990   Council Directive 90/434/EEC of 23 July 1990 on a common system of taxation applicable to mergers, divisions, transfers of assets and exchanges of shares concerning companies of different Member States OJ [1990] L 225/1   68, 86

Council Directive 90/435/EEC of 23 July 1990 on a common system of taxation applicable in the case of parent companies and subsidiaries of different Member States OJ [1990] L 225/6

Council Directive 90/605/EEC OJ [1990] L 317   361

Regulation on Mergers Reg. 4064/89 of 21 September 1990 OJ [1990] L 257/13   69, 396–7, 412, 418

Arts 1(1), (2), 3(1), 5(3), 21   418

Arts 2, 9   419

Art. 2(1)(b)   419

1991   Directive on Annual and Consolidated Accounts of Insurance Undertakings 91/674/EEC OJ [1991] L 374   361

1992   Council Directive 92/56/EEC (Collective Redundancies) OJ [1992] L 245/3 amending Dir. 75/129/EEC OJ [1975] L 48/29   465–6, 484

1993   Investment Services Directive 93/22/EEC OJ [1993] L 141/27 Art. 7   247

The Eco-Audit Regulation: EC Council Regulation No. 1836/93 OJ [1993] L 168/1   370–1

Arts 1–10   383

Art. 20   383

1994   Council Directive 94/18/EC amending Dir. 80/390/EEC OJ [1994] L 135/1   381

Council Directive 94/45/EC of 22 September 1994 on the establishment of a European Works Council or a procedure in Community-scale undertakings and Community-scale groups of undertakings for the purposes of informing and consulting employees OJ [1994] L 254/64   352–3, 376, 473, 478–9, 490

Proposed Legislation

COMPANY LAW

Proposal for a European Company COM (89) 268 Final SYN 218 and 219 25 August 1989 in OJ C 263/41 of 16 October 1989, as amended in COM (91) 174 Final SYN 218 in OJ C 176/1 8 July 1991   69, 77, 331

Draft Fifth Directive on EC Company Law OJ [1983] C 240/2 (as amended 1988, 1990 and 1991)   351, 374

Proposed Ninth Directive on Company Law   331

Proposal for a Tenth Directive on Cross-Border Mergers COM (84) 727 final 25 January 1985 OJ [1985] C 23 or EC Bulletin Supplement 1985/3   69, 86

COMPETITION LAW

Preliminary draft Commission Regulation of 30 June 1994 on the application of Art. 85(3) of the Treaty to certain categories of technology transfer agreement OJ [1994] C 178/3   415, 451

Information and Consultation of Workers

Proposal for a Directive on Procedure for Informing and Consulting Employees of Undertakings with Complex Structures, in particular Transnational Undertakings (The Vredeling Proposal) 1980: 21 ILM 422 (1982) revised 1983: see Bull EC Supplement 2/83; OJ [1983] C 217/3   351, 375

Amended proposal for a Council Directive on the establishment of a European Works Council COM(19) 345 final: OJ [1991] C 336/11   352, 375

Proposal for a Council Directive on the Establishment of European Committees etc. COM(94) 134 final–94/0113 (PRT) OJ [1994] C 135/8   375

Workers' Rights

Proposed Directive on the Protection of Posted Workers 7322/91 COM (91) 230 final   464

Proposed Directive on the approximation of the Laws of Member States relating to the safeguarding of employees' rights in the event of transfers of undertakings, businesses or parts of businesses OJ [1994] C 274/10   484

Commission Opinions and Notices

EC Commission 'Comments on US Regulations Concerning Trade with the USSR' 12 August 1982: 21 ILM 891 (1982)   128, 159

EC Commission Notice on Co-operative Joint Ventures OJ [1993] C 43/2 392–3, 416

Treaties

General
1778 US–France Treaty of Amity and Commerce   639
1883 Paris Convention for the Protection of Industrial Property (as amended)
439
       Art. 2   451
       Art. 4   440, 451
1919 Treaty of Versailles Part XIII   458
1946 US–China Friendship Commerce and Navigation Treaty   639
1948 The Havana Charter for an International Trade Organisation, 24 March
1948 (US Dept of State Pub. No. 3206, Commercial Policy Series 114,
1948)   112, 421, 574
       Art. 5   403, 605
       Arts 11, 12   605
       US–Italy Friendship Commerce and Navigation Treaty   639
1950 European Convention on Human Rights Art. 11   487
1953 US–Ethiopia Treaty of Amity and Economic Relations   635–6
1955 US–Iran Treaty of Amity, Economic Relations and Consular Rights, 15
August 1955 (284 UNTS 93) Art. IV(2)   528
Convention of 20 October 1955 Establishing EUROFIMA (378 UNTS
159)   79–80, 89
1965 The World Bank Convention for the Settlement of Investment Disputes:
see below under International Organizations, International Bank for
Reconstruction and Development.
Hague Convention on the Service Abroad of Judicial and Extra-judicial
Documents in Civil and Commercial Matters: 4 ILM 341 (1965)   135,
154, 163
1966 International Covenant on Civil and Political Rights (UNTS 171) Art.
22   470–1
1969 Vienna Convention on the Law of Treaties Art. 27   568
1972 Hague Convention on the Taking of Evidence Abroad: 9 ILM 87 (1970)
151, 153–6
       Art. 1   154
       Art. 23   154, 155
1973 US–Hungary Compensation Agreement: 13 ILM 407 (1973)   513,
530

1975 US–Chile Compensation Agreement: 14 ILM 131 (1975) 513, 530
1976 US–Germany Agreement Relating to Mutual Cooperation Regarding Restrictive Business Practices 169
1977 US–Switzerland Treaty on Mutual Assistance in Criminal Matters 152
1982 US–Australia Agreement Relating to Cooperation in Antitrust Matters 169
      US–Switzerland Memorandum of Understanding on Co-operation in the Field of Insider Trading: 22 ILM 1 (1983) 153
1984 France–Germany Agreement Concerning Cooperation on Restrictive Business Practices 26 ILM 531 (1987) 169
      US–Canada Memorandum of Understanding on Notification, Consultation and Co-operation with Respect to the Application of National Antitrust Laws: 23 ILM 275 (1984) 169
      US–Equador Investment Guaranty Agreement 28 November 1984: 24 ILM 566 (1985) 531
1985 Convention Establishing the Multilateral Investment Guarantee Agency: see below under International Organizations, International Bank for Reconstruction and Development
1986 US–Ethiopia Compensation Agreement 19 December 1986: 25 ILM 56 (1986) 513
1987 ASEAN: Agreement on Promotion and Protection of Investments: 27 ILM 612 (1988) 619, 626, 640, 647
1988 US–Canada Free Trade Agreement: 27 ILM 281 (1988) 201, 239–41, 242, 243–5
            Art. 102 239
            Art. 105 268
            Chapter 14 'Services' 239
            Chapter 16 'Investment' Arts 1601–11 239–41
            Annex 1607.3 240
            Art. 1610 270
            Arts 1701–6 268
            Arts 1806–7 241
            Art. 2005 241
            Art. 2012 268
1989 US–Poland Investment Guarantee Agreement: 28 ILM 1393 (1989) 531
1991 US–EC Agreement on the Application of Their Competition Laws: 30 ILM 1487 (1991) 169
1992 North American Free Trade Agreement: 32 ILM 289, 605 (1993) 196, 205, 238, 469
      Part Five: 'Investment', 32 ILM pp. 639–670 (1993) 241–5, 269–70
      Side Agreement on Environmental Co-operation: 32 ILM 1480 (1993) 270
      Side Agreement on Labor Co-operation: 32 ILM 1499 (1993) 270
1994 The Final Act of the Uruguay Round Negotiations Under GATT see below under International Organizations, GATT Uruguay Round

Bilateral Investment Treaties

Model Agreements

Asian African Legal Consultative Committee: Draft Model Bilateral Agreements
   on Promotion and Protection of Investments 1984: 23 ILM 237 (1984)
   618, 626, 630, 631, 640, 641, 645, 646
Netherlands Model Bilateral Investment Treaty 1987   642
US Model Bilateral Investment Treaty 1984   618, 640
                  Art. I(1)(a)   623, 642
                  Art. I(1)(c)   642
                  Art. I(3)   620
                  Art. II(1)   621
                  Art. II(2)   625
                  Art. II(5)   632
                  Art. III(1)   645
                  Art. IV   644
                  Art. VII   646
                  Art. IX   644

*Agreements Concluded (in Alphabetical Order by Capital-
exporting Country)*

Australia–People's Republic of China 1988   570, 643
Belgium Luxembourg–Indonesia 1970   643
Belgium Luxembourg–Malaysia 1982   643
Belgium Luxembourg–People's Republic of China 1984   631, 643, 645
France–Malaysia 1975   571
France–Nepal 1984   642, 643
France–People's Republic of China 1984   570, 631, 643, 645, 647
France–Rwanda 1967   641
France–Senegal 1975   571, 643
France–Sri Lanka 1963   641, 643
France–Tunisia 1972   618
Germany–Israel 1976   641, 642
Germany–Pakistan 1959   618, 641
Germany–Papua New Guinea 1980   643
Germany–Philippines 1964   644
Germany–St Lucia 1985   624, 629, 630, 640, 641, 642
Germany–Zaire 1969   643
Japan–People's Republic of China 1989   570, 631, 643, 645, 646, 647
Netherlands–Indonesia 1968   571
Netherlands–Kenya 1979   572, 642
Sweden–Malaysia 1979   571
Switzerland–Indonesia 1974   643
Switzerland–Tunisia 1961   618
UK–Bangladesh 1980   571
UK–Burundi 1990   641
UK–Egypt 1975   618

UK–Hungary 1987   630, 645, 648
UK–Indonesia 1976   641
UK–Malaysia 1981   641
UK–Papua New Guinea 1981   643
UK–People's Republic of China 1986   570, 631
UK–Philippines 1980   624, 629, 641, 642, 644, 645, 646
UK–St Lucia 1983   572
UK–Sri Lanka 1980   647
UK–Thailand 1979   644
USA–Egypt 1982   632, 641
USA–Egypt 1986 Protocol   641
USA–Panama 1982   632
USA–Russian Federation 1992   621, 641, 648
USA–Senegal 1983   571

Publications of Governments and International Organizations

Governments

Canada

Government of Canada Task Force Report: Foreign Ownership and the Structure of Canadian Industry (Ottawa, 1968)   218

Eleventh Report of the Standing Committee on External Affairs and National Defence Respecting Canada US Relations (28th Parl. 2d Sess, s. 3.01, 1970)   218

Foreign Direct Investment in Canada (Ottawa, Information Canada, 1972)   218

India

Press Information Bureau Government of India: Press Release of 24 July 1991 'New Industrial Policy Announced' reproduced in UNCTC Foreign Direct Investment and Technology Transfer in India (UN Doc. ST/CTC/117, 1992) Annex VII, p. 128   180, 209, 448, 454

Indonesia

Government Policy Statement of 22 January 1974   185

Ireland

Industrial Development Authority: Guide to Tax and Tax Reliefs in Ireland (1991)   262

Japan

Executive Office, Fair Trade Commission: The Antimonopoly Act Guidelines Concerning Distribution Systems and Business Practices (July 1991)   86, 389

Nigeria

Federal Ministry of Industries: Industrial Policy of Nigeria (1989)   207

Poland

Grounds of Justification for the Bill on Enterprises with Foreign Participation (22 February 1991)   212

Privatization in Poland: Program, Achievements and Foreign Investment Policy (Ministry of Ownership Changes, 1991)   213

Singapore
Singapore International Chamber of Commerce Investors Guide to the Economic Climate of Singapore (published annually)   263

United Kingdom
Department of Trade and Industry: Company Law Harmonisation (March 1993)   86, 375

Foreign and Commonwealth Office: Report on the Supply of Petroleum and Petroleum Products to Rhodesia (London, HMSO, 1978)   17

Inland Revenue: Unitary Tax: Review of Progress Towards Resolving the Issues (1991)   319

Inquiry into the Supervision of the Bank of Credit and Commerce International (Chairman Rt Hon. Bingham LJ, 22 October 1992)   168

Treasury and Civil Service Committee of the House of Commons Fourth Report: Banking Supervision and BCCI: International and National Regulation (HC Paper 177 1991–2)   168

United States of America
US Congress Senate Sub-Committee on Multinationals: Hearings on Multinational Corporations and US Foreign Policy 93rd Congress Second Session (1974)   17

US Department of Justice Antitrust Division: Antitrust Enforcement Guidelines for International Operations (1988)   126, 158, 161, 392, 411, 415, 417, 418

US Department of Justice Antitrust Division: Policy Statement of 3 April 1992: Press Release 92–117   389

US Department of Justice Antitrust Division: Horizontal Merger Guidelines (4 Trade Reg.Rep.(CCH) s. 13,104, 1992)   417
  ss 0.1, 1, 2, 3   419
  s. 4   419

US Department of Justice Antitrust Division/Federal Trade Commission: Draft Antitrust Enforcement Guidelines for International Operations (13 October 1994) Trade Regulation Reports No. 338, part 2, p. 37   158, 161, 162, 412, 414, 415, 418, 451

US Treasury Department: a Study of Intercompany Pricing under s. 482 of the Code (IRS Notice 88–123, 1988–2 CB 458)   291–2

International Organizations

General Agreement on Tariffs and Trade: the Uruguay Round
1986   Punta Del Este Declaration   250, 252, 255, 257

1988–9   Decisions Adopted at Mid-Term Review of Uruguay Round: 28 ILM 1023 (1989)   251, 255

1992   GATT Secretary-General: Draft Final Act of the Uruguay Round (GATT Doc. MTN.TNC/W/FA)   251

1994   The Final Act of the Uruguay Round Negotiations under GATT (GATT Doc. MTN/FA 15 December 1993) extracts in 33 ILM 1 (1994) and 33 ILM 1125 (1994) for agreements signed at Marrakesh, 15 April 1994   112, 181, 238, 251
  General Agreement on Trade in Sevices (GATS): 33 ILM 44 (1994), 33 ILM 1167 (1994)   113, 203, 252–4, 273

Arts I, XXVIII(d)   252
Arts II, III, VII, VIII, XIV, XIVbis   253–4
Art. XVI   252–3
Art. XVII   253
Art. XX   253

Agreement on Trade Related Intellectual Property Measures (TRIPs): 33 ILM 81 (1994), 33 ILM 1197 (1994)   113, 203, 255–7, 440, 441, 449

Arts 3, 4   256, 275
Art. 27(1)   275
Art. 40(2)   256
Arts 66, 67, 5   256

Agreement on Trade Related Investment Measures (TRIMS)   113, 203, 260

Arts 2, 4, 7   276

Agreement on the World Trade Organization (WTO): 33 ILM 13 (1994), 33 ILM 1144 (1994)   113, 256, 275, 461, 475

International Bank for Reconstruction and Development (IBRD or World Bank)

ICSID

Convention for the Settlement of Investment Disputes(ICSID) 4 ILM 524 (1965); 575 UNTS 159   113, 190, 243, 518, 528, 534, 541

Art. 6   564
Art. 14   565
Art. 25(1)   542, 543–4, 546, 555
(2)(a)   566
(2)(b)   544–5, 622, 623
(3)   544, 566
(4)   543, 547, 566
Art. 26   547–9, 565
Art. 27   547, 551
Arts 28–35   564
Arts 28–41   569–70
Art. 42   509, 555
(1)   549–51
(3)   510
Art. 45   570
Art. 47   549
Arts 48–49   570
Art. 52(1)   551–2
Art. 53   565
Art. 54   551, 553, 565
(2),(3)   569
Art. 55   569
Arts 59–61   570
Arts 68, 70, 73   566

Additional Facility for the Administration of Conciliation, Arbitration and Fact-Finding Proceedings (ICSID/11 June 1979)   564

MIGA
Convention Establishing Multilateral Investment Guarantee Agency (MIGA):
   24 ILM 1598–1638 (1985)   113, 515–19
      Arts 2–12(a)   532
      Art. 12(c)   518
      Art. 12(d)   602
      Arts 13–22, 58   532–3
      Art. 23(a)   616
      Art. 23(b)(ii)   603
MIGA Operational Regulations: 28 ILM 1227 (1988)   516, 532–3, 603
   para. 3.16   602
   paras 3.17, 3.33   616
MIGA Standard Contract of Guarantee and General Conditions of Guarantee
   for Equity Investments: 28 ILM 1233 (1989)   532

GUIDELINES ON FOREIGN INVESTMENT
Guidelines on the Treatment of Foreign Investment 1992: 31 ILM 1363 (1992)
   113, 120, 598–602, 603, 604, 614
      Guideline I (Relation to Existing Treaties)   599
      Guideline II (Entry and Establishment)   599
      Guideline III (Treatment of Foreign Investors)   599–600
      Guideline IV (Expropriation and Renegotiation)   600
      Guideline V (Dispute Settlement)   601

REPORTS
Annual Report 1983   88
Foreign Direct Investment in the States of the Former USSR (Washington DC,
   1992)   190, 216

International Labour Organisation
ILO Constitution Art. 3(5)   481

CONVENTIONS
No. 87 (Freedom of Association)   460
No. 98 (Right to Organise and Bargain Collectively)   460, 476
No. 111 (Discrimination in Employment)   460
No. 122 (Employment Policy)   460
No. 139 (Occupational Hazards)   475
No. 156 (Equal Opportunities and Equal Treatment)   483

TRIPARTITE DECLARATION
Tripartite Declaration of Principles Concerning Multinational Enterprises and
   Social Policy: 17 ILM 422 (1978)   457–92, 578, 590
      paras 1–12 (General Policies)   459–61, 482
      paras 13–23 (Employment)   461–3, 482–3
      paras 24–8 (Employment Security)   464–5, 483
      paras 29–31 (Training)   466–7, 485
      paras 33–5 (Wages, Benefits and Conditions of Work)   467, 485
      paras 36–9 (Safety and Health)   469–70, 486
      paras 40–57 (Industrial Relations)   470–80, 487–90

l   Governments and International Organizations

REPORTS

Recent Foreign Direct Investment in Eastern Europe: towards a Possible Role
   for the Tripartite Declaration of Principles Concerning Multinational Enter-
   prises and Social Policy (Geneva, 1991)   488
Safety and Health Practices of Multinational Enterprises (Geneva, 1984)   486
Women Workers in Multinational Corporations in Developing Countries
   (Geneva, 1985)   265
World Labour Report 1992   487, 490
World Labour Report 1993   487, 488

Organization for Economic Cooperation and Development

GENERAL

Draft Convention on the Protection of Foreign Owned Property: OECD Publi-
   cation No. 1563[6]7/Dec. 1962 reproduced 1–2 ILM 241 (1962–3); last
   revision OECD Publication No. 322081/Nov. 1967 reproduced 7 ILM 117
   (1968)   574
International Direct Investment – Policies and Trends in the 1980s (Paris, 1992)
   51
Minimizing Conflicting Requirements: Approaches of Moderation and Restraint
   (Paris, 1987)   171
Recent Trends in International Direct Investment (Paris, 1987)   52
Responsibility of Parent Companies for Their Subsidiaries (Paris, 1980)   342
Structure and Organization of Multinational Enterprises (Paris, 1987)   60,
   83–4, 341

CODES OF LIBERALIZATION

Code of Liberalization of Capital Movements 1961 (Paris, 1992)   103, 176,
   203, 238, 248–50, 586
Code of Liberalization of Current Invisibles 1961 (Paris, 1992)   238, 248–50,
   272
Introduction to the OECD Codes of Liberalization (Paris, 1987)   272
Liberalization of Capital Movements and Financial Services in the OECD Area
   (Paris, 1990)   272

GUIDELINES ON MULTINATIONAL ENTERPRISES

Multinational Enterprises and Disclosure of Information: Clarification of the
   OECD Guidelines (Paris, 1988)   373
National Treatment for Foreign-controlled Enterprises (Paris, 1985)   584–5
OECD Guidelines For Multinational Enterprises 21 June 1976: 15 ILM 961
   (1976), or OECD Guidelines 1991 Review (Paris, 1992), or OECD Guidelines for Multinational Enterprises (Paris, 1994)   13, 18, 95, 113, 116, 171,
   482, 484, 578–92, 604
National Treatment Declaration   583
   Introduction
   para. 6   580
   para. 7   580–1
   para. 8   581
   para. 9   610
   para. 10   610

Guideline on General Policies   461, 588
Guideline on Competition   589
Guideline on Disclosure   477, 582, 589
Guideline on Employment   457, 459, 463, 464, 466, 470, 471, 476, 478, 479, 484, 490, 590
Guideline on Environmental Protection   118, 467, 590
Guideline on Financing   589
Guideline on Science and Technology   590
Guideline on Taxation   589
Second Revised Council Decision on the Guidelines   587–8
Third Revised Council Decision on National Treatment   584
Council Decision on Investment Incentives and Disincentives   591
OECD Guidelines 1979 Review (Paris, 1979) reproduced 18 ILM 986 (1979) 482, 580, 591, 608, 610, 611
OECD Guidelines 1984 Review (Paris, 1984)   581, 611
OECD Guidelines 1986 Review (Paris, 1986)   482, 489, 490, 608, 610
OECD Guidelines 1991 Review (Paris, 1992)   608, 610, 611

RESTRICTIVE BUSINESS PRACTICES
'Restrictive Business Practices of Multinational Enterprises': Report of the Committee of Experts on Restrictive Business Practices (1977)   403, 422
OECD Council Recommendation Concerning Cooperation Between Member Countries on Restricitve Business Practices Affecting International Trade of 21 May 1986 25 ILM 1629 (1986)   169

TAXATION
Issues in International Taxation No. I International Tax Avoidance and Evasion (Paris, 1987)   309, 316, 320–1
OECD Committee on Fiscal Affairs: The US Proposed Regulations Dealing with Tax Aspects of Transfer Pricing Within Multinational Enterprises (10 January 1993)   294
OECD Model Tax Convention on Income and Capital (1992)   280, 288, 297, 308
    Art. 9   311
    Art. 9(2)   297–8, 316–17
    Art. 26   316
Taxation and International Capital Flows (Paris, 1990)   309
Thin Capitalization (Paris, 1987)   310
Transfer Pricing and Multinational Enterprises (1979)(New draft in preparation)   289, 303, 310, 311, 319
Transfer Pricing and Multinational Enterprises: Three Taxation Issues (1984) 311

United Nations

UNITED NATIONS CENTRE FOR TRANSNATIONAL CORPORATIONS/
TRANSNATIONAL CORPORATIONS MANAGEMENT DIVISION
An Evaluation of Export Processing Zones in Selected Asian Countries (1985, UN Doc. ST/ESCAP/395)   234, 263
Bilateral Investment Treaties (1988, UN Doc. ST/CTC/65)   639ff

Conclusions on Accounting and Reporting by Transnational Corporations (1988, UN Doc. ST/CTC/92), revised edition 1994 (UN Doc. UNCTAD/DTCI/1)   354, 367, 377, 380

Environmental Activities of Transnational Corporations: a Survey (1985)   118

Intellectual Property Rights and Foreign Direct Investment (1993, UN Doc. ST/CTC/SER.A/24)   441

International Accounting and Reporting Issues 1991 Review (UN, New York, 1992, UN Doc. ST/CTC/124)   377

International Standards of Accounting and Reporting for Transnational Corporations (1977, UN Doc. E/C.10/33, 18 October)   361-2, 373

Joint Ventures as a Form of International Economic Co-operation (1988, Doc. ST/CTC/93)   210

National Legislation and Regulations Relating to Transnational Corporations: a Technical Paper (1983, Doc. ST/CTC/35)   210, 218

National Legislation and Regulations Relating to Transnational Corporations: Volume IV (1986, Doc. ST/CTC/53)   211

National Legislation and Regulations Relating to Transnational Corporations: Volume VI (1988, Doc. ST/CTC/71)   218

National Legislation and Regulations Relating to Transnational Corporations: Volume VII (1989, Doc. ST/CTC/91)   217, 262

The New Code Environment (1990, UNCTC Current Studies Series A No. 16. UN Doc. ST/CTC/SER.A/16)   520, 596, 614

The Process of Transnationalization and Transnational Mergers (1989, UN Doc. ST/CTC/SER.A/8)   400, 417, 420

Towards International Standardization of Corporate Accounting and Reporting (1982)   380

Transnational Corporations and Industrial Hazard Disclosure (1991, UN Doc. ST/CTC/111)   383

Transnational Corporations, Services and the Uruguay Round (1990, UN Doc. ST/CTC/103)   273, 613

Transnational Corporations in World Development Trends and Prospects (1988, UN Doc. ST/CTC/89)   51, 118, 209, 215, 265

UNITED NATIONS COMMISSION ON TRANSNATIONAL CORPORATIONS

Draft UN Code of Conduct on TNCs (UN Doc. E/1990/94 of 12 June 1990)   10, 11, 14, 18, 103, 116, 373, 578, 592-6, 604, 613

Transnational Corporations in World Development: a Re-examination (1978)   17

USSR: New Management Mechanism in Foreign Economic Relations (UNCTAD/ST/TSC/10, 2 October 1987)   215

GENERAL ASSEMBLY RESOLUTIONS

Res. 1803 14 December 1962, 17 GAOR Supp. 17, p. 15 (1962)   530

Res. 3171 (XXVIII) GAOR 28th Sess. Supp. 30, p. 52 (1973)   525

Resolutions on the New International Economic Order: Res. 3201 (S-VI) 9 May 1974 The Declaration on the Establishment of the New International Economic Order; Res. 3202 (S-IV) of 16 May 1974 The Programme of Action on the Establishment of the New International Economic Order: 13 ILM 715-

766 (1974) 16, 525

Res. 3281 (XXIX) 15 January 1975 The Charter on the Economic Rights and
Duties of States: 14 (1975) ILM 251 16

Art. 2 612

Art. 2(2)(c) 524

UNITED NATIONS COMMISSION ON INTERNATIONAL TRADE LAW
(UNCITRAL)

Arbitration Rules 1976 243, 539, 563

Conciliation Rules 1980 539, 563

Model Law on International Commercial Arbitration 1985 540, 563

UNITED NATIONS CONFERENCE ON TRADE AND DEVELOPMENT
(UNCTAD)

'Concentration of Market Power Through Mergers, Takeovers, Joint Ventures
and Other Acquisitions of Control and its Effects on International Markets, in
Particular the Markets of Developing Countries' (UN Doc. TD/B/RBP/80, 22
August 1991; revised UN Doc. TD/RBP/80/Rev. 2) 417

Draft Code on Technology Transfer (as at closure of 6th Sess. of UN
Conference on an International Code of Conduct on Transfer of Technology): TD/CODE TOT/47, 20 June 1985 256, 425, 426, 444–6, 578

Chapter 1, paras 1.2, 1.3 449

Chapter 4 445

Chapter 9 445

Draft Code on Technology Transfer: Consultations of 1992 (TD/CODE TOT/
58, 22 October 1992) 448

Draft Model Law on Restrictive Business Practices (UNCTAD Doc. TD/B/
RBP/81, 12 August 1991) 422

Export Processing Free Zones of Sub-Saharan Africa (UNCTAD/ECDC/225,
1992) 264

Set of Principles for the Control of Restrictive Business Practices (UNCTAD
Doc. TD/RBP/CONF/10 Annex; UN Doc. A/C 2/35/6 of 23 October 1980,
Annex. TD/RBP/CONF/10/Rev. 1 1981): 19 ILM 813 (1980) 404, 422,
578

The Role of the Patent System in the Transfer of Technology to Developing
Countries (UN Doc. TD/B/AC 11/19, 1974) 439, 440

The Role of Trademarks in Developing Countries (UN Doc. TD/B/AC.3/3 Rev.
1, 1979) 439

World Investment Report 1993: Transnational Corporations and Integrated
International Production (1993) 52

World Investment Report 1994: Transnational Corporations, Employment and
the Workplace (1994) 52, 483

UNITED NATIONS REPORTS

Report of the Group of Eminent Persons to Study the Role of Multinational
Corporations on Development and International Relations (1974): 13 ILM
800 (1974) 5–6, 13, 16, 17

Report of the Secretary-General on Accounting for Environmental Protection
Measures (UN Doc. E/C.10/AC.3/1991/5, 11 February 1991) 369–71

Report of the Secretary-General: 'The Role of Patents in the Transfer of

Technology to Developing Countries' (UN Doc. E/3681/Rev. 1, 1964) 438

Report of UN Secretary-General: 'Transnational Corporations in the New World Economy: Issues and Policy Implications' (UN Doc. E/C.10/1992/5, 5 February 1992)   614

Preface and Acknowledgements

This book seeks to give a comprehensive introduction to the regulation of multinational enterprises (MNEs) as the principal vehicles for foreign direct investment.[1] The question of how states should respond to MNEs was first placed on the post-war political agenda in the late 1960s. Although there are numerous historical instances of concern over 'international combines',[2] the contemporary debate on MNEs has acquired a far greater political importance, for reasons that will be explored in chapter 1. This has resulted in systematic policy responses to such enterprises. It is the purpose of this book to trace the evolution of these responses since the 1960s and to highlight the considerable changes in approach to MNE regulation over the past 30 years. As such the book constitutes a study of evolution and change in international business regulation. Naturally, a book of this size cannot act as an encyclopedia of the law relating to foreign direct investment.[3] It can do no more than familiarize the reader with the principal issues and methods of MNE regulation that human endeavour has so far created. The book suggests some possible future developments in this area, but, as a result of the uncertainty that global economic and political change has generated in recent years, this aspect of the work is approached with some caution. The primary focus of the book is legal. In particular, part II sets out a relatively detailed account of the principal techniques of MNE regulation used by home and host states, while part III considers the emerging responses of international law to this type of business association. However, the book would lack coherence if it were restricted to a description of legal sources and did not relate them to the existing knowledge, possessed by other social sciences, of MNEs and their activities. Indeed, if one were to look at legal sources alone the MNE would not exist: all one would find is a series of national companies whose principal shareholder happens to be a foreign company, and/or a network of interlocking contracts between entities of different nationalities. No hint of the complex systems of international managerial control, through which the operations of the multinational group are conducted, would be discovered. Furthermore, in the absence of an interdisciplinary framework, the aims and objectives of the various legal responses to MNEs could not be properly understood. Their meaning, let alone their efficacy, could not be determined. Therefore, part I of this book is devoted to relating the knowledge of other disciplines about MNEs to the concerns of lawyers. Thereby, it is hoped to build a bridge between law and other disciplines involved in the study of MNEs, from which a valuable mutual discourse could ensue.

A book that seeks to offer an introduction to so wide-ranging a topic could not have been written without the help of others. In particular, I would like to acknowledge the assistance, over the past ten years, of my external examiners on the London University LLM course 'Multinational (Transnational) Enterprises and the Law', from which this book has evolved. They are, in chronological order, Professor Tom Hadden of Queens University of Belfast, Dr Tony Carty of Glasgow University and Professor Sol Picciotto, formerly of the University of Warwick, now of the University of Lancaster. Each has provided me with important and constructive comments upon my course and upon the ideas that I have been developing. Furthermore, each has, in turn, provided me with the opportunity to test certain thoughts and draft chapters upon audiences at their respective home universities, or at conferences organized by them. The feedback from these expositions has proved to be very valuable. In addition I would like to express my thanks to Professor William E. Butler of University College London for giving me the opportunity to present earlier drafts of chapters 15 and 17 at successive sessions of the Anglo-Soviet Symposium on Public International Law in 1990 and 1991. Again the feedback was of great value.

Furthermore, special thanks must be given to Tom Hadden for reading and commenting upon the drafts of chapters 1 to 5 and 9. Thanks are also due to the following colleagues at LSE, who have allowed me to benefit from their expertise in comments offered upon drafts of individual chapters: Professor Rosalyn Higgins QC, who read and commented upon the international legal aspects of the book; Professor Lord Wedderburn of Charlton QC, who gave me considerable assistance with and important reflections upon chapter 13; Professor Anthony Hopwood, who offered me the benefit of his expertise in international accounting by reviewing chapter 10; Professor Tom Nossiter, who read and commented upon an earlier draft of chapter 4; and Judith Freedman, who offered a valuable critique of an earlier draft of chapter 9. Naturally, I remain solely responsible for any errors that remain.

Thanks are also due to the numerous research assistants who have helped me over the years to track down materials and references. Foremost among them is my research student Amazu Asouzu, who has offered invaluable help in reading the entire draft of the manuscript, commenting critically upon my ideas, and updating and completing references. Others who have given much help include: Ruth Gordon, Elizabeth Small, Richard Pailthorpe, Matthew Logan, Tee Golvala, Deshpal Singh Panesar and Nicholas White. I would further like to thank all my students on the 'Multinationals' course who have, over the years, discussed my thoughts in class, given me important materials and subsequently corresponded with me over developments in their respective home jurisdictions. Indeed, I would like to acknowledge my debt to the LSE for providing me with a stimulating academic environment in which to bring this project to a successful conclusion. I would like to offer further thanks to the LSE Research Fund, which has supplied much of the funding for research assistance, and to the Nuffield Foundation, whose generous grant ensured that I could benefit from research assistance above and beyond the limits of in-house funding, and allowed me to defray many of the costs of preparing the manuscript. A final word of acknowledgement is due to my former employer and former colleagues at the University of Kent at Canterbury, where the first seeds for a book on the regulation of multinationals were sown, and where the first prototype for my course on multinationals was approved and tested.

I have endeavoured to state the law accurately as at 1 July 1994, but it has been possible to include some developments up to 14 October 1994, and some recent minor amendments in the paperback edition.

P. T. Muchlinski

Notes
1 Foreign direct investment is defined as follows by Professor J. H. Dunning: '(1) The investment is made *outside* the home country of the investing company, but *inside* the investing company. Control over the use of the resources transferred remains with the *investor*. (2) It consists of a "package" of assets and intermediate products, such as capital, technology, management skills, access to markets and entrepreneurship.' See J. H. Dunning, *Multinational Enterprises and the Global Economy* (Addison Wesley, 1992), p. 5, exhibit 1.2.
2 See, for example, Anthony Sampson *The Arms Bazaar* (Coronet, 1991), chapters 3 and 4, on the international arms industry. The writings of early Marxists concentrate on 'international combines': see text and references in chapter 4 at notes 22 and 23.
3 The principal collection of this kind is the World Bank publication, *Foreign Investment Laws of the World* (IBRD/Oceana, periodically updated).

Abbreviations

A	Atlantic Reporter
A. U. J. Int'l L. & Pol.	American University Journal of International Law and Policy
AC	Law Reports Appeal Cases
AFDI	Annuaire Français du Droit International
AIR	All India Reporter
AJIL	American Journal Of International Law
ALJ	Australian Law Journal
ALJR	Australian Law Journal Reports
All ER	All England Law Reports
Alta L. Rev.	Alberta Law Review
Am. J. Comp. L.	American Journal of Comparative Law
Am. J. Econ. & Soc.	American Journal of Economics and Sociology
Arb. Int'l	Arbitration International
Arb. J.	Arbitration Journal
ASIL Proc.	American Society of International Law Proceedings
BCLC	Butterworths Company Law Cases
BGHZ	Bundesgerichthofszeitung
BIFD	Bulletin for International Fiscal Documentation
Brit. J. Ind. Rel.	British Journal of Industrial Relations
Brit. J. Int. Stud.	British Journal of International Studies
Bus. Hist. Rev.	Business History Review
Bus. Law.	Business Lawyer
BYIL	British Yearbook of International Law
Cal. App. 3d	California Appeal Cases Third Series

Can. Bar Rev.	Canadian Bar Review
Can. Bus. LJ	Canadian Business Law Journal
Ch	Law Reports Chancery Division
Cmd	Command Paper
CML Rev.	Common Market Law Review
CMLR	Common Market Law Reports
Cmnd	Command Paper
Co. Law.	Company Lawyer
Col. J. Transnat. L.	Columbia Journal of Transnational Law
Col. J. World Bus.	Columbia Journal of World Business
Col. LR	Columbia Law Review
Cornell Int'l L. J.	Cornell International Law Journal
Cr. App. R.	Criminal Appeal Reports
Del. J. Corp. L.	Delaware Journal of Corporate Law
DLR 3d	Dominion Law Reports Third Series
Duke LJ	Duke Law Journal
ECLR	European Competition Law Review
Econ. J.	Economic Journal
ECR	European Court Reports
ELR	European Law Review
F. 2d	Federal Reporter Second Series
F. Supp.	Federal Supplement
Fed. Reg.	Federal Register
Fordham L. Rev.	Fordham Law Review
Ga JIL	Georgia Journal of International Law
Geo. Washington J. Int'l Law & Econ.	George Washington Journal of International Law and Economics
Hague Recueil	Proceedings of the Hague Academy of International Law
Harv. ILJ	Harvard International Law Journal
Harv. LR	Harvard Law Review
Hastings Int'l & Comp. L. Rev.	Hastings International and Comparative Law Review
HMSO	Her Majesty's Stationery Office
ICCLR	International Company and Commercial law Review
ICJ Reports	International Court of Justice Reports
ICLQ	International and Comparative Law Quarterly
ICSID Rev-FILJ	ICSID Review-Foreign Investment Law Journal
IIC	International Review of Industrial Property and Copyright Law
ILJ	Industrial Law Journal
ILM	International Legal Materials

ILR	International Law Reports
Ind. ILJ	Indian Journal of International Law
Int'l Bus. Lawyer	International Business Lawyer
Int'l J. Acctg	International Journal of Accounting
Int'l J. Soc. L.	International Journal of the Sociology of Law
Int'l Lab. Rev.	International Labour Review
Int. Org.	International Organization
Iran-US CTR	Iran-United States Claims Tribunal Reports
Israel LR	Israel Law Review
JBL	Journal of Business Law
JDI	Journal du Droit International
J. Ind. Rel.	Journal of Industrial Relations
J. Int'l Arb.	Journal of International Arbitration
J. Int'l Bus. Stud.	Journal of International Business Studies
J. Int'l Law & Econ.	Journal of International Law and Economics
J. Mart. L. & Comm.	Journal of Maritime Law and Commerce
J. Pol. Econ.	Journal of Political Economy
JWTL (JWT)	Journal of World Trade Law (now Journal of World Trade)
Law & Pol. Int'l Bus.	Law and Policy in International Business
Law and Cont. Prob.	Law and Contemporary Problems
Law. Am.	Lawyer of the Americas
Lloyds Rep.	Lloyds Law Reports
LQR	Law Quarterly Review
McGill LJ	McGill Law Journal
Mich. L. Rev.	Michigan Law Review
MLR	Modern Law Review
NCJ Int'l & Com. Reg.	North Carolina Journal of International and Commercial Regulation
NE 2d	North Eastern Reporter Second Series
NJW	Neue Juristische Wochenschrift
NR	Northern Reporter
NW J. Int'l Law & Bus.	Northwestern Journal of International Law and Business
NY 2d	New York Reporter Second Series
NYLJ	New York Law Journal
NYS 2d	New York Supplement Second Series
NYUJ Int'l Law and Pol.	New York University Journal of International Law and Policy
NYULQR	New York University Law Quarterly

	Review
NYULR	New York University Law Review
NZCLC	New Zealand Company Law Cases
OJ	Official Journal of the European Communities
OJ Sp. Ed.	Official Journal of the European Communities Special Edition
Oxford Bull. Econ. & Stat.	Oxford Bulletin of Economics and Statistics
P & CR	Property and Conveyancing Reports
P 2d	Pacific Reporter Second Series
Pol. Sci. Q.	Political Science Quarterly
Q. J. Econ.	Quarterly Journal of Economics
QB (KB)	Law Reports Queens (Kings) Bench
RADIC	African Journal of International and Comparative Law
Rutgers LR	Rutgers Law Review
SE 2d	South Eastern Reporter Second Series
SI	United Kingdom Statutory Instrument
SO 2d	Southern Reporter Second Series
SW 2d	South Western Reporter Second Series
Tax Notes Int'l	Tax Notes International
TC	Tax Cases
Texas ILJ	Texas International Law Journal
TMR	Trade Mark Review
Trade Reg. Rep.	Trade Regulation Reports
Trans. Grot. Soc.	Transactions of the Grotius Society
U. Brit. Col. LR	University of British Columbia Law Review
U. Chi. L. Rev.	University of Chicago Law Review
UKTS	United Kingdom Treaty Series
U. Miami Inter-Am. L. Rev.	University of Miami Inter-American Law Review
U. Miami L. Rev.	University of Miami Law Review
UNCTAD Rev.	UNCTAD Review
UNSWLJ	University of New South Wales Law Journal
UNTS	United Nations Treaty Series
US or S. Ct	United States Supreme Court Reports
USC	United States Code
USLW	United States Law Week
UST	United States Treaty Series
U. Toronto LJ	University of Toronto Law Journal
Va. J. Int'l L.	Virginia Journal of International Law

Vanderbilt J. Transnat. Law	Vanderbilt Journal of Transnational Law
WLR	Weekly Law Reports
Yale LJ	Yale Law Journal
YB Comm. Arb.	Yearbook of Commercial Arbitration
YBILC	Yearbook of the International Law Commission

Part I

The Conceptual Framework

1

Concern over Multinational Enterprises

Analysis of the regulation of multinational enterprises (MNEs) demands some initial scene-setting. The question of why regulation should be deemed necessary must be posed. This is best done, first, by reviewing the origins of post-war concern over MNEs. Secondly, these original concerns must be placed in their contemporary setting, as a prelude to the subject matter of this work. Thirdly, the evolving meanings given to the phrase 'multinational enterprise' should be considered, partly to satisfy the lawyer's preoccupation with definitions, but mainly to show that the concept possesses an openness and flexibility that makes it capable of covering numerous and diverse forms of international business association.

1 The Origins of Post-war Political Concern over MNEs

The origins of post-war concern over MNEs lie with specific economic, political and intellectual trends and with a growing awareness of the potential power of MNEs, as illustrated by certain sensational cases of its abuse. These trends in events and ideas created a climate which, by the early 1970s, firmly established the 'MNE issue' as a component of contemporary political debate and led to policy responses, most visibly on the international level.

1.1 The Attitudes of Countries and Regions
The physical embodiment of the modern 'MNE problem' can be traced to the rapid spread of US enterprises throughout the world since the Second World War.[1] By the 1960s a feeling gradually developed, particularly among the Europeans, that US economic power constituted a threat. This sense of unease was in part illustrated, and in part generated, by the publication in 1967 of Jean Servan-Schreiber's book *The American Challenge*.[2] The author argued

that European industry was in danger of being swamped by the overwhelming presence of US firms in the European market, particularly in crucial high technology industries. His solution was that the EEC (as it then was) should adopt a vigorous European merger policy aimed at creating European enterprises of sufficient size to be capable of matching the market power of their US competitors. Thus, US capital and business, having played a major role in the regeneration of the post-war European economy, could now hamper European economic success. US MNEs, as visible instruments of US competition, might have to be contained through the use of supranational regulation favourable to European firms.

By contrast, Japanese fears concerning MNEs did not evolve in quite the same way. The post-war Japanese economy revived behind protective trade barriers and a highly restrictive policy on inward foreign investment. Robert Gilpin explains this as the trade-off for assured US military bases on Japanese soil.[3] Thus there was no highly visible US corporate presence in Japan, although considerable US capital and know-how was brought in to revive Japanese firms, mainly in the form of loans and licensing contracts. However, by the mid-1960s, the Organization for Economic Cooperation and Development (OECD) and the USA began to prod Japan into relaxing its restrictions on direct foreign investment so as to counterbalance the large Japanese surplus in foreign trade. At the same time there were pressures from the Japanese business community to relax investment controls so as to ensure continued access to technology and export markets, to maintain the competitive edge of Japanese firms and to benefit consumers. However, the pressures towards liberalization were resisted by the state bureaucracy and by industry groups that would suffer in the short term from increased foreign competition. Among their concerns were the effect of foreign MNEs on the survival of smaller, less technologically advanced, national firms, and upon the sovereignty of Japan in national economic planning. Thus in the mid-1960s, according to Yoshino, 'the liberalization of foreign direct investment policy touched off intense debates both within the government bureaucracy and the business community. In fact, it had become a major national issue.'[4] The outcome was an easing, from 1967, of Japan's very restrictive foreign investment laws.[5]

Japanese and European concern about foreign (mainly US) MNEs in the 1960s was matched in the early 1970s by US manufacturers' concern over the competitive threat from foreign firms importing into the US domestic market, and by the fears of US labour that the growing internationalization of production by US MNEs would threaten the security of US jobs. Thus, even in the home country of the major MNEs, fear was growing as to the economic effects of large globally oriented firms. This led to moves within the USA to control the overseas investment of US firms, and the import of goods manufactured abroad. The trend culminated with the Burke–Hartke Bill of 1972. That measure included tax and tariff provisions which, it was hoped, would induce US firms to avoid relocating production in low-wage foreign economies, discourage the deferment of dividend remittances by US firms from their foreign operations and impose quotas on imports into the USA from foreign firms.[6] Although the Bill never became law, the policies that it represented have resurfaced from time to time in subsequent political debate, resulting in occasional import controls. However, at no time since Burke–Hartke has US law restricted the flow of outward investment from the country, or of inward investment into the country, save in a few strategic sectors of industry and on specific national security grounds.[7]

In the southern hemisphere, concern over MNEs took on a different economic and political character. Between 1945 and 1975 the old overseas colonies of the major European powers (including Britain, France, the Netherlands, Belgium, Spain and Portugal) were granted independence. This had a number of political and economic effects. First, the political sphere of influence of the old metropolitan powers diminished. At the same time the economic influence of these powers upon the newly independent states continued.[8] This was interpreted by many of these states as evidence of continuing economic imperialism conducted not by colonial administrators but by private firms.[9] Secondly, the newly independent states gained a voting majority in the United Nations, where they became an important pressure group, the so-called 'Group of 77.'[10] That group, supported by the then communist Eastern Bloc states, ensured that the UN would place the interests of the newly independent states at the head of its economic and social agenda. This resulted in the development of the concept of a New International Economic Order (NIEO),[11] and of the 'right to economic self-determination' which demanded the attainment of economic independence as a necessary aspect of political independence.[12]

This movement generated concern over the effects of MNEs upon the economic development of the newly independent and mostly less developed states, known collectively as the less developed countries (LDCs). The UN Secretary General was persuaded to set up a Group of Eminent Persons to study the role of MNEs on development and international relations. The Group reported on 24 May 1974.[13] The Group's report helped to lay down not only immediate UN policy in the field of MNEs, but also what could be described as the 'conventional framework' of issues generated by MNEs in their relations with developing countries. As regards the former, the

Group recommended the setting up of a UN Commission on Multi-national Corporations and a UN Centre on Multinational Corporations to oversee and develop UN policy in this area. These bodies were soon renamed the UN Commission on Transnational Corporations and UN Centre on Transnational Corporations (UNCTC), taking account of UN terminological changes in this field, which are discussed below. In 1992, the UNCTC was reorganized and re-named as the Transnational Corporations Management Division (TCMD), one of eight divisions of the United Nations Department of Economic and Social Development.

In relation to the principal substantive issues, the Group adopted a philosophy that was not opposed to investment by MNEs in LDCs, but that required the regulation of MNEs so that they could become instruments of LDC development. The vision was one of a cooperative, rather than a conflictual, relationship, coupled, however, with a recognition that powerful foreign firms could act in an abusive manner towards a developing host state. To that extent they had to be controlled. In particular, the Group accepted that the global organization, size and technological superiority of the MNE could threaten the sovereignty of the host state through the ability of the MNE to evade national regulation and taxation, to abuse its competitive power by distorting market conditions and to exploit the lack of technological know-how of the host where the latter needed modern technology to ensure the growth of its economy. Furthermore, certain undesirable non-economic abuses were singled out for control. These included subversive political intervention in the host state, the introduction of alien cultural values and lifestyles and the generation of intergovernmental confrontations between home and host states. All these abuses were to be controlled through national regulation backed up by international controls, based on the contents of an internationally agreed code of conduct. This would lay down clearly what MNEs could and could not do, and also the principles upon which the host country should formulate its policy towards MNEs.[14]

1.2   Sensational Abuses of Corporate Power by MNEs
Underlying these developments was the concern generated by revelations of sensational abuses of international corporate power by US firms. The most prominent of these was the involvement of ITT in US plans to overthrow the government of Salvador Allende in Chile,[15] and the efforts of US copper companies, nationalized by his government, to hinder Chile's economic planning through a campaign of economic disruption.[16] The Chilean case was closely examined by the US Senate Sub-Committee on Multinationals.[17] Its investigations confirmed the fears of those who believed that US

corporations were a threat to the sovereignty of host states. The Chilean investigations were followed by hearings concerning alleged corruption on the part of US firms operating abroad, particularly in the arms industry.[18] The findings of these hearings reinforced the view that US business abroad was a power that had to be controlled, and that the USA itself had a duty to check abuses by its own corporations. This resulted in the passage of the Foreign Corrupt Business Practices Act in 1977.

A climate of suspicion began to surround the operations of MNEs. Further anecdotes and verified instances of abuse continued to emerge from the USA and other countries.[19] The MNE began to be described as a challenge to the nation state, a creature with no loyalties except to itself, an entity that caused economic, social and political disruption in both the host and home countries, and aimed at global dominance. The MNE had to be tamed.

1.3 Moves towards an Economic Theory of the MNE

A third factor in the growth of concern over MNEs was the development, in the 1960s, of the first attempts to refine an economic theory of the MNE. Economists began to feel that the MNE was a unique kind of business organization, with the result that traditional economic theories concerning international capital movements and the balance of payments were no longer adequate to explain this entity.[20] During the 1950s a number of economists had concentrated on internal managerial skills, the ability of the MNE to transcend the limitations of national boundaries and its centralized control as factors which made it stand out from other types of business entity.[21] In the 1960s the first systematic theoretical explanations of MNE growth appeared.[22] This new literature, with its emphasis on the size and market power of MNEs, gave academic weight to concern over their activities. According to D. K. Fieldhouse[23] this theoretical work created a uniform concept of the MNE whose behaviour conformed to uniform and predictable patterns. This in turn generated a wave of policy-oriented literature which sought to expose the dangers of the MNE, and which suggested paths for control.[24]

A further result of theoretical interest in the MNE was the rise of empirical research into the history and patterns of behaviour of MNEs. Of particular importance is the pioneering work of the Harvard University Comparative Multinational Enterprise Project, coordinated by Raymond Vernon in the late 1960s and early 1970s. This generated the first detailed empirical studies of the growth of modern MNEs, tracing their origins in Europe and the USA back to the middle of the nineteenth century,[25] thereby undermining the view that MNEs were a very recent form of business entity. Furthermore, this work was of considerable importance in critically assessing the assumptions of the first economic theories of the MNE. The interaction between business history and economic theory has since led to some interesting reassessments as to the nature of the MNE. In particular, a more detailed appreciation of the reasons for the growth of MNEs, based on the theory of transaction costs, has emerged.[26]

1.4   The Ideological Dimension

No account of concern over MNEs would be complete without an awareness of the role of ideological positions in the field of political economy. A fuller analysis will be presented in chapter 4 as part of a wider discussion of MNE regulation. For present purposes, it is enough to note that during the 1960s and 1970s a significant current of opinion emerged that was critical of, if not openly hostile towards, the operations of capitalist firms. This was articulated in critical writings based on positions ranging from the Marxism-Leninism espoused by the then communist Eastern Bloc states to the 'managerialism' of liberals in Western states who had not abandoned capitalism, but were unhappy about its social and economic consequences and suspicious of unaccountable corporate power. This was an era in which the traditionally accepted benefits of free enterprise were in doubt, and in which socialism seemed to offer a viable alternative. Thus the ideological climate was receptive to the development of a critique of MNEs as the most developed symbols of capitalism. By contrast, neo-classical economic analysis, which sees the MNE as a beneficial entity whose growth and activities should be encouraged irrespective of particular, nationalistic, concerns was, at this time, marginalized.

1.5   Summary

The origins of modern concern over the MNE can be placed within the period of the 1960s and early 1970s. This was the period in which the economic revival of Europe and Japan generated the prospect of greater international economic competition between European, Japanese and US businesses. Foreign MNEs as agents through which such competition would, in part, take place became targets of concern. This was especially so in Europe, where the dominance of US firms seemed overwhelming (and, it appears, exaggerated[27]), and in the USA, where foreign and domestic MNEs were seen as a threat to economic security within the domestic economy. The 1960s and early 1970s were also the period when the newly independent states of the southern hemisphere coalesced into an international pressure group within the UN, and demanded the introduction, through multilateral action, of a New International Economic Order as a means of ensuring economic independence. In this context the MNE could be seen as an agent of economic dependency exploiting the LDC host. In response, the UN was encouraged to develop a comprehensive policy of MNE regulation to assist LDCs who felt powerless to act unilaterally, and who feared the more sinister effects of corporate power as witnessed by sensational cases of its abuse. Alongside these political and economic developments new theories concerning the nature and growth of the MNE appeared, giving the first theoretical explanation of the phenomenon and encouraging the view that the MNE was a uniform, unique and economically powerful entity. This spurred on a policy-oriented literature which sought to document the potential dangers of the MNE from a variety of ideological viewpoints and to suggest control-oriented policy responses. The neo-classical perspective that would become highly influential by the end of the 1980s was of limited influence at this time.

2   The Contemporary Position

Since the 1970s numerous changes have occurred in national and international approaches to MNE regulation which reflect a change of emphasis in the concerns outlined above. First, states that had previously placed restrictions on inward direct investment have relaxed these. They include, notably, the former socialist states of the now defunct Eastern Bloc. Secondly, there has been an increase in laws used by countries to attract internationally mobile projects. Indeed, the current trend in the national regulation of MNEs is moving away from highly restrictive and nationalistic responses towards a more permissive regime. At the same time states are gaining knowledge from experience and are identifying more successfully the major issues to be dealt with. Problems of ownership and control are being overtaken by new considerations regarding adequate levels of revenue from foreign investors, improved technology transfer, the better use of state bargaining power during the course of the investment, and greater specialization in the issues facing the given industry in which the host state–MNE relationship takes place. However, this trend should not be mistaken as showing a wholesale abandonment by states of interventionist and protectionist approaches to MNE issues. The change is more one of degree than quality, and a reversal of policy is always possible in a changing international economy.

On the international level there has been a retreat from the MNE 'control model' based on multilateral international organizations, as recommended by the above-mentioned UN Group of Eminent Persons. This is most prominantly shown by the failure of the UN to adopt an agreed Code of Conduct on Transnational Corporations (TNCs). This is due, largely, to an inability on the part of the developed and developing states to come to an agreement over controversial and fundamental questions. These include the meaning of 'national treatment' for TNCs, the principle of compensation to be applied in cases of nationalization, the degree of host state jurisdiction over TNCs, the scope of the prohibition on interference in internal political affairs by the TNC, the binding nature of the code and the role of public international law in defining the host state's obligations towards the TNC.

These developments can be attributed to changes in the economic and political climate since the mid-1970s and to increased knowledge about MNE operations. On an economic level, a marked slowing down of growth in the world economy since the early 1970s, especially in the manufacturing sector, combined with an increased scarcity of financial capital in the wake of the 'debt crisis' of the early 1980s, led during the 1980s to greater competition between states for foreign direct investment. Access to the best productive technology is essential for the maintenance of a state's economic well-being. As MNEs tend to be the major possessors of such technology the need to attract them and to work with them becomes all the more important. This has remained the case during the 1990s.

On a political and ideological level there have been a number of significant shifts since the 1970s, helping to create the more open approach to foreign investors. First, during the 1980s a number of states, notably the USA and UK, underwent changes in government resulting in administrations sympathetic to neo-classical political economy and its liberal approach to foreign direct investment. Secondly, the formerly socialist states of the Eastern Bloc have abandoned command economy structures and are moving towards free-market economies. Thirdly, in developing countries, external economic forces have caused a rethinking of earlier political commitments to nationalistic and state-led economic policies. Increasingly, the problem of economic efficiency is challenging governments to work out new approaches. As a consequence many states are undertaking or seriously considering the privatization of state-owned companies, some of which were previously foreign-owned, and of introducing more competition into the economy. However, the political obstacles to such change are formidable, not least because they may be seen as a denial of symbolically important national ideals, if not an outright 'sell-out' to Western interests. Fourthly, in the international arena, the fears generated by calls for a New International

Economic Order on the part of LDCs led to a reaction by developed nations. They were moved to use their leverage with the weaker developing states not only to limit the scope of the proposed UN Code of Conduct but also to bring about a new regime of bilateral investment protection treaties coupled with action aiming to establish new international institutional structures for investor protection through the World Bank and, more recently, through the Uruguay Round negotiations under the General Agreement on Tariffs and Trade (GATT).

Finally, an important contribution to contemporary thinking on MNEs has been an increase in knowledge about such firms. This has led to a shift from a highly speculative and emotional debate to more informed discussion on MNE problems. In the process a number of generalizations about MNEs have been put into doubt. First, it is clear that the MNE has not overwhelmed the nation state as a unit of power. States have responded to the issue of foreign direct investment and have used political power to coordinate economic power where necessary. The question is no longer 'can the nation state control the MNE?' but 'is the policy being pursued likely to give the benefits hoped for?' The real issue is whether the state has identified correctly the problems and advantages that a given foreign direct investment offers, and whether it has used its bargaining power successfully. Secondly, while early accounts of the MNE concentrated on its tendency towards monopoly, more recently an awareness has arisen of the highly competititive nature of the transnational economy in which MNEs operate. Thus the MNE is seen as a product of competitive forces that lead it to both defensive and attacking responses. A realization that MNEs are subject to competitive pressures can lead to better bargaining outcomes between states and corporations in given industries. However, global competition is also at the heart of many difficulties encountered by countries when dealing with MNEs. The tendency towards the globalization of the economy can have adverse welfare consequences for individual states and industries. Thirdly, the assumption can be discarded that the MNE is a uniform type of business entity whose behaviour can be predicted through logical deduction from its characteristics. Such an approach is typical of most of the thinking described in the first section. This is perhaps not surprising, since most of the research on which it was based had been done on US firms. To the extent that the results of that research were generalized into explaining all MNE behaviour, the essential diversity of the motives for, and characteristics of, foreign direct investment were blurred. Such oversimplification could not survive an increase in awareness of the reality of MNE operations.

3   *Problems of Definition*

Having considered the origins of concern over MNEs and having briefly introduced the main contemporary trends in the regulation of MNEs, by way of introduction to chapters 2 to 4, we shall now consider what, if any, progress has been made in arriving at an agreed definition of MNEs that is sufficiently sophisticated to encompass the various business forms that such firms might take.

The first use of the term 'multinational' in relation to a corporation has been attributed to David E. Lilienthal, who, in April 1960, gave a paper to the Carnegie Institute of Technology on 'Management and corporations 1985', which was later published under the title 'The multinational corporation' (MNC). Lilienthal defined MNCs as 'corporations . . . which have their home in one country but which operate and live under the laws and customs of other countries as well.'[28] This definition sees the MNC as a uninational enterprise with foreign operations. The approach is oriented towards the experience of US firms. Firms of multiple national origin, such as the Anglo-Dutch corporations Unilever and Shell, are not considered.

The existence of such firms alongside uninational MNCs has prompted a distinction to be made between these two groups of international business associations. Unfortunately, usage has not always been uniformly applied and some terminological confusion has resulted. This is particularly apparent when one compares the distinctions drawn by economists when defining the MNE with those that have entered into United Nations usage.

Economists have favoured a simple all-embracing formula, defining as a 'multinational enterprise' any corporation which 'owns (in whole or in part), controls and manages income generating assets in more than one country'.[29] This definition distinguishes between an enterprise that engages in *direct investment,* which gives the enterprise not only a financial stake in the foreign venture but also managerial control, and one that engages in *portfolio investment,* which gives the investing enterprise only a financial stake in the foreign venture without any managerial control. Thus the MNE is a firm that engages in *direct investment outside its home country.* The term 'enterprise' is favoured over 'corporation' as it avoids restricting the object of study to incorporated business entities and to corporate groups based on parent–subsidiary relations alone. International production can take numerous legal forms.[30] From an economic perspective the legal form is not crucial to the classification of an enterprise as 'multinational'.

By contrast, the United Nations (UN) has moved away from this simple formula towards a distinction between 'multinational corporations' (MNCs) and 'transnational corporations' (TNCs). In their report, the UN Group of Eminent Persons adopted the simple economist's definition of MNCs as 'enterprises which own or control production or service facilities outside the country in which they are based. Such enterprises are not always incorporated or private; they can also be co-operatives or state-owned entities.'[31] However, during discussions of the report at the Fifty-Seventh Session of ECOSOC in 1974, several representatives argued in favour of the term *transnational corporation*. This term, it was said, better expressed the essential feature of operation across national borders than did the term multinational. That term should be reserved for enterprises which were jointly owned and controlled by entities from several countries. Latin American representatives pointed out that the term multinational was being used by the Andean Group countries to refer to corporations jointly set up under Andean Group rules.[32] Such enterprises were not intended to come under UN scrutiny. They were different from uninational corporations operating across national borders.[33]

In response to such opinions, the ECOSOC adopted the term transnational corporation for the purposes of the UN programme on MNEs.[34] Henceforth, what economists call multinationals would be known as transnationals in UN parlance. Thus UN practice distinguishes between enterprises owned and controlled by entities or persons from one country but operating across national borders – the *transnational* – and those owned and controlled by entities or persons from more than one country – the *multinational*.[35]

By contrast, the politically and economically more homogeneous group of states belonging to the OECD arrived, in 1976, at an agreed definition of the MNE for the purposes of the OECD Guidelines on Multinational Enterprises. According to the OECD Guidelines, multinational enterprises

usually comprise companies or other entities whose ownership is private, state or mixed, established in different countries and so linked that one or more of them may be able to exercise a significant influence over the activities of others, and, in particular, to share knowledge and resources with the others.[36]

The crucial characteristic of a MNE is, according to this definition, the ability of one company to control the activities of another company located in another country. Other factors are not decisive. Thus, the sharing of knowledge and resources among companies or other entities would not be enough, by itself, to indicate that such companies or entities constitute a MNE.[37] The definition is broad enough to encompass both equity and non-equity based direct investment, regardless of the legal form or ownership of the dominant and servient undertakings. This definition was substantially adopted in the most recent proposed text of the now shelved UN Draft Code of Conduct on Transnational Enterprises.[38]

The above definitions should be seen as no more than broad conceptual guidelines as to which kinds of firms are MNEs and which are not. Inevitably, a certain degree of arbitrariness is involved, as exemplified in particular by the terminological debates in the UN. Much depends on the purpose for which the definition is being devised and on the available evidence of international business activities. However one wishes to define *the* MNE, a task which may not be possible with any degree of accuracy, from a regulator's perspective the major consideration remains whether certain types of international business associations are, through the nature of their activities, so distinct from uninational enterprises that they require separate regulation.

In this respect it may be helpful to show how MNEs differ from uninational enterprises that share certain of their features.[39] The first of these is the multilocation domestic enterprise. MNEs may share the following similarities with this type of enterprise. First, they own income generating assets in more than one location and use these in combination with local resources to produce goods or services. Secondly, both types of enterprise enjoy the competitive advantages of a larger economic unit when compared with single plant enterprises. However, the crucial difference between a MNE and the multilocation domestic enterprise is that the former operates its assets and controls their use across national borders, whereas the latter remains within them. Furthermore, unlike the multiplant domestic company, a MNE will organize itself into divisions whose managerial reach crosses national frontiers, and through which the national identity of the various operating companies in the group disappears, even though such identity continues on a formal level through the requirement of incorporation under the laws of the various states in which the MNE operates.[40]

The second close relation of a MNE is the domestic firm that exports part of its output. It is similar to a MNE in that it sells part of its output across national borders. However, a MNE differs in that it trades across borders in factor inputs as well as finished products, and between affiliates of the group as well as with unconnected third parties. This raises the possibility of controlling trade within a MNE to the advantage of the group as a whole, and represents one of the major competitive advantages possessed by MNEs over domestic firms.[41]

The third close relation of the MNE is the domestic firm that exports part of its factor inputs; for example, technical know-how and managerial skills. This is done by means of licensing foreign firms to develop markets abroad. MNEs can also export such knowledge, but with the difference that they usually maintain control over that knowledge by selling it only to affiliates. As will be more fully explained in chapter 2, the choice between serving the foreign market by employing a foreign licensee and serving it by setting up a foreign sales and/or production subsidiary lies at the heart of an understanding of the reasons behind the growth of MNEs.

By way of summary the following general features of MNEs should be stressed: though in many respects they resemble various types of uninational companies, MNEs differ in their capacity to locate productive facilities across national borders, to exploit local factor inputs thereby, to trade across frontiers in factor inputs between affiliates, to exploit their know-how in foreign markets without losing control over it, and to organize their managerial structure globally according to the most suitable mix of divisional lines of authority. These factors permit MNEs to affect the international allocation of productive resources, and thereby to create distinct problems in the development of economic policy in the states where they operate. Consequently, MNEs can and should be treated as a distinct type of business enterprise for the purposes of economic regulation.

4 Concluding Remarks

The remainder of this work will seek to show how the regulation of MNEs has developed and changed over the past thirty years or so, and, thereby, to explain the increasingly varied and sophisticated array of regulatory devices that has emerged. To achieve this aim it is necessary to relate the nature and operations of MNEs to legal concepts in general. The remaining chapters in part I seek to do this. Chapter 2 will describe and account for the growth of MNEs and consider what, if any, role law has had in this growth. Chapter 3 will compare business and legal forms of various common MNE structures, so as to give greater substance to the definitional issues presented in this chapter, to introduce the principal legal forms for the control of MNE operations and to highlight their limitations as devices for control. Chapter 4 will end part I by considering the nature of relations between MNEs and states, concentrating on the substantive aims and jurisdictional levels of regulation in this field.

Notes

1 For statistical data on the rise of US MNEs see Raymond Vernon, *Sovereignty at Bay* (Pelican, 1973) pp. 40–1 (oil), pp. 48–9 (non oil extractive industries), pp. 68–71 (manufacturing). According to Tugendhat the book value of US foreign direct investment rose from $7,200 million to $70,763 million between 1946 and 1969: C. Tugendhat, *The Multinationals* (Pelican, 1973), at p. 45. The reasons for this growth are discussed in chapter 2, pp. 26–8.

2 Published in English by Penguin in 1968.

3 R. Gilpin, 'The politics of transnational economic relations', in Keohane and Nye (eds), *Transnational Relations and World Politics* (Harvard, 1972), p. 48.

4 M. Y. Yoshino, 'Japan as host to the international corporation', in C. Kindleburger (ed.), *The International Corporation* (MIT Press, 1970), at pp. 358–9.

5 See further chapter 6 at p. 176.

6 S.2592, 92nd Cong., 1st Sess. (1971); H.8784, 92nd Cong., 1st Sess. (1971). See further K. H. Hughes, *Trade Taxes and Transnationals* (Praeger, 1979), chapter 2; B. Forrow, 'The multinational corporation in the enlarged European Community', 37 Law and Cont. Prob. 306 (1972). The tax aspects of the Bill are briefly discussed in chapter 8 at p. 281.

7 See further chapter 6 at pp. 175–6, and chapter 7 at pp. 224–5.

8 See Svedberg, 'Colonial enforcement of foreign direct investment', *Manchester School* (1981), p. 21.

9 This view may not be sustainable on the evidence. Svedberg, 'Colonial enforcement . . .', suggests that the continued dominance of investment from the former colonial power may be explicable on the ground that no other investors are interested in the host country. Furthermore, he suggests that such dominance appears to recede over time.

10 The Group was named after the 77 original countries that formed it.

11 The principal UN General Assembly Resolutions on the New International Economic Order are: Res. 3201 (S-VI) of 9 May 1974, The Declaration on the Establishment of a New International Economic Order; Res. 3202 (S-VI) of 16 May 1974, The Programme of Action on the Establishment of a New International Economic Order (both reproduced in 13 ILM 715–66 (1974)). These were followed by Res. 3281 (XXIX) of 15 January 1975, The Charter of Economic Rights and Duties of States (reproduced in 14 ILM 251–65 (1975)).

12 See further P. T. Muchlinski, 'The right to economic self-determination', in J. N. Adams (ed.), *Essays For Clive Schmitthoff* (Professional Books, 1983), p. 73.

13 UN Doc. E/5500/Add 1 (Part I) 24 May 1974. The report is reproduced in 13 ILM 800 (1974).

14 For a full discussion of negotiations over the Draft UN Code of Conduct on TNCs and the reasons for its non-adoption see chapter 16 at pp. 592–7.

15 See A. Sampson, *The Sovereign State: the Secret History of ITT* (Coronet, 1973), chapter 11.

16   See T. Moran, *Multinational Corporations and the Politics of Dependence: Copper in Chile* (Princeton University Press, 1977), pp. 252–3.

17   US Congress Senate Subcommittee on Multinationals, *Hearings on Multinational Corporations and US Foreign Policy*, 93rd Congress 2nd Session (US Govt Printing Office, 1974).

18   See generally Anthony Sampson, *The Arms Bazaar*, 2nd edn (Coronet, 1991).

19   For example, sales by Nestlé of unsuitable baby food in Africa which led to the World Health Organization adopting an International Code of Marketing of Breast Milk Substitutes in 1981: see G. Hamilton, *The Control of Multinationals: What Future for International Codes of Conduct in the 1980s?* (IRM Multinational Reports, IRM/Wiley, 1984), pp. 16–18; or the breaking of the UN and British oil embargo against Rhodesia by British oil multinationals: see Foreign and Commonwealth Office, *Report on the Supply of Petroleum and Petroleum Products to Rhodesia* (HMSO, 1978); M. Bailey, *Oilgate* (Coronet, 1979).

20   D. K. Fieldhouse, 'The multinational: a critique of a concept', in A. Teichova et al. (eds), *Multinational Enterprise in Historical Perspective* (Cambridge University Press, 1986), at p. 13.

21   Ibid.

22   Of particular importance was the work of Stephen Hymer, Charles Kindleberger and Raymond Vernon. See further chapter 2.

23   Fieldhouse, 'The multinational'.

24   See, for example, R. S. Barnet and R. E. Muller, *Global Reach: The Power of Multinational Corporations* (Simon and Schuster, 1974).

25   See Vernon, *Sovereignty at Bay*; M. Wilkins, *The Emergence of Multinational Enterprise: American Business Abroad from the Colonial Era to 1914* (Harvard, 1970); *The Maturing of Multinational Enterprise American Business Abroad from 1914 to 1970* (Harvard, 1974); L. Franko, *The European Multinationals* (Harper & Row 1976); and the collection of papers in 48 *Business History Review* (Autumn 1974).

26   See, for example, the collection of essays in P. Hertner and G. Jones (eds), *Multinationals Theory and History* (Gower, 1986), and see chapter 2.

27   See S. Hymer and R. Rowthorn, 'Multinational corporations and international oligopoly: the non American challenge', in C. Kindleberger (ed.), *The International Corporation* (MIT Press, 1970), p. 57; Vernon, *Sovereignty at Bay*, at pp. 30–1.

28   Quoted in Fieldhouse 'The multinational', at p. 10.

29   N. Hood and S. Young, *The Economics of the Multinational Enterprise* (Longman, 1979), p. 3. See also J. H. Dunning, *Multinational Enterprises and the Global Economy* (Addison Wesley, 1992) pp. 3–4.

30   On which see chapter 3.

31   See report of the Group of Eminent Persons, note 13 above, at p. 25.

32   See further chapter 3 at pp. 57–61.

33   See UN Commission on Transnational Corporations, *Transnational Corporations in World Development: a Re-examination* (UN Sales No. E.78.II.A.5, 1978), annex I, at p. 159.

34   Ibid.
35   See further C. D. Wallace, *Legal Control of the Multinational Enterprise* (Martinus Nijhoff, 1983), at pp. 10–13.
36   OECD Guidelines For Multinational Enterprises, 21 June 1976, introduction, para. 8. See OECD, *The OECD Declaration and Decisions on International Investment and Multinational Enterprises 1991 Review* (Paris, 1992), at p. 104.
37   Ibid., at p. 48.
38   See UN Doc. E/1990/94, 12 June 1990, para. 1, at p. 5. See further chapter 16 for a full discussion of the OECD Guidelines and Draft UN Code of Conduct for TNCs.
39   See J. H. Dunning, *International Production and the Multinational Enterprise* (Allen & Unwin, 1981), p. 7, on which the following account is largely based. This section first appeared in the author's paper, 'Lifting the corporate veil on the Western multinational corporate group', in M. A. Jakubowski (ed.), *Anglo-Polish Legal Essays*, Volume 1 (University of Warsaw Faculty of Law and Administration, 1986), pp. 159–229 at pp. 161–2. See also Hood and Young, *Economics of the Multinational Enterprise*, at pp. 5–9.
40   On which see further chapter 3.
41   See further chapter 2, at pp. 33–8.

2

The Evolution of Modern Multinational Enterprises

The present chapter seeks to describe how modern MNEs evolved, taking into account their historical and geographical origins, the economic causes for their growth and the role of legal factors in the stimulation of that growth. The sources of information for this chapter present certain difficulties. First, despite much work on the part of economists and business historians, explanations for the growth of MNEs are by no means complete. The relationship between economic theory and business history in this area has developed only recently, and considerable disagreements remain as to the interpretation of the evidence.[1] Secondly, study of legal factors in the growth of MNEs is virtually non-existent. This may be explained, first, by the understandable reluctance of economists and business historians to analyse technical legal data, and, secondly, by the generally ahistorical approach adopted by legal writers in the field of MNE regulation. They have tended to characterize the issue as new and unprecedented.[2] However, some initial attempts have been made by business historians and lawyers to consider the role of law in the growth of large national corporations,[3] from which some helpful insights can be gained.

This chapter will first outline the principal historical phases in the growth of MNEs, and secondly describe the economic causes of MNE growth, so far as they are presently understood, and relate these to legal phenomena that may be significant in assisting that growth.

1 The Principal Phases of MNE Growth

It is difficult to place a precise date on the evolution of MNEs. It is arguable that the history of the evolution of MNEs should begin with the great European colonial trading companies established in the sixteenth and seventeenth centuries.[4] Indeed, the view has been put that the chartered trading companies of the sixteenth to eighteenth centuries may differ only in the degree, not in the kind, of productive integration across borders to be found in a modern MNE.[5] However, the majority of economists and business historians place the emergence of the modern MNE in the second half of the nineteenth century. Thus, according to Mira Wilkins, American MNEs began to appear in the middle of the nineteenth century.[6] Similarly, Lawrence Franko shows that the first truly multinational European firms appeared in the mid- to late nineteenth century.[7] This period saw the development of the modern technologies, manufacturing and management processes which created the possibility of a genuine international division of production by firms.[8]

The evolution of modern MNEs can be conveniently divided into three historical periods.[9] The first begins with the emergence of the earliest internationally integrated, privately owned manufacturing firms, in about the middle of the nineteenth century, and ends in 1914 with the outbreak of the First World War. The second period begins in 1918 and ends with the outbreak of the Second World War in 1939. The third period, from 1945 to the present, encompasses the rise of foreign direct investment by MNEs to current levels and, with it, the contemporary political and legal responses that form the subject matter of this book.

1.1   The First Period: 1850–1914

During this period MNEs, as understood in contemporary economic thought, first began to emerge as part of the newly developing modern industrial economy. Britain was the world's major economic power during this period.[10] British investment was particularly prominent in railway companies throughout the world. British investments were also to be found in ranching, timber and mining. The geographical destination for these investments was primarily North America, including both the USA and Canada, Australia and Argentina. Such investments often took the form of 'free-standing' companies.[11] Typically, these companies were incorporated in the UK and comprised of a British board of directors and company secretariat which would oversee the overall operation of the company. However, their major operating assets were located and managed overseas. These companies would have no British based operations or assets. Thus they were not MNEs in the sense of contemporary definitions. The principal reason for this form of company was access to the London capital market as a means of financing overseas business projects.

In the 1890s the first market-oriented foreign investments were undertaken by British MNEs. These included Lever Brothers in soap, J. and P. Coats in cotton thread, Dunlop in tyres and the

Gramophone Company (later EMI) in records and gramophones.[12] These companies were the first truly multinational manufacturers from Britain. However, there is little agreement among business historians as to how much British investment of this period could be attributed to direct investment undertaken by MNEs. Estimates vary from 10 per cent[13] to as high as 40–50 per cent.[14]

In the same period, European MNEs began to appear.[15] In particular, German firms became dominant in chemicals, artificial textiles and electrical goods.[16] Ciba, Geigy, BASF, Hoechst, Bayer and Agfa all established new foreign operations between 1880 and 1914. In electrical goods, Siemens and AEG were the leading European companies.[17] The defeat of Germany after the First World War resulted in the expropriation of German companies overseas. The experience was to be repeated during the Second World War. Consequently, German firms did not achieve the degree of market dominance during the twentieth century attained by MNEs from other home countries.

From among other European countries, notable early MNEs included, from Sweden, the Nobel Company and SKF,[18] and, from Holland, the electrical corporation Philips, the foodstuffs manufacturer Margarine Uni (later merged with Lever Brothers of the UK to form Unilever) and Royal-Dutch Shell, which was formed by Anglo-Dutch oil interests in 1907.[19] However, it was not until after the Second World War that European firms established their most significant multinational operations. Thus, for example, French firms did not make their strongest impact as foreign direct investors until the 1950s, even though by 1914 France was the second largest foreign investor from Europe after the UK.[20]

The pre-1914 period also saw the growth of the first US MNEs.[21] Arguably, the American Singer Sewing Machine Company can be regarded as the first true manufacturing MNE.[22] It was the first successful international American manufacturing business.[23] In 1855 the company began to sell its sewing machines in France through French agents. By 1867 Singer decided to set up a factory in Glasgow, so as to meet growing demand in the UK that could no longer be supplied through imports from the USA. The factory was designed initially to assemble finished sewing machines using partly completed components imported from the USA. By 1882 Singer had decided to erect a new factory in Glasgow, which would build machines from locally manufactured components. It was the first example of a manufacturing firm moving from export sales to local production as a means of supplying a growing overseas market.

Other US firms embarked upon a strategy of international production in fields as diverse as metal products, telegraphy, telephones, phonographs, light bulbs, railway braking systems, chemicals, oil, cars and office equipment. They included such famous names as Bell, Edison, Westinghouse, Parke Davis, Eastman Standard Oil and Ford. The strongest period of growth for US enterprises abroad occurred between 1893 and 1914, at a time when the US domestic market was in recession, making foreign markets more attractive, and when a combination of stock market conditions and new anti-trust laws encouraged mergers of firms into giant corporations with interests in both home and foreign markets.[24] The principal locations for US foreign investments up to 1914 remained in Canada and Mexico. Investments in raw materials and agriculture were made in the rest of Latin America, while in Europe considerable investments were undertaken in selling, assembly, processing and manufacturing.

However, despite such rapid overseas expansion, by 1914 the USA still received more foreign investment than it exported, and the size of foreign direct investment relative to total US investment was small – some 7 per cent of US gross national product in 1914. Nevertheless, such facts should not diminish the significance of this trend. As Mira Wilkins points out, the percentage of US outward direct investment to the total US GNP has always remained at about 7 per cent, even in the mid-1960s at the height of US dominance in relation to such investment.[25] The significant fact is that US firms were willing to expand abroad and did so during this period.

The overall pattern of foreign direct investment in the forty years prior to the First World War makes this period stand out as one of MNE growth second only to the period since the Second World War.[26] The overall pattern of investments was, however, different from that experienced in the period after the Second World War. In particular, about three-fifths of foreign investment capital was directed to today's developing countries, which were, at the time, the African and Asian colonies of the principal European powers, and the newly independent capital-importing countries of Latin America. The distribution of investment across industry sectors has been estimated at about 55 per cent in primary products, 20 per cent in railways, 15 per cent in manufacture and 10 per cent in trade and distribution, with the remainder in public utilities and financial services.[27] Therefore, the pattern of foreign direct investment in this period represented a system geared primarily towards the supply of raw materials and agricultural produce from the South to meet the needs of manufacturers and growing populations in the industrialized North.

1.2   The Second Period: 1918–1939

The second period, between 1918 and the outbreak of the Second World War in 1939, is characterized by the continued development of MNEs but, by comparison with the late nineteenth and early twentieth centuries, at a slower rate owing to the general instability in the world economy during this period. This led to the pursuit of highly nationalistic economic policies by states as a means of protecting themselves against the resulting world depression. Such policies, in turn, led to an increased incidence of national cartels in key industries and to the erection of high tariff barriers to trade, as compared with the period up to 1914.

The investment environment after the First World War had undergone changes that were on the whole inimical to the expansion of foreign direct investment by firms. First, the Bolshevik Revolution took the Soviet Union outside the capitalist economic system. Although Western firms did operate in the USSR in the 1920s, as joint ventures with Soviet state enterprises under Lenin's New Economic Plan, these were liquidated by Stalin.[28] So by 1930, a major region of the world was closed off to private foreign investment. Similarly, the break-up of the Austro-Hungarian and Ottoman Empires created changes in political boundaries that made the free movement of investments more difficult.[29] Secondly, the collapse of international capital markets in the late 1920s and early 1930s brought with it economic chaos, with high inflation followed by deflation and the growth of exchange controls.[30] This led to the Great Depression in the 1930s and to a massive decline in world trade. Thirdly, in response to these economic problems, and in view of continuing fear of another war, many states turned to increasingly nationalistic economic policies. In particular, Italy and Germany adopted fascist economic policies, with their emphasis on national control over manufacturing and raw materials, and on the acquisition of foreign territory for political and economic expansion.[31]

A significant feature of the economic nationalism of the inter-war years was the growth of greater integration between firms of the same nationality. In Germany, IG Farben was founded in 1925 as a combination of Hoechst, BASF and Bayer in the chemical industry. It was to play a major role in the later expansion of German manufacturing across occupied Europe during the Second World War.[32] In 1918, Siemens, AEG and the smaller Auer interests formed Osram, a joint-venture company that came to manufacture electric lamps in numerous countries after the First World War. Similarly, Swiss dyestuffs companies invested abroad under their Interest Association, which was formed in 1918 and lasted until 1951. In Sweden, Ivar Kreuger merged domestic match making firms into a national monopoly, the Swedish Match combine, in the 1920s.[33] In Britain, Imperial Chemical Industries was formed from the merger of smaller domestic chemical companies, after an attempt by IG Farben to extend its control of the industry through the unsuccessful acquisition of the British Dyestuffs Corporation, one of the founding companies of ICI.[34]

These national combines subsequently entered into international cartels with their foreign competitors. Thus IG Farben entered into agreements with its Swiss competitors represented by the Interest Association and with ICI. The Swedish Match combine achieved market control through the related technique of obtaining a national production monopoly in host countries and taking over local competitors.[35] In the electrotechnical industry, market-sharing agreements were concluded between German and US firms.[36] Further international cartels were set up between European (including British) firms in the steel, oil and rayon markets.[37]

American firms could not cartelize their operations in the same way as European firms because of certain differences between European and American business conditions. According to Franko, these were, first, the existence of strong antitrust laws in the USA which would have rendered cartels between US firms illegal. It was not until the years following the Second World War that similar antitrust laws became established in European economies. Secondly, European businessmen had more opportunities to cartelize their operations owing to geographical proximity and the existence of stable and interrelated business elites by comparison with the USA.[38] However, legal controls within the USA did not stop US firms from joining overseas cartels. So, for example, in 1928 a cartel was formed between Shell, Anglo-Persian (now BP) and Standard Oil of New Jersey to protect their non-US interests. In 1933, US companies entered the Second International Steel Cartel with British, Chinese, Polish and Austrian companies.[39] American companies did get a concession from their government, in the Webb–Pomerene Act of 1918, which permitted US firms to enter into cartels aimed at collective export sales and to join overseas cartels provided that these had no adverse effect on competition within the USA.[40] Otherwise American firms would have been disadvantaged in world markets.

Despite the existence of international cartels and nationalistic economic policies leading to the protection of domestic industries, the inter-war period was one in which the expansion of firms through direct investment continued. By 1938, the overall stock of foreign direct investment had risen by at least 50 per cent over 1914 levels.[41] According to Professor Dunning, during this period US direct investment continued to grow, rising to 27.7 per cent of world capital stock in 1938, second only to the UK, which held some 39.8 per cent.[42] Despite the above-mentioned difficulties, firms from both countries set up subsidiaries in European host states.[43] German firms also engaged in direct investments overseas in an attempt to reconstruct their pre-war international manufacturing networks.[44]

During this period, international cartels and direct investments by firms are best seen as complementary business strategies, and not as mutually exclusive alternatives. Thus, while cartels delayed the integration of international production by MNEs, they also protected this process by enabling participating firms to undertake direct investments in regions reserved for their exclusive operation under the terms of the cartel agreement, thereby rendering the cost of the direct investment bearable by reducing the risk of damaging competition.[45]

Nevertheless, the existence of agreed and imposed restrictions on competition, as a response to prevailing market and political conditions, did affect the pattern of direct investment in the inter-war period. It was not until the 1930s that the value of direct investments exceeded the pre-war figure.[46] Furthermore, the patterns of direct investment reflected the division of world markets into spheres of influence. Thus, Canada and Latin America continued to be the most significant destinations for US direct investment, accounting for some two-thirds of the total. Similarly, during the 1930s, British firms showed a preference for investment in the Empire (or former Empire), particularly Australia, South Africa and India.[47] This is explicable in part by the fact that such markets were often allocated to British firms under international trading agreements, although it should be noted that some 39.2 per cent of British direct investments were made in Europe during this period.[48] Continental European firms remained dominant in Europe, their direct investments there accounting for 61 per cent of all direct investments by European firms.[49]

1.3   The Third Period: 1945 to the Present

The third period begins in 1945 and continues to the present. During this period the MNE has acquired unprecedented importance in international production. The growth of MNEs in this period can be divided into two phases.[50] The first is that of the rapid growth of American MNEs from the end of the Second World War to about 1960, a period in which such firms were without any appreciable international competition from countries other than Britain. The second phase, from 1960 to the present, is characterized by the relative decline of US MNE dominance, the revival of competition from European MNEs following the reconstruction of European industry after the Second World War, and the rise of new competition from Japanese MNEs. The period is further characterized by the rise of new MNEs in certain newly industrializing countries of the South and, more recently, by the opening up of new markets for

MNEs in China, the former Soviet Union and the formerly socialist countries of Eastern Europe.

1.3.1   The period of American dominance: 1945–1960   The Second World War had devastated much of the industry of Europe and Japan. The main European belligerents experienced the forced divestiture of their overseas assets. The overseas affiliates of German companies were expropriated as enemy property for the second time in a century. Similarly, British companies experienced the loss of their mainland European subsidiaries. It has been estimated that more than 40 per cent of total British overseas assets were lost owing to destruction, expropriation, nationalization or sale between 1939 and 1956.[51] The companies of other European powers had ceased trading as independent entities during the war, having been integrated into the German war effort.[52]

By contrast, US companies emerged from the war in a strong position. They had escaped the massive destruction and seizure of assets experienced in Europe. They had also been strengthened by the stimulus of war production. This had ensured highly profitable markets and had spurred the companies to the development, testing and introduction of new products and processes.[53] US firms were at that time better resourced and geared for the development of new technologies, and for the discovery of new products and markets, than their British or European competitors.[54] Thus US firms were in a unique position to expand into overseas markets, whether through exports or through direct investment.

Numerous external factors stimulated the rapid expansion of direct investment by US firms in this period.[55] First, the introduction of Marshall Aid in 1948 provided the capital basis for the reconstruction of Europe's shattered economy, which in turn opened up new opportunities for direct investment by US firms. Secondly, the new international financial and trading system established after the war through the International Monetary Fund (IMF), World Bank (IBRD) and General Agreement on Tariffs and Trade (GATT) ensured the supremacy of the US dollar as the standard currency for international transactions and favoured the gradual liberalization of the international economy through the removal of tariff barriers to trade. The removal of such restrictions allowed for the setting up of integrated production plants in more than one country. The resulting decrease in the cost of cross-border intra-firm transfers of materials, semi-finished products and finished goods was essential to the success of such a strategy.

Thirdly, the US government offered tax concessions to firms investing abroad, permitting them to credit tax paid overseas against US tax liability and to defer the repatriation of profits free of tax liability, in effect giving such firms interest-free loan capital for reinvestment abroad.[56] The US government also tackled the remaining international cartels through antitrust prosecutions brought during the 1940s and 1950s.[57] Fourthly, improvements in the speed and reliability of international communications and transport after the war ensured better control over the activities of overseas subsidiaries than had hitherto been possible.

Fifthly, European governments were enthusiastic recipients of direct investment by US firms as a means of encouraging fuller employment and higher standards of living. The establishment of the EEC in 1957 is said to have acted as a further stimulus to US direct investment.[58] While the existence of the EEC undoubtedly facilitated the extension of integrated cross-border production within the Community, it is doubtful whether the founding of the Community was a decisive factor in increasing US direct investment. Such investment would probably have occurred in any case given the size and attractions of the national markets within the various Member States, although the plants established by US firms might have been less specialized and less closely linked.[59]

In this period US firms accounted for some two-thirds of the increase in total direct investment and in the number of new subsidiaries since 1938.[60] By 1960 the USA is estimated to have held some $32.8 billion of accumulated foreign direct investment, representing 49.2 per cent of the total world stock. The UK was the second largest direct investor, with a total stock of $10.8 billion, representing 16.2 per cent of the total. France was the third largest with a stock of $4.1 billion, giving 6.1 per cent of the total. As yet Japan was a very small scale foreign direct investor with a share of 0.7 per cent of the total, while Germany held 1.2 per cent.[61]

At the same time that US firms dominated the world economy, European firms began to reappear and grow.[62] In the early 1950s the Allied administration of Germany deconcentrated the industrial combines of the Nazi era. Firms such as Bayer and Hoechst were reconstituted from IG Farben. They began to buy back confiscated foreign plants in Latin America as a first step towards full international competitiveness. Other German companies (for example, Siemens, AEG and Daimler-Benz) rebuilt their international sales networks. Italy also emerged at this time as a source of foreign direct investment. Between 1946 and 1955 Fiat and Olivetti led the way, setting up foreign manufacturing plants in Europe and Latin America. France began to make a significant impact on export markets in this period, particularly in the motor and tyre industries, which would eventually lead to a rapid increase in the establishment of foreign manufacturing plants during the 1960s and 1970s.[63]

The pattern of direct investment was beginning to display new characteristics. First, while in 1914 some two-thirds of foreign direct investment was directed towards developing countries, by 1960 this had fallen to about 40 per cent. The traditional pattern of investments by firms from Northern industrialized countries in raw material and agricultural ventures in the South, characteristic of the period prior to 1914, began to be superseded by a new pattern of investment in technologically advanced manufacturing and service industries by firms from industrially advanced countries within other industrialized countries. This reflects a growth in market-oriented investment, as opposed to the supply-oriented investment typical of the earlier colonial era. Secondly, the measure of direct investment in manufacturing had risen as the proportion taken up by agricultural and public utility investments was in decline, while mining and raw materials investments continued at levels similar to those of earlier periods.[64]

1.3.2   The period of renewed international competition: 1960 to the present   Since 1960 the share of US and UK direct investment stock has been steadily falling while that of Germany, Japan and Switzerland has been rising.[65] American dominance peaked in the mid-1970s, when some 50 per cent of foreign direct investment outflows came from the USA. By 1985 this figure had fallen to some 25 per cent. Western Europe has now taken over as the major source region for foreign direct investment, accounting for some 50 per cent of the total.[66] Direct investment to developing countries declined further over this period. According to Professor Dunning, of an estimated $293 billion invested by the seven leading home countries in 1978, 26.5 per cent was in developing countries. This was slightly higher than the 1971 figure, but below that recorded in 1960.[67] However, during the 1990s inward investment into certain newly industrializing countries rose dramatically.[68]

The period since 1960 marks the emergence of Japan as a major foreign investor. Prior to that period Japanese foreign investment was negligible.[69] Since then Japan has increased its foreign direct investment stake considerably. In 1975 it accounted for 6 per cent of the total. By 1985 this had risen to 11 per cent.[70] Until 1959 Japan's outward direct investment was restricted owing to a preoccupation with domestic reconstruction and strict governmental controls under its exchange control laws.[71] The small amount of direct investment that occurred before 1960 was centred on the textiles industry, with some investment in iron and steel production and in mining. Latin American countries, in particular Mexico, Argentina and Brazil, were the favoured locations. During the early 1960s Japanese firms began to make investments in the neighbouring countries of Taiwan, Thailand, Hong Kong and Singapore.[72] However, these were small ventures designed to overcome import restrictions and to protect access to small local markets. It was not until the mid-1960s that Japanese direct investments rose considerably in these neighbouring Asian countries, taking advantage of cheaper labour conditions than those found in Japan, and of the opportunities for exports to third countries engendered by the adoption of export-oriented industrialization policies by these countries.

Japanese direct investments grew rapidly in the early 1970s when the government liberalized, and then removed, restrictions on the export of capital as a means of stemming the appreciation of the yen.[73] Not only did Japanese firms continue to invest in the newly industrializing countries of Asia, they also began to make their first significant investments in industrially advanced countries. In 1972, investment by Japanese companies in the USA was estimated at around $1.3 billion. Manufacturing accounted for only some 10 per cent of the total, the majority being in the commercial, financial and real estate sectors.[74] An important motive for investment in local production plants was the avoidance of US restrictions on imports of Japanese goods. Similar motivations also lie behind Japanese direct investments in Europe since the early 1970s.[75] Such defensive investments in manufacturing plants in developed countries have become an increasingly significant feature of Japanese investment patterns in Western Europe and the USA since the late 1970s, as have efforts at industrial collaboration with European and American firms.[76]

However, in the 1970s the bulk of Japanese outward direct investment was still concentrated in the developing countries, such countries accounting for 56.5 per cent of all Japanese investment in 1978.[77] Apart from the above-mentioned investments in manufacturing plants in neighbouring Asian countries, much of this investment occurred in the raw materials sector. Japan is a resource scarce country. Consequently its firms have invested heavily in overseas resource extraction ventures, on the basis of a 'develop and import' policy.[78] This policy was particularly significant in the Middle Eastern oil industry during the 1970s, allowing Japan to weather the effects of increased oil prices following the actions of OPEC in 1973.[79] Japanese investment in developing countries has declined during the 1980s. In 1986 the share stood at 33 per cent of all Japanese investment.[80] In line with other major home countries, Japan has redirected investment away from developing countries towards developed countries, and in particular to the United States, where increases have occurred in both manufacturing and services investments.[81]

The sectoral composition of Japanese direct investment has also undergone change. The largest proportion of Japanese outward investment is now in the services sector, reflecting the strength of

Japanese firms in financial services and trade. Thus in 1985 services accounted for 51.8 per cent of Japan's total stock of outward direct investment, as compared to 36.2 per cent in 1975. By contrast, while manufacturing investment accounted for 32.4 per cent of the total in 1975 it now accounts for only 29.2 per cent.[82] Over 40 per cent of Japanese investments in services are located in developing countries. The bulk have been made in the developed countries, following the liberalization of international capital markets in the late 1980s.[83]

Apart from the rise of Japanese MNEs, the period from 1960 to the present is characterized by a reversal of the role played by the USA from that of the leading home country for outward investment to that of the leading host country. Between 1975 and 1986 the inward stock of foreign direct investment in the USA multiplied 7.5 times.[84] Most of this investment has come from West European firms. By 1988 the UK was the leading investor, with 31 per cent of the total stock, followed by the Netherlands with 14.9 per cent. Japan was the third largest investor with 16.2 per cent, followed by Canada with 8.3 per cent.[85] The principal reasons behind this growth during the 1980s were the relatively good prospects for the US economy at a time when the global economy as a whole had been slowing down, the rapid depreciation of the dollar from 1985, making investment in the USA relatively cheap, particularly through the purchase of existing US assets, and the liberalization of US financial markets, which encouraged the inflow of foreign firms in that sector. In addition, as noted above, Japanese firms increased their presence in response to the rise of protectionist measures and sentiment against imports from Japan.[86] However, more recently, Japanese investment has slowed down in response to the recent weakness of the US economy.[87]

At the same time US firms have reduced their outward investments, preferring to expand their domestic operations at the expense of foreign expansion. Having reached their peak in 1975, US outward investments have since declined relative to those from other home countries. In the 1980–3 period US outward investment turned down sharply, in response to sluggish world economic conditions. In particular, US firms financed the expansion of their domestic operations by borrowing funds from their overseas affiliates, thereby reversing the flow of capital funds within the firm. By this means US MNEs were able to take advantage of cheaper capital available in Eurodollar markets, relative to US financial markets, for their domestic investments.[88]

Between 1975 and 1985 Western Europe replaced the USA as the major source for outward direct investment, having been hitherto the major host region. As the USA has become the principal host to foreign direct investment, Western Europe's share has declined, reflecting slower growth prospects in the region. More limited investment prospects combined with high levels of saving by European MNEs have provided the incentive and the assets for their expansion into the US market. The major investors have come from the UK and Germany. Apart from investment in the USA, there have been numerous cross-border mergers and acquisitions within Europe, aimed at obtaining greater scale economies in preparation for the Single European Market after 1992.[89] The Single Market is expected significantly to affect investment flows into and within the EC.

Turning to the developing countries, it has already been noted that investment flows into these countries continued to decline from the 1960s. This was, in part, due to the wave of nationalizations during the 1960s and early 1970s in the natural resource industries, particularly oil. More importantly, this trend could be explained by the increasingly limited opportunities for MNEs in the least developed countries.[90] In particular a decline in demand for primary commodities, on which certain developing countries are highly dependent, high levels of external indebtedness, particularly amongst Latin American countries, and tight balance-of-payment controls all contributed to this trend. However, during the 1990s a significant rise in investment into certain developing countries, notably China, and regions, notably South East Asia and Latin America, has occurred. On the other hand countries in sub-Saharan Africa and the 48 least developed countries continue to lag behind with limited flows of inward investment.[91]

The period since 1980 has seen the rise of MNEs from developing countries.[92] Though their investments represented less than 3 per cent of the world's total stock of outward direct investment in 1985, several of these corporations own assets of over $1 billion and are a significant, if not dominant, force in their national economies. They are located mainly in Korea, Brazil, Mexico and the oil exporting countries. The most significant sector is the oil industry, where state-owned national oil corporations were formed after the nationalizations of the late 1960s and early 1970s. These have gone on to expand their activities in petroleum refining and distribution beyond the borders of their home states.[93] In manufacturing, corporations from the Republic of Korea are particularly significant.[94]

Finally, since the late 1970s there has been a marked improvement in access for MNEs to the formerly socialist states of Eastern Europe, and to China and the former Soviet Union. All these economies have revised their policies on inward direct investment, moving away from their traditional prohibitions on direct investment by foreign firms. The entry of foreign firms as partners in joint ventures with domestic enterprises was permitted, followed, in some cases, by the passing of laws permitting investment by wholly owned subsidiaries of foreign firms.[95] Some of these countries have established, or are considering, free economic zones as a further incentive to foreign investors.[96] As regards outward investment, firms from these countries have begun to operate abroad, primarily as state-owned sales and trading companies, although some direct investments in financial services and manufacturing have been made.[97]

1.3.3 Possible future developments   To conclude, certain contemporary developments should be noted as significant factors in the shaping of future patterns of foreign direct investment. First, the establishment of the Single European Market and the introduction of the Euro should make investment in the Community countries more attractive, for both EC and non-EC based firms. The removal of remaining barriers to trade and establishment in the Community should stimulate new investment opportunities in what will be the largest integrated market in the world. The relative attractions of investment in the EC and the USA should be equalized to some extent. Similarly, the creation of an enlarged North American Free Trade Area between the USA, Canada and Mexico should help to maintain and enhance the attractiveness of this region for foreign investors. It should also result in a significant reorganization of investments by firms across the region. However, such regional developments also carry the risk of increased interregional protectionism, including foreign investment controls, should global economic conditions deteriorate.

Secondly, direct investment flows to the formerly socialist states of Eastern Europe and to the former Soviet Union should increase during the 1990s as Western firms take advantage of new investment opportunities.[98] However, inward investment flows may prove not to be as high as these countries hope if they fail to make a smooth transition to a market economy, and if political instability continues.

Thirdly, technological changes may continue to make investment in developed countries more attractive than in the least developed countries. As manufacturing technology becomes increasingly computerized and automated it causes a fall in the overall costs of labour within the developed economies, thereby undercutting one of the principal competitive advantages of the least developed countries, their cheap labour. The loss of this advantage is further accentuated by the growth in demand for skilled labour. Automated production processes need highly trained staff to serve and maintain them. They also create a demand for high technology components which themselves are manufactured by skilled labour. Many developing countries cannot match the skill levels of workers in the developed economies. The MNEs may respond by relocating production back to the developed economies, thereby emphasizing the continued 'dependency' of such developing countries. However, it may be too soon to say with certainty how computerization and automation will affect the employment and investment patterns adopted by MNEs. What is certain is that MNEs will continue to act as an integrating force in the world economy.[99]

2 Explanations for the Growth of MNEs and the Role of Legal Factors Therein

Having traced the principal phases in the growth of MNEs over time and space, in this section we will summarize the major explanations for MNE growth developed by economists and relate these to legal phenomena.

2.1 Theories of MNE Growth

The economic literature on the growth of MNEs is extensive. It is not possible to discuss this in detail here. That has been done elsewhere.[100] Of importance for present purposes is the extraction, from that literature, of the major trends of economic analysis as a prelude to a discussion of the role of legal factors in the growth of MNEs. Such an exercise is of value in that economists have identified numerous factors in the growth of MNEs that have implications for legal policy responses of the kind to be considered later in this work. Thus the remainder of the present chapter seeks to link the findings of economists to the concerns of lawyers. To that extent it offers a response – albeit a very cursory one – to the call made by Professor Dunning for the adoption of a greater interdisciplinary stance in the study of the nature and causes of international production.[101]

The development of economic theory in this field can be divided into three main stages. The first theoretical developments, in the 1960s, involved the adaptation of the classical theory of the firm and the theory of imperfect or 'monopolistic' competition into the theory of MNE 'ownership- or firm-specific advantage'. In 1960 Stephen Hymer was the first to suggest that firms invested overseas so as to gain higher profits from a competitive advantage owned by them.[102] To do so they had to organize an integrated international operation so as to retain control over their advantage, and to avoid the uncertainties of operating at arm's length in an open market.

Hymer's pioneering work gave rise to subsequent refinements of the 'monopolistic' theory of multinational enterprise, notably by Charles Kindleberger. According to Kindleberger, MNEs possess competitive advantages in goods markets, through their ability to differentiate branded products, in factor markets, through their possession of superior management skills (which, when combined with advantages in goods markets or large-scale production, increase returns), in their possession of patents and trade secrets, in the economies of sale employed in production and in their access to capital.[103] Thus a MNE is most likely to emerge in industries where one or more of the following features exist: competition in branded products; the need for highly efficient management and large-scale production; research into, and development of, productive technology and products for which there is a global market; and resulting large-scale capital requirements. Consequently, MNEs are prevalent in branded products industries such as pharmaceuticals, food and beverages and cosmetics, in concentrated industries such as automobiles, chemicals, electrical goods, farm machinery or office equipment and in highly capital-intensive industries such as oil.

The 'monopolistic' theory of multinational enterprise was followed by an adaptation of the theory of international trade and location theory into the theory of 'location-specific' advantages. The starting point for 'location-specific' analysis of foreign investment is the classical economic model of international trade.[104] This model assumes that countries will specialize in the production of goods that require a high input of factors with which they are especially well endowed, and that such goods will be exported in exchange for others requiring inputs of factors with which the country concerned is poorly endowed. The model assumes that both labour and capital are internationally immobile and that in all respects the international market is perfectly competitive.

The principal significance of the classical model for analysing foreign direct investment lies in its recognition that different countries enjoy different endowments of productive resources. However, it contains a number of weaknesses that render it incapable of explaining why firms choose to produce abroad rather than trade through exports. Most importantly, the assumption of perfect competition in international markets cannot be sustained. Firms are not equally endowed with competitive assets, or with knowledge of global markets. Nor is the world economy immune from barriers to free trade. Indeed, the reverse appears to be closer to the truth, notwithstanding post-war attempts at trade liberalization. Finally, neither labour nor, more especially, capital can be assumed to be internationally immobile. The MNE is the very antithesis of this assumption.

It would be wrong to consider that there is no relationship between the economic analysis of trade and direct investment. Direct investment theory must accept that since trade and investment are complementary and, in some cases, interchangeable methods of international production the two strands of economic thought must meet. They do so by pointing to situations in which unequal resource endowments between countries cause market failure which traders or investors possessing superior competitive endowments can exploit to the detriment of other market actors. The transition from trade to investment can then be explained by reference to the transaction costs associated with arm's length sales as compared to the long-term savings in cost that can be achieved through going multinational.[105] This, too, depends upon an understanding of the relationship between the firm and the location in which it has a market.

A significant early attempt to explain the location of direct investment by MNEs along such lines was the 'product cycle' thesis, developed by Professor Raymond Vernon. This was the first comprehensive attempt to integrate firm- and location-specific factors of MNE investment within a long-run time perspective. It explained the move to foreign locations by US MNEs in terms of the gradual loss of competitive advantage experienced by a firm during the life cycle of its product. According to Professor Vernon's theory, as the product matures, demand in the domestic market becomes saturated. This necessitates the seeking out of new opportunities for profit in foreign markets which, in turn, may prompt the firm to invest in local production for such markets. Furthermore, as the life cycle of the products nears its end, the only way to remain competitive may be to reduce production costs still further. Consequently, location in low cost production areas may be necessary. This explains why locations in less developed countries may be used.[106]

The second stage of theoretical development, in the 1970s, involved the refinement of earlier work and led to greater concentration on the replacement of markets for intermediate products by the internationally coordinated division of production within the MNE. This has become known as the theory of 'internalization'. The classic concept of 'internalization' was developed in the 1930s by Ronald Coase to explain the growth of domestic multiplant firms.[107] Put simply, where the firm encounters high 'transaction costs' (the costs associated with the supply of a market through arm's length deals between seller and buyer) in procuring supplies and distributing final products through the open market, it may be able to reduce those costs by carrying out such transactions within the firm, that is, by 'internalizing' those transactions. Thereby the uncertainties of the market are replaced by the common administration of the supplier and consumer of the traded product through the vertically integrated hierarchy of the firm. Similar internalization advantages can be gained by producers at the same level of production coming together in a horizontally integrated firm through merger or takeover.

The British economists Peter Buckley and Mark Casson refined the theory of 'internalization' into a theory of MNE growth.[108] They assert that 'internalisation of markets across national boundaries generates MNEs'.[109] According to Buckley and Casson, an integrated MNE will generate flows of goods associated with production between affiliates across borders. Furthermore, transborder flows of intermediate products will take place. These include flows of semi-processed materials and, most importantly, types of knowledge and expertise embodied in patents or human capital associated with the firm's marketing, R&D, labour training, management and financial activities. The MNE will undertake such transfers so as to avoid the costs and inefficiencies of effecting such transactions at arm's length with outside suppliers and distributors, and so as to protect its 'firm-specific' advantage in productive knowledge.[110]

Furthermore, the internalization of markets for intermediate products will occur where governments intervene in international markets through tariffs or restrictions on capital movements or where there exist discrepancies between countries in rates of income and profit taxation. These interventions depend to a large degree on the valuation of internationally traded intermediate goods. In external markets the arm's length prices involved are readily available. Should the firm internalize the market the prices of the intermediate goods can be more readily controlled and so liability to taxes and tariffs may be reduced through transfer pricing techniques.[111]

Of the various markets in intermediate products the market in productive knowledge is considered to carry the strongest incentive for internalization. This is because: first, knowledge provides a 'monopolistic' advantage best exploited by the firm itself rather than through licensing; secondly, the production of knowledge requires long-term R&D and this entails lengthy appraisal and effective short-term synchronization of efforts which may be impossible at arm's length; thirdly, flows of knowledge are difficult to value and so provide an excellent basis for reductions in tax liability through transfer pricing. Buckley and Casson conclude:

There is a special reason for believing that internalisation of the knowledge market will generate a high degree of multinationality among firms. Because knowledge is a public good[112] which is easily transmitted across national boundaries its exploitation is logically an international operation; thus unless comparative advantage or other factors restrict production to a single country, internalisation of knowledge will require each firm to operate a network of plants on a world-wide basis.[113]

From this conclusion Buckley and Casson argue that the pattern of growth of MNEs since the Second World War, 'is a by-product of the internalisation of markets in knowledge'.[114] This reflects the profitability of controlling and coordinating R&D across borders, which, they maintain, is at the heart of the successful and expanding MNE.[115]

This explanation of post-war growth of MNEs is related by Buckley and Casson to factors that have increased the potential profitability of R&D. These include: the stimulation of demand for high technology goods by governments, in response to their military requirements; increased numbers of high income consumers who purchase sophisticated consumer goods; and, possibly, social factors which have increased preferences for novelty and continued improvements in product quality.[116] The shift towards the internalization of markets in knowledge may also help to explain why MNEs have tended to invest more in developed countries since the Second World War. The cost of adapting such knowledge to different market conditions, and the absence of sufficient reserves of skilled labour, capital for R&D and affluent consumers, make developing countries less attractive as locations for investments based on high technology knowledge.[117]

The third stage of theoretical development, in the late 1970s and 1980s, marks the adoption of an 'eclectic' approach in explaining international production. This most recent contribution is attributable, in large measure, to the work of Professor J. H. Dunning.[118] The 'eclectic paradigm' does not offer a single, all-embracing, explanation of international production through MNEs. Indeed, as Professor Dunning points out, 'it is not possible to formulate a single operationally testable theory that can explain all forms of foreign-owned production'.[119] Such an explanation is highly unlikely, given the range of companies and industries involved. On the other hand Professor Dunning accepts that 'it is possible to formulate a general paradigm of MNE activity, which sets out a conceptual framework and seeks to identify clusters of variables relevant to all kinds of foreign-owned output'.[120]

Professor Dunning's paradigm rests on the acceptance that, by themselves, the various theories put forward to explain international production by MNEs cannot claim to offer a complete explanation, but that they identify relevant and interrelated phenomena which, when viewed together, can lead towards a better understanding of the causes of international production by MNEs. Thus, the 'eclectic paradigm' is based on the complementary nature of theories based on firm or ownership-specific, location-specific and internalization factors, referred to as O, L and I factors.

The central hypothesis of Professor Dunning's paradigm rests on this interrelationship. He posits that the level and structure of a firm's foreign productive activities will depend on four conditions.[121] First, there is the extent to which the firm possesses sustainable ownership (O) advantages as compared to firms of other nationalities serving the same markets. Secondly, assuming that such O advantages exist, there is the extent to which the enterprise sees its interest as lying with its own exploitation of its O advantages rather than with selling them, or licensing their use, to other firms. These are the internalization (I) advantages of the firm. They may reflect the superior organizational efficiency of the firm and/or its ability to exercise monopoly power over the assets under its governance. Thirdly, assuming the above two conditions are satisfied, there is the extent to which the global interests of the firm are served by creating or using its O advantages in a foreign location. The resources needed to do this are unevenly spread out. Those countries which have them will possess a locational (L) advantage over those that do not. Fourthly, 'given the configuration of the ownership, location and internalisation (OLI) advantages facing a particular firm, [there is] the extent to which a firm believes that foreign production is consistent with its long term management strategy.'[122] Professor Dunning goes on to predict that where a country's firms possess significant O advantages, where they have significant incentives to internalize their use and where they have significant incentives to exploit these in a foreign location, the more likely they are to engage in foreign production. Equally, countries are likely to attract foreign investment by MNEs when the reverse conditions apply.[123]

The 'eclectic paradigm' provides an integrating framework around which further research can develop. For our purposes, the three core concepts of ownership, locational and internalization advantages offer a method of organizing discussion of the legal factors relevant to the growth of MNEs. Each will be considered in turn in the next section.

2.2   The Role of Legal Factors

This section is largely speculative in nature. Little research has been done to date on the role of legal factors in the growth of MNEs. Therefore, the present section does little more than provide a framework for analysis based on the principal concepts of the eclectic paradigm.

2.2.1   Ownership- or firm-specific factors   As noted above, the first attempts to explain the growth of the MNE concentrated on its ownership-specific advantages. The potential MNE should possess some unique competitive advantage which is capable of international exploitation. The foregoing discussion suggested that the MNE's evolution is attributable in large part to the possession of technological advantage and large firm size. The two are closely related. Large size may be important to successful innovation because of high research and development costs which can only be borne by a larger enterprise.[124] Furthermore, firm size is closely connected to the protection of technological advantage. As seen above, this is a factor also taken up by later theories based on the concept of internalization.

In relation to ownership- or firm-specific factors the most significant function of capitalist legal systems is to facilitate the creation and exploitation of such advantages by firms, including the MNE. Of particular importance are, first, the protection of the firm's innovations and brands as proprietary rights and, secondly, the creation of structures conducive to the growth of large corporations. The first task can be met by a system of patent and trademark protection, coupled with an effective system of contract law which can regulate the use of the firm's property in the hands of a licensee, while the second can be met by a system of company law that allows for the creation of a large joint stock fund and the ownership of shares by one company in another, without restriction as to the nationality of the shareholding company.

A system of patent law ensures the protection of the firm's competitive advantages by granting to the firm a monopoly for the exploitation of that advantage for a specified period of time. This legal right assists in the creation of a more certain environment for the extraction of a full return on the firm's investment in innovation. Patent rights will complement the MNE's protection of its innovation through the market power it enjoys as a result of its integrated international network and from the difficulty of re-creating advanced industrial technology.[125] Given the existence of such organizational and technological factors in the protection of competitive advantages, it has been argued that patent law is not used to protect those advantages, at least where MNEs are involved.[126] Therefore, the contemporary significance of patent law as a means of protecting the firm-specific advantages of MNEs is open to debate. This is exacerbated by the use in certain countries of technology transfer laws which establish controls over the manner in which the foreign firm may sell and apply its technology in the host state. On the other hand, the major capital exporting states continue to insist on the legal protection of intellectual property rights owned by their MNEs.[127]

Furthermore, the role of patent law as a historical incentive for the growth of direct investment cannot be doubted. For example, in Canada in 1872 non-Canadians were permitted for the first time to hold Canadian patents. An increase in direct investment through subsidiaries of US companies resulted. Historical evidence on individual firms suggests that patent protection played a crucial role in encouraging direct investments in the Canadian agricultural implements, electrical engineering and automobile industries.[128] There is also evidence to suggest that patent legislation was instrumental in the encouragement of inward direct investment in France, Germany and England.[129]

To the extent that size is a contributing factor to multinationality, legal conditions that permit the growth of large corporations can be seen as instrumental in the growth of MNEs. The availability of the joint stock limited liability company is, in the words of Professor Leslie Hannah, 'a necessary precondition for the widespread adoption of modern industrial organisation'.[130] It facilitates the creation of a large investment fund for the conduct of the business carried on by the company that is legally separate from the private property of the company's members, who are protected from personal liability for the debts of the company up to the limits of their respective contributions to the capital of the company.

Modern company law has evolved in a manner especially conducive to the growth of large-scale businesses. In particular, the acceptance of the holding company concept made mergers and acquisitions much simpler, and permitted the growth of corporate groups.[131] In the USA, New Jersey was the first state to authorize one corporation to hold shares in another under legislation passed in 1888. Other states subsequently followed suit.[132] In the UK a company was permitted to hold subsidiaries if their aims accorded with the aims of the parent as stated in its articles of association.[133] In Germany, the limited liability company provided an instrument for the accumulation and centralization of capital. In particular, the establishment of the supervisory board as the directing organ of the company permitted control of the enterprise by representatives of the investment banks which held widespread controlling interests in German corporations in the late nineteenth century.[134]

However, while the existence of the corporate legal form has been a necessary element in the growth of large corporate groups it is not a sufficient element.[135] Economic factors have been the primary stimulants to the development of large corporations. Thus there were discernable uniformities in the growth, during the late nineteenth and early twentieth centuries, of large enterprises in the various industrializing countries.[136] Equally, in the USA and UK rising share prices in the late nineteenth century may have stimulated the earliest mergers between firms.[137] Furthermore, in Germany, the early development of integrated corporate groups may have resulted from the relative economic underdevelopment of the country.[138] Therefore, the role of legal factors in the growth of large enterprises should be seen as being one of having influenced the form that these enterprises would take but not of causing their evolution.

Finally, considerable speculation has arisen over the role of anti-trust laws in the evolution of corporate group structures. The argument runs that the passage of antitrust laws acts as a stimulant to merger activity by blocking off the possibility of increasing monopoly power through the conclusion of cartel agreements between competing firms. While there is some evidence of a coincidence between the passage of antitrust laws and an increase in merger activity,[139] no conclusive correlation between these factors has been established.[140] Indeed, the fact that firms will enter cartels, even if they are illegal under the laws of the countries in which the participating firms operate, should make such a correlation hard to establish. Furthermore, as noted earlier, cartels and mergers may be seen as complementary and not alternative strategies.[141] In relation to the growth of MNEs between 1918 and 1939, as noted above, international cartels and foreign direct investment were complementary strategies adopted by firms. Therefore, it may not be possible to prove that antitrust considerations act as decisive factors in the growth of large national and multinational corporations, given that economic factors will determine the extent to which a firm will collude with others to control a market or internalize that market through internal expansion or the takeover of competitors.

The foregoing discussion has related legal phenomena to theories of MNE growth based on firm size and technological advantage. However, not all explanations of MNE growth concentrate on these two factors. For example, it has been argued that a firm may have to go multinational so as to coordinate and neutralize the threat posed by its competitors' decision to go multinational.[142] Other theories have concentrated on the competitive advantage enjoyed by MNEs in international capital markets as an explanation of MNE growth.[143] Another possible explanation of multinationality, related to the financial aspects of the foreign activities of firms, is that certain companies invest abroad not to achieve economies of scale and production but to diversify investment and, thereby, to reduce risk.[144] These explanations are related to competitive conditions in international capital and products markets and do not, as such, imply any significant role for legal factors as devices for the protection of firm-specific advantage.

However, there may be significant legal issues related to the regulation of the particular industry or country in which the firm operates that contribute to the overall patterns of competition in relation to

which the MNE functions. For example, Hood and Young[145] argue
that if a firm has privileged access to raw materials or minerals this
counts as a firm-specific advantage although, in general, a requirement for raw materials is a country-specific factor influencing the
location of extractive, processing or production activities. The retention of control over the raw materials concerned hinges initially on
the possession of extractive technology. This advantage is then enhanced by the market power obtained by the firm in controlling
access to the raw material and by vertical integration into production
and distribution.[146] This can explain, for example, the dominance of the oil industry by the 'oil majors'[147] or the reasons for
multinationality in the copper industry.[148] However, the possession of
access to raw materials may not be a permanent source of advantage.
External political pressures for greater host country control over
natural resources and/or drops in demand for the finished products
based on the raw material due to substitution or conservation have
caused vertical disintegration in raw materials industries. Thus, the
possession of raw materials is a firm-specific asset strongly conditioned by locational factors, including home and host state legal
regulation, and technological factors, which connote the earlier discussion on legal protection of ownership advantages. Furthermore,
the role of legal factors as elements in the MNE–host state bargaining process should not be overlooked.[149]

2.2.2 Locational factors   It follows from our earlier discussion of
economic theory that the choice of whether a firm should make a
direct investment depends on whether the costs of doing so can be
offset in the long run against the benefits. This, in turn, depends on
the interaction of O and I advantages with local conditions in prospective host locations. Relevant local factors include, *inter alia*:
whether the size and growth potential of the host's market is sufficient to justify the cost of opening a local production unit; whether
the host state provides a gateway to other markets through exports;
whether the local workforce is capable of working in the new plant;
whether wages are at a level that makes local production profitable; whether there are any public subsidies that can offset the cost
of the investment; whether the host state will set up barriers to
protect the local production unit against outside competition. If these
factors point to long-term profitability the firm will undertake a direct
investment through a subsidiary. Thus, an economic transition from
market to firm in the supply of the host state market will take place.

There can be little doubt that legal factors form an important
category of locational factors, designed to facilitate the achievement
of state economic goals whether these consist of protecting indigenous firms from foreign competition, allowing foreign firms to
enter the economy under strict controls or providing positive incen-

tives to investors in an attempt to improve the host state's advantages as a location for MNEs. In theory, therefore, the state may use its political power through law to alter its locational advantages and thereby influence the investment decisions of MNEs. The process may be illustrated by analysing the ways in which a firm might supply its products to customers in the host state. It is useful, first, to consider the issue in purely economic terms and then to examine how different legal regimes might affect the firm's choices. It is assumed that commercial conditions in the host state make it an attractive market for the foreign firm. Firms will not normally invest in the host state where this is not the case.

The simplest way to supply customers in the host state is for the firm to export its goods to the host market. This alternative will be chosen where the transaction costs of direct sales to end customers under an international sales contract are low enough not to affect the profitability of the transaction to the firm. However, the supply of the host market through direct sales will become unattractive where the volume of exports to the host is such that the transaction costs of exporting are getting too high. The transaction costs involved would include costs of negotiating individual contracts and costs of monitoring compliance. Some relief from negotiation costs could be obtained by selling in the export market through an agent. However, this too can involve transaction costs, particularly in relation to monitoring the agent's compliance with the terms of the agency agreement. Thus the firm may have to consider whether it should move to licensing local production or to making a direct investment.

In order for licensing to be chosen the host country must be endowed with a sufficient level of industrial organization and labour skills to offer suitable potential licensees for the exploitation of the foreign firm's assets. In the absence of a suitable licensee, the firm has only the choice between high cost exporting or direct investment. On the other hand, where a suitable licensee does exist, the firm must consider the cost of entering a licensing agreement over those of a direct investment in a subsidiary. As noted earlier, of prime importance here is the question of whether the licensee can be trusted to use the firm's O advantages in a manner that will not undermine their commercial worth. This is particularly significant in relation to unique technology or know-how, whose commercial value lies in its proper use and in the retention of its confidential character. A licensee may not be sufficiently capable or trustworthy, even under a strict contractual regime governed by terms favourable to the licensor, to be entrusted with the exploitation of the technology in question. In such a case, the higher cost option of establishing a local subsidiary, or the takeover of the potential licensee by the licensor, may be the only commercially effective way of protecting the foreign firm's O advantages.

Let us now consider the situation in the context of state intervention through legal regimes. The export option will only remain open as long as the host state does not pursue protectionist policies that seek to reduce the presence of foreign products in the local market. However, assuming that the host state wishes to preserve the consumption of the goods or services offered by the foreign firm, it may prefer that those products are locally produced. The host state may seek this objective by imposing high tariff barriers to trade, thereby cutting out the possibility of serving the market through exports from the home country. The foreign firm then has a choice between jumping the tariff barrier and setting up local production, through a licensee or a production subsidiary, or not investing at all. The firm may be forced to jump the tariff barrier and go multinational if the host market is too large to be ignored, or if competitors are undertaking the expense of licensing or direct investment. Indeed, 'tariff jumping' has proved to be a significant historical reason for firms setting up production subsidiaries in host countries.[150]

Alternatively, the host state may use its regulatory power to require that the foreign firm supply the market through the licensing of a local firm, or through an equity joint venture with a local firm or state entity. Here the foreign firm must decide whether the costs of compliance are outweighed by the costs of not investing at all. The market conditions in the host country, as related to the position of the firm in the global market, and to that of its competitors, will be taken into account. If it can afford to do so, the firm may decline the opportunity to invest.[151] If not it will have to sustain the cost of complying with the law and enter into the required licensing agreement or joint venture.

On the other hand, the host state may be dependent on the foreign firm to transfer its technology and know-how to the host state. In these circumstances, the host state may relinquish its power to restrict entry and establishment and may offer investment incentives to induce the MNE to invest. This raises questions relevant to the location-specific advantages of host states concerning differences between their respective regulatory environments. A MNE may choose to invest in state A rather than state B if the law of state A offers fewer regulatory constraints than the law of state B. Thus, for example, differences in, *inter alia*, disclosure requirements,[152] levels of taxation,[153] antitrust controls[154] or principles of corporate liability[155] can influence the decision of a MNE to locate in A rather than B.

From the foregoing discussion it is clear that legal factors may have a role to play in determining the locational characteristics of the host state. However, it would be wrong to assume that they are of prime significance. Ultimately, MNEs invest in a country because of its economic attractions, which, when combined with the O and I advantages of the firm, should serve to profit the latter. If they do not, investment by the MNE is unlikely.

2.2.3 Internalization factors   The legal aspects of internalization advantages in MNE growth raise perhaps the most contentious issues. The interaction between the legal aspects of locational advantages and the internalization advantages of MNEs has already been discussed. Indeed, the ability of a MNE to take advantage of differences in regulatory environments between states is seen as one of its internalization advantages. The resulting potential for the ineffectiveness of national regulation over the activities of MNEs has led certain states to apply their laws extraterritorially to non-resident units of MNEs operating within their jurisdiction. The consequence has been to encourage conflict over the exercise of such jurisdiction between the regulating state and the state in which the targeted unit of the MNE operates.[156]

The conflict caused by uncoordinated unilateral state policies has led to attempts at greater international cooperation in regulatory matters and at the evolution of an international consensus over the standards to be applied to the regulation of MNEs.[157] The supranational incorporation of MNEs has also been mooted.[158] The development of a genuine international law of foreign direct investment would serve to reduce the internalization advantages enjoyed by MNEs as a result of diversity in national regulations, through the harmonization of state policies. However, such harmonization may not produce desirable results as regards the welfare of individual states. It may not, therefore, be politically feasible.[159]

Further issues arise out of the relationship between O advantages and I advantages. In particular, the possession of a monopolistic advantage by a MNE suggests the need to control any abuse of that advantage through antitrust law. However, proponents of theories based on the concept of internalization will argue that the replacement of the market in intermediate goods with the hierarchy of the firm is an efficient outcome and the resulting competitive advantage to the firm should not be interfered with. The argument runs that the law should encourage such efficiency gains by not opposing the creation of internalization advantages. In the case of MNEs such advantages can be created either by mergers between suppliers and consumers of intermediate products, involving the takeover of a domestic firm by a foreign firm, or by the establishment of a subsidiary of a foreign firm in the host state. In the former case, the foreign nationality of the purchaser should not bar the takeover, while in the latter case, the potential threat posed by the new investment to the long-term survival or development of domestic competitors should not prevent entry. This approach is taken by countries which espouse an 'open door' to foreign inward investment.[160]

On the other hand, states may react by seeking to unbundle the internalization advantages of MNEs. According to Hood and Young,[161] a major difficulty with Buckley and Casson's above-mentioned thesis is that the long-run political or other costs of internalization may eventually make it prohibitively expensive, especially where host nations adopt discriminatory policies towards MNEs. For example, in the late 1960s and early 1970s, the wave of major nationalizations by the OPEC countries of upstream oil production facilities owned and controlled by the major oil companies effectively deinternalized those activities and replaced them with arm's length dealings between the newly formed national oil production companies that took over the nationalized assets and the oil majors: internalization gave way to interdependence between independent companies.[162]

Apart from forced divestiture, a host state could compel the sharing of firm-specific advantages with local firms through technology transfer laws or performance requirements. Again, the choice will be influenced by the host state's view of the welfare effects of inward direct investment.[163] However, in an environment geared towards investment promotion and economic deregulation, the exploitation by the MNE of its knowledge advantages within its internalized structures is more likely to be accepted and host states may refrain from regulation that interferes with this choice.

Finally, the legal response to the internalization of labour markets, identified by Cowling and Sugden as a significant competitive advantage of the MNE,[164] should be considered. Cowling and Sugden argue *inter alia* that firms become multinational in order to take advantage of lower labour costs that result from the firm's enhanced ability to 'divide and rule': 'by producing in various countries firms divide their workforce, thereby reduce labour's bargaining power, and consequently obtain lower labour costs'.[165] The ability to reduce labour costs in this way may be at least a contributory reason for the existence of some multinationals.[166]

The advantage enjoyed by the MNE over domestic firms as an exploiter of labour will depend to a significant degree on the legal conditions regarding labour relations that are imposed on it by host states. The responses of countries vary from protection of trade union rights and collective bargaining to outright repression. Thus countries may differ in the extent to which their laws will preserve the comparative advantage of MNEs over labour. The diversity of legal responses to the protection of labour rights represents, in itself, a barrier to effective cross-border trade union organization. To that extent legal factors may assist in the preservation of the MNEs advantages in this field.[167]

3   Concluding Remarks

The present chapter has sought to trace the evolution of the MNE over space and time, to summarize the leading explanations as to why the growth of such firms has occurred and to identify the most significant legal factors that may have contributed, and continue to contribute, to that growth. This is by no means a final or complete analysis. The reasons for the growth of MNEs are open to considerable debate, as reflected by the emergence of an 'eclectic' paradigm, rather than a single dominant theory of international production.

Our understanding of the contribution of legal factors to the growth of MNEs is even less advanced than economic theory. None the less, as this chapter has sought to show, the study of such factors can evolve within the same general framework as used by the eclectic paradigm. Further research is needed along these lines. On the other hand, the eclectic paradigm's concentration on firm, location and internalization factors in the growth of MNEs cannot offer a complete explanation of the origins of legal responses to MNE activities. This approach must be supplemented by reference to the relationship between the business organization and legal forms of multinational enterprise and by an understanding of the debate on the effects of MNE operations on national economies and resulting approaches to regulation. These further considerations will form the basis of the next two chapters.

Notes

1   See Peter Hertner and Geoffrey Jones (eds), *Multinationals: Theory and History* (Gower, 1986), chapter 1, 'Multinationals: theory and history', pp. 1–18. See further Geoffrey Jones, *The Evolution of International Business: An Introduction* (Routledge, 1996).

2   See, for example, D. Vagts, 'The multinational enterprise: a new challenge for transnational law', 83 Harv. LR 739 (1970).

3   See N. Horn and J. Kocka (eds), *Law and the Formation of Big Enterprises in the 19th and Early 20th Centuries* (Gottingen, 1979).

4   For the Charters of the major English trading companies see C. T. Carr, *Select Charters of Trading Corporations* (Selden Society, 1913). See, for a discussion of the sovereign immunities of the East India Company, *Nabob of the Carnatic* v *East India Co.* (1791) 1 Ves. Jr. 371; *The Ex-Rajah of Coorg* v *East India Co.* (1860) 29 Beav. 300; F. A. Mann, *Studies in*

International Law (Oxford, 1973), pp. 200–3. See further McNulty, 'Predecessors of the multinational corporation', Col. Jo. World Bus. (May–June, 1972), p. 73; Havrylyshyn, 'The internationalisation of firms', 5 JWTL 72 (1971).

5   See Ann M.Carlos and Stephen Nicholas, 'Giants of an earlier capitalism: the chartered trading companies as modern multinationals', 62 Bus. Hist. Rev. 398 (1988).

6   M. Wilkins, *The Emergence of Multinational Enterprise: American Business Abroad from the Colonial Era to 1914* (Harvard, 1970).

7   See L. Franko, *The European Multinationals* (Harper & Row, 1976).

8   On which see further A. D. Chandler, *Scale and Scope: the Dynamics of Industrial Capitalism* (Belknap/Harvard University Press, 1990). See also J. H. Dunning, *Multinational Enterprises and the Global Economy* (Addison Wesley, 1992), chapter 5.

9   See Dunning, ibid.

10 See J. Scott, *Capitalism, Corporations and Class* (1979), chapter 7, 'The internationalization of capital and the multinational company', especially at p. 160.

11 See M. Wilkins, 'Defining a firm: history and theory', in Hertner and Jones, *Multinationals: Theory and History*, especially at pp. 84–7; G. Jones, 'Origins, management and performance', in G. Jones (ed.) *British Multinationals: Origins, Management and Performance* (Gower Business History Series, 1986), at pp. 3–4.

12 G. Jones, 'The expansion of British multinational manufacturing, 1890–1939', in T. Inoue and A. Okochi (eds), *Overseas Business Activities: Proceedings of the Ninth Fuji Conference* (1984). See also: Jones, 'The performance of British multinational enterprise 1890–1945', in Hertner and Jones, *Multinationals: Theory and History*, p. 96; Jones (ed.), *British Multinationals: Origins, Management and Performance* (Gower Business History Series, 1986).

13 J. Stopford, 'The origins of British-based multinational manufacturing enterprises', 48 *Business History Review* 303 (1974). Stopford's figures have been doubted: see Jones, 'Expansion of British . . .', at p. 126.

14 See Svedberg, 'The Portfolio-direct composition of private foreign investment in 1914 revisited', 88 *Economic Journal* 763 (1978); I. Stone, 'British direct and portfolio investment in Latin America before 1914', 37 *Journal of Economic History* 690 (1977).

15 See Franko, *European Multinationals*. See the criticism of Franko's study in Hertner and Jones, *Multinationals: Theory and History*, at p. 7. See further: the contributions to Hertner and Jones in chapters 6 to 10; M. Wilkins, 'European multinationals in the United States: 1875–1914', in A. Teichova *et al.* (eds), *Multinational Enterprise in Historical Perspective* (Cambridge University Press, 1986), p. 55; M. Wilkins, *The History of Foreign Investment in the United States to 1914* (Harvard University Press, 1989).

16 See Hertner, 'German multinational enterprise before 1914: some case studies', in Hertner and Jones (note 1 above), p. 113.

17 See Hertner, 'Financial strategies and adaptation to foreign markets: the

German electro-technical industry and its multinational activities: 1890s to 1939', in Teichova *et al.* (note 15 above), p. 145.

18 See C. Tugendhat, *The Multinationals* (Pelican, 1973), at pp. 33 and 147; and see E. Hornell and J. Vahlne, *Multinationals: the Swedish Case* (Croom Helm, 1986), pp. 4–6.

19 Franko (note 7 above), at p. 52.

20 This was mainly portfolio investment: J. Savary, *French Multinationals* (Frances Pinter/IRM, 1984), pp. 1–2. However, there is no comprehensive study of the evolution of French MNEs during this period and the information appears to be rather speculative. Thus the proportion of French foreign direct investment in 1914 may in fact be higher than reported by Savary who, relying on the work of Franko (*European Multinationals*, see note 7), notes that by 1914 only one French firm had industrial subsidiaries abroad. See further contributions in Hertner and Jones (see note 1) by: Fridenson, 'The growth of multinational activities in the French motor industry 1890–1979', p. 157; Broder, 'The multinationalisation of the French electrical industry 1880–1914: dependence and its causes', p. 169.

21 See M. Wilkins, (note 6 above).

22 This claim is made by Christopher Tugendhat in *The Multinationals* (note 18 above), at p. 33.

23 See Wilkins (note 6 above), at pp. 37–45, on which the following account draws. Samuel Colt had set up a factory for the manufacture of his revolvers in the UK in 1852. However the investment failed and was sold off in 1857. According to Wilkins (p. 30) this appears to have been the first foreign branch plant of any American company.

24 See further Wilkins, ibid., at pp. 70–109; Chandler (note 8 above), at pp. 71–9.

25 Ibid., at p. 201–2.

26 See J. Dunning, 'Changes in the level and structure of international production: the last one hundred years', in M. Casson (ed.), *The Growth of International Business* (George Allen and Unwin, 1983), pp. 85–91. For an updated analysis see Dunning (note 8 above).

27 Ibid.

28 See J. Wilczynski, *The Multinationals and East–West Relations* (Macmillan, 1976), p. 108, n. 11.

29 P. Jacquemot, *La Firme Multinationale: une Introduction Economique* (Collection Gestion, Economica, Paris, 1990), p. 25. See, for example, Kernbauer and Weber, 'Multinational banking in the Danube Basin: the business strategy of the Viennese banks after the collapse of the Hapsburg monarchy', in Teichova *et al.* (note 15 above), p. 185.

30 Tugendhat (note 18 above), p. 39.

31 See, on Germany, the interesting chapter by Overy, 'German multinationals and the Nazi state in occupied Europe', in Teichova *et al.* (note 15 above), p. 299. On Italy see Denis Mack Smith, *Mussolini* (Granada, 1983), pp. 133–42, 219–20.

32 See Overy, ibid.; Chandler (note 8 above), at pp. 564–84.

33 Franko, (note 7 above), at pp. 95–6.

34   L. Hannah, *The Rise of the Corporate Economy*, 2nd edn (Methuen, 1983), p. 38. See further W. J. Reader, *Imperial Chemical Industries: a History*, Volume 1 (1970), pp. 439–66; Chandler (note 8 above), at pp. 356–66. In 1993 ICI demergered and split into two companies when its pharmaceutical, seeds, speciality and agrochemical divisions were formed into a new company, Zeneca: see *Financial Times*, 26 February 1993, p. 22.

35   Franko (see note 33 above).

36   See H. Schroter 'A typical factor of German international market strategy: agreements between US and German electrotechnical industries up to 1939', in Teichova *et al.* (note 15 above), p. 160.

37   See Tugendhat (note 18 above), at pp. 41–4. For further examples of international cartels of this period see E. Hexner, *International Cartels* (Pitman, 1946).

38   Franko (note 7 above), at pp. 97–8.

39   Tugendhat (see note 37 above).

40   Webb-Pomerene Act s. 2. See further *US* v *United States Alkali Export Association Inc.*, 86 F. Supp. 59 (1949).

41   Dunning (note 26 above), at p. 92, n. 12. and table 5.1 at p. 87.

42   Ibid.

43   On US firms in the inter-war period see M. Wilkins, *The Maturing of Multinational Enterprise: American Business Abroad from 1914 to 1970* (Harvard, 1974); on British firms see Jones (note 11 above).

44   See, for example, V. Schroter, 'Participation in market control through foreign investment: IG Farbenindustrie AG in the United States' in Teichova *et al.* (note 15 above), p. 171.

45   See Nussbaum, 'International cartels and multinational enterprises', in Teichova *et al.* (note 15 above), p. 131, especially at pp. 138–9.

46   Dunning (note 26 above), at pp. 92–3.

47   G. Jones in Inoue and Okochi (note 12 above), at p. 144.

48   Ibid.

49   Dunning (note 26 above), at p. 92.

50   Ibid., at pp. 93–4; Dunning (note 8 above), at pp. 125–33.

51   D. Shepherd, A. Silberston and R. Strange, *British Manufacturing Investment Overseas* (Methuen, 1985), p. 13.

52   See Overy (note 31 above).

53   R. Vernon, *Sovereignty at Bay* (Pelican, 1973), p. 91.

54   Ibid., at pp. 94–101.

55   See N. Hood and S. Young, *The Economics of Multinational Enterprise* (Longman, 1979), pp. 11–12; Tugendhat (note 18 above), chapter 2; Vernon, ibid., pp. 91–101.

56   Such tax privileges have since been narrowed down. See further chapter 8.

57   On which see chapter 5, at pp. 129–31.

58   See, for example, Tugendhat (note 55 above), who attributes the shift of investment by US firms from the UK to mainland Europe to the formation of the EC.

59   Vernon (note 53 above), at p. 93.

60   Dunning (note 26 above), at pp. 93–4.

61   Ibid., table 5.1, at p. 87.
62   See Franko (note 7 above), at pp. 98–104, on which the following para-
     graphs are based.
63   See Savary (note 20 above), at p. 2; C. A. Michalet and M. Delapierre, *La
     Multinationalisation des Entreprises Françaises* (Ed. Gauthier-Villars, 1973),
     pp. 18–29.
64   Dunning (note 26 above), at p. 94.
65   Ibid., at p. 96.
66   UNCTC, *Transnational Corporations in World Development: Trends and
     Prospects* (UN Doc. ST/CTC/89, 1988), at p. 74 and table V.2, at p. 77.
67   See Dunning (note 26 above), at pp. 96–7; See OECD, *International Direct
     Investment – Policies and Trends in the 1980s* (OECD, 1992). The UNCTC
     has estimated that in 1985 the figure was 23 per cent: UNCTC (note 66
     above), at p. 80.
68   See UNCTAD, *World Investment Report 1998* (United Nations, New York
     and Geneva) pp. 13–18.
69   See further M. Wilkins, 'Japanese multinational enterprise before 1914',
     60 Bus. Hist. Rev. 199 (1986).
70   UNCTC (note 68 above).
71   See M. Y. Yoshino, 'The multinational spread of Japanese manufacturing
     investment since World War II', 48 Bus. Hist. Rev. 357 at 360–1 (1974).
     On the emergence of Japanese MNEs see further: M. Y. Yoshino, *Japan's
     Multinational Enterprises* (Harvard, 1976); T. Ozawa, *Multinationalism,
     Japanese Style: The Political Economy of Outward Dependency* (Princeton
     University Press, 1979). On more recent patterns of Japanese MNE in-
     vestment, see: L. Franko, *The Threat of Japanese Multinationals – How the
     West Can Respond* (Wiley/IRM Series on Multinationals 1983); T. Ozawa
     'Japan in a new phase of multinationalism and industrial upgrading: func-
     tional integration and trade growth', 25 JWT (No. 1, February 1991) 43.
72   Ozawa, ibid., at pp. 13–14.
73   Ibid., at p. 16.
74   Yoshino (note 71 above, 48 Bus. Hist. Rev.), at p. 373.
75   See Franko (note 71 above), at p. 71.
76   See further: L. Turner, *Industrial Collaboration with Japan* (RIIA/RKP
     Chatham House Papers No. 34, 1987); M. Mason and D. Encarnation
     (eds), *Does Ownership Matter: Japanese Multinationals in Europe*
     (Clarendon Press, 1994).
77   Dunning (note 26 above), at p. 97.
78   See Ozawa (note 71 above), chapter 5.
79   Ibid., at pp. 140–53.
80   UNCTC (note 66 above), at p. 77.
81   See Fujita, 'FDI between Japan and the United States', *CTC Reporter*, No.
     29 (Spring 1990), 31.
82   UNCTC (note 66 above), table V.4, at p. 86.
83   Ibid., at p. 87.
84   UNCTC (note 66 above), at p. 74.
85   See E. Graham and P. Krugman, *Foreign Direct Investment in the United
     States* (Institute for International Economics, 1989), p. 34, table 2.2. By

1990 the figures had changed as follows: UK 26.8 per cent; Japan 20.7 per cent; Netherlands 15.9 per cent; Canada 6.9 per cent: ibid. (2nd edn, 1991), at p. 43. Figures up to 1992 are presented in ibid. (3rd edn, 1995), Table 2.2 at p. 44. These show little change from 1990.

86   UNCTC (note 66 above), at p. 75.

87   'Multinationals switch focus of investment', *Financial Times*, 16 June 1992, p. 4. On the recent slow down in the US economy see Graham and Krugman (note 85 above, 2nd edn, 1991), at pp. 21–3, (3rd edn, 1995) at pp. 20–21.

88   OECD, *Recent Trends in International Direct Investment* (OECD, 1987), p. 11.

89   UNCTC (note 66 above), pp. 79–80.

90   Ibid., p. 80.

91   South, East and South East Asia is the subregion accounting for the dominant share of FDI in developing regions in the past decade. Flows increased slightly in 1997, despite the East Asian financial crisis, with investment into China compensating for the modest decline in inward investment in the countries most affected. Latin America and the Caribbean were the leading developing regions for inward investment in 1997 attracting an additional $12bn over 1996. However continued weak demand for commodities dampened investment into Africa and the 48 least developed countries received only $1.8bn or 0.5% of world FDI inflows in 1997: see UNCTAD (note 68 above).

92   See S. Lall *et al.*, *The New Multinationals: the Spread of Third World Enterprises* (Wiley/IRM Series on Multinationals, 1983); L. Wells, *Third World Multinationals* (MIT Press, 1983).

93   For example, the Kuwait Petroleum Company, which owns refining facilities in the US and distribution facilities in the UK operating under the 'Q8' trade name: see L. Turner, *Oil Companies in the International System* (RIAA/George Allen and Unwin, 1983), pp. 237–9. Similarly Petroleos de Venezuela owns 50 per cent of the stock in the German company Ruhr Oel GmbH and two oil companies in the USA, Citgo Petroleum Corp and Nynas Petroleum: see UNCTC (note 66 above), p. 38.

94   For example, Samsung had 39 offices in 29 countries by 1980; it opened a production plant in the USA in 1984 and it plans to establish 15 overseas factories by 1990: ibid., p. 39 and box II.2.

95   See further chapter 6.

96   Tolentino, 'Overall trends of foreign direct investment', *CTC Reporter*, No. 29 (Spring 1990), p. 28.

97   See further: C. McMillan, *Multinationals From the Second World* (Macmillan, 1987); G. Hamilton (ed.), *Red Multinationals or Red Herrings?* (Frances Pinter, 1986); J. Wilczynski, *The Multinationals and East–West Relations* (Macmillan, 1976), chapter 6 at pp. 104–8 and chapter 8. It will be interesting to see how these firms will develop as their home economies transform into market economies.

98   See Tolentino (note 96 above), at pp. 28–9.

99   See John Plender, 'A bigger gap, a bigger problem', *Financial Times*, 10 August 1987, p. 8. See also L. Sklair, *The Sociology of the Global System* (Harvester Wheatsheaf, 1991), pp. 102–3. See further UNCTAD, *World*

Investment Report 1993: Transnational Corporations and Integrated International Production (UN, 1993); UNCTAD, World Investment Report 1994: Transnational Corporations Employment and the Workplace (UN, 1994).

100 See further Dunning (note 8 above), especially chapters 3 and 4. For a valuable, though now somewhat dated, introduction to the principal economic theories of the MNE and foreign direct investment see N. Hood and S. Young, The Economics of Multinational Enterprise (Longman, 1979). See also R. Caves, Multinational Enterprise and Economic Analysis (Cambridge University Press, 2nd edn, 1996); C. N. Pitelis and R. Sugden (eds), The Nature of the Transnational Firm (Routledge, 1991), especially chapter 2, 'A survey of theories of international production', by John Cantwell.

101 See J. H. Dunning, Explaining International Production (Unwin Hyman, 1988), chapter 12.

102 S. Hymer, The International Operations of National Firms, PhD thesis 1960. Published in 1976 by MIT Press.

103 C. P. Kindleberger, American Business Abroad: Six Lectures on Direct Investment (Yale University Press, 1969), pp. 14–27.

104 Commonly referred to as the Heckscher–Ohlin Model. See Dunning (note 101 above), at pp. 22–3. See further P. Samuelson and W. D. Nordhaus, Economics, 13th edn (McGraw-Hill, 1989), chapter 38.

105 See further Dunning (note 101 above), chapter 2. On the application of the transaction cost approach as an explanation of the growth of British MNEs see Nicholas, 'British multinational investment before 1939', Journal of European Economic History, 605 (1982); Nicholas, 'The theory of multinational enterprise as a transactional mode', in Jones and Hertner (note 1 above), p. 64.

106 See 'International investment and international trade in the product cycle', 80 Q. Jo. Econ. 190 (1966). This original version of the 'product cycle' thesis is further developed by Vernon in his book Sovereignty at Bay (note 53 above). The 'product cycle' thesis began to lose its relevance by the mid-1970s as Professor Vernon himself has admitted: see Vernon, 'The location of economic activity', in J. Dunning (ed.), Economic Analysis and the Multinational Enterprise (Allen & Unwin, 1974), p. 89; 'The product cycle hypothesis in a new international environment', 41 Oxford Bull. Econ. Stat. 255 (1979); Sovereignty at Bay, at p. 109. While the 'product cycle' thesis works as an explanation for the expansion of US MNEs abroad, and may still explain the entry of new US firms into international production, it is of limited relevance in explaining the behaviour of established MNEs or MNEs from other home states.

107 R. Coase, 'The nature of the firm', 4 Economica (New Series) 386 (1937). More recently the writings of Oliver Williamson have elaborated on this concept: see Markets and Hierarchies: Analysis and Antitrust Implications (Free Press 1975); The Economic Institutions of Capitalism: Firms, Markets, Relational Contracting (Free Press, 1985); Economic Organisation: Firms Markets and Policy Control (Harvester Wheatsheaf, 1986), especially pp. 158–162 on MNEs. For a critique of Williamson's approach to MNE growth see N. Kay, 'Multinational enterprise as strategic choice: some transaction cost perspectives', in Pitelis and Sugden (note 100 above), at p. 137.

108   P. J. Buckley and M. Casson, *The Future of the Multinational Enterprise* (Macmillan, 1976; revised 2nd edn with new introduction, 1991), at p. 2. (References are to the 1991 edition.)

109   Ibid., at p. 33.

110   Ibid., at pp. 37–8. For a broadly similar analysis see: Caves (note 100 above), at pp. 1–23. See also Kindleberger (note 103 above) at p. 17 for a discussion of the licensing–direct investment choice, which implies a 'transaction cost' approach.

111   On which see further chapter 8.

112   Defined by the authors as '[a good] which can be sold many times over, because the supply to one person does not reduce the supply available to others', ibid., at p. 38

113   Ibid., at p. 45.

114   Ibid., at p. 59. By comparison, before the Second World War, 'multinationality was a by-product of the internalisation of intermediate product markets in multistage production processes', particularly in the primary products industries such as food, minerals and oil: ibid., at pp. 59–60.

115   See further ibid., at pp. 56–9. Buckley and Casson thus locate the MNE's advantage not merely in the possession of a unique asset, but in the process of creating and exploiting that asset through the internalization of the relevant factor markets. They write that the MNE's principal advantages are: 'The rewards for past investment in (i) R & D facilities which create an advantage in technological fields, (ii) the creation of an integrated team of skills, the rent from which is greater than the sum of the rewards to individuals, and therefore accruing to "the firm" and within which individuals, as such, are dispensable, (iii) the creation of an information transmission network which allows the benefits of (i) & (ii) to be transmitted at low cost within the organisation but also protects such information, including knowledge of market conditions, from outsiders' (ibid., at p. 69).

116   Ibid., at p. 60.

117   Ibid., at p. 61.

118   See J. H. Dunning, *International Production and the Multinational Enterprise* (George Allen and Unwin, 1981); Dunning (note 101 above), and Dunning (note 8 above), chapter 4.

119   Dunning (note 8 above), at p. 68.

120   Ibid.

121   See ibid., at pp. 79–80, on which this summary draws.

122   Ibid.

123   Ibid. The 'eclectic paradigm' is extended to alliances of firms in J. H. Dunning, *Alliance Capitalism and Global Business* (Routledge, 1997).

124   Hood and Young (note 100 above), at p. 49.

125   See S. P. Magee, 'Information and the multinational corporation: an appropriability theory of direct investment', in J. N. Bhagwati (ed.), *The New International Economic Order* (MIT Press, 1977), p. 317.

126   See S. Lall, 'The patent system and the transfer of technology to less-developed countries' 10 JWTL 1 (1976), at pp. 8–10.

127 These issues are pursued further in chapter 12. See too chapter 7, pp. 254–7.

128 These points were made by my former colleague Greg Marchildon, now of Johns Hopkins University, in my LLM seminar at LSE in November 1988.

129 See Dunning (note 26 above), at p. 107.

130 L. Hannah, 'Mergers, cartels and concentration: legal factors in US and European experience', in N. Horn and J. Kocka (eds), *Law and the Formation of Big Enterprises in the 19th and Early 20th Centuries* (Göttingen, 1979), p. 306.

131 Ibid., at p. 308; Chandler (note 8 above), at p. 73.

132 See J. Willard Hurst, *The Legitimacy of the Business Corporation in the US 1780–1970* (Virginia University Press, 1970), at p. 69.

133 Hannah (note 130 above), at p. 308.

134 See Reich in Horn and Kocka (note 130 above), at pp. 262–71; Hopt in Horn and Kocka, at pp. 227–41; Horn in Horn and Kocka at pp. 123–89 (these chapters are published in German but contain English summaries).

135 Hannah (note 130 above), at p. 308.

136 See further A. Chandler and H. Daems (eds), *Managerial Hierarchies: Comparative Perspectives on the Rise of the Modern Industrial Enterprise* (Harvard University Press, 1980) and Chandler (note 8 above) on patterns in the USA, UK and Germany.

137 Hannah (note 130 above), at pp. 309–10.

138 See Kocka and Siegrist in Horn and Kocka (note 130 above), at pp. 55–122 (in German with English summary).

139 See Hannah (note 130 above), at pp. 311–14 on US merger boom of 1890s coinciding with the Sherman Act; Hannah, *The Rise of the Corporate Economy*, 2nd edn (Methuen, 1983), at pp. 147–9 on the increase in UK mergers after the passage in 1956 of the Restrictive Trade Practices Act.

140 See Hannah, ibid.; W. R. Cornish, 'Legal control over cartels and monopolisation 1880–1914: a comparison', in Horn and Kocka (note 130 above), at pp. 280–305.

141 Hannah, ibid., at p. 312; Kocka and Siegrist (note 130 above), at pp. 62ff.

142 Caves (note 100 above), at p. 93; F. T. Knickerbocker, *Oligopolistic Reaction and the Multinational Enterprise* (Harvard University Press, 1973). See also K. Cowling and R. Sugden, *Transnational Monopoly Capitalism* (Wheatsheaf Books, 1987), at pp. 16–22, who see such defensive behaviour as a response to competitive 'attack' coming from the firm that goes multinational first.

143 See, for example, R. Aliber, 'A theory of direct foreign investment', in C. Kindleberger (ed.), *The International Corporation* (MIT Press, 1970), p. 17, and 'The multinational enterprise in a multiple currency world', in J. H. Dunning (ed.), *The Multinational Enterprise* (George Allen & Unwin, 1971), p. 49. For a critique of Aliber's theory see: Hood and Young (note 100 above), at p. 51; P. Buckley and M. Casson, *The Future of the Multinational Enterprise*, 2nd edn (Macmillan, 1991), at p. 71.

144 See Kopits 'Multinational conglomerate diversification', 32 Econ. Int. 99

145 (1979). See also Caves (note 100 above), at pp. 19–22.

145 Hood and Young (note 100 above), at p. 53.

146 See, for example, T. A. B. Corley, 'Strategic factors in the growth of a multinational enterprise: the Burmah Oil Company 1886–1928', in M. Casson (ed.), *The Growth of International Business* (George Allen & Unwin, 1983), p. 214.

147 These are the largest seven oil companies: Exxon, Mobil, Texaco, Gulf, Socal (Chevron), Shell and BP.

148 See T. Moran, *Multinational Corporations and the Politics of Copper in Chile* (Princeton University Press, 1977).

149 See Muchlinski, 'Law and the analysis of the international oil industry', in J. Rees and P. Odell (eds), *The International Oil Industry: an Interdisciplinary Perspective* (Macmillan, 1987), p. 142. See further chapter 4 below.

150 See, for example, the case of British MNEs in the inter-war years: Jones (note 12 above). For the effect of tariff barriers to trade on US MNEs see M. Wilkins, *The Emergence of Multinational Enterprise: American Business Abroad from the Colonial Era to 1914* (Harvard, 1970), especially pp. 78–109. The industrialization of Canada and Australia through inward direct investment owes much to the use of tariff barriers to trade: see Caves (note 100 above), at pp. 34–5 and references there cited.

151 For example, when, in 1973, India introduced a foreign ownership limit of 40 per cent in Indian subsidiaries of foreign firms, IBM and Coca-Cola decided to leave the Indian market rather than compromise their policy of investing abroad only through wholly owned subsidiaries. See further chapter 6 at pp. 179–80.

152 See chapter 10.

153 See chapter 8.

154 See chapter 11.

155 See chapter 9.

156 See chapter 5.

157 See further part III.

158 See chapter 3.

159 See further chapter 4.

160 See, for example, the UK's policy on foreign takeovers discussed in chapter 11.

161 Hood and Young (note 100 above), at p. 57.

162 See further P. Odell and J. Rees (eds), *The International Oil Industry* (Macmillan, 1987), especially papers by Penrose at p. 9, Zakariah at p. 107, Muchlinski at p. 142.

163 See further chapter 4.

164 Cowling and Sugden (note 142 above).

165 Ibid., at p. 62.

166 See further R. Sugden, 'The importance of distributional considerations', in Pitelis and Sugden (note 100 above) p. 168.

167 See further chapter 13.

3

Business and Legal Forms of Multinational Enterprise: towards a Theory of Control

This chapter deals with the relationship between the business organization and legal form of MNEs. The chapter will first consider the principal types of business organization and control structures commonly found in modern MNEs. Secondly, the main kinds of legal forms adopted by MNEs will be described. Thirdly, the chapter will end with an assessment of the interrelationship between these two elements. This will offer insights into a crucial matter in the regulation of MNEs: namely, where does control over the activities of the enterprise lie, and do the legal forms into which MNEs are expected to fit adequately reflect the allocation of decision-making power in the firm? As will be seen below, legal forms may not coincide with the business organization of the firm. This may lead to a mismatch between the firm's control structures and the legal structures through which the firm is sought to be regulated, to the detriment of effective regulation.

The chapter will proceed on the basis of two assumptions: first, that the business form of the enterprise tends to reflect the market strategy taken by it, in accordance with the 'strategy and structure' thesis of Alfred Chandler;[1] secondly, that the legal form adopted will aim at the most cost-effective accommodation between the corporation's business needs and the regulatory requirements to which it is subject.[2] Here, a significant factor will be the degree of freedom as to the choice of legal form given to the MNE in its various operating jurisdictions.

1 MNEs as Transnational Business Organizations

In common with other large multilocation enterprises, MNEs have outgrown the simple managerial structure of the entrepreneurial corporation.[3] Corporate growth demands a greater specialization and division of labour within the firm. At first, growth may be piecemeal, with new subsidiary corporations being formed as the need for new functions arises and as new products or services are developed. Eventually, however, a major rationalization may take place, with a reorganization of the company along divisional lines of control based on managerial functions, products and areas of operation.[4] This process of 'divisionalization' has been defined as follows:

Divisionalisation is the process by which the structure of a group of companies is changed from the traditional relationship of parent company and subsidiary company to one where all the operating functions of several, or possibly all of the wholly-owned subsidiaries are performed within one corporate entity, and the discreet functions are organised within separate divisions of that company. The previous structure in which each function had a separate formal and legal corporate existence is dispensed with.[5]

Within the MNE such reorganization may involve a restructuring of the global functions of the group. The principal lines of control will differ according to the type of firm and the kinds of markets in which it operates. They will also evolve over time. Thus it is not uncommon for a firm to have begun on its path to multinational organization with an export department, which is then superseded by an international division responsible for all the firm's overseas activities, including exports and direct investments, which, in its turn, may be replaced by a global divisionalization of the firm.[6]

Space prevents a detailed analysis of the different models of global divisionalization. This has been done elsewhere.[7] However, certain valid generalizations can be usefully made. For example, a company, such as an oil company, which locates, extracts, processes, transports and distributes raw materials, will tend to organize around global functional divisions. On the other hand, a company with an undiversified line of products or services, operating in more than one country or region, will tend to organize around a global area divisional structure, while a company with a highly diversified line of products or services will tend to organize around global product or service divisions.[8] If such a diversified company also operates in many different geographical markets it may adopt a matrix structure in which lines of management based on product and area divisions cross. In such cases the management of the firm may become a complex process with competition and conflict emerging between the various lines of command.[9]

Ultimately, divisional structures should represent the most effective communication system between the decision-making centres of the firm and the market(s) in which it operates. In a mature MNE, the size and complexity of the managerial structure could itself become a hindrance to such communication. In response to this probiem MNEs have begun to experiment with more decentralized forms of organization. According to Professor Dunning, the global firm must bear in mind two types of balancing act in this process.[10] The first is that between the international integration of production within the firm and the responsiveness of individual affiliates to the needs of the national economies within which they operate.[11] This may require greater input from local managers in corporate decision-making and greater exchange of information among affiliates. The second is that of obtaining the advantages of geographical and product based organizational structures while avoiding their weaknesses. This may lead to a shift of emphasis away from a hierarchical, vertical, control structure, to a 'heterarchical' network of cooperative and lateral relationships.[12]

The trend towards 'heterarchy' may lead firms to spread certain functions geographically across the enterprise. Thus R&D need not remain tied to the parent company, as has been the trend in past years. Similarly, certain divisional head offices could be relocated outside the home state. Furthermore, the firm itself could be reorganized into smaller, self-standing units of decision-takers who will come together in a mix that fits the business tasks that the firm faces, without creating permanent organizational structures. The role of the head office will then be transformed from that of the ultimate policy-maker and directing 'brain' to that of coordinator and identifier of new business opportunities and the creator of task force networks within the firm. This function may extend beyond the firm to outside bodies possessing the required business and/or technological expertise to realize a business project. Thus, not only will hierarchical structures within the firm be subject to greater organizational flexibility, but the organizational boundaries between individual firms themselves will begin to blur, as increased numbers of strategic alliances are formed.[13]

This new approach to corporate organization has been followed in recent years by several leading MNEs. A commonly cited example is the Italian office equipment manufacturer Olivetti, which sources an increasing proportion of its products from suppliers and operates a network of joint ventures and alliances with small and medium-sized companies around the world, as well as with larger firms such as AT&T of the USA and Canon of Japan.[14] Other firms have been decentralizing specific divisional functions. Thus, in 1991, IBM relocated the headquarters of its communications systems business from New York to near London.[15] Similarly, Hewlett Packard moved the global headquarters of its personal computer product group from California to France, while other firms, notably Electrolux and APV, the British food processing company, have shifted divisional responsibilities to host countries as a result of acquisitions of competitors at similar levels of expertise to themselves.[16] However, as Christopher Lorenz of the *Financial Times* has pointed out, these examples are still rare exceptions and the 'headquarters effect', whereby skills and senior decision-takers are concentrated around the parent company, remains true for many firms.[17] This trend may, therefore, not yet represent the norm, but only an indication of what the future might look like. Indeed, in certain industrial sectors decentralization and 'networking' may be inappropriate, as it would create costs and uncertainties akin to those of an arm's length market, which, as noted in chapter 2, has led to the internalization of functions within the centrally organized MNE. Nevertheless, the trend towards 'networking' and 'heterarchy' must be considered as a significant modification to the conventional notion of the MNE as a unitary pyramid of decision-takers, one which has important implications for discussions of legal regulation and liability, given the changing structures of control that may be involved.

Finally, before we go on to the legal forms of multinational enterprise, it is necessary to consider the degree of centralized control that the head office of a MNE might exercise over local affiliates. While each firm will determine the degree of centralization/decentralization required in accordance with its perception of the most cost-effective and efficient strategy, empirical studies have shown up certain common patterns among MNEs.[18] The findings have concentrated on two sets of factors: first, the general influences on the locus of decision-taking; secondly, the degree of influence commonly exercised by the parent in relation to particular types of decisions.

As to the first, after an extensive review of significant empirical studies the OECD offered the following conclusions:

a foreign subsidiary may be seen as having relatively little autonomy if it belongs to a large multinational group established in many foreign countries; if it manufactures fairly standardised products; if the activities of the members are largely integrated, with important interflows of products between them (this holds true especially for the investment and finance function); if it has been created to serve a market larger than the country in which it is established; or if the parent company holds a large portion of the equity. On the other hand, a subsidiary may be seen as more autonomous if it was acquired to serve mainly the local market; if it belongs to a small group; if it has interchange of products with the rest of the group and is operating in an activity slightly different from that of other members (the opposite holds true for the marketing function); if an important part of its common shares is held by local investors; and if the whole concern pursues a growth strategy.[19]

To these factors may be added: the nationality and resulting business culture of the parent (for example, there is some evidence to suggest that US firms tend to be more centralized than non-US firms); the age of the subsidiary, in that centralization may decrease over time; the method of entry into the host state, in that a new establishment may be more closely controlled than an acquired local company; the industrial sector in which the firm operates, in that some industries will be more globally integrated and centralized than others; the performance of the subsidiary, in that poor performance increases central control; and the tendency of geographically organized MNEs to be less centralized than functional, product or matrix-organized firms.[20]

As to the second, Professor Dunning points out that centralized decisions are more likely in areas that are: 'perceived as being culture free, in those which offer substantial economies of common governance, and those which are likely to be more efficiently implemented by the parent firm'. He cites R&D, capital expenditure plans and dividend policy as examples. By contrast, decisions confined to the affiliate, or matters needing sensitivity to local environments and relationships, such as personnel and labour relations or sales promotion, are likely to be made on a decentralized basis.[21]

Following from the above, for the purposes of discussing control and regulation of MNEs, a distinction will have to be made, first, between hierarchically and heterarchically integrated MNEs, and, secondly, between integrated MNEs and 'transnational networks' involving free-standing firms. Furthermore, the actual degree of control exercised by a parent over its affiliates will vary in accordance with a significant range of factors. This makes the prediction of parent company control for regulatory purposes dependent on specific market and organizational conditions, requiring often difficult economic and commercial analysis. This may lead to the use of presumptions of control as a device for the formulation of legal structures for MNEs, and for the activation of substantive regulations against non-resident units of the MNE. It is an issue that will recur in a number of areas discussed in this work.

2   Legal Forms of Multinational Enterprise

This section offers an attempt at a comprehensive classification and analysis of the principal types of legal structures employed by MNEs in the course of their operations. The legal structure used will be the product of a number of factors, including the nature of the business activity in question and the transaction costs involved,[22] the extent to which the law will require the use of a particular structure and the principal national characteristics of the firm and those of the legal cultures from which and within which it operates. The underlying aim is to create a legal structure that will offer the fewest regulatory burdens while permitting the maximum operational flexibility that is permissible under the law of the state in which the legal structure resides. The resulting legal structure may or may not correspond to the business structure of the enterprise concerned. Much depends on particular circumstances and on the extent to which the hand of management may be involved in an attempt to reduce regulatory burdens.

The classification used divides MNE legal structures into those based on contract, equity based corporate groups, joint ventures between independent firms, informal alliances, publicly owned MNEs and supranational forms of international business.[23] The first three are the most common forms of legal organization open to privately owned and operated firms, the fourth emerges from the observable tendency of MNEs to adopt business alliances that have no clear legal form but which may generate legal liabilities, the fifth considers the distinct legal features of state-owned MNEs and the last considers examples of existing forms of supranational business entities developed by regional organizations of states and briefly contrasts the publicly owned MNE with the so-called 'public international corporation', a creature of the public sector and international treaty which may perform business functions similar to those carried out by MNEs.

2.1   Contractual Forms

As noted in chapter 1, the OECD definition of multinational enterprise is not limited to equity based groups, but extends to any enterprise in which one entity can exert a significant influence over another.[24] Furthermore, as noted in chapter 2, the supply of foreign markets may be achieved through business forms that fall short of setting up an owned and controlled subsidiary in the host state. The legally binding contract offers various options in this respect, ranging from simple one-off export sales to complex and permanent international consortia. Discrete export sales can be disregarded for the purposes of this work, given the incidental and arm's length nature of such transactions. However, in other cases where international business is carried on by means of contract, there may emerge a relationship of control and dominance by one party which creates a degree of business integration that would come within the OECD definition of a MNE. Thus it is appropriate to consider such 'controlled' contractual relations as a legal form of multinational enterprise.

Such enterprises may lie beyond the normal distinction between corporation and contract, forming a distinct type of business association that applies both corporate and contractual methods of organization. Gunther Teubner has described such associations as 'network organizations'.[25] Contractual linkages can be divided between those aimed at distribution and those aimed at production.

2.1.1 Distribution agreements   The simplest form of such relations arises where a producer in the home state enters into a distribution agreement with a distributor in the host state.[26] In return for sole or exclusive selling rights in the host state and, possibly, other territories, the distributor will be obliged to purchase the producer's products and to use its best efforts to sell them. This may involve the transfer of intellectual property rights, such as trade marks, and know-how, so that the seller can maintain the identity and quality of the product. This offers a useful route into a foreign market for the producer without the need for the expenditure associated with the establishment of a sales subsidiary.

A similar effect may be achieved through the establishment of a distribution franchise. This differs from a simple distribution agreement in that the producer in the home state (the franchisor) transfers to the local distributor (the franchisee) a complete business format, including relevant intellectual property rights and know-how, in return for the capital contribution needed to establish the outlet from the franchisee. The degree of control exercised by the franchisor over the franchisee is considerably greater than that which normally occurs in an ordinary distribution agreement, where the distributor is usually free to sell goods as it sees fit after purchase of stocks from the producer. This is because, under a franchise, the franchisor seeks to expand its products and brand image abroad in a uniform business format, which helps to develop its presence as an international business.[27] This method of internationalization has been used, in particular, by retail chains offering specialized goods, such as, for example, computer hardware and software, cosmetics or wedding attire, for which there is a uniform international demand but where the manufacturer or retailer (which may be the same entity) lacks, or does not wish to commit, the capital to set up subsidiaries or branches in every foreign sales location.

2.1.2 Production agreements   Should overseas demand for a product manufactured in the home state be such as to make overseas production desirable, a number of contractual options present themselves. First, the producer (the licensor) may license a local manufacturer (the licensee) to produce the product in the host state. This will involve the transfer of patented technology and know-how to the local manufacturer, who will be bound to use the technology in a manner that protects the licensor's competitive advantage in the technology. The licence may form part of a wider production franchise package where, in return for the capital contribution of the local producer, the patented technology is accompanied by a business format and by close franchisor control over the acts of the franchisee.

Such arrangements may raise questions as to whether any anti-competitive effects are created by restrictive clauses in the licensing agreement or franchise. In developing states a further question arises regarding the benefits of the technology transfer to the local economy. These matters will be considered in chapter 12. It should be noted that licensing is an option open only where a suitable local producer can be found, and where the risk of damaging interference by third parties in the patented technology and secret know-how is small. If these difficulties exist, the producer in the home state may have little alternative but to set up a manufacturing subsidiary in the host state.

The most advanced contractual form of MNE is the international consortium. This is defined as 'an organisation which is created when two or more companies co-operate so as to act as a single entity for a specific and limited purpose'.[28] At their most complex, international consortia can act as integrated international production enterprises, hardly distinguishable in economic terms from equity based international groups. Indeed the legal form may take that of an incorporated joint-venture company or partnership. Such forms are most often used for specific, large-scale construction or engineering projects that require the skills and resources of companies from more than one state for their successful realization. Examples include the discovery, in 1970, of the North Sea oil fields by a multinational consortium of four companies led by Phillips Petroleum, the joint development and production of Concorde by Sud Aviation of France and the British Aircraft Company of the UK,[29] and Airbus Industrie.

Airbus Industrie is of particular interest, representing, as it does, the major European civil aircraft manufacturer.[30] It is composed of four original participating companies from Germany (Deutsche Airbus, 37.9 per cent), France (Aerospatiale, 37.9 per cent), the UK (British Aerospace, 20 per cent) and Spain (CASA, 4.2 per cent). Each participant manufactures parts of the aircraft in its home country. Those parts are then transported by Airbus's own aircraft to the production line at Toulouse for final assembly. The legal form of the consortium is that of a French *groupement d'intérêt économique* (GIE), which offers the advantages of joint partnership and legal personality, but without the regulatory or fiscal burdens of full incorporation.[31] Given that Airbus is developing into a large-scale multinational manufacturing enterprise, its current legal form is inadequate to deal with the resulting problems of accountability (in that the GIE does not have to produce financial results) and unlimited liability that are a consequence of using the French GIE form. Thus it is planned to convert Airbus Industrie into a free-standing corporation, though the partner companies have not yet resolved the details.

2.2 Equity Based Corporate Groups

The most commonly held image of a MNE is that of a closely controlled group of companies linked by shares held by the parent company and its intermediate holding companies. While this is an acceptable staring point, it fails to describe the considerable variations of structure that can be developed through the use of the parent–subsidiary relationship. In particular, there exist noticeable differences between groups from different countries and regions. The group structure adopted is a product of the business and legal environment from which the firm has grown. It is, therefore, legitimate to classify group structures along national or regional lines. This approach will be adopted below, where some of the most common and distinctive structures will be described. However, the resulting classification should not be treated as immutable. As noted in section 1 of this chapter, the process of group organization is a dynamic one, and, as firms become more global in their operations and business culture, new group forms will develop. These will result in changes in group legal structures. Therefore, this section will end with some thoughts on the likely legal consequences of such changes.

2.2.1 The Anglo-American 'pyramid' group This type of structure consists of a parent company which owns and controls a network of wholly or majority-owned subsidiaries, which may themselves be intermediate holding companies for sub-groups of closely held subsidiaries. The resulting structure is that of a 'pyramid' with the parent company at its apex. As noted above, when the pyramid crosses borders, this represents the 'classic' conception of the MNE which underlies much of the thinking on MNE regulation.

Although the pyramid structure of ownership and control is widely used throughout the major capital-exporting states other than Japan (which will be considered below), it is especially typical of US and UK held MNEs.[32] For example, the US auto manufacturer, Ford, has traditionally operated through 100 per cent owned overseas subsidiaries. In Europe, Ford of Europe has replicated this structure across the continent since it combined its then separate UK and German companies in 1967.[33] However, where necessary Ford will subscribe to less than 100 per cent ownership. Thus in Japan Ford owns 25 per cent of Mazda; in Taiwan it owns 70 per cent of its Lioho joint venture, the remaining 30 per cent being held by local interests in accordance with Taiwan's foreign investment law; in Brazil Ford was the joint owner, with Volkswagen, of Autolatina. Similarly, IBM has been organized hitherto as a closely held US group coordinating its global activities through IBM World Trade Corporation, which acts as the holding company for IBM's wholly owned regional holding companies, which in turn act as holding companies for regional and national sub-groups of wholly owned subsidiaries.[34]

In common with US MNEs, British MNEs have tended to organize along extended lines of closely held parent–subsidiary relationships. In a study of the legal and business organization of three British corporate groups up to 1979 (Bowater, Reckitt and Colman and the Rank Organisation[35]) Professor Hadden observed the large size and complexity of the groups. At that time, Bowater had some 420 companies, of which almost 200 were registered in the UK alone, some held at three levels of remove from the ultimate parent;[36] the Rank group contained some 220 companies excluding those jointly held by Rank-Xerox;[37] Reckitt and Colman contained some 170.[38] The major reason given for this proliferation was the expansion of these companies by way of acquisition. It led to different patterns of overseas sub-groups. Some were organized around an intermediate holding company in a particular country, such as, for example, Reckitt and Colman Australia or Bowaters of Canada, while other groups were operated through subsidiaries of the principal British operating company for the given line of business. By contrast the fourth company in the study, IBM (UK), had a simple corporate structure involving a single UK holding company and four operating subsidiaries.[39] Furthermore, Professor Hadden found that some firms were using 'agent only' companies as a means of reducing the administrative burdens of full disclosure. These duties were avoided by the transfer of a subsidiary's assets to its holding company, leaving the subsidiary to trade as the agent of the holding company, obliged only to produce a formal balance sheet in which its capital would be typically offset by a loan to the holding company.[40]

2.2.2   European transnational mergers   A number of large MNEs have been created through what Channon and Jalland call 'transnational merger'.[41] These structures represent a border between corporate groups headed by one parent and joint ventures between independent companies. In some cases such entities started as joint ventures and then developed an integrated international structure. In other cases the legal characteristics of the joint venture form have remained. Transnational mergers have occurred in both the private and public sectors of industry. This type of MNE is especially common in Europe, where the integration of national companies across borders into larger enterprises, offering new economies of scale and scope, is a well established phenomenon.

According to Professor Schmitthoff, four factors influence the choice of legal and managerial structure in the transnational

merger.[42] First, the national stock exchange quotation of each participating company must not be affected. The usual solution is the
creation of a twin holding company located in each home state, based
on joint shareholding by the founding parent companies, and the
transfer of operating activities to subsidiaries that may be jointly or
separately owned and controlled by the holding companies. An example is the Anglo-Dutch oil company Royal Dutch Shell. This firm
consists of a Dutch parent (Royal Dutch Petroleum Co.) and a
British parent (Shell Transport and Trading Co.) who own and
control Dutch and British holding companies in a ratio of 60/40, with
Royal Dutch holding the majority share. The national holding companies share a unified management board. Each national holding
company in turn owns and controls its nationally based operating
subsidiaries as separate sub-groups. A similar approach was taken by
Agfa Gevaert when this company was formed by Agfa, the German
parent, and Gevaert, the Belgian parent, in 1964. Each parent owned
50 per cent of the shares in the two national holding companies.
Since 1981 the group has had only one shareholder, Bayer AG of
Germany. It has transformed itself into a unified MNE.[43] The twin
holding company approach has also been adopted by Eurotunnel,
which consists of jointly held French and English holding companies,
Eurotunnel SA and Eurotunnel plc, each of which owns respectively
the French and English concessionary companies France Manche
SA and the Channel Tunnel Group Ltd. This is an example of the
twin holding company approach being used to establish a new
transnational enterprise as opposed to the case of a merger between
two existing enterprises.

Secondly, the aim of the merger is usually the achievement of
greater economies of scale and scope than the founding companies
could achieve by themselves. This will lead to an international
divisionalization of the firm and to the creation of new transnational
management structures, such as, for example, a joint management
committee composed of senior managers from each of the founding
firms. Such an approach was taken by Unilever in the 1920s when the
UK consumer products company, Lever Brothers, joined with the
Dutch margarine producer, Margarine Uni, to create one of the first
transnational mergers. The group is run by a management committee
known as the Special Committee composed of the chairmen and
vice-chairmen of both the UK and Dutch companies. In addition,
the directorate of the firm must not exceed twenty-five and must
represent a balance between British and Dutch directors, which is
achieved through each national holding company's right to nominate
directors.[44]

Thirdly, the dividend rights of shareholders must be protected.
This may lead to a share equalization agreement, whereby the

founding firms agree to equalize any differences in dividends payable to shareholders in each home state. Such an agreement was pioneered by Unilever. This is a unique arrangement that other firms have not chosen to adopt.[45] For example, the Anglo-Dutch publishing group, Reed-Elsevier, whose merger took effect on 1 January 1993, has chosen a 50/50 joint ownership structure, without any premium or cash payment to either set of shareholders and with the retention of separate stock market listings. The operating subsidiaries are grouped under a UK holding company, while finance subsidiaries are grouped under Elsevier Reed Finance, a Dutch company.[46]

Finally, the merger must take account of its fiscal consequences. Indeed, the structure adopted by Reed-Elsevier was prompted in large measure by such considerations. It offers tax saving effects as the Dutch holding company is in a better position to benefit from tax havens, in that it is entitled to earn tax-free interest on such deposits.[47] The fiscal barriers to transnational mergers may have distorting effects on international competition, preventing the development of efficient transnational groups. Within the EC, this has been identified as a possible source of competitive disadvantage between companies based in one Member State, and companies from more than one Member State, that wish to merge. To remedy the situation the EC Council has adopted a Directive on a common system of taxation applicable to mergers, divisions, transfers of assets and exchanges of shares concerning companies of different Member States.[48]

However, despite the above-mentioned successes in transnational mergers, such entities are subject to intense centrifugal forces that may lead to their break-down.[49] In particular, if the merger does not develop a suitable internal control and coordination system it is likely to fail. The differing corporate cultures and national backgrounds of the participating firms may prevent such an organizational development from taking place. Equally, if one of the firms involved is economically weaker, it may disappear into the stronger firm. This may not be acceptable to the home state of the weaker partner, which may act to prevent the merger from taking place. The difficulties involved have been graphically illustrated by the failure of the proposed merger in 1992 between British Airways and KLM Royal Dutch Airlines. Considerable fears were expressed at the time that BA would overwhelm the smaller Dutch airline.[50] The merger negotiations came to a standstill over the profit shares that each airline would take from the merged company. KLM had insisted on a 40 per cent stake, which proved unacceptable to the larger British airline.[51]

On the other hand, in 1991, Renault and Volvo successfully entered a joint venture by means of a 20 per cent shareholding acquired by Volvo in Regie Nationale des Usines Renault, the Renault car company, and a 45 per cent shareholding in Renault Vehicles Industriels, the Renault commercial vehicles company, while Renault took a 25 per cent share in the Volvo Car Corporation and a 45 per cent share in the Volvo Truck and Bus Company. The exchange of shares was matched with closer cooperation between both companies through joint management committees.[52] A complete merger of the two companies' operations was agreed in 1993, with the French government initially holding 51 per cent of the new holding company, Renault-Volvo Automotive.[53] However, the merger did not take place owing to opposition from Volvo's principal institutional shareholders against what they saw as a takeover by a foreign state-owned firm. This prompted a revolt by a majority of Volvo's board against the merger.[54] In the wake of the failure of the proposed merger, both firms dismantled their cross-shareholding arrangements, stressing again the difficulties inherent in transnational mergers.[55]

The development of transnational mergers in Europe is inevitably going to be influenced by the industrial and competition policies of the EC. It has always been the aim of EC policy to encourage the development of European transnational firms. This aim underlies the proposal for a European Company, revived in 1989 as part of the Single Market programme.[56] It has also motivated the above-mentioned tax Directive and a proposed Directive on cross-border mergers.[57] However, the draft Directive has encountered strong opposition and no steps have been taken to date to implement it.[58] On the other hand, the EC competition authorities will strike down any cross-border merger that is likely to impede competition by enhancing a dominant position in the common market within the terms of the EC Merger Regulation.[59]

2.2.3 The Japanese keiretsu   The legal character of Japanese corporate groups is strongly influenced by the requirements of the Law on Prohibition of Private Monopoly and Ensuring of Fair Trade (Anti-Monopoly Law) of 1947.[60] This law was introduced by the Allied occupying powers through the Supreme Commander for Allied Powers (SCAP), as part of a wider programme for the decentralization of economic power in Japan.[61] Prior to the Second World War, the Japanese economy was dominated by major business groups, the *zaibatsu*, headed by a family holding company, each with its own bank and international trading house.[62] These groups were dissolved by law in 1945 and 1946.[63]

The Anti-Monopoly Law sought to prevent the re-emergence of *zaibatsu* by the prohibition, in article 9 of the Law, on the creation of a holding company, which is defined as a company whose primary business is to control the business activities of another company by holding its shares. This does not prohibit the holding of shares by one company in another provided that the parent company is also engaged in some form of business activity.[64] Furthermore, large joint-stock companies engaged in business other than financial services whose assets exceed thirty billion yen or that have a capital of more than ten billion yen are prohibited from acquiring or holding shares in other companies beyond set limits. Companies engaged in financial services are prohibited from owning more than 5 per cent (10 per cent in the case of insurance companies) of the outstanding stocks of other companies.[65]

As a result of these provisions Japanese groups have evolved unique structures which seek to avoid the prohibitions in the Anti-Monopoly Law. These groups, or *keiretsu*, are characterized by small, intra-group cross-shareholdings coupled with strong coordinated management organized around inter-company management conferences. Thus control over satellite companies of the *keiretsu* is not exercised by means of formal voting powers, but by means of managerial coordination. The *keiretsu* may be divided into two principal types.[66] The first consists of the post-war descendants of the *zaibatsu* (Mitsubishi, Mitsui and Sumitomo) and the three *keiretsu* centred on banks (Fuji Bank, Sanwa Bank and the Daiichi Kangyo Bank). The second consists of the industrial *keiretsu* and contains at least one hundred groups, including major groups like Toyota.[67] These have a structure more akin to a pyramid group, with a controlling holding company and subordinate subsidiaries. In order to comply with the 1947 Act, the principal holding company should carry on its own business and restrict its holdings in subsidiaries and associated companies to a maximum of 50 per cent of its assets and must restrict its dividend income to a similar extent. Thus, controlling holdings are possible, although 100 per cent ownership is unusual. This allows for substantial external shareholdings in group companies.[68]

As a result of the flexibility offered by the *keiretsu* system for the creation of joint ventures, Japanese companies have been more ready to use such an approach to overseas establishment. When investing abroad, a number of firms from the group may join together into a joint venture, which may also include partners from the host state. This approach was widely used by the textile and steel industries when they were setting up production facilities abroad. By contrast, the electrical and electronics industries developed their own sales and service subsidiaries followed by manufacturing subsidiaries in which the Japanese parent retained a higher share of ownership, with local joint-venture partners restricted to distribution or agency functions. This approach was required to retain control over the parent company's technology and to protect the brand name.[69]

2.2.4   Changes in business organization and effects on equity based structures   The above-mentioned equity structures have developed around groups that were initially national firms but that expanded abroad through internal expansion or by way of foreign acquisitions, or through transnational merger. As such they represent the legal forms of developing MNEs, in which centralized managerial control may be facilitated by the concentration of voting rights at the level of the parent through closely held subsidiaries.

However, once firms have become established as integrated international businesses, the major pressures are, as noted in section 1 of this chapter, towards the maintenance of global competitiveness through increased international coordination and local responsiveness. This may lead, in appropriate cases, to a degree of decentralization in the business structures of the firm, with smaller business units and some demergering of activities. In legal terms, this process could result in the gradual replacement of closely held subsidiaries with free-standing companies linked to the parent by contract. While not representing a return to arm's length legal relations between former affiliates, this process entails an increased incidence of what were earlier referred to as 'control contracts', arrangements whereby economic integration between dominant and servient enterprises is achieved by contractual rather than equity links. Indeed, the experience of Japanese MNEs suggests that equity based links can coexist with looser forms of legal relation, such as joint ventures between jointly managed firms and with local partners, although such links may be harder to achieve in states with strict controls over anti-competitive agreements or concerted practices.

Nevertheless, it would be wrong to consider that such developments herald the end of legal linkages based on equity in MNEs. Certain industry sectors may continue to require a high level of integrated control over subordinate enterprises which makes the use of parent–subsidiary relations preferable to 'control contracts'. This may be the case where the use by the subordinate enterprise of innovative and highly valuable technology belonging to the parent is involved, as contract may be an inadequate method for ensuring compliance with parent company demands for quality and secrecy. Equally, the preservation of an international equity-based network can offer advantages in relation to the limitation of liability, or the avoidance of regulatory requirements and the manipulation of earnings flows across borders through transfer pricing transactions, that would be harder to achieve through 'control contracts'. Thus there may be significant benefits from the equity group form that will ensure its continued use by MNEs.

2.3   Joint Ventures

The term 'joint venture' has no precise legal meaning. It can refer to any agreement or undertaking between two independent firms.[70] However, certain features are commonly associated with the concept.[71] In particular, the joint venture involves the cooperation of two or more otherwise independent parent undertakings which are linked, through the venture, in the pursuit of a common commercial, financial or technical activity.[72] Unlike a parent–subsidiary relationship, in which there is control by a single dominant undertaking, the joint venture normally involves shared control by the parent undertakings, and is often treated as an associated undertaking for accounting purposes. Nevertheless, one undertaking may exercise a dominant influence over the venture, as where it holds 51 per cent or more of the equity (or of the contribution, in the case of a contractual joint venture). In such cases the joint venture may be treated as a subsidiary for accounting purposes by the dominant undertaking.

The precise nature of that control, the proportionate contributions of the joint venture partners, their respective participation in profits and losses, the legal form of the venture, including its legal relation to its parent undertakings, and the conditions for dissolution are matters for determination in the joint venture agreement between the parent undertakings.[73] The agreement is subject to the requirements of the law governing the joint venture.[74] The joint venture itself will be subject to regulation under the relevant system of competition law applicable to it.[75]

The joint venture may take the legal form of a contract, partnership or limited liability company. In some legal systems, such as that of England and Wales, each alternative is freely available. In others more limited choices may be available.[76] As will be seen in chapter 6, in certain states, notably, until recently, the former socialist states of Eastern Europe and the former USSR, entry and establishment by direct foreign investors had been permitted only through the adoption of a joint venture between the foreign undertaking and a local joint venture partner, in accordance with the local law on joint ventures involving foreign capital participation. However, such laws are now less common as the liberalization of entry conditions for foreign investors has become more generalized.

The incidence of international joint ventures between firms from more than one country is common. Some joint ventures have acquired a permanence which is hard to distinguish in economic terms from an integrated group. However, full merger in legal terms has been avoided for reasons of policy. Examples can be found in many industries. For example, joint ventures are now common in the steel industry.[77] Major joint ventures have also been established in electrical engineering,[78] aeroengines[79] and pharmaceuticals,[80] to name but a few.[81]

A unique joint venture structure is furnished by Scandinavian Airline Systems (SAS).[82] In order to capture economies of scale and scope which would be unavailable to the parent companies individually, the major national airlines of Sweden (AB Aerotransport), Norway (Det Norske Luftfartselskap A/S) and Denmark (Det Danske Luftfartselskab A/S) entered into an agreement, in 1951, to establish an international joint venture in the provision of civil aviation services. The current consortium agreement runs until 31 December 2005.

The agreement sets up the 'SAS Consortium' owned by the three parent companies in the following proportions: three-sevenths Swedish, two-sevenths Norwegian and two-sevenths Danish. The parent airlines have transferred responsibility to the Consortium for scheduled air services. They have also set up a second consortium, Scanair, to operate charter services, and a third, SAS Commuter, which operates certain routes for the SAS Consortium. In addition, the SAS Consortium owns several subsidiaries and affiliates. The Consortium is managed by the Assembly of Representatives, composed of the parent companies' boards of directors. This body appoints the consortia's boards of directors, approves financial statements and decides on the amount of profit to be transferred to the parent companies.

The SAS Consortium has no legal personality separate from the parent companies. However, its activities are facilitated by the co-operation of the Swedish, Danish and Norwegian governments, which are 50 per cent stakeholders in their respective national parent companies. The Consortium is subject to the national laws of the three countries, and can enter into private contracts. The parent companies accept unlimited liability for the activities of the Consortium.

In many ways, the SAS Consortium is unique, combining as it does elements of a contractual joint venture with integrated group management, and public sector involvement. Yet it is less than a full transnational merger. It continues on the basis of a renewable agreement between the parent companies, and thus fits better into the joint venture classification.

2.4   Informal Alliances between MNEs

Thus far the legal forms of intercorporate alliance have been considered from the perspectives of contractual links, transnational mergers and joint ventures. The reasons behind the choice of these various legal forms depend, *inter alia*, on the degree of integration required for the realization of the alliance's objects, and on the regulatory burdens associated with each form. Thus, an inter-corporate alliance will take the form of a transnational merger where the parent firms wish fully to integrate their business operations, and where the joint holding of group assets requires the use of equity based structures to facilitate the international integration of owner-ship and to ensure the benefits of limited liability. The contractual route is most likely where the alliance is set up for a specific commer-cial aim, such as distribution or R&D, which does not involve a high level of integration between the parties and where the risks are small enough not to require limited liability. A contractual relationship is more rarely used for the joint production of a specific product or the joint provision of a service where the level of integration and risk may be higher. Thus, cases like Airbus Industrie or SAS may be seen as exceptional in this respect. In such cases a joint-venture company is more likely to be established, so as to give the parent companies a measure of insulation from the venture, although a measure of limited liability can be achieved through contract by the apportionment of liability between the parent companies on a joint and several basis. On the other hand, a contractual joint venture may avoid duties of corporate disclosure and allow for less transparency than an equity joint venture. Indeed, Airbus has been frequently accused by US critics of concealing the true measure of public subsidy that it receives because of the more limited disclosure re-quirements imposed by French law on a GIE, as compared to a joint-stock company.

By contrast to the above-mentioned legal forms some inter-corporate alliances may, in fact, lack clear legal structures. Tricker describes these as 'federations of companies'. He gives the following simplified example, based on actual practice:

> Three PLC's, each quoted on different stock exchanges around the world, have cross-holdings of each other's shares between 27 and 30%. This is sufficient to provide interlocking directorships, but the companies are not subsidiaries or associates that would make any member a subordinate company.[83]

Tricker concludes that in this situation the common directors and chief executives of the various subsidiaries in the three groups can exercise joint influence over areas of common concern such as bids, tenders, pricing, products, research and financial strategy. Thus col-lective decisions affecting shareholders and outsiders can be made in the absence of any legal form that identifies the federated area of concern, and through which the regulatory requirements of the rel-evant law would be imposed.

In such a case, it would appear that managerial structures operating across the federation are not legally accountable. This raises two questions: first, whether there should be a duty on the participating companies to establish a legally identifiable joint entity, such as a consortium or joint venture company; secondly, whether such a structure should be struck down by competition law as tending towards a reduction of normal commercial risks between otherwise independent firms.

2.5 Publicly Owned MNEs

No classification of MNE structures would be complete without reference to public ownership. Despite the contemporary emphasis on privatization, there remain sufficient numbers of significant MNEs that are either partly or wholly state-owned. Indeed, some of the examples used in preceding sections involve firms with a measure of public ownership. Thus Aerospatiale, the French partner in Airbus Industrie, and CASA, the Spanish partner, are both state-owned, at 100 and 72 per cent respectively. The three parent companies of SAS are 50 per cent state-owned. Renault is 80 per cent state-owned. In order to participate in the share exchange with Volvo in 1990, its legal status had to be changed by law from a *régie* of the French state into a public limited company.[84] Despite the failure of the proposed Renault–Volvo merger, the company is to be partially privatized, with a planned overall reduction of the French government's shareholding to just above 50 per cent.

Publicly owned MNEs can arise through one of two routes: either a state-owned enterprise adopts a strategy of international expansion, or an existing MNE is nationalized.[85] The former is more likely to occur in developing home states, where private capital and entrepreneurship are in short supply, making state entrepreneurship the only option for international expansion.[86] This is occurring in a number of industrial sectors. For example, the national petroleum companies of a number of developing countries are evolving international investment strategies.[87] Similarly, Embraer of Brazil is establishing itself as an international aerospace company. By contrast, the nationalization route has been taken mainly in developed countries, as the principal home states of major MNEs. In particular, the French nationalizations of 1982 brought some very large multinational groups into public ownership.[88]

The principal question affecting the legal structures of publicly owned MNEs is the relationship between the state and the enterprise, and, in particular, the degree of control that the former wishes to exercise over the latter.[89] Normally, the enterprise will be incorporated as an entity separate from the state, with the state as the majority or exclusive shareholder. In some states ownership is effected through a state holding company, rather than by direct shareholding.[90] The state may have directors on the board, and may impose obligations of direct reporting to the minister responsible for the industrial sector concerned. Additionally, or in the alternative, accountability may be ensured as a result of the state's control over the financing of the company. The position of the state as principal shareholder makes the enterprise dependent on grants from the state, offering the latter a powerful weapon of control.[91]

A further significant element in the control system is the setting of objectives for the enterprise. This can be done by way of statements of objects in the legislation establishing the corporation. In France, following the 1982 nationalizations, the government effected this aim through separate 'planning contracts' with the eleven nationalized groups. These were to last for four years. They set agreed obligations and targets for the group concerned in relation to its strategic options, employment trends, financial requirements and future financial commitments. By this means the French government sought to harmonize state policy with the strategy of the major publicly owned groups.[92] However, despite such contractual controls, the French government continued to respect the managerial autonomy of the nationalized groups, which were free to pursue their commercial and international strategies as they saw fit.

However, even with such an approach, the presence of a state interest in a MNE may be counterproductive. Limits on available finance could undermine a commercially necessary policy of internationalization, and the fact of state ownership could create the perception that the enterprise is no more than an emanation of the home government. Thus the reduction, if not the removal, of state involvement may be required for internationalization to succeed. However, the state may be a useful partner where the private sector is virtually non-existent, as in developing countries,[93] or where it provides insufficient capital for the expansion of a business. Indeed, the French nationalizations provided much needed new capital and credit to France's MNEs, and can be seen as a positive step in their international strategies.[94] Therefore, a role for continued state ownership in MNEs is foreseeable but, perhaps, not inevitable.

2.6 Supranational Forms of International Business
The final category in this classification of MNE legal structures involves entities that are formed under laws adopted by regional organizations of states, aimed at the furtherance of cooperation between firms from more than one member state. It also distinguishes

the 'public international corporation' from the publicly owned MNE, so as to avoid confusion between these two distinct international business forms.

2.6.1 Forms adopted by the European Community The proposed Statute for the European Company has already been briefly mentioned above. At the time of writing it is yet to be adopted, as there is considerable opposition to its proposals on worker participation. The draft Statute will be discussed in more detail in chapter 9.

Of greater immediate significance is the European Economic Interest Grouping (EEIG), which was introduced by Regulation in 1985.[95] Based on the French GIE, but none the less distinct, the EEIG seeks to create a supranational form of business association that will facilitate cross-border cooperation between business entities operating within the EC. It is of limited commercial scope, its purpose being

to facilitate or develop the economic activities of its members and to improve or increase the results of those activities; its purpose is not to make profits for itself. Its activity shall be related to the economic activities of its members and must not be more than ancillary to those activities.[96]

Consequently the EEIG is disqualified from certain commercial activities. These include: the exercise of a power of management over the activities of its members or of another undertaking; the holding of shares in a member undertaking (though it may hold shares in any other undertaking where this is necessary for the attainment of its objects and the shares are held on its members' behalf); the use of the EEIG for the making of intracorporate loans to directors or transfers of property between a company and a director or connected person, save to the extent allowed by the company laws of Member States; and membership of another EEIG.[97] It is clear, therefore, that the EEIG is not to be used as a management or holding company for the members, or as a conduit company for the members' benefit. Furthermore, the EEIG must not employ more than 500 persons. Thus it is unlikely to be used for large-scale manufacturing operations. Indeed, the EEIG is most likely to be used for joint R&D or distribution, or for other forms of smaller-scale intercorporate cooperation. It has also proved popular as a method of creating transnational legal practices, given that the membership of an EEIG extends not only to companies but also to natural persons providing, *inter alia*, professional services.[98]

The EEIG is formed by the conclusion of a contract by the participants,[99] who must be either companies with their central administrations in different Member States, natural persons carrying on their principal activities in different Member States or a combination of companies and natural persons from different Member States.[100] Upon registration and establishment in accordance with the Regulation in a Member State,[101] the EEIG shall have full legal capacity. However, the legal personality of the grouping falls to be determined by the laws of the Member States.[102] The internal organization of the EEIG is governed by the law of the Member State in which the official address is situated.[103]

The EEIG is run by the members acting collectively and the manager or managers.[104] Each member shall have one vote although more than one vote may be given in the constitutive agreement, provided that no member holds a majority of the votes.[105] The profits shall be deemed to be those of the members and shall be shared among them in the proportions laid down in the contract.[106] They shall be taxed in accordance with national tax laws.[107] The members shall have joint and unlimited liability, the consequences of which fall to be determined by national law.[108]

2.6.2   *The Andean Multinational Enterprise adopted by the Andean Common Market (ANCOM)*[109]   In the early 1980s ANCOM introduced the Andean Multinational Enterprise (AME) as a means of creating supranational regional enterprises aimed at the furtherance of joint industrial development.[110] The legal form of the AME is that of a company with capital contributions from national investors from more than one Member State that together exceed 60 per cent of the capital of the company.[111] It is domiciled in the territory of one of the Member Countries or in the country where the enterprise is transformed into an AME, through the sale of part of its stock to subregional investors, or created through merger between two or more national or mixed companies.[112]

According to article 7 of the Law on Andean Multinational Enterprises (the Code), the laws governing the enterprise are, in descending order of importance: its articles of incorporation, which must be in accordance with the Code; the Code in respect of matters not stipulated in the articles; in respect of matters not governed by either the articles or the Code, the legislation of the country of principal domicile, which would normally be the country of incorporation (in certain cases, not listed by the Code, the legislation of the country where the AME establishes a legal relationship or in which the legal acts of the enterprise will take effect in accordance with the applicable rules of private international law).

AMEs are entitled to special treatment under the laws of the Member Countries. In particular, they are entitled to: national treatment (article 9); free circulation of capital contributions (article 10); free import and export of goods constituting part of the capital contribution (article 11); access to export incentives (article 12); freedom to participate in sectors reserved for national enterprises under Member Countries' laws (article 14); rights to establish branches in other Member Countries (articles 15 and 16); freedom for foreign participants to repatriate earnings (article 17); national treatment in taxation matters and freedom from double taxation (articles 18 to 20); free choice of personnel and free movement of investors, promoters and executives (articles 21 and 22); and privileged application of technology transfer rules (article 23).

2.6.3 *Public international corporations* Finally, it is necessary to distinguish between a publicly owned MNE and a public international corporation.[113] The latter is an entity set up by two or more states through an international treaty. It will perform a specific economic function that is of importance to the public policy of the founding states, and that can be better carried out by means of intergovernmental cooperation. Such corporations have been set up in, *inter alia*, the atomic energy field,[114] transportation[115] and satellite communications.[116] More recently, the concept of a joint intergovernmental corporation has been used by the Yemen Arab Republic and the People's Democratic Republic of Yemen to develop oil reserves lying along the border between the two states.[117]

The legal regimes of corporations identified by lawyers as public international corporations are many and varied. Some are no more than joint ventures between publicly owned corporations from more than one country, and may be better seen as publicly owned MNEs (for example, SAS), while others are close in character to intergovernmental organizations. There is little conclusive agreement on the precise border between these two types of public sector enterprise.[118] According to Professor Kahn, the crucial question revolves around the legal regime that governs the enterprise.[119]

The essential difference between a public international corporation and a publicly owned MNE is that the former will be governed by a regime based on its constitutive treaty rather than on any system of national law. Although a public international corporation may have a seat in one of the participating states, the law of the seat will not apply where a matter is dealt with by the treaty. Thus, for example, the Treaty establishing Eurofima, the intergovernmental corporation set up to administer the common servicing of rolling stock among fourteen European railway companies, states in article I:

The Governments which are party to the present Convention approve the Company's constitution which will be governed by the Statutes attached to the present Convention (hereinafter called 'the statutes') and, residually, by the law of the Headquarters' State in so far as the present Convention does not derogate therefrom.[120]

Accordingly, although Eurofima's headquarters are in Switzerland, and it is established as a corporation under Swiss law, Swiss law will be subordinated to the Treaty regime. This is reinforced by article II(a), which gives effect to any variations in the Statutes notwithstanding that these may contradict the law of Switzerland as the headquarters state.

In addition, a public international corporation may be identified where it is closely administered by governmental officials from the participating states rather than by commercial managers, where it enjoys a measure of diplomatic immunity not normally given to a commercial corporation, and where the dispute settlement provisions in the constitutive treaty envisage international rather than national procedures. This may involve a special tribunal set up by the participating states or, as in the case of Eurofima, by recourse to the International Court of Justice.[121]

3   Concluding Remarks: Business and Legal Forms and the Control of MNE Activities

In section 1 of this chapter, it was seen that, in common with most large multilocation enterprises, MNEs have outgrown the simple managerial structure of the entrepreneurial corporation and have reorganized along divisional lines of control based on managerial functions, products and areas of operation. However, unlike a multiplant domestic company, a MNE will organize itself along divisional lines whose managerial reach crosses national frontiers, and through which, for business purposes, the national identity of the various operating companies in the group disappears. At the same time, in legal terms, the group remains a collection of commonly held companies possessing the nationality of their country of incorporation. Similarly, in the case of a transnational network (TNN), control over the operations of a local enterprise, and participation in the creation of the products or services offered by it, may involve several associated entities both within and outside the jurisdiction, linked by contractually based managerial control systems.

From the regulator's perspective the major question is whether the resulting legal structure corresponds with the firm's decision-making structure, and places it within the organizational presumptions underlying the legal form from which its legal duties stem. It is clear that existing legal forms of business organization, essentially contract and corporation, were simply not designed to correspond with such extensive business structures as MNEs. Contract assumes an arm's length relationship between otherwise independent entities of equal bargaining power, while the corporation assumes a single unit enterprise owned and controlled by its members. Neither form contemplates the linking of legally separate entities into unified business structures, whether through 'control contract' or divisional management.

Regarding contractual structures, the possibility of managerial control by one firm over another raises the question of whether the contract should be disregarded for regulatory purposes: whether the 'contractual veil' should be lifted so that the dominant undertaking can be made liable for the acts of the subordinate undertaking, regardless of the contractual allocation of risk between them. Similarly, in relation to equity based structures the question arises: when should the regulator be free to disregard the corporate separation between parent and subsidiary and lift the 'corporate veil' so as to allocate responsibility with the ultimate decision-maker along the line of management in the group? As will be shown in detail in chapter 9, these questions may prove inadequate as methods of dealing with MNE regulation. What may be needed is a radical rethinking of the very legal forms themselves, and their replacement with new legal forms better able to correspond with the decision-making boundaries of firms.

For the present it is enough to outline some possible answers to these problems. First, as regards the legal structures in equity based multinational corporate groups, two broad approaches to reform can be identified. The first, favoured by Professor Hadden, is structural. The corporate entity should be reformed in a way that more closely corresponds to its business organization, and ensures the existence of a relevant unit for accounting, fiscal and other regulatory purposes. In this Professor Hadden favours the retention of the most useful characteristic of the corporate legal form, the creation of an identifiable legal representation of the underlying business activity, and its adaptation to modern realities.[122] This may entail new group enterprise forms for equity based groups, and raises the question of whether informal alliances should be forced to adopt corporate legal form. The structural approach will be considered in greater detail in chapter 9.

The second approach, favoured by Tricker, is operational. He advocates leaving the present version of the company legal form intact, but increasing the obligations placed directly upon establishments or divisions within the group. In particular, Tricker favours the introduction of greater divisional disclosure through the concept of an 'accountable business activity', whereby managers would be responsible for disclosing information according to the actual lines of decision-making in the enterprise, rather than relying on the limits of the legal obligation to disclose, which is attached to incorporated entities only.[123] Issues of improved disclosure and governance will be considered in chapter 10.

As regards the limits of control in contractual situations, possible responses are to be found in the idea of 'network liability' put forward by Professor Teubner,[124] which will be considered in chapter 9, and in the use of antitrust laws to protect the business independence of the weaker contracting party and third parties that may be denied access to markets controlled by network organizations. These matters will be considered in chapter 11.

The above questions arise mainly in relation to privately owned groups, as publicly owned groups may be presumed to have stronger public controls over their decision-making, at least as far as the home state is concerned. In relation to regulation by the host state, however, publicly owned MNEs may create not only the regulatory problems associated with the limits of contract and corporation, but also the problem of dealing with the home state as the ultimate owner and controller of the enterprise. Thus further problems of a highly political nature may emerge in such cases, possibly requiring negotiated diplomatic solutions. These are beyond the scope of the present work.

Notes

1 See further A. D. Chandler, *Strategy and Structure: Chapters in the History of the American Industrial Enterprise* (MIT Press, 1962); *The Visible Hand: the Managerial Revolution in American Business* (Harvard, Belknap, 1977); *Scale and Scope: the Dynamics of Industrial Capitalism* (Harvard, Belknap, 1990).

2 On which see further R. Vernon and L. T. Wells, *The Economic Environment of International Business*, 4th edn (Prentice-Hall, 1986), chapter 2.

3 See generally the works of Chandler (note 1 above).

4 See further M. Wilkins, *The Maturing of Multinational Enterprise: American Business Abroad From 1914 to 1970* (Harvard, 1974), chapter 15; L. Franko, *The European Multinationals* (Harper, 1976), chapter 8.

5 Deloitte, Haskins and Sells, Corporate structure – subsidiaries or divisions? (August 1983), cited in R. I. Tricker, *Corporate Governance* (Gower, 1984) at p. 145.

6 See further, on evolutionary patterns of MNE structural growth following Chandler's 'strategy and structure' thesis: J. Stopford and L. Wells Jr, *Managing the Multinational Enterprise* (Basic Books, 1972), part I. For a different, but complementary, approach based on conflicts in decision-making: M. Z. Brooke and H. Lee Remmers, *The Strategy of the Multinational Enterprise*, 2nd edn (Pitman, 1978), chapter 2.

7 See D. Channon and M. Jalland, *Multinational Strategic Planning* (Macmillan Press, 1978), chapters 2 and 3; S. Robock and K. Simmonds, *International Business and Multinational Enterprises*, 4th edn (Irwin, 1989),

chapter 11; J. H. Dunning, *Multinational Enterprises and the Global Economy* (Addison Wesley, 1992), chapter 8.

8   Dunning, ibid. at p. 217.

9   See further C. A. Bartlett and S. Ghoshal, *Managing Across Borders: The Transnational Solution* (Century Business, 1989), pp. 31–2.

10   Note 7 above at pp. 218–19, on which this paragraph draws.

11   On which see further Y. Doz, *Strategic Management in Multinational Companies* (Pergamon Press, 1986).

12   See further: Ghoshal and Bartlett (note 9 above), and 'The multinational corporations as an interorganizational network', 15 Academy of Management Review 603 (1990); Doz and Prahalad, 'Managing DMNCs: a search for a new paradigm', 12 Strategic Management Journal 145 (1991); Hedlund and Kogut, 'Managing MNCs: the end of the missionary era', in G. Hedlund (ed.), *TNCs and Organizational Issues* (UN Library on Transnational Corporations/Routledge, 1992); R. Van Tulder and G. Junne, *European Multinationals in Core Technologies* (Wiley/IRM, 1988), chapter 3.

13   For an extensive account of this thesis see R. Reich, *The Work of Nations: Preparing Ourselves for 21st Century Capitalism* (Simon and Schuster, 1991). See also Bartlett and Ghoshal (note 9 above); K. Ohmae, *Triad Power: the Coming Shape of Global Competition* (Free Press, 1985) and *The Borderless World* (Fontana, 1991); Brooke, 'Multinational corporate structures: the next stage', *Futures*, April 1979, p. 111; Dunning (note 7 above), chapter 9.

14   See R. Van Tulder and G. Junne (note 12 above), at p. 43; Christopher Lorenz, 'The trouble with the "networked" company', *Financial Times*, 22 May 1989, p. 40. The EC Commission approved, under EC competition law, the cooperation agreement between Olivetti and Canon, whereby the Italian firm would gain access to the technology of the Japanese firm in the field of copying machines: Olivetti/Canon OJ [1988] L 52/51; [1990] 4 CMLR 832.

15   Christopher Lorenz, 'IBM joins the ranks of "transnationals" ', *Financial Times*, 10 December 1990, p. 11. IBM intended reorganizing still further by breaking up its operating divisions into free-standing companies linked to the corporation by contract. See: *IBM Think* No. 5, 1992, 'Special report: creating a new IBM'; 'IBM's global overhaul aims at agility', *Financial Times*, 6 December 1991, p. 26; Jack Schofield, 'The chips are down at Big Blue', *The Guardian 2*, 12 January 1993, pp. 2–3. However, the incoming Chief Executive, Lou Gerstner, stopped these plans, although the goal of decentralizing management has not been abandoned: 'IBM chief halts plans to break up computer group', *Financial Times*, 17 May 1993, p. 1.

16   Christopher Lorenz (note 15 above, 10 December 1990), p. 11.

17   See Christopher Lorenz, 'More grist to the transnational mill', *Financial Times*, 15 March 1991, p. 13. This effect may be reinforced by the competitive advantages of the home state. See further M. Porter, *The Competitive Advantage of Nations* (Macmillan, 1990).

18   See further: OECD, *Structure and Organization of Multinational Enterprises*

(Paris, 1987); Dunning (note 7 above), at pp. 222–32; Martinez and Jarillo, 'The evolution of research on co-ordination mechanisms in multinational corporations', 20 Journal of International Business Studies 489 (1989). On control over decision making in UK subsidiaries of foreign-owned firms see: M. Steuer *et al.*, *The Impact of Foreign Direct Investment on the United Kingdom* (Dept of Trade and Industry, 1973), chapter 7; S. Young, N. Hood and J. Hamill, *Decision-making in Foreign Owned Multinational Subsidiaries in the UK* (ILO Working Paper No. 35, 1985).

19   OECD, ibid. at p. 35.

20   Dunning (note 7 above), table 8.1 at p. 225, using Young, Hood and Hamill (note 18 above) as source.

21   Dunning (note 7 above), at p. 226.

22   See chapter 2.

23   The classification emerges from the following sources: R. E. Tindall, *Multinational Enterprises* (Oceana, 1975), chapter 4; C. M. Schmitthoff, 'The multinational enterprise in the United Kingdom', in H. R. Hahlo, J. Graham Smith and R. W. Wright, *Nationalism and the Multinational Enterprise* (Sijthoff/Oceana, 1977), pp. 22–38 and appendices at pp. 343–65; ibid., *The Export Trade*, 9th edn (Stevens, 1990), chapters 15–18; C. D. Wallace, *Legal Control of the Multinational Enterprise* (Martinus Nijhoff, 1983), pp. 13–16; R. I. Tricker (note 5 above), at pp. 149–150.

24   See p. 13.

25   See G. Teubner, 'The many-headed hydra: networks as higher-order collective actors', in J. McCahery, S. Picciotto and C. Scott (eds), *Corporate Control and Accountability* (Oxford, Clarendon Press, 1993), p. 41. See further: G. Teubner, 'Unitas multiplex: corporate governance in group enterprises', in D. Sugarman and G. Teubner (eds), *Regulating Corporate Groups in Europe* (Nomos, 1990), pp. 67–104; G. Teubner, 'Beyond contract and organization? The external liability of franchising systems in German law', in C. Joerges (ed.), *Franchising and the Law: Theoretical and Comparative Approaches in Europe and the United States* (Nomos, 1992), p. 105.

26   See further Schmitthoff, *Export Trade* (note 23 above), at pp. 260–71.

27   See further J. N. Adams and K. V. Prichard Jones, *Franchising: Practice and Precedents in Business Format Franchising*, 3rd edn (Butterworths, 1990). For the position of distribution and service franchises under EC law see V. Korah, *Franchising and the EEC Competition Rules* (ESC Publishing, 1989).

28   Schmitthoff, *Export Trade* (note 23 above), at p. 343.

29   Examples taken from Tindall (note 23 above), at p. 75.

30   See further I. McIntyre, *Dogfight: the Transatlantic Battle over Airbus* (Praeger, 1992), chapter 5; K. Ellis, 'Ahead together' 42 *Air International* 92 (February 1992), and 'Airbus – the family expands', 42 *Air International* 133 (March 1992).

31   See Ordonnance No. 67-821, 23 September 1967. For commentary see: P. Merle, *Droit Commercial: Sociétés Commerciales* (Précis Dalloz, 1988), pp. 579–92.

32   On the other hand, according to Professor Hadden, in Canada and Australia 'it is more common for major groups to be structured in a more

complex manner, with interlocking webs of majority and minority holdings which make it more difficult to assess accurately the profitability and solvency either of the group as a whole or of its constituent companies or to identify those who are formally responsible for their operations': 'The Regulation of Corporate Groups in Australia', in 15 UNSW L. J. 61 at 64 (1992). On Canada see: T. Hadden, R. Forbes and R. Simmonds, *Canadian Business Organizations Law* (1986), chapter 9.

33 See Ford Motor Company, *The Making of Ford in Europe* (Public Affairs Doc. No. 2.5/589).

34 See Angello, 'Multinational corporate groups', 125 Hague Recueil (1968 III) 447 at pp. 503–4; T. Hadden, *The Control of Corporate Groups* (IALS, 1983) pp. 73–6. However, as noted above, more decentralization of managerial functions may take place in the future.

35 Hadden, ibid. The fourth company studied was IBM (UK) Ltd. See previous note. A more recent example is the Irish group Guinness plc. It operates through two core companies, United Distillers, the group's spirits company, and Guiness Brewing Worldwide, which brews Guinness stout throughout the world. It also owns Cruzcampo, making Guinness Spain's largest brewer: see *Guinness plc Fact File* (1992).

36 However, this group appears to have undergone considerable changes since the time of the Hadden study. See, for a recent list of principal operating companies, Bowater Annual Report and Accounts 1991, at pp. 54–6.

37 For a more recent list of principal subsidiary and associated undertakings of the Rank Organization see Annual Report and Accounts 1991, at pp. 41–4.

38 Note 34 above, at p. 9 and appendices.

39 Ibid., p. 11.

40 Ibid., at p. 13. See further Osunbor, 'The agent-only subsidiary company and the control of multinational groups', 38 ICLQ 377 (1989); Tricker (note 5 above), at pp. 66–7.

41 Note 7 above, at p. 45.

42 See Schmitthoff in Hahlo, Smith and Wright (note 23 above), at pp. 32–3.

43 See Agfa publication, *Agfa* (1992) at pp. 3, 35.

44 Schmitthoff, in Hahlo, Smith and Wright (note 23 above), at p. 34. See also *Unilever Annual Review 1992*, pp. 26–8 for composition of the current Special Committee and Board.

45 According to the Unilever Equalization Agreement, 'The principal object of the Equalization Agreement is to ensure that, in principle, it does not make any difference to a shareholder whether he holds shares in NV or PLC. The agreement achieves this by securing that the rights attaching and benefits accruing to each unit of ownership in NV evidenced by F1.12 nominal amount of ordinary capital and the rights attaching and benefits accruing to each unit of ownership in PLC evidenced by £1 nominal amount of ordinary capital shall as nearly as possible be the same as if each such unit formed part of the ordinary capital of one and the same company.' The Equalization Agreement provides that if the current profits of

either company shall be insufficient to meet its preference or ordinary dividends, the other company shall or may, respectively, be called upon to provide the amount required for this purpose. To date neither company has been called upon to do so as each company has been able to meet such obligations from its own current profits. The author is grateful to Unilever plc for supplying a summary of the principal terms of the Equalization Agreement.

46   See 'Overlapping umbrellas', *Financial Times*, 18 February 1993, p. 34.

47   Ibid.

48   Council Directive 90/434/EEC of 23 July 1990 OJ [1990] L 225/1.

49   See Bayer, 'Horizontal groups and joint ventures in Europe: concepts and reality', in K. Hopt (ed.), *Legal and Economic Analysis on Multinational Enterprises, Vol. II: Groups of Companies in European Laws* (1982), chapter 1; Wallace (note 23 above), at pp. 185–6. A classic example of the breakdown of a transnational merger is the now defunct Dunlop–Pirelli union, described by Bayer at p. 12.

50   'BA looks at going Dutch with KLM', *Financial Times*, 20 November 1991, p. 25, by Charles Leadbeater.

51   'The airline deal that did not fly', *Financial Times*, 28 February 1992, p. 17.

52   'Alliance drives a smooth course', *Financial Times*, 19 November 1991, p. 27. For an official description of the shareholding exchange and cooperation agreement between Volvo and Renault see *Renault Rapport Annuel 1990*, pp. 12–14, 45–7.

53   For details see 'The Renault–Volvo merger', *Financial Times*, 7 September 1993, p. 28.

54   See 'Volvo abandons Renault merger', *Financial Times*, 3 December 1993, p. 1.

55   See 'Renault and Volvo move to end their cross-shareholdings', *Financial Times*, 17 February 1994, p. 21.

56   See further text at p. 77 below.

57   EC Commission Draft Tenth Directive on Cross-border Mergers of PLCs: OJ [1985] C 23 25 January 1985; EC Bulletin Supplement 1985/3. For analysis see F. Wooldridge, *Company Law in the United Kingdom and the European Community* (Athlone Press, 1991), pp. 41–3.

58   See DTI, *Company Law Harmonisation* (March 1993), p. 7.

59   On which see further chapter 11 at pp. 396–7.

60   Law No. 54, 1947.

61   See T. Blakemore and M. Yazawa, 'Japanese commercial code revisions concerning corporations', 2 Am. Jo. Comp. L. 12 (1953).

62   The major *zaibatsu* were Mitsubishi, Mitsui, Sumitomo and Yasuda.

63   Imperial Ordinances No. 65 of 1945 and No. 23 of 1946.

64   See H. Oda, *Japanese Law* (Butterworths, 1992), at pp. 347–8; M. Matsushita, *International Trade and Competition Law in Japan* (Oxford, 1993), pp. 124–6; J. W. Rowley and D. I. Baker (eds), *International Mergers: the Antitrust Process* (Sweet & Maxwell, 1991), chapter 10 at pp. 867–8; Executive Office, Fair Trade Commission of Japan, *The Antimonopoly Act Guidelines Concerning Distribution Systems and Business*

Practices, 11 July 1991, chapter 7. The prohibition on holding companies was to be abolished in 1997.

65 Ibid., article 11, Antimonopoly law.

66 See T. Hadden, 'Regulating corporate groups: an international perspective', in McCahery *et al.* (note 25 above), at pp. 352–4. See further M. Hayakawa, 'Zum gegenwartigen Stand des Konzernrechts in Japan', in E. J. Mestmacher and P. Behrens (eds), *Das Gesellschaftsrecht der Konzerne im Internationalen Vergleich* (Nomos, 1991); R. Clark, *The Japanese Company* (Yale University Press, 1979), pp. 73–87; K. Miyashita and D. Russell, *Keiretsu: Inside the Hidden Japanese Conglomerates* (McGraw-Hill, 1994).

67 See ibid. at p. 354.

68 Ibid. at p. 353.

69 See Yoshino, 'The multinational spread of Japanese manufacturing investment since World War II', 48 Bus. Hist. Rev. 357 (1974).

70 See Brodley, 'Joint ventures and antitrust policy', 95 Harv. L. R. 1523 at pp. 1525–7 (1982). Brodley includes the creation of significant new enterprise capability in terms of new productive capacity, new technology, a new product or entry into a new market as part of his definition of a joint venture for antitrust purposes.

71 For a fuller discussion see: E. Herzfeld, *Joint Ventures*, 3rd edn (Jordans, 1996).

72 Joint ventures may be established between affiliates belonging to the same group. As noted above this is not uncommon among Japanese companies when setting up foreign operations.

73 See Schmitthoff, *Export Trade* (note 23 above), at pp. 339–40.

74 On which see Herzfeld (note 71 above), chapter 5.

75 On which see: Brodley (note 70 above); F. L. Fine, *Mergers and Joint Ventures in Europe: the Law and Policy of the EEC*, 2nd edn (Graham and Trotman, 1992). The treatment of R&D joint ventures under EC competition law is dealt with in V. Korah, *Technology Transfer Agreements and the EC Competition Rules* (Oxford, Clarendon Press, 1996).

76 See Herzfeld (note 71 above), at pp. 35–6.

77 See 'World steelmakers forge new cross-border links', *Financial Times*, 24 January 1990, p. 33.

78 GEC-Alsthom: 'Welding two cultures into a world force', *Financial Times*, 19 March 1990, p. 19.

79 Examples include General Electric–Snecma, Rolls Royce–BMW, Pratt and Whitney–MTU: 'Modest alliance between two pioneers', *Financial Times*, 4 May 1990, p. 23.

80 Sanofi-Sterling: 'Building bridges over troubled waters', *Financial Times*, 10 January 1991, p. 21.

81 For further examples see K. Ohmae, *Triad Power and Borderless World* (note 13 above).

82 See Scandinavian Airlines System Annual Report 1991 at pp. 44–6; Angello (note 34 above), at pp. 494–5. SAS was recently engaged in negotiations with KLM, Swissair and Austrian Airlines aimed at setting up a jointly owned company in which SAS, KLM and Swissair would own 30 per cent and Austrian 10 per cent. These negotiations have not been

successful: see *Financial Times*, 12/13 June 1993, p. 14; *Financial Times*, 22 November 1993, p. 1.

83   Tricker (note 5 above), at pp. 148–9.

84   'Renault status changed for Volvo alliance', *Financial Times*, 30 April 1990, p. 3.

85   J.-P. Anastassopoulos, G. Blanc and P. Dussauge, *State-owned Multi-nationals* (Wiley/IRM, 1987), at pp. 12–13.

86   Certain enterprises from the former socialist states of Eastern Europe and the former USSR display the characteristics of emerging MNEs. Assuming they continue to develop international operations, these enterprises will have started their path to multinationality as state-owned entities. See further: C. H. McMillan, *Multinationals from the Second World* (Macmillan, 1987); G. Hamilton (ed.), *Red Multinationals or Red Herrings?* (Frances Pinter, 1986).

87   Examples include Petrobras (Brazil), Pemex (Mexico), Kuwait Oil Company, Petroleos de Venezuela. See Anastassopoulos *et al.* (note 85 above), at pp. 183–4; L. Turner, *Oil Companies in the International System*, 3rd edn (RIIA/George Allen and Unwin, 1983), at pp. 237–9.

88   These included St Gobain (reprivatized in 1986), Pechiney, Rhône-Poulenc, Thomson, Cie Générale d'Electricité (reprivatized in 1987). See further J. Savary, *French Multinationals* (IRM/Frances Pinter, 1984), supplement, pp. 155–91; Anastassopoulos *et al.* (note 85 above), at pp. 121–4.

89   See further Khan, 'Some legal considerations on the role and structure of state oil companies: a comparative view', 34 ICLQ 584 (1985); Wälde, 'Restructuring and privatization: viable strategies for state enterprises in Developing Countries?', *Utilities Policy* (October 1991), pp. 412–17.

90   For example, in Italy the oil company Agip is controlled by Ente Nazionale Idrocarburi (ENI). ENI is to privatized in the near future: *Financial Times*, 14 April 1993, p. 21; *Financial Times*, 15 June 1993, p. 19.

91   See further Anastassopoulos *et al.* (note 85 above), at pp. 69–72.

92   See: Savary (note 88 above), at pp. 161–2; Anastassopoulos *et al.* (note 85 above), at p. 40.

93   Developing countries may retain public ownership where the alternative is domination of an industry by foreign capital. However, in the long term the pressures of state control may force privatization to occur. Short of privatization reforms aimed at increasing managerial efficiency may be taken. See World Bank, *Annual Report 1983*, chapter 8.

94   Anastassopoulos *et al.* (note 85 above), at p. 181.

95   Council Regulation No. 2137/85 of 25 July 1985 OJ [1985] L 199/1. This Regulation has been implemented into UK law by means of Statutory Instrument: SI 1989 No 638; SI 1989 216 (N. Ireland). For analysis see Wooldridge (note 57 above), at pp. 103–17; S. Israel, 'The EEIG – a major step forward for Community law', 9 Co. Law 14 (1988); M. Anderson, *European Economic Interest Groupings* (Butterworths, 1990). See also Companies House, *European Economic Interest Groupings: a Guide for Business* (Companies House, 1993).

96   Ibid., article 3(1).

97   Ibid., article 3(2).
98   Ibid., article 4(1). See 'EC framework finally comes into its own', *Financial Times*, 19 June 1989, p. 27.
99   Ibid., article 1(1). The law governing the formation contract is the law of the Member State in which the official address is situated: article 2.
100 Ibid., article 4(2).
101 On which see ibid., Arts. 6–12.
102 Ibid., article 1(2) and (3).
103 Ibid., article 2(1).
104 Ibid., article 16(1).
105 Ibid., article 17(1).
106 Ibid., article 21(1).
107 Ibid., preamble, recital 14.
108 Ibid., article 24(1).
109 On which see further chapter 16 at pp. 575–7.
110 Andean Commission Decision on Andean Multinational Enterprises (16–18 March 1982), 21 ILM 542 (1982); as amended by ANCOM Decision 292 (21 March 1991), 30 ILM 1295. All references in text are to the 1991 Decision. The official Spanish term is 'Empresa Multinacional Andina' (EMA).
111 Ibid., article 1.
112 Ibid., and articles 5–6.
113 See further: I. Brownlie, *Principles of Public International Law*, 5th edn (Oxford, 1998), at pp. 67–8; D. Ijalaye, *The Extension of Corporate Personality in International Law* (Oceana, 1978), chapter III; Schmitthoff, 'The international corporation', 30 Trans. Grot. Soc. 165 (1944); Kahn, 'International companies', 3 JWTL 498 (1969); Mann, 'International corporations and national law', in *Studies in International Law* (Oxford, 1973), p. 553 or in (1967) BYIL 145.
114 E.g. Eurochemic: see Khan (note 113), at p. 504.
115 E.g. Air Afrique: see Ijalaye (note 113 above), at pp. 81–4.
116 E.g. INTELSAT: ibid., at pp. 91–6.
117 See Onorato, 'Joint development in the international petroleum sector: the Yemeni variant', 39 ICLQ 653 (1990).
118 As is revealed by a comparison of approaches taken by the authorities cited in note 113 above.
119 Note 113 above, at pp. 503–11.
120 Convention of 20 October 1955: 378 UNTS 159.
121 Ibid., article XIV.
122 Hadden, *Control of Corporate Groups* (note 34 above), at pp. 44–5.
123 See Tricker (note 5 above), at pp. 156–9.
124 See writings cited in note 25 above.

4

Relations between MNEs and States: towards a Theory of Regulation

The preceding chapters have offered certain building blocks for understanding the nature of MNE regulation. The focus has been, first, on the reasons for MNE growth, including the role, if any, of legal factors in its promotion, and, secondly, on the relationship between the business and legal forms of MNEs, as an introduction to the problems of control through legal forms of business association. However, a developed understanding of the regulation of MNEs requires a further dimension. This stems from the interaction of MNEs with the political communities in which they operate, namely nation states.

In this respect, it is necessary to consider two sets of questions. First, the substantive content of any regulatory agenda must be ascertained. This can be done in the light of the perceived effects of MNEs on home and host states. Secondly, the principal jurisdictional levels and methods of regulation must be determined, so as to describe the range of policy choices open to regulators. Neither set of issues is capable of value-free discussion. Therefore, an inevitable feature of this chapter will be the elaboration of certain ideological themes briefly introduced in chapter 1.

1 Developing a Regulatory Agenda: Interactions between MNEs and Home and Host States

The discussion of relations between MNEs and states has involved a significant shift in international relations theory away from a state-centred 'balance of power' paradigm, in which the objects of study are nation states and their respective political, diplomatic and military interactions, and towards a 'transnational relations' analysis, which allows for the recognition of the role of non-state transnational actors in the international system, and emphasizes that the actions of such actors may increase international economic interdependence.[1]

The MNE figures prominently among such non-state actors. Indeed, MNEs can be seen as participants in a tripartite system of international interactions in an increasingly global economy involving the relations of governments to governments, governments to corporations and corporations to corporations.[2]

The implication for policy-makers in nation states is that, when developing national economic policy, they must evolve approaches to the operations of MNEs which serve to increase the benefits that their state can obtain from interactions with such firms. This raises the question of what those benefits may be. At this point difficulties of evaluation arise. As yet too little is known of the activities of MNEs and their effects on national economies to provide absolute answers. However, in terms of economic theory, a broadly beneficial effect is predicted from increased flows of direct investment, in that these may make available a wider range of goods at lower cost than would be possible in a world of closed national markets.[3] None the less, examples of economic gains from foreign direct investment can usually be met by counter-examples of losses caused by the same process. The point can be illustrated by reference to four factors commonly mentioned in discussions of the costs and benefits of direct investment by MNEs: namely, employment levels, balance of payments considerations, technology and skills transfer, and competitive effects in the local economy.[4]

Regarding employment effects, it is argued that MNEs can enhance employment levels in a host state by importing new jobs. However, this must be weighed against possible job losses in less competitive domestic firms. Equally, the stability of the imported job must be taken into account. Is the job likely to be long-term, or is it merely a short-term job given the extent of the foreign firm's commitment to the local economy? Furthermore, from the home state perspective, it is arguable that local jobs may be lost as domestic MNEs relocate employment to more advantageous foreign locations.[5] On the other hand, the creation of overseas jobs may stimulate job creation in the home state as the MNE's international linkages develop.

With regard to balance of payments considerations, a host state's balance may be improved by the inflow of new capital represented by a direct investment. However, this initial effect must be weighed against the longer-term outflow of capital through repayments of loans and through dividend remittances. Should these exceed the initial investment, then a net loss to the balance of payments will result. A similar result may occur if the local affiliate is highly integrated into the international production network of the MNE and is obliged to purchase inputs from affiliates in other states to an amount that exceeds the initial inflow of capital. However, such effects may be offset by a positive export performance from the MNE affiliate. The temptation may be for the host state to impose export requirements on the foreign firm as a condition of entry. Similarly, costly imports of inputs may be controlled by requiring the local affiliate to use locally produced inputs. As will be seen in chapter 7, such performance requirements have become objects of considerable dispute between capital-exporting and capital-importing states.

On the question of technology and skills transfer, it is argued that MNEs, as the principal holders of advanced productive technology and managerial skills, can enhance a host economy through the transfer and dissemination of such competitive benefits. This argument depends on the willingness of the MNE to share its competitive advantages with local firms and workers. If the technology and know-how involved are unique, it is unlikely that the MNE will readily give up its lead by disseminating its knowledge. It would be most likely to set up a wholly owned subsidiary in the host state, so as to control the use of its technology and skills. Alternatively, it might enter into licensing agreements that impose restrictive terms on the licensee as to the use and dissemination of the technology. In either case employees using the technology may be subjected to restrictive covenants as to subsequent employment with competitors. These issues will be considered further in chapter 12.

Finally, on the question of the competitive effects of foreign direct investment on the host economy, it is often asserted that MNEs will spur domestic firms into greater efficiency by exposing them to new competition. However, as Brech and Sharp point out, in the absence of significant spill-over effects that make new techniques available to local firms, and in the absence of adequate investment capital for local firms to develop, the net result may be that the foreign firm will drive the local competition out. Given the highly concentrated nature of many of the markets in which MNEs operate, significant anti-competitive effects may result.[6]

Given the uncertainties that surround the evaluation of MNE effects on home and host states' economies, there has evolved a significant ideological conflict over this issue, resulting in differing conceptions of the political economy of foreign investment, and in distinct policy prescriptions. Four major ideological strands can be identified. These are the 'neo-classical market analysis' of the MNE, the 'orthodox post-war economic' perspective, the 'Marxist' perspective and the 'nationalist' perspective.[7] They have each made significant contributions to the MNE debate since the 1960s. More recently, new perspectives in the debate have emerged, of which two appear to have long-term significance. These are the 'environmental' perspective and a developing concept of 'global consumerism'.[8] Each will be considered in turn.

1.1   The Neo-classical Perspective

This starts from the assumption that the market, as the most efficient allocator of resources, should be allowed to operate with as little regulatory interference as possible. In the sphere of international economics, this leads to a preference for an 'open' international economy with minimal state or international regulation. States should then be free to specialize in the production and sale of those commodities which they can make most efficiently, and to trade them for other commodities made more cheaply by other states. This should lead to a globally efficient economy and to a rational international division of labour.

In this process the MNE is an important 'medium for integrating and organising resource utilisation on a global scale'.[9] It acts as a means by which different national economies, with different comparative advantages in skills, labour, raw materials and know-how, can be integrated through the international division of labour within the enterprise. Crucial to this is a world economy in which the MNE is free to set up affiliates whenever and wherever it wishes, to engage in uninhibited intra-firm trade and trade with third parties. Given such conditions the MNE's operations are presumed to improve global welfare.

Although many states have pursued an 'open door' approach to foreign investment,[10] the MNE does not operate in a world free from restrictions on its activities even in so-called 'open door' economies. This fact has prompted neo-classical economists to dismiss intervention in the form of restrictions on foreign investment as being very wasteful of resources both nationally and internationally. Furthermore, they argue that such restrictions would fail to achieve the major economic objective of foreign direct investment, namely the transfer and acquisition of productive knowledge.[11] However, such views have been criticized for failing to appreciate the difficulties involved in securing an equal international spread of benefits from foreign direct investment. This issue is taken up by the 'orthodox economic' school on policy towards MNEs, to which we now turn.

1.2   The Orthodox Post-war Economic Perspective

This approach goes beyond the neo-classical perspective's faith in a free and unregulated market as the ultimate source of economic efficiency and human welfare. Rather, the orthodox perspective argues that markets can become imperfect allocators of resources because they are distorted by the costs of technology and the costs associated with the distribution of resources and products. This leads to a non-coincidence in the market between the supply of and demand for products, resulting in distributional conflicts. Such conflicts must be diminished or, if possible, eradicated by selective public sector intervention in the economy.

The large, managerially controlled corporation is identified as a major source of market failure. Through its size and technological capability the large corporation can monopolize and distort product markets, undermine consumer choice through advertising, avoid stock market regulation by becoming self-financing through reinvestment of profits, and avoid making losses that smaller firms cannot avoid. Thus, the corporation must be regulated to prevent these consequences. Such regulation could take a 'low intervention' or 'high intervention' perspective. At the low end the so-called 'managerialists' suggest that corporate managers could be expected to take public interest, as well as profit-oriented, decisions, thereby ensuring that firms act in a socially responsible way.[12] On an intermediate level the state itself can direct corporate policy through legal reforms of corporate structures and duties, ensuring that the interests of groups affected by corporate decisions will be taken into account. This is the idea of 'corporate governance'. Finally, at the 'high intervention' end there is the policy of 'corporatism', where the interests of capital, labour and society interact through public bodies, composed of governmental, business and labour interests, that are dedicated to national economic planning. At this point the market is greatly curtailed as the major source of economic organization.

During the late 1960s and early 1970s many of the ideas developed by this school formed the basis of the mainstream critique and policy response to the rise of MNEs. The orthodox economic critique of the MNE sees this type of corporation as carrying the monopolistic and anti-competitive tendencies identified in large national corporations on to an international stage. There it reproduces the same dangers of market failure. This requires selective and flexible state intervention for the minimization of the costs of MNE operations. Furthermore, should state control be ineffective, measures of supranational control through regional and universal international organizations may be required.[13] However, it is accepted that MNEs may bring net benefits to the world economy along the lines suggested in neo-classical analysis. Thus over-restrictive controls are seen as self defeating. The result is a policy of accommodation between the MNE and the nation state.

Within this general perspective both 'low intervention' and 'high intervention' policies have been proposed and/or pursued. The 'low intervention' approach is manifested in existing and draft voluntary codes of conduct concerning MNEs promulgated by international organizations.[14] These are replete with exhortations for good corporate citizenship on the part of MNEs *vis-à-vis* their host countries. The intermediate 'corporate governance' perspective can be seen in numerous EC proposals for greater disclosure, accountability and worker participation in MNEs[15] or in national laws requiring indigenous involvement in the ownership and control of local subsidiaries of foreign corporations.[16]

The high intervention 'corporatist' solution also finds its place. The demands put forward in the 1970s by the UN Group of 77, for rights to control national economic policy and to the free use of national resources, belong to this approach.[17] Similarly, on the international level, calls for greater public international control through international organizations and the setting up of special bodies to deal with MNEs can be said to have been inspired by 'corporatism' in a broad sense. For example, the OECD Guidelines on Multinational Enterprises of 1976 were the product of negotiations between the member governments and the Trades Union and Business Advisory Committees of the OECD. Although the Guidelines are a 'low intervention' compromise, which the unions thought was a weak response to MNEs,[18] they do represent a product of tripartite consultation, a key element of 'corporatism'. Furthermore, the Guidelines are periodically reviewed by the OECD Committee on International Investment and Multinational Enterprises. This is made up of officials from the member governments, who consult closely with the Trades Union and Business and Industry Advisory Committees. As a result, numerous trade union and governmental grievances on particular instances of MNE behaviour have been aired before this Committee.[19] In these circumstances, it is fair to regard the OECD Guidelines as displaying at least a tendency towards 'corporatist' solutions to MNE regulation.

Thus, orthodox economic analysis has had a marked influence upon the evolution of MNE control policy. In some respects its more radical recommendations (such as nationalization or strict entry controls over foreign investors) are hard to distinguish from those advocated by adherents of the 'Marxist' school. To this we now turn.

1.3   The Marxist Perspective

This approach centres on the exploitative aspects of capitalism in the international economy.[20] Building upon Marx's theories of the concentration of capital, labour exploitation and the division of labour in society,[21] subsequent writers have developed theories of 'monopoly capitalism' and 'imperialism' to explain the operation of international capitalism.[22] The thesis is that the tendency of national capitalist industry to move towards 'monopoly' (used here to denote not single firm dominance but market concentration in general) prompts the export of capital. The character of the capital exported is significant. It is described as 'finance capital', a term denoting the merger between 'financial capital' (money capital dealt with by banks and other financial enterprises) and 'industrial capital' (capital employed by productive enterprises). This fusion of concepts, introduced by Hilferding, permits the view that, for the purposes of international investment, the functions of financing and controlling the investment can be united in a single enterprise. As Anthony Brewer notes, 'if this generalisation of the concept is accepted, it opens the way to regarding the large multinational companies of today as part of finance capital',[23] since such companies engage in both of the above-mentioned functions.

The early Marxist model of capitalist imperialism does not address certain modern concerns. In particular, it has little to say about the impact of capitalism on underdeveloped countries, other than a vague expectation of capitalist development within them. Nor does it consider in detail the role of MNEs in the world economy, although, as noted above, the concept of 'finance capital' could extend to such enterprises. More recent writings of Marxists from Western and Southern states have attempted to fill the gap.[24] Their starting point is the concept of a division in the world economy between the advanced 'core' countries of the capitalist North and the underdeveloped 'periphery' countries of the economically dependent South. The latter are said to be in a position of permanent disadvantage owing to the particular way in which they have been linked to the advanced capitalist economies.

The MNE has been fitted into this 'centre–periphery' model of underdevelopment. By means of its international integration the MNE is said to act as an agent of underdevelopment. It has the power to control both the flow of commodities and products out of the LDC and the degree of inward investment, because of its monopolistic control of the market(s) concerned. Furthermore, Hymer has argued that the MNE reproduces 'centre–periphery relations' within itself through the hierarchical division of authority in the firm between the highest levels of management in the home country of the parent, intermediate management in regional sub-centres and the lowest levels of management in the branch plants located in LDCs. This management structure re-emphasizes 'core country' control through the increasing exclusion of 'peripheral country' nationals from managerial posts higher up the corporate hierarchy. At the lower levels, managers in the LDCs form a local interest group that can influence national economic policy in favour of the MNE, at the expense of the host state's real interests.[25]

These views have been the subject of extensive critical writing since the early 1970s. Two major strands of criticism are worth noting. First, some writers on the left have felt that the conventional Marxist analysis presented above has underestimated the extent to which capitalist penetration of the 'peripheral' countries has in fact led to economic growth.[26] Secondly, others have criticized this approach as paying too much attention to relations between states. In the process the 'new international division of labour', which serves to internationalize the class conflict between capital and labour, is ignored. Furthermore, this division of labour occurs not only through the medium of the MNE but also through transnational subcontracting between firms.[27] Thus a MNE-oriented model of international capital exploitation is seen as incomplete.

In the early 1970s the monopolistic and imperialistic theory of the MNE held sway on the left and with it a nationalistic policy response was recommended. In particular, the extensive nationalization of the 'commanding heights' of the national economy was recommended, with the result that the parent companies of the leading home-based MNEs and the major subsidiaries of foreign-owned MNEs would be brought into public ownership.[28] This approach will now be contrasted with other theories of nationalism as a theoretical foundation for MNE regulation.

1.4   The Influence of Nationalism[29]

The debate on MNEs cannot be regarded in exclusively economic terms. It contains the further issues of national independence, self-determination and cultural autonomy. The underlying fear is that large foreign firms have sufficient power, first, to undermine the host state's political and economic independence,[30] and, secondly, to threaten cultural identity by displacing locally created tastes and values with imported substitutes, spurred on by advertising through the transnational media corporations.[31] Consequently states may impose controls on MNEs that are not justifiable in economic terms, at least on a neo-classical analysis.

According to neo-classical economists the issue to be explained is why it is valuable to have certain kinds of production controlled by resident nationals rather than foreigners. Albert Breton offered a tentative explanation in his paper 'The economics of nationalism', published in 1964.[32] Breton's hypothesis is that a society can choose to invest resources in 'nationality or ethnicity', by means of the purchase or nationalization of foreign owned assets or by the imposition of tariffs, taxes, subsidies or other instruments to make foreign ownership of property less attractive. The return on this investment is both monetary and non-monetary. The monetary reward comes with an increase in the availability of high-income jobs for members of the national or ethnic groups in question, when such jobs are transferred from foreigners to that group. This redistribution of jobs favours middle-class occupations and so represents a redistribution of existing national wealth rather than an overall addition to it. The non-monetary reward is 'of a psychic order and is usually referred to as pride, sense of identity and the like'.[33]

Professor Johnson points out that such nationalism may risk damaging the competitiveness of the economy, through the replacement of highly skilled foreigners by less skilled nationals, excessive numbers of employees, excessive stress on 'prestige' manufacturing industries at the cost of industries in which the country has a genuine comparative advantage, and undue stress on state planning in place of the market.[34] The implication is that public welfare would be better served by a cosmopolitan 'open-door' and non-interventionist approach to national economic policy. However, this assumption may not always be borne out in practice. Indeed, Professor Johnson places certain preconditions upon the assumption for it to be true: the foreign nationals employed in the economy must be receiving no more than a fair price for their skilled qualifications and there cannot be discrimination against similarly qualified local nationals. He is content to assume that in most cases these preconditions are met.[35] Therefore, Professor Johnson assumes away what may be the major motivation behind a nationalistic economic programme – the acquisition of control over the means of production by local nationals where they have been previously excluded from such control. Short-run economic losses are irrelevant given the prospect of long-term national economic power.

The neo-classical critique of economic nationalism contains an important warning. If a nationalistic economic programme is adopted it must be kept within the bounds of economic reality. Otherwise an even greater degree of national dependency and weakness will be created – 'nationalism' cannot justify economic disaster. This sentiment is shared by the critics of neo-classical economics and should be taken seriously.[36]

The neo-classical approach to economic nationalism may be contrasted with the pro-nationalistic sentiments of 'dependency theory'. This label covers a wide range of writings and in no way reflects a common ideological position.[37] Rather, it is an expression bringing together writers of differing political and economic backgrounds who agree on the basic thesis that the underdeveloped nations of the 'Third World' are in a relation of economic dependency towards the rich nations of the North, and can only achieve true economic development by greater national control over the economy, whether by means of the greater regulation of foreign trade and investment within the capitalist system, or, as recommended by Marxists, through withdrawal from that system.[38]

The aspiration towards economic and political sovereignty has been a continuous theme throughout the MNE debate. It serves to explain why an 'economically inefficient' response has been taken in certain cases. Furthermore, 'nationalism' informs state policy in both capitalist and non-capitalist states and regions. It cuts across the traditional 'left–right' axis of political economy, and introduces a complementary 'national–international' axis. This results in ideological discontinuities and paradoxes which help to explain why both capitalists and Marxists may espouse nationalistic policies despite the avowed 'internationalism' of their economic theories (the international freedom of capital on the one hand, and international class conflict on the other).[39] It can produce curious alliances. For example, in Chile, during the early 1950s, not only the political left, informed by ideas of 'neo-colonialism', supported the increase of control over US copper companies but also the political right, who felt that without greater national control over the economy, they could never enjoy the benefits of capitalism to the full. Indeed, by the late 1960s, a broad political spectrum favoured the outright nationalization of the copper companies. The process began in the mid-1960s with the 'Chileanization' of these companies through increased public share-ownership and state control initiated by the centre-right government of Eduardo Frei. Salvador Allende's Marxist government brought this process to its logical conclusion when the US copper companies were fully nationalized in 1970–1.

The preceding discussion should not be interpreted as saying that all controls over MNEs are inspired by nationalism. Equally, not all states have pursued restrictive policies on MNEs as an outcome of nationalistic planning. Some have chosen to follow the neo-classical prescription that an 'open door' to foreign firms is the best way to serve the national interest. Significant examples exist of spectacular economic growth, and rising living standards for the mass of the population, in countries that have followed this approach.[40] Indeed, such states pose a challenge to the traditional prediction of 'dependency theory' that peripheral economies are doomed to permanent underdevelopment, and suggest that state-inspired entrepreneurship can produce growth.

1.5   The Environmental Perspective

In more recent times a further dimension has emerged in the debate on MNEs. This concentrates on the ecological effects of their international operations. In particular, MNEs are criticized for paying

inadequate attention to the environmental damage that their operations can cause, and for relocating environmentally hazardous processes into countries with lax or non-existent environmental controls.
The role of MNEs in the control of pollution and resource depletion
is also a major concern.[41] The principal regulatory questions that
have been raised in this context concern the development of group
liability for damage caused by environmental hazards under the
control of a MNE, a matter highlighted by the accidents at Seveso
and Bhopal,[42] the development of improved disclosure on environmental matters[43] and better provision for compensation in the case of
accidents.[44] As yet, this perspective is more concerned with specific
technical issues regarding improved environmental regulation of
MNEs. However, it carries within itself the potential for developing
a new general framework for the evaluation of business activities.[45] As
such it may become a significant ideological current influencing
future policy.

1.6 'Global Consumerism'

This concept, developed by, among others, Leslie Sklair in his book
Sociology of the Global System,[46] seeks to identify the social and cultural effects of the expansion of global firms producing goods for
private consumption. It posits the creation of an emergent global
culture based on the goods and services offered by MNEs, which
form a lifestyle distinct from that traditionally experienced by the
population in a host state. Of particular significance is the role of
transnational media and advertising corporations as the creators of
images that encourage the development of consumer tastes which fit
with the products and services offered by MNEs.

In response to the threat of foreign cultural domination, many
states have seen fit to protect their cultural industries – in particular
the mass media – from foreign control, either by means of restrictions
or by outright prohibitions on foreign ownership. On the other hand,
as consumer choices move towards the acquisition of globally mar-
keted products, policy-makers may be more concerned about the
satisfaction of such wants, rather than their curtailment, especially if
the consumers in question form a politically influential section of the
community. This will be the case in lower income societies, where
only the more affluent and more influential may be in a position to
buy such goods and services.[47]

This last point leads to a significant general concern. In order to
fuel the continued development of global consumerism, sufficient
income levels must be generated to provide adequate disposable
income for expenditure on consumer goods, and for the creation of
new mass consumer markets. In this respect a major consideration

arises regarding the creation and maintenance of long-term employment for the consuming public. Therefore, employment stability may be a policy consequence of furthering consumerism as a desirable goal. Failure in this respect may serve to undermine support for consumerist policies in the future, given their emphasis on the satisfaction of material wants. The emerging ideology of 'global consumerism' lies in contrast to the environmental perspective, given its continued faith in economic growth and increasing consumption as a valid goal of economic and social policy.

1.7 Synthesis: Framework for a Regulatory Agenda

Each of the above-mentioned ideological positions posits an answer to the issue of MNE regulation that rests on its beliefs as to the manner in which wealth is generated in the international economy. Thus there appears a contrast between the 'neo-classical' and 'orthodox' positions, with their essentially benign attitude to MNE activities, and the 'Marxist' perspective, with its assumption that MNEs reproduce exploitative economic relations on an international scale.

Within the capitalist system the choice lies between 'open door' and 'regulated' access to the national economy for the MNE. The choice is conditioned by adherence to economic and political beliefs that range from the 'neo-classical' to 'corporatist' models described above. The results have been diverse, with differing degrees of openness and protectionism being followed by states. On the other hand, there is a general recognition that the potentially anti-competitive effects of large MNEs should be addressed. Thus control through competition law has generally been accepted. The above-mentioned ideas have influenced laws and regulations in this field. Examples of laws and regulatory policies displaying 'neo-classical', 'orthodox economic' and/or 'nationalistic' characteristics will be seen in part II.

By contrast, 'Marxist' analysis leads to the conclusion that the state should extract itself from exploitative capitalist economic relationships, nationalize its economy and reduce contact with capitalist enterprises to a minimum. Law serves here as an instrument of 'decoupling' by means of extensive nationalizations of foreign-owned property, and of prohibitions on the entry of new foreign capital. Such policies were pursued until the 1970s by the former socialist states of the Eastern Bloc, as will be briefly described in chapter 6.

Since the mid-1970s there has been a significant reappraisal of policies towards MNEs, caused by changes in international economic and political conditions, already mentioned in chapter 1. This has led to changes in international and national regulatory environments. The trend has been away from 'investor control' towards 'investor promotion and protection', among both developed and less developed countries espousing free market or mixed economies. At the same time, the socialist system is disintegrating, as hitherto socialist states adopt policies of transformation into market economies. Consequently, in these states, there has been a move away from hostility towards MNEs, towards a policy of less restricted entry by means of joint ventures and, more recently, by wholly foreign owned enterprises.

On the international level, intergovernmental organizations have committed themselves to a policy of controlling abuses of market and/or political power by MNEs, while accepting their utility as contributors to national economic development. This represents an intermediate response between ideological extremes, although greater emphasis is now placed on the promotion of foreign direct investment than in the 1970s. This policy shares equal status with that of controlling abusive practices by MNEs.

As yet, the environmental movement has made only tentative inroads into MNE regulation, of the kind outlined above. However, its influence is growing, with the possible result that policies based on the promotion of economic growth *per se* may eventually disappear. Thus the environmental movement may curb the current preference for the growth of global consumerism as a dominant regulatory theme.

The principal features of, and reasons for, the above-mentioned changes in policy will be described and analysed in parts II and III. However, before that is done we must turn to the question of jurisdictional levels and methods of regulating MNEs.

2   Jurisdictional Levels and Methods of MNE Regulation

This section considers the implications of the transnational business structure of MNEs on the levels of jurisdiction at which regulation can take place, and on the methods by which it can be carried out. It is here that the relationship between state and corporate power will be analysed, and the boundaries of effective state action ascertained. The discussion will commence with a determination of state objectives in the regulation of MNEs, focusing on differences in the priorities of home and host states. It will continue by considering the issue of bargaining over controls between host states and MNEs, seeking to identify how far each participant may enjoy the power to structure a regulatory environment favourable to its concerns. The discussion will end by considering the choice of jurisdictional levels open to states as frameworks for regulation, distinguishing between unilateral regulation at the national level, bilateral interstate regulation through a treaty regime, regional regulation through supranational organizations of states and global regulation by multilateral treaty and/or through intergovernmental organizations.

2.1   The Regulatory Priorities of Home and Host States

While each state's policy should be viewed as unique, certain generalizations are possible as to the broad regulatory goals of home and host states respectively. As regards home states, their traditional concerns have centred on, *inter alia*, the protection of domestic labour against the export of jobs abroad, adequate revenue from the repatriation of dividends earned by overseas subsidiaries of home-based parent companies, the promotion and protection of technological leads enjoyed by home-based MNEs and access to raw materials in short supply in the home state.[48] These concerns have prompted unilateral action designed to preserve the conditions of the national economy in the face of outward investment,[49] notably through the use of exchange controls[50] or through restrictions on foreign tax credits.[51]

New concerns have emerged for home states as a result of the increased integration of the international economy. In particular, as the principal home states have also become leading host states, they have had to consider the need for the equal and reciprocal treatment of inward and outward investment. This has led to the gradual acceptance of policies aimed at the progressive liberalization of entry conditions and the harmonization of treatment standards, as evidenced by OECD Codes in these fields.[52] The leading home states are concerned to extend these principles to all host states, as shown by their bargaining positions before the UN concerning the now shelved draft Code of Conduct on Transnational Corporations,[53] and regarding the investment-related aspects of the Uruguay Round of the GATT Negotiations.[54] That they should do so indicates an increasing willingness on the part of these states to use their political and economic power to protect the global interests of their corporations. It is an important feature in the emerging new international regulatory framework, which will be considered further below.

In addition, home states may increasingly adopt policies that seek to strengthen the competitiveness of home based MNEs. This could range from the giving of political and diplomatic support for new investment opportunities by way of improved relations with potential host states, to the monitoring of host state policies that give rise to discrimination against home firms, and to more general matters, such as the improvement of education and infrastructure in the home state, that act as a means of preserving the competitive advantage of home based firms.[55]

With regard to host states, their regulatory priorities stem from the fact that, regardless of their level of economic development, inward direct investment may be needed to supply new capital, technology, goods or services that no locally based firm can supply at equivalent or lower cost. Thus, host states will generally encourage the entry of firms that can bring these factors into the economy. However, host states will wish to guard against some of the difficulties, mentioned earlier, that can result if inward direct investment is permitted. Thus, conditions may be imposed on the entry of a foreign firm. These may relate to the legal form that the local enterprise must take, the level, if any, of local ownership in the new enterprise, and any performance requirements that the enterprise must fulfil, regarding, for example, import levels, technology and skills transfer, job levels, export levels or long-term investment strategy. Alternatively, foreign firms may be prohibited completely from certain sensitive sectors of the host economy. Apart from entry requirements, the host may impose measures to ensure adequate revenue from the investment by way of taxation. It will also normally subject the local affiliate of the MNE to the general system of business regulation in force within the host state. The extent and degree of regulation imposed on the local affiliate of a MNE will depend on the relative bargaining power of the firm and the host state. To this we now turn.

2.2   Bargaining between Host States and MNEs

The relationship between the host state and a MNE will be the outcome of a bargaining process between them. In this regard the formal content of the host state's laws and regulations should be viewed as a starting point for negotiation, as an initial statement of the host's regulatory goals. How far that system is actually applied in a given case will depend on the outcome of bargaining at the stage of entry. This, in turn, depends on the relative bargaining strength of the host state and the MNE.

Though generalization on such a case-specific issue is difficult, certain theories have emerged concerning the relativity of bargaining power between MNEs and host states. In the previous section of this chapter one such theory, the 'dependency' theory, has already been encountered. It predicts that less developed host states are in a permanently weaker bargaining position in relation to MNEs as a result of the unequal conditions of trade and investment in the international economy, and because of the willingness of local ruling elites to submit to the interests of foreign capital. Thus, dependency theory posits a picture of exploitation of less developed host states by MNEs which cannot easily be remedied.

In contrast to the pessimism of dependency analysis, the 'bargaining' theory of host state–MNE relations posits that there can be situations in which even a developing host state has the stronger bargaining position. This approach was first developed, in the context of the copper industry in Chile, by Professor Theodore Moran.[56] Having examined the continuing relationship between US copper companies and the Chilean state between 1945 and the overthrow of Salvador Allende's government in 1973, Professor Moran concluded that a slow shift in the balance of power had occurred in favour of the host state, which led to the eventual nationalization of the copper companies by President Allende's government in 1970. Professor Moran suggested that the bargaining power of the MNE was at its strongest on entry, because of the uncertainties surrounding the future prospects of a natural resource investment, but that it weakened over time as the actual profitability of the investment became apparent and as the host state moved up the learning curve of negotiating, operating and supervisory skills. However, the balance of power would shift back to the MNE on those occasions when the host state needed new investment in production or processing facilities, the technology for which was owned and controlled by the MNE. Furthermore, in determining whether the host state was likely to use its theoretical bargaining power to the full, account had to be taken of certain local variables. In particular, these included: the prominence of the targeted industry in the national economy; the setting for negotiations, especially the host state's perception of the costs and benefits of the investment as compared to the cost of replacing or of doing without it; the process of policy formation, taking into account the value of retaining or removing the foreign investment to various interest groups and their ability to influence public policy in line with their interests.[57]

Professor Moran's initial work was restricted to the natural resources industry. In relation to manufacturing industries a different pattern of bargaining power appears to apply.[58] First, the MNE may be in a weak position at the point of entry given the host state's control over terms of access to the local market. However, once admitted, the firm may gain in power over time as it forges alliances with local suppliers, distributors and creditors.[59] Secondly, where the industry concerned is characterized by continuous technological change and/or dynamic markets, the MNE is likely to possess a lasting bargaining advantage over the host state. This is because the firm is in a better position to control access to the relevant technology and international markets. However, even where the host state acquires an independent technological base it may find itself in a situation of technological dependency given that new developments vital to the well-being of the national industry will happen outside its borders. Thus, the host state may have to attract foreign firms possessing the latest technology even where it has a domestic presence in the field.[60]

To conclude, in manufacturing industries the host state appears to be in a weaker position than the foreign firm, unless the firm is operating in a mature industry that is not reliant on new technology. In such cases the foreign firm may be vulnerable as its contribution to the host economy may be easy to replicate locally.

Given the foregoing emphasis on technology as the major source of bargaining power, the distinction between manufacturing and natural resources industries may not be so great, in that technological dependency can also arise in the latter. As already noted, when Chile needed technology and investment for new mining ventures in the copper industry the bargaining power of the US copper companies increased. Furthermore, after nationalization the Chilean copper industry remained vulnerable to pressure from US firms by means of an embargo on spares and new technology.

As regards service industries, host states appear to be in a relatively strong position, given the traditionally high degree of prudential regulation in such sectors. Furthermore, many states have instituted public monopolies in the provision of services, to the exclusion of foreign firms. Certain services, deemed vital to the national economy, may in addition be classified as sectors restricted to foreign investors. In this area, liberalization by way of privatization and the reduction of entry barriers may have to occur before the issue of host state–MNE bargaining can be considered in the light of extensive experience. At present, these matters have been the subject of debate as part of the Uruguay Round negotiations.[61]

The above comments should not be taken as anything more than broad general propositions. They arise from specific studies of countries and/or industry sectors, concentrating on natural resources and manufacturing. This empirical work is far from complete. Moreover, much of it is concerned with a rather inconclusive debate over the continuing relevance, if any, of dependency analysis, offering evidence both in support of and against this position. However, as Professors Stopford and Strange point out, the traditional concern of dependency theory with the unequal economic situation of less developed states may have been supplanted by a more complex dependency that affects both developed and less developed states alike. This rests on the constraint of governmental policy choices, in an increasingly integrated global economy, through the independent decisions of the dominant firms in industry sectors regarding such matters as the location of production or R&D, product development and marketing and choice of technology.[62] In a world where all governments suggest that they are committed to increasing the welfare of their citizens, responding to these decisions while attempting to meet these social objectives may entail a significant limitation of state power.[63]

On the other hand, this should not imply that cooperative approaches to MNE–host state relations are impossible. Indeed, Professors Stopford and Strange suggest that such cooperation is not only desirable but possible, given that firms are themselves in a weaker bargaining position as a result of increased international competition between firms, which offers host states the opportunity to trade firms off against one another.[64] Of significance in this respect would be access on the part of host states to information about firms and the international markets in which they operate. Here states with more developed databases and professional analytical skills will be at an advantage. Inevitably, the poorer states will be at a relative disadvantage.[65] Thus neo-dependency may manifest itself in the inability to formulate an effective bargaining position due to a lack of relevant information. This dimension of state power should not be overlooked. It may be remedied by the use of multilateral rather than unilateral approaches to regulation, a matter to be considered in the next section.

2.3 Jurisdictional Levels of Regulation
The international scope of MNE operations offers, in theory, a choice between three major levels of regulation: the national level, which can be subdivided between unilateral governmental regulation and bilateral regulation based on a treaty concluded between the home and host states; the regional level, involving a supranational regulatory authority established by a group of states sharing common economic interests in a defined geographical area; and the international level, involving regulation by a substantial majority of the world's states acting through multilateral intergovernmental organizations.[66] Each level will be considered, taking into account the economic interests that it may be able to serve and the legal problems that may be associated with it. Through this process certain models of regulatory systems will be built up as a guide to understanding the evolving structures of MNE regulation.

2.3.1 National regulation   At present, this is the most significant level of regulation. As will be seen below, emergent regional and international regulatory orders are still insufficiently developed to replace the nation state as the principal focus for the regulation of MNEs, though such a development cannot be ruled out for the future. As noted in sub-section 2.1, the main aim of regulation at the national level is to secure the greatest economic and social benefits from the activities of MNEs, whether as a home or host state. In economic terms this unilateral approach may result in what Hood and Young term 'beggar-thy-neighbour' policies.[67]

In the pursuit of their national interests states will not consider the impact of their regulatory policies on the economic welfare of other states. Unilateral national regulation tends to create a global market divided by different policy regimes, leading to distortions in investment patterns caused by the extensive adoption of second-best policies based on state intervention. Each state will seek to attract the greatest advantages from relations with MNEs, resulting in competition over investment incentives which can act as a form of protectionism. It is a system in which the weaker states will be increasingly disadvantaged and in which much public expenditure may be wasted in attracting MNEs for little economic gain. Furthermore, differences in regulatory regimes can be exploited by MNEs to their benefit, without any corresponding gain being transmitted to the states in which they operate, as already outlined in chapter 2.

The principal legal problem attached to unilateral regulation by the state arises from the fact that the MNE operates across the limits of national legal jurisdiction. The integrated character of its business activities will result in a mismatch between, on the one hand, the managerial and operational reach of the firm and, on the other, the jurisdictional reach of the state that seeks to regulate the MNE. This may result in situations where regulation exclusively within the territorial jurisdiction of the regulating entity may be ineffective.[68] The response of the state may be to extend the operation of its laws outside its territorial jurisdiction, that is, to apply its laws extraterritorially.

Thus, the legislature may wish to prescribe laws that apply to the whole of the MNE group regardless of its presence in another jurisdiction. For example, the home state may seek to protect its strategic interests by prohibiting companies possessing its nationality from trading with potential enemy powers. Such a prohibition would apply to the parent by reason of its nationality of incorporation. It could be made to extend to its overseas subsidiaries by reason of the nationality of the parent, on the basis of the control that it exercises over its subsidiaries. This disregards the legal nationality of the subsidiary as a juristic person incorporated under the law of the host state, and extends the law of the home state to its actions. To take another example, where the home state of a MNE imposes disclosure requirements on the parent, whether for the purposes of company law or taxation, the latter may seek to avoid those requirements by locating the relevant information abroad with a subsidiary incorporated under a legal system that protects the confidentiality of commercial information. In these circumstances the home state will order the production of the information only if it is prepared to extend the reach of its court orders into the host country of the subsidiary.[69] Equally, where a foreign parent company incorporates an operating subsidiary in the host country, and that subsidiary eventually becomes insolvent as a result of negligent decisions made by the parent, the liquidator of the subsidiary may only be successful if it can persuade the courts of the host state to issue process out of the jurisdiction against the parent corporation in an action for negligence.[70]

In each of these cases the court must be prepared not only to pierce the corporate veil between parent and subsidiary to establish liability, but also to pierce the 'jurisdictional veil' between them and seek to make the law of the forum apply to the foreign-based unit of the enterprise. Furthermore, in each of the above-mentioned cases, the regulating state seeks to make the overseas unit of the MNE act in accordance with the law that governs the activities of the unit present within the regulating state. In the home state, that will involve the regulation of an overseas subsidiary through the imposition of legal duties on the parent to direct the acts of the subsidiary in the required manner. In the host state, that will involve the imposition of legal duties on the foreign parent through the physical presence of the subsidiary within the jurisdiction. This may have the effect that obedience to one legal system will result in a violation of the law of the other, or, at least, in the imposition of legal standards not accepted under the law of that other.

The extraterritorial application of law can have serious political effects. First, it can be seen as an attempt by the regulating state to impose its policies upon others, disregarding the interests of the target state. Secondly, the target state's exclusive territorial sovereignty will have been infringed. This can lead to diplomatic conflict and to retaliatory measures against the regulating state. The perception that the target state's sovereignty has been disregarded can escalate the seriousness of the conflict, regardless of the actual damage inflicted on the economic interests of the target state.[71] Relations between the regulating and target states may deteriorate.

Attempts to exercise extraterritorial jurisdiction are a manifestation of the regulating state's power and confidence in the validity – if not superiority – of its policies. Generally, weak states do not attempt such an exercise. Indeed, the history of extraterritoriality disputes is closely related to the recent history of American power. Attempts by the USA, since the Second World War, to extend the reach of its laws have led to the majority of such disputes. These have arisen *inter alia* in relation to the scope of US anti-trust and securities laws, its national restrictions over exports to potential enemy countries, federal rules of disclosure and attempts to impose worldwide freezes on assets of countries suspected of supporting international terrorism held by the overseas branches of US banks.[72]

Such disputes have occurred between the USA and its principal trading partners from within the OECD. They have not involved the developing countries. These states are more likely to accept the extraterritorial operation of foreign laws as a price to be paid for foreign aid and investment. Furthermore, as the evolution of international direct investment involves increased cross-investment between the USA, Europe and Japan, conflicts over the right to regulate the activities of MNEs are more likely to emerge among the developed market economies. It is mainly a problem of the developed countries coming to terms with the emergence of an integrated global economy.[73]

On the other hand, developing host states may seek to engage the protection of their interests through a process of 'reverse extraterritoriality' where the laws of the home state impose higher standards of regulation over the parent company than those imposed on the locally incorporated subsidiary. Thus, during the American proceedings in the *Bhopal* case,[74] the private plaintiffs and the Indian government argued that the USA was the appropriate forum for the conduct of the litigation, and that US law was the applicable law, on the grounds *inter alia* that Indian law was procedurally and substantively incapable of dealing with such complex issues of liability. By comparison, US law offered the prospect of less delay and greater damages. The US courts rejected this argument. The host state should not be permitted to invoke US law in preference to its own law in the case of an accident that occurred on its own territory; US law would not apply globally to the overseas subsidiaries of US companies in determination of liability for tortious acts.

The emergence of extraterritoriality conflicts has led to calls for greater coordination between states in the development and enforcement of regulatory and procedural standards. Extraterritoriality issues underlie many of the regulatory techniques to be considered in part II. Accordingly, the next chapter will consider these matters in more detail as an introduction to part II.

Some of the problems of regulatory diversity between states can be solved on a bilateral level through the use of treaties based on reciprocity between the parties. Bilateral treaties have been concluded to control numerous commercial matters of direct concern to the signatory states, including double taxation,[75] recognition of corporations and transportation. Increasingly, as will be shown in chapter 17, capital-exporting and capital-importing states are entering into bilateral investment treaties (BITs) which establish minimum standards of treatment for investors from the other contracting state in the territory of the host state. Such treaties may limit the absolute discretion of the host state in setting the standards by which foreign investors are to be regulated. According to Siqueiros, such bilateral regimes can work only if entered between states of broadly similar economic development. Otherwise the reciprocity on which the treaty is based will be illusory.[76] In such cases the treaty may in fact impose the regime favoured by the stronger party on to the weaker party. This may be particularly true of BITs, bearing in mind the fact that these are usually based on a standard form model developed by the capital-exporting party. In any case, bilateral treaties offer no more than a limited solution to problems of regulatory diversity, as they represent specific regimes applicable only to the signatory states.

2.3.2 Regional regulation   One alternative to unilateral state regulation is for states with common economic interests in a coherent geo-political region to form a joint economic organization for the coordination of their economic policies. This may take the form of a free trade area, in which customs duties between the participating states are progressively removed, or of a developed common market, in which not only free trade but also full economic integration is pursued. Such policies may or may not involve the broader aim of full political union. In relation to MNE operations, such a development has the advantage of creating a harmonized economic policy area in which MNEs can organize their international network without having to confront differences in regulatory regimes. This should result in greater economic efficiency.

In relation to MNE regulation, the regional approach should increase the bargaining power of individual states through collective action (on the assumption that a common policy on direct investment is pursued), and reduce the mismatch between the territorial limits of jurisdiction and the geographical scope of MNE operations, at least as regards firms operating exclusively within the territory of the participating states. However, in relation to firms operating both within and outside the territory of the regional organization, the problem of jurisdictional limitation will re-emerge. Indeed, the regional organization may have to apply its own laws extraterritorially in order to ensure effective regulation over firms operating across its borders. In this it is no more than a 'superstate'.

Further problems may emerge in the evolution of a common policy on MNEs. The participating states may disagree over the content of such policy.[77] The organization may not even have a comprehensive policy in this area. Thus the success of such an approach depends on political agreement about regulatory goals.

Nevertheless, the regional approach to regulation may grow in significance, particularly if the global economy succumbs to the protectionist pressures created by economic recession, to damaging international competition between MNEs from different home regions and to political instability. The resulting model may involve a world of competing, self-contained, regional and interregional economic blocs, which increase economic interdependence within their boundaries while decreasing interdependence with other blocs.[78]

2.3.3 International regulation Neo-classical economic analysis points to the development of international regulation as the most efficient solution to the control of MNEs.[79] The area of control would coincide with the global market, allowing for the progressive removal of national regulatory barriers to foreign investment and intra-firm trade. Competition would be ensured by the establishment of global anti-trust regulation, while externalities could be regulated internationally through universal environmental and resource transfer laws. Incentives for MNEs to exploit differences in national regulations could be removed by the harmonization of tax laws, disclosure standards, labour regulations and corporate liability regimes. International incorporation for MNEs could be instituted as well as a multilateral agreement for the protection and promotion of investment. The system would require the establishment of multilateral institutions that would police and develop the system. This model requires the restriction of state sovereignty in the economic sphere through the acceptance of the right of the international system to regulate matters previously within the exclusive domain of state jurisdiction. Such a system has been periodically promoted, as under the abortive Havana Charter of 1948, which sought to set up the International Trade Organization as part of the post-war multilateral economic order.[80] Its most recent manifestation comes with the initiatives of the OECD and the World Bank in the field of foreign investment, and in the contents of the Final Act of the GATT Uruguay Round, which will be considered below.

The above-mentioned model has been challenged by an international model which seeks to protect host state sovereignty in the control of foreign investors. Such was the purpose behind the now defunct proposals for the creation of a New International Economic Order (NIEO) in the 1970s, which was briefly discussed in chapter 1 as one of the motivating factors in the development of concern over the activities of MNEs. The assumption behind this model is that MNEs have sufficient power to undermine the economic policies of the weaker, less developed, capital-importing states. Consequently, such states need to have their political power enhanced through the recognition, by international law, of their rights to control the entry, establishment and operation of MNEs in their territories. The NIEO approach thus presents international law as a system for the protection of state rights against powerful non-state actors.

The liberalization model, on the other hand, sees international law as a system for the restriction of state power where its exercise can lead to distortions in the global economy. The latter model is, not surprisingly, favoured by the major home states of MNEs as a goal to be strived for. As suggested above, there is at present some evidence to show that the major capital-exporting states are seeking the support of the international community in the development of a liberal 'New International Order for Trade and Investment' through the major multilateral economic and trade institutions. In particular, the World Bank has established an International Centre for the Settlement of Investment Disputes (ICSID), which provides a forum for delocalised dispute settlement, a Multilateral Investment Guaranty Agency (MIGA), which establishes an international system of investment insurance and acts as a body for the analysis of investment policies in general. The common aim of these institutions is to create structures that will aid in the reduction of risk to foreign investors and, thereby, contribute to an improved investment climate in participating states, while at the same time providing protection to host states against abuses of diplomatic protection by home states.[81] The structure and operation of these bodies will be considered in part III.

In the field of standard setting, the OECD issued its own Guidelines on Multinational Enterprises in 1976, while the now shelved draft UN Code of Conduct for Transnational Corporations has moved from its initial NIEO-inspired goal of MNE control to an accommodation between this aim and the aim of protection and promotion of foreign investment, favoured by the major capital-exporting states. The World Bank has also issued, in 1992, Guidelines on the Treatment of Foreign Direct Investment as a contribution to the on-going debate on international standards in this area.[82] These developments will be discussed, along with other multilateral guidelines, in chapter 16.

Finally, the Uruguay Round of multilateral negotiations under the GATT has resulted *inter alia* in the adoption of a new General Agreement on Trade in Services (GATS) and new Agreements on Trade Related Intellectual Property issues (TRIPs) and on Trade Related Investment Measures (TRIMs). The extension of the GATT into these areas has prompted the conclusion of an Agreement establishing a new World Trading Organization (WTO) to oversee the administration of this system. The WTO has embarked on the creation of a new institutional structure for the international regulation of trade and investment, which alongside the above-mentioned World Bank institutions might go some way to regulating the international system along liberal economic lines. The course of the Uruguay Round negotiations in these areas and the main features of the above-mentioned Agreements are discussed in chapter 7.

It is significant that these developments are occurring outside the UN and its specialized agencies. These bodies were given the responsibility of creating the institutional structures for the establishment and administration of the NIEO. As seen in chapter 1, the UN Centre and Commission for Transnational Corporations were designated as the bodies responsible for the conclusion of the UN Code of Conduct on TNCs, and for the furtherance of research and consultancy in the field of TNC activities. They have not, however, taken a leading role in the most recent international initiatives, perhaps because of their association with the NIEO model. In any case, as already noted in chapter 1, in 1992 the UNCTC was downgraded. Its functions have been modified and are now performed by the Division on Investment, Technology and Enterprise Development (DITE) which is part of UNCTAD.

On the other hand, in October 1990 fifteen leading developing countries suggested the establishment of an International Trade Organization within the UN system, as a response to the proposed WTO under GATT. The proposed UN body would have responsibility *inter alia* for the development of rules on foreign investment that recognized the right of less developed countries to impose conditions on foreign investors that would promote development and enhance competition.[83] Thus, debate over the appropriate international regulatory model is by no means over. There remains considerable reluctance on the part of states to part with their sovereign powers, even in the face of an increasingly international economy, where the economic and social success of a state is closely related to the development of beneficial relationships with MNEs.

3 Concluding Remarks

The opening chapters of this work have laid the conceptual ground for the study of the legal phenomena surrounding the operations of MNEs. The significance of particular issues to the more detailed analysis that follows has been highlighted where necessary by way of cross-referencing. It remains to explain the sequence of chapters in parts II and III. Part II begins, in chapter 5, with a detailed analysis of the limits of national jurisdiction. Chapter 6 will then go on to discuss controls over entry and establishment. Chapter 7 deals with 'open door' policies and incentives for investors, and considers attempts at the bilateral, regional and multilateral levels to liberalize conditions for the entry and establishment of foreign investors. Chapters 8 to 13 then discuss specific issues of post-entry regulation that have become objects of concern in relation to MNEs. These are taxation and tax avoidance, group liability and the liability of directors, accountability and disclosure, anti-trust problems, technology transfer and labour relations. Part III will then discuss the issues surrounding the evolution of a new international law relating to foreign investment by MNEs. Chapter 14 begins with a discussion of the issues in MNE–host state relations that have most commonly been regulated by international law, namely the renegotiation of international investment agreements and the expropriation of property and assets belonging to MNEs. Apart from analysing the applicable substantive law, this chapter also considers alternative methods of dealing with such risks through bilateral negotiations leading to lump sum compensation agreements and through national and multilateral investment insurance schemes, highlighting the scheme established by MIGA. Chapter 15 then turns to the issues surrounding the settlement of investment disputes through international methods. In particular, it examines the procedures of ICSID. Chapter 16 contains a discussion, in a historical context, of attempts to codify the substantive international law applicable to foreign investor–host state relations. It concentrates on attempts to develop international codes of conduct for MNEs and shows how, in recent years, the tendency has been to emphasize the promotion and protection of foreign investment over the rights of host states to control such investment. Chapter 17 continues this theme with a detailed examination of BITs and their significance in relations between capital-exporting and capital-importing states.

Notes

1   See generally: R. O. Keohane and J. S. Nye, *Transnational Relations and World Politics* (Harvard, 1972); S. Strange, *States and Markets*, 2nd edn (Pinter, 1994), chapter 1.

2   See further J. Stopford and S. Strange, *Rival States, Rival Firms* (Cambridge University Press, 1991).

3   See M. Brech and M. Sharp, *Inward Investment: Policy Options for the United Kingdom* (RIIA/RKP, 1984), at p. 30.

4   For an extensive discussion of the economic effects of MNEs on these four variables see J. H. Dunning, *Multinational Enterprises and the Global Economy* (Addison-Wesley, 1992), part 3. See also J. M. Stopford and L. Turner, *Britain and the Multinationals* (Wiley/IRM, 1985), chapters 6 and 7.

5   See, for a UK based study along these lines, F. Gaffikin and A. Nickson, *Jobs Crisis and the Multinationals: De-industrialisation in the West Midlands*

(Birmingham Trade Union Group for World Development, 1983).

6   Brech and Sharp (note 3 above), at pp. 37–8.

7   'Neo-classical market analysis' refers to theories based on classical market theory of value; 'orthodox post-war economic perspective' refers to the dominant economic theories used by post-war governments to direct their economic policy, based on Keynesian cost-of-production theories; 'Marxist perspective' refers to theories based on the Marxist concepts of labour surplus value and monopoly; the 'nationalist perspective' refers to economic policies designed to strengthen national wealth and sovereignty. For a fuller analysis of the ideological dimension of international political economy see C. Edwards, *The Fragmented World* (University Paperbacks, 1985) and L. N. Hood and S. Young, *The Economics of Multinational Enterprise* (Longman, 1979), chapter 8.

8   On which see in particular L. Sklair, *Sociology of the Global System* (Harvester Wheatsheaf, 1991), chapter 3.

9   Hood and Young (note 7 above), at p. 327.

10   See chapter 7 for examples.

11   See, for example, H. G. Johnson, 'The efficiency and welfare implications of the international corporation', in C. Kindleberger (ed.), *The International Corporation* (MIT, 1970), p. 35.

12   See, for example, A Bearle and G. Means, *The Modern Corporation and Private Property* (Harvest Books, 1968), pp. 309–13; J. K. Galbraith, *The New Industrial State* (Pelican, 1972).

13   See R. Vernon, *Sovereignty at Bay* (Pelican, 1973), at pp. 260–71.

14   See, for example, OECD Guidelines on Multinational Enterprises 1976 and the Draft UN Code of Conduct on Transnational Corporations, both discussed in detail in chapter 16.

15   See chapter 10.

16   See examples in chapter 6.

17   See the UN Resolutions cited in chapter 1, note 11, and see chapter 14.

18   See J. Robinson, *Multinationals and Political Control* (Gower, 1983), p. 119.

19   See chapter 13.

20   For a full discussion see A. Brewer, *Marxist Theories of Imperialism*, 2nd edn (Routledge and Kegan Paul, 1990).

21   See K. Marx, *Capital, Volume I* (Lawrence & Wishart, 1970), pp. 350–68 and chapter XXV.

22   The connection between 'monopolies' and 'imperialism' was explained by R. Hilferding in *Finance Capital* (1910, published in English by Routlege and Kegan Paul, 1981). See also N. Bhukarin, *Imperialism and World Economy* (1917, published in English by Merlin 1972). Their theories were made popular by V. I. Lenin in his pamphlet *Imperialism: the Highest Stage of Capitalism*, in V. I. Lenin, *Selected Works* (English edition, Moscow, 1952, volume 1, part 2; or Foreign Languages Press Peking, 1975).

23   Brewer (note 20 above), at p. 93.

24   Among the leading works in this context are P. Baran, *The Political Economy of Growth* (Pelican, 1973; first published 1957); A. G. Frank, *Capitalism and Underdevelopment in Latin America* (Modern Reader Paperbacks, 1969; first published 1967); S. Amin, *Unequal Development* (Monthly Review Press,

1976; originally in French, 1973). For full discussion see Brewer (note 20 above).

25 The multinational corporation and the law of uneven development', in H. Radice (ed.), *International Firms and Modern Imperialism* (Pelican, 1975), p. 37; or in J. Bhagwati (ed.), *Economics and World Order from the 1970s to the 1980s* (1972), p. 113.

26 See Bill Warren, 'Imperialism and capitalist industrialisation', *New Left Review*, No. 81 (1973), p. 3; *Imperialism: Pioneer of Capitalism* (New Left Books, 1980). See also J. Petras and D. Engbarth, 'Third World industrialisation and trade union struggles', in R. Southall (ed.), *Trade Unions and the Industrialisation of the Third World* (Zed Books, 1988), p. 81.

27 See Olle and Scholler, 'Direct investment and monopoly theories of capitalism', 16 *Capital and Class* 41 (1982); K. Cowling and R. Sugden, *Transnational Monopoly Capitalism* (Wheatsheaf Books, 1987); F. Frobel, J. Heinrichs and O. Kreye, *The New International Division of Labour* (Cambridge University Press, 1980).

28 See Stuart Holland, *The Socialist Challenge* (Quartet, 1976). This book represents the thinking that influenced the British Labour Party's Alternative Economic Strategy in the 1970s.

29 This section is a revised version of a paper entitled 'Economic nationalism and the regulation of multinational enterprises', given at the Development Studies Association Annual Conference, University of Glasgow, September 1990. That paper has been published in A. Carty and H. Singer (eds), *Conflict and Change in the 1990s* (Macmillan, 1993), p. 38.

30 Through, for example, the manipulation of markets, employment and sympathetic social groups and politicians.

31 On which see further: A. Mattelart, *Transnationals and the Third World: the Struggle for Culture* (Bergin and Garvey Inc., 1983); L. Sklair, *Sociology of the Global System* (Harvester Wheatsheaf, 1991), chapter 5.

32 *Journal of Political Economy* LXXII (1964) 376–86.

33 Ibid., at p. 379.

34 H. G. Johnson, 'A theoretical model of economic nationalism in new and developing states', *Political Science Quarterly*, LXXX (June 1965), p. 169.

35 Ibid., at p. 179.

36 See, for example, Dudley Seers, *The Political Economy of Nationalism* (Oxford University Press, 1983).

37 For a full analysis of 'dependency' theories see Gabriel Palma, 'Dependency and development: a critical overview', in D. Seers (ed.), *Dependency Theory: a Critical Reassessment* (Frances Pinter, 1981), p. 20.

38 The foreign investment policy of the Andean Common Market (ANCOM) offers a good example of a policy based on the non-Marxist version of 'dependency' analysis. See the original version of the Andean Foreign Investment Code: 11 ILM 126 (1972) revised text 16 ILM 138 (1977), discussed in chapter 16. The Andean Pact represents what the late Dudley Seers called 'extended nationalism': see note 36 above.

39 See further Seers (note 36 above), chapter 2.

40 For example, Singapore, Taiwan, Hong Kong. See further M. Smith et al., *Asia's New Industrial World* (Methuen, 1985); L. Turner and N. McMullen (eds), *The Newly Industrializing Countries: Trade and Adjustment* (RIIA/

George Allen & Unwin, 1982).

41   See L. Sklair, 'Global sociology and global environmental change', in M. Redclift and T. Benton (eds), *Sociology and Global Environmental Change* (Routledge, forthcoming); UNCTC, *Transnational Corporations in World Development* (UN, 1988), chapter XV; UNCTC, *Environmental Aspects of the Activities of Transnational Corporations: a Survey* (UN, 1985); UNCTC, 'Transnational corporations and issues relating to the environment' (UN Doc. E/C.10/1991/3); C. S. Pearson (ed.), *Multinational Corporations, Environment and the Third World: Business Matters* (Duke University Press, 1987); OECD, *The OECD Declaration and Decisions on International Investment and Multinational Enterprises 1991 Review* (Paris, 1992), Guideline on Environmental Protection, at pp. 107–8, analysis at pp. 52–4.

42   On which see generally chapter 9.

43   On which see chapter 10, pp. 368–71.

44   On which see further P. T. Muchlinski, *The Right to Development and the Industrialisation of Less Developed Countries: the Case of Compensation for Major Accidents Involving Foreign-owned Corporations* (Commonwealth Secretariat, Human Rights Unit Occasional Paper, 1989).

45   See, for example, T. Lang and C. Hines, *The New Protectionism* (Earthscan, 1993).

46   Sklair (note 8 above).

47   See UNCTC (1988, note 41 above), at pp. 222–5. See also Bennett and Sharpe, 'Agenda setting and bargaining power: the Mexican state versus transnational automobile corporations', 32 *World Politics* 57 at 76 (1979–80). Bennett and Sharpe argue that, in relation to consumer tastes in cars, the Mexican middle classes 'wanted what they had become accustomed to: modern, US style products. A Mexican car would not have been acceptable. The relationship of the Mexican state to its national bourgeoisie thus demanded that Mexico needed the sort of automobile industry that only transnational firms could provide'. In the former communist states of Eastern Europe, increased access to globally branded goods is popularly seen as a yardstick for measuring the success of the transition to market economies. Again it is the newly rich entrepreneurial classes that are in the best position to satisfy their wants. See Guy de Jonquieres, 'From bare shelves to blue jeans', *Financial Times*, 10 June 1992, p. 18.

48   See, for example, the discussion of US interests in C. Fred Bergsten, T. Horst and T. Moran, *American Multinationals and American Interests* (Brookings Institution, 1978); on UK interests, Stopford and Turner (note 4 above), chapter 8; on Swedish interests, E. Hornall and J. Vahlne, *Multinationals: the Swedish Case* (Croom Helm, 1986); on Japanese interests, Dunning (note 4 above), at pp. 568–9.

49   See further Gardner, 'The transnational corporation and the home country', 15 Col. J. Transnat. L. 369 (1976).

50   As under the now repealed UK Exchange Control Act 1947, on which see Hood and Young (note 7 above), at pp. 307–10.

51   See chapter 8 at pp. 280–1.

52   See further chapter 7 at pp. 248–50 and chapter 16 at pp. 578–92.

53   See chapter 16.

54 See chapter 7. This is also the case in relation to a possible future multilateral agreement on investment.

55 On which see further M. Porter, *The Competitive Advantage of Nations* (Macmillan, 1990). See also, on the power of MNEs to influence the economic policy agenda of home states by way of their 'embeddedness' in the state–finance–industry–labour policy networks of the home state, R. Sally, 'Multinational enterprises, political economy and institutional theory: domestic embeddedness in the context of internationalisation', 1 *Review of International Political Economy* 161 (Spring 1994).

56 T. H. Moran, *Multinational Corporations and the Politics of Dependence: Copper in Chile* (Princeton University Press, 1974). See also Moran, 'Multinational corporations and dependency: a dialogue for dependistas and non-dependistas', 32 Int. Org. 79 (1978); Leonard, 'Multinational corporations and politics in developing countries', *World Politics* 454 (1980); Dunning (note 4 above), at pp. 551–4; D. Lecraw, 'Multinational enterprises and developing countries', in P. J. Buckley (ed.), *New Directions in International Business* (Edward Elgar, 1992), p. 28.

57 Copper in Chile, at p. 217. See, for example, Bennett and Sharpe (note 47 above).

58 See generally T. Moran (ed.), *Multinational Corporations: the Political Economy of Foreign Direct Investment* (Lexington, 1985).

59 See further G. Gereffi, *The Pharmaceutical Industry and Dependency in the Third World* (Princeton University Press, 1983), at pp. 159–60.

60 See, for example, the cases of the Indian and Brazilian computer industries: Greico, 'Between dependency and autonomy: India's experience with the international computer industry', 36 Int. Org. 609 (1982); Adler, 'Ideological guerilas and the quest for technological autonomy: Brazil's domestic computer industry', 40 Int. Org. 673 (1986); Evans, 'State, capital and the transformation of dependence: the Brazilian computer case', 14 *World Development* 791 (1986). On the legal details behind these policies see chapter 12.

61 See chapter 7 at pp. 250–60.

62 Stopford and Strange (note 2 above), at p. 229.

63 Thus, for example, the UK government was constrained in its bargaining, during the 1970s, with the Chrysler Corporation over the latter's investment in the Linwood car manufacturing plant in Scotland because of the pressure to maintain employment in what was a region of high unemployment. See: N. Hood and S. Young, *Multinationals in Retreat: the Scottish Experience* (Edinburgh University Press, 1982), pp. 61–80; L. Grunberg, *Failed Multinational Ventures* (1981), chapter 5.

64 Stopford and Strange (note 2 above), at pp. 214–27. See also J. M. Kline, 'The role of transnational corporations in Chile's transition: beyond dependency and bargaining', 1 *Transnational Corporations* 81 (No. 2, August 1992) and *Foreign Investment Strategies in Restructuring Economies: Learning From Corporate Experiences in Chile* (Greenwood Press, Quorum Books, forthcoming).

65 See, for an example of how such problems might be overcome with the assistance of international organisations, Fui S. Tsikata (ed.), *Essays from*

the Ghana-Valco Renegotiations 1982–85 (Ghana Publishing Corporation, 1986).

66   See generally: Siqueiros, 'The juridical regulation of transnational enterprises', in *New Directions in International Trade Law Volume I* (UNIDROIT, 1978), p. 281; D. Vagts, 'The multinational enterprise: a new challenge for transnational law', 83 Harv. LR 739 (1970); C. D. Wallace, *Legal Control of the Multinational Enterprise* (Martinus Nijhoff, 1983), chapter 2.

67   Hood and Young (note 7 above), at p. 244.

68   See further, on the relationship between the MNE's business organization and its amenability to control by the state, L. Wells Jr, 'The multinational business enterprise: what kind of international organisation?', in Keohane and Nye (note 1 above), p. 97.

69   See, for example, *Lonrho v Shell Petroleum* [1980] 1 WLR 627 (HL).

70   This is a simplified version of the facts that occurred in the English case of *Multinational Gas and Petrochemical Co. v Multinational Gas and Petrochemical Services Ltd* [1983] Ch. 258, [1983] 2 All ER 563. (CA).

71   See Litvak and Maule, 'Conflict resolution and extraterritoriality', 13 *Journal of Conflict Resolution* 305 (1969).

72   See further chapter 5.

73   See Picciotto, 'Jurisdictional conflicts, international law and the international state system', 11 Int'l Jo. Soc. L. 11 (1983).

74   In *Re Union Carbide Gas Plant Disaster at Bhopal India* 634 F. Supp. 842 (SDNY, 1986), 25 ILM 771 (1986); aff'd as modified 809 F. 2nd 195 (2nd Cir 1987), 26 ILM 1008 (1987); cert. den. 108 S. Ct 199 (1987).

75   See further chapter 8.

76   Siqueiros (note 66 above), at p. 288.

77   See, for example, the case of ANCOM discussed in chapter 16.

78   See further L. Thurow, *Head to Head: the Coming Economic Battle among Japan, Europe and America* (Morrow, 1992). For a contrary view see P. Krugman, *Pop Internationalism* (MIT Press, 1996).

79   Hood and Young (note 7 above) at pp. 238–9.

80   On which see further chapter 11 at p. 403; chapter 16 at p. 574.

81   See I. F. I. Shihata, 'Towards a greater depoliticisation of investment disputes: the roles of ICSID and MIGA' (ICSID, 1992).

82   World Bank, *Report to the Development Committee and Guidelines on the Treatment of Foreign Direct Investment*, 21 September 1992: 31 ILM 1363 (1992).

83   The 15 states were: Algeria, Argentina, Brazil, Egypt, India, Indonesia, Jamaica, Malaysia, Mexico, Nigeria, Peru, Senegal, Venezuela, Yugoslavia, Zimbabwe. See *Financial Times*, 2 October 1990, p. 8.

Part II

Regulation by Home and Host States

5

The Jurisdictional Limits of Regulation through National or Regional Law

In chapter 4 it was seen that the principal jurisdictional level for the regulation of MNEs remains the nation state. Given the international nature of MNE organization and management, this situation creates the problem of extraterritoriality. The present chapter will consider in more detail the principal legal issues that have emerged from attempts to exercise extraterritorial jurisdiction over MNEs. This issue has been extensively documented in legal literature.[1] However, this work would be incomplete without an analysis of the principal trends in legal and diplomatic practice that have emerged in this area. The chapter will begin with an overview of the legal bases for the exercise of extraterritorial jurisdiction. These rest on the rules of public international law concerning state jurisdiction. It will then go on to consider state practice in this area, examining how the various bases of extraterritorial jurisdiction have been used in the fields of prescriptive, personal and enforcement jurisdiction. In relation to enforcement jurisdiction, particular attention will be given to the problem of the disclosure of evidence in proceedings involving a MNE. The chapter will conclude with an analysis of how extraterritoriality conflicts can be limited by way of legal and diplomatic initiatives.

1 The Legal Bases for the Extraterritorial Regulation of MNEs

The legal regulation of state jurisdiction is covered by rules of public international law. These are based on the exclusive sovereignty of each state over the territory it controls. Given that all states are equal in the eyes of international law, this power is to be enjoyed without let or hindrance from another sovereign state. Therefore, each state has a reserved domain of domestic jurisdiction. This has as its corollary a duty of non-intervention on the part of other states.[2]

Should the territorial principle of state jurisdiction be observed to the letter, any assertion of extraterritorial jurisdiction by a state would amount to a violation of international law. Such a view might be unduly restrictive of a state's legitimate interest in the effective enforcement of its laws against MNEs. This raises the question of whether the territorial principle can be modified to justify a measure of extraterritorial jurisdiction. According to Professor Brownlie, international law is developing in the light of the need to modify the territorial principle.[3] Consequently, alternative bases of jurisdiction have been put forward as exceptions to the territorial principle of jurisdiction, subject to the reservation that these must preserve a substantial and genuine connection between the subject matter of jurisdiction and the territorial base, and reasonable interests, of the state seeking to exercise jurisdiction.[4] Of the various exceptions put forward three are of particular relevance to the regulation of MNEs: the nationality, protective and objective territorial principles.

1.1   Nationality

It is accepted that in certain cases a state can assert jurisdiction over its nationals abroad.[5] In accordance with this principle, the home state of a MNE could seek to justify jurisdiction over the activities of an overseas unit in a number of situations. First, the managers of an overseas subsidiary, by reason of their home country nationality, could be subjected to home country legal requirements. Secondly, where there are no home country nationals on the board of the subsidiary, or they are in a minority, the home state could require the parent company to order its overseas subsidiaries to act in compliance with home country laws, by reason of the nationality of the parent company as the principal shareholder in the foreign subsidiary. This effectively disregards the foreign nationality of incorporation of the subsidiary. Such an assertion of jurisdiction has caused considerable difficulties in practice, as will be seen in the context of US trade embargoes addressed to the overseas subsidiaries of US firms. Thirdly, where the parent company operates abroad through unincorporated branches, these will retain the nationality of the parent and could, therefore, be subjected to the direct jurisdiction of the home country by reason of their corporate nationality. This has been a matter of significance in the extraterritorial regulation of the overseas branches of US banks.[6]

1.2   Protective Jurisdiction

Nearly all states accept the right of a state to exercise extraterritorial jurisdiction over acts done abroad which adversely affect the vital interests of the regulating state.[7] For example, in relation to customs, fiscal immigration or sanitary regulations, a coastal state is entitled to exercise the control necessary to enforce such regulations over a zone on the high seas contiguous to its territorial waters.[8] On an analogy with the contiguous zone concept, it might be possible to argue that the exercise of jurisdiction over the foreign units of a MNE is acceptable when it is required to secure vital national interests in areas of public governmental regulation. A convincing example would be the control of tax avoidance by the parent company through the use of transfer price manipulations between itself and its foreign subsidiaries.[9] On the other hand, it is debatable whether the mere protection of economic advantage on the part of the regulating state, at the expense of the target state, could be seen as the protection of 'vital interests'. It may be necessary to draw a distinction – not unlike the distinction between sovereign and commercial acts in the context of state immunity – between acts pursued in the genuine public interests of the regulating state and those designed to favour its commercial interests at the expense of other states.

1.3   Objective Territorial Jurisdiction

The question of a modification to the strict territorial principle of jurisdiction arises where the elements of a criminal offence are commenced in one state and are completed in another. This has given rise to the assertion by states of an objective territorial jurisdiction over offences initiated abroad and completed within the jurisdiction.[10]

The objective principle was accepted as a valid basis for the exercise of state jurisdiction in criminal matters by the Permanent Court of International Justice (PCIJ) in the *Lotus* case.[11] In that case, the Turkish courts had convicted, on a charge of involuntary manslaughter, the officer of the watch on a French ship that had collided with a Turkish ship on the high seas, causing the death of Turkish nationals on board the Turkish ship. The PCIJ held that Turkey was entitled to exercise its criminal jurisdiction on the basis that the effects of the offence were produced on the Turkish vessel. The Turkish vessel could be regarded as a place assimilated to Turkish territory, and, therefore, the offence was committed within Turkish territory, even though the perpetrator was, at the relevant time, aboard the French ship. The PCIJ held that the territoriality of criminal law was not an absolute principle of international law and by no means coincided with territorial sovereignty.[12] The Court further held that states retained a wide measure of discretion in respect of the application of their laws and the jurisdiction of their courts to persons, property and acts outside their territory.[13] The Court did not clarify the limits of this discretion, leaving the precise scope of the objective territorial principle unclear and open to interpretation by states. On the other hand, subsequent decisions of the International Court of Justice (ICJ) have laid stress on the need for a genuine connection between the subject matter of the jurisdiction and the territory of the state seeking to exercise its jurisdiction.[14] Therefore, an unlimited discretion on the part of states to assert jurisdiction on the basis of the objective principle cannot be presumed. Furthermore, according to Neale and Stephens,[15] the application of the objective principle gives rise to at least two main areas of dispute. First, the conduct involved may be regarded as criminal in the state where it is completed but not in the state where it was initiated. Such differences in the law may be particularly common in the areas of economic and business regulation. Secondly, there is the problem of establishing a sufficient causal connection or nexus between the initiation and completion of the crime to justify applying the objective principle. A state determined to extend the scope of its laws will give a broad interpretation to the relevant chain of causation, taking remote rather than immediate causes as the justification for its action.

2   The Extraterritorial Regulation of MNEs in State Practice

Having considered the main exceptions to the strict territoriality principle in international law, in this section of the chapter we will describe how state practice has evolved in relation to the extraterritorial regulation of MNEs. A state's legal jurisdiction can be divided between the jurisdiction to prescribe laws, to adjudicate disputes and to enforce legal orders and judgments.[16] Each area of claims to jurisdiction will now be considered.

2.1   Jurisdiction to Prescribe

The United States has led attempts to extend its laws to non-resident units of MNEs.[17] This has been justified on the basis of the need for regulatory effectiveness in major fields of economic and public policy. For example, in relation to US antitrust laws, 'Conduct relating to US import trade that harms consumers in the United States may be subject to the jurisdiction of the US anti-trust laws regardless of where such conduct occurs or the nationality of the parties involved.'[18] Similarly, under US securities laws, prescriptive jurisdiction exists over transactions occurring outside the USA which have, or can be expected to have, a significant effect on the US securities market.[19] Furthermore, the USA has, over the years, asserted the power, *inter alia*:[20] to restrict exports of goods by the overseas subsidiaries of US firms operating in third countries so as to prevent the avoidance of US trade embargoes against unfriendly powers; to freeze the assets of unfriendly powers held in bank accounts located in the overseas branches of US banks;[21] and to criminalize the making of corrupt payments to foreign government officials by US companies under the Foreign Corrupt Practices Act 1976–7.

Throughout these areas there runs a common theory of jurisdictional competence, that is seen, at least by American lawyers, as being compatible with international law.[22] According to this theory, a state has jurisdiction to prescribe on the basis of territorial control, effects within the jurisdiction, the nationality of the person or entity subject to control and the protective principle. In relation to the regulation of MNEs the nationality and effects principles have been of particular importance as justifications for the assertion of US jurisdiction. Their application in controversial cases will be considered first, followed by an analysis of the limitations on the exercise of extraterritorial prescriptive jurisdiction developed under US law in response to resulting interstate conflicts. This section will then end with a consideration of how prescriptive jurisdiction could be asserted over the non-resident parent of the MNE by reason of the presence of a subsidiary within the jurisdiction.

2.1.1 Nationality links   The nationality principle was applied by the USA in the *Fruehauf* case.[23] During the 1960s the USA restricted trade with the People's Republic of China (PRC) under its Trading with the Enemy Legislation. Fruehauf France SA, a company two-thirds owned and controlled by its American parent, Fruehauf International, entered into a major contract to supply the French truck maker Berliet with trailers that would be exported along with Berliet tractor units to the PRC. The US Treasury Department ordered the American parent company to stop the sale. An order to this effect was passed on to the French subsidiary. Berliet refused to accept the termination of the contract and threatened to sue the French subsidiary. Thereupon, the French directors of the subsidiary, who were in a minority of three to five in relation to the American nominees, applied to the courts claiming that, under French law, the purported termination was an abuse of rights (*abus de droit*) by the majority of American directors, whose decision had been motivated by the threat of personal liability under US law, and was not in the company's best interests, given the large potential liability for the breach. The Paris Court of Appeal affirmed the decision of the commercial court of Corbeil that a temporary administrator should be appointed to oversee the performance of the contract, as the decision of the board not to perform was indeed not in the interests of the company. Thereupon the US Treasury Department accepted that the French subsidiary was not under the control of its US parent and withdrew the order.[24]

The US government again sought to exercise extraterritorial jurisdiction on the basis of, *inter alia*, the nationality principle in the Soviet gas pipeline affair.[25] On 22 June 1982 the US Department of Commerce, at the direction of the President, extended existing controls on the export and re-export of goods and technical data relating to oil and gas exploration, exploitation, transmission and refinement.[26] The regulations prohibited the export of oil and gas equipment and technical data needed for the construction of a new gas pipeline from the Soviet Union to Western Europe. To the extent that the regulations prohibited direct exports of such equipment and data from the USA they were unobjectionable. However, they extended the prohibition to the re-export of such goods and data, where these were of US origin, by persons in third countries. Furthermore, the re-export of non-US goods and data by a person 'subject to the jurisdiction of the United States' was conditional on permission from the US Office of Export Administration. Finally, no person in the USA or in a foreign country could export or re-export to the USSR foreign products based on US technical data where any person subject to the jurisdiction of the USA received royalties for, or had licensed the use of, the technical data concerned. The effect of the Regulations was to extend the operation of US export controls to companies not possessing US nationality but using US technology under licence, and to the overseas subsidiaries of US companies by reason of their US ownership or control.

According to the Commission of the European Communities, these Regulations went beyond what was acceptable under international law,[27] first on the grounds that they violated the territorial principle of jurisdiction in that they purported to regulate the activities of companies in the EC, not under the territorial competence of the USA,[28] and, secondly, because there could be no support for the scope of the Regulations under the nationality principle. As regards the EC-based subsidiaries of US companies, the Regulations purported to impose US nationality on companies contrary to their nationality of incorporation and place of registered office, these being the tests of corporate nationality accepted as general principles of international law by the ICJ in the *Barcelona Traction* case.[29] As regards the companies whose only tie to the USA was through the use of licensed technology, or the possession of US origin goods, the Commission stated that 'Goods and technology do not have any nationality and there are no known rules under international law for using goods or technology situated abroad as a basis for establishing jurisdiction over the persons controlling them.'[30] These violations of the nationality principle were seen by the Commission as exacerbating the infringement of the territoriality principle.

The US Regulations elicited widespread protests from European states. Some European states applied blocking measures that required the companies covered by the US orders to fulfil their contracts.[31] In response, in November 1982, President Reagan rescinded the Regulations and the 'sanctions' that had been imposed on companies that had continued to perform their contracts. However, there has been no formal change in the US position on jurisdiction in the field of export controls.[32] Thus the potential for conflict remains, although it must be considerably diminished in view of the US government's failure in respect of the Soviet gas pipeline embargo.

2.1.2   The 'effects' doctrine   This doctrine evolved in the context of US anti-trust law to deal with overseas cartels which interfere with the US market to the detriment of the US consumer in violation of s. 1 of the Sherman Act.[33] By s. 1 of the Sherman Act, 'every contract, combination in the form of trust or otherwise, or conspiracy in restraint of trade or commerce among the several states or with foreign nations' is illegal and a felony. By s. 2 of the Act, 'every person who shall monopolize, or attempt to monopolize any part of the trade or commerce among the several states or with foreign nations, shall be deemed guilty of a misdemeanour'. The wide language of these provisions suggests that they apply not only to impugned transactions or conspiracies within the USA but also to such activities when they occur outside the USA.

Initially, the US Supreme Court observed the limits of US territorial jurisdiction in this area.[34] This did not, however, prevent the application of the Sherman Act to a conspiracy which, while involving the acts of a foreign sovereign, also involved deliberate anti-competitive acts by the conspirators within the USA.[35] The most significant American case in this area is *US v Alcoa*,[36] decided in 1945. There, the US Court of Appeals for the Second Circuit established the principle that the Sherman Act extended to the activities of non-nationals abroad where this produced anti-competitive effects within the USA. The case concerned anti-trust proceedings that had been instituted against the Aluminum Company of America (Alcoa) and Aluminum Limited (Limited), a Canadian corporation. Limited had been incorporated in 1928 to take over all the non-US assets of Alcoa. By 1935 the two corporations had become completely separate. In 1931 Limited joined an international cartel in the aluminium market, which, by 1936, included imports into the US market. The trial court held that Alcoa itself had no part in these agreements. The remaining question was, therefore, whether Limited could be held to have violated the Sherman Act.[37]

The Appeal Court held that Limited could be held liable under the Sherman Act. The Court's opinion was delivered by Judge Learned Hand. On the question of jurisdiction the Judge said:

> It is settled law . . . that any state may impose liabilities, even upon persons not within its allegiance, for conduct outside its borders that has consequences within its borders which the state reprehends; and that these liabilities other states will ordinarily recognize.[38]

On its true construction, the Sherman Act was held to impose liability on the conduct of persons not in allegiance to the USA for conduct occurring outside its territory. The jurisdiction of the USA under the Sherman Act was limited to those cases in which an anticompetitive agreement made by non-US parties outside US jurisdiction was intended to affect US imports or exports, and its performance was shown actually to have had some effect upon them.[39] On this issue, as soon as the intent to affect imports or exports had been established, on the basis of the foreseeability of the effects of the agreement in question, the burden of proof shifted to the defendant to show that no appreciable effects had in fact occurred.

This case laid the foundations for the more extensive application of the Sherman Act to foreign cartels, which was to lead to the first major conflicts over US extraterritorial jurisdiction. However, since *Alcoa*, US antitrust enforcement policy has been such that applications of the 'effects doctrine' have been rare.[40] Most cases have involved American companies, as participants in illegal cartels, over whom jurisdiction was never in doubt. Furthermore, foreign companies have not usually been named as defendants in suits initiated by the US authorities unless the express purpose of the restrictive agreement concerned had been to divide up world markets, with the US market being preserved for the US party in return for its exclusion from overseas markets. Direct interference with the US market is clear in such cases.[41]

Major conflicts over the application of the 'effects doctrine' did occur in two leading cases, each of which involved a direct challenge to the economic policy of the target state.[42] The first was the *Swiss Watchmakers* case.[43] In that case, the US courts attacked the Swiss watch industry's government sponsored cartel, whose aim was the protection of the industry against damaging competition from both within and outside Switzerland. The court held that the conduct of the Swiss industry in Switzerland was itself a violation of US antitrust laws and ordered changes in the organization of that conduct. That resulted in diplomatic protest from Switzerland, leading to the intervention of the State Department, and to a modification of the court's order so as to exclude actions undertaken by Swiss defendants that were not contrary to Swiss law.[44] Similarly, in *Zenith Radio Corp.* v *Hazeltine Research Inc.*[45] a private treble damages action was successfully brought by the plaintiff corporation against the defendant on the ground that the latter, along with other US firms supplying the Canadian domestic appliances market, had entered a patent pool in Canada which had the effect of hampering competition from imports into Canada. The patent pool had been encouraged by the Canadian government as part of its domestic economic policy favouring the local production of consumer goods for the Canadian market. The decision engendered protest from the Canadian government.[46]

An apparent change of direction occurred in the case of *Timberlane* v *Bank of America*,[47] where the US Court of Appeals for the Ninth Circuit restated the effects doctrine in the light of the need to take account of the legitimate interests of foreign states. According to the judgment of the Court, delivered by Judge Choy, 'a tripartite analysis seems to be indicated'.[48] The antitrust laws require:

in the first instance that there be *some* effect – actual or intended – on American commerce before the Federal courts may legitimately exercise subject matter jurisdiction under those statutes. Second, a greater showing of burden or restraint may be necessary to demonstrate that the effect is sufficiently large to present a cognizable injury to the plaintiffs and, therefore, a civil violation of the antitrust laws. . . . Third, there is the additional question which is unique to the international setting of whether the interests of, and links to, the United States – including the magnitude of the effect on American foreign commerce – are sufficiently strong vis-a-vis those of other nations, to justify an assertion of extraterritorial authority.[49]

The elements to be weighed in this process include: the degree of conflict with foreign law or policy; the nationality or allegiance of the parties and the locations or principal places of business of corporations; the extent to which enforcement by either state can be expected to achieve compliance; the relative significance of effects on the USA as compared with those elsewhere; the extent to which there is an explicit purpose to harm or affect American commerce; the foreseeability of such effect and the relative importance to the violations charged of conduct within the USA as compared with conduct abroad.

In *Mannington Mills* v *Congoleum Corp.*,[50] the Third Circuit Court of Appeals added four further factors that should be considered in the balancing process. These were: the possible effect on foreign relations if the court exercises jurisdiction and grants relief; if relief is granted, whether a party will be placed in the position of being forced to perform an act illegal in either country or be under conflicting requirements by both countries; whether an order for relief would be acceptable in the USA if made by a foreign nation under similar circumstances; whether a treaty between the affected nations has addressed the issue.[51]

The balancing test laid down in *Timberlane* and *Mannington Mills* is further supplemented by the doctrines of sovereign immunity and 'foreign sovereign compulsion' as a means of reducing conflicts over the extraterritorial application of antitrust laws.[52] Thus in *International Association of Machinists* v *The Organization of Petroleum Exporting Countries*[53] an anti-trust action brought against the member states of OPEC failed on the ground that the defendants were sovereign states entitled to immunity from suit for their actions as members of the said organization, in that these actions were undertaken in pursuit of sovereign purposes. As regards 'foreign sovereign compulsion', the US Department of Justice will not prosecute conduct that has been compelled by a foreign sovereign in circumstances where a refusal to comply with the foreign sovereign's command would give rise to the imposition of penalties or other severe sanctions. However, private anti-competitive conduct that is merely encouraged, or permitted by, or consistent with the laws and policies of the foreign sovereign will not offer a defence to an antitrust action, although measures short of compulsion may be relevant in a comity analysis, as described below.[54]

Finally, mention should be made of the Foreign Trade Antitrust Improvements Act 1982. This limits the operation of the Sherman Act to conduct involving trade or commerce, other than import trade or commerce, with foreign nations unless such conduct has a direct, substantial and reasonably foreseeable effect on US domestic trade or commerce, or on import trade or commerce with foreign nations, or on US exporters.[55] The effect of this provision is to reduce the number of antitrust cases involving foreign defendants through its exclusion of import commerce, although its effect on the balancing test may be to narrow its scope in cases where the statute applies.[56]

It is notable that US law has evolved its own doctrines to meet the criticism of an excessive assumption of extraterritorial jurisdiction.[57] The above-mentioned developments in US antitrust law have been reflected and generalized beyond the field of antitrust in s. 403 of the Third Restatement.[58] By s. 403(1), 'even when one of the bases of jurisdiction listed in s. 402 is present, a state may not exercise jurisdiction to prescribe law with respect to a person or activity having connections with another state when the exercise of such jurisdiction is unreasonable.' This principle has been applied by some US courts as a requirement of comity, that term being understood not merely as an act of discretion and courtesy but as reflecting a sense of obligation among states.[59] Whether the exercise of jurisdiction is unreasonable depends on an evaluation of all the relevant factors including those listed in s. 403(2)(a) to (h).[60] These considerations are not exhaustive; nor are they listed in any order of priority.[61]

Conflicting exercises of jurisdiction by two states are dealt with by s. 403(3). This recommends that where two states could each reasonably exercise jurisdiction over a person or activity, but the prescriptions by the two states are in conflict, each state is obliged to evaluate its own as well as the other state's interest in exercising jurisdiction in the light of all the relevant factors. A state should defer to the other state where that state's interest is clearly greater. The scope of s. 403(3) has been reviewed by the US Supreme Court in the case of *Hartford Fire Insurance Co. et al.* v *California*.[62] Certain London based reinsurers were alleged to have engaged in unlawful conspiracies with US based primary insurers and reinsurers to affect the terms upon which reinsurance for commercial general liability cover would be available on the US domestic market. The London reinsurers argued that the claims against them should have been dismissed as improper applications of the Sherman Act to foreign conduct. The US Supreme Court dismissed this argument. It held that a US court should only decline to exercise Sherman Act jurisdiction on the grounds of international comity where there was a true conflict between the requirements of domestic and foreign law. According to s. 403(3) such a conflict did not exist 'where a person subject to regulation by two states can comply with the laws of both'.[63] Following this prescription, the Supreme Court held that the London reinsurers were subject to US jurisdiction in that they did not argue that British law required them to act in some fashion prohibited by US law, or that their compliance with the laws of both countries was otherwise impossible. Thus there was no relevant conflict with British law. In so holding the Supreme Court rejected the argument of the UK government, as *amicus curiae*, that it had established a comprehensive regulatory regime over the London reinsurance market and that the conduct of the London reinsurers was perfectly consistent with British law and policy. The fact that their conduct was lawful in the UK was not, in itself, a bar to the application of US antitrust laws.[64]

2.1.3 Links of ownership and control Finally, the possibility of asserting prescriptive jurisdiction over a foreign parent company based on the presence of its subsidiary within the host state should be considered. Such a basis for prescriptive jurisdiction is suggested in the US Restatement.[65] The assertion of jurisdiction on this basis involves disregarding the corporate separation between parent and subsidiary. Consequently, often difficult enquiries would have to be made regarding the extent of control exercised by the overseas parent over the acts of its subsidiary, to determine whether the two corporations can be regarded as a single entity for the purposes of legal regulation by the state seeking prescriptive jurisdiction. The issue of disregarding corporate separation between resident and non-resident units of a MNE has arisen mainly in relation to the question of personal jurisdiction over the non-resident unit, and will be further considered in that context.

2.2   Personal Jurisdiction

The starting point for the assertion of personal jurisdiction is the presence of the defendant within the jurisdiction for the purpose of issuing process against him.[66] However, every advanced legal system accepts a power to issue process against a non-resident defendant, provided that there are sufficient factors connecting that defendant with the forum, which can justify the assertion of personal jurisdiction over him or it.[67]

On the other hand, even if a sufficient connection is found to justify the exercise of personal jurisdiction over the non-resident unit of the MNE, the courts of the forum must consider whether, taking into account the interests of the parties to the proceedings and the implications for international comity between states, they should in fact do so. Thus the analysis of personal jurisdiction over non-resident units of MNEs involves not only questions of fact concerning the existence of relevant connecting factors, but also questions of discretion regarding the appropriateness of the forum as the place for determining the dispute before it. Each will be considered in turn.

2.2.1   Establishing a sufficient connection between the forum and the non-resident unit of the MNE   In relation to the service of process against non-resident units of a MNE, the major question is whether the non-resident unit can be brought before the courts of the forum despite its absence from their territory. As noted above, this depends on the establishment of sufficient links between the non-resident unit and the actions that are the subject matter of proceedings before the forum jurisdiction. Clearly, where the non-resident unit has acted directly on its own behalf within the jurisdiction, no difficulty should arise in exercising jurisdiction over it.

More problematic is the case where the non-resident unit acts outside the jurisdiction, but those acts have damaging effects on persons within the forum jurisdiction. At this point the assertion of jurisdiction over the non-resident unit will have to be based either on the presence of an affiliated enterprise within the forum jurisdiction and, in particular, on the links of ownership and control between the resident and non-resident affiliates, or on other significant business contacts with the jurisdiction, such as the presence within the forum jurisdiction of officers of the non-resident entity, or of products made by that entity.

The mere presence of an affiliate within the jurisdiction may not be sufficient, of itself, to establish personal jurisdiction over the non-resident entity. The crucial question is whether the *linkages between the resident and non-resident entities* are such that the two can be regarded as a single unit for the service of process. This involves, first, an analysis of the legal form of the entity within the jurisdiction and, secondly, an ascertainment of the way in which business activities between the two entities are organized.

The legal form of the entity within the forum jurisdiction may be crucial in determining the amenability of the non-resident unit to suit. In particular, the legal distinction between establishment through a branch or a subsidiary may be of considerable practical importance given that a branch does not possess separate legal personality from that of its parent whereas a subsidiary does. For example, under the English Companies Act 1985, where a company incorporated outside the United Kingdom (an oversea company) establishes an unincorporated place of business within the UK[68] it will be amenable to suit before the English courts as long as it has an identifiable place of business within the jurisdiction to which process may be served or sent.[69] The effect is 'to protect a foreign company's British creditors by obtaining for them ab initio the means of serving process in this country, free from the inconvenience of seeking out the foreign company in its country of incorporation.'[70] In this respect the foreign company is placed on the same footing as an English company. In striking contrast, where a foreign parent chooses to incorporate an English subsidiary, rather than operate through a branch or office, the English courts will look first and foremost to the English subsidiary as the relevant corporate unit, respecting the corporate separation between the parent and subsidiary. Thus service of process on the local subsidiary will not normally amount to service on the foreign parent company.[71]

On the other hand, US law will normally accept as valid the service of process on the foreign parent company through its US subsidiary.[72] There is no requirement to the effect that the foreign defendant should be served under the procedures established by the Hague Convention of 1965 on the Service Abroad of Judicial and Extra-judicial Documents in Civil and Commercial Matters.[73] On the other hand, it was held in *Federal Trade Commission* v *Compagnie de Saint Gobain Pont à Mousson*[74] that where a subpoena effecting compulsory process is served by direct mail on a foreign company in a foreign jurisdiction, the failure to use established channels of international judicial assistance will render such service invalid under US law, as it violates accepted principles of territorial sovereignty at international law.

Having considered the legal form of the relationship between parent and local affiliate, we must now analyse the business relationship between them to determine whether the acts of the affiliate within the jurisdiction can be attributed to the non-resident parent. Where a local branch is involved this should not be difficult. However, where a local subsidiary is involved an analysis of fact will have to be undertaken which is not dissimilar to 'lifting the corporate veil' for the purposes of establishing the liability of the parent company for the acts of its subsidiary.[75] This involves consideration of the extent to which the parent controls the acts of its subsidiary within the jurisdiction, so that the acts of the latter can be seen as either the direct acts of the foreign parent or acts which create parent company responsibility on the basis of agency.[76] However, it seems well settled that the mere ownership of shares in the subsidiary is not a sufficient connecting factor between the parent and the jurisdiction. A further connection must be found.[77] The burden of proof falls on the party seeking personal jurisdiction over the non-resident parent. The standard of proof may be lower than that required to establish the substantive liability of the non-resident parent.[78] In relation to a non-resident affiliate other than the parent company, the major question is whether the degree of economic integration between itself and the entity within the forum is sufficient to see the latter as the agent of the former for the purpose of the actions that are subject to legal proceedings. In this respect US courts have been relatively liberal in establishing the requisite economic links between affiliates.[79]

By contrast to US law, English law remains highly territorial in its approach to personal jurisdiction over MNEs. Thus in *Multinational Gas and Petrochemical Services Co.* v *Multinational Gas and Petrochemical Services Ltd*,[80] the Court of Appeal refused to accept jurisdiction over American, French and Japanese parent companies, the sole shareholders in a joint venture operating within the jurisdiction through an agent company, in a claim brought against them by the liquidator of the joint venture. The Court of Appeal held *inter alia* that the foreign parent companies could not be regarded as proper parties to the action, in that the joint venture was a separate enterprise for whose acts the parent companies had no responsibility in accordance with the doctrine established in *Salomon's*[81] case and culminating in *Re Horsley and Weight Ltd.*[82] In any case, were the foreign parent companies to be joined in the action, they 'would . . . be faced with an action in this country involving novel propositions of law as well as lengthy and expensive investigation of the facts'.[83] That weighed against the granting of leave to serve process outside the jurisdiction. This decision illustrates the difficulties of taking litigation to the 'centre' of a MNE located outside the jurisdiction. The liability to suit of the non-resident parent company can be avoided by reference to traditional doctrines of company law, which fail to disclose a cause of action. It is an instance of allowing the logic of the single unit enterprise to shield the directing units of a corporate group from potential liabilities which were, arguably, created by their mismanagement of the joint venture.

The question of extending forum jurisdiction to non-resident units of MNEs has also arisen under EC law, in the context of articles 85 and 86 of the Treaty of Rome, which are the foundations of Community competition law.[84] The issue arises where a non-EC based parent company, operating within the EC through a subsidiary, is suspected of anti-competitive conduct occurring within the territory of the Community that has an adverse effect on EC trade and competition.

In order to establish its jurisdictional authority over non-EC based parent companies in anti-trust matters, EC law applies an 'enterprise entity' test to prove a territorial connection between the non-EC parent and the jurisdiction through the presence of its subsidiary within the Community.[85] The dicta of the Court and Commission suggest that the very existence of a parent subsidiary relationship is *prima facie* sufficient to establish jurisdiction over the non-resident parent, although, as Merkin and Williams point out, it is unclear from the judgments of the European Court of Justice whether the true basis of extraterritoriality is 'the notion that the conduct of EEC subsidiaries is imputed to their foreign parents or that all companies within the same group are treated as a single "economic entity"'.[86]

The approach taken in the early leading cases has been confirmed more recently by the Commission in the *Wood Pulp*,[87] *Zinc Producer Group*[88] and *Aluminium Imports from Eastern Europe*[89] cases. These cases have also extended the scope of EC anti-trust jurisdiction. In particular, the reach of EC competition law has been extended to non-EC firms that export directly to, or do business within, the Community, irrespective of whether they have an established corporate presence within the Community. This extension of jurisdiction was approved by the European Court of Justice in the appeal against the Commission's decision on jurisdiction in the *Wood Pulp* case.[90] In the course of its judgment, the ECJ noted that the conclusion of an agreement which had the effect of restricting competition in the Common Market consisted of conduct made up of two elements, the formation of the agreement and its implementation. The applicability of EC competition law could not be made to depend on the place where the agreement was formed but on whether it was implemented within the Common Market. Otherwise undertakings would have an easy way of evading the law. On the facts the wood pulp producers had implemented their pricing agreement (which had been concluded outside the Community) though selling to purchasers within the Community at coordinated prices. The Court concluded that 'it is immaterial in that respect whether or not they had recourse to subsidiaries, agents, sub-agents or branches within the Community in order to make their contacts with purchasers within the Community'.[91]

This decision caused some commentators to believe that the Community has accepted a broad 'effects doctrine', similar to that espoused in the USA.[92] However, it appears that the Community's jurisdiction is limited only to non-EC firms with direct or indirect trading links within the EC. Thus in the *Zinc Producer* case, the Commission noted that where a restrictive agreement involved firms that would make no significant contribution to improving competition in the Community in the absence of the agreement, such firms were outside the scope of Community law. Any further extension of extraterritorial jurisdiction is unlikely given the difficulties of enforcing EC law against non-EC companies, and the lack of any procedure for compelling disclosure of relevant information from such firms.[93]

From the above examples, it is clear that different legal systems will take different positions on the extent to which they will 'lift the corporate veil', disregard the legal separation between resident and non-resident units of a MNE and establish personal jurisdiction over the non-resident unit by virtue of the presence of its affiliate within the jurisdiction. Much depends on the legal culture involved and, in particular, on the extent of its support for the territorial principle of jurisdiction in the face of the potential ineffectiveness of its laws in relation to MNEs.

A further factor is whether the legal system is prepared to go beyond the logic of corporate separation between affiliated enterprises in a MNE and adopt the 'economic entity' principle, making the MNE group as a whole subject to the personal jurisdiction of the forum. Here, a presumption of control by the parent over the subsidiary is involved. Such a presumption can serve as notice to the foreign parent that, on setting up a subsidiary within the host state's jurisdiction, it is subject to all the liabilities that a locally incorporated parent company may bear. For example, article 10 of the Argentinian Draft Code of Private International Law states:

Multinational Enterprises, such as conglomerates or holding companies, operating within the jurisdiction of several countries, despite the pluralistic nature of their legal personality, shall be considered economic units, and their activities shall be evaluated in the light of economic realities respecting their subjection to Argentine law.[94]

This provision makes clear that the activities of MNEs shall be regulated in accordance with Argentine law, on the basis of their economic unity and regardless of the legal separation between the various companies within the group.

Similarly, in the case of a parent company incorporated in the forum jurisdiction, a presumption of control may serve as notice of its responsibility before the courts of its home state for the acts of its overseas subsidiaries, where these would give rise to liability if they occurred locally. Such reasoning appears to be implicit in the US case-law in various fields on establishing jurisdiction over the foreign subsidiaries of US corporations. Although the courts have not departed from the language of corporate separation, the fact of such separation has not been allowed to interfere with the reach of US law to the subsidiary.

Apart from links based on ownership and control between the resident and non-resident units of the MNE, *other possible bases of personal jurisdiction* include the presence of officers of the non-resident unit within the jurisdiction and/or the presence of products manufactured by the non-resident unit within the jurisdiction, whether as a result of direct sales from abroad or of trade through third parties within the jurisdiction.

Under English law, it would appear that the temporary presence, within the jurisdiction, of officials of a foreign firm carrying on business on its behalf will suffice to establish personal jurisdiction over it.[95] Under US law, the question has arisen whether it is within the principle of due process to issue proceedings against a defendant who is temporarily present in the jurisdiction. This has been answered to the effect that transient presence is a sufficient basis for the exercise of personal jurisdiction.[96] This approach has since been upheld by the US Supreme Court, albeit in a non-commercial case.[97] These cases show a varied approach to the question of whether a non-resident corporation can be validly impleaded through the temporary presence of its officers in the jurisdiction. However, where such an officer is within the jurisdiction on the business of the foreign entity, it may be possible to serve that entity through him or her, despite the tentative nature of the contact involved, provided that the subject matter of the suit has a sufficient connection with the forum jurisdiction.

In recent years, courts in various jurisdictions have been asked to assert personal jurisdiction over non-resident manufacturing enterprises on the basis of the presence of their products within the jurisdiction. The issue has arisen in the context of actions for personal injuries caused by accidents occurring within the jurisdiction involving foreign manufactured products. This is likely to become a more frequent phenomenon in litigation, as the manufacture of consumer products becomes increasingly internationalized. A number of situations can be distinguished.

The first involves finished goods that have been imported into the jurisdiction by the foreign manufacturer and distributed through a local sales subsidiary. In such a case, as noted above, personal jurisdiction could be asserted on the basis of presence through the subsidiary. Secondly, there is the case where the goods enter the jurisdiction through an independent third party distributor. It may be desirable to sue the manufacturer where the third party excludes liability for defects in the goods, or where it has insufficient assets to compensate the claimant under the contract of sale. Under English law the foreign corporation will be amenable to suit in such a case only if the distributor within the jurisdiction has been carrying on the foreign corporation's business, and not merely its own business, through the introduction of the foreign corporation's products into the jurisdiction. This demands an analysis of the functions the distributor has been carrying out and all aspects of the relationship between it and the foreign corporation. Significant questions include: whether the distributor has acquired business premises to enable it to act on behalf of the foreign corporation; whether the foreign corporation pays for the distributors business overheads or only pays a contractual commission; the extent to which the foreign corporation controls the distributor in the conduct of its business; whether the distributor is allowed to display the foreign corporation's name and/or trademark; whether the distributor enters contracts of sale on its own behalf or as agent of the foreign company and, if so, whether the distributor is capable of binding the foreign company contractually.[98] Under US law such contacts may also be sufficient to establish personal jurisdiction over the non-resident company.[99]

Thirdly, a more difficult situation arises where there is no direct or indirect business presence on the part of the manufacturer in the jurisdiction and the product is brought in by the consumer himself. A still harder case arises where an accident is caused by the failure of a component manufactured by a non-resident company which is then incorporated into the finished product by another independent foreign company. If national laws are to protect the consumer effectively in such cases, then jurisdiction over foreign manufacturers may have to be asserted on the basis of the presence of their products alone.

Though certain US judges appear to be sympathetic to this view, as witnessed by the vigorous dissenting judgments in the US Supreme Court in *World-Wide Volkswagen Corporation* v *Woodson*[100] and *Asahi Metal Industry Co.* v *Superior Court of California*,[101] US law has not gone quite so far. The current state of US law is well summarized in *Asahi*. Relying on the long established US test of personal jurisdiction over foreign corporations, first laid down by the US Supreme Court in the seminal case of *International Shoe Co.* v *Washington*,[102] as interpreted in the *World-Wide Volkswagen* case, and on the authority of *Burger King Corp.* v *Rudzewicz*,[103] the Supreme Court held:

The placement of a product into the stream of commerce, without more, is not an act of the defendant purposefully directed toward the forum State. Additional conduct of the Defendant may indicate an intent or purpose to serve the market in the forum State, for example, designing the product for the market in the forum State, advertising in the forum State, establishing channels for providing regular advice to customers in the forum State, or marketing the product through a distributor who has agreed to act as the sales agent in the forum State. But a defendant's awareness that the stream of commerce may or will sweep the product into the forum State does not convert the mere act of placing the product into the stream into an act purposefully directed towards the forum State.[104]

On balance, the policy of US courts appears to be to allow jurisdiction save in the most exceptional cases. Where the defendant is a MNE with a business presence in the USA, this seems reasonable. For, if the corporation enters the 'stream of commerce' within US jurisdiction, and enjoys the protection of US law, this privilege carries with it a responsibility to respond to suits which are brought against the corporation as a result of its activities within the jurisdiction.[105] The line to be drawn is between a fortuitous, albeit theoretically foreseeable, presence of products in the forum jurisdiction – whether brought about by the acts of consumers after purchase or through incorporation into other products by intermediate manufacturers who then bring the finished product into the jurisdiction – and a purposeful strategy of market penetration, whether involving the presence of a local affiliate or not.[106] The above-mentioned American cases offer excellent illustrations of the jurisdictional problems involved in transnational product liability litigation, and of possible solutions to them which stretch, but ultimately do not destroy, the concept of a connection between the territory of the forum jurisdiction and the subject matter of the claim against the non-resident manufacturer.

2.2.2 The doctrine of forum non conveniens *as applied to non-resident units of MNEs* Even where the non-resident unit of the

MNE is amenable to the personal jurisdiction of the forum in accordance with the above-mentioned principles, in a common law jurisdiction the court may conclude, under the *forum non conveniens* doctrine, that the exercise of jurisdiction is inappropriate, in view of the inconvenience that the proposed litigation would cause to the parties and to the proper administration of justice. In relation to litigation involving the activities of MNEs this question will be of particular significance where the facts leading to the dispute have occurred in a foreign host jurisdiction, at the hands of a subsidiary, but the plaintiff is seeking the procedural advantage of litigating before the forum jurisdiction of his choice, whether the home jurisdiction where parent company is present, or a third jurisdiction where an affiliate is present.[107] This is known as 'forum shopping'.

Until recently, the American courts were favoured in cases where an American-made product or industrial process had caused injury abroad to a non-US claimant. The hope was that the US forum would be made available to the foreign plaintiff against the US corporation responsible for the product or process, thereby giving the plaintiff the advantage of US personal injuries litigation with low legal costs based on the contingency fee system,[108] liberal rules of pre-trial discovery, trial by jury and the prospect of a high damages award. However, in recent years the US courts have restricted the availability of US jurisdiction in such cases.[109] The US courts will not entertain a claim where an appropriate foreign forum exists, even though it may be less advantageous to the plaintiffs than a US forum. Where an adequate alternative forum exists, the American court will weigh the relevant private and public interest factors to determine whether dismissal is appropriate.[110] Furthermore, where the plaintiff is foreign his or her choice of forum deserves less deference, as the very object of the inquiry is to ensure that the trial is convenient.[111]

The above-mentioned principles were applied in the *Bhopal* case to deny US jurisdiction to the Indian victims of the gas leak disaster of 2–3 December 1984 at Union Carbide's pesticides plant in Bhopal.[112] The Indian plaintiffs, with the Government of India, had argued for US jurisdiction against Union Carbide Corporation (UCC), the parent company of Union Carbide of India (UCIL), on the grounds: first, that the Indian legal system was inadequate to meet the demands of such complex litigation;[113] secondly, that UCC, 'a monolithic multinational, controlled the design, construction and operation of the Bhopal plant through its global network of corporate planning, direction and control',[114] and was therefore responsible for the acts of its Indian subsidiary at the plant and should be sued in the USA, because the relevant evidence as to its liability lay in the USA; thirdly, that there was an overwhelming US public interest in retaining the case, in view of potential dangers to the American public from similar industrial processes used at Bhopal's sister plant at Institute, West Virginia, and because the USA, as the world's foremost industrial nation, had an interest in encouraging 'American multinationals to protect the health and well being of peoples throughout the world'.[115]

At first instance Judge Keenan rejected these arguments on the grounds that: India was an adequate forum, possessing a legal system and remedies based on the English law of tort; India was a proper forum on private interest considerations, in that the accident had occurred there and all the principal witnesses could be found there; and the overriding public interest in the litigation lay with the Indian jurisdiction as the jurisdiction possessing the superior regulatory interest in the case.[116] Therefore, Judge Keenan dismissed the case to India. He was upheld on this finding by the US Court of Appeals for the Second Circuit.[117]

Judge Keenan saw the *Bhopal* case as one of an accident whose *locus* was in India, and so refused to characterize the issues in the case as arising out of the control exercised by the US parent over its Indian subsidiary. Therefore, it was inevitable that he should conclude that the balance of interests pointed to the Indian forum. This decision suggests that there may be little purpose in a foreign plaintiff who has suffered an injury at the hands of an overseas subsidiary of a US MNE seeking to sue the parent in the USA, unless there is clear proof of the direct involvement of the parent company in the wrongdoing, and there is a clear US interest in the litigation. On both issues the foreign plaintiff will have a hard burden to discharge. The US courts are not willing to become a global forum for litigation brought against US MNEs.

In recent years the English courts have also sought to control the practice of 'forum shopping'.[118] However, the approach of the English courts to the question of *forum non conveniens* appears to have been constrained by the Brussels Convention on Jurisdiction and the Enforcement of Civil and Commercial Judgments 1968. Section 49 of the Civil Jurisdiction and Judgments Act 1982 (which incorporates the Brussels Convention into English law) states that: 'Nothing in this Act shall prevent any court in the United Kingdom from staying, sisting, striking out or dismissing any proceedings before it, on the ground of *forum non conveniens* or otherwise, where to do so is not inconsistent with the 1968 Convention.' The scope of s. 49 has been the subject of recent litigation. It has been held, in two first instance decisions involving insurance claims arising out of policies entered into in the London market by foreign insurers covering foreign risks, that where the Convention points to the English forum as a mandatory forum, it would be contrary to the purposes behind the Convention to permit any residual discretion over forum in the English courts, even though the facts of the case may point to the forum of a non-contracting country as the appropriate forum.[119] In this respect, English law is showing signs of moving away from Anglo-American doctrine and of coming closer to European doctrine, under which no discretion over the exercise of jurisdiction by a national court is recognized.[120]

However, the Court of Appeal has restricted the scope of these rulings in *Re Harrods (Buenos Aires) Ltd.*[121] In an action between the two Swiss corporate shareholders of Harrods (Buenos Aires), a company incorporated in England but whose business as a department store was carried on exclusively in Argentina, the Court of Appeal held that article 2 of the 1968 Convention did not mandate English jurisdiction over the dispute simply because the Harrods company was domiciled in the UK. On the facts Argentina was clearly the more appropriate forum. This case has been strongly criticized as being contrary to the true meaning of the Brussels Convention.[122]

2.3   Jurisdiction to Enforce[123]

Where a legal system has accepted jurisdiction to prescribe laws concerning the activities of non-resident units of MNEs, the effectiveness of such a policy must ultimately depend on its ability to enforce any judgments made against the non-resident. At this point the problem of extraterritoriality is at its most acute, as the judgment against the non-resident entity attempts to regulate its conduct within the territory of another sovereign state. The exercise of extraterritorial enforcement jurisdiction can take place where the enforcing jurisdiction makes direct orders against the foreign units of the MNE, or takes non-judicial measures within its jurisdiction against the assets of the foreign entity, or denies to it certain privileges usually accorded to enterprises engaged in the same business, such as import licences, tax credits or access to government tenders.[124]

The most serious disputes over exorbitant US claims to enforcement jurisdiction have arisen in antitrust cases.[125] As seen above, in certain such cases, the US courts have been forced to amend the extraterritorial aspects of their orders after diplomatic intervention by the foreign state concerned.[126] Attempts to enforce US judicial decisions against non-resident entities of MNEs have been met not only with diplomatic measures of opposition from target states but also with legal responses. Thus numerous countries have passed so-called 'blocking statutes' which have the effect *inter alia* of refusing recognition to foreign judgments that adversely affect the trade or commercial policy of the legislating state,[127] or principles of international law or comity.[128]

Equally, the corporate separation between parent and subsidiary in a multinational corporate group could be used as a justification by the courts of the home state for refusing to enforce a judgment issued against a subsidiary in a foreign host jurisdiction, with the aim of holding its parent company liable. Thus in *Adams* v *Cape Industries plc*,[129] the Court of Appeal refused to 'lift the corporate veil' between a British parent company and its American sales subsidiary, or to treat the two companies as a single 'economic entity', so as to permit the enforcement, in the UK, of a US default judgment given against the parent. However, this case should not be interpreted as laying down a principle that corporate separation is an absolute bar to the enforceability of a foreign judgment against a UK based parent company. On the facts, the judge in the American proceedings had not assessed the defendant's liability to each individual plaintiff, but had merely awarded a total sum to be divided among the plaintiffs by their counsel. This constituted a breach of natural justice under English law, making the award unenforceable before the English courts. In these circumstances, the refusal of the Court of Appeal to 'lift the corporate veil', or to see the presence of affiliated companies in the USA as the presence of the British parent, is understandable.

2.4 The Disclosure of Evidence in Proceedings Involving a MNE

A particularly contentious issue in the field of extraterritorial jurisdiction has been the assertion, again by US courts, of powers to order the disclosure of evidence located abroad with the foreign affiliates or associates of companies operating within US jurisdiction.[130] By contrast the English courts have been unwilling to 'lift the corporate veil' and to order the disclosure of documents located in the overseas subsidiaries of British firms.[131]

The general principles observed by US courts in this respect have been summarized in s. 442(1) of the Third US Restatement on Foreign Relations Law.[132] The Restatement states that a court or agency of the USA, when authorized by statute or rule of court, may order a person subject to its personal jurisdiction to produce documents, objects or other information relevant to an action or investigation, where the information or the person in possession of the information is outside the USA.[133] In deciding whether to make such an order the court or agency should take into account:

the importance to the investigation or litigation of the documents or other information requested; the degree of specificity of the request; whether the information originated within the United States; the availability of alternative means of securing the information; and the extent to which noncompliance with the request would undermine important interests of the United States, or compliance with the request would undermine important interests of the state where the information is located.[134]

Failure to comply with an order to produce the requested information may subject the person to whom the order is addressed to sanctions including a finding of contempt, dismissal of a claim or defence, or default judgment, or may lead to a determination of fact favourable to the opposing party.[135] These general principles have been applied in numerous areas. However, orders for the discovery of documents in antitrust cases, and in areas covered by foreign secrecy laws, have engendered the greatest hostility from target states and deserve closer scrutiny.

2.4.1　Disclosure of evidence in US antitrust proceedings　In this area, foreign defendant corporations have been subjected to the broad requirements of US antitrust investigations and pre-trial disclosure rules on numerous occasions since the late 1940s.[136] Of particular significance were attempts, in the early 1960s, to control the use of liner conferences on routes between the USA and Europe,[137] and the more recent uranium cartel litigation of the 1970s.[138] Each series of cases led to the adoption of 'blocking statutes' by several target states, aimed at restricting compliance with wide-ranging US disclosure orders by companies located within their respective jurisdictions.

The experience of the uranium cartel litigation led to the adoption of the UK Protection of Trading Interests Act 1980.[139] By this Act the Secretary of State for Trade and Industry can issue orders to persons carrying on business in the UK not to comply with measures taken, or to be taken, by any overseas country for the regulation or control of international trade, where it appears to the Secretary of State that those measures apply extraterritorially to persons carrying on business in the UK, and are damaging, or threaten to damage, the trading interests of the UK.[140] The Secretary of State is further empowered to issue orders prohibiting compliance, by a person in the UK, with a request made by any court, tribunal or authority of an overseas country to produce before it any commercial document that is not within the territorial jurisdiction of that country or to furnish any commercial information to any such court, tribunal or authority.[141]

These powers were reviewed by the House of Lords in *British Airways Board* v *Laker Airways Ltd.*[142] This case arose out of the collapse, in 1982, of Laker Airways (Laker), which had been running a low-fare transatlantic air service between the UK and USA. Shortly after going into liquidation, Laker commenced US antitrust proceedings before the Federal District Court in Washington DC against a number of airlines who were members of the International Air Transport Association and others, alleging a conspiracy between them to eliminate Laker by charging predatory air fares which forced Laker out of business, and claiming treble damages and punitive damages of more than $2 billion. In the course of the US proceedings, Laker sought extensive pre-trial discovery of documents and answers to far reaching interrogatories from British Airways (BA) and British Caledonian (BCal). The latter applied to the English courts for an injunction to restrain the US proceedings. The judge refused to grant the relief sought and BA and BCal appealed. Before the appeal could be heard the Secretary of State for Trade and Industry issued an order, in June 1983, under ss 1 and 2 of the 1980 Act prohibiting BA and BCal from complying with any request or prohibition imposed upon them under the US antitrust laws as a result of a judgment in the US action, and prohibiting compliance with any request for the production of documents or commercial information in the US action without the Secretary of State's consent. Laker sought to challenge this order on judicial review. The Court of Appeal allowed the appeal against the refusal of injunctions restraining the US proceedings, on the basis of the Secretary of State's order, but dismissed Laker's application for judicial review.[143] Both issues were appealed to the House of Lords.

The House of Lords rejected Laker's application for judicial review. Their Lordships also rejected the appeal of BA and BCal. An injunction against the US proceedings would not be issued on the ground that to do so would deprive Laker of a remedy against these airlines under US antitrust law, which fell within the jurisdiction of the Federal District court in Washington DC, within whose territory both BA and BCal had premises and carried on business. No equivalent remedy was available under English law and so this was not like a *forum non conveniens* action. Either the US proceedings could continue or Laker would have no cause of action. Furthermore, contrary to the view expressed by the Court of Appeal, the House of Lords held that the Minister's order was not decisive in favour of granting an injunction.

This decision shows that the English courts will respect the right of a foreign court to determine a cause of action arising under its law against a UK based defendant, where that cause of action arises out of activities carried on by the defendant within the foreign jurisdiction. In such a case an order under the Protection of Trading Interests Act will not be construed as an absolute bar to those proceedings. In this respect the House of Lords decision in *Laker* conforms to a territorial conception of jurisdiction, in that it avoids giving to the order of the Secretary of State the power effectively to terminate proceedings legitimately brought by the plaintiff before the courts of a foreign country.[144] On the other hand, where such proceedings are sought against a defendant who has no relevant connection with the foreign jurisdiction, the English courts will enjoin the foreign proceedings. Thus, in *Midland Bank* v *Laker Airways Ltd*,[145] the mere existence of a parent–subsidiary relationship between an enterprise based in the UK and its foreign affiliate was held not to be sufficient to prove the presence of the UK based company in the foreign jurisdiction for the purposes of adjudication. Consequently the Court of Appeal issued an injunction against antitrust proceedings that were to be brought against the Midland Bank by Laker Airways. The *British Airways* case could be distinguished on the grounds that: Midland's connection with Laker arose out of banking transactions in England governed by English law and intended to be so governed; there was no connection between Midland and any of the airlines operating in the USA; Midland had done nothing in the USA that could have been governed by the US antitrust laws; the Midland Bank's subsidiary bank in California had a separate legal existence, was not managerially controlled by its parent and had no connection of any kind with the airlines involved in the liquidator's antitrust suit; and such banking activities as were carried on in the USA by Midland's subsidiary, Thomas Cook, were incidental to the group's tourist business and had no relevance to the facts in issue. It followed that the Midland Bank had not submitted itself to the jurisdiction of US antitrust legislation in the same way that BA and BCal had done.

2.4.2   US disclosure orders and foreign secrecy laws   Another significant source of conflict between the USA and other states has arisen in cases where the US authorities seek evidence located abroad with the affiliates or associates of litigants, or with third parties (often the litigant's foreign bank), and that evidence is subject to secrecy laws in force in the target jurisdiction.

The applicable principles are summarized in s. 442(2) of the US Restatement on Foreign Relations Law, which draws upon the leading decision of the US Supreme Court in *Société Internationale* v *Rogers*.[146] By s. 442(2):

If disclosure of information located outside the United States is prohibited by a law, regulation, or order of a court or other authority of the state in which the information or prospective witness is located, or of the state of which a prospective witness is a national,

(a) a court or agency in the United States may require the person to whom the order is directed to make a good faith effort to secure permission from the foreign authorities to make the information available;

(b) a court or agency should not ordinarily impose sanctions of contempt, dismissal, or default on a party that has failed to comply with the order for production, except in cases of deliberate concealment or removal of information or failure to make a good faith effort in accordance with paragraph (a);

(c) a court or agency may, in appropriate cases, make findings of fact adverse to a party that has failed to comply with the order for production, even if that party has made a good faith effort to secure permission from the foreign authorities to make the information available and that effort has been unsuccessful.[147]

This provision applies not only to cases involving foreign secrecy laws but also to cases where a 'blocking statute' prohibits disclosure in accordance with the trading interests of the target state.

The US courts have interpreted the *Société* decision as requiring a 'balancing approach'.[148] This involves taking account of the factors listed in s. 442(1)(c) of the Restatement and, in particular, comparing the importance of the US interest in disclosure against the interest of the target state in retaining the confidentiality of the information or documents in question.

This approach has been applied in cases involving requests for information from both US and foreign based MNEs by the US Internal Revenue Service (IRS), where that information is located in overseas subsidiaries or in the foreign parent company and is subject to commercial secrecy laws.[149] The US courts have generally held that the US interest in disclosure outweighs the target state's interest in preserving commercial confidentiality. These cases can be justified on the ground that, in the absence of strong extraterritorial disclosure requirements, MNEs can use their international network of companies not only to avoid the payment of tax but also to resist legitimate investigations by the IRS. Arguably, had the relevant records remained within the US jurisdiction, no issue of extraterritorial law enforcement would have arisen.

However, such decisions have met with protests from foreign governments. For example, the government of Japan made such a protest when a US District Court in California held that a summons for information issued by the IRS against the US sales subsidiary of the Japanese Toyota Corporation was sufficient to effect service on the Japanese parent company.[150] According to the Japanese government such service violated international law. However, the Court held that service was effected within the bounds of international law, it having applied the requirements of the Third Restatement to conclude that there was a strong American interest in obtaining the information and there was no reasonable alternative means of obtaining it.

Harder to justify are cases where the order for disclosure is made against an innocent third party, such as a bank, which holds information relevant to an investigation by US agencies. Here too, the US courts have resorted to a balancing test.[151] However, the precise limits of permissible discretion have not been clearly drawn. Much depends on the nature of the investigation involved and on the weight to be given to good faith efforts at disclosure in the face of penal confidentiality laws. For example, in the area of grand jury investigations into drug related crimes, the discretion to require disclosure from third parties operating in 'secrecy havens' has been widely interpreted.[152] No doubt a finding that the third party has not acted in good faith is a significant consideration. However, even where the third party does act in good faith it can face impossible choices. The courts of other jurisdictions have often refused to give effect to US extraterritorial disclosure orders.[153] None the less, the US courts may still require compliance with the US order. For example, in *US* v *Chase Manhattan Bank*[154] the US District Court held the Chase Manhattan Bank to be in civil contempt for failure to comply with an order to disclose to the IRS records held by its Hong Kong branch where the disclosure of those records had been prevented by an order of the Hong Kong courts. Chase's good faith argument, based on the revised Restatement, was found to be unpersuasive in the balancing process. The Restatement did not require the court to refrain from imposing a contempt order where the bank had acted in good faith, it gave it a discretion to do so. Furthermore, the order in the present case was a court order, not a rule of law or a regulation.[155] By contrast, in *US* v *First National Bank of Chicago*[156] the Court of Appeals for the Seventh Circuit held that where the bank can establish with certainty that the release of information pursuant to an IRS summons would subject its employees in a foreign jurisdiction to the risk of imprisonment, this should weigh significantly in the court's application of the balancing test. However, such a finding did not bar a court from compelling production of the information where this could be obtained without endangering the liberty of the foreign employees. The bank was still obliged to undertake a good faith effort to secure the information.

Thus, US law leaves a considerable measure of discretion in the issuing of extraterritorial orders for the disclosure of evidence held by third parties. By comparison English law will not permit the issue of orders for the discovery of documents located in the foreign branches of UK or foreign banks that are doing business within the English jurisdiction. In *MacKinnon* v *Donaldson Lufkin & Jenrette Securities Corp.*[157] Hoffmann J rejected a request for an order under s. 7 of the Bankers Books Evidence Act 1879, requiring access to the banking records of the defendant corporation which were held at the head office of Citibank in New York. Such an order would infringe the sovereignty of the USA. In the course of his judgment Hoffmann J specifically rejected the adoption of a balancing test to weigh the respective interests of the English and American jurisdictions, on the ground that this would carry little conviction outside the forum. However, the Bank of England may override a court order restraining a bank from disclosing documents to a foreign bank regulator, or to any third party, where it reasonably requires those documents for the discharge of its supervisory functions under s. 39(3)(a) of the Banking Act 1987. This may include cases where the foreign bank regulator and the Bank of England have a shared interest in the information and the Bank of England is willing to cooperate in securing the information for itself and for the foreign regulator.[158]

2.4.3   The reduction of conflicts over demands for disclosure of evidence located in a foreign jurisdiction   The major objection to over-broad US discovery orders has been the fact that they infringe the sovereignty of the target jurisdiction. On the other hand, the motives behind such orders are often justifiable. MNEs should not be able to take advantage of their international network of companies to evade their legal duties under US law. Thus the US authorities do have a legitimate interest to protect. The problem is not so much one of ends as of means. In recent years the US authorities have become more sensitive to this issue and numerous techniques for the reduction of conflicts over extraterritorial discovery have gradually been adopted, with, it must be said, varying degrees of success. The techniques involved can be divided between bilateral methods of cooperation and the multilateral approach adopted by the Hague Convention on the Taking of Evidence Abroad of 1970.

The evolution of *bilateral cooperation* is well illustrated by the experience of the US Securities and Exchange Commission (SEC) in dealing with insider trading investigations involving requests for information from Swiss banks.[159] In the early 1980s two cases arose in which SEC investigations were hampered by Swiss bank secrecy laws. The first concerned an investigation into possible insider dealing in the course of the takeover of St Joe Minerals Corporation by Joseph E. Seagram and Sons in 1981. The SEC issued a subpoena to a Swiss bank, the Banca della Svizzera Italiana (BSI), for documents related to purchases of St Joe shares that it had carried out through its subsidiary in the USA on the day before the takeover was announced. Informal attempts to ascertain the identity of the bank's principal in these transactions had failed, owing to the Swiss bank secrecy laws to which BSI was subject. In October 1981, the SEC filed a motion seeking to compel the production of the required information under Rule 37 of the Federal Rules of Civil Procedure. After concluding that the US interest in the enforcement of its securities laws could not be thwarted by the use of a foreign bank account subject to foreign secrecy laws, the Federal District Court for the Southern District of New York granted the motion ordering BSI to disclose the identity of its customer or risk a fine of $50,000 for every day of non-compliance and a ban on trading in US markets.[160] Confronted with these sanctions, BSI obtained a waiver of the secrecy laws from its customer and produced the requested information. However, had this not occurred it would have been difficult to secure the information given the clash between the US order and Swiss law.

The second case involved suspected insider dealing associated with the merger between Kuwait Petroleum Corporation and the Santa Fe International Corporation. Again, certain purchases of Santa Fe stock had been made by the US branches of Swiss banks, acting on behalf of unknown principals, in the week prior to the announcement of the merger. The SEC decided to apply for judicial assistance from the Swiss authorities in discovering the identity of the unknown purchasers, under the 1977 Switzerland US Treaty on Mutual Assistance in Criminal Matters. A request was made on 22 March 1982. The Swiss Federal Tribunal rejected the request as falling outside the terms of the 1977 Treaty.[161] In particular, as Swiss law did not recognize at that time an offence of insider dealing, there was no precisely equivalent offence under the Swiss Penal Code that could require the compulsory assistance of the Swiss authorities in accordance with article 4(2)(a) of the Treaty. The only similar offence under Swiss law was that of violation of trade secrets, which was inapplicable to insider dealings in the absence of special circumstances, such as disclosure to third parties for profit. Such circumstances were not indicated in the request. Therefore no measures of cooperation could be ordered. Relying on this opinion, the SEC filed a second Treaty request to learn the customer's identities, adding new facts which disclosed a violation of Swiss law relating to trade secrecy under article 162 of the Criminal Code. On 16 May 1984, the Swiss Federal tribunal granted the SEC's request and the identity of the customers was obtained.[162]

Although the SEC was successful in these cases, each resulted in less than a ideal solution from the regulator's point of view. The BSI case generated tensions between the USA and Switzerland, and in the Santa Fe case the request for information was delayed for thirty months. These experiences led the SEC, in 1984, to advocate the enactment of a 'waiver by conduct' law, whereby the mere fact of executing a securities transaction in the USA would amount to a waiver of foreign bank secrecy laws and to an implied consent to the disclosure of information and evidence relevant to the transaction for the purposes of the enforcement of Federal securities laws.[163]

This proposal met with widespread criticism. It would have increased opposition to SEC investigations from foreign states. Furthermore, it would have been easy to avoid the application of the principle by use of a chain of foreign intermediaries, preventing any investigation from identifying the true facts. The 'waiver by conduct' approach was superseded in 1988 by the Insider Trading and Securities Fraud Enforcement Act, which offers far-reaching assistance to foreign securities authorities which believe that information about securities violations in their country can be found in the USA, in return for reciprocal cooperation being offered to the SEC.[164]

This more cooperative approach also became manifest in Swiss–US relations after the BSI case. On 30 August 1982 a Memorandum of Understanding to establish mutually acceptable means for improving international law enforcement and cooperation in the field of insider trading was signed on behalf of the Swiss and US governments.[165] Furthermore, Switzerland has made insider dealing a crime under its law, thereby removing some of the difficulties experienced by the SEC in the Santa Fe case.[166] It has also used article 3 of the Banking Law, which requires that a bank's managers 'enjoy a good reputation and thereby assure the proper conduct of business operation', to make investigations into banks alleged to be involved in foreign insider trading transactions.[167]

In the field of antitrust the US government has also concluded non-binding memoranda of understanding[168] or binding agreements on cooperation with other governments,[169] and with the EC,[170] based on good faith principles of mutual assistance, as recommended by the OECD Council.[171] Other OECD member countries have concluded similar bilateral cooperation treaties.[172] Such agreements offer a structure for cooperation between the signatories. However, requests for information are generally subject to a power of refusal on the part of the requested state where its substantial economic or other vital interests are threatened by the communication of such information.[173] Thus something reminiscent of a balancing of interests test is present.

The *Hague Convention on the Taking of Evidence Abroad in Civil or Commercial Matters 1970*[174] is designed to assist in the gathering of evidence required in civil or commercial matters that is situated outside the forum jurisdiction. Among its procedures is that of issuing 'letters of request'. The judicial authority that requires evidence located in another jurisdiction will issue a letter of request addressed to the authority in the other jurisdiction designated to receive such requests.[175] The letter of request specifies the details of the evidence required.

The Convention places few limits on the power to issue letters of request. Only three general qualifications appear in article 1 of the Convention. First, the issuing authority must act in accordance with the provisions of its governing law. Secondly, a letter shall not be used to obtain evidence which is not intended for use in judicial proceedings, commenced or contemplated. Thus general fishing expeditions unconnected with judicial proceedings are outside the Convention. Thirdly, the Convention does not extend to the service of judicial documents, the issuance of any process of execution or enforcement, or provisional or protective measures. These are covered by the Hague Convention of 1965 on the Service Abroad of Judicial and Extra-judicial Documents in Civil and Commercial Matters.[176] In sum, the Hague Evidence Convention is limited to requests for evidence arising in the course of actual litigation.

By article 23 of the Convention, 'a Contracting State may, at the time of signature, ratification or accession, declare that it will not execute Letters of Request issued for the purpose of obtaining pre-trial discovery of documents as known in Common Law countries'. Numerous Contracting States have made reservations to this effect.[177] In its reservation, the UK has gone further and has specified what it understands to be included in the discovery of documents. According to the UK reservation a letter of request issued for the purpose of pre-trial discovery of documents includes any letter of request which requires a person: '(a) to state what documents relevant to the proceedings to which the letters of request relate are, or have been, in his possession, custody or power; or (b) to produce any documents other than particular documents specified in the letter of request as being documents appearing to the requested court to be, or to be likely to be, in his possession, custody or power.' This wording echoes s. 2(4) of the Evidence (Proceedings in Other Jurisdictions) Act 1975, which implements the scheme of the Convention into English law. Section 2(4) was interpreted by the House of Lords in the *Westinghouse* case as excluding general 'fishing expeditions'.[178] Thus the UK reservation clearly seeks to prevent the Convention from being misused as a cover for unacceptable US pre-trial discovery procedures. Indeed, the Convention as a whole 'was intended primarily to apply to "evidence" in the sense of material required to prove or disprove allegations at trial. It was not intended to apply to discovery in the sense of the search for material which might lead to the discovery of admissible evidence.'[179]

Against this background, the recent judicial controversy in the USA surrounding the relationship between the Hague Convention and US pre-trial discovery rules will be examined. The issue arose in a series of cases involving the tortious liability of European manufacturers for deaths and injuries suffered by US citizens, caused by accidents involving their products, that took place within the US jurisdiction. By the mid-1980s a disagreement had emerged among lower level US courts as to whether there was a requirement to proceed first under the Hague Convention[180] or whether the US court could proceed under US discovery rules alone, without this constituting a threat to the sovereignty of the foreign state in which the evidence is located.[181]

The issue went up to the US Supreme Court in the joined cases of *Anschuetz GmbH* v *Mississippi River Bridge Authority* and *Messerschmitt Bolkow Blohm* v *Walker*. These cases were settled after argument had been submitted and so no judgment resulted.[182] However, the Supreme Court did deliver a judgment in the case of *Société Nationale Industrielle Aerospatiale* v *US District Court for the Southern District of Iowa*.[183] The Supreme Court held that an American court should resort to the Convention when it deemed that course of action appropriate after considering the position of the parties before it as well as the interests of the foreign state concerned. However, the Supreme Court declined to articulate specific rules to guide this 'delicate task of adjudication'. In this the Supreme Court followed the argument of the US government in its *amicus* brief, which saw the Convention as an optional method for obtaining discovery that should apply when considerations of comity and the facts of the given case warranted it. On the other hand, the Supreme Court rejected the view of the Court of Appeals that the Convention simply did not apply to discovery sought of a foreign litigant subject to the jurisdiction of a US court. In arriving at this conclusion, the Supreme Court rejected the petitioner's argument that the Convention should be treated as a mandatory procedure to be used in preference to US rules of discovery by an American court. In the Supreme Court's view, this was contrary to the language and history of the Convention.

Thus, under US law, it is possible to persuade a US court that the Hague Convention procedure should be used in preference to US rules of pre-trial discovery. However, as noted above, the Hague Convention was not specifically designed to provide for pre-trial discovery. Moreover, as most of the Contracting States have made reservations under article 23, refusing to recognize letters of request made for the purposes of US-style pre-trial discovery, it is hard to see how the Convention can assist the US litigant. Therefore, it is likely that in cases where a US court is faced with a request for pre-trial discovery against a foreign party over which it has subject matter and personal jurisdiction, it will conclude that US rules should apply. As Collins has noted, the real problem lies not with discovery but with the consequences of the assumption of wide rules of personal juris-diction by the US courts.[184] It is the latter that give rise to the problem of extraterritoriality which is consummated by the request for discovery. On the other hand, given the unsuitability of the Hague Convention procedure for dealing with US-style pre-trial discovery, insistence upon its use by foreign defendants is hard to justify on grounds other than the desire to deprive the US plaintiff of a legitimate procedural advantage before the US courts. Such an argument may be no more than a delaying tactic that seeks to protect a foreign manufacturer, whose products or acts have injured a US citizen, from proof of liability.[185]

3   Concluding Remarks: the Limitation of Extraterritoriality Conflicts

The present chapter has considered the legal consequences that follow when a state or supranational organization adopts a unilateral policy of extending jurisdiction extraterritorially to the foreign units of a MNE. That the USA has been the most assertive state in this respect is, perhaps, not surprising. Not only has it been, until recently, the dominant political power in the international economy, it also has a legal experience based upon the creation of a unified transcontinental economy that has conditioned its legislators, administrators and judges towards an easy acceptance of extraterritorial jurisdiction in all its forms. However, the conflict generated by US assertions of extraterritorial jurisdiction has given rise to numerous attempts at minimizing its incidence, both on a unilateral level by the US courts and on a bilateral and multilateral level through diplomatic agreements and initiatives. Indeed, the recent growth of inward investment into the USA may make it more sensitive to retaliatory pressure against US firms, requiring a further reappraisal of its attitude to the assertion of extraterritorial jurisdiction.[186]

As noted earlier, on a unilateral level, US courts have adopted the 'balance of interests' approach, inspired by successive revisions of the US Restatement on Foreign Relations Law. However, the effectiveness of this approach as a means of minimizing conflicting requirements being placed upon MNEs is open to question. As Judge Wilkey stated in *Laker Airways* v *Sabena*:

Domestic courts are created by national constitutions and statutes to enforce primarily national laws. The courts of most developed countries follow international law only to the extent it is not overridden by national law. Thus courts inherently find it difficult neutrally to balance competing foreign interests. When there is any doubt, national interests will tend to be favoured over foreign interests. This partially explains why there have been few times when courts have found foreign interests to prevail.[187]

In this respect, it has been suggested that extraterritoriality conflicts could be avoided by the adoption of a 'shared values' approach.[188] Thus, where a state wishes to apply extraterritorially a mandatory rule of its internal economic law, should that law express the shared values of both states, the courts of the target state ought to apply it. They should only prevent the application of the enforcing state's law where there is a genuine threat to the national interests of the target state in the specific circumstances of the case. The mere fact that the sovereignty of the target state has been interfered with should not be decisive, if its vital economic interests are not threatened. This approach appears to add little to the 'balancing test'. It will always be open for the court in the target state to see the existence of a threat to vital national interests where the enforcing state seeks to infringe the former's sovereignty. Moreover, it is a mistake to assume that the economic policies of the major Western states are converging, so that 'shared values' can be identified.

On the other hand, the state-centred model of international business regulation can be supplanted as states agree to develop new harmonized standards of international economic regulation, and create new conflict avoidance procedures.[189] Developments in the EC, such as the 1968 Brussels Convention and the various programmes for the development of a uniform substantive economic law of the Community, exemplify the alternative. However, success in these initiatives, let alone in the globalization of economic regulation, is far off. For the foreseeable future the administration, by states, of competing systems of economic regulation will continue to generate conflicts of jurisdiction in cases involving the activities of MNEs.

Notes

1 See further: D. Rosenthal and W. Knighton, *National Laws and International Commerce: the Problem of Extraterritoriality* (Chatham House Papers No. 17, RIIA/RKP, 1982); A. Neale and M. Stephens, *International Business and National Jurisdiction* (Oxford, 1988); M. Sornarajah, *The International Law on Foreign Investment* (Grotius Publications, 1994), chapter 4. A useful discussion can be found in Roth, 'Reasonable Extraterritoriality: Correcting the "Balance of Interests"', 41 ICLQ 245 (1992).

2 See further: I. Brownlie, *Principles of Public International Law*, 5th edn (Oxford, 1998), chapters XIV–XV; D. P. O'Connell, *International Law*, 2nd edn (Stevens, 1970), Vol. II, chapter 19; Akehurst, 'Jurisdiction in international law', 46 BYIL 145–257 (1972–3); F. A. Mann, *Studies in*

International Law (Oxford, 1973) chapter I; or 111 Hague Recueil 1 (1964 I).

3   Brownlie (note 2 above), at p. 301.

4   Ibid.

5   For example, under English law, a British subject can be prosecuted before the English courts for a number of offences committed abroad, including treason and murder: *R* v *Casement* [1917] 1 KB 98 (treason); Offences against the Person Act 1861 s. 9 (murder). See further D. J. Harris, *Cases and Materials on International Law*, 5th edn (Sweet & Maxwell, 1998), p. 267; O'Connell (note 2 above), vol. II, pp. 824–6.

6   See references at note 21 below.

7   See e.g. *DPP* v *Joyce* [1946] AC 347 (acts of treason committed by an alien abroad are within the jurisdiction of the British courts); *Molvan* v *Attorney-General for Palestine* [1948] AC 351 (PC) (an alien involved in acts of illegal immigration committed on the high seas is subject to British jurisdiction). See also *Attorney-General of the Government of Israel* v *Eichmann* 36 ILR 5 (1961)(District Court Jerusalem).

8   See the Geneva Convention on the Territorial Sea and the Contiguous Zone 1958, article 24 (UKTS 3 (1965); Cmnd 2511; 516 UNTS 205; UN Convention on the Law of the Sea 1982 article 33 (UN. Doc. A/CONF.62/122); 21 ILM 1261 (1982).

9   See chapter 8.

10 See Brownlie (note 2 above), at pp. 303–4. See further Harvard Research Draft Convention on Jurisdiction with Respect to Crime 1935: 29 AJIL Supp. 443 at pp. 484–7.

11 (1927) PCIJ, Ser. A. No. 10, p. 23.

12 Ibid., at p. 20.

13 Ibid., at p. 19.

14 See *Nottebohm Case*, ICJ Reports (1955) p. 4 (jurisdiction to confer nationality on individuals must be exercised in the light of effective links between the individual and the state); *Anglo-Norwegian Fisheries Case*, ICJ Reports (1951) p. 116 (jurisdiction to delimit territorial sea must be exercised in the light of a genuine connection between the land domain and the sea). These cases lay the basis for Professor Brownlie's opinion on the development of international law in this area referred to at note 4 above.

15 Neale and Stephens (note 1 above), at p. 15.

16 See *The Third Restatement of the Foreign Relations Law of the United States* (American Law Institute, 1987), s. 401. The author favours the use of the American classification as the clearest conceptualization of the questions involved. In practice, however, issues of jurisdiction usually involve a mix of the heads of jurisdiction mentioned in the text.

17 See further Rosenthal and Knighton (note 1 above).

18 US Department of Justice Antitrust Division, *Antitrust Enforcement Guidelines for International Operations* (10 November 1988), s. 4.0 at p. 29. See now draft *Antitrust Enforcement Guidelines for International Operations* (13 October 1994), Trade Reg. Rep. No. 338, part 2, p. 37, s. 3.1 at p. 47: 'Anticompetitive conduct that affects US domestic or foreign commerce may violate the US antitrust laws regardless of where such conduct occurs or the nationality of the parties involved.'

19 See US Restatement (note 16 above), s. 416 at pp. 295–6 and see Comment (a) at p. 297.

20 See US Restatement (note 16 above), s. 414 and Reporter's Notes 3–8 at pp. 269–82.

21 See: US Restatement (note 16 above), s. 414, Reporter's Note 6, pp. 279–80; Heininger, 'Liability of US banks for deposits placed in their foreign branches', 11 Law & Pol. Int'l Bus. 903 (1979). According to the Restatement, two groups of issues have emerged in litigation in the USA and elsewhere: (a) to what extent may the US courts or government agencies require production of records of foreign branches of banks whose headquarters are situated in the USA or restrict the transfer of funds deposited at such branches; (b) to what extent are home offices liable for obligations entered into or deposits made at branch banks in foreign states. The first issue will be considered below. See text at notes 149–56 below. The second issue is extensively discussed by Heininger and need not detain us. On the response of the English courts to attempts by the US authorities to freeze the assets of foreign governments held in the UK branches of US banks see: *Libyan Arab Foreign Bank* v *Bankers Trust Co.* [1988] 1 Lloyds Rep. 259; [1989] 3 All ER 252; *Libyan Arab Foreign Bank* v *Manufacturers Hanover Trust Co.* [1988] 2 Lloyds Rep. 494; [1989] 1 Lloyds Rep. 608.

22 See s. 402 of the Third Restatement (note 16 above).

23 *Société Fruehauf* v *Massardy* [1968] D. S. Jur 147 [1965] JCP II 14 274 bis (Cour d'Appel, Paris), English translation: 5 ILM 476 (1966). See: C. D. Wallace, *Legal Control of the Multinational Enterprise* (Martinus Nijhoff, 1983), pp. 100–3; Craig, 'Application of the Trading with the Enemy Act to foreign corporations owned by Americans: reflections on Fruehauf v Massardy', 83 Harv. LR 579 (1970).

24 See Rosenthal and Knighton (note 1 above), at p. 63.

25 For a chronology of the affair see: G. Hufbauer and J. Schott, 'The Soviet–European gas pipeline: a case of failed sanctions', in T. Moran (ed.), *Multinational Corporations: the Political Economy of Foreign Direct Investment* (Lexington Books, 1985), at pp. 225–39. For analysis see: D. Morse and J. Powers, 'US export controls and foreign entities: the unanswered questions of pipeline diplomacy', 23 Va. JIL 537 (1983); H. Moyer and L. Marby, 'Export controls as instruments of foreign policy: the history, legal issues and policy lessons of three recent cases', 15 Law & Pol. Int'l Bus. 1 (1983); Ellicott, 'Extraterritorial trade controls – law, policy and business.' Private investors abroad – Problems and Solutions', in *International Business in 1983 vol. 1* (1983).

26 The relevant regulations appear in 21 ILM 864 (1982). The regulations were upheld by the US courts in *Dresser Industries Inc.* v *Baldridge* 549 F. Supp. 108 (1982).

27 See Commission of the European Communities, 'Comments on the US regulations concerning trade with the USSR', 12 August 1982: 21 ILM 891 (1982).

28 Ibid., para. 5, at p. 3.

29 ICJ Reports 1970, p. 3, at p. 43 (see further Chapter 15 below). Cited ibid., para. 7, at p. 4. The Dutch courts applied the principle in *Barcelona Traction* to limit the effect of the US orders in relation to Dutch

subsidiaries of US firms: see *Compagnie Européenne de Pétroles* v *Sensor Nederland BV* 22 ILM 320 (1983).

30 Ibid., para. 8, at p. 4.

31 See e.g. United Kingdom: the Protection of Trading Interests (US Reexport Control) Order 1982 S. I. 1982 No. 885, 30 June 1982, made under the Protection of Trading Interests Act 1980 rendering the US Regulations measures which were damaging to UK trading interests. On 2 August 1982, the Secretary of State for Trade and Industry, Lord Cockfield, issued directions under s. 1(3) of the Protection of Trading Interests Act to four British companies forbidding them to comply with the American embargo.

32 Neale and Stephens (note 1 above), at pp. 158–9; Ellicott (note 25 above), at pp. 30–2.

33 Given the extensive and instructive literature on this subject it is unnecessary to offer more than an introductory account in this work. For more detailed analysis see: Rosenthal and Knighton (note 1 above). chapter 2; Neale and Stephens (note 1 above), chapters 3–8; J. Atwood and K. Brewster, *Antitrust and American Business Abroad*, 2nd edn (McGraw-Hill, 1981, and supplement); W. Fugate, *Foreign Commerce and the Antitrust Laws*, 4th edn (Little Brown & Co., 1991).

34 See *American Banana Company* v *United Fruit Co.* 213 US 347 (1909).

35 See *US* v *Sisal Sales Corporation* 274 US 268 (1927). For comment see: Rosenthal and Knighton (note 1 above), at p. 24; Neale and Stephens (note 1 above), at p. 87.

36 148 F. 2d 416 (1945).

37 *In personam* jurisdiction had been established over Limited because it ran an important administrative office in New York. This could have been its actual headquarters.

38 Ibid., at 443.

39 Ibid., at 444.

40 See M. Sornarajah, 'The extraterritorial enforcement of US antitrust law: conflict and compromise', 31 ICLQ 127 (1982).

41 See further Neale and Stephens (note 1 above), chapter 5 and their discussion of *US* v *National Lead Co.* 63 F. Supp. 513 (SDNY 1945), 332 US 319 (1947); *US* v *General Electric Co.* 82 F. Supp. 753 (1949), 115 F. Supp. 835 (1953); *US* v *United States Alkali Export Association Inc.* 86 F. Supp. 59 (1949); *Timken Roller Bearing Co.* v *US* 83 F. Supp. 284 (1949), 341 US 593 (1951).

42 See also *US* v *ICI* 100 F. Supp. 504 (SDNY 1951) and 105 F. Supp. 215 (SDNY 1952), as reviewed by the English courts in *British Nylon Spinners* v *Imperial Chemical Industries* [1953] 1 Ch. 19 (CA) and [1955] 1 Ch. 37.

43 *US* v *Watchmakers of Switzerland Information Center Inc.* 1963 Trade Cases CCH, para. 70600, 1965 Trade Cases CCH, para. 71352.

44 See 1965 Trade Cases, para. 71352 and Neale and Stephens (note 1 above), at pp. 156–7.

45 395 US 100 (1969).

46 Rosenthal and Knighton (note 1 above), at p. 31.

47   549 F. 2d 597 (1976 Ninth Circuit). See further Neale and Stephens (note 1 above), chapter 6.

48   Ibid., at p. 613.

49   Ibid.

50   595 F. 2d 1287 (1979).

51   Ibid., at pp. 1297–8.

52   See further Neale and Stephens (note 1 above), chapter 7; Sornarajah (note 40 above), at pp. 138–47.

53   649 F. 2d 1354 (Ninth Circuit, 1981).

54   US Department of Justice, *Antitrust Division Antitrust Enforcement Guidelines for International Operations* (10 November 1988) para. 6, at p. 33. See also the draft Guidelines of 13 October 1994 (note 18 above), s. 3.32, p. 56. See further: *Continental Ore Co.* v *Union Carbide and Carbon Corp.* 370 US 690 (1962); *Interamerican Refining Corp.* v *Texaco Maracaibo Inc.* 307 F. Supp. 291 (D. Del 1970); *Matsushita Electric Industrial Co.* v *Zenith Radio Corp.* 475 US 574 (1986).

55   15 USC s. 6a. See also US Department of Justice Antitrust Guidelines 1988 (note 18 above), at pp. 30–1; draft Guidelines of 13 October 1994 (note 18 above), ss 3.13.1–3.13.4, pp. 49–52.

56   Roth (note 1 above), at p. 259.

57   The extent to which this balancing approach can be effective in avoiding conflict will be considered at the end of this chapter. By contrast, the German system of antitrust law, which also espouses an 'effects doctrine' modelled on US precedents, has approached the issue of excessive jurisdictional claims by way of a two-tier test. First, there must be clear proof of harm to the domestic competitive system within Germany that amounts to a violation of the particular substantive provisions involved. Secondly, the compatibility of the proposed exercise of jurisdiction will be tested by reference to the principles of international law. Thus German law is evolving in the context of an explicit reference to the controlling authority of international law. See further Gerber, 'The extraterritorial application of the German antitrust laws', 77 AJIL 756 (1983).

58   Third restatement . . . (note 16 above), at p. 244.

59   Ibid., comment (a), p. 246.

60   The factors listed are: '(a) the link of the activity to the territory of the regulating state i.e. the extent to which the activity takes place within the territory, or has substantial, direct and foreseeable effect upon or in the territory; (b) the connections, such as nationality, residence, or economic activity, between the regulating state and the person principally responsible for the activity to be regulated, or between that state and those whom the regulation is designed to protect; (c) the character of the activity to be regulated, the importance of regulation to the regulating state, the extent to which other states regulate such activities, and the degree to which the desirability of such regulation is generally accepted; (d) the existence of justified expectations that might be protected or hurt by the regulation; (e) the importance of the regulation to the international political, legal or economic system; (f) the extent to which the regulation is consistent with the traditions of the international system; (g) the extent to which another

state may have an interest in regulating the activity; and (h) the likelihood of conflict with regulation by another state.'

61   Ibid., comment (b), p. 246.
62   Decided 28 June 1993, to be reported at 113 S. Ct 2891. I am grateful to my former student, Peter J. Stocks of the US Department of Justice, for supplying me with a copy of this opinion.
63   Third Restatement (note 16 above), s. 403 comment e, p. 247.
64   The majority opinion was met with a dissenting opinion, led by Scalia J, which asserted that, although the Sherman Act undoubtedly had extraterritorial scope, the balancing analysis required under s. 403 of the Third restatement pointed to the conclusion that the UK had a heavy interest in regulating the activity in question under s. 403(2)(g). The USA should defer to that overriding interest, especially as the activity relevant to the counts in issue took place primarily in the UK, the defendants were British corporations and British subjects having their principal place of business or residence outside the USA (see s. 403(2)(a) and (b)). Furthermore, the majority's interpretation of s. 403(3) was contrary to earlier case-law and would bring the Sherman Act and other laws into sharp and unnecessary conflict with the legitimate interests of other countries. The draft Guidelines 1994 (note 18 above) support the majority interpretation of the comity analysis: see s. 3.2 at pp. 53–4.
65   See Third restatement (note 16 above), s. 414, comment h, at p. 273. See also *Commonwealth* v *Beneficial Finance Co.* 275 NE 2d 33 (Sup. Ct Mass. 1971) cert. denied 407 US 914 (1972). In this case, the Supreme Court of Massachusetts held that prescriptive and adjudicatory jurisdiction over an out-of-state (though not alien) parent company could exist where the subsidiary within the jurisdiction has committed an offence within the jurisdiction as an agent of the parent: 275 NE at 56–7.
66   See under English law, *Sirdar Gurdyal Singh* v *Rajah of Faridkote* [1894] AC 670 at 683–4 per the Earl of Selbourne LC; under US law, *Pennoyer* v *Neff* 95 US 714 at 717 (1878), *Hanson* v *Denkla* 357 US 235 at 250–1 (1958).
67   See s. 421 US Restatement (note 16 above), at pp. 305–6.
68   See The Companies Act 1985 s. 691 (as amended by the Companies Act 1989, s. 145), s. 695.
69   For the meaning of 'a place of business' under s. 695 see: *South India Shipping Corporation* v *Export Import Bank of Korea* [1985] 2 All ER 219 (CA); *Re Oriel* [1985] 3 All ER 216 at 223 per Oliver LJ (CA). On what constitutes valid service under s. 695(1) see *Rome* v *Punjab National Bank* [1989] 1 WLR 1211.
70   South India Shipping, ibid., per Ackner LJ at pp. 224a–b.
71   In order for the foreign parent to become a party to English proceedings, where the parent is domiciled outside the EC, it must be shown that the parent is a proper party to be served in accordance with one or more of the heads of Order 11 Rule 1(1) of the Rules of the Supreme Court. Where the parent company is domiciled within the EC, service of process will be subject to the provisions of the Brussels Convention on Jurisdiction and Enforcement of Judgments in Civil and Commercial Matters 1968 incorporated into English law by the Civil Jurisdiction and Judgments Act

1982. The Convention imposes new mandatory rules of jurisdiction on English courts in cases where service is sought against a defendant domiciled in an EC Member State. On the Brussels Convention and the Civil Jurisdiction and Judgments Act see further: L. Collins, *The Civil Jurisdiction and Judgments Act 1982* (Butterworths, 1983); T. Hartley, *The Civil Jurisdiction and Judgments Act 1982* (1983); P. Kaye, *Civil Jurisdiction and Enforcement of Foreign Judgments* (1987). For a shorter analysis see P. M. North and J. J. Fawcett, *Cheshire and North's Private International Law*, 12th edn (Butterworths, 1992), chapter 14.

72 See *Volkswagenwerk AG v Schlunk* 468 US 694 (1988); 27 ILM 1092 (1988).

73 Ibid. The Convention came into effect on 10 February 1969. For text see: 4 ILM 341 (1965).

74 636 F. 2d 1300 (DC Cir 1980).

75 See further chapter 9.

76 See Fawcett, 'Jurisdiction and subsidiaries', [1985] JBL 16. See for the US position: *Wells Fargo & Co. v Wells Fargo Express Co.* 556 F. 2d 406 (9th Cir 1977); *Bryant v Finnish National Airlines* 15 NY 2d 426; 260 NYS 2d 625; 208 NE 2d 439 (1965); *Taca International Airlines v Rolls Royce* 204 NE 2d 329 (1965); *J. M. Sachlein Music Co. Inc. v Nippon Gakki Co. Ltd* 197 Cal App 3d 539 (1987 1st dist); *Rollins Burdick Hunter Inc. v Alexander & Alexander Services Inc.* 206 Cal App 3d 1 (1988 2nd dist). In antitrust cases, the US courts have applied the same general principles of jurisdiction as apply in other cases. In doing so the courts act under the statutory authority granted by s. 12 of the Clayton Act and s. 7 of the Sherman Act to bring antitrust proceedings against a corporation in any district in which it is 'found' or 'transacts business'. It is enough to show that the corporation transacted business within the jurisdiction, either from abroad, or through a US subsidiary: *US v Scophony Corporation of America* 333 US 795 (1948). There must be some evidence of control going beyond the mere existence of the parent–subsidiary relationship. However, as was pointed out in *Akzona v Du Pont* 607 F. Supp. 227 at 238–40 (Dist. Ct Del. 1984), the standards of jurisdiction under s. 12 of the Clayton Act are more leniently applied, so as to give effect to the policy of the antitrust acts. Thus the presence of separate corporate formalities will not prevent jurisdiction from being exercised where, in fact, the US subsidiary is controlled by the foreign parent for the purposes of antitrust violations.

77 See e.g. the US case *Cannon Manufacturing Co. v Cudhay Packing Co.* 267 US 333, 45 S. Ct 250, 569 L Ed 634 (1925). See also: *Walker v Newgent* 583 F. 2d 163 (5th Cir. 1978); *Product Promotions Inc. v Cousteau* 495 F. 2d 483 (5th Cir. 1974); 36 Am Jur 2d s. 347.

78 See *Hargrave v Fireboard Corp.* 710 F. 2d 1154 at 1161 (5th Cir. 1983).

79 See, for example, *Frummer v Hilton Hotels International Inc.* 227 NE 2d 851 (1967); affirmed but distinguished in *Delagi v Volkswagenwerk AG* 29 NY 2d 426, 278 NE 2d 895, 328 NYS 2d 653 (1972).

80 [1983] Ch. 258; [1983] 2 All ER 563; [1983] 3 WLR 492 (CA).

81 [1897] AC 22.

82 [1982] Ch. 442.

83   [1983] 2 All ER 563 at p. 588(f).

84   See further R. Whish, *Competition Law*, 3rd edn (Butterworths, 1993) chapter 11; R. Merkin and K. Williams, *Competition Law: Antitrust Policy in the United Kingdom and the EEC* (Sweet & Maxwell, 1984) at pp. 471–3; D. G. Goyder, *EEC Competition Law*, 3rd edn (Clarendon Press, 1998), pp. 545–53; Whatstein, 'Extraterritorial application of EC competition law – comments and reflections', 26 Israel LR 195 (1992).

85   See *Re Cartel in Aniline Dyestuffs* (Commission Decision 69/243, 24 July 1969) [1969] CMLR D. 23. Upheld in Case 48/69 *ICI* v *Commission* [1972] CMLR 557, [1972] ECR 619. Case 61/72 *Continental Can* v *Commission* [1973] ECR 215; [1973] CMLR 199. Case 6 and 7/73 *Commercial Solvents* v *Commission* [1974] 1 CMLR 309.

86   Note 84 above, at p. 472.

87   *Re Wood Pulp* [1985] 3 CMLR 474.

88   *Re the Zinc Producer Group: The Community* v *Rio Tinto Zinc Corporation plc and Others* [1985] 2 CMLR 108.

89   [1987] 3 CMLR 813.

90   Case 89/85 [1988] 4 CMLR 901.

91   Ibid., para. 17, at p. 941.

92   See e.g. A. Hermann, 'EC joins extraterritoriality club', *Financial Times*, 13 October 1988, p. 39. This view was criticized by Sir Alan Neale, co-author of Neale and Stephens (note 1 above), in a letter to the *Financial Times* published on 23 November 1988 at p. 29. He sees the case as offering a stricter test, requiring proof of anti-competitive acts within the Community. This view appears to be borne out by other cases discussed in the text below.

93   Merkin and Williams (note 84 above), at pp. 472–3.

94   The full text of the Code can be found in 24 ILM 269 (1985). For background see Goldschmidt (1972) II Hague Recueil 201.

95   See *Dunlop Pneumatic Tyre Co. Ltd* v *AG für Motor und Motorfahrzeugbau vorm Cudell & Co.* [1902] 1 KB 342 (CA).

96   See *Amusement Equipment* v *Mordelt* 779 F. 2d 264 (5th Cir. 1985).

97   *Burnham* v *Superior Court of California* 110 S. Ct 2105 (1990) (a New Jersey resident was validly served by his wife, who was resident in California, with court summons and divorce petition in California, while he was there on a temporary visit for business purposes and to see his children).

98   See *Adams* v *Cape Industries plc* [1991] All ER 929 at 1014–15 per Slade LJ (CA). See too the UK Product Liability Act 1987 s. 2(2)(C).

99   See *International Shoe* v *Washington* 326 US 310; 90 L Ed 95 (1945); *Waters* v *Deutz Corporation* 460 A 2d 1332 (Del. Sup. Ct, 1983); *Worldwide Volkswagen Corporation* v *Woodson* 444 US 286 (1980). See, in the context of antitrust actions: *Hoffman Motors Corp.* v *Alfa Romeo* 244 F. Supp. 70 (SDNY 1965), *US* v *Aluminum Company of America* 20 F. Supp. 13 (1937), *Akzona Inc.* v *E. I. Du Pont de Nemours & Co.* 607 F. Supp. 227 esp. at 236–40 (Dist. Ct Del. 1984).

100 444 US 286 (1980).

101 107 S. Ct 1026, 74 L. Ed. 2d 92 (1987) and 26 ILM 702 (1987) (Slip

Opinion).

102   326 US 310, 90 L Ed 95 (1945)

103   471 US 462 (1985).

104   26 ILM 702 (1987) Slip Opinion at p. 8.

105   See *Galle* v *Allstate Insurance Co.* 451 SO 2d 72 at 75 (Lo 4th Cir. 1984).

106   On the other hand, the isolated contacts of an alien corporation with the US jurisdiction, such as a single contract negotiating session, or the purchase of products for use abroad, or the training of personnel within the jurisdiction for employment abroad, is not a contact of a continuous and systematic nature within the principle of *International Shoe*. See *Helicopteros Nacionales de Colombia* v *Hall* 466 US 408, 104 S. Ct 1868, 80 L. Ed. 2d 404 (1984).

107   Under US law, even where the cause of action does not arise out of or relate to the foreign corporation's activities in the forum state, that corporation can be subjected to the personal jurisdiction of the forum when there are sufficient contacts between the foreign corporation and the forum, as where, for example, the foreign corporation maintains an office within the jurisdiction. See *Perkins* v *Benguet Consolidated Mining Co.* 342 US 437 (1952).

108   Whereby the claimant's US attorney will not take fees for his services but will be remunerated only on the basis of a percentage of any award of damages.

109   See the leading case of *Piper Aircraft* v *Reyno* 454 US 235 (1981). See further Muchlinski, 'The Bhopal case: controlling ultrahazardous industrial activities undertaken by foreign investors', 50 MLR 545, at pp. 553–4 (1987). But see the Texas Supreme Court case, *Texas Dow and Shell Oil* v *Alfara* (1990). For comment see Sir Michael Ogden, 'Hope for world litigants in the best little courthouse in Texas', *Financial Times*, 9 July 1990, p. 23.

110   See *Gulf Oil* v *Gilbert* 330 US 501 (1947). On the essentially similar English doctrine of *forum non conveniens* see: *MacShannon* v *Rockware Glass* [1978] AC 795; *The Abidin Daver* [1984] AC 398; *Spiliada Maritime Corporation* v *Cansulex Ltd 'The Spiliada'* [1986] 3 WLR 972 per Lord Goff at p. 985F: 'The basic principle is that a stay will only be granted on the ground of forum non conveniens where the Court is satisfied that there is some other forum having competent jurisdiction, which is the appropriate forum for the trial of the action, i.e. in which the case may be tried more suitably for the interests of all the parties and the ends of justice.' The factors to be weighed in the exercise of the court's discretion are summarized by Lord Goff at pp. 895G–7G and 991D–2E. Lord Goff's judgment was cited and summarized with approval by Bingham LJ in *Du Pont de Nemours & Co. and Endo Laboratories Inc.* v *I. C. Agnew K. W. Kerr and Others* [1987] 2 Lloyds Rep. 585 at 588 (CA). See also *Ronleigh Ltd* v *MII Exports Inc.* [1989] 1 WLR 619 (CA).

111   See *Piper Aircraft* (note 109 above), at 256.

112   *In Re Union Carbide Gas Plant Disaster at Bhopal India* Opinion and Order 12 May 1986: 634 F. Supp. 842 (SDNY 1986), 25 ILM 771 (1986) For analysis of the US litigation over jurisdiction see: Muchlinski (note 109

above); Indian Law Institute, *Inconvenient Forum Convenient Catastrophe: the Bhopal Case* (1986).

113 On which see further Galanter, 'Legal torpor: why so little has happened in India after the Bhopal tragedy', 20 Texas ILJ 273 (1985).

114 Plaintiff's Executive Committee, 'Memorandum in opposition to Union Carbide Corporation's motion to dismiss on grounds of *forum non conveniens*', 6 December 1985, p. 3.

115 Ibid., at p. 88.

116 See for full discussion Muchlinski (note 109 above), at pp. 555–60.

117 809 F. 2d 195 (USCA 2d Cir), 26 ILM 1008 (1987), cert. denied 108 S. Ct 199 (1987). The USCA rejected two conditions that Judge Keenan had attached to his dismissal of the case, concerning the monitoring of due process before the Indian courts by the US District Court, and the application of Federal pre-trial discovery to UCC alone. The Court of Appeals upheld the condition that UCC voluntarily submit to Indian personal jurisdiction, without which India would not have provided an adequate alternative forum. For discussion see Muchlinski (note 109 above), at pp. 560–3.

118 See Schuz, 'Controlling forum shopping: the impact of MacShannon v Rockware Glass Ltd', 35 ICLQ 374 (1986); *Smith Kline & French* v *Bloch* [1983] 2 All ER 72 (CA); *SNI Aérospatiale* v *Lee Kui Jak* [1987] 3 All ER 510 (PC).

119 See *S and W Berisford plc* v *New Hampshire Insurance Co.* [1990] 2 QB 631; [1990] 2 All ER 321 (Com. Ct); *Arkwright Mutual Insurance Co.* v *Bryanston Insurance Co. Ltd* [1990] 2 QB 649 [1990] 2 All ER 335 (Com. Ct).

120 See the *Berisford* case, ibid., at [1990] 2 All ER, p. 332a–e, citing the Schlosser Report on the 1968 Convention: 1979 OJ C 59 pp. 97–9, paras 76, 78; and see *Cheshire and North's Private International Law* (note 71 above), at pp. 331–4.

121 [1992] Ch. 72; [1991] 4 All ER 334 (CA).

122 See *Cheshire and North's Private International Law* (note 71 above), at pp. 333–4.

123 Enforcement jurisdiction includes the issue of jurisdiction to apply measures to entities that enjoy sovereign immunity. Such a question may conceivably arise where a state-trading enterprise is involved, but it is not relevant in cases concerning privately owned corporations. It is therefore not discussed.

124 See further US Restatement (note 16 above), s. 431, comment c, at pp. 321, 322. Under US law, non-judicial enforcement measures are subject to judicial review for fairness: ibid., comment e.

125 See, for example, *British Nylon Spinners* v *Imperial Chemical Industries* [1953] 1 Ch. 19 (CA); [1955] 1 Ch. 37 (Dankwerts J).

126 See the *Swiss Watchmakers* and *Zenith Radio* cases (notes 42–6 above) and Neale and Stephens (note 1 above), at pp. 156–7.

127 See: UK, Protection of Trading Interests Act 1980 (c. 11) ss. 5, 6; Canada, Combines Investigation Act as amended by Stats. Can. 1974/75 c. 76 s. 12, ss 31.5, 31.6; Australia, Foreign Antitrust Judgments (Restriction of Enforcement) Act 1979 No. 13 of 1979 s. 3.

128 See Australia: ibid.

129 [1991] 1 All ER 929 (CA) affirming Scott J (ChD). Leave to appeal refused by Appeal Committee of the House of Lords 24 October 1989.

130 See *In re Grand Jury Subpoena Duces Tecum* 72 F. Supp. 1013 (1947); *In Re Investigation of World Arrangements with Relation to . . . Petroleum* 13 FRD 280 (1952); and see US cases on disclosure by banks of records held by branches in foreign jurisdictions at notes 151–4 below.

131 See: *Lonrho* v *Shell Petroleum* [1980] 2 WLR 367 (CA) aff'd [1980] 1 WLR 627 (HL); *Re Tecnion Investments Ltd* [1985] BCLC 434 (CA).

132 Note 16 above, at pp. 348–9.

133 Ibid., s. 442(1)(a).

134 Ibid., s. 442(1)(c).

135 Ibid., s. 442(1)(b).

136 For early controversies in the antitrust field see the cases cited in note 130 above.

137 On the liner conferences dispute and blocking legislation see: Picciotto, 'Jurisdictional conflicts, international law and the international state system', 11 Int'l Jo. Soc. L. 11 at pp. 19–21 (1983); Neale and Stephens (note 1 above), at pp. 110–14. The UK passed the Shipping Contracts and Commercial Documents Act 1964 (c. 87) to block US measures in this area. Other states passed similar legislation during the mid to late 1960s. These included Germany, France, Norway, Belgium and Sweden. For full references to these laws see US Restatement (note 16 above), s. 442 Reporter's Note 4, at p. 358.

138 See *In re Westinghouse Uranium Contract* [1978] AC 547 (HL); *Re Westinghouse Electric and Duquesne Light Co.* (1977) 78 DLR (3d) 3 (Ont. H. C.). See also *Gulf Oil Corporation* v *Gulf Canada Ltd* (1980) 111 DLR (3d) 74 (Sup. Ct Can.).

139 For analysis of the Act see: Lowe, 'Blocking extraterritorial jurisdiction: the British Protection of Trading Interests Act 1980', 75 AJIL 257 (1981) and Lowenfeld's reply in ibid., p. 629; Marston, 14 JWTL 461 (1980). See also the annotated version of the Act in *Current Law Statutes* 1980 (c. 11). For examples of similar blocking statutes in other jurisdictions see: Australia, Foreign Proceedings (Prohibition of Certain Evidence) Act 1976 replaced by Foreign Proceedings (Excess of Jurisdiction) Act 1984, Austl. Acts No. 3; Canada, Foreign Extraterritorial Measures Act, Stat. Can. 1984 c. 49; France, Law No. 80–538 of July 16 1980 [1980] Journal Officiel 1799, English translation 75 AJIL 382 (1981); South Africa, Second General Law Amendment Act 94 1974 ss 2, 12 Stat. S. Africa 602.

140 Ibid., s. 1.

141 Ibid., s. 2(1).

142 [1984] 3 WLR 413, [1984] 3 All ER 39 (HL). For analysis see Neale and Stephens (note 1 above), at pp. 117–27.

143 [1983] 3 All ER 375 (QBD and CA).

144 This objection was raised by Judge Wilkey in *Laker Airways Ltd* v *Sabena* 731 F. 2d 909 at 930 (DC Cir. 1984), over the effect of the Court of Appeal's ruling in the Laker case, in the course of his judgment restraining two European airlines, Sabena and KLM, from seeking recourse to foreign courts against the US antitrust proceedings. That judgment was given

before the House of Lords decision in Laker, which meets many of Judge Wilkey's objections against the restraining injunction granted by the Court of Appeal.

145 [1986] 1 All ER 526 (CA).

146 357 US 197, 78 S. Ct 1087, 2 L Ed 2d 1255 (1958).

147 US Restatement (note 16 above), at pp. 348–9.

148 See In Re *Westinghouse Electric Corp. Uranium* 563 F. 2d 992 at 997 (1977).

149 See *US* v *Vetco Inc.* 644 F. 2d 1324 (9th Cir. 1981) cert. den. 454 US 1098 (1981); *Marc Rich & Co AG* v *US* 707 F. 2d 663 (2nd Cir 1983).

150 *US* v *Toyota Motor Corporation* 569 F. Supp. 1158 (1983).

151 See *First National City Bank* v *IRS* 271 F. 2d 616 (2nd Cir. 1959)(taxation); *In re Application of Chase Manhattan Bank* 297 F. 2d 611 (1960)(taxation); *US* v *First National City Bank* 396 F. 2d 897 (2nd Cir. 1968)(antitrust); *SEC* v *Banca della Svizzera Italiana* 92 FRD 111 (SDNY 1981)(insider dealing).

152 See *US* v *Bank of Nova Scotia II* 740 F. 2d 817 (11th Cir. 1984) cert. den. 469 US 1106 (1985). See also *US* v *Bank of Nova Scotia I* 691 F. 2d 1384 (11th Cir. 1982) cert. den. 103 S. Ct 3086 (1983).

153 See England, *XAG and others* v *A bank* [1983] 2 All ER 464 (QBD Com. Ct); Germany, *Krupp Mak Maschinenbau GmbH* v *Deutsche Bank AG* (Landgericht Kiel 6/30/82) 22 ILM 740 (1983).

154 590 F. Supp. 1160 (SDNY 1984). See for the original order *US* v *Chase Manhattan* 584 F. Supp. 1080 (SDNY 1984). See also parallel cases arising out of the same facts: *Garpeg Ltd* v *US* 583 F. Supp. 789 (SDNY 1984), motion to vacate denied 583 F. Supp. 799 (SDNY 1984) and see 588 F. Supp. 1237 (SDNY 1984); *Vanguard International Manufacturing Inc.* v *US* 588 F. Supp. 1229 (SDNY 1984).

155 590 F. Supp. at 1162.

156 699 F. 2d 341 (7th Cir. 1983).

157 [1986] 1 All ER 653 (ChD) applying *R* v *Grossman* (1981) 73 Cr. App. R. 302 (CA)

158 See *A and others* v *B Bank, Bank of England Intervening* [1992] 1 All ER 778 (QBD Com. Ct Hirst J). See further, on the problems of international cooperation in international bank supervision: *Inquiry into the Supervision of the Bank of Credit and Commerce International* (Chairman Rt Hon. Bingham LJ, 22 October 1992) esp. chapter 3; Treasury and Civil Service Committee of the House of Commons Fourth Report, *Banking Supervision and BCCI: International and National Regulation* (HC Paper 177, 1991–2).

159 For a fuller recent account of these matters see Baltic, 'The next step in insider trading regulation: international cooperative efforts in the global securities market', 23 Law & Pol. Int'l Bus. 167 (1991–2).

160 *SEC* v *Banca Della Svizzera Italiana* 92 FRD 111 (SDNY 1981)

161 The decision appears in unofficial English translation in 22 ILM 785 (1983).

162 See 24 ILM 745 (1985). For a background account of how this case was solved and settled see 'Cutting the Swiss web' by Terry Dodsworth in the *Financial Times*, 10 April 1986.

163 See SEA 1934 Release No. 21186 File No. S7-27-84, 'Request for comments concerning a concept to improve the Commission's ability to investigate and prosecute persons who purchase or sell securities in the US markets from other countries'.

164 Public Law No. 100–704 102 Stat. 4677 (1988).

165 See 22 ILM 1 (1983) and note 'Insider trading laws and Swiss banks: recent hope for reconciliation', 22 Col. J. Transnat'l L. 303 (1984). Similar agreements have been concluded with the UK, Japan, the Canadian Provinces of Ontario, Quebec and British Columbia, Brazil, Italy, the Netherlands and France: see Baltic (note 159 above), at p. 191.

166 Insider dealing was prohibited by article 161 Swiss Penal Code enacted 1 July 1988.

167 As was done in the case of the investigation against Bank Leu by the Swiss Federal Banking Commission in 1987 in connection with transactions involving the purchase of 41 million Guinness shares under an indemnity against loss granted by Guinness: 'Swiss banking: a hole in the heart', *Financial Times*, 3 February 1987, p. 22.

168 See US–Canada Memorandum of Understanding as to Notification Consultation and Co-operation with Respect to the Application of National Anti-trust Laws of 9 March 1984: 4 Trade Reg. Rep (CCH) s. 13,503, 23 ILM 275 (1984).

169 See US–Australia Agreement Relating to Cooperation in Antitrust Matters 29 June 1982, TIAS No. 10365 4 Trade Reg Rep (CCH) s. 13,502; US–Germany Agreement Relating to Mutual Cooperation Regarding Restrictive Business Practices 23 June 1976, 27 UST 1956, TIAS No. 8291, 4 Trade Reg. Rep. (CCH) s. 13,501.

170 European Communities–United States Agreement on the Application of Their Competition Laws: 30 ILM 1487 (1991). The legality of this agreement was the subject of proceedings brought by France in Case C-327/91 *France v EC Commission*. The European Court of Justice has held that the agreement was unlawful as the Council and not the Commission should have concluded it. The Council is expected to approve the agreement; 'EU court overturns antitrust accord with US', *Financial Times*, 10 August 1994, p. 1.

171 See OECD, *Council Recommendation Concerning Cooperation between Member Countries on Restrictive Business Practices Affecting International Trade*, OECD Doc. No. C(86)44 Final 21 May 1986, reproduced in 25 ILM 1629 (1986). The USA has recently passed new legislation which allows US antitrust authorities to conclude bilateral agreements for the provision of information concerning antitrust enforcement matters to countries which agree to share their own information in this field on the basis of reciprocity: see International Antitrust Enforcement Assistance Act 1994 (s. 2297 and HR4781 103rd Cong., 2nd Sess., 1994); noted in 'US antitrust law will aid foreign co-operation', *Financial Times*, 11 October 1994, p. 8.

172 See France–Germany Agreement Concerning Cooperation on Restrictive Business Practices 28 May 1984: 26 ILM 531 (1987).

173 For example, France–Germany, ibid., article 5.

174   Cmnd 6727 reproduced 9 ILM 87 (1970). See also the Report of the US
       delegation to the preparatory conference: 8 ILM 785 (1969), Amram 63
       AJIL 521 (1969); Report of Second Meeting of Special Commission on
       the Operation of the Convention: 24 ILM 1668 (1985).
175   Ibid., articles 1 and 2.
176   See note 73 above.
177   For example, Denmark, Finland, France, Norway, Portugal and Sweden
       from among the original ratifying states, subsequently joined by
       Germany. All the ratifying states except the USA, Barbados, Israel and
       Czechoslovakia have made a reservation under article 23.
178   Note 138 above. For the limits of permissible requests under English law
       see further: *Re Asbestos Insurance Coverage Cases* [1985] 1 WLR 331; *Re
       State of Norway's Application (Nos 1 and 2)* [1989] 1 All ER 745 (HL);
       Panayiotou v Sony Music Entertainment (UK) Ltd [1994] 1 All ER 755
       (ChD).
179   Collins, 'The Hague Evidence Convention and Discovery: a serious mis-
       understanding?', 35 ICLQ 765 at 783 (1986). This article presents con-
       vincing evidence in support of the thesis referred to and accepted in the
       text.
180   As held by, for example, the Supreme Court of West Virginia in *Eickhoff
       Maschinenfabrik v Starcher* 328 SE 2d 492 (1985).
181   As held in *Anschuetz & Co. v Mississippi River Bridge Authority* 754 F. 2d
       602 (5th Cir. 1985); *MMB v Walker* 757 F 2d 729 (5th Cir. 1985); *Re
       Société Nationale Industrielle Aérospatiale* 788 F. 2d 1408 (9th Cir. 1986);
       *Société Nationale Industrielle Aérospatiale v US District Court for the District of
       Iowa* 782 F. 2d 120 (8th Cir. 1986).
182   The principal briefs of the parties are reproduced in 25 ILM 803ff (1986).
       The US government, as *amicus*, had argued that the courts had a dis-
       cretion to use either the Convention or US rules of discovery in the light
       of considerations of international comity; the petitioners, supported by
       amicus briefs from the German, French and British governments, argued
       that the Hague Convention procedure should apply first and that the
       application of US pre-trial discovery rules was a violation of international
       law in that they failed to acknowledge the judicial sovereignty of foreign
       states in which evidence was located.
183   107 S. Ct 2542 (1987); 26 ILM 1021 (1987). The parties' principal briefs
       are reproduced in 25 ILM 1475ff (1986).
184   Note 179 above at p. 785. See further Oxman, 37 U. Miami L. Rev. 733
       at 740–2 (1983); Jennings, 33 BYIL 146 at 171 (1957) and Collins,
       'International law aspects of obtaining evidence abroad', in C. Olmstead
       (ed.), *Extraterritorial Application of Laws and Responses Thereto* (ILA/ESC,
       1984), at p. 186.
185   However, as Collins points out, the Convention may be of use in produc-
       ing evidence where, for example, a foreign codefendant fails to appear and
       its evidence is essential to prove the case against the codefendants, or to
       facilitate a site inspection: ibid., at p. 784.
186   See D. E. Rosenthal and W. M. Knighton (note 1 above), at p. 9. See also
       A. D. Neale and M. L. Stephens (note 1 above). They argue that a policy

of aggressive extraterritoriality creates more costs than benefits; they advocate a reassertion of the territorial principle of jurisdiction.

187   *Laker Airways* v *Sabena*, at 951. See further Maier, 'Interest balancing and extraterritorial jurisdiction', 31 Am. J. Comp. L. 579 (1983); Rosenthal and Knighton (note 1 above), at pp. 25–8; Roth (note 1 above). Note also the views of Hoffmann J on the balancing test in *MacKinnon* v *Donaldson Lufkin and Jenrette Securities Corp.* (note 157 above). Judge Wilkey's view appears to have been borne out by the outcome of the recent *Insurance Antitrust Litigation* 723 F. Supp. 464 (ND. Ca 1989); 938 F. 2d 919 (9th Cir. 1991) upheld on appeal by the US Supreme Court (note 62 above).

188   See Grossfeld and Rogers, 'A shared values approach to jurisdictional conflicts in international economic law', 32 ICLQ 931 (1983).

189   See further the Australian proposal for a mechanism for the reduction of conflicting requirements in national laws, and reactions thereto, in OECD, *Minimizing Conflicting Requirements: Approaches of Moderation and Restraint* (Paris, 1987), p. 24 and annex V. See also OECD, *The OECD Declaration and Decisions on International Investment and Multinational Enterprises 1991 Review* (Paris, 1992), chapter 4 and annex II(4).

6

The Control of Inward Investment by Host States

This chapter deals with the principal techniques used by host states to control the entry and establishment of foreign direct investment. These techniques represent policy responses that seek to preserve national economic independence against possible threats from the activities of foreign investors. They range, at one extreme, from the complete exclusion of foreign investors to techniques of controlled access to the host state's economy. In the next chapter techniques for the encouragement of foreign direct investment will be considered both at the level of the host state and at the bilateral and multilateral levels, thereby completing the continuum of policy choices from controlled access to open access and investment incentives. Before we turn to specific techniques of control, certain general points should be made concerning the possible constraints on a host state's discretion in the regulation of inward direct investment stemming from international law. This is of particular significance in view of the increased concern shown by international organizations, and in the recently completed negotiations under the Uruguay Round of the GATT regarding the development of a liberal international investment order.[1]

1 The Scope of Host State Discretion

Host state control over inward investment can be divided into three major areas. First, there may be restrictions excluding such investment from the state as a whole or from specific sectors and/or industries. Secondly, foreign direct investment may be permitted after a review process, which may or may not place conditions upon the foreign investor in return for permission to enter the host state. Thirdly, once the foreign investment has been established, the activities of the investor will be subject to the general laws of the land.

The first and second areas operate at the stage of entry. Here the host state exercises its sovereign right to control the presence of aliens within its territory. In terms of international law, the host state has an unlimited discretion at this stage, subject only to restraints voluntarily undertaken in international economic agreements. Thus it is highly important to consider how far a given host state has accepted international obligations to guarantee access for foreign investors into its territory. It may be unlawful under the applicable international treaty regime for the host to adopt the kinds of measures to be discussed below.

The third area represents the post-entry phase, when the foreign investor has subjected itself to the laws of the host state. In general, the laws applicable at this stage are the same as those applied to domestic enterprises. However, the operation of these laws may be affected by the nature of the MNE's business organization and activities, and may result in the creation of new legal responses aimed at MNEs in particular. Again, according to established principles of state sovereignty under international law, the host state has a theoretically unlimited discretion to regulate the activities of the foreign investor.[2] However, the question arises whether international minimum standards for the treatment of foreign investors should control the extent of this discretion.[3] Not surprisingly, capital exporting countries favour this approach. By contrast, capital importing countries have traditionally opposed the control of their discretion in this area by international law. On the other hand, certain host states have submitted to international minimum standards through the conclusion of bilateral investment treaties (BITs), as the price to be paid for access to foreign capital and technology. Where this is so, the content and effect of host state laws on the legal rights of foreign investors may be subject to review in accordance with the standards contained in the applicable treaty. The legal effects of BITs are discussed at length in chapter 17. However, it should be stressed that BITs do not normally restrict the host state's discretion to control the entry and establishment of foreign investors. In general, this discretion is explicitly preserved by the terms of the BIT, which usually leaves the matter to regulation under the applicable law of the host state.[4] This emphasizes that the major concern behind such treaties is the protection of foreign investors after entry into the host contracting state.

2   Techniques for Restricting Entry and Establishment

In the discussion of such techniques an initial problem arises over the adoption of a suitable system of classification. Some writers have distinguished between the policies of developed and developing host states.[5] This distinction is of little help when describing legal (or, indeed, economic and political) phenomena associated with the contemporary international division of labour, and will not be followed here.[6] In practice, the legal techniques used by developing and developed countries to control the entry and establishment of MNEs do not differ very much in nature, only in degree. Furthermore, given the gradual move away from restrictive policies on inward investment by less developed countries (LDCs), the post-socialist states and the remaining socialist states, such a distinction appears no longer to reflect reality. It is primarily of historical value as an explanation of the motives behind legal developments in the 1960s and early 1970s. A second approach is to classify control techniques according to their ideological origins.[7] The importance of this approach lies in its stressing the need for an interdisciplinary understanding of foreign investment controls. However, excessive stress on ideology can lead to a blurring of the distinct legal questions that different degrees of control over entry and establishment create, regardless of the political motives behind them. In the light of these observations the approach adopted here is one of considering techniques of control along the continuum from total exclusion to conditional entry, identifying the policy origins of the various techniques involved and the principal legal issues that each technique raises.

2.1   Total Exclusion and Sectoral Exclusion of Foreign Investors

2.1.1   Total exclusion   The most restrictive legal response to foreign investors is the imposition of a complete prohibition on inward direct investment. Such a response has been advocated by the more radical forms of economic nationalism and dependency theories.[8] However, this approach can now be viewed as obsolete, given the economic costs it entails. It isolates the host state from access to foreign capital and technology and requires the development of substitute domestic products and technology, which can prove to be unattainable and/or financially ruinous.[9] Nevertheless, in the past, certain states have practised a policy of total exclusion for a variety of reasons. The most prominent among these were the then socialist states of Eastern Europe led by the USSR, and the People's Republic of China (PRC). The Eastern European states and the Soviet Union had had access to Western technology up until the onset of the Cold War in the late 1940s, when the USA and its Western allies introduced restrictions on trade with these states.[10] This, coupled with the non-participation of the Eastern Bloc states in the Bretton Woods

System, led to economic disintegration between East and West and to the establishment of an independent and self-sufficient Eastern trading area organized around the now defunct Council for Mutual Economic Assistance (CMEA).[11] This resulted in a gradual diminution of trade with Western nations. Only contractual transfers of goods and technology not restricted by Western embargoes were possible. Direct investment by Western firms was impossible until the more recent liberalization of the Eastern European economies, first through the introduction of joint venture laws, then in some countries by the introduction of laws permitting direct investment through wholly owned subsidiaries.[12] Similarly, China closed its doors to Western direct investment from the Revolution of 1949 until 1979, when joint ventures were first permitted by law, with wholly owned foreign enterprises being permitted to invest after the introduction of new legislation in 1986.[13]

2.1.2 *Sectoral exclusion*   Short of complete exclusion, inward direct investment can be excluded from certain sectors of the host state's economy. Most states have adopted either total or partial restrictions in what are perceived as 'key sectors' in the economy.[14] These areas generally encompass industries relevant to national security and defence, for example shipbuilding or aerospace, culturally significant industries, such as film and broadcasting, and public utilities.[15] The general use of such laws suggests that they pose few problems for states in their international economic relations, representing a recognized 'reserved domain' for national ownership and control.

However, difficulties can arise when a host state so interprets its vital national economic and security interests as to create a discriminatory regime for the exclusion of foreign investors from sectors where national firms are under threat from foreign competition. For example, in the USA, during the 1980s pressures increased in Congress, given the recent wave of Japanese and other acquisitions of US companies,[16] to extend the definition of 'national security' to include US economic interests.[17] However, such pressures were resisted in the revised Exon-Florio amendment, which empowers the US President to prohibit the takeover of a US firm by a foreign firm where there exists 'credible evidence that the foreign interest exercising control might take action that threatens to impair national security'.[18] Under the implementing Regulations companies voluntarily notify the Committee on Foreign Investment in the USA (CFIUS) of a proposed takeover of an American company. The Committee has thirty days to decide whether to undertake an investigation into the proposed acquisition. If it does investigate the inquiry must be completed within forty-five days. A recommendation is then made to the

President, who has fifteen days to announce his decision, and from which there is no right of appeal. 'National security' is not defined in the Regulations, but the General Discussion of the Regulations makes clear that only transactions that involve products, services and technologies important to US national defence requirements are covered.[19] To date only one takeover has been blocked, that of the US aircraft parts manufacturer Mamco by the China National Aero-Technology Import and Export Company.[20] However, the law has resulted in several deals being restructured to meet CFIUS objections.[21] In one case, CFIUS approved the takeover of Semi-Gas, a small Californian semiconductor production equipment supplier, by the New Jersey based subsidiary of the Japanese company Nippon Sanso KK. However, Sematech, the US semiconductor industry consortium, argued that the sale would place newly developed semiconductor technology into foreign hands. It urged the US Justice Department to oppose the sale on antitrust grounds. This challenge was rejected by the courts.[22] At the level of US states, local legislatures have been seeking to adopt restrictive laws to protect local companies from foreign takeover. These developments caused anxiety in the OECD over increasing US protectionism in the field of inward investment, which, for a time, hindered the adoption of a new instrument on 'national treatment' designed to minimize unreasonable discrimination against foreign firms operating within OECD countries.[23]

Japan too has traditionally reserved certain sectors from foreign investors.[24] Such reservations have since been replaced by a system of discretionary screening, which subjects intended investment projects to possible revision or cancellation where they are found to be injurious or damaging to national security or public order and public safety, or are to be made in the exceptional industries of agriculture, forestry, fisheries, mining, petroleum, leather and leather products, or where a project bypasses regulations on capital transactions.[25] This law represents an on-going process of liberalization in Japanese inward investment regulation,[26] emphasized in the Japanese Cabinet's decision of 26 December 1980, that the inward investment screening procedure shall be applied in conformity with the OECD Code on the Liberalization of Capital Movements.[27] However, a wide measure of ministerial discretion is retained. The manner in which that discretion is exercised will determine the extent to which the law will act as a device of protection against foreign competition. In this the Japanese law is little different from the investment screening laws of other countries, which are considered in section 2.4.

The reservation of specific sectors from foreign investors has been used by developing countries to protect indigenous industries from foreign domination, on the basis of the so-called 'infant industry' argument. Thus, a newly established national enterprise is seen as entitled to protection from the full effect of market forces, where these could expose it to fatal competitive pressures from established foreign firms, and so deny to the country concerned an opportunity to create its own industrial base in the relevant industrial sector. This was the aim behind South Korea's recently restrictive policy on inward investment.[28] Similarly, in recent years both Brazil and India have restricted foreign investors from their mini- and microcomputer industries. Brazil now feels able to reduce these restrictions, so as to ensure that its recently established national industry is not deprived of the latest foreign informatics technology. India too has liberalized its technology import controls.[29]

The reservation of certain industrial and commercial sectors for exclusive equity ownership by the nationals of the host state can be used to develop an indigenous capital base. For example, under the now repealed Nigerian Enterprises Promotion Decrees (since 1991 redesignated as Acts) of 1972, 1977 and 1989[30] certain industrial and commercial activities that were deemed to be within the technical and managerial competence of Nigerian citizens were reserved exclusively for Nigerians.

2.2 Laws Restricting Foreign Shareholdings in National Companies

In this context an initial distinction can be made between laws that merely require local financial participation in what would otherwise be a wholly owned subsidiary of a foreign parent company, and equity joint venture laws. The latter require not only local shareholding but also local participation in the management of a locally incorporated joint enterprise with the foreign investor. These laws seek to restrict not only foreign ownership but also foreign control over the investment and are, therefore, of particular importance to states that wish to retain direct control over the activities of the foreign investor. Joint venture laws have for this reason been especially significant in socialist states. They are considered in more detail in section 2.3.

The present section considers laws restricting foreign shareholdings in locally incorporated companies. In recent years, restrictions on foreign shareholding have been used for numerous purposes by host states. This section concentrates in particular on 'indigenization' laws and on restrictions associated with privatization programmes in various countries. Of relevance too are restrictions on the takeover of host state firms by foreign investors, based on the application of national antitrust laws. These are considered in chapter 11.

2.2.1 Indigenization laws   A major purpose behind legal restrictions on foreign ownership in local companies has been to secure the 'indigenization' of foreign owned companies, that is, to transfer the ownership of shares in the company concerned to nationals of the host state. This should not be confused with 'nationalization' or 'expropriation' in that the shares of the foreign owned company are not forcibly divested in return for compensation, but are placed on the market for local investors to purchase at market prices.[31]

A leading example of such a policy is the series of Nigerian Enterprises Promotion Acts passed in 1972, 1977 and 1989.[32] These successive laws developed the Nigerian indigenization programme, setting up the institutional structure for the transfer of shares from foreign to Nigerian ownership,[33] and laying down the criteria for indigenization. The method adopted was to classify industrial sectors into separate schedules, each of which specified a different limit to foreign ownership.

Under the 1977 Act there were three schedules.[34] Schedule 1 specified sectors which required little capital to set up and operate, such as cake making or hairdressing, or involved particular national interests, such as radio and TV broadcasting, and which were deemed to be within the competence of Nigerians to operate and own. These sectors were reserved for exclusive Nigerian ownership.[35] Schedule 2 listed enterprises in which Nigerians were able to participate, but where foreign capital contributions and managerial expertise were considered valuable; for example, banking, beer brewing, construction, mining and book publishing. In these sectors Nigerian ownership could not be less than 60 per cent.[36] Schedule 3 listed enterprises involving highly complex operations for which foreign capital and know-how were essential. These included distilling and blending of spirits, pharmaceuticals, manufacture of engines and turbines, motor vehicles and aerospace. Here Nigerian ownership could not be less than 40 per cent.[37]

Under the 1989 Act these schedules were reduced to one. The sectors listed there were reserved for exclusive Nigerian ownership.[38] They encompassed broadly the same areas as schedule 1 of the 1977 law. In all other sectors foreign investors were free to set up wholly owned subsidiaries, except in the separately regulated areas of banking, insurance, petroleum prospecting and mining. Even in scheduled sectors foreign investors could own enterprises if the capitalization involved was not less than 20,000,000 naira[39] and prior approval was received from the Securities and Exchange Commission.[40]

These changes were introduced as part of Nigeria's policy for stimulating increased investment, both domestic and foreign, which had slumped in recent years.[41] Furthermore, a liberalization of the indigenization laws was required to make effective Nigeria's privatization programme, initiated in 1988, and its debt conversion scheme.

Under that scheme, holders of dollar denominated promissory notes could change them into naira denominated notes, giving an average debt-conversion discount of some 50 per cent, and then invest the proceeds in new or existing enterprises, including those offered for privatization.[42] Without liberalization there would have been too few investment opportunities.[43]

Comparable restrictions on foreign equity participation were introduced in India under the Foreign Exchange Regulation Act of 1973 (FERA).[44] By s. 29 of the Act as it stood in 1973:

a company (other than a banking company) which is not incorporated under any law in force in India or in which the non-resident interest is more than forty per cent or any branch of such company, shall not, except with the general or special permission of the Reserve Bank [of India], –

(a) carry on in India a branch, office or other place of business for carrying on any activity of a trading, commercial or industrial nature, other than an activity for the carrying on of which permission of the Reserve Bank has been obtained under section 28; or

(b) acquire the whole or any part of any undertaking in India of any person or company carrying on any trade, commerce, industry or purchase the shares in India of any such company.

This provision sought, first, to contribute to the conservation of India's foreign exchange reserves by controlling the outflow of foreign currency through its limitation of foreign equity participation in Indian companies, resulting in reduced remittances of earnings abroad. Secondly, by restricting the foreign ownership of Indian companies, s. 29 sought to increase indigenous participation in industrial development.

Section 29 was supplemented by Guidelines for its administration.[45] These laid down qualifications to the general ownership requirements of s. 29(1). Under the original version of the Guidelines, Indian companies with more than 40 per cent foreign holding were permitted to carry on business in areas requiring sophisticated technology[46] or in a predominantly export-oriented industry (in which minimum exports are 60 per cent of total production), provided they reduced the foreign holding to 74 per cent. Where a firm exported 100 per cent of its production it was entitled to more than 74 per cent foreign equity on the merits of its case. A diversified company would be given individual consideration. If most of its activity was in 'core' areas of the economy,[47] it would be entitled to foreign equity participation not exceeding 74 per cent.

The imposition of foreign ownership limits under FERA resulted, during the 1970s, in a substantial dilution of shareholding by MNEs, which had until then controlled some one-fifth of India's corporate

180 Regulation by Home and Host States

assets.[48] Some companies, notably IBM and Coca-Cola, refused to dilute their holdings and left India.[49] However, the majority complied, fearing loss of access to a major market owing to India's strict controls over imports and the possibility that a competing company would take over the existing company's market share.[50] On the other hand, MNEs were not without power in this new environment. They still retained control over the resulting jointly owned companies. In many cases local ownership was so dispersed as to provide no controlling influence against the foreign firm. Furthermore, foreign equity was often turned into foreign debt, thereby preserving both the income flow of the foreign firm and its control over the Indian company. Moreover, the control that they possessed over technology and access to foreign markets ensured that MNEs would retain a strong bargaining position.

Thus, the effect of FERA was to permit the retention of MNE control over operations in 'core' areas of the economy and in the export-oriented industries, while reducing overall levels of foreign ownership in the Indian economy. A further effect was the stimulation of domestic business houses to enter industries hitherto dominated by MNEs and to develop indigenous substitute technologies, thereby reducing dependence on foreign capital and technology. None the less, this policy has not provided India with the kind of industrial development it had hoped for, sparking debate over whether India should retain a restrictive policy on foreign participation.[51]

That debate has resulted in the Congress government of 1991 recommending the liberalization of FERA, as part of a wider programme to introduce greater deregulation and competition into the Indian economy.[52] The reforms came amid discussions between the Indian government and the IMF about a long-term loan of some $5 to 7 billion. The reforms have included the amendment of s. 29 of FERA, through the removal of the words, 'or in which the non-resident interest is more than forty per cent', thereby terminating any statutory control over the maximum level of foreign shareholding by a foreign investor in an Indian company.[53] This measure, coupled with the abolition of state controls over stock market issue prices, has led foreign firms to increase their stakes in their Indian subsidiaries up to 51 per cent to secure control, at discounts of up to 90 per cent of market prices. This has, in turn, led to the outlawing of preferential issues to small groups of shareholders, amid protests from leading MNEs.[54]

In both India and Nigeria, the principal social and economic effect of indigenization appears to have been an extension of equity ownership among the better-off sections of society,[55] without any major increase in control over the operations of the MNEs involved, and at the cost of shortages of new technology and investment capital. This is particularly pressing in the present period, when both countries face acute balance-of-payments difficulties and possess a relatively uncompetitive industrial base. Consequently, the economic nationalism of earlier years is being relaxed in favour of increased access to the national economy by MNEs as a source of new investment capital. However, there are some signs of a growing disquiet with economic liberalization in both countries. In 1994 the new military government of Nigeria announced the reintroduction of foreign exchange controls,[56] while in India leading local businessmen have expressed concern over the growing role of foreign investors in the economy and politicians have organized mass protests against the Final Act of the Uruguay Round negotiations.[57]

2.2.2 Restrictions on foreign ownership in privatized companies In recent years numerous governments have initiated privatization programmes designed to introduce greater competition and private investment into economic sectors hitherto dominated by publicly owned enterprises.[58] Given that publicly owned enterprises have predominated in strategic industries such as transport, public utilities, natural resources, energy, financial services and defence, the unregulated sale of such enterprises to the private sector raises the possibility of their falling under foreign ownership and control, thereby threatening existing national control over vital economic interests. Consequently, privatizations of publicly owned companies have often involved restrictions on foreign ownership. To illustrate the techniques of control employed, the examples provided by the UK and French privatization programmes will be considered.

In the UK, the government has retained control over certain matters in recently privatized companies by way of the so-called 'golden share'. By this device, the government retains one special rights redeemable preference share of £1 held by itself or its nominee in the privatized company. The company's Articles of Association then specify that certain matters are deemed to be a variation of the rights of the special share and can only be effective with the consent in writing of the special shareholder.[59] In certain strategically significant companies the 'golden share' has been used specifically to restrict foreign ownership. Such restrictions have been introduced for British Aerospace, British Airways and Rolls-Royce in their Articles of Association, where the approval of the British government is required for any material disposal of assets. In addition British Aerospace and Rolls-Royce both limited foreign ownership to 15 per cent in their Articles, while the British Airways Articles contained a general restriction on foreign ownership.

These restrictions raised objections from the European Commission on the grounds that they could be used as a means of discriminating against the participation of nationals from other EC Member States in the capital of the British companies, contrary to article 221 of the Treaty of Rome. Although restrictions on foreign shareholding may be lawful under the EEC Treaty in relation to the activities in which these companies were involved,[60] the Commission was uneasy about the size of the limits imposed. After extensive negotiations with the British government it was agreed that the ceiling for foreign ownership would be raised for British Aerospace and Rolls-Royce to 29.5 per cent,[61] subject to review by the Commission in 1992 in the light of changes in the structure of the European defence industry,[62] while the British Airways 'golden share' will only be used if the Secretary of State determines that the airline's operating rights are threatened by a loss of ownership or control to foreign investors.[63] Thus, as far as EC Member States are concerned, excessive limitations on foreign ownership in privatized firms will be struck down by the Commission. Indeed, the Commission has recently opened infringement proceedings against the UK over the shareholding limits in British Aerospace and Rolls-Royce, in order to re-examine their compatibility with the Treaty of Rome.[64]

Apart from the 'golden share' the UK government can control the build-up of foreign shareholdings in strategic British companies through its competition policy. Most notably, such a strategy was adopted after the sale of the government's holding in BP when the Kuwait Investment Office built up an unacceptably high shareholding stake in BP. This case will be considered in chapter 11, as part of a general examination of UK policy on foreign takeovers of British companies.

Finally, it should be noted that under the Industry Act 1975, the Secretary of State for Trade and Industry retains the power to prevent the transfer of control of 'important manufacturing undertakings'[65] to non-residents where they build up a share of over 30 per cent in the undertaking.[66] However, these powers have never been used. This is not surprising. The Secretary of State retains a discretion in the matter. Thus if he or she supports the takeover, or has ideological objections to state interference in the market for corporate control, the power will not be used. Secondly, given the high qualifying percentage, many cases simply fall outside the power. A holding of less than 30 per cent will often be sufficient to ensure control. Thirdly, it may be difficult to discover that a transfer of control has in fact taken place, as where a number of shareholders agree to buy a series of small shareholdings, acting in accordance with a common plan to take over the targeted UK company, or where a number of apparently unconnected shareholders buy as nominees of an undisclosed buyer who seeks to control the company.[67] Therefore, the powers under the Industry Act 1975 are something of a dead letter as regards control over foreign participation in UK manufacturing companies, and will not be effective in preserving privatized companies under British control.

In France, after the widespread nationalizations of 1981–2 effected by the then socialist government, the right-of-centre government of Jacques Chirac introduced a major programme of privatization in 1986. As part of this policy, the control of foreign participation in privatized companies was enshrined in statute. By articles 9 and 10 of Law No. 86-912 of 6 August 1986,[68] no individual or corporation could acquire more than 5 per cent of the shares transferred at the time of sale of the shares by the state, and the sum total of the shares sold directly or indirectly by the state to foreign individuals or corporations, or to those under foreign control, should not exceed 20 per cent of the capital of the enterprise. This limit was acceptable to the European Commission, after it had objected to the original proposed limit of 15 per cent.[69] However, the 20 per cent limit could be lowered by decree of the Minister if the protection of national interests were required. Under the most recent privatization programme, initiated by the new centre-right government of 1993, the prime minister, Edouard Balladur, had hoped to abolish all restrictions on foreign investment in the new privatization legislation. However, following a Senate amendment, a 20 per cent limit on foreign investment in privatized companies by non-EU investors was reintroduced.[70]

Article 10 of Law No. 86-912 continued by laying down the legal regime for the creation of a governmental 'golden share' in newly privatized companies. This governed foreign shareholdings in privatized companies after the initial sale of shares by the state. For each company subject to the Privatization Law of 1986[71] the Minister of the Economy, after consultation with the privatization commission, would determine by decree whether the protection of national interests 'requires that a common share held or acquired by the government be transformed into an extraordinary share bearing rights defined in this present article'. The principal right attached to the extraordinary share was that of permitting holdings by one or several individuals or corporations acting in concert to exceed 10 per cent of the capital. The extraordinary share could be converted back to a common share at any time by ministerial decree. It lapsed by operation of law after five years. In areas covered by articles 55, 56 and 223 of the EEC Treaty,[72] holdings of more than 5 per cent by persons or corporations subject to article 10 were subject to the agreement of the Minister of the Economy. Acquisitions in violation of the provisions of article 10 would invalidate the voting rights attached to the shares so purchased and the shares had to be sold within three months. The extraordinary share was less powerful than the British 'golden share', given its limited duration and the absence of powers to block disposals of assets.[73] Furthermore, it was not used as often.[74] The golden share was revived for the new wave of privatizations. It was more powerful than its predecessor as it was of indefinite duration.[75]

2.2.3 Concluding remarks Following our consideration of two areas in which controls over foreign shareholdings in locally incorporated companies have been instituted, given the diverse objectives involved it may not appear possible to offer any useful generalizations about the nature of present trends in inward investment policy. Yet there is an underlying unity of purpose emerging from these seemingly diverse illustrations. As Nigeria and India are liberalizing their investment controls, so too the UK and France are seeking to open up sectors previously closed to investors from abroad. In its own way, each country is increasing its integration into the international division of production, by increasing the possibilities for foreign capital participation. With this participation certain sectors may eventually fall under foreign control. On the other hand, in an increasingly open international economy, the desirability of foreign control may in future fall to be decided by reference to antitrust law, with its emphasis on encouraging competition, rather than by reference to a presumption as to its undesirability, embodied in laws restricting foreign shareholding. Much depends on how states will view their national security requirements in the future.

2.3   Laws Regulating Equity Joint Ventures between Foreign and Local Enterprises

A policy of integration into the international division of labour may be combined with a desire to retain local managerial control over the enterprise in which the foreign investor participates. One attempt to create such a compromise is embodied in laws regulating the establishment of equity joint ventures between foreign and local enterprises. The basic technique of control involved is to make the entry of the foreign investor into the host state conditional upon the substantial involvement of local participants in the ownership and control of the investment project in question. The local participant may be a private or public sector entity, depending on the circumstances of the case and on the prevailing economic system and policy of the host state. Such laws go beyond the indigenization laws studied in the previous section in that the local participant not only owns a share of the equity in the joint venture, which by itself may be insufficient to ensure control, but also participates in its management.

Such arrangements are not, however, a guarantee of local control. First, local management may not be able to manage the project effectively. Indeed, a major reason for bringing in the foreign partner may be to enhance local managerial skills and technical knowledge. Thus the local partner is likely to be dependent on the foreign partner for major decisions, at least in the early stages of the joint venture.[76] Secondly, where the foreign partner is a MNE, the joint venture will be dependent on the international network of that partner for its success. For example, the joint venture will depend on the production and marketing organization of the MNE for supplies of inputs and access to export markets. Similarly, the foreign partner may control the know-how and technology needed for the joint venture. Consequently, the foreign partner may exercise effective business control over the joint venture, even where it holds a minority share of the equity.

None the less, joint ventures have become increasingly common in developing host countries and in the socialist and post-socialist states. There are significant advantages for both the MNE and the host state.[77] Briefly put, for the MNE, a joint venture offers an opportunity to enter a new market with the advantage of the local business know-how of the local partner, which may prove invaluable in an unfamiliar, if not hostile, business environment. Furthermore, the foreign nationality of the MNE can be subsumed behind the local nationality of the joint venture, thereby reducing the risk of its being identified as a 'foreign' corporation and being subjected to discriminatory treatment.

For the host state, the joint venture offers a means of introducing new capital and technology into the domestic market, while at the same time retaining the legal form, if not the commercial substance, of control over the foreign investor. Consequently joint venture laws have been of particular importance in states espousing economic development policies in a strongly nationalistic political environment. For example, in Indonesia, under a Government Policy Statement of 22 January 1974 all new foreign investment in Indonesia should have Indonesian participation of not less than 30 per cent. All new foreign investment had to be initiated as a joint venture, with Indonesian participation being raised to 51 per cent within a period of ten years.[78] In 1986 Indonesia relaxed its previously strict rules over majority Indonesian equity participation in joint ventures with foreign firms, allowing a more flexible period within which the requirement of 51 per cent local ownership was to be met. Thus in the case of large, high risk, investments made in remote areas or where the joint venture would export at least 85 per cent of its products, an initial foreign shareholding of 95 per cent was permitted, with local equity participation being increased to 20 per cent within five years, increasing to 51 per cent in the following ten years. Enterprises setting up in a bonded zone were permitted up to 95 per cent foreign ownership and were exempted from the 51 per cent 'fade-out' requirement. New guarantees and incentives for foreign investors were also introduced and certain sectors of the economy were opened up to foreign capital for the first time.[79] Further measures of liberalization were introduced in 1987.[80] In 1992, 100 per cent foreign ownership was allowed for the first time since independence.[81] Other countries and regions espousing joint venture policies have also progressively liberalized restrictions on foreign participation.[82]

The ability of joint venture laws to legitimate inward direct investment within a politically unfavourable environment has made them particularly attractive to socialist states, which, as was noted above, had been previously opposed to foreign direct investment within their borders. Since the early 1970s the member states of the now defunct CMEA, and other socialist states outside Eastern Europe, have passed laws permitting Western capital to enter on the basis of joint ventures with domestic state enterprises and, more recently, as wholly owned foreign enterprises. As they lagged increasingly behind the West in technological capability and productivity, particularly in the civilian sector, the socialist states became less able to satisfy the growing demands of their populations for material consumption or to earn sufficient returns from exports. Somehow the introduction of new, Western, productive knowledge into domestic civilian production had to be assured and, at the same time, the domestic economy had to be protected against uncontrolled capitalist penetration. This was achieved through the use of joint venture laws.

The first to adopt such a law was Hungary in 1972.[83] Yugoslavia,[84] Poland,[85] Romania[86] and Bulgaria[87] followed during the 1970s. In 1979, the People's Republic of China (PRC) adopted its so-called 'open door' policy of attracting foreign capital by means of the new law on Chinese–foreign joint ventures and its accompanying Regulations.[88] During the 1980s Czechoslovakia decided to enact a joint venture law,[89] as did Ethiopia, North Korea, Cuba and Vietnam.[90] Most notably, the Soviet Union changed its policy on Western investment and passed a joint enterprises law in January 1987,[91] in line with the new policy of restructuring (*perestroika*) in foreign economic affairs. Only the German Democratic Republic resisted the adoption of such laws until the communist government lost power in 1989. Albania, the last socialist state to pursue a policy of economic autarchy, decided in 1991 to permit inward investment through joint ventures.[92]

An exhaustive discussion of the above-mentioned joint venture laws is beyond the scope of this work.[93] For present purposes a distinction will be made between, first, the post-socialist states of Eastern Europe, secondly, the former Soviet Union and its successor states, and, thirdly, the PRC. Each country or region is facing distinct economic and political problems that have influenced and continue to influence policy on their regulation of inward investment. Thus while all three are moving broadly in the direction of a free market economy, the speed and direction of each is unique.

2.3.1   The post-socialist states of Eastern Europe   In these states, the incidence of joint venture laws is best seen as a transitional phase towards an open free market economy in which wholly owned subsidiaries of foreign firms are, in principle, welcome. Indeed, more recent legislation from these countries has already moved in this direction. For example, in Poland Law No. 325 of 23 December 1988, which came into force on 1 January 1989, dropped a previous condition that Polish partners in a joint venture should hold a majority share and empowered the Polish investment authorities to permit inward direct investments through wholly owned subsidiaries.[94] This law has since been replaced by the 1991 Foreign Investment Act.[95] According to the Polish Parliament, the new law aims at the creation of legal conditions for foreign investors that are comparable to those pertaining in other states, that accord with the principles of a market economy and that end the socialist legal tradition of treating inward foreign investment as an 'enclave' within the economy.[96] The principal changes introduced under the 1991 Act reflect these aims. First, the Act removes the need for case-by-case screening of all investment proposals and limits the requirement for a permit to activities in five designated areas (the operation of sea and airports; dealing in real estate or acting as an intermediary in such transactions; defence industries that are not covered by licensing requirements; wholesale trading in imported consumer goods; the provision of legal services),[97] to transactions where a state legal person is to make a contribution in kind to the company being set up, such as real estate or a plant,[98] where a foreign party acquires shares in an existing company and that company carries on activities in one of the listed areas or needs a licence or permit under separate regulations,[99] and where a state legal person makes a contribution in kind to an existing company with foreign participation.[100] Secondly, the 1991 Act introduces new investor protection provisions. These include the payment of full compensation for expropriation,[101] tax concessions[102] and rights to the repatriation of profits in foreign currency.[103]

Other Eastern European states have also introduced laws liberaliz-ing the foreign investment environment. Since 1991, Hungary has permitted the establishment of foreign-owned enterprises, or the acquisition by foreigners of a share in an existing Hungarian enter-prise, without official permission.[104] The rules concerning repatri-ation of profits have been further liberalized,[105] and substantial tax concessions are available.[106] Similarly, Czechoslovakia enacted a new Foreign Investment Law in 1990.[107] This law opened up all sectors of the Czechoslovak economy except for areas relating to defence and national security.[108] It further introduced protection against expro-priation and state interference.[109] However, a general screening pro-cedure for all foreign investments was retained.

Such developments have been accompanied by mass privatization programmes aimed specifically at attracting foreign investors. Thus, for example, in Czechoslovakia fifty leading enterprises were offered as candidates for privatization in June 1991. By 1996, the Czech car manufacturer Skoda will be 70 per cent owned by Volkswagen of Germany.[110] Enterprises with more than 30 per cent foreign owner-ship will be subject to a preferential tax regime of 40 per cent flat rate on profits, as compared to 55 per cent on firms with under 30 per cent foreign ownership.[111] Since the break-up of Czechoslovakia further privatizations have been announced by the Czech govern-ment.[112] In Poland 400 state owned factories, representing 25 per cent of the country's industrial sales, were offered for sale in 1991. These companies will remain with a 30 per cent state shareholding but will be able to enter into joint venture and management con-tracts. Shares will be available to Polish and foreign investors. How-ever, it appears that ultimate control is to remain in Polish hands.[113] In May 1993 new legislation provided for the privatization of a further 600 state enterprises.[114] In Hungary, privatization com-menced in 1990 with state-owned enterprises in the retail, restaurant and consumer services sectors. In 1991 other state-owned enterprises were added through the use of 'shell companies', to which the state-owned enterprise transfers its assets.[115]

2.3.2   The People's Republic of China   Since 1979 China has pro-gressively liberalized the legal environment for foreign investment. However, the administrative environment remains one of strict con-trol and supervision. Consequently, too much weight should not be placed on legal developments alone when assessing the true degree of liberalization that has taken place. The whole issue is still very much in the realms of divided debate in China. The trend is, however, towards a more open economy.[116] The principal legislation affecting inward direct investment remains the equity joint venture law of 1979 as amended in 1990.[117] This is complemented by the contractual joint venture law of 1988[118] and the law on wholly-owned foreign enterprises.[119] These will be briefly considered.

The contractual and equity joint venture laws share many features in common. Thus the following discussion will concentrate on the equity joint venture law and reference to the contractual joint venture law will only be made where there are significant differences. The purposes behind the equity joint venture law are stated in article 1 as being, *inter alia*, the expansion of international cooperation and technological exchange, and the enabling of foreign companies and individuals to incorporate themselves within the territory of the PRC. This is the first Chinese law to create the possibility of incorporation as an entity other than a state enterprise. The joint venture takes the form of a 'limited liability company' governed by the laws of the PRC.[120] A contractual joint venture also acquires the status of a 'legal person' in accordance with Chinese law.[121] These terms are uncertain in their scope. Limited liability is not defined under Chinese law,[122] although under the joint venture law the risks are shared by the participants in accordance with their respective contributions.[123] The term 'legal person' is defined by the General Principles of Civil Law of 12 April 1986 as including the right to own, use and dispose of property, the right to carry on management and productive activities independently and the right to sue and be sued. However, according to Moser, there remain many uncertainties as to how this definition applies to joint ventures.[124]

Both equity and contractual joint ventures are subject to approval by the relevant Chinese authorities before they can operate. The approval procedure involves the submission of a joint venture contract and articles of association to the reviewing authority, which must decide within a prescribed period. For equity joint ventures the relevant authority is the Ministry of Foreign Economic Relations and Trade (MOFERT) or lower level authorities to which the task is delegated by MOFERT.[125] Approval will be denied *inter alia* where the proposed joint venture appears to be detrimental to Chinese sovereignty, to violate Chinese law, to be incompatible with China's national economy, to be likely to cause environmental pollution or to contain obvious inequity in the agreements, contracts or articles of association.[126] Once approval has been given, the joint venture shall apply to the relevant authorities to register and will obtain an operating licence.[127]

An equity joint venture must contain at least 25 per cent foreign capital, although there is no upper limit on the foreign contribution. Profits are shared by the participants in proportion to their respective contributions.[128] Each party to the venture can contribute cash, capital goods or industrial property rights. Where the foreign party contributes technology this must be advanced technology that is appropriate to China's needs. Should the foreign party intentionally provide outdated equipment or technology it shall pay compensation for any resulting losses. The Chinese party can contribute the right to use a site as part of its contribution.[129]

The joint venture shall have a board of directors with a composition stipulated in the articles of association. The chairman and one or two vice-chairmen shall be chosen 'through consultation by the parties or through election by the board of directors. If the Chinese side or the foreign side assumes the office of chairman, the other side shall assume the office(s) of the vice-chairman or chairmen.'[130]

Profits are distributed in accordance with the respective shares of the parties in the venture after payment of income tax on gross profits.[131] The foreign party can then remit its net profits abroad through the Bank of China in accordance with the foreign exchange regulations in force and in the foreign currencies stipulated in the joint venture contract.[132] The joint venture can set up a foreign exchange account in its own name with a bank or any other financial institution which is permitted to handle foreign exchange transactions.[133]

By article 14 of the 1979 law disputes between the joint venture participants which the board of directors fails to settle through consultation may be settled through conciliation or arbitration by an arbitral body of China or through arbitration by an arbitral body agreed upon by the parties. It is not clear whether the arbitral body must be a body subject to Chinese law, or whether an international arbitral body can be selected. The 1983 Regulations on Joint Ventures[134] make no mention of international arbitration but urge arbitration by the Foreign Economic and Trade Arbitration Commission of the China Council for the Promotion of International Trade in accordance with its arbitration rules,[135] or, in the absence of an arbitration agreement between the parties, recourse to the Chinese People's Court.[136] However, Chinese bilateral investment treaties do contemplate international arbitration.[137] Indeed, the PRC has recently ratified the Washington Convention on the Settlement of Investment Disputes 1965 as a first step towards the acceptance of the International Centre for the Settlement of Investment Disputes (ICSID) as a means of international arbitration and conciliation in disputes with foreign investors.[138]

The operation of joint ventures in the PRC has been beset with problems. As noted above, a major difficulty lies with the high levels of control exercised by the Chinese authorities over industrial and commercial activities. In particular, significant regulations are classed as 'internal' (*neibu*) and may not be revealed to foreigners.[139] Thus not all the relevant administrative rules are always accessible. Further problems have arisen in relation to labour relations, land use and regulation of purchases of inputs.[140] However, the authorities have made considerable efforts to ease problems.[141] Furthermore, in an attempt to reinforce China's commitment to an open door policy the 1990 amendment to the Joint Venture Law introduced a new article 2(3) whereby 'the state shall not nationalize or requisition any joint venture. Under special circumstances, when public interest requires, joint ventures may be requisitioned in accordance with legal proceedings and appropriate compensation shall be made.'

As an alternative to a joint venture the foreign investor is able to set up a wholly owned subsidiary in accordance with the 1986 Law on Wholly Foreign-Owned Enterprises and its implementing regulations. Approval for such an enterprise is required from MOFERT or other authorities designated by the State Council of the PRC.[142] To obtain approval the enterprise must 'be conducive to the development of China's economy', and 'shall use advanced technology and equipment or market all or most of [its] products outside China'.[143] Should the enterprise fail to invest in China within a designated period after approval, its licence to operate will be revoked.[144]

Where the enterprise fulfils the conditions for being considered a legal person under Chinese law it shall be so considered.[145] This is a rather obscure provision given the absence of a comprehensive company law in the PRC.[146] However, the law itself offers certain guarantees to the enterprise. Thus, by article 4 of the law, 'The investments made by a foreign investor in China, the profits he earns and his other lawful rights and interests shall be protected by Chinese law.' Furthermore, the enterprise is protected from expropriation except under 'special circumstances . . . should it prove necessary to do so in the public interest', in which case 'legal procedures will be followed and reasonable compensation will be made'.[147] This protection should be enhanced by the terms of investment protection treaties entered into by the PRC and by access to ICSID, given that China has agreed to the jurisdiction of the Centre in disputes over compensation resulting from expropriation and nationalization.[148]

As long as the enterprise acts in accordance with its approved articles of association, it will be free from interference in its operations.[149] Profits legitimately earned from the enterprise may be remitted abroad.[150] On the other hand the enterprise is obliged to employ Chinese workers as well as foreign workers,[151] set up account books in China and submit to independent audit,[152] pay taxes in China,[153] insure with Chinese insurers[154] and observe Chinese foreign exchange regulations.[155] Liquidation of the enterprise will be subject to regulations.

As a result of the adoption of an 'open door' policy towards foreign investment the PRC managed to attract some $20 billion of approved investment projects by 1987.[156] However, the Chinese authorities have on occasion expressed disappointment that much of the investment has not been in priority high technology or export-oriented industries.[157] More recently, the suppression of anti-government protests in 1989, culminating in the Tiananmen Square massacre in June of that year, raised the question of China's political stability as a host to foreign investment. The USA, Europe, Japan and the World Bank imposed sanctions on China in response to this outrage, but by early 1990 these were being relaxed.[158] Furthermore, the events of 1989 do not seem to have had a significant short- or long-term deterrent effect on inward investment into the PRC.[159] The Chinese economy is just too great a market to ignore, regardless of internal political developments. Indeed, foreign investment has recently increased, with 47,000 joint ventures being established in 1992 alone, bringing the total value of foreign investment in China to date to US$37 billion.[160]

2.3.3   The Soviet Union and its successor states   Following on the heels of liberalization in China and Eastern Europe, the Soviet Union also embarked on a transition to a market economy, commencing with a reversal of its long-standing prohibition of foreign inward investment through the enactment of the 1987 law on joint enterprises.[161] The aim behind the international aspects of Soviet economic reforms was to ensure the increased involvement of the Soviet Union in the international division of labour.[162] The 1987 Law represented the first step towards a market economy in which foreign investors are encouraged. It served as a learning experience for the Soviet authorities, who constantly sought to improve its terms through reforms. On the other hand, although by the beginning of 1990 there were more than 1,000 joint enterprises planned or in operation they did not provide the economic development that was hoped for.[163]

A new legal regime for foreign investment was introduced by the Russian Soviet Federated Socialist Republic Law of 4 July 1991.[164] Although former Soviet legislation has been declared void in the new Russian Republic, it will take many years for future Russian laws to supplant old Union legislation. Thus the 1991 law may continue to indicate the principal lines of Russian legal theory in the field of foreign investment for the immediate future.[165] The 1991 law permits, for the first time, the establishment of wholly foreign-owned enterprises in the Russian Republic.[166] Furthermore, it introduces guarantees as to the protection of foreign investments. These include: the right to national treatment;[167] guarantees against nationalization, except in the case of extraordinary events and in the public interest, whereupon the foreign investor is entitled to 'the payment of swift, adequate and efficient compensation';[168] the right of resort to international dispute settlement centres if an international treaty in force in the Republic so provides;[169] the right of repatriation of funds after the payment of required taxes;[170] the right to reinvest funds in the Russian Republic.[171] The law establishes a procedure for the creation and liquidation of enterprises with foreign investment.[172] It requires that all enterprises with foreign investment be registered in accordance with the procedures laid down for this purpose.[173] State registration can only be denied for failure to observe the law relating to the creation of such an enterprise. Denial of registration may be appealed to a court of law.[174] The law goes on to delineate the types of activities that enterprises with foreign investment may undertake,[175] the conditions for the acquisition by foreign investors of ownership shares in other enterprises, specifically permitting their participation in privatization,[176] rights to land use and acquisition,[177] and the conditions of foreign investment in Free Economic Zones.[178]

Other former Soviet republics have enacted foreign investment laws. These have been the object of a recent World Bank study.[179] That study found the following features to be displayed by the laws that it analyses.[180] Most require registration of foreign investments with a designated authority, usually the Ministry of Finance. In some cases several different authorities must be approached. The laws all specify certain standards of treatment. A common feature is the provision for national treatment. Transfers of capital appear to be allowed but the World Bank found that many provisions were unclear in this respect. Rights of expropriation are generally very narrowly drawn, being limited to exceptional situations such as epidemics or natural disasters, and compensation is payable for the loss suffered by the foreign investor. Recourse to international arbitration is generally authorized but the laws were frequently unclear on this topic. Of the former Soviet Republics, apart from Russia, Belarus, Estonia, Lithuania and Kazakhstan have signed the ICSID Convention and Belarus, Estonia and Lithuania have also ratified. All the former Soviet Republics have applied for membership of the Multilateral Investment Guarantee Agency. They have also started to sign BITs.[181]

2.3.4 Concluding remarks   From the above, it can be seen that the socialist and post-socialist countries have moved a long way from their previous policy of 'decoupling' and separate development from the capitalist system. They have used equity and contractual joint venture techniques, coupled with close regulation and strict approval procedures, as a means of introducing controlled foreign investment into their economies. From this starting point all these states have progressively liberalized their economies towards a free market system welcoming inward direct investment by foreign firms. The states of Eastern Europe have travelled furthest and fastest along this route, progressively abandoning their connection with socialist principles of economic, political and social organization, which had been imposed upon them since the Second World War. The result is a legal regime for foreign investors that is increasingly open in character, though as yet more restrictive than may be normal in the OECD countries. For China the move away from a command economy model in the field of foreign investment has been similar to that experienced in Eastern Europe during the 1980s. However, it has not been accompanied by the abandonment, at least at the levels of national government, of socialist principles. The aim still appears to be the creation of a 'socialist market economy' within the framework of a Communist Party-led political order. This may change when the existing generation of Chinese leaders is replaced. By contrast, the former Soviet Union has been a late starter in the progressive dismantling of command economy structures in the field of foreign investment, as reflected by the recent date of the Soviet joint enterprise law. The long-term aim is the creation of a market economy. However, the political environment remains unstable and it is difficult to predict the future evolution of the law, whether in Russia or in the several new republics. On the other hand, investment in the region is slowly increasing.[182]

2.4   'Screening Laws'

'Screening laws' involve the case-by-case review of proposed foreign investments by a specialized public authority in the host state that is charged with the task of establishing whether or not a given proposal is in accordance with the economic and social policies of the host state. As we have seen in the foregoing sections, 'screening' procedures are often established in association with restrictive regimes regulating the ownership and control of foreign investments. On the other hand, screening may be used as the sole technique of regulation, unaccompanied by any statutory requirements concerning permissible limits of foreign ownership and/or control, and be aimed only at ensuring official scrutiny and approval of proposed investments. In many cases the screening process will empower the reviewing authority, or the minister or government department to which it is answerable, to impose operational conditions, usually referred to as performance requirements, upon the investor as the price for approval.

The screening of foreign investments is one of the most widely used techniques for controlling the entry and establishment of MNEs in host states.[183] This approach has been favoured by states that welcome foreign owned and controlled investments, but are concerned about the loss of economic sovereignty or adverse economic consequences that may accompany such investments in particular cases. Both economically advanced and less developed countries (LDCs) have adopted screening laws.

2.4.1 Screening laws in LDCs Certain LDCs have adopted this technique, often in association with the imposition of performance requirements and/or access to investment incentives, as an alternative to strict restrictions on foreign ownership and control of inward direct investments. Two typical examples of this approach are the laws of Mexico and Ghana.

In 1984 and again in 1989 Mexico, which had hitherto imposed strict limitations on foreign investment under the 1973 Act on Foreign Investment, liberalized its previous ceiling of 49 per cent on foreign ownership outside restricted sectors and introduced automatic approval procedures based on certain conditions that the foreign investor must fulfil.[184] The 1989 reforms were effected through Regulations. This raised some uncertainty as to their legality under the regime of federal law as reflected in the 1973 Act. Consequently, for the avoidance of uncertainty and as a further measure of liberalization, the 1989 Regulations have been formally codified and developed in the new Foreign Investment Act of 1993 (the Act).[185]

The Act has limited screening procedures to certain economic activities, listed in article 8, where the foreign investor is seeking a participation of more than 49 per cent,[186] and to foreign acquisitions of over 49 per cent in Mexican corporations where the total value of the stated capital exceeds 85 million new pesos.[187] Screening is to be carried out by the National Commission of Foreign Investments.[188] In evaluating applications for approval under the above provisions, the Commission must take into account: the impact upon the employment and training of workers; the technological contribution; compliance with environmental provisions; and, in general, the contribution of the proposed investment to the increased competitiveness of Mexico's factories and businesses.[189] Unlike the 1989 Regulations, which imposed specific performance requirements, the 1993 Act only permits the Commission to impose requirements which will not distort international trade.[190] On the other hand, the Commission may prohibit acquisitions by foreign investment for reasons of national security.[191]

Outside those areas requiring screening by the Commission, the Act guarantees freedom of foreign investment: in any proportion of capital; in the acquisition of fixed assets; in entry into new areas of economic activity or in the manufacture of new lines of products; in the opening and management of commercial entities; or in the expansion or relocation of those already in existence. This general freedom is excluded where the Act reserves certain listed activities for the state,[192] or for Mexicans or Mexican corporations.[193] In addition, article 7 of the Act lists several economic activities where foreign investment is limited by percentages, ranging from 10 up to 49 per cent, but where approval by the Commission is unnecessary. The listed areas include, *inter alia*, domestic air transportation, cable TV, fishing and insurance. The listed areas were previously reserved for Mexicans. The scheme of the 1993 Act ensures that national treatment is accorded to foreign investors in all fields save those specifically reserved for Mexican participation. This ensures that Mexican foreign investment law is in line with the requirements of the North American Free Trade Agreement.[194]

A similar approach to screening has been adopted by the Ghana Investments Centre under the Investment Code of 1985, which liberalized the restrictive conditions of entry for foreign investors under the 1981 Investment Code.[195] In areas other that those reserved exclusively for Ghanaian investors,[196] or in insurance and banking, where enterprises must be jointly owned with Ghanaians,[197] or in petroleum, which is subject to a separate statutory regime, the Centre will approve an enterprise wholly owned by a non-Ghanaian if it involves an investment of foreign capital or equivalent goods worth at least US$100,000 and it is a net foreign exchange earning enterprise.[198] The approval procedure requires an appraisal of the capacity of the enterprise to contribute to any of the following objectives: development of the productive sectors of the economy; efficient utilization, expansion and diversification of the productive capacity of existing enterprises; utilization of local materials, supplies and services; creation of employment opportunities in Ghana; real increase in national export earnings; real savings on national imports; development and transfer of advanced technology, including the upgrading of indigenous technology; country-wide distribution of viable enterprises; and such other objectives as the Centre may consider relevant for achieving the objects of the Code.[199]

The application procedure requires that the prospective investor obtains an application form from the Centre and submits the completed form to the Centre, including a short statement on how the proposed investment meets the above-mentioned criteria.[200] On receipt of the form, the Centre shall submit within fourteen days a copy to the ministry, government department or agency under whose administrative competence the enterprise falls.[201] That body shall submit to the Centre comments on the proposal within twenty-one days of its receipt from the Centre. The Centre will take such comments into account when deciding whether to approve the proposal.[202] In granting approval for an investment, the Centre shall have due regard to the need to generate constructive competition among enterprises and shall avoid a tendency to establish monopolies.[203] It shall also consider the environmental effects of the proposed enterprise.[204] When the Centre resolves to approve an enterprise, it must notify the applicant promptly in writing. The applicant must, in turn, confirm in writing to the Centre within twenty-one days that he or she intends to proceed with the enterprise.[205]

Should the Centre approve the investment it shall issue a certificate of approval, which has the legal force of a manufacturing licence under the Manufacturing Industries Act 1971 in the case of a manufacturing investment, or of an establishment licence in other cases.[206] The certificate may stipulate certain conditions that the investor must comply with on pain of the suspension or cancellation of the approval. These conditions may deal with: the amount and source of capital; the nationality and number of shareholders; the project size; the training of Ghanaians in administrative, technical, managerial and other skills related to the operation of the enterprise; the period of time to commence the implementation of the enterprise; reporting on the implementation of the project and operation; the prevention and control of any damage to the environment; the utilization of local raw materials; and any other matter that is appropriate with regard to the objects of the Code.[207] The approval of a proposed investment will also entitle the investor to the various fiscal and other benefits that are available under the 1985 Code to approved enterprises.[208] Certain industrial sectors that are regarded as particularly important to the economy are given special benefits and incentives.[209]

2.4.2 Screening laws in economically advanced countries
Screening laws are frequently found in economically advanced states that do not espouse an 'open door' approach to foreign investment. Examples include Japan,[210] France,[211] Spain,[212] Australia[213] and New Zealand.[214] The most comprehensive example of inward investment regulation through screening laws in an economically developed country is to Professor be found in the Canadian experience since the early 1970s.

Canada has long been a major location for foreign direct investment, particularly from the USA. The considerable levels of investment by US firms have created a close economic relationship between the two countries. They have also led to a sense of dependency and loss of national identity on the part of Canadians, which periodically manifests itself in nationalistic calls for the reduction of US influence in Canada.[215] Such sentiments were prominent in the late 1960s and early 1970s in relation to the then growing debate on the effect of MNEs on Canadian society and its economy. Between

1968 and 1972 three government reports on direct investment in Canada helped to create an environment of concern over the increasing domination of MNEs, especially from the USA, over the Canadian economy.[216] Of these the most important was the last, the so-called 'Gray Report'. This Report recommended the setting up of a new investment screening agency which would act as a bargaining agent with MNEs and prevent monopolistic foreign ownership in Canadian industry.

In January 1973, the newly elected Liberal government led by Pierre Trudeau introduced the bill that was to become the Foreign Investment Review Act (FIRA). The Liberals had lost their overall majority in the House of Commons and had to rely on the left-wing New Democrat Party for support. Consequently, the provisions of the Bill were tougher on foreign investors than the government would have liked.[217] Furthermore, it was one part of a wider policy aimed at increasing Canadian participation in the national economy.[218] The Act became law on 12 December 1973.[219] Following the recommendation of the Gray Report, the Act established the Foreign Investment Review Agency (the Agency) as a screening body for the approval of new inward investment on the basis of its being or likely to be 'of significant benefit to Canada',[220] as defined by reference to the criteria listed in s. 2(2) of the Act and subsequent regulations.[221] The Act applied to two forms of inward investment: the acquisition of control of existing Canadian enterprises and the establishment of new businesses in Canada.[222] It did not limit the internal expansion of foreign owned enterprises already operating in Canada, which, according to Professor Rugman, accounted for most new direct investment recorded in Canada.[223]

The review procedure set up by FIRA involved an initial assessment by the Agency followed by a report to the Minister of Industry, Trade and Commerce. The Minister would then assess whether the investment represented a significant benefit to Canada. If it did, the Minister would recommend to the Cabinet that the investment be approved. If it did not, the investor would be given more time to provide further information and to make further representations. The Cabinet would then decide whether the investment met the statutory test of significant benefit to Canada. The approval could be made conditional on the acceptance of specific commitments by the investor, which would become legally binding upon the granting of approval by the Cabinet.[224] This procedure was to be completed within sixty days.[225] It was a closed procedure, involving as it did the highest executive organ in the country. This made the likelihood of judicial review more remote, given the immunity of the Cabinet from such an action.[226]

In practice the majority of applications under FIRA were approved.[227] However, the Act engendered opposition both from within Canada and from the US government. Within Canada, the administrations of the provinces saw the legislation as inhibiting their power to attract inward investment.[228] Meanwhile, in the USA, the free market oriented Reagan administration adopted a policy of opposition to the Canadian legislation.[229] In 1982, the US government made a request before the GATT Council that it set up a panel to examine matters concerning the administration of FIRA. The USA complained about undertakings given by foreign investors under FIRA in relation to the purchase of Canadian goods and the maintenance of export levels. It is important to stress that the complaint did not relate to the compatibility of the screening procedure *per se* with the GATT, but to the adverse and discriminatory effects on international trade between the USA and Canada that were allegedly created by the above-mentioned undertakings. The panel concluded that Canada had violated GATT principles through the adoption of such undertakings. The Canadian government responded by discontinuing the practice of accepting undertakings from investors which gave preferential treatment to Canadian goods and services over imported goods.

In 1984, the new Conservative administration led by Brian Mulroney promptly repealed FIRA and replaced it with the Investment Canada Act 1985 (the 1985 Act).[230] This introduced a less stringent screening procedure applicable only to larger investment proposals, which was conducted by lower levels of government. The new government was concerned to change the perception of foreign investors as to Canada's attitude to foreign direct investment. Thus, according to s. 2 of the 1985 Act,

Recognizing that increased capital and technology would benefit Canada, the purpose of this Act is to encourage investment in Canada by Canadians and non-Canadians that contributes to economic growth and employment opportunities and to provide for the review of significant investments in Canada by non-Canadians in order to ensure such benefits to Canada.

The 1985 Act requires that non-Canadians[231] making an investment to establish a new Canadian business, or an investment to acquire control of a Canadian business in any manner specified in the Act, must provide notice of such investments to the Investment Canada Agency (the Agency), which replaces the Foreign Investment Review Agency.[232] This requirement does not apply to the exempt transactions listed in s. 10(1) of the 1985 Act. The 1985 Act does not clarify the purpose of the notification procedure,[233] but it appears from the terms of s. 13(3) that notification is required so that the

Agency can determine whether the investment is reviewable under the Act or, alternatively, is exempt from review. The Agency must send a notice for review to the prospective investor within twenty-one days after the certified date upon which notice of the investment was given.[234]

The establishment of a new business in Canada by a non-Canadian[235] is not reviewable unless it involves the commencement of a business that falls within a prescribed specific type of business activity that is related to Canada's cultural heritage or national identity.[236] Whether a business activity is related to Canada's cultural heritage or national identity falls to be determined by regulations made under the 1985 Act. The acquisition of control of a Canadian business[237] is subject to review depending on the mode of acquisition involved and the value of the assets of the targeted Canadian enterprise. Section 28(1) of the 1985 Act designates five types of acquisition relevant to the Act:

(a) the acquisition of voting shares of a corporation incorporated in Canada carrying on the Canadian business;
  (b) the acquisition of voting interests of an entity that:
    (i) is carrying on the Canadian business, or
    (ii) controls, directly or indirectly, another entity carrying on the Canadian business
where there is no acquisition of control of any corporation;
  (c) the acquisition of all or substantially all of the assets used in carrying on the Canadian business; or
  (d) the acquisition of voting interests of an entity that controls, directly or indirectly, an entity carrying on the Canadian business, where
    (i)   there is no acquisition of control, directly or indirectly, of a corporation incorporated elsewhere than in Canada that controls, directly or indirectly, an entity in Canada carrying on the Canadian business, or
    (ii) there is an acquisition of control described in sub-paragraph (i).

The acquisition can be effected by a chain of transactions provided one of the above results is achieved.[238] The acquisition of control is presumed, for the purposes of s. 28, where a majority of the voting shares in the Canadian corporation are acquired, but not where fewer than one-third of the voting shares are acquired. Where more than one-third but fewer than a majority of the voting shares are acquired control is presumed unless it can be proved that the acquirer does not in fact control the corporation through its acquisition.[239]

Once an acquisition of control by any of the above methods has taken place the review procedure will come into operation only if the value thresholds laid down in the statute are met. By s. 14 of the 1985 Act, where the investment involves the acquisition of direct control of a Canadian business or of its assets,[240] review is required where the asset value of the Canadian business is C$5 million or more. Where the investment involves the acquisition of indirect control over a Canadian business[241] the threshold for review is C$50 million or more, unless the value of the assets of the Canadian business concerned amounts to more than 50 per cent of the value of the total assets acquired by the non-Canadian, in which case the threshold is lowered to C$5 million. These limits have been removed for US investors as a result of the USA–Canada Free Trade Agreement, which will be considered in the next chapter.[242] It is of some significance to note that, as far as review of indirect acquisitions is concerned, this involves an extraterritorial exercise of jurisdiction. Under FIRA the Canadian courts were willing to defend the exercise of such jurisdiction.[243] The 1985 Act appears to have preserved such jurisdiction in cases where the acquisition of a Canadian business forms a major part of a larger foreign takeover.[244]

After receipt of an investment notification, should the Agency decide that the investment falls within a reviewable category, the application is forwarded to the Minister of Regional Industrial Expansion as the Minister responsible for the administration of the 1985 Act.[245] The Minister will then decide whether the proposed investment is likely to be 'of net benefit to Canada'.[246] The level of decision-making is thus lowered from that of the Cabinet. Furthermore, the 'net benefit' test introduces a lower requirement for approval than the 'significant benefit' test under FIRA. However, the statutory criteria for consideration of a 'net benefit' are similar to those found in FIRA in connection with the former test. Thus, the Minister must consider the effect of the investment on economic activity in Canada, including: its effect on employment, resource processing, use of parts, components and services produced in Canada and on exports; the level of Canadian participation in the investment and in the industry where the investment occurs; the likely effects on productivity, efficiency, technological development and product innovation; the effect of the investment on competition; its compatibility with federal and provincial industrial, economic and cultural policies and its effect on Canada's ability to compete in world markets.[247]

The Minister must make the required decision within forty-five days from the certified date of receipt of the application. If no decision is made within this period, the Minister must notify the applicant that he or she is unable to complete his or her consideration of the investment. There remains a further thirty day period for decision that may be extended by mutual agreement. Should that period run out without a decision being made, the investment is automatically allowed.[248] If the Minister decides that the investment does not comply with the 'net benefit' criterion the applicant may be requested to make further representations or to enter into undertakings.[249] Thereupon the Minister makes a final determination as to the 'net benefit' of the investment. If the investment is disallowed the applicant shall not implement it or, if it has been implemented, control of the Canadian business that is the subject of the investment must be relinquished through divestment.[250] Failure to comply with the procedures or with a decision under the 1985 Act renders the non-Canadian subject to compliance orders and to penalties for non-compliance.[251]

Compared to FIRA, the Investment Canada Act allows a wider range of inward investments to be made without approval, has lowered the criterion for approval from 'significant' to 'net' benefit, has shortened the review period and has located the centre of decision making at ministerial level. Furthermore, the 1985 Act appears to have stimulated a subsequent increase in inward investment.[252] However, these changes are not as radical a departure from the spirit of FIRA as they appear to be. Although the emphasis has shifted from investment control to investment promotion,[253] it is clear that the Canadian government did not abandon its right to review investment it considers to be 'of national sensitivity or significance'.[254] Indeed, in a rare exercise of its powers under the 1985 Act, in June 1991 the Canadian government turned down a proposal by Aerospatiale of France and Alenia of Italy to buy De Havilland of Canada from the US aerospace company Boeing unless certain assurances as to significant Canadian participation, continued research and the long-term commercial viability of the Canadian company would be given.[255]

Furthermore, the 1985 Act contains little to protect the investor's rights against a decision of the Minister to refuse permission for a proposed investment. First, despite removing decision-making power from the Cabinet the Act has retained the confidentiality provisions of FIRA almost intact.[256] Thus disclosure to the investor remains limited. Secondly, while there is a statutory right of appeal against court orders made against the investor under s. 40 of the 1985 Act, there is no corresponding right to judicial review of a Ministerial decision to refuse approval for an investment. According to Paterson, the investor is left to the general law on judicial review, where it might be extremely difficult to make out a case in view of the tradition of not giving reasons for the disallowance of an investment.[257] Thirdly, the drafting and structure of the Act leaves much to be desired in terms of clarity. The giving of advice on the basis of the Act is difficult, and therefore compliance costs are likely to be high. Equally, legal planning may avoid the review process, again at cost to the investor.[258]

2.4.3 Concluding remarks The above-mentioned examples of screening laws share certain essential features. They all use a specialized investment review agency to deal with the administration of the host state's foreign investment policy, with final decision making power being located either with the agency or with a higher level of government. The decision-making process tends to be highly discretionary, and is commonly exercised in the absence of effective judicial review against decisions unfavourable to the foreign investor. This problem, mentioned in the context of the Canadian legislation, is common to many jurisdictions.[259]

Arguably, judicial review is inappropriate in such cases. Major investment decisions may be unique given variations in the nature of the foreign investor, the size and characteristics of the proposed investment and the industrial sector involved. Thus a case-by-case approach is almost inevitable, and a clear indication as to the likelihood of a proposal being accepted may not always be possible. Nevertheless, there are few safeguards against the unreasonable exercise of ministerial or administrative discretion in national investment laws. Host states wishing to encourage inward investment, but, equally, wishing to retain a foreign investment screening procedure, could consider offering rights of judicial review to investors against unfavourable decisions by the screening authorities. Additionally, clear administrative guidelines should be issued from which investors could reasonably predict what the response of host state authorities to a particular proposal would be. The investment promotion literature of the host state should serve to fill this role.

A more significant issue concerns the mounting efforts by capital-exporting states to introduce multilateral controls over host state restrictions on the entry and establishment of foreign investors. The above-mentioned US reaction to the contractual undertakings extracted from foreign investors under the Canadian FIRA is a case in point. This approach is echoed in the OECD Code on the Liberalization of Capital Movements and in the newly concluded Agreements on Trade in Services (GATS), Trade Related Investment Measures (TRIMs) and Trade Related Intellectual Property Measures (TRIPs) under the Final Act of the GATT Uruguay Round. These developments will be considered in the next chapter.

3   Concluding Remarks: the Movement towards Liberalization of Controls over Foreign Investors

The present chapter has described the major techniques of inward investment control that have been used by host states to prevent the domination of their national economies by foreign investors. Such techniques were at the forefront of the policy response to MNEs in the 1970s, when levels of foreign investment in host state economies were reasonably high and considerations of economic nationalism and self-determination were at their height. However, as the international division of labour evolves so the cost of economic nationalism is perceived to be too great to sustain, given the resulting loss of access both to investment capital and to the most modern productive technology. Increasingly, both economically advanced and less developed countries are turning away from the strict regulation of foreign ownership and control of investment and are permitting such investment on less stringent terms. The progressive liberalization of indigenization laws is perhaps the best example of this trend. Similarly, investment screening laws are being applied less restrictively. Furthermore, the policies of outright prohibition of foreign investment pursued in the past by socialist states are virtually obsolete.

Given the widespread adoption of privatization programmes, the range of industrial sectors reserved for public ownership is decreasing and a corresponding increase in investment opportunities is being created. While reservations and controls over levels of foreign investment in privatized companies are a common feature of such programmes, in many countries the very purpose of privatization is to increase the overall level of inward foreign investment in the economy. Thus privatization policies are clearly within the trend towards liberalization of foreign investment even though they offer good examples of controls over foreign ownership.

The remaining prohibitions on foreign investment are to be found in sectors of the national economy relevant to national security. In this connection, the question remains whether states are willing to extend the meaning of 'national security' to include 'national economic security'. This offers a possible future avenue for protectionism in an otherwise increasingly deregulated environment for foreign investment.

Notes

1 See further chapter 7 and part III. See also M. Sornarajah, *The International Law on Foreign Investment* (Grotius Publications, 1994), chapter 3.
2 See C. D. Wallace, *Legal Control of the Multinational Enterprise* (Martinus Nijhoff, 1983), at p. 84.
3 See further chapter 14.
4 See further Parra, 'Principles governing foreign investment, as reflected in national investment codes', 7 ICSID Rev-FILJ 428 at 429–35 (1992).
5 See A. E. Safarian, *Governments and Multinationals: Policies in the Developed Countries* (British–North American Committee, 1983), pp. 53–4. Safarian

notes that the LDCs have taken actions which go beyond those taken by developed countries in protecting their economic sovereignty. Professor Safarian has recently published a more extensive study of developed host state policies in this area, entitled *Multinational Enterprise and Public Policy: a Study of the Industrial Countries* (Edward Elgar, 1992).

6   See further N. Harris, *The End of the Third World: Newly Industrializing Countries and the Decline of an Ideology* (Pelican, 1986).

7   See e.g. Seidman, 'Foreign private investors and the host country', 19 JWTL 637 (1985). Seidman, in this comparative study of LDC foreign investment laws, has distinguished between 'investor protection codes', which are inspired by a pro-capitalist economic policy and seek to offer an 'open door' to foreign investors, 'investment codes', which seek to reconcile a 'mishmash' ideology involving adherence to a market economy with a 'socialist' social welfare programme, and 'investor control codes', which seek to involve MNEs in the host state economy only under conditions of strict regulation as to the form and conduct of an investment, often requiring the setting up of a joint venture controlled by the partner from the host state.

8   See chapter 4 above.

9   However, the survival of the Rhodesian economy during the period of UDI from 1965 to 1979 is often cited as a counter-example of successful economic autarchy.

10   See D. Campbell (ed.), *Legal Aspects of Joint Ventures in Eastern Europe* (Kluwer, 1981), pp. 4–5.

11   Set up in 1949, the CMEA included the Soviet Union, Czechoslovakia, East Germany, Hungary, Poland, Bulgaria and Romania. Mongolia and Cuba joined in 1962 and 1972 respectively. Yugoslavia had associate status.

12   See further text at notes 83–115 below.

13   See further text at notes 116–159 below.

14   See Wallace (note 2 above), at pp. 45–8.

15   For example, US Federal laws restrict foreign investment in the following sectors: public broadcasting and telecommunications, coastal and internal shipping, internal air traffic (though liberalization is being considered), minerals exploitation on public lands and atomic energy. State laws restrict out-of-state banks from operating within their jurisdictions (here too liberalization is being considered): see Wallace, ibid., at p. 47. See also US, Canadian and Mexican reservations to the North American Free Trade Agreement: 32 ILM 605 at pp. 704–80 (1993). The emergency US government commission on the airline industry has recommended that up to 49 per cent of the voting stock in a US airline could be owned by a foreign airline. 'US airlines may be opened to more foreign investment', *Financial Times*, 20 July 1993, p. 14. Current restrictions prohibit more than a 25 per cent holding of voting stock in a US airline: Federal Aviation Act 1958 49 USC App. Ch. 20 s. 1301 (16), Department of Transportation Order 91-1-41 January 23, 1991. Thus, for example, British Airway's original bid for a 44 per cent stake in US Air was blocked. However, a renewed bid for a 19.9 per cent stake in US Air was given temporary approval. British Airways has increased its holding in US Air to 24.6 per

cent and intends further to increase its holding should the maximum foreign-ownership limits be raised: 'BA buys 19.9 per cent stake in US Air', *Financial Times*, 22 January 1993, p. 15; 'BA wins temporary approval for US Air link-up', *Financial Times*, 16 March 1993, p. 1; 'BA buys additional US Air stock and maintains 24.6 per cent holding', *Financial Times*, 27 April 1993, p. 21. BA disposed of its holding in US Air in 1997.

16   See further E. M. Graham and P. R. Krugman, *Foreign Direct Investment in the United States*, 3rd edn (Institute for International Economics, 1995).

17   See *Financial Times*, 31 May 1991, p. 3: 'Congress set to attack Bush's investment open door'.

18   See the US Omnibus Trade and Competitiveness Act 1988, s. 5201 Public Law 100–418 August 23, 1988, 102 Stat. 1107 reproduced in 28 ILM at p. 460 (1989). Reinstated by Defense Production Act Extension Amendments Public Law 102–99, 105 Stat. 487, August 17, 1991. US Treasury regulations implementing this provision were introduced on 21 November 1991: 31 ILM 424 (1992). For analysis see Holmer, Bello and Preiss, 'The final Exon–Florio regulations on foreign direct investment: the final word or prelude to tighter controls?', 23 Law & Pol. Int'l Bus. 593 (1992).

19   Regulations, ibid. at 31 ILM p. 429 col. 2.

20   *Financial Times*, 6 February 1990, p. 6.

21   See Holmer *et al.* (note 18 above), at pp. 610–14; Graham and Krugman (note 16 above), at pp. 126–32.

22   'US court rejects attempt to block sale to Japanese', *Financial Times*, 28 March 1991, p. 27.

23   See *Financial Times*, 31 January 1991, p. 6: 'OECD presses for more liberal rules on investment'. For a full discussion of the 'national treatment instrument' see chapter 16 at pp. 583–7.

24   See Wallace (note 2 above), at pp. 45–6. See also M. Y. Yoshino, 'Japan as host to the international corporation', in I. Frank (ed.), *The Japanese Economy in International Perspective* (Johns Hopkins University Press, 1975), p. 273.

25   See Foreign Exchange and Foreign Trade Control Law (Law No. 228, December 1, 1949 as amended) chapter V, articles 26–30; Cabinet Decision Concerning Policy Applications on Inward Direct Investments (Decision of Cabinet Meeting of 26th Day of December 1980), in *Japan: Laws, Ordinances and Other Regulations Concerning Foreign Exchange and Foreign Trade* (Chuo Shuppan Kikaku Co., 1990) at (A)-20 to (A)-27 and (A)-206. See also Sakamoto, 'Japan's outward and inward FDI', *The CTC Reporter*, No. 27 (Spring 1989), at p. 67; M. Matsushita, *International Trade and Competition Law in Japan* (Oxford, 1993), pp. 241–7.

26   According to Dr Wallace, Japan's liberalization of foreign investment laws has had a limited effect, many measures being introduced as 'token moves' in response to criticisms from the USA: note 2 above. In fact the Japanese authorities are making considerable efforts to attract inward investment. The major barriers to inward investment remain in the complexity of the Japanese market and culture, over which legislators and government officials have no real control. See further: L. Turner, *Industrial Collaboration with Japan* (Chatham House Papers No. 34, RIIA/RKP 1987), pp. 103–4;

C. Higashi and G. Peter Lauter, *The Internationalisation of the Japanese Economy*, 2nd edn (Kluwer, 1990), pp. 222–9.

27 Note 25 above. On the OECD Code see chapter 7 at pp. 248–50.

28 See D. Encarnation, *Dislodging the Multinationals: India's Strategy in Comparative Perspective* (Cornell University Press, 1989), at pp. 204–13; Westphal *et al.*, 'Foreign factors in Korea's industrialization', in Changsoo Lee (ed.), *Modernization of Korea and the Impact of the West* (East Asian Studies Center, University of Southern California, 1981); Hayward, 'Foreign investment and licensing in Korea', 23 U. Brit. Col. LR 405 (1989).

29 See further Greico, 'Between dependency and autonomy: India's experience with the international computer industry', 36 Int Org. 609 (1982); Adler, 'Ideological guerillas and the quest for technological autonomy: Brazil's domestic computer industry', 40 Int Org. 673 (1986); Evans, 'State, capital and the transformation of dependence: the Brazilian computer case', 14 *World Development* 791 (1986). The legislative basis of Brazil's informatics policy and its subsequent liberalization are described in chapter 12 at pp. 448–9. The liberalization of India's technology licensing policy is described in the same chapter at pp. 447–8.

30 See note 32 below.

31 On 'nationalization' and 'expropriation' see chapter 14. On the distinction between these concepts and 'indigenization' see Beveridge, 'Taking control of foreign investment: a case study of Nigeria', 40 ICLQ 302 at pp. 305–6 (1991); Akinsanya, 'Host governments' responses to foreign economic control: the experience of selected African countries', 30 ICLQ 769 at pp. 776–8 (1981).

32 Nigerian Enterprises Promotion Act 1972 (No. 4 of 1972) [1972] Official Gazette Fed. Rep. Nig. 123 A11 (Supp. Part A); Nigerian Enterprises Promotion Act 1977 (No. 3 of 1977); Nigerian Enterprises Promotion Act 1989 (No. 54 of 1989) [1989] Official Gazette Fed. Rep. Nig. 76 A809 (Supp. Part A); CAP 303 Laws of the Federation of Nigeria vol. 23 (rev. edn, 1990). For analysis of the 1972 and 1977 Decrees see: Megwa, 'Foreign direct investment climate in Nigeria: the changing law and development policies', 21 Col. J. Transnat'l L. 487 (1983); Osunbor, 'Nigeria's investment laws and the state's control of multinationals', 3 ICSID Rev-FILJ 38 (1988); Beveridge, 40 ICLQ 302 (1991); T. J. Biersteker, *Multinationals, the State, and Control of the Nigerian Economy* (Princeton University Press, 1987). For the background to the 1989 Act see: Nigerian Federal Ministry of Industries, *Industrial Policy of Nigeria (Policies, Incentives, Guidelines and Industrial Framework)* (January 1989), pp. 41–5. The 1989 Act was repealed by the *Nigerian Investment Promotion Commission Decree* 1995 (No. 16, 16 January 1995).

33 First through the Nigerian Enterprises Promotion Board set up by the 1972 Act (ibid.) and now through its successors, the newly established Nigerian Securities Exchange Commission and/or the Minister of Industries: 1989 Act (ibid.), explanatory note and ss 3–5. See now the powers of the Industrial Development Co-ordination Committee, which now acts as the principal screening authority for pre-investment approvals under the

1989 Act: Industrial Development Co-ordination Act 1988 s. 4. (No. 36, 1988), CAP. 178 Laws of the Federation of Nigeria vol. 10 (rev. edn, 1990), p. 6953.

34   For analysis see Osunbor (note 32 above), at p. 52.

35   1977 Act (note 32 above), s. 4.

36   Ibid., s. 5.

37   Ibid., s. 6.

38   1989 Act (note 32 above), s. 1(1).

39   Ibid., s. 1(2).

40   Ibid., s. 3(2). This task may now be performed by the Industrial Development Co-ordination Committee.

41   See *Industrial Policy of Nigeria* (note 32 above); *Financial Times Survey: Nigeria*, 7 March 1988, p. VI: 'How multinationals may be tempted'.

42   *Financial Times*, 17 January 1989, p. 3: 'Nigeria eases curbs on foreign investment', and *Financial Times Survey: Nigeria*, 6 March 1989, p. 3: 'An auction with discounts' and p. 5: 'A formidable timetable'.

43   Ghana has also liberalized its indigenization laws. Compare the 1981 Investment Code (Law No. 437 of 11 August 1981) with the 1985 Code (Law No. 116 of 13 July 1985) and the 1994 Ghana Investment Promotion Centre Act (Act 748, 29 August 1994). See also Laryea, 39 ICLQ 197 (1990).

44   Act 46 of 1973. See AIR 1973 Acts or S. R. Roy, *The Foreign Exchange Regulation Act 1973*, 3rd edn (Kamal Law House, 1989), pp. 148–97. For comment see Saxena and Kapoor, 13 JWTL 170 (1979). For the Act as amended by Act 29 of 1993 see *Baharat's Foreign Exchange Regulation Act 1973* (Baharat Law House, 1994).

45   See Roy, ibid., pp. 178–87.

46   Defined in the Guidelines by reference to criteria such as, *inter alia*, '(i) whether the technology is used for the manufacture of products that would otherwise necessitate imports, (ii) whether the discontinuance of the manufacture of products with the technology would have adverse impact on the economy etc.'

47   As defined by the lists of industrial activities contained in appendix I of the Industrial Licensing Policy, February 1973.

48   See further D. J. Encarnation (note 28 above), on which the following paragraphs are based.

49   Coca-Cola has since returned: 'India clears way for entry of big foreign companies', *Financial Times*, 25 June 1993, p. 6. IBM has returned in a joint venture with Tata Industries, Tata Information Systems, to make computer systems and to develop software: 'IBM returns to India for joint computer venture', *Financial Times*, 4 February 1992, p. 3.

50   As happened in the computer industry after IBM pulled out, and more generally in the electronics and electrical goods sectors. See Greico, 'Between dependency and autonomy: India's experience with the international computer industry', 36 Int. Org. 609 (1982); Encarnation, ibid., at pp. 166–9.

51   See Encarnation (ibid.) chapter 5, and see further P. Bardhan, *The Political Economy of Development in India* (Basil Blackwell, 1984); I. J. Ahluwalia, *Industrial Growth in India: Stagnation Since the Mid-sixties* (Oxford Univer-

sity Press, 1985).

52 See Press Information Bureau, Government of India, Press Release of 24 July 1991, 'New industrial policy 1991 announced', reproduced in UNCTC, *Foreign Direct Investment and Technology Transfer in India* (UN Doc. ST/CTC/117, 1992), annex VII, p. 128; Financial Times, 2 July 1991, p. 6: 'India moves to ease industrial controls'; *Financial Times*, 25 July 1991, p. 20: 'India eases foreign investor rules'.

53 See s. 29(1) Foreign Exchange Regulation Act 1973 as amended by the Foreign Exchange Regulation (Amendment) Act 1993 (Act 29 of 1993), in *Baharat's Foreign Exchange Regulation Act 1973* (Baharat Law House, 1994).

54 'Foreign companies protest at Indian plan', *Financial Times*, 6 April 1994, p. 26; 'India bans foreign share discounts', *Financial Times*, 26 April 1994, p. 7.

55 On India see Swamy, *Multinational Corporations and the World Economy* (Alps, 1980) chapter 1. On Nigeria see A. Akinsanya, 'The indigenisation of the economy and power relations in a developing economy: the Nigerian experience', paper delivered at the 13th World Congress of the International Political Science Association, Paris, 15–20 July 1985; C. Ake, 'Indigenisation: problems of transformation in a neo-colonial economy', in C. Ake (ed.) *The Political Economy of Nigeria* (Longman, 1985), chapter 9.

56 'Reversal of economic reform angers lenders', *Financial Times*, 12 January 1994, p. 4; 'Nigerian government to control allocations of foreign exchange', *Financial Times*, 29/30 January 1994, p. 3. However, in January 1995, the government reversed this policy by abolishing exchange controls and the Nigerian Enterprise Decree: 'Nigeria in policy V-turn', *Financial Times*, 16 January 1995, p. 4.

57 'Coca-cola invasion starts to worry businessmen', *Financial Times*, 9 November 1993, p. 6; 'Protests grow in India over GATT accord', *Financial Times*, 7 April 1994, p. 6.

58 On the British and French programmes see Cosmo Graham and Tony Prosser, *Privatizing Public Enterprises* (Clarendon Press, 1991). On privatization in developing countries see: UNCTC, *Transnational Corporations and World Development: Trends and Prospects* (UN Doc. ST/CTC/89, 1988), pp. 264–5; V. V. Ramanadham (ed.) *Privatisation in Developing Countries* (Routledge, 1989); P. Cook and C. Kirkpatrick (eds), *Privatisation in Less Developed Countries* (Wheatsheaf Books, 1988).

59 Graham and Prosser, ibid., p. 141. A full analysis of the use of the 'golden share' by the British government can be found in Graham and Prosser at pp. 141–51.

60 See EEC Treaty articles 55, 56 and 223, which permit limitations on ownership of shares by nationals of other EC Member States in cases of activities connected, even occasionally, with the exercise of public authority (article 55), on the grounds of public policy, public security and public health (article 56), and where this is required for the protection of essential interests of state security in connection with the production of or trade in arms, munitions and war material.

61 In 1993, the foreign holding limit for Rolls-Royce was breached and the

foreign shareholders concerned were asked to relinquish their purchases: 'Rolls-Royce foreign holding breached', *Financial Times*, 6 July 1993, p. 23.

62   See *Financial Times*, 4 August 1989, p. 18.

63   Graham and Prosser (note 58 above), at p. 144. See further article 44(A) of the British Airways Articles of Association of 26 January 1987, which ensures that as long as, and to the extent that, the holding or enjoyment by British Airways or any subsidiary thereof of any operating right is conditional on the company being to any degree owned or controlled by United Kingdom nationals, the company is so owned and controlled.

64   'Brussels warns on foreign curbs', *Financial Times*, 8 March 1994, p. 11.

65   Defined by s. 11(2) of the 1975 Act as 'an undertaking which, in so far as it is carried on in the United Kingdom, is wholly or mainly engaged in manufacturing industry and appears to the Secretary of State to be of special importance to the United Kingdom or to any substantial part of the United Kingdom.'

66   See ss 11–20.

67   Such activities were initially suspected in the Westland affair although the Stock Exchange inquiry into the case exonerated the major participants of such impropriety. See further: Joanna Gray and Ross Denton, 'Some company law problems arising from the Westland case', in D. Oliver (ed.), *Political Aspects of the Westland Affair* (University College London, Faculty of Laws, Working Papers No. 3, April 1986), p. 42; *Second Report from the House of Commons Trade and Industry Committee: Westland plc* HC 176 (1986–7), paras 15–20.

68   English translation in 26 ILM 1399–1401 (1987).

69   Graham and Prosser (note 58 above), at p. 151.

70   'Foreigners restricted in French sell-off ', *Financial Times*, 2 July 1993, p. 2.

71   Law No. 86-793 of 2 July 1986.

72   See note 60 above.

73   Graham and Prosser (note 58 above), at p. 152.

74   See ibid. at pp. 152–3.

75   See 'France to retain protective share of Elf-Aquitaine', *Financial Times*, 26 July 1993.

76   See further UNCTC, *Joint Ventures as a Form of International Economic Cooperation* (1988 UN Doc. ST/CTC/93) at pp. 68–73; Asante, 'Restructuring Transnational Mineral Agreements' 73 AJIL 335 (1979).

77   See Wallace (note 2 above), at pp. 75–7; UNCTC, Joint Ventures (ibid.), at pp. 48–68; Franko, 'International joint ventures in developing countries: mystique and reality', 6 Law & Pol. Int'l Bus. 315 (1974).

78   See UNCTC, *National Legislation and Regulations Relating to Transnational Corporations: a Technical Paper* (1983 UN Doc. ST/CTC/35) at pp. 73–6; see further the Law on Foreign Capital Investment Law No. 1 of 1967 under which joint ventures are established.

79   See Sunaryati Hartono, 'Indonesia's laws and policies on foreign investment' (mimeo, 1990), paper presented at the Singapore Conference on International Business Law: International Investment, Westin Plaza, August 1990.

80 Ibid.

81 See 'Indonesia to allow foreign ownership', *Financial Times*, 24 April 1992, p. 4; 'Indonesia in a bind over foreign investment policy', *Financial Times*, 19 May 1992, p. 4; *Financial Times Survey: Indonesia*, 24 June 1992, p. IV. The required conditions for full foreign ownership are that the investment exceeds US$50 million in Java and Sumatra, but can be less in remote areas. See further Halverson, 'Foreign direct investment in Indonesia: a comparison of industrialized and developing country investors', 22 Law & Pol. Int'l Bus. 75 (1991).

82 See, for example, South Korea, which in 1984 increased the number of sectors in which foreign investments are allowed: UNCTC, *National Legislation and Regulations Relating to Transnational Corporations Volume IV* (1986, UN Doc ST/CTC/53), pp. 198–200; Kim, 'Legal aspects of foreign investment in Korea', 15 Hastings Int'l & Comp. L. Rev. 227 (1992). See also the reform of the Andean Investment Code in chapter 16 at pp. 575–7.

83 Decree of the Minister of Finance No. 28/1972 on economic associations with foreign capital participation, amended by Decree no. 7/1977 of 6 May 1977: 17 ILM 1451 (1978). Comment: Lorinczi and Dorian, 10 Law & Pol. Int'l Bus. 1205 (1978); Szasz, 10 Int'l Bus. Lawyer 99 (1982). Superseded by Decree Law No. 34 of 1986 on Some Aspects of the Rules on Economic Associations (Presidential Council).

84 Associated Labour Act of 25 November 1976; Law on Investment of Resources of Foreign Persons in Domestic (Yugoslav) Organisations of Associated Labour 7 April 1978: 18 ILM 230 (1979) as amended: 24 ILM 315 (1985). Comment: Grozdanic, 9 Yugoslav Law 59 (1982); Loughlin, 17 JWTL 12 (1983); Artisien and Buckley, 18 JWTL p. 163 (1984). A law permitting wholly foreign owned enterprises was passed in 1989: Law on Foreign Investments of 8 January 1989: 28 ILM 1543 (1989).

85 In Poland foreign investment was initially limited to so-called 'Polonia' investments by persons of Polish origin resident outside Poland under the Decree of 14 May 1976 of the Polish Council of Ministers, later replaced by Decree No. 146 of 1982 on principles for conducting business by foreign legal and physical persons in Poland in the field of small industry. Large-scale joint ventures were permitted for the first time under the law of 23 April 1986 on companies with foreign capital participation. See further: Scriven, 14 JWTL 424 (1980); Burzynski and Juergensmeyer, 14 Vanderbilt Jo. Transnat. Law 17 (1981); Greenberg, 16 Geo. Washington Jo. Int'l Law & Econ. 377 (1982); Weralski, 23 European Taxation 144 (1983); Jadach, 18 Cornell Int'l Jo. 63. (1985); Mahmassani, 3 ICSID Rev-FILJ (1988), p. 286.

86 Decree No. 424 of 2 November 1972 and see Decrees on Regulation and Taxation of Joint Companies: 12 ILM 656, 657 (1983).

87 Edict No. 535 concerning economic collaboration between Bulgarian juridical persons and foreign juridical and physical persons of 25 March 1980: 19 ILM 992 (1980). comment: Kuiper, 20 European Taxation 293 (1980). Bulgaria liberalized its foreign investment law to allow for foreign ownership of Bulgarian enterprises and wholly owned foreign enterprises

212 Regulation by Home and Host States

in 1992: 'Bulgaria eases curbs on foreign investment', *Financial Times*, 10 February 1992, p. 2.

88 The Law on Joint Ventures of 1 July 1979: 18 ILM 1163 (1979) as amended on April 4 1990: *Beijing Review*, 7–13 May 1990, pp. 27–8; Regulations for Implementation of Law on Joint Ventures of Sept. 20, 1983: 22 ILM 1033 (1983).

89 *Financial Times*, 12 February 1987, p. 5: 'Czechs plan to bring in joint venture law', and ibid. 9 October 1987, p. 23.

90 Ethiopia: Joint Venture Establishment Proclamation No. 235/1983, Negarit Gazeta 1983, p. 22. North Korea: Joint Venture Law of 1985: 24 ILM 806 (1985). North Korea recently passed a new foreign investment law which allows foreign companies to set up wholly owned facilities in special economic zones: 'N. Korea unveils law on foreign investment', *Financial Times*, 21 October 1992, p. 6. Cuba: Legislative Decree No. 50 on Economic Association between Cuban and Foreign Entities of 15 February 1982: 21 ILM 1106 (1982). comment: Zorn and Mayerson, 21 Col. Jo. Transnat. Law 273 (1983). Vietnam: Law on Foreign Investment, with Amendments and Additions 29 December 1987, 30 June 1990: 30 ILM 930 (1991); Decree Regulating in Detail the Implementation of the Law on Foreign Investment 6 February 1991: 30 ILM 942 (1991).

91 Decree on Joint Enterprises with Western and Developing Countries 13 January 1987: 26 ILM 749 (1987).

92 *Financial Times*, 10 May 1991, p. 6: 'Albania starts to lift barriers in investment drive'.

93 For an earlier comparative account see: D. Campbell and M. Miller (eds), *Legal Aspects of Joint Ventures in Eastern Europe* (Kluwer, 1981); see also UNCTC, Transnational Corporations in World Development (note 58 above), chapter XVIII, 'Joint venture policies of the socialist countries of Eastern Europe'.

94 Journal of Laws (Dziennik Ustaw Polskiej Rzeczpospolitej Ludowej) No. 41 of 28 December 1988, item 325, effective 1 January 1989; English translation: 28 ILM 1518 (1989). See: Piontek, 'Polish Foreign Investment Law 1988' 23 JWT 5 (No. 5, 1989). The 1988 Law was amended in 1990: see further Gordon, 'The Polish Foreign Investment Law of 1990', 24 Int'l Law 335 (1990).

95 Act of 14 June 1991, Journal of Laws (Dziennik Ustaw Rzeczpospolitej Polskiej) [1991] No. 60, 4 July 1991, item 253; English translation 30 ILM 871 (1991). For commentary see Allen and Overy, *Key Legal Facts for the Foreign Investor in Poland* (1991).

96 'Grounds of Justification for the Bill on enterprises with foreign participation' (Uzasadnienie) Sejm Rzeczpospolitej Polskiej X kadencja Prezes Rady Ministrow Print (Druck) No. 765 of 22 February 1991 (RM 10-292-91), at p. 1. I am grateful to Mr Grzegorz Namiotkiewicz of the Polish Bar for supplying a copy of this document.

97 1991 Act, article 4(1).

98 Ibid., article 4(2).

99 Ibid., article 6(1).

100 Ibid., article 6(3)–(4). The procedure for application and approval of permits is set out in articles 12–19. The conduct of activities that require

a permit without such authorization may lead to a court petition for the invalidation of such acts: article 20.

101　Ibid., article 22.

102　Ibid., article 23.

103　Ibid., articles 25, 26.

104　Hungary Act No. XCVIII (1990) s. 1. See further Pogany, 'Recent developments in the law relating to foreign investment in Hungary', 6 ICSID Rev-FILJ 114 (1991). The current framework of the law relating to foreign investment in Hungary was laid down in Act XXIV of 1988 which is reproduced in English in 4 ICSID Rev-FILJ 148 (1989). See further Pogany, 'The regulation of foreign investment in Hungary', 4 ICSID Rev-FILJ 39 (1989); Eichmann, 'Legal aspects of doing business in Hungary', 24 Int'l Law 957 (1990). Act XXIV of 1988 was amended by Act No. XLIV (1989); Act No. V (1990); and Act No. XCVIII (1990). Further amendments were introduced in 1994: see European Bank of Reconstruction and Development, *Transition Report* (October 1994), p. 126.

105　Ibid., s. 10.

106　See Pogany, 'Recent developments' (note 104 above), at pp. 116–17.

107　Act No. 173 of 1988 as amended by Act No. 112 of April 19, 1990. See further Mahmassani, 'The legal framework for foreign investment in Czechoslovakia', 6 ICSID Rev-FILJ 65 (1991). These laws have now been superseded by Part I, chapter II, of the 1991 Commercial Code (Act No. 513 of 5 November 1991): see European Bank of Reconstruction and Development, *Transition Report* (October 1994), p. 124.

108　Ibid., article 7(2).

109　Ibid., articles 22 and 9.

110　'Profile Skoda Automobilova', *Financial Times Survey: Czech Republic*, 24 March 1993, p. IV.

111　*Financial Times*, 14 June 1991, p. 2: 'Czechs hang "for sale" sign on 50 of republic's key companies.' See further R. Frydman *et al.*, *The Privatization Process in Central Europe* (Central European University Press, 1993), pp. 38–92.

112　'Czechs plan second wave of privatisation', Financial Times, 11 March 1993, p. 4. Slovak investors will be allowed to own shares in privatised Czech enterprises: 'Czechs allow transfer of shares to Slovakia', *Financial Times*, 13 May 1993, p. 2.

113　*Financial Times*, 28 June 1991, p. 3: 'Poles publish details of mass privatisation'. See further Dr K. Bandyk, *Privatization in Poland: Program, Achievements and Foreign Investment Policy* (Ministry of Ownership Changes, 1991). The legal basis for Poland's privatization programme can be found in the Act on the Privatization of State-Owned Enterprises of 13 July 1990. See further Frydman *et al.* (note 111 above), at pp. 146–207.

114　'Warsaw clear to privatise 600 ventures', *Financial Times*, 1/2 May 1993, p. 2.

115　See Act LXXIV of 1990 on Privatization of State-owned Enterprises; on 'shell companies' see the Transformation Act (Act VI of 1988 as amended and Act No. XIII of 1989). See further Frydman *et al.* (note 111 above), at pp. 93–145.

116　As witnessed by the Provisions of the State Council Encouraging Foreign

Investment of 11 October 1986, *Beijing Review*, No. 43, 27 October 1986, pp. 26–8.

117   Note 88 above. For full analysis see: M. J. Moser (ed.), *Foreign Trade, Investment and the Law in the People's Republic of China*, 2nd edn (Oxford University Press, 1987); comment Rich, 15 Int'l Lawyer 183 (1981); Topp, 14 Jo. of Int. Law & Econ. 133; Therowy, 14 Jo. of Int. Law & Econ. 185; Jaslow, 31 (1983) Am. Jo. Comp. L. 209; Rui Mu, 22 (1983–4) Col. Jo. Transnat. L. 61; Fenwick, 40 Bus. Law 839 (1985); Wei, *Beijing Review*, No. 22, 2 June 1986, pp. 4–5.

118   Law on Chinese–Foreign Contractual Joint Ventures 13 April 1988, *Beijing Review*, 20–26 June 1988, p. 29.

119   Law on Enterprises Operated Exclusively with Foreign Capital, 12 April 1986, *Beijing Review*, No. 18, 5 May 1986, p. 16.

120   1979 Joint Venture Law articles 4 and 2.

121   1988 Law article 3. An equity joint venture is also referred to as a 'legal person' in article 2 of the 1983 regulations (note 88 above).

122   See, however, the Opinions on Standards for Companies Limited by Shares of 19 June 1992 and Opinions on Standards for Limited Liability Companies promulgated by the State Commission for Restructuring the Economy of 22 June 1992 discussed in Wohlgemuth, 'Joint stock and limited liability companies in the law of the People's Republic of China' [1993] 1 ICCLR 12.

123   1979 Law article 4.

124   Moser (note 117 above), at p. 102.

125   See the 1983 Regulations (note 88 above), chapter II, articles 8–10. For the procedures applicable to contractual joint ventures see 1988 Law article 5, which lays down a 45-day limit for the making of a decision.

126   1983 Regulations ibid., article 5.

127   1979 Law article 3; 1988 Law article 6.

128   1979 Law article 4.

129   Ibid., article 5.

130   Ibid., article 6, as amended. The original provision required that the chairman be appointed by the Chinese participant.

131   Ibid., article 7.

132   Ibid., article 10.

133   Ibid., article 8, as amended. Under the 1979 law such an account could only be opened with the Bank of China.

134   Note 88 above.

135   Ibid., article 110.

136   Ibid., article 111.

137   See further chapter 17 at p. 633.

138   On ICSID see chapter 15 at pp. 540–60. The PRC accepts ICSID jurisdiction only in relation to disputes over the level of compensation payable upon expropriation of foreign owned property. See further Koa, 'The International Bank for Reconstruction and Development and dispute resolution: conciliating and arbitrating with China through the International Centre for the Settlement of Investment Disputes', 24 NYUJ Int'l Law and Pol. 439 (1991).

139 See Moser (note 117 above), at p. 102.

140 See ibid. at pp. 111–16.

141 See *Financial Times Survey: China*, 14 December 1988, p. 4.

142 1986 Law article 6. Detailed Rules for the Implementation of the Law on Wholly Foreign Owned Enterprises in China of 28 October 1990, article 8: see *China Economic News Supplement* 1991, 3.4, or SC 12/12/90 [1991] China Law and Practice 35; see also MOFERT PRC, *Wholly Foreign Owned Enterprise Law Implementing Rules Explanation 6 December 1991* [1992], China Law and Practice 30.

143 1986 Law article 3.

144 Ibid., article 9.

145 Ibid., article 8.

146 Moser (note 117 above), at p. 127. But see Wohlgemuth (note 122 above).

147 Ibid., article 5.

148 See ICSID, News Release of 7 January 1993; News from ICSID, Vol. 10, No. 1 (Winter 1993), p. 1.

149 Ibid., article 11.

150 Ibid., article 19.

151 Articles 12–13.

152 Article 14.

153 Article 17.

154 Article 16.

155 Article 18.

156 See UNCTC, *Transnational Corporations in World Development* (note 58 above), at pp. 84–5, box V.1. See further M. M. Pearson, *Joint Ventures in the People's Republic of China* (Princeton University Press, 1992).

157 See *Financial Times*, 30 January 1986: 'Foreign investment commitments fail to satisfy Chinese'.

158 See *Financial Times*, 11 January 1990, p. 4: 'China prepares to woo Western financiers' and 'World Bank likely to resume lending within a few weeks'.

159 See generally the survey of business opinion from several countries exporting direct investment capital to the PRC in the *Financial Times*, 30 June 1989, p. 8.

160 'Lure of the billion-buyer market', *Financial Times*, 14 June 1993, p. 2.

161 Note 91 above. See further M. M. Boguslavskii, *Joint Ventures with the USSR* (I. B. Tauris & Co., 1992).

162 See further UNCTAD Consultant Study, 'USSR: new management mechanism in foreign economic relations', UNCTAD/ST/TSC/10, 2 October 1987; The Economist, 9 April 1988: 'A survey of the Soviet economy'; Jerry F. Hough, *Opening up the Soviet Economy* (Brookings Institution, 1988).

163 *Financial Times*, 11 January 1990, p. 3: 'West slow in reforging Soviet industry'.

164 English translation in 31 ILM 397 (1992).

165 See the Introductory note to the Russian law by W. Frenkel (ibid.) at p. 397.

166   Ibid., article 3.
167   Ibid., article 6.
168   Ibid., article 7. By article 8 this compensation must be proportional to the real value of the expropriated investment, must be paid without delay and must be paid by the expropriating entity.
169   Ibid., article 9. This is significant given the fact that Russia has concluded several BITs with Western states and has signed the Washington Convention on the Settlement of Investment Disputes on 16 June 1992: see ICSID, *Annual Report 1992*, annex 1 at p. 13.
170   Ibid., article 10.
171   Ibid., article 11.
172   Ibid., articles 12–15, 19.
173   Ibid., articles 16, 17.
174   Ibid., article 18.
175   Ibid., chapter 4 (articles 20–34).
176   Ibid., chapter 5 and article 37 thereof. The Russian privatization programme is governed by the Law on Privatization of State and Municipal Enterprises in the Russian Federation 1991 as amended 5 June 1992. See further R. Frydman *et al.*, *The Privatization Process in Russia, Ukraine and the Baltic States* (Central European University Press, 1993), pp. 1–82.
177   Ibid., chapter 6 (articles 38–40).
178   Ibid., chapter 7 (articles 41–2). In the FEZ foreign investors are entitled to a simplified registration procedure, and advantageous tax regime, lowered rates of compensation for land use, lower customs duties on imports and exports and simplified entry and exit procedures for foreign nationals. St Petersburg (formerly Leningrad) has been designated as a FEZ.
179   See World Bank, *Foreign Direct Investment in the States of the Former USSR* (Washington DC, 1992). The World Bank study does not claim to be definitive. As a result considerable uncertainty remains as to the scope and effect of the laws surveyed. The study deals with the foreign investment laws of Azerbaijan, Belarus, Estonia, Kazakhstan, Kirghizia, Latvia, Lithuania, Russia, Ukraine and Uzbekistan. Obviously it is beyond the scope of this work to offer more than a brief summary based on the World Bank study. For a more recent survey see European Bank of Reconstruction and Development, *Transition Report* (October 1994), chapter 9.
180   See ibid., pp. 22–37.
181   Ibid., at pp. 36–7.
182   See 'Investors see a new star rising slowly in the east', *Financial Times*, 5 January 1993, p. 17.
183   Wallace (note 2 above), at p. 61.
184   For the 1984 reforms see Sandra F. Maviglia, 'Mexico's guidelines for foreign investment: the selective promotion of necessary industries', 80 AJIL 281 (1986). For the 1989 reforms see Etienne, 'The new investment opportunity: Mexico', BIFD (September 1992), p. 419.
185   Published in Diario Oficial de la Federacion, 27 December 1993, first section, pp. 92–9; English translation in 33 ILM 207 (1994).
186   The economic activities listed in article 8 are: port services to vessels engaged in internal navigation; shipping corporations engaged exclusively

in high seas operations; administration of air traffic terminals; private education at all levels; legal services; credit information services, securities rating institutions; insurance brokers; cellular telephones; oil pipeline construction; drilling of oil and gas wells.

187   Ibid., article 9 and tenth transitory article. The threshold figure will be reviewed annually.

188   Ibid., article 26(II).

189   Ibid., article 29.

190   Ibid.

191   Ibid., article 30.

192   See ibid., article 5, which lists e.g. petroleum, electricity, railroads, posts and telecommunications.

193   See ibid., article 6, which lists e.g. national land transportation, radio and television other than cable TV and retail gasoline sales.

194   See Canada–Mexico–United States North American Free Trade Agreement 17 December 1992, Part Five, Investment, Services and Related Matters: 32 ILM 605 at pp. 639–70 (1993). See further chapter 7 at pp. 239–45.

195   Ghana Investment Code 1985 (PNDC Law 116, 17 July 1985) summarized in UNCTC, *National Legislation and Regulations Relating to Transnational Corporations, Volume VII* (1989 UN Doc. ST/CTC/91) pp. 21–24; comment Laryea (note 43 above). For similar screening laws in other African countries see: Zambia, Investment Act, 1991 (No. 19 of 1991); Uganda, Investment Code, 1991 (Statute No. 1, 1991); Tanzania, National Investment (Promotion and Protection) Act (Act No. 10 of 1990) reproduced in 6 ICSID Rev-FILJ 292 (1991) or 3 RADIC 840 (1991), see also Peter 'Promotion and protection of foreign investments in Tanzania: a new investment code', 6 ICSID Rev-FILJ 42 (1991); Nigeria, Industrial Development Co-ordination Committee Act 1988 (note 33 above); Cameroon, Kofele-Kale, 'Investment codes as an instrument of economic policy: a Cameroon case study', 25 Int'l Law 821 (1991). See also Parra (note 4 above).

196   See Investment Code 1985 s. 16 and Schedule; UNCTC, ibid., at pp. 25–6 for the list of reserved enterprise sectors.

197   Insurance requires at least 60 per cent Ghanaian participation; banking requires at least 40 per cent Ghanaian participation.

198   Investment Code 1985 s. 21(1) and (3).

199   Ibid., s. 22(1).

200   Ibid., s. 24.

201   Ibid., s. 25(1).

202   Ibid., s. 25(2).

203   Ibid., s. 23.

204   Ibid., s. 22(4).

205   Ibid., s. 26(1).

206   Ibid., s. 21(4) and (5).

207   Ibid., s. 26(2).

208   Ibid., ss 12–15, ss 18–20; summarized in UNCTC (note 195 above), at pp. 29–33.

209   For details see ibid., s. 12(1).

210 See text at notes 24–27 above.
211 See Law No. 66-1008 of 28 December 1966 [1966] Journal Officiel 11621; Decree No. 67-78 of 1967 [1967] Journal Officiel 1073 and 1074; Decrees Nos 71-143 and 71-144 of 1971 discussed in Wallace (note 2 above), at pp. 63–5; Decrees Nos 80-617 and 80-618 of 4 August 1980 concerning Community Investments. See further UNCTC, *National Legislation and Regulations Relating to Transnational Corporations: a Technical Paper* (UN Doc. ST/CTC/35, 1983), pp. 316–32; Safarian (note 5 above).
212 See Royal Decree 1265/1986 of 27 June 1986 chapters II, VI, VII and VIII as amended 1991; Royal Decree 2077/1986 of 25 September 1986 sections II, VI, VII and VIII. English translation in 26 ILM 727–44 (1987).
213 See Foreign Acquisitions and Takeovers Act 1975 as amended at 30 November 1991 (PRA 26/91) – Cat No. 91 4742 2. See further Breit, 'Australian multinationals: growth or survival?' 10 JWTL 265 (1976); Ryan, 'Foreign investment in Australia and New Zealand', 54 ALJ 443 (1980); Hamilton, 'New foreign investment rules for Australia', 50 ALJ 574 (1976); D. Flint, *Foreign Investment Law in Australia* (Law Book Co., 1985). The Act has been appplied in an increasingly relaxed manner in recent years. The Foreign Investment Review Board approves 95 per cent of applications from overseas companies to acquire stakes of over 15 per cent in Australian companies in accordance with the requirements of s. 18 of the Act: 'Australia faces an identity crisis', *Financial Times*, 14 December 1992, p. 21.
214 Overseas Investment Act 1973 (No. 14, 1973) reprinted as on 1 August 1989: Reprinted Statutes Vol. 24, p. 617; Overseas Investment Regulations 1985: 1985/256 Statutory regulations Vol. 3, p. 1287; Overseas Investment Exemption Notice 1985: 1985/272; UNCTC, *National Legislation and Regulations Relating to Transnational Corporations Volume VI* (1988 UN Doc. ST/CTC/71), at pp. 132–6.
215 See Turner, 'Canadian regulation of foreign direct investment', 23 Harv. ILJ 333 at 335–7 (1983). See also Franck and Gudgeon, 'Canada's foreign investment control experiment: the law, the context and the practice', 50 NYULR 76 at 77–84 (1975).
216 These were: (a) the Government of Canada Task Force Report, *Foreign Ownership and the Structure of Canadian Industry* (Queen's Printer, 1968) commonly referred to as the 'Watkins Report' after the head of the Task Force; (b) the *Eleventh Report of the Standing Committee on External Affairs and National Defence Respecting Canada–US Relations*: 28th Parl. 2d Sess. s. 3.01 (1970), commonly referred to as the 'Wahn Report'; (c) *Foreign Direct Investment in Canada* (Information Canada, 1972), commonly referred to as the 'Gray Report' after Herbert Gray, the head of the Governmental Working Group set up to review Canada's policy on direct investment. For a discussion of these reports see: Franck and Gudgeon (note 215 above), at pp. 98–105; A. Rugman, *Multinationals in Canada: Theory, Performance and Economic Impact* (Martinus Nijhoff, 1980), chapter 9, reprinted from 10 JWTL 171–6 (1976); Leckow and Mallory, 'The relaxation of foreign investment restrictions in Canada', 6 ICSID Rev-FILJ 1 at 1–11 (1991).

217 See Franck and Gudgeon (note 215 above), at p. 107; Rugman, ibid., at p. 129.
218 Ibid., at pp. 108–111.
219 Chapter 46, 1973–4 Statutes of Canada 620 amended by chapter 52, 1976–7 Statutes of Canada 1274. For an analysis of the provisions of FIRA see: Turner (note 215 above), at pp. 338–41; Franck and Gudgeon (note 215 above), at pp. 111–42; Donaldson and Jackson, 'The Foreign Investment Review Act: an analysis of the legislation', 52 Can. Bar. Rev. 171 (1975).
220 Ibid., s. 2(1).
221 The criteria listed included *inter alia* the effect of the investment on employment, resource processing, exports from Canada, productivity, competition, technological and product development, the degree of Canadian participation, and general national industrial and economic policy goals.
222 The Act came into operation in two phases: the first came into effect on 9 April 1974 concerning the takeover of existing Canadian firms by foreign investors, the second on 15 October 1975 concerning the setting up of new businesses in Canada.
223 Rugman (note 216 above), at p. 129.
224 Undertakings could be agreed with investors in five areas: the production of export goods; the location of research and development in Canada; the processing of raw materials in Canada; the hiring of Canadian managers and directors; and the purchasing of Canadian goods and services.
225 Ibid., ss 10–11.
226 R. K. Paterson, *Canadian Regulation of International Trade and Investment* (Carswell, 1986), at p. 299.
227 See Turner (note 215 above), at p. 341; Rugman (note 216 above), at pp. 134ff, reprinted from 11 JWTL 322–33 (1977).
228 Turner (note 215 above), at pp. 336–7.
229 See Turner (note 215 above), at pp. 344–6. For a fuller account of this proceeding see Paterson (note 226 above), at pp. 300–4, on which the next paragraph is based. The Report of the GATT Panel was adopted on 7 February 1984 (L/5504): see BISD 30th Supplement, p. 140 (1984).
230 Statutes of Canada 1985 c. 20. See Paterson (note 226 above), at pp. 316–17 for a note of the political background to this statute. For analysis of the Act see further: Paterson, ibid., pp. 317–35; Glover, New and Lacourciere, 'The Investment Canada Act: a new approach to the regulation of foreign investment in Canada', 41 Business Lawyer 83 (1985); Grover, 'The Investment Canada Act', 10 Can. Bus. LJ 475 (1985); Rose, 'Foreign investment in Canada: the new Investment Canada Act', 20 Int'l Law 19 (1986); Arnett, 'From FIRA to Investment Canada', 24 Alta L. Rev. 1 (1985); Evans, 'Canada for sale: the Investment Canada Act', 21 JWTL 85 (1987); Leckow and Mallory (note 216 above).
231 A 'non-Canadian' is defined by s. 3 of the 1985 Act as 'an individual, a government or an agency thereof or an entity that is not Canadian'. 'Canadian' is defined by s. 3 as (a) a Canadian citizen; (b) a permanent resident of Canada who has been resident in Canada for not more than

one year after the time at which he first became eligible to apply for Canadian citizenship; (c) a federal, provincial or local government of Canada or an agency thereof; (d) a corporation, partnership, trust or joint venture determined in accordance with s. 26 of the Act to be Canadian controlled. By s. 26 Canadian control is established by the existence of a Canadian voting majority in the company, or by *de facto* Canadian control despite a non-Canadian majority of voting shares as where the Canadian minority is the controlling group or two-thirds of the board has Canadian members.

232   Investment Canada Act 1985, s. 11. The Investment Canada Agency is set up under ss 6–9 of the Act.

233   See Grover (note 230 above), at pp. 476–7.

234   Ibid., s. 13(1)(b)(ii).

235   S. 3 of the 1985 Act defines a 'new Canadian business' as a business that is not already being carried on in Canada by the non-Canadian and that, at the time it is established, is either unrelated to any other business being carried on in Canada by the non-Canadian, or is related to another business being carried on in Canada by that non-Canadian but falls within a prescribed specific type of business activity that, in the opinion of the Governor in Council, is related to Canada's cultural heritage or national identity.

236   Ibid., s. 15.

237   Defined in s. 3 of the 1985 Act as a business that (a) has a place of business in Canada; (b) has an individual or individuals in Canada that are employed or self-employed in connection with that business; and (c) has assets in Canada used in carrying on that business.

238   Ibid., s. 29.

239   Ibid., s. 28(3).

240   That is, the cases listed in s. 28(1)(a)–(d)(i) above.

241   As defined in s. 28(1)(d)(ii) above.

242   See chapter 7 at pp. 240–1.

243   See *Dow Jones & Co. Inc.* v *Attorney-General of Canada* (1980) 113 DLR (3d) 395 aff'd 122 DLR (3d) 731 (FCA 1981); *A-G of Canada* v *Fallbridge Holdings Ltd* 63 NR 17 (FCA 1985) cited in Paterson (note 226 above), at pp. 324–6; see further O'Laughlin, 'Extraterritorial application of Canadian Foreign Investment Review', 8 NW J. Int'l Law & Bus. 436 (1987); Romer, 'Was the sigh of relief premature? the Investment Canada Act', 19 Vand. J. Transnt'l Law 613 (1986).

244   Paterson, ibid., at p. 325.

245   Ibid., s. 21(1) and Glover *et al.* (note 230 above), at p. 95.

246   Ibid.

247   Ibid., s. 20.

248   Ibid., s. 22(2)–(3).

249   Ibid., s. 23(1).

250   Ibid., s. 24.

251   Ibid., ss 39–41.

252   See *Financial Times*, 22 December 1987, p. 27: 'Tide turns as inflows rise and barriers fall'. According to this source, in 1981 gross inflows of capital

into Canada amounted to C$4.8 billion. In 1986 gross inflows amounted to C$7.5 billion, giving a net foreign direct investment figure of C$1.6 billion after deducting outflows.

253 The 1985 Act contains statutory duties placed upon the Minister to encourage business investment in Canada: s. 5(1).

254 Glover *et al.* (note 230 above), at p. 98.

255 *Financial Times*, 21 June 1991, p. 23: 'Canada blocks de Havilland sale to European groups'.

256 See Paterson (note 226 above), at p. 331 and s. 36 of the 1985 Act.

257 Paterson, ibid., at p. 334.

258 See further Grover (note 230 above), esp. at pp. 480–1.

259 See for further examples Seidman, 'Foreign private investors and the host country', 19 JWTL 637 at 651–4 (1985).

7

Measures for the Encouragement of Inward Direct Investment

In chapter 6 techniques for the control of inward direct investment were considered. The present chapter considers the positive promotion of foreign investment as an aspect of the liberalization of investment conditions identified in the previous chapter. It looks, first, at host states' techniques for ensuring open access for investors and for encouraging investment through incentives. Secondly, it goes beyond unilateral measures taken by host states and looks at bilateral and multilateral initiatives for the liberalization of controls over entry and establishment by foreign investors. These developments must be examined as a potential, if not actual, source of restraint on the absolute sovereignty of nation states over the entry and establishment of foreign investors within their jurisdiction.

1 The Encouragement of Inward Direct Investment by Host States

This section considers the principal techniques used by host states seeking to ensure an 'open door' to foreign investors. The prerequisite for such an approach is the absence of onerous administrative measures for the approval of foreign investments and the general absence of ownership, control or performance requirements as a condition of entry. In addition to the absence of such controls, certain states may offer investment incentives in the form of new opportunities for investment as a result of deregulation and privatization policies, fiscal or other benefits associated with inward investment, and the creation of special economic zones for export-oriented investment. The content of national laws in areas relevant to foreign investors, such as planning regulations, corporate disclosure requirements or labour relations, may also be framed in a manner that is attractive to their interests. Finally, states may offer constitutional guarantees for the peaceful enjoyment of private property and may reinforce these by the conclusion of bilateral investment treaties (BITs), which subject the host contracting state's treatment of investors from the other contracting state to the international minimum standards of treatment contained in the treaty.[1] However, as shown in chapter 6, even in states espousing an 'open door' to foreign investors, there are likely to be sectors that are excluded from foreign investment. Furthermore, in the absence of privileged concessions, foreign investors will be subjected to the principle of 'national treatment'[2] and will be expected to follow the general commercial and other applicable laws of the land. In this sense, foreign investors are never absolutely free to invest or act as they please. Finally, it should be stressed that 'open door' policies may be espoused by states following a policy of high governmental regulation in the economy. In this sense, the techniques described below are not exclusively associated with free-market economies.

1.1   Host States without Specialized Controls on Inward Direct Investment

Numerous states have adopted an 'open door' policy on inward direct investment.[3] In particular, the Member States of the OECD have pledged themselves to the progressive removal of restrictions on inward investment under the Code for the Liberalization of Capital Movements.[4] The majority of the OECD states espouse this approach, though not without reservations. Of these the UK and USA have among the most liberal regimes.

The UK has traditionally welcomed inward direct investment under successive Conservative and Labour administrations.[5] Under the present Conservative government policy has swung decisively towards the encouragement of inward investment. In 1979, the then newly elected Conservative government suspended controls over inward capital movements under the Exchange Control Act of 1947.[6] The Exchange Control Act was itself repealed in 1987, thereby removing the only significant restrictions on inward and outward investment under UK law. The only remaining powers relevant to the control of inward investment are those given to the Secretary of State for Trade and Industry under the scheme of 'golden shares' in privatized companies and under the Industry Act of 1975, both discussed in chapter 6, and under the merger control provisions of the Fair Trading Act 1973, which may be used to prevent the takeover of a British company by a foreign investor where this is deemed to be against the public interest. These powers will be considered in chapter 11.

The general policy of the former Conservative government was outlined in 1982 by the then Secretary of State for Trade and Industry, Patrick Jenkin, in terms that are still of relevance today:

> The government is committed to maintaining and strengthening the operation of market forces in order to improve the country's economic performance. A free flow of inward investment contributes to this central policy objective by introducing additional productive capacity to compete with established sources in the UK and with imports as well as to raise exports. Such investment, often bringing new technological skills and managerial expertise, thus tends to increase both the quality and quantity of output and employment in this country.[7]

British policy on inward investment has involved not only the removal of exchange controls but also the positive encouragement of investors through the activities of regional and national investment promotion agencies, the selective use of industrial aid and the setting up of enterprise zones and free ports. These will be considered in more detail in the next section.

Like the UK, the USA adopts an 'open door' to inward investment on the ground that free market forces in the global circulation of capital promote economic efficiency and should be encouraged.[8] The freedom of entry and establishment into the USA is enshrined in the network of friendship, commerce and navigation (FCN) Treaties concluded since the Second World War by the USA with its principal trading partners from among the developed nations.[9] This freedom is protected in FCN Treaties by the principle of 'national treatment', whereby the foreign corporation is entitled to the same treatment within the USA as is accorded in like situations to US corporations.[10] This includes the right to form a locally incorporated subsidiary, which will then enjoy the same rights, and be subject to the same duties, as a US corporation. FCN Treaties do not provide for treatment better than national treatment for the US subsidiaries of foreign MNEs, but merely assure to them 'the right to conduct business on an equal basis without suffering discrimination based on their alienage'.[11] Such treaties can override conflicting provisions of US law as they are generally deemed to be 'self-executing', thereby possessing the force of a superior rule of law within the US legal system.[12]

On the other hand, as seen in chapter 6, the 'open door' principle is not unqualified under US law. Legal restrictions on foreign ownership in given sectors,[13] and the controls imposed by the Exon-Florio amendment,[14] have been introduced. Furthermore, foreign investors face not inconsiderable levels of regulation under US domestic laws in accordance with the principle of 'national treatment' and permissible exceptions thereto. Thus, the investor is subject to disclosure requirements in the areas of company law, securities regulation and taxation.[15] Specialized disclosure requirements cover acquisitions of agricultural land by foreign investors under the Agricultural Foreign Investment Disclosure Act 1978.[16] Furthermore, foreign investors are subject to specific reporting requirements under the International Investment and Trade in Services Survey Act of 1976.[17] By this statute, a foreign national or corporate entity or other foreign person who creates, buys or sells a 10 per cent or greater voting interest in a US business enterprise or in US real estate must submit a report to the Bureau of Economic Analysis of the Department of Commerce. The report must be filed within forty-five days of the acquisition being made and must contain information as to: the legal interest established or transferred; the identity of the transferor, the transferee and the beneficial owner of the interest; the enterprise or property in which the interest is held; the management and financial structure of the US affiliate and the composition of its debts assets and income; and, finally, the extent of transnational trade in goods or services conducted or to be conducted by the US affiliate.[18] In addition to such transactional reporting requirements, the 1976 Act introduced a duty to make annual reports and five yearly reports on the investment.[19] A quarterly report is required from any US affiliate exceeding an exemption level of $10 million.[20] Thus, US disclosure requirements recognize the special need for information concerning the acquisition of US enterprises by foreign investors. However, even with these requirements, the USA remains one of the most open economies in the world.

1.2 Investment Incentives

Several states employ incentives to attract internationally mobile foreign investors. These may be available only after the official approval of a project by the relevant screening agency, or they may be available as of right once the foreign investor has decided to invest. The justification for incentives is that they may reduce risk to investors, thereby making the host state more attractive to them. This can be achieved either through direct subsidies (e.g. waiver of export or import duties, concessions from indirect taxes, rates or other charges, or industrial development grants) or by way of income tax incentives.[21] Such policies are likely to be favoured by countries that would otherwise be of marginal interest to foreign investors on purely economic grounds.

One of the pioneers of an incentive-led inward investment policy has been the Republic of Ireland. Since 1958, the Republic has offered fiscal incentives to manufacturers.[22] Currently, the major incentive consists of a 10 per cent maximum corporate tax rate for manufacturing profits until 31 December 2010. The maximum rate for profits earned in other ways is 40 per cent.[23] This has resulted in Ireland being used by foreign MNEs as a 'tax haven' jurisdiction. MNEs have structured their operations so as to take full advantage of the lower tax rates, either by the use of off-shore holding companies controlling an unincorporated entity in Ireland, thereby allowing Irish profits to be reinvested abroad without subjection to tax in the home state of the parent company, or by using international transfer pricing manipulations to inflate the profits of Irish subsidiaries.[24] More recently, new incentives have been introduced to encourage the location of international funds management in Ireland, in competition with Luxembourg and other locations.[25]

Similarly, Singapore has offered incentives to foreign manufacturers since the 1960s. At that time the government of Lee Kuan Yew adopted a growth strategy based on an expansion of export-oriented manufacturing dominated by MNE investors.[26] To achieve this objective the government established free zones offering tariff, tax and regulatory reliefs to businesses located therein. These zones permitted firms to trade without restriction with the rest of the world, to process goods for export at low cost and to benefit from offshore banking facilities free from exchange controls. In addition the government established tax incentives for so-called 'pioneer industries' to set up new capital and technology intensive projects in the country. Other tax allowances were made available as incentives for, among other things, expansion of investments or exports, for the setting up of technical service and research and development activities or for construction projects.[27]

Economically developed countries may use investment incentives to attract internationally mobile investors to the less developed regions of the country. UK policy in this field offers a good illustration. Selective assistance to foreign and domestic investors is available both on a local and on a regional level. The basic approach is to provide financial incentives through discretionary grants and aids to industry, as well as selective concessions on fiscal and other legal obligations that would otherwise extend to the investor. In this there is an element of industrial planning aimed at alleviating the economic and social problems caused by the decline of traditional industries in certain regions and cities of the UK.

On the local level, local authorities are empowered under part III of the Local Government and Housing Act 1989 to promote the economic development of their areas. In so doing, they may provide local assistance to industry in the way of: grants, loans or guarantees of borrowing to the investor; investing in a person's undertaking by acquiring share or loan capital in that body; or providing persons with property, services or other financial benefit. Further assistance is available to reclaim derelict land under the Derelict Land Act 1982. There are also a number of schemes for inner city regeneration, including the City Grant as a means of encouraging private capital to redevelop inner urban sites, the Urban Programme of central government assistance to local authorities, local assistance in the creation of 'improvement areas' under the Inner Urban Areas Act 1978 and assistance to industry from Urban Development Corporations.[28] Furthermore, certain inner city and docklands areas have been designated 'enterprise zones', areas in which the usual planning and local revenue requirements do not apply.[29]

On the regional level, regional development agencies have been set up for Scotland, Wales and Northern Ireland to further economic development in their regions. Of these, the Industrial Development Board for Northern Ireland deserves special mention. It is responsible for the promotion of inward investment into the region, and is empowered to offer assistance which is more generous than that available for other regions of the UK, in view of the higher than average rates of unemployment in the region and the difficulties caused by the local political situation. Thus, tax-free grants of up to 50 per cent of the cost of new factory buildings, machinery and equipment may be available depending on location; management incentive grants are available to attract managers, and training grants are available for blue-collar workers. Preferential tax incentives apply to new investments in the region. Furthermore, in appropriate cases, government loans and various forms of equity participation may be agreed.[30]

For other regions of the UK the government offers assistance to areas, known as 'Assisted Areas', that are in need of investment to revitalize their economies.[31] The main type of assistance is the 'Project Grant'. This is a discretionary grant made to an investor in a manufacturing or service industry where the investment: has a good chance of paying its way; will create or safeguard employment in the Assisted Areas; will benefit the regional and national economy and needs assistance to go ahead. This last criterion is of considerable importance as no assistance will be given if the project has already begun with the help of private sector finance.[32] The amount of grant to be negotiated will be the minimum necessary for the project to go ahead on the proposed basis. This approach has replaced the earlier policy of the Regional Development Grant Scheme, which gave automatic assistance to projects located in Assisted Areas of up to 15 per cent of the cost of capital expenditure on new assets and £3,000 for every new job created.[33]

The principal danger with investment incentive policies is that they may, in fact, be ineffective in attracting useful, long-term investment. A foreign investor may be happy to take advantage of the host state's incentives, and, as soon as these run out, to disinvest. A major concern behind any investment incentive scheme should be, therefore, to avoid the encouragement of such short-term, opportunistic investment. A balance must be sought between the legitimate reduction of high start-up costs for the foreign investor by means of incentives and a wasteful public subsidization of private gain. At heart, the decision to invest is still motivated by factors, such as market size and location, that cannot be altered by legislation. This should militate against over-generous incentives offered by countries that have good comparative advantages in such areas. There is evidence to show that the UK is taking such a market-oriented view through its selective approach to financial assistance and through making such assistance conditional upon the degree to which the foreign investor is willing to invest. The assistance offered to Nissan for its project to establish a car factory in North-East England offers a good illustration. Only if the project reached a specified output of cars would public finance become available to the Japanese firm.[34] On the other hand, the more recent decision of the Toyota company to set up a car factory in Derbyshire attracted no assistance from the government, as this was regarded as unnecessary.[35] By contrast, countries like Ireland or Singapore, which enjoy fewer natural comparative advantages as locations for foreign investment, can be expected to continue offering much greater incentives. However, even in such states, caution must be exercised against using public money without effect.

A further danger behind such incentive-based policies is that they may lead to a distortion of the international economy. Competition over incentives to foreign investors amounts to a protectionist policy, especially when there is less internationally mobile capital to go round. Within the EC, state aids to investment will be contrary to the provisions of article 92 of the Treaty of Rome where they interfere with trade between the EC Member States and do not fall within the permissible categories of state aids listed in article 92.[36] By contrast, there exists no general international regulation of excessive public subsidies to investors. Thus, in the world economy as a whole, competition over investment incentives is likely to continue for as long as governments believe that fiscal and other incentives can compensate for the shortcomings of their states as locations for inward investment.

1.3   Export Processing Zones (EPZs) and Related 'Policy Enclaves' within the Host State

1.3.1   The evolution of EPZs   The EPZ represents a specialized form of investment incentive regime that has played a significant role in the evolution of globalized production by MNEs. Such a zone has been defined as 'a designated specialized industrial estate which produces mainly for export and which constitutes an enclave from the trade and customs regime of a country in which free trade applies'.[37] Thus the EPZ is a legally defined 'policy enclave' within the host state's territory, to which a distinct regime of customs and trade regulations applies. This may be coupled with a package of investment incentives, designed to attract internationally mobile inward direct investment, preferably in the manufacturing sector.[38]

In essence, the EPZ has grown out of a compromise between two conflicting strategies of economic development pursued by LDCs. During the late 1960s and 1970s, numerous LDCs adopted policies of import substituting industrial development, which aimed at the creation of an independent domestic industrial base by means of, *inter alia*, restrictions on imports and inward foreign investment. However, such policies were strongly biased against export activity. The result was that these countries failed to earn adequate returns on domestic investment. By way of response, in the 1970s certain LDCs, not wishing to abandon import substituting policies entirely, introduced EPZs as a means of partial and limited liberalization.[39] The aim was to attract MNEs into the EPZ by means of favourable customs regulations and other incentives, so that these firms would set up production facilities in the zone. From these, they would service global export markets in both finished and intermediate products. Thereby, it was believed, the host state could earn increased export earnings. Furthermore, investment in EPZs by MNEs was thought likely to bring further benefits in the form of increased employment opportunities, improved training and skills for the workforce and the transfer of modern productive technology.[40] However, as will be seen below, actual performance has not always lived up to these expectations.

The EPZ phenomenon has been viewed as an evolution of the ancient 'free port' concept.[41] This is correct in so far as both approaches involve the creation of a 'policy enclave'. Nevertheless, a crucial difference between a 'free port' or 'free trade zone' (FTZ) and an EPZ is that, while both are created by a special customs regime, the former aims mainly at the encouragement of free trade in finished products and commodities, while the latter is specifically concerned with encouraging export-oriented manufacturing investment. This is not to suggest that elements of a 'free port' cannot coexist with an EPZ. Nevertheless, the aim of encouraging inward investment by MNEs has clearly been the dominant motive for setting up EPZs.

The first EPZ was established in Ireland in 1956 with the creation of the Shannon Free Zone around Shannon Airport.[42] However, the principal developments in this policy have occurred in LDCs, particularly in East Asia. Thus, *inter alia*, India, Taiwan, Malaysia, the Philippines and South Korea have all adopted EPZs.[43] In Africa, the first EPZ was created in Mauritius in 1970.[44] Other Sub-Saharan countries have since established EPZs.[45] In North Africa, Egypt has established similar zones as part of its *infitah* (open door) policy.[46] In Latin America Puerto Rico was the first to adopt the EPZ concept in 1962.[47] In Mexico, a unique policy based on EPZ principles has emerged as a means of stimulating industrial development along the US–Mexican border. US firms have, for some years, been taking advantage of conditions in ss 806.30 and 807 of the US Tariff Schedule. These allow for the export of goods from the USA for assembly abroad and for their reimportation at favourable rates of tariff, in that import duties are only levied on the value added abroad.[48] These regulations have made it profitable for US firms to export labour-intensive production activities to low labour-cost areas. The low labour costs attract low reimportation tariffs owing to the low value added. Indeed, such tariff concessions may be seen as a significant home country contribution to the growth of EPZs in LDCs. In 1965, the Mexican government introduced the Border Industrialization Programme to encourage US industrial investors to exploit this concession in US tariffs by locating labour-intensive production in Mexico. Special customs concessions were introduced for the importation of parts and raw materials required for the processing, assembly and finishing of products destined entirely for export, within a 20 kilometre strip parallel to the international border or to the coast line.[49] Since the 1960s the in-bonded factories of the so-called *maquila* industry have extended hundreds of miles inland from the border, thereby straining the 'enclave' character of the original border zone.[50]

1.3.2   The principal legal and administrative features of EPZs in developing host states   The most important legal and administrative features of an EPZ are: the applicable incentive regime and facilities offered to investors; pre- and post-entry administrative procedures and the relationship between the EPZ and the rest of the host state, referred to as the domestic tariff area (DTA). Each will be considered in turn.

The major incentives offered in EPZs relate to tax exemptions and duty-free imports. These are usually supplemented by exemptions from import quotas and the freedom to import capital and to remit profits. There may also be non-fiscal financial incentives, such as export allowances or subsidized interest rates.[51] Where the host country has a comparative advantage in the production of commodities for which there is a world demand, such incentives should be enough to attract the required investment. However, in certain cases it may be necessary to develop the infrastructure required for the desired industries to evolve.[52] Thus, many EPZ projects include the provision of facilities in the form of transport links, factory buildings, commercial services and housing and social services for the workforce. In areas of low population, it may also be necessary to bring in workers from other regions.[53] The development of such facilities is particularly characteristic of EPZs that are aimed at the industrialization of underdeveloped regions of the host state.[54]

Of especial significance to the evolution of EPZs is the harnessing of the major locational advantage of less developed host states, namely low-cost labour. Thus, the legal control of labour relations within the EPZ acquires considerable importance as a means of preserving this advantage. Consequently, it is not uncommon to find that the employment rights of workers, and the right to establish trade unions or to take industrial action, are more limited within the EPZ than in the DTA.[55] This has led to debate over the benefits of EPZs for the local workforce. On the one hand, the restriction of labour rights is seen as a disadvantage, while, on the other, the compensating advantage of new employment, often at higher rates of pay than those experienced in the DTA,[56] is emphasized.[57] Further controversy has also centred on the fact that the majority of workers in EPZs are young, single, females. It has been suggested that this may depress overall wage rates and create a more docile workforce, less inclined to espouse trade union membership, which, traditionally, has been geared to male concerns. On the other hand, women may in fact have opportunities for employment and pay within the EPZ that far surpass anything they could otherwise have expected.[58]

It is common for the administrative regime of an EPZ to establish eligibility criteria for investments. Most often, these include a combination of one or more of the following: the export-orientation of the investment; limited or no local equity participation; substantial foreign capital investment; significant local content in production; employment promotion effects and possibilities for technology transfer.[59]

The authorization required for entry into the EPZ will usually be within the power of a specialized agency set up to administer the EPZ on behalf of the host state government. Some countries have a central authority for this purpose.[60] Others have established separate authorities for the administration of EPZs.[61] Ideally, the relevant authority will have sufficient links with government departments to enable it to act as a 'one stop' service for the foreign investor, thereby reducing administrative inconvenience. In this way the EPZ authority can be used to bypass bureaucratic delays. Apart from administering the entry of foreign investors, the authority will usually have responsibility for the provision of infrastructure and services within the EPZ, the promotion and marketing of investment opportunities within the zone and the recruitment of workers.

The funds for developing and operating EPZs usually come from central government. Thus, in order to be successful, an EPZ should generate returns over and above the public funds provided. Whether this is the case will be considered in sub-section 1.3.3.

As noted earlier, the essential feature of an EPZ is its status as an enclave within the host state bounded by a distinct customs regime. In effect, the EPZ is outside the territory of the host state for trade and investment purposes. Thus, a common feature of EPZs is that they are bounded by two frontiers: the political, fiscal and excise frontier between the host state and the rest of the world; and an internal fiscal and excise frontier between the zone and the rest of the host state (the DTA). This has significant effects upon the manner in which relations between the EPZ and DTA are arranged. In order to preserve the enclave status of the EPZ, certain states have, as already noted, specified the total or partial exclusion of local capital from investment in the EPZ, although the policies of individual states differ in this respect. More significantly, the local authorities must ensure that goods entering the zone are employed for the purposes of consumption or production within it, and are not smuggled into the DTA. Smuggling has proved to be one of the undesired, but perhaps inevitable, side-effects of EPZs.

In order to protect domestic producers from adverse competition, and to preserve the export orientation of the zone, firms operating in the EPZ may be prohibited or restricted from selling in the domestic market of the host state.[62] However, there may be schemes that permit sales into the local market. For example, in India, EPZ located firms are permitted to sell 25 per cent of their output on the local market provided all necessary import licences have been obtained and duties paid.[63] Similarly, the Egyptian Foreign Investment Law of 1989[64] states in article 32 that 'Customs' taxes shall be paid on goods imported from the free zone into the local market as if they were imported from abroad.' By contrast, sales by local producers to firms within the EPZ are generally encouraged. These will be treated as deemed exports from the DTA, and may attract fiscal and/or other benefits for EPZ firms as incentives to utilize local sources of supply.[65]

Finally, it should be noted that the enclave status of the EPZ may be diluted over time. First, the geographical unity of the EPZ may be weakened if the fiscal and other advantages offered in the EPZ are extended to firms operating outside it. As noted above, this has happened in Mexico in relation to *maquila* factories. Similarly, in

Egypt, firms were encouraged to locate on the outskirts of EPZs by having the benefits of the zone apply to their operations, creating individual 'private free zones'.[66] Secondly, the EPZ system can be eroded where the regime for foreign investment applicable to the DTA is liberalized. This may undermine the economic rationale behind the EPZ, and encourage firms to invest in the DTA. For example, a significant reason behind the failure of the Bataan EPZ in the Philippines appears to have been the extension of the bonded warehouse scheme, at first initiated exclusively within the zone, to other EPZs, coupled with the easier availability of investment incentives to investors outside the zone.[67]

1.3.3 The performance of EPZs   As devices for attracting inward investment by MNEs, EPZs have met with considerable success. Since the 1960s such zones have become locations for the more labour-intensive stages of production undertaken by MNEs. Taking advantage of the lower labour costs found in EPZs, MNEs in assembly-type industries (particularly consumer electronics, light machinery, clothing, textiles and resource processing) have established plants therein. These investments have increased jobs in the host countries and have contributed to export promotion, in that most of the production in EPZs has been oriented towards supplying developed country markets. According to Wall, the success of pioneering EPZs in Ireland, South Korea and Taiwan may have led many LDCs to believe that this was attributable to the zone instrument itself and not to the inherent attractions of those countries to export-oriented investment.[68] This may explain why the idea has since been emulated by so many countries. However, the results have not been uniformly good in terms of the objectives behind such zones.

First, although employment has been generated in EPZs, the contribution of EPZs to resolving the labour surplus problem may be marginal in most countries.[69] Secondly, although EPZs may contribute to an increase in the export of manufactured goods from a country, this may be at the cost of considerable imports that may counterbalance, and even extinguish, any resulting foreign exchange surplus.[70] Thirdly, while firms in EPZs will develop backward linkages with DTA firms, the incidence of such cooperation may be limited.[71] Fourthly, the nature of EPZ production, concentrating as it does on labour-intensive assembly work, is unlikely to ensure any significant transfer of modern technology into the host country's economy.[72] Fifthly, there have been instances in which the costs of setting up the EPZ have not been recouped owing to poor decisions on location, contradictory policies and the lack of effective marketing to potential investors.[73] As Kumar points out, a major difficulty with EPZs has been that they have been given a multiplicity of incompatible goals to achieve. It may not, in fact, be possible to do more than achieve a net increase in foreign exchange and employment through the establishment of EPZs. The wider goals of developing economically backward regions should, in his view, be dropped.[74]

However, certain more fundamental weaknesses in the EPZ concept are emerging. First, as improvements in manufacturing technology cause a fall in the overall costs of labour within the developed economies, one of the principal competitive advantages of the EPZs is thereby undercut. The loss of this advantage is further accentuated by the growth in demand for skilled labour. Automated production processes need highly trained staff to serve and maintain them. They also create a demand for high technology components which themselves are manufactured by skilled labour. Most LDCs in which EPZs are located cannot match the skill levels of workers in the developed economies. The MNEs may respond by relocating production back to the developed economies, thereby emphasizing the continued 'dependency' of the LDCs.[75] Secondly, as more developing host states liberalize investment conditions within the country as a whole, the justification for retaining special economic enclaves within the economy is weakened. As noted at the beginning of this section, EPZs were set up as exceptions to a general policy of import substituting growth through the encouragement of domestic enterprises. Once the host country abandons such a policy and the conditions prevailing in the EPZ become generalized, the need for an EPZ is less apparent.

Such zones do, however, continue to attract the attention of countries and analysts. Thus the UN Economic and Social Commission for Asia and the Pacific, despite identifying most of the shortcomings listed above, still recommends the use of EPZs as a means of attracting internationally mobile foreign direct investment.[76] In recent years the idea of setting up special economic zones to attract foreign investors has been mooted in the former Soviet Union,[77] and has led to the passing of enabling provisions in the Russian Foreign Investment Law of 1991.[78] In the People's Republic of China (PRC), the EPZ concept has been studied and elaborated into a unique policy device, the 'special economic zone'. To this we now turn.

1.3.4   The Chinese 'special economic zone' policy   The Chinese 'special economic zone' (SEZ) policy aims not only at encouraging inward direct investment by MNEs but, more importantly, at the creation of a capitalist economic enclave within the PRC, which can act as a testing ground for the creation of a new Chinese 'socialist market economy'. Thus, in the PRC, the EPZ and FTZ concepts have been adapted into a new kind of administrative regime for the reorganization of socialist relations of production. This forms a pivotal part of China's wider 'open door' policy, leading eventually, it is hoped, to that country's integration into the international division of labour, while at the same time preserving its socialist ideological perspective.[79]

The first SEZs were created in 1979 in the municipalities of Shenzhen, Zhuhai and Shantou in Guangdong province in southeast China. These were followed in 1980 by Xiamen in Fujian province. In 1983 Hianan Island in southern China was elevated to a special administrative zone under the jurisdiction of the Guangdong Provincial People's Government, displaying many of the features of a SEZ. In May 1984 fourteen coastal cities were opened up to foreign trade and investment, and in 1985 three special delta economic zones were established in the Pearl River and Yangtze areas.[80] The provinces of Guangdong and Fujian were chosen as the sites for SEZs in view of their coastal locations, their traditional links with expatriate Chinese, from whom considerable investment could be expected, and their proximity to Hong Kong with its financial infrastructure and resources. Furthermore, the economic development of these regions is part of the PRC's preparation for their integration with Hong Kong in 1997. The whole region is then likely to enjoy a special political, administrative and economic status in the PRC.[81]

The original regulatory framework for the Guangdong SEZs comes from the Regulations on Special Economic Zones in Guangdong Province, adopted by the Fifteenth Session of the Standing Committee of the Fifth National People's Congress on 26 August 1980.[82] The Xiamen SEZ is governed by five regulations on the registration of enterprises, land use, labour management, the import of technology and association with inland parts of China.[83] Similar specific regulations have also been passed in relation to the Guangdong SEZs.[84]

This regulatory framework does not create a distinct regime from the national laws of the PRC. Thus article 2 of the Guangdong Regulations states that 'The enterprises and individuals operating in the special zones must abide by the laws, decrees and relevant regulations of the People's Republic of China.' However, article 2 continues by making an exception to this general rule in relation to special provisions as stipulated in the regulations. Therefore, the specific provisions in the SEZ regulations supersede national law in the matters covered by them.[85] Thus, for example, the regulations permit the setting up of joint ventures in the SEZ. However, they are silent on the detailed regulation of such ventures. This must, therefore, be provided by the national law on joint ventures, except where the SEZ regulations differ, as, for example, on the question of taxation. It is not possible to provide here a comprehensive analysis of all the Chinese SEZ regulations. This has, in any case, been done elsewhere.[86] Rather, the Guangdong Regulations will be briefly reviewed to consider the similarities and differences between the SEZ concept and EPZs in capitalist LDCs.

The objectives of Chinese SEZs differ from those of EPZs in capitalist LDCs. While the latter are concerned mainly with the encouragement of export-oriented industry, the SEZs in Guangdong are involved in 'all undertakings which have a positive meaning in international economic cooperation and technical exchange including the fields of industry, agriculture, animal husbandry, breeding, tourism, housing and other construction work and advanced technological research and manufacturing work. They may also engage in other business which is of interest to both sides.'[87] Nevertheless, there are broad similarities between SEZs and EPZs in the incentives and preferential treatment given to foreign investors.

Thus the foreign investor has the right to set up an independently owned and operated enterprise in the SEZ,[88] a right not extended to the rest of China until the passing of the Law on Enterprises Operated Exclusively with Foreign Capital of 12 April 1986.[89] Secondly, machinery and equipment, spare parts, raw and semi-processed materials, means of transportation and other capital goods required for production imported by enterprises in the SEZ are exempt from import duties.[90] The income tax rate within the zone is 15 per cent,[91] as compared to 30 per cent for the taxable income of joint ventures and foreign enterprises in the rest of China.[92] Furthermore, preferential treatment is given to enterprises established within two years of the promulgation of the regulations, enterprises with an investment of US$5 million or more and enterprises involving higher technologies or having a longer cycle of capital turnover.[93] Thirdly, there is free remittance of profits after payment of income tax.[94] Fourthly, upon reinvestment of profits in the SEZ for five years, the foreign trader may apply for a reduction or exemption of income tax on profits so reinvested.[95] Fifthly, entry and exit procedures are to be simplified for foreigners.[96] These are now covered by the specific regulations mentioned above.

Further similarities with EPZs are contained in the requirement that the commodities produced by enterprises in the SEZ are to be sold on the international market.[97] Sales to the domestic Chinese market can only be made with the permission of the SEZ administrative committee and on payment of customs duty.[98] Thus the export enclave status of the SEZ is preserved. On the other hand, purchases by SEZ firms of raw materials and other supplies from Chinese producers are encouraged.[99] The enclave status of SEZs has been further emphasized in subsequent regulations on entry and exit.

In particular, on 1 April 1986, new regulations were introduced to reinforce the internal border or 'control line' between Shenzhen SEZ and the rest of China, so as to reduce the incidence of smuggling and black market activities.[100]

The administration of the Guangdong SEZs is carried out by the Administrative Committee of the Special Economic Zones of Guangdong Province (ADCOM). This is given broad powers of action over the operation of the zone.[101] These include the approval of proposed investments,[102] the preparation of the infrastructure[103] and the operation of personnel recruitment services either directly or through labour service companies.[104] In order to assist in the economic activities of the zone the Guangdong Provincial Special Economic Zones Company has been established. Its functions include the accumulation of funds and trust and investment work, cooperation with foreign investors in setting up joint ventures, assisting in procurement and marketing work with units in China and consultancy services.[105] Thus the principal administrative organs of the SEZs carry out many of the same functions as their counterparts in capitalist LDCs.

In all, it can be concluded that the Guangdong SEZs share many of the operational features of EPZs. The principal difference lies in the broader range of economic activities sought to be encouraged in the SEZs, in the underlying policy objective of developing a capitalist economy within an enclave of a socialist country and preparing the region for reunification with Hong Kong.

The Chinese experiment with SEZs has met with a mixed reception. In the mid-1980s, the Chinese authorities felt that the SEZs had not lived up to their expectations. In particular, there was disappointment on the relative lack of export production and the rise of profiteering, smuggling and currency crime.[106] On the other hand, the SEZs, and in particular Shenzen, have continued to grow and to attract foreign investment. The SEZs and the other special coastal zones account for the largest share of direct investment into China.[107] Thus, the doubts of earlier years have been quelled.

In one respect, the SEZ experiment has altered a fundamental aspect of socialist economic relations, namely the protection of the worker. A significant feature of the SEZ system is a shift towards more performance related rewards for workers and towards an employment contract system of labour regulation.[108] This has in turn led to increased pressure for the dismissal of unsatisfactory workers.[109] Equally, there are many job opportunities in the SEZs. Workers come to them from other parts of China. This has brought with it the problems of exploitation associated with temporary urbanization: child labour, poor living conditions and excessive compulsory overtime. Although officials and employers deny the existence of such problems, they have been documented in the local and foreign press. On the other hand, workers in the Shenzhen SEZ have the best social security package in China after local authorities imposed this on employers. Finally, there is some evidence of growing labour unrest in the Shenzhen SEZ.[110] Therefore, it appears that the experiment in capitalist production is beginning to alter a fundamental feature of socialist political economy, and to introduce the prospect of class conflict.[111]

2   Bilateral and Multilateral Measures for the Encouragement of Direct Investment

As noted at the beginning of this Chapter, the encouragement of direct investment should be considered not only from the perspective of unilateral policies undertaken by host states, but also from that of interstate initiatives. The US network of FCN treaties, which guarantee the freedom of entry and establishment for investors from each contracting party, has already been alluded to above.[112] It remains, in this section, to consider, first, certain contemporary regional initiatives for increased economic integration and investment liberalization. The discussion will concentrate on North America and Europe as illustrative cases.[113] Secondly, two highly significant multilateral initiatives on investment liberalization will be studied. These are the OECD Codes on the Liberalization of Capital Movements and Current Invisible Operations, and the investment related provisions of the Final Act of the Uruguay Round of GATT negotiations.

2.1   Regional Arrangements Dismantling Barriers to Inward Investment

Under this heading attention will be paid to the emergent North American Free Trade Area (NAFTA) and to the Single European Market (SEM) of the European Community (EC). In theory, these initiatives illustrate two distinct approaches to trade and investment liberalization. The NAFTA sets out, in principle, to do no more than ensure freer access for trade and investment between the participating states, which retain their national powers of economic regulation subject to the principle of national treatment.[114] By comparison, the SEM goes further in that the EC aims at creating a single common market, governed by harmonized supranational regulations, and aiming at eventual economic and monetary union between the Member States.[115] In practice, however, the two approaches may not have very different results in that they both tend towards the economic convergence of the states concerned. In particular, the NAFTA contains provisions not commonly found in a mere free trade agreement, including provisions on services, investment, intellectual property and bilateral dispute settlement mechanisms.[116] It may therefore be proper to regard the NAFTA as a 'halfway house to a North American common market'.[117] Each approach will be considered in turn.

2.1.1   The North American Free Trade Area   The NAFTA aims at the closer integration of the economies of the USA, Canada and Mexico by means of a single trilateral free trade agreement. It has been preceded by bilateral negotiations. Thus, the USA and Canada ratified a bilateral Free Trade Agreement (FTA) between them in the autumn of 1988. It entered force on 1 January 1989.[118] In addition, the USA agreed a framework understanding on bilateral trade with Mexico in 1987.[119] Since then bilateral negotiations continued between the USA and Mexico on sectoral matters.[120] A framework agreement between Canada and Mexico was also being negotiated.[121] It is instructive to consider briefly the investment related provisions of the USA–Canada FTA before looking at the provisions of the NAFTA, especially as the former are already in force.[122]

Article 102 of the USA–Canada FTA makes clear that the objectives of the agreement are to eliminate barriers to trade in goods and in services, and to 'liberalize significantly conditions for investment within this free trade area'. Furthermore, in the field of financial services, Chapter Seventeen of the Agreement ensures the continued integration of the US and Canadian markets and commits the Parties to their respective programmes of liberalization in this field.[123] Central to the services and investment rules in Chapters Fourteen and Sixteen is the requirement of national treatment.[124] This may be departed from only where: '(a) the difference in treatment is no greater than that necessary for prudential, fiduciary, health and safety, or consumer protection reasons; (b) such different treatment is equivalent in effect to the treatment accorded by the Party to its investors for such reasons; (c) prior notification of the proposed treatment has been given in accordance with Art. 1803.'[125]

Chapter Sixteen of the FTA enumerates obligations that the host Party must observe in its dealings with investors from the other Party. First, minimum local equity requirements cannot be imposed on investors by the host Party.[126] Nor can the host Party require the sale or other disposal of an investment made by an investor from the home Party by reason of its nationality.[127] Secondly, the host party shall not impose performance requirements as a condition of permitting investment in its territory, or as a means of regulating the conduct or operation of a business enterprise located in its territory.[128] Thirdly, investments made by investors from the other party are guaranteed against direct or indirect nationalization or expropriation, or a series of measures tantamount to an expropriation, except '(a) for a public purpose; (b) in accordance with due process of law; (c) on a non-discriminatory basis; and (d) upon payment of prompt, adequate and effective compensation at fair market value.'[129] Fourthly, the Agreement guarantees the free transfer of profits, royalties, fees, interest or other earnings from an investment or any proceeds of sale of all or any part of an investment or from the partial or complete liquidation of such investment.[130] Fifthly, any new taxation measure or subsidy that constitutes a means of arbitrary or unjustifiable discrimination between investors of the Parties or a disguised restriction on the benefits accorded to investors under Chapter Sixteen comes within the scope of its protective provisions.[131] Furthermore, where a Party feels that a tax measure or subsidy has the effect of impairing or nullifying any benefit reasonably expected to accrue to that Party directly or indirectly from the Agreement, that Party may institute the consultation or, if appropriate, the dispute settlement provisions of the Agreement or, with the consent of the other Party, proceed to arbitration.[132]

Of particular significance in Chapter Sixteen are the provisions that affect the content of Canadian foreign investment law. Annex 1607.3 of the FTA effectively amends certain provisions of the Investment Canada Act as from the date of entry into force of the Agreement. First, in relation to a direct acquisition of control of a Canadian business by an investor of the USA, the review threshold in the Act is raised from the statutory C$5 million to C$25 million in 1989, C$50 million in 1990, C$100 million in 1991 and C$150 million in 1992.[133] Thereafter the threshold will be raised in accordance with the formula set out in the agreement.[134] Secondly, in relation to the indirect acquisition of control of a Canadian business by a US investor, the current statutory review threshold of C$50 million is increased to C$100 million in 1989, C$250 million in 1990 and C$500 million in 1991. Since 1 January 1992 such acquisitions have ceased to be reviewable. Thirdly, where a Canadian business controlled by an investor of the USA is being acquired by an investor of a third country, the acquisition remains reviewable provided that the gross value of the assets of the business is not less than the thresholds applicable to US investors.[135] This facilitates sales of US owned Canadian businesses. However, investors of a third country acquiring Canadian businesses controlled by Canadians will continue to be subject to existing statutory thresholds.[136] Fourthly, guidelines or regulations made pursuant to the Investment Canada Act must be amended to ensure that they comply with the provisions on minimum levels of local equity, divestiture and performance requirements in the FTA.[137] Except for the restriction on divestiture, none of the amendments to the Investment Canada Act apply to the oil and gas and uranium mining industries.[138] Furthermore, cultural industries[139] are exempt from the Agreement to the extent provided for in article 2005.[140] In relation to Chapter Sixteen, this introduces an obligation on Canada to offer compensation to a US investor who has been required to divest from a Canadian cultural industry pursuant to a review of his or its indirect acquisition of a business therein. The amount of compensation must accord to a fair market value, as determined by an independent, impartial assessment.[141] These provisions are quite remarkable in that they introduce an amendment of Canadian legislation by treaty. They achieve what the USA has been attempting to do for some considerable time, namely the substantial removal of Canadian controls over US inward direct investment.[142]

Chapter Sixteen also contains provisions on the settlement of investment disputes. These are to be conducted in accordance with the provisions of Chapter Eighteen of the Agreement, which sets up a bilateral arbitration procedure under articles 1806 and 1807.[143] The only additional requirements introduced in Chapter Sixteen are that the arbitral panel should be composed of individuals experienced and competent in the field of international investment, and that the panel should take into consideration how investment disputes are normally dealt with by internationally recognized rules for commercial arbitration.[144]

Part Five of the NAFTA contains essentially the same types of provisions on investment, services (including financial services) and related matters as the USA–Canada FTA, and extends these to the three Contracting Parties.[145] Chapter Eleven of Part Five contains the provisions that deal specifically with investment. Chapter Eleven, Section A, provides the framework of guarantees for investors and principles of state action that are designed to liberalize the North American investment environment. Thus, investors of another Party and their investments are entitled to national treatment[146] and Most-Favoured-Nation (MFN) treatment.[147] As between these standards the one that offers the better treatment to investors shall be applied.[148] Investors shall also enjoy the protection of minimum standards of treatment under international law, including fair and equitable treatment and full protection and security, and non-discrimination with respect to measures relating to losses suffered as a result of armed conflict or civil strife.[149] Performance requirements are prohibited. Apart from the familiar list of prohibited export and import requirements, local content and procurement rules and local sales quotas, the NAFTA includes within the prohibition requirements to transfer technology, production processes or other proprietary knowledge except when this requirement is imposed by a court, tribunal or competition authority as a result of an alleged violation of competition laws, or to act in a manner not inconsistent with the Agreement.[150] This is no doubt to prevent Mexico continuing with any future technology transfer controls that do not accord with the Western model of technology transfer regulation.[151]

Furthermore, no nationality requirement may be imposed as to the composition of the board of directors of a local enterprise that is an investment from another Contracting Party, although a Party may require that the majority of the board be of a particular nationality, or resident in the territory of that Party, provided that this does not materially affect the ability of the investor to exercise control over its investment.[152] The Parties may make reservations to the operation of national treatment and MFN standards, and to the prohibitions on performance requirements and board membership requirements, as regards any existing non-conforming measures at the levels of federal, state or local government. Thus a 'standstill' on new restrictions is introduced.[153] Chapter Eleven continues with a guarantee on the free transfer of profits, proceeds of sale, contractual payments compensation payments and arbitral awards connected with the investment.[154] Regarding expropriation, the same standard as exists in the USA–Canada FTA is applied. Thus, expropriation must be for a public purpose, non-discriminatory, in accordance with due process of law and international law, and on payment of compensation equivalent to the fair market value of the expropriated investment immediately before the expropriation took place.[155]

Apart from laying down standards for the treatment of investors, Chapter Eleven, section A, also establishes certain rights of action in relation to investment for the administrative authorities of the Contracting Parties. Thus, the Parties may adopt measures that prescribe special formalities in connection with the establishment of investments by investors from another Party, provided these do not materially impair the protection given under the Agreement, and require that the investor supplies routine information concerning the investment.[156] Likewise, the Agreement permits measures that are considered appropriate to ensure that investment activity in the territory of a Party is undertaken in a manner sensitive to environmental concerns, as long as these measures are otherwise consistent with the Agreement.[157] The Parties stress that it is inappropriate to encourage investment by relaxing domestic health, safety and environmental measures. Thus they undertake not to weaken such measures as a means of encouraging investment. Should one Party feel that another is carrying out such a policy, it may request consultations with a view to avoiding such encouragement.[158] This provision is designed to meet one of the fears expressed by opponents of the NAFTA, namely that it could permit US and Canadian firms to relocate to Mexico and take advantage of the lower environmental and health and safety standards to be found there.[159]

Chapter Eleven, section B, establishes a detailed system for the settlement of investment disputes between a Party and an investor from another Party, based on the principles of international reciprocity and due process before an impartial tribunal.[160] An investor may make a claim on its own behalf, or on behalf of an enterprise owned and controlled by it, against the host Party on the basis of a violation by the host Party of any of the guarantees or protective principles in Chapter Eleven, Section A, or where a state enterprise or state sanctioned private monopoly is alleged to have acted in violation of those standards.[161] The claim should first be settled by consultation or negotiation.[162] Where this fails the claim may be submitted for arbitration under the terms of the Agreement. Arbitration can take place under the ICSID Convention, where both the disputing Party and the Party of the investor are parties to the Convention, the Additional Facility Rules of ICSID, where only one of the Parties concerned is a party to the ICSID Convention, or the UNCITRAL Arbitration Rules.[163] The Agreement provides detailed rules for the submission of a claim, the composition of the arbitral tribunal, the conduct of proceedings, the place of arbitration, the governing law, evidence, interim measures and the finality and enforcement of the award.[164] Both Canada and Mexico have excluded from the scope of the dispute settlement provisions a decision following a review, under the relevant national laws, as to whether or not to permit an acquisition that is subject to review.[165]

The USA–Canada FTA and the NAFTA have both created controversy as regards their effects on regional and international trade and investment. In relation to regional effects, numerous studies suggest that the USA–Canada Agreement will act to the general benefit of Canada and the USA, and that the NAFTA will benefit North America as a whole. In both cases it has been argued that more jobs will be created than lost through the ensuing restructuring,[166] and that firms will reorganize production on a continental basis with resulting cost savings that will ensure their increased ability to compete on a global scale.[167] On the other hand, Canadian critics of the USA–Canada FTA have predicted extensive divestment by US firms from Canada, on the ground that inward investment by US firms would no longer occur. The Canadian market could be served from US production locations, where the overall costs of production are lower. This process could result in extensive job losses for Canadians.[168] Similar fears have been voiced over the effects of the NAFTA.

US labour unions are concerned that US firms will relocate to Mexico to take advantage of lower environmental standards and pay rates, while in Mexico the fear is that new high-technology production methods will reduce the amount of inward investment from the USA. Neither concern can be clearly supported or refuted.[169] However, there has been considerable pressure on President Clinton to call for supplementary agreements on the enforcement of labour laws and environmental standards by Mexico so as to avoid the relocation of jobs to that country.[170] Supplemental agreements in these areas have since been concluded.[171]

As regards the implications of the NAFTA for the global process of trade and investment liberalization, opinion is divided. It is not clear whether the NAFTA is a spur to such liberalization or a brake upon it. This issue first surfaced in the context of the USA–Canada FTA. Proponents of the former view have argued that the USA–Canada FTA has kept the momentum for liberalization going, in that the parties to the world's largest bilateral trading relationship have adopted a policy of such liberalization between them, and have thereby created a model for multilateral negotiations to follow.[172] A similar argument could be made for the NAFTA, in that it would be instrumental in creating a single market for the whole of North America including, for the first time, a major newly industrializing country of the South. It could offer a new model of cooperation between developed and developing countries. However, that assumes that Mexico will be more than merely a low-cost labour market and will develop an advanced consumer society similar to that enjoyed by its northern partners. It is as yet unclear whether such a consequence is possible.[173]

By contrast, it is arguable that the USA–Canada FTA and NAFTA represent a form of bilateral and trilateral protectionism, offering reciprocal preferential treatment for US, Canadian and Mexican traders and investors, to the exclusion of their competitors from outside North America. Significantly, a GATT working party on the USA–Canada FTA reported to the GATT Council that it was unable to agree over whether the FTA was consistent with the aims of the GATT, and described it as having the potential of undermining the GATT system's credibility in that third party interests were not clearly protected.[174] The 1992 dispute between the USA and Japan and Canada over North American content requirements for Honda cars produced in Ontario is a case in point.[175] However, the NAFTA should act as a spur to liberalization if non-North American firms are able to benefit from its provisions merely by reason of their presence in the region. In principle this should be the case. The definition of 'investor of a Party' includes an enterprise of a Party, and 'enterprise of a Party' is defined as 'an enterprise constituted or organized under the law of a Party, and a branch located in the territory of a Party and carrying out business activities there'. This is wide enough to encompass a North American subsidiary or branch of a non-North American parent.[176] On the other hand, despite its welcoming attitude to the NAFTA, fears have been expressed by the EC that European firms may lose market share in financial services and in services generally, fall foul of the rules of origin requirements in the auto and textiles industries and lose shares in some agricultural sectors. These matters may raise issues under the GATT.[177] Furthermore, should international competition become too intense in the region, the privileges of the NAFTA could, in future, be reserved for corporations of North American origin, regardless of their presence in the region. It remains to be seen what future political processes will create.

2.1.2   The Single European Market   The Treaty of Rome (EEC Treaty) ensures that restrictions on the freedom of establishment, or the freedom to supply services, are removed for natural and legal persons possessing the nationality of a Member State.[178] Consequently, as between the Member States, existing restrictions on direct investment, or on the provision of cross-border services, by nationals of Member States are being progressively abolished and no new restrictions can be introduced.[179] In relation to the operations of companies or firms, article 58 of the EEC Treaty provides:

Companies or firms[180] formed in accordance with the law of a Member State and having their registered office, central administration or principal place of business within the Community shall, for the purposes of this chapter, be treated in the same way as natural persons who are nationals of Member States.

The right of establishment, as it applies to companies and firms, includes 'the right to take up and pursue activities as self-employed persons and to set up and manage undertakings, in particular companies or firms within the meaning of the second paragraph of Art. 58,[181] under the conditions laid down for its own nationals by the law of the country where such establishment is effected, subject to the provisions of the chapter relating to capital.'[182] Article 66 of the EEC Treaty extends article 58 to the provision of services, ensuring that companies can also benefit from the freedoms accorded in that area to natural persons. Article 58 suggests two possible routes into another Member State: first, the establishment of a new company, or the transfer of an existing company, from one Member State to another, known as 'primary establishment'; secondly, the establishment of an office, branch or subsidiary in another Member State, termed 'secondary establishment'.[183]

Regarding primary establishment, it has been made clear by the European Court of Justice (ECJ) in *R v HM Treasury, ex p Daily Mail and General Trust plc*,[184] that a transfer of the central management and control of a company from one Member State to another, while that company retains its status as a company incorporated under the legislation of the first Member State, does not amount to 'establishment' for the purposes of articles 52 and 58.[185] Consequently, in the absence of harmonized Community law concerning the retention of legal personality in the event of the transfer of the registered office of a company from one Member State to another, the home state is free to introduce national laws that regulate the consequences of such a move.[186] However, the ECJ also held that the home Member State must not hinder the establishment in another Member State of one of its nationals or of a company incorporated under its legislation and having its registered office, central administration or principal place of business within the Community. Otherwise the rights guaranteed by articles 52ff would be rendered meaningless.[187] This complements the duty on the host Member State to ensure that foreign nationals and companies are treated in the same way as nationals of that State.

The most common method whereby companies from one Member State enter a host Member State is through the establishment of an office, agency, branch or subsidiary. In these cases, the host Member State must not impose discriminatory provisions, such as tax provisions, which would limit the freedom for companies to choose the appropriate legal form for their activities within the host Member State.[188] Where the company seeks to enter a host Member State through secondary establishment methods, it must show a real and continuous link with the economy of a Member State to qualify as a beneficiary of this right.[189]

The benefits of the right to establishment and freedom to provide services are available subject to the derogations contained in article 56. This permits the special treatment of foreign nationals on grounds of public policy, public security or public health. This provision is interpreted in the same manner as the restrictions on the free movement of workers under article 48(3) of the EEC Treaty.[190] It should be noted that the possibility of tax avoidance and the risk of revenue loss to Member States have been considered insufficient to create an additional derogation to the above-mentioned freedoms.[191]

It is clear from articles 58 and 66 that the right to establishment and the right to provide services in another Member State can only be enjoyed by a company formed in accordance with the law of a Member State and having its registered office, central administration or principal place of business within the Community. This is wide enough to cover the EC-based subsidiaries of non-EC parent companies. However, the EEC Treaty does not guarantee these rights to companies that have no legally recognized EC presence in the sense of article 58. Therefore, it is not possible for, say, a US or Japanese based company to invoke the EEC Treaty if it is denied access to the economy of a Member State whether for the purpose of establishing a place of business or for the provision of cross-border services.

In the absence of a common Community policy on inward investment from outside the EC, individual Member States retain a discretion over their policy towards investors from outside the EC. In general, the Member States of the EC espouse an 'open door' to non-EC investors, so there should be little real disadvantage to such investors. However, in the field of financial services, considerable unease has been expressed by non-EC firms over conditions of access to the SEM.[192] This centres on the concept of 'reciprocity', whereby non-EC firms will only be permitted to enter the European market if EC-based firms are offered reciprocal rights of entry into non-EC markets. Initially, it was feared that new EC provisions in the financial services field would establish a 'mirror-image' concept of reciprocity, in that access to the SEM for non-EC firms would depend on their home jurisdictions offering identical terms of access for EC-based firms. However, these fears have been somewhat allayed by the adoption of a modified concept of reciprocity, based on national treatment standards. For example, in the Second Banking Directive,[193] should a non-EC state fail to grant national treatment to EC credit institutions, a subsidiary of a credit institution from that country may be denied an EC banking licence. On the other hand, lack of equivalent treatment will lead to negotiations between the state concerned and the EC Council but not to the denial of licences.[194] A similar approach has been adopted in the Investment Services Directive.[195]

2.2 Multilateral Arrangements Dismantling Barriers to Inward Investment

The major capital-exporting countries have maintained a policy *inter se* of progressively dismantling barriers to inward investment through multilateral arrangements. Initially, this was manifested in the OECD Codes on the Liberalization of Current Invisible Operations and on the Liberalization of Capital Movements, which were adopted by the OECD Council on 12 December 1961.[196] More recently, the major capital exporters, led by the USA, have sought to limit the powers of non-OECD host states in controlling the entry and establishment of foreign investors in the Uruguay

Round of the GATT Negotiations. Each will be considered in turn.

2.2.1 The OECD Codes of Liberalization   The two OECD Codes deal, respectively, with the progressive abolition of obstacles to trade and investment in the fields of current invisibles, covering the major service industries,[197] and capital movements, which include *inter alia* all other areas where direct investment may occur.[198] The Codes have the legal status of an OECD Decision which is binding on all Members. Although they cover distinct subjects, the two Codes are governed by similar general principles and monitoring procedures. The Codes enshrine the principle of liberalization by means of a reciprocal duty to abolish any national restrictions upon the transfers and transactions to which the Codes apply.[199] This is reinforced by a positive duty to grant any authorization required for the conclusion or execution of the transactions or transfers covered,[200] and by a duty of non-discrimination in the application of liberalization measures to investors from other Member States.[201]

However, the Codes permit Members to lodge reservations in relation to matters on which full liberalization cannot be immediately achieved, thereby stressing the progressive nature of the liberalization involved.[202] Furthermore, the obligation to liberalize is not peremptory. It is qualified by the Member's reasonable public interest concerns. Thus, article 3 of each Code states that a Member is not prevented from taking action which it considers necessary for '(i) the maintenance of public order or the protection of public health, morals and safety; (ii) the protection of essential security interests; (iii) the fulfilment of its obligations relating to international peace and security.'

The obligation to liberalize is further qualified by the preservation, in each Code, of the powers of Members to verify the authenticity of transactions or transfers and to take any measures required to prevent evasion of their laws or regulations.[203] Moreover, where the economic and financial situation of a Member justifies such a course, the Member need not take all the measures of liberalization provided for in the Code.[204] Similarly, where the member has taken such measures of liberalization, it may derogate from those measures where these result in serious economic and financial disturbance or where there exists a seriously deteriorating balance-of-payments situation.[205] Again, as in the case of reservations, the derogation provisions permit for a gradual liberalization of restrictions in situations where unconditional liberalization may be against a Member's immediate interests.

The lodging of a reservation or derogation does not disentitle the Member concerned from the right to benefit from measures of liberalization offered by other Members, provided the notification and examination procedures laid down in the Codes are complied with.[206] These procedures are administered by the Committee on Capital Movements and Invisible Transactions.[207] Under the Invisibles Code the examination is conducted in relation to subject matter, the reservations of all Member countries being considered at the same time, whereas under the Capital Movements Code examinations are by each Member country in turn. This reflects differences in the approach to restrictions in each field. Under the Invisibles Code, most restrictions are concentrated in a small number of unrelated service sectors, while under the Capital Movements Code restrictions are often closely related to one another and to the macroeconomic policy and performance of each country concerned.[208] Upon completing its examination, the Committee reports to the OECD Council, which may endorse a Member's decision to withdraw or amend a reservation by means of a legally binding decision, or may make non-binding recommendations to a Member on further measures of liberalization.[209]

In relation to direct investment and establishment, the Capital Movements Code is of primary significance. In Annex A to the Code, direct investment is defined as 'investment for the purpose of establishing lasting economic relations with an undertaking such as, in particular, investments which give the possibility of exercising an effective influence in the management thereof'. The Code extends to both inward and outward investment effected by means of the creation or extension of a wholly owned enterprise, subsidiary or branch, the acquisition of full ownership of an existing enterprise, participation in a new or existing enterprise or a long-term loan of five years or longer.

In 1984 the Capital Movements Code was extended to include the right of establishment.[210] Thus Annex A continues:

The authorities of the Members shall not maintain or introduce:

Regulations or practices applying to the granting of licences, concessions, or similar authorizations, including conditions or requirements attaching to such authorizations and affecting the operations of enterprises, that raise special barriers or limitations with respect to non-resident (as compared to resident) investors, and that have the intent or the effect of preventing or significantly impeding inward direct investment by non-residents.

This definition of the right to establishment is wide enough to cover most policies that restrict, or make conditional, access to non-resident investors. They are subject to the above-mentioned public policy exemptions to the Code.

The Invisibles Code protects the right of establishment and operation for branches and agencies of foreign insurers.[211] While host countries remain entitled to regulate the establishment of foreign insurers, this must be done in accordance with the general principle of equivalent treatment for national insurers and insurers from other OECD Member States, so that the latter shall not be liable to heavier burdens than those imposed on the former. Therefore, equivalent authorization provisions must apply to both. Furthermore, financial guarantees and deposits must be as low as possible and equivalent for both types of insurers.

Finally, the Liberalization Codes must be read alongside the National Treatment Instrument in the OECD Guidelines on Multinational Enterprises.[212] While the Liberalization Codes cover rights of establishment for non-resident investors, the National Treatment Instrument covers the standards applicable to already established enterprises owned or controlled by non-residents. It requires that such enterprises be treated in a manner no less favourable than that accorded to domestic enterprises in a similar situation. The National Treatment Instrument is reviewed by the OECD Committee on International Investment and Multinational Enterprises. Together, the various OECD Codes provide an integrated set of principles by which the progressive liberalization of investment and establishment can be furthered among the OECD Member States. They establish the OECD Member's general policy on investment, a policy which gives an indication of the kinds of regulatory principles that these states are seeking to apply to the global economy as a whole.

2.2.2   *The Uruguay Round and direct investment issues*   The Uruguay Round of multilateral trade negotiations has, for the first time, introduced investment related issues into the GATT agenda. New areas of negotiation have been instituted concerning: the freedom of cross-border trade and rights of establishment in relation to services; the protection of intellectual property against counterfeiting and host country technology transfer measures; and the limitation of trade-related investment measures, such as performance or equity requirements, imposed by host states on foreign investors. These issues came to be on the negotiating agenda as a result of pressure from the major capital-exporting countries, and from the USA in particular.[213] The underlying aim of the capital exporters is to remove what they perceive as impediments to the growth of an integrated global economy, in which the activities of MNEs would be free from restrictive regulation, enabling them to act on purely economic considerations to the presumed benefit of all states.

The Uruguay Round was launched at the Special Session of GATT Contracting Parties held at Punta del Este, Uruguay, between 15 and 20 September 1986. The meeting ended with the adoption of the Punta del Este Declaration, which sets out the agenda for the Round.[214] In relation to investment issues, the Declaration embodied a compromise between the capital-exporting states and the LDCs, which were concerned that excessive liberalization in the fields under review could result in their economies being swamped by foreign MNEs to the detriment of domestic firms.[215] While trade related intellectual property issues (TRIPs) and trade related investment measures (TRIMs) were included as negotiating items within the GATT framework, services were to be negotiated separately. This was a compromise worked out to accommodate the LDCs comprising the so-called Group of Ten, led by Brazil and India,[216] who remained opposed to any extension of the GATT beyond pure trade issues.[217]

The Round proceeded to a mid-term review in December 1988 and April 1989.[218] In 1990, negotiations broke down as a result of major disagreements over agriculture between the EC and the USA. Negotiations continued in December 1991, after the EC and USA worked out an initial compromise on the differences that separated them. In January 1992 it was hoped that the Round could be concluded on the basis of final texts drawn up by the Secretary-General of the GATT in all major areas, including those of concern to this work.[219] The negotiations finally came to an end in December 1993, when the Final Act Embodying the Results of the Uruguay Round of Multilateral Trade Negotiations was drawn up for signature.[220] The Final Act was opened for signature on 15 April 1994 in Marrakesh, Morocco. Against this background each of the three investment-related areas of negotiation will be considered.

In recent years trade and direct investment in *services* have become increasingly significant features of the world economy.[221] The principal providers of services are firms located in the major capital exporting countries. In order to exploit the potential international market for their activities, service-oriented MNEs need open access to host countries, whether through cross-border trade or, where necessary, through establishment within the host country. However, the areas in which service enterprises work (e.g. financial services, insurance, transport, media, tourism) are among the most highly regulated of business sectors.[222] Consequently, markets are fragmented along national lines. Business environments in host states will often favour local providers over foreign competitors, or exclude them altogether. Furthermore, national markets may be controlled by local private or public monopolies, making liberalization particularly difficult. It is against such restrictions that the capital-exporting countries launched their initiative on services in the Uruguay Round. They argued that the GATT should cover all traded commodities, which must now include services as well as goods. The capital exporters partially succeeded in this aim. Although services would not be discussed under the GATT, parallel negotiations leading to an eventual international agreement on services would take place.[223]

According to part II of the Punta del Este Declaration, the aim of negotiations in this area was 'to establish a multilateral framework of principles and rules for trade in services, including the elaboration of possible disciplines for individual sectors, with a view to the expansion of such trade under conditions of transparency and progressive liberalization and as a means of promoting economic growth of all trading partners and the development of developing countries.' This statement is wide enough to cover not only trade in services but also the right of establishment. Furthermore, the Mid-Term Review Decision stated that 'foreign services may be supplied according to the preferred mode of delivery', suggesting that any agreement should allow a service provider the freedom to choose between cross-border trade and establishment within the host state.[224]

The General Agreement on Trade in Services (GATS) envisages the possibility of a right of establishment.[225] By article I thereof, trade in services is defined as the supply of a service *inter alia* through the commercial presence of a service supplier of one Member in the territory of any other Member.[226] Furthermore, by article XXVIII(d) 'commercial presence' is defined as meaning 'any type of business or professional establishment, including through (i) the constitution, acquisition or maintenance of a juridical person, or (ii) the creation or maintenance of a branch or a representative office within the territory of a Party for the purpose of supplying a service.' This definition is consistent with the existence of a right of establishment. Such a right will exist where a member of the GATS makes specific commitments on market access under article XVI of the GATS. Article XVI goes on to state that, in sectors where the Member undertakes market access commitments, it is prohibited from imposing certain listed limitations on the supply of services, unless it expressly specifies that it retains such limitations. These limitations include measures that would affect access through *inter alia* direct investment. Thus, in the absence of express reservation, the Member cannot restrict or require specific types of legal entity or joint venture through which a service could be provided, or impose limits for the participation of foreign capital drawn up in terms of limits on maximum foreign shareholding or total value of individual or aggregate foreign investment.[227]

The wording of article XVI makes clear that the receiving state is entirely free in determining the extent of its market access commitments, and that it may expressly reserve powers to limit the mode of supply; there is no general obligation to remove all barriers concerning the entry and establishment of service providing firms. Each Member of the GATS is obliged to do no more than set out the specific market access commitments that it is prepared to undertake in a schedule drawn up in accordance with article XX of the GATS. Thereafter, Members shall enter into subsequent rounds of negotiations with a view to achieving progressively higher levels of liberalization.[228] Thus, the GATS stops short of guaranteeing rights of establishment in all cases. Indeed, a blanket abolition of national controls over services would have been impossible to negotiate. Consequently, a slower, progressive approach to liberalization has been adopted by all the participating states.[229]

The gradual nature of the GATS is further exemplified by the scope of the obligations that must be observed by receiving states in relation to those sectors in which market access commitments have been made. Thus, under article XVII, national treatment is guaranteed to services and service suppliers of any other Member in the scheduled sectors, but is made subject to 'any conditions and qualifications set out therein'.[230] Any additional commitments that are not subject to scheduling under articles XVI or XVII, including those relating to qualifications, standards or licensing matters, are left to negotiation between GATS Members.[231] On the other hand, certain obligations attach automatically when a member makes a specific commitment. Thus, Members must apply domestic regulations in sectors where specific commitments have been undertaken in a reasonable, objective and impartial manner,[232] and establish legal procedures that will provide the service supplier with 'prompt review of, and where justified, appropriate remedies for, administrative decisions affecting trade in services'.[233] In addition, a Member must not apply restrictions on international payments and transfers for current transactions relating to its specific commitments,[234] unless there exist serious balance-of-payments and external financial difficulties or the threat thereof.[235] These obligations can only be terminated through the termination of the underlying specific commitment.

Apart from specific commitments made under the above-mentioned provisions, the GATS introduces certain general obligations binding upon Members as a result of signing the Agreement. Thus Members are bound *inter alia* to: extend Most-Favoured-Nation (MFN) treatment to all other members (article II); offer transparency in the publication of laws and regulations pertaining to trade in services (article III); work towards the progressive recognition of national qualifications in the field of services (article VII); and ensure that monopoly suppliers of services act consistently with the MFN principle and with Members' specific commitments (article VIII).

These general obligations are subject to public order, public health and national security exceptions (articles XIV, XIVbis). Furthermore, Members are allowed to declare exemptions lasting up to ten years from the MFN standard.[236] Thus the general obligations are rather weak.

Finally, it should be noted that the GATS contains provisions relating to LDCs. The Preamble recognizes the particular need of developing countries to exercise the right to regulate the supply of services within their territories in order to meet national policy objectives. Equally, article IV(1) encourages the negotiation of specific commitments by different Members relating to: the strengthening of the domestic services capacity of LDCs, their efficiency and competitiveness through, *inter alia*, access to technology on a commercial basis; the improvement of LDC access to distribution channels and information networks; and the liberalization of market access in sectors and modes of supply of export interest to LDCs. Furthermore, developed country Members are encouraged, by article IV(2), to establish contact points designed to facilitate LDC service suppliers in obtaining relevant commercial and technological information. Thus, the GATS is cautious not to subject LDCs to immediate liberalization and offers certain general obligations to ensure that service suppliers from LDCs can compete in international markets.[237] However, these are rather weak commitments which do not impose positive duties to open up markets for such suppliers.

For some years MNEs have been pressing their home governments for increased action over the protection of their technological advantages against copyright abuses in countries where such rights have not been respected.[238] In particular, US firms from the computer, chemical and automobile industries formed the Intellectual Property Committee to press for increased controls over international copyright 'piracy' and 'counterfeiting' of goods.[239] This led the USA, supported by other capital-exporting countries, to press for the inclusion of *trade related intellectual property measures* (TRIPs) into the Uruguay Round.[240]

The capital exporters argue that the non-observance of intellectual property rights by certain host states serves to distort trade and to impede investment in these countries. Such non-observance is said to act as a disincentive to firms that have tied up large sums in the development of new technology and products as they may be unwilling to risk that advantage being freely taken by competitors in the host state. The assumption behind this argument is that, unless the creators of new technology are assured a monopoly rent from their innovation, technological development and investment based on the most modern technology will be impaired. However, this theoretical position may not stand up to empirical scrutiny. As I. K. Minta of the UNCTC points out, the level of intellectual property protection in a host state is not necessarily a determinant of investment. There are cases of high investment levels amid low levels of such protection, and cases of non-exploitation of patents when these are granted.[241]

Notwithstanding these difficulties, the Punta del Este Declaration proceeded on the basis of the capital exporters' theoretical assumptions and placed the elaboration of new rules and disciplines in the area of TRIPs on the negotiating agenda. The aim was to 'reduce the distortions and impediments to international trade', and the Declaration emphasized the need 'to promote effective and adequate protection of intellectual property rights, and to ensure that measures and procedures to enforce intellectual property rights do not themselves become barriers to legitimate trade'. The Declaration went on to mandate negotiations for the development of a new multilateral framework to deal with trade in counterfeit goods, and stressed that the GATT negotiations would be without prejudice to initiatives taken in the World Intellectual Property Organization (WIPO) or elsewhere.

From the outset, negotiations became embroiled in disputes over the extent of this mandate. The LDCs were opposed to any discussion of substantive standards in the GATT. Such matters should, in their view, be discussed in international organizations with competence in this area. The GATT negotiations should be limited only to a clarification of the relevant GATT provisions.[242] By the Mid-Term Review, this disagreement had not been resolved.[243] However, ministers agreed to continue negotiations on: the applicability of the basic principles of the GATT and of relevant international intellectual property agreements or conventions; the provision of adequate standards and principles concerning the availability, scope and use of trade related intellectual property rights; the provision of effective and appropriate means for the enforcement of trade related intellectual property rights, taking into account differences in national legal systems; the provision of effective and expeditious procedures for the multilateral prevention and settlement of disputes between governments, including the applicability of GATT procedures; and transitional arrangements aiming at the fullest participation in the results of the negotiations.[244] Ministers further agreed to take into account concerns raised by participants related to the underlying public policy objectives of their national systems for the protection of intellectual property, including developmental and technological objectives.[245] Negotiations over counterfeit goods would also continue.[246]

The dispute over GATT jurisdiction in relation to TRIPs has been resolved in the Final Act by giving the Agreement on TRIPs separate administrative status from the GATT.[247] The Agreement will have its own council acting under the umbrella of the new World Trade Organization (WTO). This organization will also encompass the GATT and the GATS, which, too, will have its own administrative council.[248]

The TRIPs Agreement accepts the principle that intellectual property rights are private rights deserving protection.[249] Thus it accords national treatment[250] and MFN/non-discrimination standards to foreign firms.[251] Patents are to be protected for twenty years,[252] and designs for integrated circuits for ten years.[253] Computer programs will be protected as literary works under the Berne Convention.[254] The TRIPs agreement also accepts the 'special needs of the least-developed country Members in respect of maximum flexibility in the domestic implementation of laws and regulations in order to enable them to create a sound and viable technological base'.[255] Accordingly, developing countries will be allowed to delay product patent protection for up to ten years.[256]

However, the TRIPs Agreement is likely to have the effect of weakening the technology transfer policies of developing host states. Some have introduced specialized technology transfer laws which may have to be modified in the light of the new agreement. In particular, by article 40(2), Members are permitted to regulate licensing practices or conditions that may constitute an anti-competitive abuse of intellectual property rights. However, there is no mention of the regulation of such practices or conditions where they may not be anti-competitive but may, none the less, be viewed as undesirable in the light of national economic policy. The latter approach is typical of LDC technology transfer laws. Furthermore, under article 67, developed countries are encouraged to cooperate with LDCs in the preparation of domestic intellectual property legislation. There is no mention of specialized technology transfer laws. On the other hand, article 66 of the TRIPs Agreement allows LDCs up to ten years' grace before they are required to apply the agreement, except for their obligations under articles 3, 4 and 5.[257] In addition, developed countries shall provide incentives to enterprises and institutions in their territories for the purpose of promoting and encouraging technology transfer to least developed country members in order to enable them to create a sound and viable technological base.[258]

Thus, there is some recognition in the TRIPs Agreement of the need to ensure adequate technology transfer. However, the emphasis on competition and intellectual property law as the principal means of regulating technology transfer questions echoes the model preferred by developed technology-exporting countries. This model has been opposed by less developed technology-importing countries both through the development of specialised technology transfer laws and through the proposed Code of Conduct on Transfer of Technology, which is the subject of currently deadlocked negotiations under the auspices of UNCTAD. The TRIPs Agreement may serve further to undermine the negotiations on this Code.[259] These issues will be discussed more fully in chapter 12.

The final area of investment related negotiations concerns *trade related investment measures* (TRIMs). There is no commonly accepted definition of what constitutes a TRIM. This lack of clarity is apparent from the Punta del Este declaration, which states that, 'following an examination of the operation of GATT Articles related to the trade restrictive and distorting effects of investment measures, negotiations should elaborate, as appropriate, further provisions that may be necessary to avoid such adverse effects on trade.' From this statement it is not apparent what TRIMs are. All that is clear is that certain types of investment measures may have an effect on trade, and, where that effect is to restrict or distort trade, new provisions should be negotiated to avoid such effects. The capital exporting countries sought to have TRIMs included in the Uruguay Round in the light of their belief that the investment policies of certain developing and developed host states were too restrictive to permit investment decisions being made on purely economic grounds. This increased the costs of investment for MNEs and distorted international investment flows, which in turn distorted international flows of trade in intermediate products.

In particular, the capital exporters object to the use of investment incentives, which, they claim, introduce distorting subsidies for inward direct investment, and performance requirements, which operate as disincentives to investment, imposing burdens that would not be undertaken by firms if they were free to make investment decisions on economic grounds alone. The most common TRIMs to which objection has been taken are incentives by way of tax concessions, subsidies or investment grants that influence the location of investments, and performance requirements that include, *inter alia*: local equity requirements restricting foreign ownership of investments; licensing requirements and technology transfer rules requiring the transfer of foreign firms' technology; remittance and foreign exchange restrictions limiting external financial transfers; manufacturing limitations restricting production levels; domestic sales, local content and manufacturing requirements that seek to displace imports; and export requirements seeking to increase the export performance of the host state.[260]

Such measures have been taken mainly by less developed host states in order to secure the investments required for their development needs and priorities, to protect their balance-of-payments situation against distortions caused by profit remittances or payments for goods and services, and to control possible restrictive business practices on the part of foreign firms related to their market power and ownership of technology.[261] They have also been used by developed countries as part of their investment policies.[262] For example, in the European Community, governments make cash grants of up to 60 per cent of the cost of investment in priority sectors. The average effective rate is 19 per cent.[263] Fears have also been expressed by non-EC firms that EC rules concerning the Community origin of goods could act as local content requirements. For example, in response to the impending commencement, in October 1988, of exports to mainland Europe of Nissan cars assembled in Britain, France, Italy and Spain decided not to treat such cars as goods in free circulation, but as goods subject to national quota restrictions on Japanese cars, on the ground that to qualify as Community goods entitled to free entry the cars should have a content of European made components of 80 per cent. As the cars manufactured in Britain had a local content of no more than 70 per cent it was argued that they did not qualify.

The British government duly asked the Commission to intervene and to clarify the situation. It had invested considerable sums by way of industrial development assistance in the British Nissan plant in Sunderland and wished to reduce the uncertainty created by the French moves, especially as other Japanese firms were interested in setting up production plants in the UK.[264] The Commission eventually persuaded the French government to accept the British built Nissans as products of European origin under Regulation 802/68,[265] whereby products are deemed to have originated in the country in which 'the last substantial process or operation that was economically justified was performed, having been carried out in an undertaking equipped for the purpose, and resulting in the manufacture of a new product or representing an important stage of manufacture'.[266] Italy did not accept this interpretation at first. However, she reached an arrangement with Britain to allow British built Nissans to enter freely while continuing to claim that they were Japanese cars.[267] The EC Commission is unwilling to impose specific local content rules on EC assembled Japanese cars. This position was confirmed at the Uruguay Round when, in 1990, the EC finally acknowledged that local content rules were an inadmissible barrier to foreign investment. This was seen as a significant victory for Japan, which had been increasingly worried over the implications of potential local content rules on its European industrial investments.[268]

Similarly, in the USA individual states offer grants to foreign investors. Thus Michigan offered US$120 million in state and local incentives to attract Mazda in 1984 ($14,000 per job); Indiana offered US$110 million to Subaru-Isuzu in 1986 ($51,000 per job); Kentucky offered US$325 million to Toyota in 1989 ($108,000 per job).[269] Furthermore, the Federal Reserve Bank of St Louis has found a positive correlation between the international investment promotion expenditures of individual states and exports from those states.[270]

Thus, even developed states find it useful to ensure adequate levels of investment for the fulfilment of their economic plans through TRIMs. On the other hand, the US government has been willing to take a stand against TRIMs applied by foreign host states to foreign investors, as shown by the bringing of a case before the GATT Panel against Canada concerning performance requirements agreed with investors under FIRA.[271] Furthermore, s. 301 of the 1974 Trade Act, as amended in 1988, has been invoked against countries that deny access to US firms on the basis of TRIMs.[272] The USA applied s. 301 against India, in respect of what it saw as that country's excessive restrictions on foreign investment and, in particular, on the establishment of foreign service industries.[273]

As with the other areas of investment related negotiating issues, the debate on TRIMs has been strongly influenced by neo-classical economic analysis. Under this paradigm, perfect competition is assumed. It follows that TRIMs, as second-best economic policies, are in principle distortive and must be removed so as to ensure the survival of conditions of perfect competition. However, as noted in chapter 2, the very existence of MNEs results from the failure of perfect competition in international markets. Thus, economic policymakers will tend to introduce measures that combat the adverse effects of imperfect competition as conducted by MNEs. In this sense TRIMs attempt to minimize the adverse effects on the host state's economy of structural imbalances in the distribution of investment and technology. The empirical evidence suggests that there is some merit in the use of TRIMs and that the neo-classical objections are overstated.[274] Although import-substituting TRIMs may have adverse effects on the host state's economy if they merely shelter inefficient producers from competition, export performance TRIMs may actually benefit the host by ensuring a higher return from exports to world markets and encouraging backward and forward linkages that enhance economic development.[275] Therefore, the need for strict controls over TRIMs may have been overestimated by the capital-exporting states.

The Final Act contains an Agreement on TRIMs.[276] This specifies that certain categories of TRIMs offend the principles of the GATT. TRIMs that are inconsistent with the GATT are said to be measures that are mandatory or enforceable under domestic law or under administrative rulings, or compliance with which is necessary to obtain an advantage. The TRIMs Agreement identifies two groups of TRIMs that offend the GATT. The first consists of TRIMs that offend the national treatment principle in article III(4). These TRIMs either require the purchase or use by an enterprise of locally produced products or impose import restrictions on the enterprise that relate the amount of imports permitted to the volume or value of local products exported by it.[277] Secondly, the TRIMs Agreement lists other TRIMs that are equivalent to quantitative restrictions prohibited by article XI(1) of the GATT. These include: restrictions on the importation by an enterprise of products used in or related to its local production whether generally or in proportion to the amount that it exports; the achievement of such import restrictions by limiting the enterprise's access to foreign exchange; export requirements specified in relation to certain products, the volume or value of products or as a proportion of local production.[278] Developing countries will be free to deviate temporarily from these provisions to the extent that they are allowed to deviate from articles III and XI of the GATT under article XVIII thereof.[279] Thus the TRIMs Agreement offers some recognition of LDC arguments over the utility of TRIMs as a means of protecting infant industries and the balance of payments, these being the two main grounds of derogation from the GATT principles allowed under article XVIII. The TRIMs Agreement is to be administered by a committee whose responsibilities shall be assigned to it by the Council for Trade in Goods, one of the new councils to be established under the auspices of the WTO.[280]

3   Concluding Remarks

The present chapter has considered policies of investment liberalization and promotion both at the level of unilateral measures undertaken by host states and at regional and multilateral levels. In each case, the policy aim has been to remove regulatory barriers to the free flow of inward direct investment in the belief that this is likely to offer the most positive economic gains to both the national and the global economy. However, the removal of host state controls cannot automatically guarantee adequate levels or useful kinds of inward investment; nor will it guarantee an equitable international distribution of the benefits of such investment. Furthermore, competition over investment incentives between states may create economic distortions between them with little positive gain to their economies. None the less, the reduction of barriers to direct investment and the use of investment incentives stand to benefit MNEs in that they can establish operations over a wider geographical space and can enjoy reduced investment risks.

Against this background, using their ability to influence home state policy,[281] MNEs have ensured that the leading home states place the reduction of barriers to foreign direct investment on to the agendas of regional and multilateral economic organizations. In this way they hope to influence the content of host state policy away from restrictive controls over direct investment and towards an increasingly deregulated environment. This strategy has met with some success. Regional bodies such as the NAFTA and the EC have been willing to reduce barriers to direct investment within their territories. In principle, the opening up of such regional markets has been extended not only to firms already established within the region but also to those established outside it. However, the fear remains that such regional organizations can become protectionist and introduce restrictive and discriminatory regulations against the entry and establishment of firms from outside the region. By contrast, the results of the Uruguay Round have offered few concrete commitments to liberalization. The limited rights of entry and establishment under the GATS are a case in point. On the other hand, the TRIPs and TRIMs Agreements offer a potentially stronger regime of protection for foreign investors, although even these Agreements allow for substantial delays on the part of Member States before they need to be implemented.

Notes

1   See further chapter 17.

2   On which see further chapter 16.

3   For examples of developing countries espousing an 'open door' approach see Seidman 'Foreign private investors and the host country', 19 JWTL 637 at pp. 638–42 (1985). On early post-independence 'open door' policies in Nigeria see Megwa 'Foreign direct investment climate in Nigeria: the changing law and development policies', 21 Col. J. Transnat'l L. 487 at 488 (1983).

4   See further below at notes 197–212.

5   See for the period 1964–70 and a brief discussion of the 1970–4 Conservative Government M. Hodges, *Multinational Corporations and National Governments: a Case Study in the United Kingdom's Experience 1964–70* (Saxon House, 1974); for the 1974–9 Labour Government and the early years of the former Conservative Government see A. M. Gamble and S. A. Walkland, *The British Party System and Economic Policy 1945–83*

(Clarendon Press, 1984), pp. 132–40. See further M. Brech and M. Sharp, *Inward Investment: Policy Options for the United Kingdom* (Chatham House Papers No. 21, RIIA/RKP 1984); J. Stopford and L. Turner, *Britain and the Multinationals* (IRM/Wiley, 1985) esp. chapters 6, 7 and 9.

6　See part III of the Exchange Control Act 1947; suspended by SI 1979/1333 and SI 1979/1660. See Hodges, ibid., at pp. 76–86 for an analysis of the regulatory scheme under the 1947 Act.

7　Quoted in *British Business*, 26 February 1982.

8　See UNCTC, *National Legislation and Regulations Relating to Transnational Corporations, Volume VII* (1989, UN Doc. ST/CTC/91), at p. 280. See generally R. Turcon, *Foreign Direct Investment in the United States* (Sweet & Maxwell, 1993).

9　FCN Treaties are no longer concluded, having been superseded in relation to developing countries by BITs. See further chapter 17 at pp. 617–18 and see C. D. Wallace, *Legal Control of the Multinational Enterprise* (Martinus Nijhoff, 1983), at pp. 51–5.

10　The principle is also guaranteed under the right of equal protection under US laws to resident aliens. See: *Bethlehem Motors* v *Flynt* 256 US 421 (1921). See also D. Vagts, 'The United States of America and the multinational enterprise', in H. R. Hahlo *et al.* (eds), *Nationalism and the Multinational Enterprise* (Sijthoff Oceana, 1977), at pp. 15–16.

11　See *Sumitomo Shoji America Ltd* v *Avagliano* 21 ILM 970 at 976–7 (1982); 638 F. 2d 552 (2d Cir 1981) vacated 457 US 176 (1982).

12　See *Kalamazoo Spice Extraction Co.* v *The Provisional Military Government of Socialist Ethiopia* (US 6th Cir 1984) 729 F. 2d 422 (1984); 78 AJIL 902 (1984); 23 ILM 393 at 398–9 (1984). See further Wallace (note 9 above), at p. 51, n. 42 and pp. 53–4.

13　Listed in chapter 6 at note 15.

14　See at pp. 175–6.

15　UNCTC (note 8 above), at pp. 301–3; Wallace (note 9 above), at pp. 140–4; Scarborough, 'The foreign investor in the United States: disclosure, taxation and visa laws', 19 Int'l Law 85 (1985). See further chapter 10 at pp. 362–3 (disclosure) and chapter 8 at p. 296 (taxation).

16　Title 7 USC Cap 66 ss 3501–8 (1978). See Scarborough, ibid., at pp. 94–7; UNCTC, ibid., at p. 302.

17　Public Law No. 94-472 90 Stat. 2059 codified at Title 22 USC Cap 46 ss 3101–8 (1976). See Scarborough, ibid., at pp. 87–94; UNCTC, ibid., at p. 301; see also Wallace (note 9 above), at pp. 94–5.

18　22 USC s. 3104(b).

19　22 USC s. 3103(b).

20　Introduced in 1984: 49 Fed. Reg. 3174.

21　See further Y. Hadari, 'The role of tax incentives in attracting foreign investments in selected developing countries and the desirable policy', 24 Int'l Law 121 at 125–9 (1990). A good example of a country using tax incentives to attract inward direct investment is Israel. See G. Klugman, *Transnational Taxation of Foreign Investments in Israel* (Yacov, Salomon, Lipschutz & Co., 1992), chapter 2.

22　See the Industrial Development (Encouragement of External Investment) Act 1958.

23　See Finance Act 1990. See further Industrial Development Authority, Ireland, *Guide to Taxes and Tax Reliefs in Ireland* (July 1991), at pp. 3–5.

24　See T. Hadden, 'Controlling the multinationals: experience in Ireland and abroad', paper read at a conference on 'Multinationals in Ireland', Faculty of Law, University College, Galway, Ireland 13 June 1986.

25　See s. 18, Finance Act 1989 as amended by the Finance Act 1991. See further 'Dublin as a location for collective investment fund management' (Industrial Development Authority, Ireland, February 1991).

26　See further Hafiz Mirza, *Multinationals and the Growth of the Singapore Economy* (Croom Helm, 1986), chapter 3.

27　For the most recent incentive regime see *Investor's Guide to the Economic Climate of Singapore* (1991 edition, published annually by the Singapore Chamber of Commerce), chapter 5.

28　For fuller details see Invest in Britain Bureau Data Sheet, 'Local assistance to industry' (Ref: 0073a, 25 August 1992).

29　See Local Government Planning and Land Act 1980 s. 179 and Schedule 32; Invest in Britain Bureau, 'Enterprise zones' (Ref: 1076a, 8 September 1992); Lloyd and Botham, 'Ideology and implementation of enterprise zones in Britain', 8 *Urban Law and Policy* 33 (1985).

30　For fuller information see Invest in Britain Bureau Data Sheet, 'Incentives in Northern Ireland' (Ref: 0057a, 10 May 1993).

31　The UK government, in 1993, redesignated the areas that qualify as 'assisted areas'. For the first time areas of hitherto affluent South East England were designated: see 'Cartography of distress redrawn', *Financial Times*, 24/25 July 1993, p. 5; Invest in Britain Bureau Briefing on Britain (1993, Issue 3), p. 15.

32　See further Invest in Britain Bureau Data Sheet, 'Regional assistance' (Ref: 0172a, 7 September 1992).

33　See s. 4(1)(a) Industrial Development Act 1982 as amended by the Co-operative Development Agency and Industrial Development Act 1984 s. 5 and Schedule 1, and Statutory Instrument SI 1984/1845. Regional Development Grants were terminated after 31 March 1988 by the Regional Development Grants (Termination) Act 1988 (c. 11 1988) The DTI's policy behind this change can be seen in 'DTI: the Department for Enterprise' (Cm 278, 12 January 1988).

34　John Stopford and Louis Turner, *Britain and the Multinationals* (Wiley/IRM, 1985), p. 239. The specified output of cars was reached and the money was provided: see *Financial Times*, 15 December 1987, p. 1. A more recent example of assistance is the offer of some £58 million in grants and loans to the Korean company Samsung for its new factory at Wynyard, Cleveland: 'Samsung to invest £450 million in UK', *Financial Times*, 18 October 1994, pp. 1 and 12.

35　See *Financial Times*, 19 April 1989, p. 12: 'Young hails investment decision "landmark" '.

36　For analysis of the applicable case-law see D. Wyatt and A. Dashwood, *European Community Law*, 2nd edn (Sweet & Maxwell, 1993), chapter 18.

37　ESCAP/UNCTC, An Evaluation of Export Processing Zones in Selected Asian Countries (United Nations, ESCAP/UNCTC Publication Series B, No. 8. 1985), p. 1. (cited hereafter as ESCAP, 1985).

38   See further Wall, 'Export Processing Zones', 10 JWTL 478 (1976).
39   See R. Kumar, India's Export Processing Zones (Oxford University Press, 1989), at pp. 4–6.
40   See further ESCAP (1985), at pp. 15–21.
41   ESCAP (1985), at pp. 9–10.
42   On which see further L. Sklair, 'Foreign investment and Irish development: a study of the international division of labour in the Midwest region of Ireland', *Progress in Planning*, 29, 149–217 (1988). See also *Financial Times Survey: Ireland*, 1 November 1991, p. 3: 'Emphasis on service sector'.
43   See ESCAP (1985), table 1–7 at p. 45. On India's EPZs see Kumar (note 39 above).
44   See Mauritius Export Processing Zone Act (No. 51) 1970 as amended by Acts Nos 50 of 1975 and 13 of 1980. See further P. G. Alter, *Export Processing Zones for Growth and Development: the Mauritian Example* (1990); P. Hein, 'Structural transformation in an island country: the Mauritius Export Processing Zone (1971 to 1988)', 1 UNCTAD Rev. 41 (No. 2, 1989).
45   These include Senegal, Liberia, Ghana, Zaire, Togo and Madagascar, Cameroon and Kenya. For details see: UNCTAD, *Export Processing Free Zones of Sub-Saharan Africa* (UNCTAD/ECDC/225, 1992). More recently, Nigeria passed legislation in this field. See: Nigeria Export Processing Zones Decree 1991 (Decree No. 34 13 June 1991) repealed and replaced by Nigeria Export Processing Zones Decree (No. 63, 1992) of 19 November 1992: *Federal Republic of Nigeria Official Gazette*, No. 62, Vol. 79 of 1992. This decree empowers the President of Nigeria to designate areas of the country as EPZs. It also establishes the Nigeria Export Processing Zones Authority to manage, control and coordinate all activities within the Zones. The Authority has control over all goods deposited or manufactured in the Zones and power to demarcate areas within the Zones as customs territory. The first Nigerian EPZ was set up in Calabar, the capital of Cross River State. See 'Goose with the golden egg', *Newswatch Magazine*, 16 March 1992, p. 29.
46   See Law No. 230 for 1989 of 20 July 1989: unofficial English translation in 4 ICSID Rev-FILJ at pp. 376–95 (1989); comment by Marchais at p. 297. For a discussion of the origins and effects of the original Free Zones established under Law 43 of 1974, which Law 230 of 1989 replaces, see L. Sklair, 'The costs of foreign investment: the case of the Egyptian Free Zones', in Elie Kedourie and Sylvia G. Haim (eds), *Essays on the Economic History of the Middle East* (Frank Cass, 1988), p. 132.
47   ESCAP (1985), at p. 10.
48   See N. Hood and S. Young, *The Economics of Multinational Enterprise* (Longman, 1979), at p. 207.
49   See L. Sklair, *Assembling for Development: the Maquila Industry in Mexico and the United States* (Unwin Hyman, 1989, updated US publication by the Center for US–Mexican Studies, University of California, San Diego, 1993), at p. 45.
50   See Sklair, ibid., chapter 7.

51   ESCAP (1985), at pp. 21–7. See also UNCTC, *Transnational Corporations in World Development Trends and Prospects* (1988, UN Doc ST/CTC/89), box XVII.2 at pp. 274–5 (Cited hereafter as UNCTC, 1988).

52   Wall (note 38 above), at p. 481.

53   See ESCAP (1985), at pp. 30–2.

54   See, for example, the Kandla Free Trade Zone in India described by Kumar (note 39 above), at pp. 36–7 and the Bataan EPZ in the Philippines described in ESCAP (1985), at pp. 220–45.

55   ESCAP (1985), at p. 33. See further: International Confederation of Free Trade Unions, Trade Unions and the Transnationals, Information Bulletin, Special Issue No. 3, 'Export Processing Zones' (ICFTU, 1983), esp. paras 35–55. See for a discussion of the position in India's EPZs Kumar (note 39 above), at pp. 112–23.

56   *Per contra*, Kumar (ibid., pp. 120–1) shows that wage rates in the Indian EPZs are in fact only two-thirds of those in the DTA.

57   See L. Sklair, *Sociology of the Global System* (Harvester Wheatsheaf, 1991), at pp. 93–6; UNCTC (1988), at p. 275.

58   See further Sklair, ibid., at pp. 96–101; UNCTC (1988), box XIII.2 at p. 216; UNCTC/ILO, *Women Workers in Multinational Corporations in Developing Countries* (Geneva, 1985).

59   ESCAP (1985), at pp. 33–4.

60   For example, South Korea and Thailand: ESCAP (1985), at p. 34.

61   See ESCAP (1985), at pp. 35–8 for a comparative analysis.

62   ESCAP (1985), at pp. 28–9.

63   See Kumar (note 39 above), at pp. 47–8.

64   Note 46 above.

65   ESCAP (1985), at pp. 29–30.

66   See further Sklair (note 46 above).

67   See ESCAP (1985), at pp. 240–41.

68   Wall (note 38 above), at p. 485.

69   ESCAP (1985), at p. 71.

70   Ibid., at p. 75.

71   Ibid., at p. 81.

72   Ibid., at pp. 82–3.

73   See, in particular, Kumar's analysis of the relative failure of the Kandla Free Trade Zone in comparison to the Santa Cruz Electronics Export Processing Zone in India (note 39 above), and the reasons given for the failure of the Bataan EPZ in the Philippines in ESCAP (1985), at pp. 240–4.

74   Kumar (note 39 above), at pp. 184–5.

75   See John Plender, 'A bigger gap, a bigger problem', Financial Times, 10 August 1987, p. 8. See also ESCAP (1985), at p. 99.

76   ESCAP (1985), at pp. 98–106.

77   'Soviet call for moves to boost joint ventures', Financial Times, 21 April 1988.

78   See chapter 6 at note 178.

79   On the relationship between economic policy and ideology in the PRC's policy on SEZs see: T. Chan, E. K. Y. Chen and S. Chin, 'China's Special

Economic Zones: ideology, policy and practice', in Y. C. Jao and C. K. Leung (eds), *China's Special Economic Zones: Policies, Problems and Prospects* (Oxford University Press, 1986), chapter 5; V. Sit, 'The Special Economic Zones of China: a new type of export processing zone?', *The Developing Economies*, XXIII-1 (March 1985), p. 68; L. Sklair, 'Problems of socialist development: the significance of Shenzhen Special Economic Zone for China's open door development strategy', 15 *International Journal of Urban and Regional Research* (No. 2, 1991), Special issue 'Urbanisation in the Hong Kong–South China region', p. 197.

80   See E. Pow and M. J. Moser, 'Law and investment in China's Special Investment Areas', in M. Moser (ed.), *Foreign Trade, Investment and the Law in the People's Republic of China*, 2nd edn (Oxford University Press, 1987), p. 199; L. Sklair (note 57 above), at pp. 178–81.

81   Pow and Moser, ibid., at pp. 201–2.

82   English translation: *China's Foreign Economic Legislation* (Beijing, Foreign Language Press, 1982), vol. I, pp. 193–200; or *East Asian Executive Reports*, Vol. 2, No. 10. (15 October 1980), pp. 26–8. (Cited hereafter as Guangdong Regulations. The citations in the text are from the East Asian Executive Reports translation.) For analysis see: K. Herbst 'The regulatory framework for foreign investment in the Special Economic Zones', in Yao and Leung (note 79 above), at pp. 124–37; Pow and Moser, in Moser (note 80 above), at pp. 205–11; S. Nishitateno, 'China's Special Economic Zones: experimental units for economic reform', 32 ICLQ 175 (1983).

83   English translations: *China Economic News*, 25 March 1985, Registration Regulations and Labour Management Regulations; 15 April 1985, Land Use Regulations and Regulations on Economic Association Between the Xiamen SEZ and Inland Areas of China; 22 April 1985, Regulations on Technology Imports. See further Pow and Moser, ibid., at pp. 211–30.

84   Ibid. See also Herbst (note 82 above), at pp. 126–7. These were adopted on 17 November 1981. English translations: China's Foreign Economic Legislation (1982) vol. I, at pp. 207–11 (Entry and Exit Regulations); 223–8 (Labour and Wage Regulations); 215–19 (Business Registration Regulations); 233–9 (Land Registration Regulations). In 1992 the Shenzhen SEZ was given legislative autonomy thereby allowing more localized rule making than was hitherto possible under the regulatory powers of the government of Guangdong Province: *Financial Times*, 3 July 1992, p. 6.

85   Pow and Moser (note 80 above), at p. 205.

86   See in particular Pow and Moser (note 80 above).

87   Guangdong Regulations (note 82 above), article 4.

88   Guangdong Regulations, ibid., article 10.

89   English translation in *Beijing Review*, No. 18, 5 May 1986, pp. 16–17.

90   Guangdong Regulations (note 82 above), article 13.

91   Guangdong Regulations, article 14. Income Tax Law of the People's Republic of China for Enterprises with Foreign Investment and Foreign Enterprises, 1 July 1991, article 7. English translation in Beijing Review, 24–30 June 1991, p. 23.

92 See 1991 Income Tax Law, ibid., article 5.

93 Guangdong Regulations (note 82 above), article 14.

94 Ibid., article 15.

95 Ibid., article 16.

96 Ibid., article 18.

97 Ibid., article 9.

98 Ibid.

99 Ibid., article 17.

100 See Pow and Moser (note 80 above), at pp. 212–14.

101 See Guangdong Regulations (note 82 above), article 23.

102 Ibid.

103 Ibid., article 5.

104 Ibid., article 19.

105 Ibid., article 25.

106 'Peking reviews "open door" policy', *Financial Times*, 19 August 1985.

107 For a comparative account of the main SEZs see Pow and Moser (note 80 above), at pp. 202–4; for a comparison of their economic performance relative to each other and to the rest of the PRC see Kueh, 'Foreign investment and economic change in China', 131 *China Quarterly* 637 (1992). On Shenzhen see Sklair (note 79 above) and ESCAP (1985), at pp. 114–42.

108 See Pow and Moser (note 80 above), at pp. 215–19 for a comparison of the Provisional Regulations of the Special Economic Zones of Guangdong Province Governing Labour and Wages for Business Enterprises of 1 January 1982 and the corresponding national regulations for labour management in joint ventures.

109 See Sklair (note 79 above), at pp. 205–08, on which the following passage is based.

110 Ibid., at p. 208.

111 On which see Sklair, ibid., at pp. 208–13.

112 See text at notes 9–12 above; see also chapter 17 below.

113 These are by no means the only initiatives among states for closer economic cooperation. Others include ASEAN (South East Asia), see Framework Agreement on Enhancing ASEAN Economic Cooperation of 28 January 1992: 31 ILM 506 (1992); ANCOM (Venezuela, Bolivia, Colombia, Chile, Ecuador), see further chapter 16; Mercosur (Brazil, Argentina, Paraguay, Uruguay), see 30 ILM 1041 (1991); ECOWAS (West Africa), see 14 ILM 1200 (1975). Other relevant bodies include Caribbean Economic Community (CARICOM), EFTA–EEC European Economic Area (Europe) and the Magreb Association (North Africa). Space constraints prevent a full discussion of all initiatives in respect of investment taken by these bodies.

114 See Canada–Mexico–United States: North American Free Trade Agreement, 17 December 1992, Parts One–Three, 32 ILM 289 (1993); Parts Four–Eight, 32 ILM 605 (1993) (cited as NAFTA).

115 See H. Crookell, *Canadian–American Trade and Investment under the Free Trade Agreement* (Quorum Books, 1990), at pp. 19–21. See further P. Robson, *The Economics of International Integration*, 3rd edn (Allen &

Unwin, 1987), chapter 2. See also the Maastricht Treaty, 7 February 1992, text in 31 ILM 247 (1992). Whether the scheme for monetary union envisaged by this Treaty will come into operation is still open to question at the time of writing.

116   See NAFTA (note 114 above), Parts Five, Six and Seven.

117   D. Cameron, 'Striking a deal', in D. Cameron (ed.), *The Free Trade Deal* (James Lorimer & Co, 1988), at p. 23.

118   See 27 ILM 281 (1988). For a guide to the provisions of the Agreement see J. R. Johnson and J. S. Schachter, *The Free Trade Agreement: a Comprehensive Guide* (Canada Law Book Inc., 1988). For policy commentary see: Crookell (note 115 above); Cameron (note 117 above); J. J. Schrott and M. G. Smith (eds), *The Canada–United States Free Trade Agreement: the Global Impact* (Institute for International Economics, 1988); P. Morici (ed.), *Making Free Trade Work: the Canada–US Agreement* (Council on Foreign Relations, 1990); M. Gold and D. Leyton Brown, *Trade-offs on Free Trade: the Canada–US Free Trade Agreement* (Carswell, 1988); C. Reynolds, L. Waverman and G. Bueno, *The Dynamics of North American Trade and Investment: Canada, Mexico and the United States* (Stanford University Press, 1991).

119   See 27 ILM 438 (1988).

120   See Reynolds, Waverman and Bueno (note 118 above), at p. 3; 'New links across the border', *Financial Times*, 13 December 1991, p. 4, and 'Political will boosts hopes of N. America trade pact', *Financial Times*, 17 December 1991, p. 5. For an analysis of Mexico's position in the light of the US–Canada FTA see Weintraub, 'The impact of the agreement on Mexico' in Morici (note 118 above), p. 102.

121   Reynolds *et al.*, ibid.

122   See further Raby, 'The investment provisions of the Canada–United States Free Trade Agreement: a Canadian perspective', 84 AJIL 394 (1990).

123   Articles 1701–6. See further Johnson and Schachter (note 118 above), chapter 6.

124   By article 105: 'Each Party shall, to the extent provided in this Agreement, accord national treatment with respect to investment and to trade in goods and services.'

125   Articles 1402.3, 1602.8.

126   Article 1602.2.

127   Article 1602.3.

128   Article 1603.1. This provision singles out requirements concerning export levels or percentages of goods or services, import substitution of goods or services, local supply purchasing and domestic content percentages. Performance requirements cannot be imposed on investors from third countries where these would have a significant impact on trade between the US and Canada.

129   Article 1605.

130   Article 1606.

131   Article 1609.1, 1609.2.

132   Ibid., referring to article 2011.

133   Annex 1607.3.2(a)(i) A–E.

134 Annex 1607.3.2(c)(i).

135 Annex 1607.3.2(b).

136 Johnson and Schachter (note 118 above), at p. 106.

137 Annex 1607.3.3.

138 Annex 1607.3.4.

139 Defined by article 2012 as enterprises engaged in: (a) the publication, distribution or sale of books, magazines, periodicals, or newspapers in print or machine readable form but excluding the sole activity of typesetting; (b) the production, distribution, sale or exhibition of film or video recordings; (c) the production, distribution, sale or exhibition of audio or video music recordings; (d) the publication, distribution or sale of music in print or machine readable form; or (e) radio communication in which the transmissions are intended for direct reception by the general public, and all radio, television and cable television broadcasting undertakings and all satellite programming and broadcast network services.

140 Under NAFTA, as between the USA and Canada, any measures adopted in relation to cultural industries continue to be governed by the terms of the US–Canada FTA, save for those provided for by article 302 of the NAFTA and any measure of equivalent effect thereto. The rights and obligations between Canada and any other Party to NAFTA with respect to cultural industry measures shall be identical to those that apply between Canada and the USA: NAFTA (note 114 above), annex 2106.

141 Article 1607.4.

142 See chapter 6. See also Cameron (note 117 above), at p. 88, where he quotes US officials' briefing notes for the then US Treasury Secretary James Baker and US Trade Representative Clayton Yeutter to the effect that 'We could not end the life of Investment Canada, but we greatly circumscribed the scope of its activities.' But see Raby (note 122 above), who feels that significant Canadian controls over US inward investment remain.

143 Article 1608.4. The scope of the dispute settlement procedure is determined by articles 1608.1–1608.3.

144 Ibid. See further chapter 15.

145 Part Five is at 32 ILM, pp. 639–70 (1992). See also Part Eight, Chapter Twenty-one: Exceptions (ibid., at pp. 699–702); annex I (Reservations for Existing Measures and Liberalisation Commitments), pp. 704–48; annex II (Reservations for Future Measures), pp. 748–59; annex III (Activities Reserved to the State), pp. 759–60 (concerning Mexico only); annex IV (Exceptions For Most-Favoured-Nation Treatment), pp. 760–1.

146 Ibid., article 1102. This provision includes a prohibition on minimum national equity or indigenization requirements: article 1102.4.

147 Ibid., article 1103.

148 Ibid., article 1104.

149 Ibid., article 1105.

150 Ibid., article 1106.1.

151 On which see further chapter 12.

152 Ibid., article 1107.

153 Ibid., article 1108.

154 Ibid., article 1109.

155   Ibid., article 1110.
156   Ibid., article 1111.
157   Ibid., article 1114.1.
158   Ibid., article 1114.2.
159   Indeed, on 30 June 1993, a US District Court ruled that the Office of the US Trade Representative should carry out an environmental impact assessment of the NAFTA, in response to a petition by US environmental groups: *Public Citizen* v *Office of US Trade Representative* 30 June 1993, US District Court DC No. 92–2102. This ruling has since been overturned by the Federal Appeals Court, and by the US Supreme Court: 'Environmental case against Nafta rejected', *Financial Times*, 25/26 September 1993, p. 2; 'Nafta appeal rejected', *Financial Times*, 11 January 1994, p. 6.
160   Ibid., article 1115.
161   Ibid., articles 1116 (Claim by investor on its own behalf), 1117 (Claim by investor on behalf of an enterprise).
162   Ibid., article 1118.
163   Ibid., article 1120. Mexico and Canada are not yet parties to the ICSID Convention.
164   See ibid., articles 1119, 1121–38.
165   Ibid., annex 1138.2.
166   See on the US–Canada FTA: Wonnacott 'Labour and Canada–US Free Trade' in Gold and Leyton-Brown (note 118 above), p. 376; Robb, 'The Canada–US Free Trade Agreement: employment effects and adjustment in the labour market', in ibid., p. 383. On the NAFTA see G. Hufbauer and J. Schott, *NAFTA: an Assessment*, rev edn (Institute for International Economics, 1993), chapter 2.
167   See on the US–Canada FTA: Crookell (note 115 above), chapter 5; A. E. Safarian, 'Direct investment strategies and the Canada–US Free Trade Agreement', in Reynolds *et al.* (note 118 above), p. 147. On the NAFTA see Hufbauer and Schott, ibid., chapter 4, esp. pp. 79–84.
168   See M. Watkins, 'Investment', in Cameron (note 117 above), at pp. 88–90. There is some evidence that this has happened, though it is not conclusive: 'There are some flies in the Nafta ointment', *Financial Times Survey: Canada*, 9 December 1992, p. 3.
169   See further Sklair Assembling for Development (note 49 above), chapter 11.
170   'Clinton gets tips on fine-tuning Nafta', *Financial Times*, 18 February 1993, p. 3.
171   For the texts of both side agreements see 32 ILM 1480 (Environmental Cooperation), 1499 (Labor Cooperation) (1993). See further: Hufbauer and Schott (note 166 above), addendum; *Financial Times Survey: North American Free Trade*, 12 May 1993, pp. 1, 3, 4; 'Pact may clear way to free trading in N. America', *Financial Times*, 14/15 August 1993, p. 1.
172   Indeed, in article 1610 of the Agreement, the USA and Canada have pledged their intention in the Uruguay Round and in other international forums to improve multilateral arrangements and agreements with respect to investment. Although the provisions of the Agreement cannot be automatically transported into the GATT negotiations, they offer a statement

of a common US–Canadian position. See further J. Schott, 'Implications for the Uruguay Round', in Schott and Smith (note 118 above), p. 159.

173   See Sklair (note 169 above).

174   See 'FTA could undermine credibility of Gatt system', *Financial Times*, 13 November 1991.

175   In 1992 the US Customs Service had ruled that Honda cars produced in Ontario did not qualify for duty-free benefits under the US–Canada FTA, as they did not contain the 50 per cent North American content required for such treatment. Accordingly a 2.5 per cent import duty was levied upon such cars. See Cantin and Lowenfeld, 'Rules of origin, The Canada–US FTA, and the Honda case', 87 AJIL 375 (1993).

176   See the NAFTA (note 114 above), article 1139.

177   'EC positive about Nafta agreement', *Financial Times*, 13 May 1993, p. 6.

178   See EEC Treaty, articles 52–66. See also, for illustrations of the types of restrictions to be abolished: General Programme for the Abolition of Restrictions on Freedom of Establishment OJ [1974] Sp. Ed. 2nd Series IX, p. 7; General Programme for the Abolition of Restrictions on Freedom to Provide Services JO 32/62; OJ [1974] Sp. Ed. 2nd Series IX, p. 3. For a recent commentary on the applicable legal principles see D. Wyatt and A. Dashwood, *European Community Law*, 3rd edn (Sweet & Maxwell, 1993), chapter 10.

179   Thus Spain and Portugal were bound to liberalize their restrictive foreign investment screening laws on entry into the EU, as will be prospective new Member States possessing such laws, e.g. Sweden.

180   Article 58 goes on to define 'companies or firms' as 'companies or firms constituted under civil or commercial law, including co-operative societies, and other legal persons governed by public or private law, save those which are non-profit making.'

181   See previous note.

182   EEC Treaty, article 52.

183   See *R* v *HM Treasury, ex p Daily Mail and General Trust plc* [1989] 1 All ER 328 at 343 d-g per Advocate-General Darmon.

184   Ibid. For comment see Lever, 26 CMLR 327 (1989). See also *Re Expatriation of a German Company* (Case 3Z BR 14/92, Bayerisches Oberstes Landesgericht) 7 May 1992 [1993] 2 CMLR 801. The German court applied the *Daily Mail* case to prevent the relocation of the seat of a German company to London.

185   Ibid., at p. 349, paras 21–5.

186   Ibid., at pp. 348–9, paras 19–20.

187   Ibid., at p. 348, paras 15–16.

188   See *EC Commission* v *French Republic* Case 270/83 [1986] ECR 273; [1987] 1 CMLR 401; *R* v *Inland Revenue Commissioners ex parte Commerzbank AG* [1993] 3 CMLR 457; [1993] 4 All ER 37 (ECJ).

189   See General Programme for the Abolition of Restrictions on Freedom of Establishment OJ Sp. Ed. 2nd Series IX, p. 7. Title I; Case 79/85 *Segers* [1986] ECR 2375.

190   On which see further: Wyatt and Dashwood (note 178 above), at pp. 293, 311; Directive 64/221 of February 25 1964 JO [1964], 850.

191   *EC Commission* v *French Republic* (note 188 above), at para. 25.
192   See C. H. Golecombe and D. S. Holland, 'Banking and securities', in G.
      C. Hufbauer (ed.), *Europe 1992. An American Perspective* (Brookings Insti-
      tution, 1990), p. 65.
193   89/646/EEC OJ [1989] L 386/1 30 December 1989. This Directive en-
      tered into force on 1 January 1993.
194   Ibid., article 9.
195   Council Directive on investment services in the securities field 93/22/EEC
      OJ [1993] L 141/27 article 7. See further Cremona, 'A European passport
      for investment services', [1994] JBL 195.
196   Code on the Liberalization of Current Invisible Operations [OECD/
      C(61)95] (hereafter Invisibles Code); Code on the Liberalization of Capi-
      tal Movements [OECD/C(61)96] (hereafter Capital Movements Code).
      The Codes are regularly updated by Decisions of the OECD Council to
      reflect all changes in the positions of Members. The updated Codes are
      periodically republished. The current editions at the time of writing are
      those of 1992, to which all subsequent references pertain. For background
      to the Codes see: OECD, *Introduction to the OECD Codes of Liberalization*
      (June 1987), esp. chapter 2; OECD, *Liberalization of Capital Movements
      and Financial Services in the OECD Area* (1990).
197   See Invisibles Code, annex A, for list of current invisible operations
      covered.
198   See Capital Movements Code, annex A, list A (I) and (II), which deal with
      the freedom to make and to liquidate direct investments.
199   See article 1, 'General undertakings' in the respective Codes.
200   Ibid., article 2, 'Measures of liberalization'.
201   Ibid., article 9, 'Non-discrimination'.
202   Ibid. These reservations are set out in annex B to each Code. They offer
      a good periodic indicator of how far liberalization has actually progressed
      among the OECD Member States.
203   Both Codes, article 5(a), 'Controls and formalities'.
204   Ibid., article 7(a), 'Measures of derogation'.
205   Ibid., sub-paras (b) and (c).
206   Ibid., article 8, 'Right to benefit from measures of liberalization'. For the
      notification and examination procedure in relation to reservations see both
      Codes, article 12; for the notification and examination procedure in re-
      lation to derogations see both Codes, article 13.
207   See both Codes, part III, 'Terms of reference', for the composition and
      functions of the Committee.
208   See *Introduction to the OECD Codes of Liberalization* (note 196 above), at p.
      15.
209   Ibid.
210   See further *Introduction to the OECD Codes of Liberalization* (note 196
      above), at pp. 22–4.
211   See Invisibles Code, annex I to annex A, part III.
212   See chapter 16 at pp. 583–7.
213   For a full analysis of the background to the Uruguay Round negotiations
      see C. Raghavan, *Recolonisation: GATT, the Uruguay Round and the Third
      World* (Zed Books, 1990), chapters 1–4.

214 The Declaration is reproduced in ibid., annex 1; or 25 ILM 1623 (1986).

215 For a forceful statement of the LDC position see generally Raghavan, ibid. For a critical examination of India's approach to the Uruguay Round negotiations see Desai, 'India in the Uruguay Round', 23 JWTL 33 (No. 6, 1989). There is now mounting popular opposition in India against the signing of the Final Act of the Uruguay Round: 'Protests grow in India over Gatt accord', *Financial Times*, 7 April 1994, p. 6.

216 The other members were Argentina, Cuba, Egypt, Nicaragua, Nigeria, Peru, Tanzania and Yugoslavia. Argentina detached itself from the group prior to the Special Session, while Kenya and Zimbabwe joined.

217 See Randihawa, 'Punta del Este and after: negotiations on trade in services and the Uruguay Round', 21 JWTL 163 at pp. 163–4 (No. 4, 1987); *Financial Times*, 18 September 1986, p. 5: 'Gatt ministers seek a draw in wrestling match over services'.

218 For the decisions adopted at the conclusion of the mid-term review, 8 April 1989, see GATT Focus, *Newsletter*, No. 61 of May 1989 reproduced in 28 ILM 1023 (1989).

219 GATT Secretary-General Draft Final Act of the Uruguay Round (GATT Doc. MTN. TNC/W/FA).

220 See GATT Doc MTN/FA 15 December 1993 (UR-93-0246). Extracts in 33 ILM 1 (1994). For the largely unchanged agreements signed at Marrakesh on 15 April 1994 see extracts in 33 ILM 1125 (1994) (referred to below as the 'April Agreements').

221 See UNCTC, *Transnational Corporations, Services and the Uruguay Round* (1990, UN Doc. ST/CTC/103); UNCTC (1988, note 51 above), part five; UNCTC, 'The role of transnational corporations in services, including transborder data flows' (UN Doc. E/C. 10/1987/11) summarized in *The CTC Reporter*, No. 23 (Spring 1987), pp. 18–21.

222 See further Klodt, 'International trade, direct investment and regulation of services', 12 *World Competition* 49 (No. 2, 1988); Putterman, 'Transnational production in services as a form of international trade', 16 *World Competition* 123 (No. 2, 1992).

223 See Raghavan (note 213 above), chapter 5.

224 See part II, 'Negotiations on trade in services', para. 7(e): 28 ILM 1023 at 1037 (1989). Raghavan argues that the right to establishment is not covered by the Mid-Term Review Decision on the basis that the issues singled out for further negotiation in part II, para. 4 of the Decision do not specifically list it: Raghavan (note 213 above), at pp. 255–6, referring to part II, para. 4(a)–(d) of the Mid-Term Review Decision. This argument fails to take account of the fact that para. 4 states that work on a definition of services should proceed on the basis that the multilateral framework may include inter alia the, 'cross-border movement of factors of production where such movement is essential to suppliers'. This connotes an establishment in the host state that uses supplies of intermediate factors of production obtained from abroad.

225 GATT Doc. MTN/FA II-A1B; 33 ILM 44 (1994) (December Agreement); 33 ILM 1167 (1994) (April Agreement).

226 Ibid., article 1(c).

227 Ibid., article XVI (2)(e)–(f).

228 Ibid., article XIX(1). This process is to begin no later than five years after the date of entry into force of the Agreement Establishing the World Trade Organization (See GATT Doc. MTN/FA II, 33 ILM 13 (1994) (December Agreement); 33 ILM 1144 (1994) (April Agreement)).

229 See, for analysis of this negotiating problem, Jackson, 'Constructing a constitution for trade in services', 11 *The World Economy* 2 (1988). For a more radical, prescriptive approach see Nicolaides, 'Economic aspects of services: implications for a GATT agreement', 23 JWTL (No. 1, 1989) 125. See also 'Slender success in attacking barriers', *Financial Times*, 16 December 1993, p. 4.

230 GATS (note 225 above), article XVII(1).

231 Ibid., article XVIII.

232 Ibid., article VI(1).

233 Ibid., article VI(2).

234 Ibid., article XI(1).

235 Ibid., article XII.

236 Ibid., article II(2) and annex on article II, Exemptions, para. 6.

237 The OECD recommends the liberalization of services in LDCs as a positive stimulus to development. See OECD, *Trade in Services and Developing Countries* (1989).

238 The UNCTC has estimated the losses resulting from such abuses as around US$60 billion. See I. K. Minta, 'Intellectual property rights and investment issues in the Uruguay Round', *The CTC Reporter* No. 29 (Spring 1990), p. 43. See also UNCTC report on the subject to the 16th Session of the UN Commission on TNCs: UN Doc. E/C. 10/1990/13.

239 See *Financial Times*, 8 September 1986: 'A question of patent unfairness'.

240 The USA had already taken unilateral measures against such abuses by means of s. 301 of the Trade and Tariff Act 1984 (strengthened by the Omnibus Trade and Competitiveness Act 1988), whereby the US Trade Representative (USTR) kept a 'watch list' of countries that were identified as indulging in unfair intellectual property practices that adversely affected US trading interests. Listing would be followed by bilateral negotiations, which, if unsuccessful in resolving the matter, would be followed by retaliatory measures taken by the USTR against the listed country. On s. 301 generally, see further J. Bhagwati and H. Patrick (eds), *Aggressive Unilateralism: America's 301 Trade Policy and the World Trading System* (Harvester Wheatsheaf, 1991).

241 Minta (note 238 above). Minta cites case studies from the Turkish pharmaceutical industry and a survey of patent exploitation by MNEs in Nigeria to support his argument. See Kirim, 'Reconsidering patents and economic development: a case study of the Turkish pharmaceutical industry', 13 *World Development* 227 (1985); Adikibi, 'The multinational corporation and monopoly of patents in Nigeria', 16 *World Development* 517 (1988).

242 Raghavan (note 213 above), at p. 128.

243 Ibid., at pp. 257, 260.

244 Mid-Term Review Decision (note 218 above), at ILM p. 1030.

245 Ibid.

246 Ibid., ILM p. 1031.
247 Agreement on Trade Related Aspects of Intellectual Property Rights, Including Trade in Counterfeit Goods: GATT Doc. MTN/FA II-A1C; 33 ILM 81 (1994) (December Agreement); 33 ILM 1197 (1994) (April Agreement).
248 Ibid., part VII. See also the Agreement Establishing the World Trade Organization (note 228 above), especially article IV.
249 Note 247 above, preamble.
250 Ibid., article 3.
251 Ibid., article 4.
252 Ibid., article 33. By article 27(1), 'patents shall be available for any inventions, whether products or processes, in all fields of technology, provided that they are new, involve an inventive step and are capable of industrial application.' The protection is to be available regardless of the place of invention or whether the products are imported or locally produced. Article 27(3) permits the exclusion from patentability of: (a) diagnostic, therapeutic and surgical methods for the treatment of humans and animals; and (b) plants and animals other than micro-organisms and essentially biological processes for the production of plants or animals other than non-biological and microbiological processes.
253 Ibid., article 38.
254 Ibid., article 10(1).
255 Ibid., preamble.
256 Ibid., article 65.
257 These relate to national treatment, MFN treatment and provisions of multilateral agreements concluded under the auspices of the World Intellectual Property Organization.
258 Ibid., article 66(2).
259 Raghavan (note 213 above), at p. 135.
260 See Minta (note 238 above), table at p. 45. For an explanation of the principal types of investment measures taken by LDCs see Raghavan (note 213 above), at pp. 148–51. See also T. Moran, *The Impact of Trade-related Investment measures (TRIMs) on Trade and Development: Theory, Evidence and Policy Implications* (UNCTC, 1991), chapter II. A shorter summary can be found in Moran, 'The impact of TRIMs on trade and development', 1 *Transnational Corporations* (No. 1, 1992), pp. 55–65.
261 See Raghavan, ibid., at pp. 147–8.
262 See, for example, Irish and UK investment incentives described at pp. 225–6 and 226–7 above; See also the policy behind Canada's FIRA in chapter 6.
263 See S. Guisinger, 'Investment related measures', in M. W. Finger and A. Olechowski (eds), *Handbook on Multilateral Trade Negotiations* (World Bank, 1987).
264 These included Mitsubishi and Toyota. Toyota decided to invest in an assembly plant at Burnaston near Derby. See *Financial Times*, 19 April 1989, p. 1: 'Toyota invests £700m in UK assembly plant'. See ibid., p. 8, for a full analysis of the project. Similar developments have occurred in other sectors. For example, in the microchip industry Fujitsu announced

plans to establish a factory at Newton Aycliffe, County Durham. See *Financial Times*, 12 April 1989, p. 1: 'Fujitsu picks UK for chip plant'. It appears that the UK is the favoured location for direct investment by Japanese firms wishing to set up a European manufacturing base in preparation for the SEM.

265 OJ [1968] L 1148/1 as supplemented and amended.

266 Ibid., article 5. On the details of the French acceptance of this interpretation of Regulation 802/68 see *Financial Times*, 18 April 1989, p. 1: 'France backs down over UK-built Nissan cars'.

267 See *Financial Times*, 2 May 1989, p. 20: 'Italy and UK reach deal over Nissans'.

268 See *Financial Times*, 8 January 1990, p. 2: 'Gatt prepares to see fair play in trade as 1992 approaches'.

269 Moran (note 260 above), at p. 97.

270 C. C. Coughlin, *The Competitive Nature of State Spending on the Promotion of Manufacturing Exports* (Federal Reserve bank of St Louis, May/June 1988).

271 See chapter 6 at p. 199.

272 Trade and Tariff Act 1974, 88 Stat. 1978, 19 USC s. 2411ff as amended by the Omnibus Trade and Competitiveness Act of 1988 Public Law No. 100-418, 102 Stat. 1107 s. 1301. This provision lapsed in 1990 but has recently been revived in a more limited form. See 'Not so super 301 after all', *Financial Times*, 6 October 1994, p. 4.

273 See Raghavan (note 213 above), at p. 146. See also 'US versus India', *Financial Times*, 12 June 1989, p. 19. India has since proposed a partial liberalization of its foreign investment law: see chapter 6 at p. 180.

274 Minta (note 238 above), at p. 46. See further T. Moran and C. Pearson, *Trade-related Investment Performance Requirements* (OPIC, 1987); Moran and Pearson, 'Tread carefully in the field of TRIP measures', 11 *The World Economy* 119 (1988).

275 See Moran (note 260 above), chapters III, IV.

276 Agreement on Trade-related Investment Measures: GATT Doc. MTN/FA II-A1A-7; not reproduced in ILM.

277 Ibid., article 2 and annex, para. 1.

278 Ibid., article 2 and annex, para. 2.

279 Ibid., article 4.

280 Ibid., article 7.

281 On which see chapter 4.

8

Taxation Problems Associated with MNEs

As in the case of a purely domestic company, the principal aim behind the taxation of MNEs is to collect revenue on the undistributed profits of the company and upon the distributions of profits made to shareholders, in accordance with the rules applicable to the taxing jurisdiction concerned.[1] However, the taxation of MNEs involves further issues arising out of the internationally integrated operations of the firm, the legal relations between its affiliates and the territorial limits of national revenue laws. Of the many tax issues relevant to MNEs,[2] this chapter concentrates on three areas that illustrate the particular difficulties faced by tax-paying MNEs and the states that seek to collect revenue from them. The first concerns problems of international double taxation encountered by MNEs. Secondly, the ways in which home and host states can influence the location of MNE activities by use of their tax systems is considered as a prelude to the third issue, which deals with the opportunities for tax avoidance enjoyed by MNEs as a result of their integrated international operations.

1 International Double Taxation and MNEs

Where a domestic firm carries on business as an economically integrated unit through a network of separately incorporated companies, each company will be assessed to tax as a separate tax-payer. Thus, a subsidiary is liable to tax on its undistributed profits and the parent is liable to tax on the profits remitted to it by its subsidiary. This may result in the risk of double taxation where a subsidiary pays a dividend out of its profits to the parent company. The risk arises as the remitted profits would already have been included in the calculation of the subsidiary's own tax liability. Such a result may be avoided by use of group income provisions.[3] Secondly, trading losses occurring in one company may not be set off against profits occurring in another. To avoid this result domestic tax laws normally allow for certain group reliefs.[4]

By contrast, the MNE experiences further, distinctive, tax difficulties associated with its international operations. In particular, it is prone to suffer international double taxation. This differs from the double taxation to which a domestic corporate group is exposed in that the latter involves the risk of 'an income flow being subjected to more than one charge to tax within the *same* domestic tax system'.[5] International double taxation, on the other hand, arises from 'a profit being subjected to more than one charge to tax because that profit would . . . be within charge to tax under the system of two or more countries'.[6] International double taxation can arise in the case of MNE operations because both the host and the home state will claim a charge to tax on the profits of the company.[7] The host state will tax the profits of the subsidiary on the basis that these arise, or have their 'source', within the host's territory. Furthermore, the host may impose a withholding tax on dividends that are remitted out of the subsidiary's profits to the parent company. Likewise, the home state will charge the remitted profits to tax as part of the worldwide profits of the parent company, the home state's jurisdiction to tax being based on the residence of the parent company in the home country.

Were this income flow to remain subject to international double taxation, companies would face considerable disincentives against the making of foreign investments. A major investment outlay might not be returned in the form of adequate net profits. It has been argued that this result would be economically inefficient, in that there would be unequal tax treatment between domestic and foreign investment, causing a distortion in international investment and resource allocation patterns.[8] The effect would be contrary to that predicted under a state of 'tax neutrality' where, ideally, tax rates for domestic and foreign investment would be the same and taxation would thereby cease to be an important factor in investment decision-making.[9]

In order to combat international double taxation, the tax laws of most capital-exporting countries include rules for its alleviation. This can be done either by unilateral relief measures under the state's internal tax laws or by rules contained in bilateral double taxation conventions. Unilateral relief is granted irrespective of whether any other state grants reciprocal relief, while bilateral relief is granted under the reciprocal regime contained in the tax treaty concluded by the two signatory states.[10]

There are two principal methods of relieving double taxation, used in both unilateral and bilateral systems.[11] The first is the tax credit system. Under this method the parent company is permitted to set off the taxes paid by its subsidiary in the host state against its tax liability to the home state on its remitted worldwide profits. This has the effect of subjecting the MNE to the home country rate of tax as long as it is equal to, or higher than, the combined rate charged by the host state on the subsidiary's profits under corporation tax and on dividend remittances under withholding tax.

Thus, for example, where the subsidiary earns profits of 100 in the host state (H) and is taxed at a rate of 50 per cent, the remaining 50 is remitted to the parent company. This is then 'grossed up' by the amount of tax paid in H, that is, 50 + 50 = 100. The grossed up figure is then subjected to home country tax, say 50 per cent, which results in a tax liability for the parent of 50. The 50 paid in tax in H is credited against this liability, which in this case results in the elimination of further tax liability in the home state. If the home state tax were, say, 60 per cent, the parent company's liability to tax would be 10.[12] Such a system is used by the UK, Canada, Japan and the USA.[13] It achieves tax neutrality between domestic and outward foreign investors in the home state. However, where the host state tax rate is higher than that of the home state, the credit system will not protect the foreign investor against the higher foreign tax liability thereby incurred. It merely avoids the same income flow being taxed twice by the home and host state.[14]

The second method of double taxation relief is the exemption method. By this system, the home state exempts the profits of the foreign subsidiary from domestic taxation when they are remitted to the parent company. Only when the parent company distributes those profits as a dividend to its shareholders will the home state derive any revenue from them. Given that the profit remittance from the subsidiary will have been subjected to a withholding tax in the host state, and the shareholders will have been charged to full personal income tax on their received dividends without any relief for the host state withholding tax, this system retains an element of unrelieved international double taxation.[15]

However, the MNE as a whole will have been subjected only to the host state rate of tax. This results in a lower burden of tax on foreign investments than on domestic investments, provided that the tax rate in the host state is lower than that applicable in the home state.[16] It is therefore an attractive method for investors who have income from low tax countries. This has led to criticisms that the exemption method encourages investment in low tax countries and the use of tax havens.[17] On the other hand, it is an easy system to administer and, unlike the credit system, which is limited to relief from foreign income taxes, capital gains taxes or corporation taxes, it permits account to be taken of foreign taxes that do not correspond to such taxes.[18] Among the countries using this method are the Netherlands, Belgium, France and Switzerland.[19]

As noted above, apart from adopting unilateral measures, states may enter into bilateral tax treaties which regulate the incidence of international double taxation experienced by *inter alia* firms operating in both countries. According to Davies, given that most developed states offer unilateral reliefs against international double taxation that are virtually identical to treaty reliefs, it is arguable that tax treaties have only a minor role in relieving double taxation.[20] In his opinion, the major function of such treaties lies in the assistance of commercial relations between treaty partners by enabling them to divide between themselves tax revenues in respect of income falling to be taxed in both jurisdictions.[21] The result will reflect the relative economic strength of the parties. Thus where both parties enjoy equivalent reciprocal flows of trade and investment, each stands to benefit to a similar extent from the treaty. However, where the flow of trade and investment is from one party to the other, as is the case in relation to developed and less developed countries, the bulk of the benefits will flow to the capital-exporting state party.[22] The majority of bilateral tax treaties are between developed states and are based, in large measure, on terms similar to those found in the OECD Model Double Taxation Convention. It is not proposed to discuss these terms, save to the extent that they establish bilateral approaches to the problems of tax avoidance by MNEs.[23]

2   Location of Investments and Tax Considerations

In chapter 7 it was seen how host states may seek to influence the locational decisions of MNEs by offering tax incentives. Equally, home states may introduce tax incentives for domestic firms to invest abroad, as where a tax credit or exemption system operates. Alternatively, home states may introduce tax penalties against foreign direct investment where the outflow of domestic capital is believed to harm domestic investment, employment and/or balance-of-payments.[24]

A foreign tax deduction system will be attractive to a home state that wishes to discourage outward direct investment by its corporations, in that it subjects foreign investment to a higher tax liability than domestic investment. Under this method foreign tax is allowed as a deduction against the profit liable to tax in the home state. Thus the tax paid in the host state is deducted from the tax base of the parent company, unlike under the foreign tax credit system, where foreign tax is credited against the parent company's tax liability on gross profits. Thus, for example, where a subsidiary earns profits of

100 in the host state and is taxed at a rate of 50 per cent, the remaining 50 is remitted to the parent company. This is then subjected to home country tax, say 50 per cent, which results in a tax liability for the parent of 25. The total tax paid is thus 75: 50 in the host state and 25 in the home state. By comparison, as shown above, the same example yielded no parent company liability to tax under the foreign tax credit system, the total liability to tax being the 50 paid in the host state. From this example it can be seen that a deduction system will usually result in little or no relief from double taxation. It does no more than prevent the total burden of home and host state taxes from exceeding 100 per cent.[25]

A deduction system was proposed in the USA in the early 1970s under the Burke–Hartke Bill.[26] It aimed to replace the foreign tax credit and to act as an incentive for US firms to invest more in the domestic economy. However, if it had been implemented the effect on cutting outward direct investment may not have been very great, as US MNEs would have turned from the export of domestic capital to foreign capital for the expansion of their overseas operations. Furthermore, the abolition of the foreign tax credit would have subjected US firms to increased risks of international double taxation as compared to their foreign competitors, which would have put them at a long-term competitive disadvantage.[27]

Inevitably, competition for investment and revenue will continue in the international economy, despite the regulatory effects of bilateral tax treaties. Differences in national tax regimes can be expected to remain. Given these continuing differences tax considerations will be a vital factor in MNE investment decisions.[28] The outcome of numerous decisions will hinge on the applicable tax conditions. Examples include: the decision whether to operate through a permanent establishment that is subject to local taxation, or through a representative office or agent-only company that enjoys tax advantages; whether the subsidiary in a high tax host state should have a high debt structure that could involve loans from tax haven finance companies affiliated to the MNE group; whether sales to affiliates or to third parties should be channelled through conduit companies located in low tax jurisdictions;[29] whether leasing, licensing, royalty and service payments should be structured so as to channel funds to low tax jurisdictions; or whether research and development (R&D) activities should be located in the home country or overseas so as to take maximum advantage of available R&D expense allowances.[30] Thus, tax considerations will affect the economic and legal nature of a MNE's presence in a country, and will provide the background to international tax avoidance mechanisms employed by MNEs.

3   Tax Avoidance and MNEs

One of the most contentious issues arising from the operations of MNEs has been their apparent ability to avoid, or even to evade,[31] tax through the use of their integrated international business networks. In particular two issues have given rise to concern: the so-called 'transfer pricing' problem and the use of 'tax havens' by MNEs.

3.1   The 'Transfer Pricing' Problem

In chapter 2 it was seen that, according to the proponents of the 'internalization' theory of MNE growth, one of the principal features of the MNE is its ability to replace cross-border, arm's length, markets in intermediate factors of production with an intra-firm 'market'.[32] This permits the transfer of goods, services and know-how between affiliates of a MNE without the uncertainties of arm's length transactions, under a system of planning in the allocation and pricing of such transfers. Thereby, the overall costs of production to the MNE can be reduced, enhancing its efficiency as a producer.

When such integration of production flows occurs across national borders, not only can the MNE organize production around the more efficient internal 'market' in inputs, it can also control that market across national jurisdictions, so as to minimize the group's exposure to liability under the fiscal and excise regimes of the countries in which it operates. Thus, for example, where a subsidiary in country A is subject to a corporation tax rate of 40 per cent and a subsidiary in country B is subject to a rate of 20 per cent, the prices charged for transfers of inputs between them can be manipulated so as to ensure that the bulk of the profits earned by the two related undertakings appears in the books of the subsidiary in B. This can be done, first, by under-invoicing B for the cost of inputs bought by it from A, thereby reducing the profits made by A from sales to B, and increasing the profits of B by reason of cheaper inputs from A. Alternatively, should B supply inputs to A, A can be over-invoiced for the cost thereof, resulting in a reduction in A's profits, and in a corresponding transfer of the inflated purchase price to B's profit account. From the firm's perspective this is an efficient outcome, as the group's overall liability to tax is reduced. From country A's perspective this amounts to a loss of revenue from the business activities of subsidiary A, by reason of A's profits being relocated to subsidiary B through the internal 'market' of the MNE. From country B's perspective, it is a gain to the revenue from profit-generating activities that take place outside its jurisdiction.

From this simple example it is clear that the internal administration of transfer prices by a MNE can create significant regulatory conflicts. First, country A may seek to control the manipulation of internal transfer prices by the MNE, so as to ensure that profit-generating activities carried on by the MNE within its borders are effectively and fully taxed. Secondly, country A may seek the co-operation of country B in reducing the incentive for tax avoidance that the latter's lower rate of tax offers. This may entail the opposition of country B, in that it stands to gain from such avoidance as long as country A's tax rates are higher, and on the ground that country A may be interfering with country B's sovereign power to set and administer taxation within its own jurisdiction.

In order to understand how such regulatory conflicts arise, and the types of measures that have been devised to combat the problem of tax avoidance by MNEs, this section of the chapter considers, first, how transfer prices are established within the internal 'market' of a MNE. Secondly, the incentives that prompt firms to engage in transfer price manipulations, and the costs of so doing, are identified. Too often, discussion on the activities of MNEs simply assumes that because the possibility of manipulating transfer prices exists it will always be taken. However, in practice the costs may outweigh the advantages, and the firm will not engage in such manipulations. The existing empirical evidence on the incidence of transfer price manipulations by MNEs will be briefly considered in this connection. After these matters have been dealt with, the two principal approaches to the control of transfer price manipulation will be described. These are the so-called 'arm's length' and 'formula apportionment' approaches. This will include an analysis of the new US approach based on the 'comparable profit interval' (CPI).

3.1.1 *Establishing transfer prices in MNE networks* Under this heading two matters will be described: first, the principal methods for establishing transfer prices within a MNE network; secondly, the principal types of transactions through which transfer price manipulations can occur.

The pricing of transfers of goods and services within a MNE network creates considerable managerial and accounting problems. In particular, while the management of individual plants and divisions may be carried out on a decentralized basis, and is made accountable by means of separate accounts for each 'profit centre', the collective interests of the group enterprise may require the formulation of a centralized financial strategy. This often results in the centralized setting of transfer prices over which each profit centre will have no control. The ability of individual profit centres to maximize their profits could be compromised in the process. Thus, to avoid the creation of disputes over pricing between profit centres, or between central and local management, the enterprise must establish transfer prices in a rational way.[33] Furthermore, the pricing mechanism must be such as to allow for the setting of optimal prices on internal flows of goods and services. Failure to do so could result in misallocations of resources, and in distortions in the final prices of products.[34]

To meet these requirements MNEs have used a variety of mechanisms to set internal transfer prices. Two basic methods are used, although there are numerous individual variations.[35] The first is the 'cost-plus' method. This starts with the basic cost of the item to be transferred, calculated according to one of a number of possible costing criteria, to which is added a percentage mark-up, allowing a margin of profit to accrue to each seller in the chain. The second is the 'sales-minus' method. Here the final price of the finished product is the starting point. From this a percentage discount is subtracted, leaving the buyer with a margin of profit on the transfer, based on the assumption that the affiliated buyer will add value to the product prior to resale at the final price.

From a purely economic perspective both approaches have been criticized.[36] The cost-plus method has been criticized for condoning avoidable high cost production techniques, for not taking into account the price a final product might fetch and for the fact that the mark-up percentage can at best be determined by a rule of thumb. Furthermore, there is serious disagreement as to the type of costing criterion that should be adopted. One of three main criteria may be applied: marginal or direct costing, which charges only the direct costs of labour and raw materials to the transaction, the overheads being charged against the parent company's profit and loss account; full costing, which allocates overhead costs to the various products being transferred; and standard costing, which allocates costs based on anticipated costs per unit of output. The sales-minus approach, while acknowledging the final price of finished products, does not avoid the other drawbacks of the cost-plus formula. Furthermore, the final price might be artificially inflated by the monopolistic position of the enterprise in its market, thereby making it only remotely connected with the true costs of production. Moreover, if the final retail price were inflated by the marketing division, its profits could rise at the expense of production division profits.

Given these drawbacks the question arises as to whether open market prices for the items transferred may be used. In principle, such prices should offer the most efficient and accurate valuation system. Furthermore, market prices would appear to be suitable for use in a divisionalized enterprise operating through profit centres, in that they would create incentives for profit centre managers to reduce costs and maximize profits. However, the realities of MNE operations limit the utility of open market prices. First, the use of such prices assumes that profit centres are free to purchase inputs on the open market rather than through the MNE network. This may not be the case, even for commonly available inputs. Secondly, the market pricing approach assumes that all the relevant productive inputs are freely available on open markets at arm's length prices. Where a MNE possesses specialized productive technology or managerial know-how, it is highly unlikely that comparable and/or compatible alternative inputs can be purchased in an open market. Thus no open market may exist in which an arm's length price can be established.[37]

Furthermore, it might be wrong to assume that open market prices are somehow more objective and less arbitrary than internally determined transfer prices. The existence of perfectly competitive markets in intermediate products cannot be assumed. In cases where a free market does not exist an internally determined transfer price may be the best approximation of its value.[38] Even where a comparable free market price can be established, it will benefit the firm to use internally set transfer prices so as to achieve the various efficiency objectives that the manipulation of such prices can offer.[39] In this respect the general preference has been to use cost based methods, although market price based approaches have also had wide application.[40]

The transfer of financial payments and flows within a MNE can occur in a variety of ways. The conduit chosen for such purposes will have important implications for ensuring an efficient allocation of money payments among the component companies of the MNE, given that different financial flows will incur different rates of tax liability. Therefore, MNEs will use different conduits to channel funds depending on their relative profitability to the group. For example, a subsidiary can remit profits to its parent by way of a dividend payment, which would become subject to withholding tax in the host state and to corporation tax in the hands of the parent. However, should the parent make a loan to the subsidiary, the remittance of interest by the latter to the parent may not incur the same level of tax liability. The payment of interest by the subsidiary would not normally incur liability to withholding tax in the host state, and the interest repayments would be tax deductible in the hands of the subsidiary. Furthermore, the interest rate can be set to achieve the best profit shifting effect. Consequently, the overall tax burden of the group can be reduced, provided the repayment complies with the home and host states' anti-avoidance laws as a genuine repayment and not a deemed dividend, and the interest rate charged is not questioned.[41] Additionally, certain channels may be preferred over others because transfer price manipulations will be harder to detect.

Thus, payments for services may be preferred to payments for goods, as arm's length prices for services rendered may be harder to ascertain.[42]

The principal conduits for transfer pricing manipulations can be classified as follows.[43] First, trade related payments may be used in the form of payments for goods and payments of interest on trade credits. Secondly, as noted in the above-mentioned example, intra-firm loans can be used, as where a short- or long-term loan is made to an affiliate and the interest rate is fixed for maximum profit shifting effect. Thirdly, service payments can act as conduits. These may include payment fees for use of patents and trademarks, payments of overhead costs and payments for specific services rendered by one affiliate to another. Financial flows within the enterprise also occur through equity related payments. These may be made by the parent, through its equity contribution to the subsidiary, and by the subsidiary, through its dividend remittances to the parent. Here the MNE may have little flexibility in manipulating transfer prices owing to high levels of legal regulation, but the amount of remittance and reinvestment may be controlled by the parent, thereby ensuring a more efficient distribution of finance throughout the group. These flows may be particularly important in relation to the use of tax haven holding companies.

3.1.2 Incentives, disincentives and empirical evidence for transfer price manipulations   According to Sanjaya Lall incentives for transfer price manipulations can be classified under two broad heads: those which maximize the present value of the MNE's overall profits and those which minimize the present and future risk of uncertainty about the value of profits.[44] Under the first heading come manipulations aimed at: the reduction of tax or tariff liability by taking advantage of differences in national tax and tariff rates; the avoidance of restrictions on the remittance of profits by overpricing imports into the jurisdiction; exchange rate speculation involving the removal of profits from a devaluing currency into a stronger one; and the reduction of dividends payable to local shareholders by way of reducing the profitability of a local subsidiary through the overpricing of imports.[45] Under the second heading come manipulations aimed at minimizing the exposure of the firm's profits to governmental threats of expropriation or to threats from trade union activism, or at reducing the apparent profitability of a subsidiary as a method of deterring competitors from making an entry into the subsidiary's market.[46]

As mentioned above, whether or not a MNE will take advantage of such possibilities depends upon the actual profitability of such manipulations to the enterprise. Merely because the theoretical opportunity to engage in transfer price manipulation exists, this does not mean that it will take place. According to Plasschaert, given the actual operation of the international taxation system, with tax credits, exemptions and limited deferral rules being employed by states, the actual possibilities of making significant savings to tax are relatively limited, except in the case of tax haven jurisdictions. However, even such jurisdictions may offer only temporary advantages as profits remitted there will have to be repatriated to the home country to sustain dividend payments and, as will be seen below, several home states have adopted laws controlling the use of tax havens.[47]

Furthermore, the costs of running an effective transfer pricing operation may be too great given the specialist tax and other expertise involved, the possibility of conflicts between central management and local profit centre managers (which may require two sets of accounts to be drawn up, one for internal and one for external use)[48] and the rate at which local tax and excise conditions change, requiring complex computer modelling of the international tax situation of the firm. In such circumstances it may be better to establish stable internal transfer prices, even if this results in the loss of marginal gains against tax liability.

In addition to such internal costs, the increasing use of transfer pricing controls by national revenue authorities may increase the external limitations on transfer price manipulations.[49] Indeed, the detection of such tax avoidance (or evasion) could seriously harm the reputation of the firm. Therefore, the firm must consider the likelihood of being detected before it engages in tax reducing manipulations. This depends on the extent to which the country in question can effectively operate its anti-avoidance legislation. In this respect the developed home states of MNEs are likely to be more effective than less developed host states, with their more limited resources.[50]

Finally, the extent to which MNEs actually engage in transfer price manipulations should be briefly considered. The major sources of evidence for such practices consist of a number of empirical studies,[51] whose general representativeness has been questioned,[52] and reports of cases involving transfer price abuses. Of these, the most extensive report is that of the UK Monopolies and Mergers Commission (MMC) into the pricing practices of the Swiss pharmaceutical firm Hoffman–La Roche during the 1960s. This concerned inter alia the transfer prices charged by the Swiss company for imports of Librium and Valium to its UK subsidiary during that time. The MMC found that considerable overpricing of the imported active ingredients had occurred. It ordered the company to reduce the prices of its final products, to repay the UK government for earlier overpricing of the products sold to the National Health

Service and to pay some £1.58 million in additional tax.[53] This report was made in the context of a monopolies investigation, and, as such, the tax avoidance issues were incidental to the major questions of market dominance and overpricing of finished products. The outcome of the investigation shows how these issues can be interrelated.[54] In one respect, the MMC Report is exceptional. As far as Inland Revenue investigations into transfer pricing abuses are concerned, it is not usual for findings to be published. The procedure is confidential and subject to strict prohibitions against disclosure.[55] Furthermore, the Inland Revenue prefers a negotiated approach to transfer pricing issues and litigation in open court has not occurred. Thus, little officially reported information on transfer pricing practices is available in the UK.

By contrast, the US transfer pricing control system, with its emphasis on detailed rules and regulations, is more likely to result in litigation. Thus, a significant source of information over transfer pricing manipulations has come to light in reported US cases.[56] However, these cases concern evidence of past practices in specific industries under particular tax conditions. Thus, even these sources cannot offer conclusive general data as to the nature and incidence of transfer pricing.

Nevertheless, given the fact that the tax authorities of most of the major capital-exporting countries, and not insignificant numbers of capital-importing countries,[57] are prepared to set up transfer price monitoring units, and to empower tax commissioners to reallocate income from transfers of value between related entities, it can be presumed that transfer price manipulations are likely to be taken up by MNEs in the absence of the deterrent effect of these regulatory structures.

3.1.3   The regulation of transfer price manipulations: arm's length and comparable profit interval (CPI)   This sub-section describes the principal regulatory approaches to international transfer price manipulations by MNEs.[58] It concentrates on US federal and state laws as these offer the most developed and open illustrations of the various approaches in operation. UK practice will also be referred to where useful.[59]

The *arm's length approach* is the principal method used for the reallocation of income between related enterprises for tax purposes. It is the approach accepted by the OECD Member States in the OECD Model Double Taxation Convention.[60] Essentially, the arm's length approach seeks to allocate the profits and losses on a transfer between entities under common ownership or control by reference to the prices charged in a comparable transaction undertaken by uncontrolled entities dealing at arm's length with each other. Thereby, the tax authorities can make a reallocation which reflects, as far as possible, the allocation that would have occurred if the related parties had themselves been dealing at arm's length.

The arm's length standard underlies the UK approach to transfer pricing controls. Section 770 of the Income and Corporation Taxes Act 1988 lays down the applicability of the arm's length standard to the review of prices charged for transfers of property between a resident and non-resident body of persons when one controls the other or both are under common control.[61] The approach of the UK Inland Revenue to transfer pricing matters can be gleaned from periodic press releases.[62] The Inland Revenue will be guided by the considerations set out in the 1995 OECD Transfer Pricing Guidelines in its application of the arm's length standard.[63]

The best illustration of the arm's length method of income allocation is offered by US federal tax law, as it stood prior to 1993. The basic power to reallocate income between related entities is set down in s. 482 of the US Internal Revenue Code:

In any case where two or more organizations, trades or businesses (whether or not incorporated, whether or not organized in the United States, and whether or not affiliated) owned or controlled directly or indirectly by the same interests, the Secretary may distribute, apportion, or allocate gross income, deductions, credits, or allowances between or among such organizations, trades, or businesses, if he determines that such distribution, apportionment, or allocation is necessary in order to prevent evasion of taxes or clearly to reflect the income of any such organizations, trades, or businesses. In the case of any transfer (or license) of intangible property (within the meaning of section 936(h)(3)(B)), the income with respect to such transfer or license shall be commensurate with the income attributable to the intangible.[64]

Regulations prescribing the criteria to be used for the control of income allocations falling under s. 482 were passed in 1968, and were revised in 1993.[65] The 1968 Regulations established that the aim of s. 482 was to 'place a controlled taxpayer on a tax parity with an uncontrolled taxpayer, by determining, according to the standard of an uncontrolled taxpayer, the true taxable income from the property and business of each of the controlled taxpayers.'[66] The Regulations went on to make clear that s. 482 could be used not only to combat the avoidance or evasion of tax by way of transfer price manipulations but also in cases where internal transfer pricing did not aim to reduce the MNE's overall liability to US and foreign tax, but had the inadvertent effect of reducing the US share of that tax.[67] Thus s. 482 is a significant revenue gathering provision which may be particularly attractive to a US administration in a recession and/or in a political climate hostile to increases in personal income tax.

In order to reallocate income under s. 482, the Commissioner must establish, first, that the entities involved are owned or controlled directly or indirectly by the same interests and, secondly, that the allocation of income between the related entities is other than that which could be expected where the transaction had been effected between uncontrolled entities dealing at arm's length. The Commissioner's discretion in these matters is broad.[68] Only where the Commissioner makes a reallocation that is arbitrary, capricious or unreasonable will it be overruled.[69] 'Controlled' for the purposes of s. 482 is defined as 'any kind of control, direct or indirect, whether legally enforceable, and however exercisable or exercised. It is the reality of control which is decisive, not its form or the mode of its exercise. A presumption of control arises if income or deductions have been arbitrarily shifted.'[70] To come within the scrutiny of s. 482, the controlling interest must have complete power to shift income among its subsidiaries.[71]

Under the 1968 Regulations the arm's length allocation methods to be used by the Commissioner were laid down in a strict order of application.[72] By way of illustration, two significant cases will be considered: first, the allocation of income in sales of tangible property between members of a group of controlled entities; secondly, allocations in the case of the transfer or use of intangible property, such as intellectual property rights, a matter that has grown in significance in recent years.

In the case of sales involving tangible property, the Commissioner was obliged to use one of three allocation methods prescribed in the Regulations. He was first obliged to consider the transaction under the comparable uncontrolled price method.[73] This required the Commissioner to establish the arm's length price of a controlled sale by reference to the price paid in a comparable uncontrolled sale.[74] This method had to be used wherever there were comparable uncontrolled sales.[75] However, where there were no comparable uncontrolled sales, the resale price method had to be used.[76] Where there were no comparable uncontrolled transactions and the resale price method was inappropriate, the Commissioner had to use the cost-plus method. Typically, this would be appropriate where 'a manufacturer sells products to a related entity which performs substantial manufacturing, assembly or other processing of the product or adds significant value by reason of its utilization of its intangible property prior to resale in uncontrolled transactions.'[77]

Should none of these methods be reasonably applicable to the facts of a particular case, the Commissioner could use some other appropriate method of pricing.[78] In certain cases this entailed the determination of an appropriate 'profit split' between the related entities. In *Eli Lilly & Co.* v *CIR*, the Court of Appeals for the Seventh Circuit described the profit split method as one that 'divides combined revenues based on an ad hoc assessment of the contributions of the assets and activities of the commonly controlled enterprises'.[79] The Court of Appeals went on to criticize it as an inherently imprecise method of allocation. Indeed the outcome may be largely determined by bargaining between the fiscal authorities and the tax-paying company.[80]

The profit split approach has been used in a number of cases involving the transfer of intangibles between related entities, an area in which the ascertainment of arm's length prices is often fraught with difficulty, owing to the relative absence of comparable uncontrolled transactions from which an arm's length price can be determined.[81] A profit split may be more appropriate in dealing with transfers of intangibles between related enterprises because, to the transferor, the income stream from the transfer will consist not only of the consideration payable for the intangible by the related transferee but also the enhanced value of its direct or indirect equity interest in the related transferee. Thus an unmodified arm's length pricing approach may not show clearly the true economic value of the transaction.[82]

To meet such difficulties, s. 482 was amended by the Tax Reform Act 1986. This added the last sentence, which introduces the 'commensurate with income' standard to cases involving the transfer or licence of intangible property.[83] According to McDaniel and Ault, 'this language was intended to mandate a profit splitting approach which looks to the actual profit generated by the intangible and the relative economic contributions which each of the related parties involved has made to the income which has been generated.'[84] In 1988 the US Treasury Department issued a White Paper to review the application of the 'commensurate with income' standard.[85] The White Paper introduced four different approaches to the allocation of income from intangibles, each of which aims at ascertaining a price as close as possible to an arm's length price. The first two approaches, the 'exact comparable' and the 'inexact comparable' methods, echoed the arm's length method. The price of the intangible transferred in the related party transaction would be determined by comparison with an exactly comparable transaction between unrelated parties, if such a transaction existed, or, in the absence of an exactly comparable transaction, with an inexactly comparable transaction which was sufficiently similar in economic terms to permit reasonable comparison.[86]

Where no exact or inexact comparable transactions existed, the White Paper advocated the use of the 'basic arm's length rate of return' (BALRM) method. This method involved an allocation of profits between the related entities which sought to distinguish between profit that was attributable to the use of tangible assets and that which was derived from the use of intangibles. This was achieved by ascertaining the market rate of return on the tangible assets and factors of production used by each entity, through a comparison with similar functions and assets employed by unrelated entities, and allocating that rate of return to the entity using the asset or factor of production in question. The remaining income would then be allocated to the intangible and was thereby allocated to the owner of the intangible, the related transferor.[87] In cases where the related transferee also owned intangibles that were used in exploiting the transferred intangible the 'BALRM plus profit split' method would apply. The method would operate as follows. First, each party would be allocated a return on the functions performed through the application of the BALRM method. The remaining income, representing the residual income from the use of intangibles, would then be split according to the relative value of the intangibles of each party. The White Paper recognizes that the splitting of intangible income will largely be a matter of judgment.[88]

In addition to defining the principles by which the 'commensurate with income' standard should be applied, the White Paper considered how that standard could be applied to cost-sharing arrangements. A cost-sharing arrangement was defined in the White Paper as 'an agreement between two or more persons to share the costs and risks of research and development as they are incurred in exchange for a specified interest in any property that is developed'.[89] Such arrangements were permitted by the s. 482 Regulations provided they were made in good faith.[90] The White Paper concluded that *bona fide* cost-sharing arrangements would continue to be acceptable, as long as any new participant compensated existing parties to the arrangement for the value of any intangibles already developed.[91]

The White Paper of 1988 represents a significant attempt to tackle the inherent weaknesses of the arm's length approach, in particular the assumption that comparable sales between uncontrolled entities exist from which an arm's length price can be determined. This leads to an air of unreality where no comparables exist. In such cases it may be unfair to the tax-payer to subject it to a comparison with inexactly comparable third party transactions, or to second guess internal transfer pricing decisions which may have been made upon commercially justifiable grounds, taking account of the competitive conditions in a particular industry and of differences in the efficiency of firms in the industry.[92] It is against the background of the White Paper that the US Internal Revenue Service (IRS) proposed, in 1992, a modification of the arm's length standard that supplements it with the CPI method.

The proposed IRS Regulations of 1992[93] sought to extend the 'commensurate with income' principle in s. 482 to related party transfers of tangibles as well as to intangibles, by way of the general adoption of the *comparable profit interval* (CPI) method.[94] This method involves a comparison of the tax-payer's allocation of profits between related entities with the range of profits that would have been earned by similarly situated uncontrolled tax-payers engaging in comparable uncontrolled transfers. It requires a complex six step analysis.[95] First, the controlled party whose profits are to be tested must be identified. The tested party may be any affiliated business that is a party to the controlled transaction, including an entity not under examination by the IRS. This may include a foreign party not subject to US taxation. Secondly, the comparable uncontrolled businesses whose profitability will be used to establish the CPI must be identified. This requires identification of comparable uncontrolled businesses with the most similar functions to those of the tested party. Failure to identify a proper comparable will undermine the whole analysis.[96] Thirdly, the 'constructive operating income' of the tested party will be computed on the basis of a comparison of the profits of the uncontrolled parties and the controlled tested party. Fourthly, the CPI is determined by identifying those amounts of constructive operating income derived from the comparable uncontrolled businesses which converge to form a range that is 'reasonably restricted in size'. Such convergence around a similar level of profitability is an indication of the level of profitability that the tested party could be expected to achieve if it were operating at arm's length. Fifthly, the 'most appropriate point' within the CPI will be determined to set the tested party's arm's length income. The CPI offers a profit period from which the most appropriate point for comparison may be selected. This offers a degree of flexibility in determining the income allocation for s. 482 purposes. Selection is made either based on statistical techniques measuring the central tendency or by reference to qualitative criteria relating to the degree of comparability of the uncontrolled party and the reliability of the profit level indicators used to generate the constructive operating income. The sixth, and final step, converts the 'most appropriate point' within the CPI into the transfer price for the controlled transaction(s).

The proposed Regulations did not seek to replace the existing methods of allocation under s. 482. The comparable uncontrolled price method would still have first priority, and the resale price, cost-plus and 'fourth' methods would remain.[97] However, where an allocation was made under any of these three latter methods, the CPI method would be used to validate the resulting transfer price by showing that it produced a level of operating income for the controlled party that was within the CPI.[98] As regards the treatment of transfers of intangibles, the proposed Regulations kept intact the broad approach of the White Paper. The exact comparable method was renamed the 'matching transaction method', the inexact comparable method was renamed the 'comparable adjustable transaction method', and the BALRM and BALRM plus profit split methods were amended by the CPI method.[99] The proposed regulations also contained new rules relating to cost-sharing arrangements.[100]

The original version of the proposed Regulations was received with criticism from international business circles, on the grounds *inter alia* that: companies would be forced to disregard actual contractual terms agreed on commercial principles and apply artificial pricing rules based on hypothetical profits; this would introduce arbitrary additional tax costs; vast amounts of detailed information would have to be amassed about the confidential affairs of US and foreign companies; this information would often be unavailable and, as a result, the IRS would have to make subjective judgments about profit comparisons; international double taxation would be increased to an unprecedented scale.[101] In January 1993, the OECD Committee on Fiscal Affairs reported on the proposed US reforms.[102] It was critical of the USA for departing from the classical arm's length approach and for risking increased international double taxation if other states did not accept the new US approach. The OECD committee expressed a preference for transaction-based or profit-split approaches, with CPI being used as a method of last resort. It urged the USA to make substantial amendments to this effect in the proposed Regulations, and to introduce them on a temporary basis only.

In line with these criticisms the USA issued new Regulations, effective from April 1993, on a temporary basis.[103] In relation to transfers of tangible property, the 1993 Regulations have abandoned the insistence in the 1992 proposals on the CPI method as a method of priority. Furthermore, they have abandoned the approach of the 1968 Regulations in that there is no longer a strict hierarchy of methods. Instead, the 1993 Regulations provide that the method that best gives the most accurate arm's length result should be applied. This is referred to as the 'best method rule'.[104] The Regulations then provide for a functional analysis in determining whether uncontrolled transactions are comparable to the transaction under investigation,

taking account of the functions performed, the risks involved, contractual terms adopted, applicable economic conditions and property
or services involved in the transaction.[105] They also permit for an
arm's length range of prices to be considered as the basis of comparison, rather than expecting a single price to be arrived at.[106] As for
pricing methods, the 1993 Regulations retain the comparable uncontrolled price, resale price and cost-plus methods used in the 1968
Regulations.[107] To these is added the CPI method as a non-manda-
tory alternative.[108] Where none of the other methods can reasonably
be applied any other method may be used provided that the tax-payer
discloses that method in its tax return.[109] There is a new sixth method
proposed that is based on a profit-split.[110] The 1993 Regulations
go on to provide separate treatment for transfers of intangible
property.[111] They retain the matching transaction and comparable
adjustable transaction methods from the 1992 proposals, but no
longer make the results subject to confirmation using the CPI
method. They also retain use of the CPI method and permit another
method to be used on the same terms as for transactions involving
tangible property. The 1993 Regulations deal with a particular problem relating to restrictions on payments under foreign laws and their
effects on IRS allocations under s. 482.[112] New penalties for under-
statement of tax arising from a substantial valuation misstatement are
introduced.[113]

Despite these apparent concessions to the criticisms of the 1992
proposals, the 1993 Regulations have themselves been criticized by
the International Chamber of Commerce (ICC) Commission on
Taxation.[114] The ICC Commission feels that the arm's length standard remains the only legitimate approach for determining intercompany transfer prices in cross-border transactions and that the 1993
Regulations still give the CPI method too high a status. The Commission rejects that a comparison of profits is a reliable guide in
determining whether the contractual terms in a given controlled
transaction are terms to which uncontrolled tax-payers would have
agreed.[115] Furthermore, the 'best method rule' suggests that CPI will
be used in a large number of cases in relation to both tangibles and
intangibles, as the Regulations presume that it will ordinarily, 'provide an accurate measure of an arms-length result'.[116] The apparent
bias towards the CPI method is seen as having been reinforced by the
fact that the profit-split method is outside the 'best methods' rule.[117]
Thus, the Commission concludes that the 1993 Regulations remain
essentially the same in terms of methodology as the 1992 proposals,
and are open to the same objections on grounds of impracticality
as well as on the grounds of incompatibility with the arms-length
principle.[118]

Despite differences in the formal content of laws, certain *common problems concerning the administration of a transfer pricing control system* will emerge. First, it may be hard to identify that a MNE is engaging in tax avoidance through transfer price manipulations. The tax authorities will have to infer facts from annual tax returns. Initial indications of such practices may appear in the form of consistent losses made over a period of years in an associated enterprise. However, there may be good reasons for such a situation, such as the existence of strong political or social pressures to keep the enterprise open, or the hope that eventually it will become a profitable venture.[119] Other indications might include the receipt of goods or services from a related enterprise for little or no payment.[120] Again, the authorities must be satisfied that there are no sound commercial reasons for such a practice, and that the main purpose of the transactions is the shifting of liability to tax. To assist in the determination of appropriate arm's length prices, the tax authorities of various countries have conducted periodic industry-wide studies, thereby enhancing their general knowledge of pricing practices.[121]

Secondly, there will be problems in obtaining the relevant information from the taxpaying MNE. Once the authorities are satisfied that an investigation should be mounted, they will request further information about the MNE's commercial organization, its production and distribution systems and any other matters that will help in determining whether the internal transfer prices used by the firm are compatible with the arm's length standard. Such information can usually be ordered for disclosure if the firm does not supply it voluntarily.[122] Two problems bear specific mention in this respect. First, the tax-paying corporation may not retain sufficient documented information for use by the authorities. To avoid this difficulty the US Internal Revenue Service Regulations[123] demand annual information returns in respect of 'reportable transactions'[124] with related persons from all US corporations that are 25 per cent foreign owned, foreign corporations engaged in a US business that are 25 per cent foreign owned and any foreign corporation that is engaged in a US business even if it is not foreign owned. Failure to comply results in monetary and non-monetary penalties.[125] Other countries also require periodic disclosure of information for transfer pricing control.[126] In the UK no special reporting requirements exist. The tax-payer must submit its annual tax return to the Inland Revenue with accompanying accounts and computations that substantiate the return. Where no return is made, or where the Inspector of Taxes is dissatisfied with the return, the Inspector is empowered to assess liability to tax on the basis of his or her own estimate of profits. The tax-payer can appeal to the Tax Commissioners against this assessment but must disprove the correctness of the assessment.[127] Secondly, problems of extraterritoriality may arise if the information required lies outside the jurisdiction of the taxing state. The problems involved have already been considered in chapter 5, in relation to the use of US extraterritorial disclosure orders in IRS investigations.[128] The UK position on disclosure of information from non-resident related companies is laid down in s. 772(2) of the Income and Corporation Taxes Act 1988. This empowers the Inland Revenue to order the disclosure, by a UK-resident parent company, of relevant information located with any company that it controls[129] regarding transactions between the parent and any of its 51 per cent held non-resident subsidiaries, or between such a non-resident subsidiary and a UK-resident 51 per cent held subsidiary. This section seeks to avoid extraterritoriality conflicts by restricting the order to the UK-resident parent company alone.

The possibility of jurisdictional conflicts over disclosure can be diminished, though not entirely eliminated, where a bilateral double taxation treaty exists between the home and host states of the MNE. This will usually contain a provision requiring the exchange of information necessary for carrying out the provisions of the treaty or the domestic tax laws of the contracting states.[130] However, under the OECD Model Convention the duty to exchange information does not include any obligations: to carry out administrative measures at variance with the laws and practices of one or other contracting state; to supply information that is not obtainable under the laws or in the normal course of the administration of one or other contracting state; or to supply information which would disclose any trade secrets or trade processes, or information the disclosure of which would be contrary to public policy (ordre public).[131] Therefore difficulties may still arise over whether the information requested is within the ambit of the duty to exchange or lies outside its scope.

A third difficulty associated with the regulation of transfer price manipulations is that of international double taxation. This may arise where a reallocation decision results in the shifting of income from one country to another. For example, if the taxable income split on a transaction between the parent and its foreign subsidiary is stated by the parties as being 25/75 per cent, and the home state reallocates this to 50/50 per cent, unless the host state tax authorities make a corresponding downward adjustment of 25 per cent on the taxable income of the subsidiary, there is a risk of economic double taxation on the group as a whole. To alleviate this possibility article 9(2) of the OECD Model Double Taxation Convention recommends that the host state makes the necessary adjustment to the tax charged on the subsidiary's profits. However, the article 9(2) procedure is not compulsory, which weakens it considerably. Where the host state refuses to make an adjustment, as where it disagrees with the application of the arm's length valuation made by the home state, the two states should enter into consultations through their competent authorities with a view to resolving their differences.[132] A provision based on article 9(2) is contained in many, but not all, bilateral double taxation treaties.[133]

A more developed system of double taxation control in disputes regarding transfer price adjustments has recently been developed by the European Community. In 1990 the EC adopted a Convention on the elimination of double taxation in connection with the adjustment of profits of associated enterprises.[134] This introduces a compulsory procedure for the settlement of such disputes. Any tax-paying enterprise that feels it has been subjected to unrelieved double taxation as a result of an arm's length reallocation of income may complain to the competent authority of the Contracting State of which it is an enterprise or in which its permanent establishment is situated.[135] The competent authority will then seek to reach a mutual agreement with the competent authority of any other Contracting State concerned. If the competent authorities fail to reach such agreement within two years from the date that the tax-paying enterprise first submitted its complaint, they shall set up an advisory commission charged with delivering its opinion on the elimination of the double taxation in question.[136] The commission shall consist of an independent chairman, two representatives of each competent authority concerned and an even number of independent persons of standing to be appointed by mutual agreement from a list of independent persons nominated by the Contracting States.[137] The commission shall deliver its opinion not more than six months from the date on which the matter was referred to it.[138]

Thereupon the competent authorities party to the dispute shall take a decision by common consent which will eliminate the double taxation complained of within six months of the date of the commission's opinion. They are free to take a decision that deviates from the commission's opinion, as long as they apply the arm's length standard.[139] However, if they fail to reach agreement within the requisite period, they shall be obliged to act in accordance with that opinion.[140] This procedure deals with double taxation only after it has occurred. The EC Commission is currently studying how double taxation caused by differing income allocations could be prevented. A uniform system of EC transfer price controls could eventually emerge.[141]

A fourth difficulty arises in tax systems that permit a credit against foreign tax, in that a reallocation may affect the entitlement of the parent company to foreign tax credit. Under US law provisions exist to ensure that foreign tax credit is not used by the US tax-paying parent as a means of reducing the tax effect of any reallocation of income to it. Only where the parent can show that all efforts by its foreign subsidiary, in seeking a repayment of foreign taxes on the reallocated income, have been exhausted without success will any foreign tax credit be allowed against the tax already paid on the reallocated income.[142] Otherwise, any foreign taxes paid will be assumed to have been made as a voluntary contribution to the host state not eligible for foreign tax credit.

Inevitably, an element of uncertainty can creep in to the control of transfer pricing in related party transactions. It is in response to such uncertainty that the US IRS has proposed a new system of Advanced Determination Rulings, whereby the tax-payer can approach the IRS for a ruling that a proposed system of internal transfer pricing meets the requirements of s. 482.[143]

3.1.4 Formula apportionment Much of the discussion above centred on the difficulties inherent in establishing appropriate arm's length prices for related party transactions. Critics of the arm's length approach argue that such an enquiry is bound to fail where the transaction occurs between affiliates of an internationally integrated MNE. The arm's length standard simply does not conform to the economic reality of the group, and imposes an artificial 'separate entity' analysis upon its operations.[144] As an alternative, the formula apportionment approach is recommended.

The formula apportionment or unitary business method has been applied to tax-paying MNEs under the laws of certain states of the USA, most notably in California.[145] The essence of this approach was described by the US Supreme Court in *Container Corporation of America* v *Franchise Tax Board*.[146] The Court held that the unitary business/formula apportionment approach rejects geographical or transactional accounting and instead calculates the local tax base of corporations operating in more than one jurisdiction by means of a two step approach: first, the scope of the 'unitary business', of which the tax-paying enterprise's activities in the taxing jurisdiction form one part, must be ascertained; secondly, the total income of the unitary business between the taxing jurisdiction and the rest of the world must be ascertained and apportioned on the basis of a formula taking into account objective measures of the corporation's activities within and outside the jurisdiction.

The basic US constitutional requirement that entitles a state to tax income on a unitary basis is that there be some 'nexus' between the taxing state and the tax-payer. This is fulfilled by the conduct of some part of the corporation's business within the jurisdiction.[147] Assuming that such a nexus exists the question of whether the business involved is a 'unitary business' arises. In determining whether a unitary business exists the tax authorities must undertake an economic analysis of the activities of the MNE, and ascertain the extent to which its affiliates act as a unified business entity.[148] The approach is reminiscent of cases involving the 'lifting of the corporate veil' between parent and subsidiary, and not dissimilar criteria of analysis are employed to show that actual control over the business activities of the group is exercised by the parent company.[149]

In the *Container Corporation* case,[150] the US Supreme Court made two general observations on the evidence required to find a unitary business. First it left open the question of whether any one factor indicating control would be sufficient, by itself, to prove the existence of a unitary business. Secondly, the Supreme Court held that it was unnecessary to show a substantial flow of goods between enterprise units to prove a unitary business. The prerequisite to an acceptable finding of a unitary business was a 'flow of value, not a flow of goods'.[151] Thus the Court adopted a broad approach which could include evidence of dividend flows, royalty fees, management charges or intra-corporate loans in the determination of the existence of a unitary business.

The burden is on the tax-payer to disprove the existence of a unitary business where the state's assessment is challenged.[152] This can be done by showing that the income assessed to tax was derived from activities unrelated to the tax-payer's business within the taxing jurisdiction. In adjudicating the issue the court will look to the 'underlying economic realities of a unitary business' and must be satisfied that the income derives from an 'unrelated business activity' which constitutes a 'discreet business enterprise', if the tax-payer is to succeed.[153]

Once the existence of a 'unitary business' has been established, the tax authorities will require evidence of the worldwide profits of that business, from which the proportion of profits chargeable to tax in the taxing jurisdiction will be calculated. This is done by applying a formula based on the proportion of total payroll, property and sales of the unitary business that are located within the taxing jurisdiction. Under US law, for an apportionment to stand, it must be applied fairly by the taxing state and must not result in discrimination against interstate or foreign commerce, in breach of the US Constitution.[154] This requires that the application of the formula should not lead to double taxation. Furthermore, within the context of US state and federal relations, the application of the formula must not impair the need for federal uniformity in matters of foreign commerce.[155]

The formula apportionment method has engaged considerable opposition, from US and foreign MNEs, from the US government and from a number of foreign states, including the United Kingdom. Indeed, the UK has introduced, under s. 54 of the Finance Act 1985, a power of retaliation against US companies operating in the UK, if any British company is subjected to tax on the unitary principle.[156] The major basis of opposition is that the unitary tax system inevitably leads to double taxation. Furthermore, as far as the US government is concerned, the use of worldwide unitary taxation methods by states of the Union prevents it from speaking with one voice in matters of international trade, given the wide adoption of 'water's edge', that is source-based, approaches to corporate taxation by other countries, and by the USA in international tax treaties.[157]

As to the issue of double taxation, where a payroll, property and sales formula is used, it will tend to allocate a higher proportion of income to jurisdictions where wage rates, property values and sales prices are higher. Thus it has an inevitable double taxation effect, in that a high proportion of income already taxed at source in a foreign jurisdiction will be reallocated to the taxing jurisdiction, provided it is more economically developed than the foreign jurisdiction.[158] For example, on the facts of *Container Corporation*,[159] some 13 per cent of the appellant US corporation's worldwide income from its unitary business was allocated to its operations in Latin America. This was less than half of the arm's length total. Thus profits taxed at source in Latin American host states would again be taxed in California.

In *Container Corporation* a US based company with a business presence in California sought to challenge the constitutionality of California's use of the unitary tax system in relation to its cardboard package manufacturing business, which took place in California and in several Latin American affiliates. The US company did not succeed. The Supreme Court was satisfied that the Californian tax authorities had acted constitutionally. However, the Supreme Court explicitly left open the question whether the application of worldwide unitary tax to the US subsidiary of a foreign parent company would be constitutional.[160]

More recently, cases challenging unitary tax assessments against US subsidiaries of foreign parent companies have reached US courts. In particular, the US Supreme Court has had occasion to consider the extent to which a foreign parent company has standing before the federal and state courts to challenge a state's method of determining tax. In *Franchise Tax Board of California* v *Alcan Aluminum et al.*[161] the Supreme Court accepted in principle that the foreign parent of a US subsidiary that had been subjected to a worldwide unitary tax assessment could be said to have suffered an actual financial injury such as would give it standing to bring a case under the Foreign Commerce Clause of the US Constitution. However, the Supreme Court did not feel it necessary to offer standing before the US federal courts on the ground that, in the first instance, any challenge against the application of state taxation laws should be made before state courts. Furthermore, it was held that the foreign parent need not have an independent right of action before the state courts. The US subsidiary could plead injury to the parent company's interests on the latter's behalf, by virtue of the control exercised by the parent over its subsidiary. Thus, while not giving an unqualified right of action to foreign parent companies, and thereby avoiding a decision as to whether this was an appropriate case for direct shareholder rights of action,[162] this case appears to have moved a little beyond earlier decisions, made in certain Circuits of the US Court of Appeals, to the effect that unitary tax does not cause direct or independent harm to the foreign parent company.[163]

Significantly, in California, changes in the law appear to be moving away from the use of worldwide unitary taxation in the case of foreign parent companies and their US subsidiaries. In 1988, California allowed foreign based MNEs the option of computing their California taxes according to the 'water's edge' principle, on payment of a fee into the California Unitary Fund.[164] Furthermore, in November 1990 the California Court of Appeals held, in the case of *Barclays Bank International Limited* v *Franchise Tax Board*,[165] that California's unitary tax law, as applied to foreign based unitary businesses, was unconstitutional, being in violation of the Foreign Commerce Clause. However, the Supreme Court of California reversed this ruling.[166] The US Supreme Court has since upheld this decision.[167] Equally, US based corporations have also continued to challenge the application of California's unitary tax to their international operations.[168] Alongside these developments in litigation, the UK government stepped up the pressure on the Clinton administration by threatening to apply the retaliatory powers under the 1985 Finance Act from 1 January 1994. The US Treasury has apparently put pressure upon California to reform the law further so as to meet the UK's objections. A reform Bill was passed by the Californian legislature in September 1993, although the UK is still not satisfied that it meets those objections.[169]

The above-mentioned developments show that, on purely political grounds, the use of formula apportionment/unitary tax methods creates difficulties. In addition, there are significant policy problems created by this approach, which make it hard to say conclusively that it is a better method than the arm's length principle in dealing with the taxation of flows of value between related entities in a MNE. The first problem, that of enhanced double taxation, has already been broached. Unless all countries agree, contrary to current practice, to abandon 'water's edge' approaches and to replace these with an agreed unitary tax formula, double taxation and confusion are bound to continue. Even if all states were agreed on the worldwide adoption of a uniform formula apportionment system,[170] should the currently most popular payroll, property and sales formula be used, it would not avoid the resulting inequality of revenue distribution between developed and less developed tax jurisdictions that was pointed out by the dissenting judges in *Container Corporation*.[171] Secondly, as the OECD has stated, formula apportionment demands 'a complex analysis of the different functions of the various associated enterprises and a sophisticated weighing up of the different risks and profit opportunities in the various different stages of manufacturing, transportation, marketing and so on. Nor would the information necessary for such an assessment be readily available or, in many cases, available at all.'[172] The obtaining and analysis of the relevant information would demand considerable resources that would not be available to many countries. Furthermore, it would put MNEs to considerable expense in providing the information. The additional costs may not be justifiable in terms of the marginal improvements in profit allocation analyses that formula apportionment might offer over the arm's length approach.[173]

3.2 The Use of 'Tax Havens' by MNEs

A further advantage arising out of the MNE's international network is its ability to set up and use controlled subsidiaries in 'tax haven' jurisdictions as conduits for various transactions which have the effect of channelling funds to the tax haven subsidiary. To understand the value of a tax haven to a MNE, and to appreciate the nature of regulatory responses from non-tax haven states in which the MNE operates, it is necessary, first, to describe the concept of deferral in the international tax system.[174]

In the major capital-exporting countries, tax on income generated by overseas subsidiaries only becomes due when it is repatriated to the parent company in home country. Until such time, therefore, tax on the unremitted income is deferred. Should the home country tax rate be higher than that of the host country a saving to tax results. This is equal to the unremitted income times the rate differential for the period of deferral. The deferral benefit amounts to an investment subsidy by the home country to its foreign investor, in that it offers an incentive for the reinvestment of foreign sourced profits into foreign operations. This enables firms from countries not using an exemption method of double tax avoidance to compete on equal terms with firms from such countries, in that both groups of firms then effectively pay only the host country rate until the eventual remittance of profits by the firm from the country not employing an exemption for foreign source income. Tax deferral may thus achieve 'capital import neutrality' in the host country, in that all foreign firms pay the same effective rates of tax, at least until remittance to the home country.

The possibility of tax deferral has contributed to the rise of tax haven jurisdictions.[175] Tax havens are characterized by little or no taxation. They are, typically, small communities with independent tax authorities, though they are not necessarily independent states. They are usually located close to major economic areas. Their principal source of income rests in the administration charges levied for the use of tax haven facilities, such as company registration fees, and in the private income generated by the demand for specialist commercial, legal, accounting and other services.[176] A further advantage of tax havens is their common adherence to standards of strict commercial confidentiality. This has given rise to conflicts over disclosure of evidence in litigation involving, in particular, multinational banks operating branches in tax havens.[177]

MNEs may use tax haven subsidiaries in a number of ways. First, the firm may locate an offshore holding company in a tax haven to benefit fully from deferral possibilities. Dividends will be paid into this company, which will then be free to redistribute financial resources throughout the international network of the firm. This is known as 'primary sheltering', as the character of the income flow remains unaltered. The separate legal personality of the tax haven company shelters the income from home country tax. According to the OECD, this is the most common use to which tax havens are put by MNEs.[178]

Secondly, the MNE may use transfer pricing manipulations involving the tax haven subsidiary to shelter income arising from sales to affiliates and to final customers. This may be achieved by means of 'cross-invoicing'. A subsidiary in a high tax jurisdiction may channel a sale to an affiliated or unaffiliated purchaser in another country through an affiliated tax haven base company. Thus what would normally have been a single sales transaction is divided into two steps. First, a sale to the tax haven company will be effected at undervalue. Secondly, a sale will be effected between the tax haven company and the eventual purchaser at the agreed contract price, as where the buyer is an unrelated entity, or even at overvalue where the buyer is an affiliate in a high tax country. In either case the profit on the sale accrues to the tax haven subsidiary.[179]

Thirdly, a MNE may use tax haven subsidiaries to alter the character of the income to take advantage of exemptions provided for by tax treaties or domestic laws in the home country. This is known as 'secondary sheltering'.[180] This result may be achieved in a number of ways. For example, an income flow from an overseas subsidiary may be channelled to a tax haven subsidiary which then makes a loan to the parent company, thereby altering what should have been a dividend remittance taxable at the hands of the parent into a loan, the principal and interest being repayable to the tax haven without further liability to tax in the home country. For this purpose the tax haven subsidiary may be set up as a financial services corporation. A similar result may be achieved by the use of a 'captive' insurance company. The MNE may set up a wholly owned insurance company in a tax haven, which deals with the insurance of the parent company's risks. In return the parent pays premiums to the insurance company. Not only will income be thereby diverted to the tax haven, but the parent will be able to deduct the premiums from home country tax. The premium will be set for the best possible tax saving effect.[181] Further savings may be obtained by the use of captive management services companies located in a tax haven. Profits can be shifted from affiliates in high tax jurisdictions to the tax haven as fees for services rendered by the captive service company.[182]

The control of tax avoidance involving tax haven affiliates can be carried out in at least two principal ways. First, where transfer pricing manipulations result in an artificial shifting of profits to the tax haven subsidiary from the parent company or its affiliates, the home or host country can apply transfer pricing controls to reallocate those profits back to the company within its jurisdiction. Secondly, specialized laws that seek to control both primary and secondary sheltering may apply. Primary sheltering is controlled by denying any deferral advantage to income that is in the hands of a tax haven affiliate, treating it as income taxable in the hands of its parent company as the principal shareholder. Secondary sheltering is controlled by denying the tax deductible status of a given transaction and treating any income attributed to the tax haven subsidiary as the taxable income of its parent company.

The original model for such legislation was developed by the US under the so-called 'Subpart F' provisions of the Internal Revenue Code.[183] These were introduced in 1962 and can be found in ss 951ff of the Code.[184] These provisions created the concept of a 'controlled foreign corporation' (CFC). This is defined as a foreign corporation in which 'United States shareholders'[185] own more than 50 per cent of the 'total combined voting power' of all classes of stock or more than half of the 'value' of the stock.[186] These provisions are not applied mechanically.[187] Thus where US shareholders devise schemes of indirect ownership, or sell stock to foreign interests so that the US share falls below 50 per cent, the foreign corporation will none the less be regarded as a CFC where the foreign shareholders are, in effect, the instruments of the US shareholders.[188] The test is one of substance and not form.[189] Thus, relevant factors to be considered include *inter alia*: the consideration paid by the foreign shareholders for the US shareholders' shares, the relationship between the US and the foreign shareholders, the powers of the foreign shareholders and the incidence of dissent and debate over the future activities of the foreign corporation.[190] Even where a US parent company apparently sells a foreign subsidiary to an independently owned foreign holding company, the true relationship between the US seller and the foreign purchaser must be examined to determine whether the transaction is no more than a scheme for the retention of US control designed to avoid the burden of Subpart F.[191]

Once it is established that the foreign corporation is a CFC the Subpart F provisions require the US shareholder to report as a dividend its *pro rata* share of the CFC's 'Subpart F income' and its 'increase in earnings invested in United States property'.[192] Subpart F income consists of insurance income arising from premiums on policies covering risks outside the CFC's tax haven country,[193] and 'foreign base company income' (FBCI).[194] FBCI covers profits accruing to the tax haven subsidiary as a result of 'cross-invoicing' transactions or service payments. It also includes payments for shipping or other transport services, or oil related income, where the tax haven company is set up as a base for the profits accruing from these classes of activity.[195] However, if the CFC purchases property from a related party and substantially transforms it prior to sale, or includes it in a substantial manufacturing operation prior to sale, or where the company's conversion costs in connection with the use of such property account for 20 per cent or more of the total cost of the goods sold, the income derived from those sales will accrue to the CFC and will not be included in the US tax-payer's FBCI.[196] Otherwise, the US parent would be liable to tax on the earnings of its overseas subsidiaries regardless of the nature of their operations. Only transactions that are set up to avoid US tax should come within Subpart F scrutiny. Difficulties over distinguishing between genuine manufacturing activities and tax avoidance operations are likely, and adequate information over the precise nature of an activity may not always be forthcoming.[197]

The second category of CFC income relates to transactions whereby a dividend remittance to the parent is transformed into an otherwise non-taxable investment or flow of funds, the clearest example being a loan from the tax haven subsidiary to the parent. The Code treats such investments or flows as a dividend in that amount paid to the US shareholder and then taxed as current income in the hands of the shareholder. 'United States property' for this purpose includes any tangible property located in the USA, stock in related corporations, obligations of a US person and the right to use US patents acquired or developed by the CFC for use in the USA.[198]

The overall effect of these provisions is to ensure that the genuine overseas business activities of US MNEs enjoy the deferral subsidy, while mere tax avoidance schemes are controlled. However, as McDaniel and Ault point out, Subpart F provisions lose much of their relevance if the home country tax rate is significantly lowered, as the incentive to defer remittances is then much reduced.[199] On the other hand, according to the OECD, Subpart F type laws have led to an increase in taxable income in the countries using such laws.[200] Much, no doubt, depends on the relative tax rates in place at any time, upon the effectiveness of tax administrations in investigating tax avoidance schemes successfully, and upon the ingenuity of tax-paying corporations in devising new schemes to avoid the existing legislation.[201]

4 Concluding Remarks

This chapter has sought to introduce some of the best known taxation problems surrounding the activities of MNEs. It has shown how the integrated operations of such firms can offer opportunities for efficient tax planning that may not be open to purely domestic firms, and how national tax authorities may seek to control any resulting tax avoidance. The international character of the income generating activities of MNEs, the national reach of individual tax administrations, increased international competition over attracting inward direct investment and the need to obtain sufficient revenue returns from MNEs has led, inevitably, to calls for the reform of the international tax system.[202] For the present, however, the primary locus for regulation remains with national tax authorities applying systems of taxation designed to further national policy goals. A significant degree of harmonization may occur in the near future in the EC. However, even here, national control over tax policy can be expected to remain significant for some years to come.

Notes
1 On the domestic tax treatment of companies see J. D. R. Adams and J. Whalley, *The International Taxation of Multinational Enterprises in Developed*

Countries (Institute of Fiscal Studies/Associated Business Programmes, 1977) chapter 2; on UK company taxation see J. H. Farrar *et al.*, *Farrar's Company Law*, 4th edn (Butterworths, 1998), chapter 21.

2   For a full treatment of the taxation of MNEs see S. Picciotto, *International Business Taxation* (Weidenfeld and Nicolson, 1992).

3   See e.g. UK Income and Corporation Taxes Act 1988, s. 240.

4   See e.g. ibid., ss 402–3.

5   Adams and Whalley (note 1 above), at p. 41.

6   Ibid.

7   See ibid., at pp. 42–3; see also S. Plasschaert, *Transfer Pricing and Multinational Corporations: an Overview of Mechanisms and Regulations* (Gower, Saxon House, 1979), chapter 10. Appendix 1, paras 10.4–10.5, at p. 112.

8   See Adams and Whalley (note 1 above), at pp. 66–8.

9   See further Gumpel, 'The taxation of American business abroad – is further reform needed?', 15 J. Int'l L. & Econ. 389 (1981); R. Caves, *Multinational Enterprise and Economic Analysis* (Cambridge University Press, 2nd edn, 1996), chapter 8, esp. pp. 189–200.

10   Adams and Whalley (note 1 above), at pp. 44–5.

11   See ibid., at pp. 45–6; Plasschaert (note 7 above), at paras 10.7–10.12, pp. 113–14; D. R. Davies, *Principles of International Double Taxation Relief* (Sweet & Maxwell, 1985), paras 1.03–1.05.

12   For examples of the application of a foreign tax credit see Adams and Whalley, ibid., at pp. 75–6.

13   Davies (note 11 above), para 1.03. On the US system see R. L. Kaplan, *Federal Taxation of International Transactions* (West Publishing Co., 1988), chapter 3 (new edition in preparation); P. McDaniel and H. Ault, *Introduction to United States International Taxation*, 3rd edn (Kluwer, 1989), chapter 6.

14   McDaniel and Ault, ibid., at pp. 88–9.

15   Adams and Whalley (note 1 above), at p. 74

16   Plasschaert (note 7 above), at para 10.10.

17   Davies (note 11 above), at para 1.05.

18   Ibid., para 1.04.

19   Ibid.

20   Davies (note 11 above), para. 1.06. See further Owens, 'Double taxation treaties: their role in relieving double taxation', 17 Rutgers LR 428.

21   See also McDaniel and Ault (note 13 above), at pp. 173–4. In addition to the avoidance of double taxation, tax treaties also frequently proclaim their purposes as including the avoidance of tax evasion and the promotion of trade and investment. See P. Baker, *Double Taxation Conventions and International Tax Law (a Manual on the OECD Model Tax Convention on Income and on Capital, 1992)*, 2nd edn (Sweet & Maxwell, 1994), paras B-07 to B-12.

22   See further Irish, 'International double taxation agreements and income taxation at source', 23 ICLQ 292 (1974).

23   OECD Model Convention 1992, latest revision 1997. For a comprehensive commentary see: *OECD Model Tax Convention on Income and Capital (Report of the Committee on Fiscal Affairs)* (1992, updated); Baker (note 21 above) and Davies (note 11 above), who also discusses UK practice. The

1992 Model Convention is a revised version of the 1977 Model Convention which was based on a Draft Convention published in 1963. For a Comparison of the 1963 Draft and the revised 1977 Model Convention see: International Fiscal Association, *The Revised OECD Model Double Taxation Convention on Income and Capital* (Kluwer, 1978) or *IFA Yearbook 1977*. For a comparison of the 1977 OECD Model Convention with the UN Model Convention of 1980 and the US Model Treaty see Davies (note 11 above) at paras 3.15–3.21. See also, on US practice, McDaniel and Ault (note 13 above), chapter 11, and Kaplan (note 13 above), chapter 8.

24 See further Park, 'Fiscal jurisdiction and accrual basis taxation: lifting the corporate veil to tax foreign company profits', 78 Columbia LR 1609 (1978). R. Vernon, *Storm over the Multinationals* (Macmillan, 1977), pp. 123–8; Adams and Whalley (note 1 above), chapter 12. OECD, *Taxation and International Capital Flows* (1990). This study notes that tax incentives are relatively ineffective in attracting inward direct investment, but that more countries are using them.

25 Adams and Whalley (note 1 above), at p. 46.

26 S. 2592 92d Cong. 1st Sess. (1971); H. 8784 92d Cong. 1st Sess. (1971). See K. Hughes, *Trade, Taxes and Transnationals* (Praeger, 1979), at pp. 23–35.

27 See C. Bergsten, T. Horst and T. Moran, *American Multinationals and American Interests* (Brookings Institution, 1978), at p. 112, n. 20, pp. 208–10 and p. 179; N. Hood and S. Young, *The Economics of Multinational Enterprise* (Longman, 1979), at pp. 302–5.

28 See D. F. Channon and M. Jalland, *Multinational Strategic Planning* (Macmillan, 1978), chapter 6; A. C. Shapiro, *Multinational Financial Management*, 4th edn (Allyn and Bacon, 1992), pp. 556–9.

29 On which see further OECD, *International Tax Avoidance and Evasion Issues in International Taxation No. 1* (1987), pp. 88–106.

30 This was a contentious issue in the USA in the early 1980s when Congress instituted a moratorium on the allocation of R&D expenses to foreign source income of US firms, resulting in its allocation to US source income. This caused a reduction of revenue to the USA as the reallocation of R&D expenditures from foreign to domestic income increased the amount of taxable foreign source income that could be credited against US taxation. The beneficiary firms argued that the moratorium would act as an incentive to locate R&D investment in the USA. Critics saw this as special pleading for lower tax liability. See Kaplan (note 13 above), at pp. 68–80.

31 According to Davies, 'The concepts of tax avoidance and tax evasion are notoriously difficult to define, but in general terms both involve a reduction or elimination of tax liability through either legitimate/legal means (avoidance) or through illegitimate/illegal means (evasion)' (note 11 above), at para. 1.09.

32 See pp. 35–8.

33 See Plasschaert (note 7 above), at para. 3.2, p. 29 and pp. 24–6. See also D. K. Eiteman and A. I. Stonehill, *Multinational Business Finance*, 5th edn (1989), at pp. 558–9.

34 Plasschaert, ibid.

35 See J. Arpan, 'International transfer pricing', in C. Nobes and R. Parker (eds), *Issues in Multinational Accounting* (Philip Allan Publishers, 1988), at p. 163.

36 See Plasschaert (note 7 above), paras 3.10–3.11 at p. 33, from which the following remarks are taken.

37 See Plasschaert, ibid., paras 3.7–3.9 at pp. 31–2.

38 Arpan (note 35 above), at pp. 163–4.

39 See further text at notes 44–46 below.

40 Arpan, ibid. See further J. S. Arpan, *International Intracorporate Pricing: Non-American Systems and Views* (Praeger, 1972).

41 See Schapiro (note 28 above), at pp. 365–73. See further OECD, *Transfer Pricing and Multinational Enterprises* (1979) at paras 183–91. On the question of whether a loan payment between associated enterprises in a MNE should be treated as an equity payment for tax purposes see further: OECD, *Thin Capitalization Issues in International Taxation No. 2* (1987).

42 Plasschaert (note 7 above), at para. 4.21.

43 See ibid., paras 4.15–4.22. See further OECD, 1979 (note 41 above).

44 S. Lall, *The Multinational Corporation* (Macmillan, 1980), at p. 112.

45 Ibid., at pp. 113–14; see also: Channon and Jalland (note 28 above), at pp. 155–7; Arpan (note 35 above), at pp. 164–71. On the use of transfer price manipulations in relation to local shareholder interests see Fitzpatrick, 'Transfer pricing, company law and shareholders' interests', [1975] JBL 202.

46 Lall, ibid., at pp. 115–16.

47 Plasschaert (note 7 above), at paras 5.6–5.16.

48 See Eiteman and Stonehill (note 33 above), at p. 560. But see Lall (note 44 above), at p. 118, who feels that this restraint on transfer price manipulation is overstated.

49 For an introductory selection of literature on national transfer pricing laws see Baker (note 21 above), at para. 9-02, n. 3 and 4. See further note 59 below.

50 See further Lall (note 44 above), at pp. 146–151; Irish, 'Transfer pricing abuses and less developed countries', 5 *Asian Pacific Tax and Investment Bulletin* (1987) 227–37, 298–313.

51 See in particular C. Vaitsos, *Intercountry Income Distribution and Transnational Enterprises* (Oxford University Press, 1974); Lall (note 44 above), at pp. 120–7, 144–6. For a recent summary of the principal empirical studies in this field see J. H. Dunning, *Multinational Enterprises and the Global Economy* (Addison Wesley, 1992), at pp. 516–21. The pharmaceutical industry has been a major source of empirical data on transfer pricing: see G. Gereffi, *The Pharmaceutical Industry and Dependency in the Third World* (Princeton University Press, 1983), at pp. 193–8.

52 See R. Vernon, *Storm over the Multinationals* (Macmillan, 1977), at pp. 154–8; A. Rugman, *Multinationals in Canada: Theory, Performance and Economic Impact* (Martinus Nijhoff, 1980), chapter 7.

53 Monopolies and Mergers Commission, *Chlordiazepoxide and Diazepam: a Report on the Supply of Chlordiazepoxide and Diazepam* (HMSO, 1973).

54 See further C. R. Greenhill and E. O. Herbolzheimer, 'International transfer pricing: the restrictive business practices approach', 14 JWTL 232 (1980).

55 See Inland Revenue Press Release, 26 January 1981 (7), 'The transfer pricing of multinational enterprises', para. 12.

56 According to Judge Nims, Chief Judge of the United States Tax Court, in 1990 there were then over 200 cases before the Tax Court filed by the US Internal Revenue Service involving alleged transfer pricing manipulations with reported profit deficiencies ranging from $10 million to $6 billion: *Tax Notes Today*, 6 November 1990, cited by Prof. Williams in D. W. Williams (ed.), *Tax on the International Transfer of Information* (Longman Special Report, 1991), at p. 3. For an example of a 'classic' instance of profit shifting between jurisdictions for tax advantages see *E. I. Du Pont De Nemours & Co. v United States* 608 F. 2d 445 (Ct Cl. 1979); for a more recent example see *Seagate Technology Inc. v Commissioner* 102 TC No. 9, summarized in *IBFD Tax News Service*, TNS-139 (1994).

57 See A. Devoy, 'Recent transfer pricing developments around the world', *The Tax Journal*, 19 March 1992, p. 15, where Korea, Pakistan, Mexico and Brazil are mentioned as developing countries with controls over transfer pricing. The People's Republic of China has introduced transfer pricing rules, under the 1991 Income Tax Law for Enterprises with Foreign Investment and Foreign Enterprises, which require arm's length dealing between affiliated enterprises: see Notice on Implementation Measures for the Administration of Transactions Between Affiliated Enterprises 1992 (Guo Shui Fa 237 of 29 October 1992) noted in *IBFD Tax News Service*, TNS-423 (1993).

58 For an extensive discussion of the policy behind the arm's length and formula apportionment approaches see Surrey, 'Reflections on the allocation of income and expenses among national tax jurisdictions', 10 Law & Pol. Int'l Bus. 409 (1978); and see Picciotto (note 2 above), chapter 8.

59 For a regularly updated survey of national transfer pricing regulations see: IBFD, *The Tax Treatment of Transfer Pricing* (1987, with supplements). For a survey of 25 countries see W. Lawlor (ed.), *Cross-border Transactions between Related Companies* (Kluwer, 1985). For French practice see article 57 of the Code General des Impôts analysed in Pascal Picault, *Fiscalité Française des Investissements à l'Etranger* (Dunod, 1986), pp. 97–125; see also C. D. Wallace, *Legal Control of the Multinational Enterprise* (Martinus Nijhoff, 1983), pp. 128–30. For German practice see A. Radler and F. Jacob, *German Transfer Pricing* (Kluwer, 1984).

60 See article 9. For Commentary on article 9. See OECD (note 23 above) at C(9)-1 to C(9)-8; Baker (note 21 above), paras 9-01 to 9-26; Davies (note 11 above), chapter 14. For the OECD's views on the control of transfer pricing generally see OECD (1979) (note 41 above) and OECD, *Transfer Pricing and Multinational Enterprises: Three Taxation Issues* (1984). The OECD 1979 Report on Transfer Pricing was recently reviewed. New draft guidelines were published on 8 July 1994. After a process of consultation a final version of the new OECD transfer pricing guidelines was

published in June 1995: OECD *Transfer Pricing Guidelines For Multinational Enterprises and Tax Administrations* (1995 with annual updates).

61   S. 770 of the ICTA 1988 (formerly s. 485 ICTA 1970) provides:

(1)   Subject to the provisions of this section and section 771, where any property is sold and –

(a)   the buyer is a body of persons over whom the seller has control or the seller is a body of persons over whom the buyer has control or both the buyer and the seller are bodies of persons over whom the same person or persons has or have control; and

(b)   the property is sold at a price ('the actual price') which is either –

(i)   less than the price which it might have been expected to fetch if the parties to the transaction had been independent persons dealing at arm's length ('the arm's length price'), or

(ii)   greater than the arm's length price, then, in computing for tax purposes the income, profits or losses of the seller where the actual price was less than the arm's length price, and of the buyer where the actual price was greater than the arm's length price, the like consequences shall ensue as would have ensued if the property had been sold for the arm's length price.

(2)   Subsection (1) above shall not apply –

(a)   in any case where –

(i)   the actual price is less than the arm's length price, and

(ii)   the buyer is resident in the United kingdom and is carrying on a trade there, and

(iii)   the price of the property falls to be taken into account as a deduction in computing the profits or gains or losses of that trade for tax purposes; or

(b)   in any case where –

(i)   the actual price is greater than the arm's length price, and

(ii)   the seller is resident in the United Kingdom and is carrying on a trade there, and

(iii)   the price of the property falls to be taken into account as a trading receipt in computing the profits or gains or losses of that trade for tax purposes; or

(c)   in relation to any transaction in relation to which section 493(1) or (3) applies; or

(d)   in relation to any other sale, unless the Board [of the Inland Revenue Commissioners] so direct.

(3)   [. . .].

Subsections (2)(a) and (b) make clear that a reallocation of income will only occur in cases where there is a loss to UK revenue. In both of these cases there is a gain to the revenue from increased taxation.

62   See e.g. note 55 above.

63   'Plans to update rules will protect revenues', *Financial Times*, 3 July 1997,

p. 23 and see note 60 above.

64 US Internal Revenue Code: 26 USCA s. 482.

65 See, for the last version to adopt a pure arm's length approach, *Federal Tax Regulations 1991* (West Publishing Co.) Vol. 2, ss 1.482-1 and 1.482-2. The revised regulations were introduced in April 1993 on a temporary basis. They were made permanent in July 1994, and are discussed below in the text at notes 103–113. For analysis of the 1968 Regulations see: Jenks, 'Treasury regulations under section 482', 23 *Tax Lawyer* 279 (1970); Baker and Hartline, 'Recent developments concerning Internal Revenue Code s. 482', 11 Houston LR 89 (1973); comment, 8 Texas Int'l LJ 219 (1973); Madere, 'International pricing: allocation guidelines and relief from international double taxation', 10 Texas Int'l LJ 108 at pp. 111–20 (1975); note 89 Harv. LR 1202 (1976); Schindler and Henderson, 'Intercorporate transfer pricing', 29 Tax Notes 1171 (1985); McDaniel and Ault (note 13 above), chapter 8; Kaplan (note 13 above), chapter 5.

66 Treas. Reg. s. 1.482-1(b)(1).

67 Treas. Reg. s. 1.482-1(c).

68 See *Charles Town Inc.* v *CIR* 372 F. 2d 415 (CA Md 1967) (finding of common control will not be reversed unless clearly erroneous); *Peck* v *CIR* 752 F. 2d. 469 (9 Cir. 1985) (Commissioner has a broad discretion to place controlled taxpayers in the same position as uncontrolled taxpayers dealing at arm's length).

69 *Eli Lilly & Co.* v *CIR* 856 F. 2d 855 (7th Cir. 1988).

70 Treas. Reg. s. 1.482-1(a)(3). See *Forman & Co. Inc.* v *CIR* 453 F. 2d 1144 (2d Cir. 1972).

71 *CIR* v *First Security Bank of Utah* 405 US 394 (1972). See also *Proctor & Gamble Co.* v *Commissioner* 95 TC 323 (1990) aff'd 961 F. 2d 1255 (6th Cir. 1992); *Exxon Corp.* v *Commissioner* (TCM 1993-616), noted *IBFD Tax News Service*, TNS-56 (1994).

72 See Treas. Reg. s. 1.482-2. It is not proposed to discuss all the principal situations in which an arm's length allocation is possible. The transactions not discussed are: loans (see Treas. Reg. s. 1.482-2(a)); performance of services for another (see Treas. Reg. s. 1.482-2(b)); use of tangible property under lease or other arrangement (see Treas. Reg. s. 1.482-2(c)).

73 Treas. Reg. s. 1.482-2(e)(2).

74 Treas. Reg. s. 1.482-2(e)(2)(ii). 'Uncontrolled sales' were defined as '(a) sales made by a member of the controlled group to an unrelated party, (b) sales made to a member of the controlled group by an unrelated party, and (c) sales made in which the parties are not members of the controlled group and are not related to each other.'

75 Treas. Reg. s. 1.482-2(1)(ii).

76 Ibid.

77 Treas. Reg. s. 1.482-2(e)(1)(ii).

78 Treas. Reg. s. 1.482-2(e)(1)(iii).

79 856 F. 2d 855 at 871 (7th Cir. 1988).

80 See Plasschaert (note 7 above), at para. 11.7.

81   McDaniel and Ault (note 13 above), at p. 140. See also the following cases
     for the complexities of trying to apply the arm's length standard to trans-
     fers of intangibles: *Hospital Corporation of America v CIR* 81 TC 520 (US
     Tax Ct 1983) (held: 75/25 per cent split of income from use of intan-
     gibles); *Eli Lilly & Co.* v *Commissioner* 84 TC 996 (1985) modified in part
     856 F. 2d 855 at 871–873 (7th Cir. 1988) (held: 45/55 per cent split);
     Ciba-Geigy Corp. v *Commissioner* 85 TC 172 (1985); *G. D. Searle & Co.* v
     Commissioner 88 TC 252 (1987); *Seagate Technology Inc.* v *Commissioner*
     102 TC No. 9, noted *IBFD Tax News Service*, TNS-139 (1994).

82   See further Staff of the Joint Committee on Taxation, *General Explanation
     of the Tax Reform Act of 1986* (1987), pp. 1015–17, reproduced in Kaplan
     (note 13 above), at pp. 160–3.

83   Under s. 482 intangible property includes: a patent, invention, process,
     know-how, copyright, trade-mark, franchise, method, system or technical
     data. See Internal Revenue Code s. 936(h)(3)(b); see also Treas. Reg. s.
     1.482-2(d)(3), which omits 'know-how' from the list. The 1993 Regu-
     lations include, under intangible property: patents, inventions, formulae,
     processes, designs, patterns, know-how; copyrights and literary, musical or
     artistic compositions; trademarks, trade names or brand names; fran-
     chises, licences and contracts; methods, programmes, systems, pro-
     cedures, campaigns, surveys, studies, forecasts, estimates, customer lists
     or technical data; other similar items: Treas. Reg. 1.482-4T(b).

84   McDaniel and Ault (note 13 above), at p. 140.

85   A Study of Intercompany Pricing under s. 482 of the Code IRS Notice 88–
     123, 1988–2 CB 458. See further D. W. Williams (ed.), *Tax on the
     International Transfer of Information* (Longman Special Report, 1991),
     papers by Prof. Karen P. Brown at p. 27 and Rom Watson at p. 75; J. E.
     Bischel, 'The S.482 White Paper and superroyalties: existing and pro-
     posed transfer pricing methods', *BIFD* (February 1990), p. 83.

86   See White Paper at 486–7 and Brown, ibid., at pp. 29–30; Bischel, ibid.,
     at pp. 84–5.

87   See Bischel (note 85 above), at p. 85; McDaniel and Ault (note 13 above),
     at p. 141. McDaniel and Ault offer the following example of the appli-
     cation of BALRM: 'P has developed a patent for the manufacture of a
     product which will be manufactured under a licence granted to a foreign
     affiliate. The transaction will generate 500 of income and, at a market rate
     of return on the tangible assets involved, 150 of the income would be
     allocated to the tangible assets held by the subsidiary and 150 to the
     tangible assets of the parent. The remaining 200 would be allocated to P
     as the commensurate amount of income from the patent.'

88   Brown (note 85 above), at p. 31, referring to White Paper at 490–1.

89   Note 85 above at 492. For a full analysis of cost-sharing arrangements and
     their use as tax avoidance devices see: OECD (1979, note 41 above) at
     paras 102–24, pp. 55–62.

90   See Treas. Reg. s. 1.482-2(d)(4).

91   McDaniel and Ault (note 13 above), at p. 142.

92   Jenks (note 65 above), at p. 310. See also Bird, 'Shaping a new inter-
     national tax order', *BIFD* (July 1988), at p. 294.

93 Proposed Treasury Regulations s. 1.482 57 Fed. Reg. 3571 (1992). For analysis see: Weizman, 'US transfer pricing: grim prospects for multinational companies', [1992] 5 ICCLR 163; *BIFD* (June 1992), pp. 271–306.

94 See Quigley, 'A commentary on how the proposed regulations affect the general principles of section 482 as described in the existing regulations and in case law', *BIFD* (June 1992), 281 at pp. 282–4. Quigley doubts whether s. 482 authorizes the IRS to extend the 'commensurate with income' standard to transfers of tangible property.

95 Prop. Treas. Regs. s. 1.482-2(f)(3)–(9).

96 Cole and Rubloff, 'Proposed transfer pricing regulations under s. 482 of the Internal Revenue Code', *BIFD* (June 1992), 292 at p. 296.

97 Prop. Treas. Reg. s. 1.482-2(e)(1)(ii).

98 Prop. Treas. Reg. s. 1.482-2(e)(1)(iii),(iv).

99 Prop. Treas. Reg. s. 1.482-2(d)(3)–(5).

100 See further Prop. Treas. Reg. s. 1.482-2(d)–(g), discussed by Weizman (note 93 above), at pp. 168–9.

101 See the Joint Paper of the Business and Industry Advisory Committee to the OECD and the International Chamber of Commerce on the Proposed Intercompany Pricing Regulations (May 1992): (1993) *Tax Notes International* 103–13.

102 OECD Committee on Fiscal Affairs, 'The US proposed regulations dealing with tax aspects of transfer pricing within multinational enterprises', Report of 10 January 1993: see Executive Summary in *BIFD* (January 1993), pp. 21–5.

103 Treas. Reg. 1.482-1T to 1.482-6T: TD 8470, Notices of Proposed Rule Making IL 21–91 and IL 401–88. See Ruchelman, 'Transfer pricing regulations issued in the United States', *BIFD* (April 1993) 187. A summary of the new Regulations, and how they differ from the proposed Regulations of 1992, can be found in IRS Bulletin 1993–10, 8 March 1993. The 1993 Regulations were made permanent in July 1994.

104 Treas. Reg. s. 1.482-1T(b)(2)(iii)(A).

105 Treas. Reg. 1.482-1T(c)(1)(i). See Ruchelman (note 103 above), at pp. 189–90 for a fuller explanation.

106 Treas. Reg. s. 1.482-1T(d)(2)(i)(A)and(B).

107 Ibid. s. 1.482-3T(a).

108 Ibid. s. 1.482-5T(a)–(d).

109 Ibid. s. 1.482-3T(e)(2)(i).

110 Proposed Treas. Reg. 1.482-6T described in Ruchelman (note 103 above), at pp. 195–7.

111 Ibid. s. 1.482-4T(a)–(e).

112 See Proposed Treas. Reg. 1.482-1T(f) discussed in Ruchelman (note 103 above), at pp. 198–9.

113 Proposed Treas. Reg. 1.6662-5 discussed in Ruchelman, ibid., at pp. 199–201.

114 (1993) *Tax Notes International* 103.

115 Ibid., para. 10.

116 Treas. Reg. 1.482-5T(a) cited ibid., para. 27.

117 Ibid., paras 26 and 30.

118 Ibid., para. 33.
119 See OECD (1979, note 41 above), at para. 28, p. 21 and para. 42, p. 31.
120 Ibid., para. 40, p. 29. See also *Hospital Corporation of America* v *CIR* 81 TC 520 (US Tax Ct 1983).
121 OECD (1987, note 29 above), at paras 96–7, pp. 41–2.
122 See e.g. UK ICTA 1988 s. 772.
123 See Treas. Reg. s. 1.6038A (effective for taxable years beginning after July 10, 1989) published US Federal Register Vol. 56, No. 118 (19 June 1991), pp. 28056–75, with corrections Vol. 56, No. 164 (23 August 1991), p. 11792; reproduced in 30 ILM 1320 (1991).
124 Including sales and purchases, rents, royalty payments, service payments, loan payments, and transactions involving nonmonetary consideration or less than full consideration: Treas. Reg. s. 1.6038A-2(a)(3) and (4).
125 See Treas. Reg. s. 1.6038A-4 and s. 1.6038A-7. On 27 January 1994 new temporary penalty regulations relating to transfer pricing documentation requirements were introduced. See Treas. Reg. ss 1.6662-5T-6T, 1.6664-4T(d). For analysis see: Krupsky, 'New IRS transfer pricing documentation requirements', *BIFD* (June/July 1994), p. 321; Burge and Lowell, 'How to avoid US transfer pricing penalties', *BIFD* (April 1994), p. 180.
126 Australia requires the periodic conclusion of special-purpose questionnaires: OECD (1987, note 29 above), para. 94, p. 41. Canada introduced reporting requirements similar to those used by the USA under the 1987 tax reforms: Borden, Elliot, Howard, Mackie, *Barristers and Solicitors Report For Non-residents*, Vol. 1, Issue 1, Winter 1990, p. 1.
127 Inland Revenue Press Release (note 55 above), para. (8).
128 See chapter 5 text at notes 149–156 and, in particular, *US* v *Vetco* 644 F. 2d 1324 (9th Cir. 1981); *US* v *Toyota Motor Corp.* 569 F. Supp. 1158 (1983); *Marc Rich & Co. AG* v *US* 707 F. 2d 663 (1983).
129 'Control' is defined under s. 840 ICTA 1988: s. 773(2) ICTA 1988; see also s. 772(3) ICTA 1988 (attribution to controller of powers of nominees and connected persons).
130 See OECD, *Model Double Taxation Convention* (1992, note 23 above), article 26.
131 Ibid., article 26(2).
132 Article 9(2) states: 'Where a Contracting State includes in the profits of an enterprise of that State – and taxes accordingly – profits on which an enterprise of the other Contracting State has been charged to tax in that other State and the profits so included are profits which would have accrued to the enterprise of the first-mentioned State if the conditions made between the two enterprises had been those which would have been made between independent enterprises, then that other State shall make an appropriate adjustment to the amount of the tax charged thereon on those profits. In determining such adjustment, due regard shall be had to the other provisions of this Convention and the competent authorities of the Contracting States shall if necessary consult each other.' Even though article 9(2) says that the other state shall make the appropriate adjustment, the OECD Commentary to the Model Convention makes clear that the making of such an adjustment is discretionary and not mandatory and depends on the other state agreeing with the reallocation made by the first

state. See: OECD (1992, note 23 above), at C(9)3, paras 5–6; Baker (note 21 above), at para. 9–23. For comment on article 9(2) generally see: Baker, ibid., at paras 9–13 to 9–19; Davies (note 11 above), at paras 14.05–14.06; OECD (1984, note 60 above); Madere, 10 Texas Int'l LJ 108 at 126–32 (1975).

133 See e.g. US Model Income Tax Treaty of 16 June 1981, article 9(2). However, Belgium, Finland, Norway, Portugal and Switzerland have all reserved the right not to include article 9(2) in their tax conventions: OECD Commentary, para. 16 reproduced in Baker, ibid., at 9–26.

134 Convention (90/463/EEC) OJ [1990] L 225/10.

135 Ibid., article 6(1).

136 Ibid., article 7(1). Under article 8 of the Convention, the mutual agreement procedure need not be initiated where one of the enterprises concerned is liable to a serious penalty as a result of its transfer pricing practices, and where judicial or administrative proceedings, which may result in the imposition of such a penalty, have been instituted and are being conducted simultaneously with proceedings under the Convention the latter proceedings may be stayed until the judicial or administrative proceedings have been concluded.

137 Ibid., article 9(1), (4).

138 Ibid., article 11(1).

139 Ibid., article 12(1); article 12(4) (which requires use of the arm's length standard in allocating profits on related party transactions).

140 Ibid., article 11(1).

141 Goergen, 'Harmonization of enterprise taxation in the European Community', *BIFD* (July/August 1991) 312 at p. 315. The author, who was at the time of writing this article the Director for company law and direct taxation in the EC Commission, writes: 'The ideal solution . . . would be the adoption and uniform application of common transfer pricing rules. However, this is a long-term objective. In the meantime, less ambitious measures can be envisaged, i.e. the organization of simultaneous or joint tax audits of multinational companies having branches or subsidiaries in different member states and the development of advance rulings.' See also Council Directive 90/435 of 23 July 1990 on a common system of taxation applicable in the case of parent companies and subsidiaries of different Member States: OJ [1990] L225/6.

142 Rev. Rul. 76–508, 1976–2 Cum. Bull. 225; Rev. Rul. 80–231, 1980–2 Cum. Bull. 219, cited by McDaniel and Ault (note 13 above), at pp. 146–7.

143 For full text of the draft IRS procedure: 2 *Tax Notes Int'l* 565 (June 1990); comment, McIntyr, 2 *Tax Notes Int'l* 545 (June 1990); Brown, in Williams (note 85 above), at pp. 35–7. Canada also uses an advance agreement system: see Advance Pricing Agreement Process, Revenue Canada Release of 29 July 1993 noted in *Tax News Service*, TNS-338 (1993).

144 See Schindler and Henderson, 'Intercorporate transfer pricing', 29 *Tax Notes* 1171 at 1172–3 (1985).

145 For a comprehensive analysis see G. Harley, *International Division of the Income Tax Base of Multinational Enterprises* (1981). The most significant worldwide unitary tax law has been that of California. See California

Revenue and Taxation Code s. 25101–25141 West's Annotated California Codes, 1989 Cumulative Pocket part, chapter 17. But see amendments below at note 169.

146   463 US 159 (1983); Slip Opinion reproduced 22 ILM 855 (1983). Comment Heising, 16 Law & Pol. Int'l Bus. 299 (1984). See also *Chicago Bridge and Iron Co.* v *Caterpillar Tractor Co.* 103 S. Ct 3562 (1983); *Anaconda Corp.* v *Franchise Tax Board of California* 103 S. Ct 3563 (1983).

147   See *Container Corporation of America* v *Franchise Tax Board* at ILM p. 858 citing *Exxon Corporation* v *Wisconsin Department of Revenue* 447 US 207 at 210–220 (1980) and *Mobil Oil* v *Commissioner of Taxes of Vermont* 445 US 425 at 436, 437 (1980).

148   The meaning of a 'unitary business' has been considered in the following US Supreme Court decisions: *Mobil Oil* v *Commissioner of Taxes of Vermont* 445 US 425 (1980); *Exxon Corporation* v *Wisconsin Department of Revenue* 447 US 207 (1980); *F. W. Woolworth & Co.* v *Taxation and Revenue Department of the State of New Mexico* 458 US 354 (1982); *ASARCO INC.* v *Idaho State Tax Commission* 458 US 307 (1982); *Container Corporation of America* v *Franchise Tax Board* (note 146 above).

149   The leading cases cited in note 148 establish the following conditions for a valid finding of a 'unitary business' for the purposes of liability to tax. (a) It must involve substantially the same business activity. A diversified firm cannot therefore be a 'unitary business' when viewed as a whole. (b) The existence of unified business activity will be determined by reference to functional business criteria. Thus mere passive ownership, or unusual potential for control, is insufficient. Evidence of actual control is required and mere economic benefit is not enough. (c) Evidence of actual control involves an examination of the parent – subsidiary relationship. The following criteria have been considered: stock ownership, the nature and identity of the management, the degree of centralization of the business, the degree of autonomy given to the subsidiary, including the extent of its financial and technical dependence on the parent, and the interchangeability and powers of personnel. (d) Legal and divisional separation, as well as internal accounting procedures, can be disregarded for the purposes of establishing control. (e) No one criterion is decisive and each case involves an analysis of its own facts.

150   Note 146 above.

151   Ibid., ILM p. 865.

152   *Mobil Oil* v *Commissioner of Taxes of Vermont* 445 US 425 at 439 (1980); *Exxon Corporation* v *Wisconsin Department of Revenue* 447 US 207 at 221 (1980).

153   *Mobil Oil* v *Commissioner of Taxes of Vermont* 445 US 425 at 439 (1980).

154   Container Corporation (note 146 above).

155   *Japan Line Ltd* v *County of Los Angeles* 441 US 434 (1979). See also *Reuters Ltd* (NY State CA), noted *Tax News Service*, TNS-8 (1994).

156   On US government attitudes see: P. Winship, 'State taxation of multinational business: the unitary tax debate' [1985] JBL 179; *Alcan Aluminum Ltd et al.* v *Franchise Tax Board of California* Brief Amicus Curiae of the United States: 25 ILM 683 (1986). The US government proposed legis-

lation banning states from applying worldwide unitary taxation; see 25 ILM 704–15, 739–59 (1986). The UK position and s. 54 of the Finance Act 1985 are reproduced in 25 ILM 734–8 (1986). See further Inland Revenue and US Treasury, *Unitary Tax: Review of Progress towards Resolving the Issues* (Inland Revenue, 1991).

157 For a valuable summary of the principal arguments against the imposition of unitary tax on the worldwide profits of MNEs see: *Container Corporation v Franchise Tax Board of California* (note 146 above), dissenting opinion of Powell, O'Connor JJ, Burger CJ.

158 Ibid.

159 Note 146 above.

160 *Container Corporation v Franchise Tax Board* (note 146 above) at 189, n. 26, and at 195, n. 32; ILM pp. 870, 873.

161 107 L. Ed. 2d 696 (1990)

162 As was held by the US Court of Appeals for the Seventh Circuit in this case: 860 F. 2d 688 at 696–7 (1988).

163 See: *Shell Petroleum NV v Graves* 709 F. 2d 593, 595 (9th Cir.) cert. den. 464 US 1012 (1983); *EMI v Bennett* 738 F. 2d 994, 997 (9th Cir.) cert. den. 469 US 1073 (1984); *Alcan Aluminum Ltd v Franchise Tax Board* 558 F. Supp. 624, 626–9 (SDNY) aff'd 742 F. 2d 1430 (2nd Cir., 1983) cert. den. 464 US 1041 (1984).

164 Senate Bill 85 of 1986 which entered force after 1 January 1988. See Rothschild, 'California unitary tax update', *BIFD* (February 1991), p. 71.

165 Noted in Rothschild, ibid.

166 Case S019064 Judgment of 11 May 1992.

167 Judgment of 20 June 1994: 'US judges dismiss Barclays' challenge on unitary taxation law', *Financial Times*, 21 June 1994, p. 1. See for background Rothschild, 'California's new "water's edge" election enhances business opportunities for foreign investors: the US Supreme Court to rule in Barclays case', *BIFD* (January 1994), p. 3.

168 See Rothschild (note 164 above), at p. 73.

169 Senate Bill 671 enacted 10 September 1993, signed by Governor Wilson on 6 October 1993. For analysis see Rothschild (note 167 above). See also 'UK still unhappy with California tax proposals', *Financial Times*, 21/22 August 1993, p. 2. The principal changes enacted by SB 671 are that: firms electing to be taxed under the 'water's edge' principle shall no longer be subject to an election fee; they will no longer be required to produce a domestic disclosure spreadsheet; the election period is extended to seven years, with automatic annual renewal unless the taxpayer notifies non-renewal; and the Franchise Tax Board cannot disregard a water's edge election.

170 For a view supporting the adoption of a new international tax order for direct foreign investment based on a uniform unitary tax system see Bird, 'Shaping a new international tax order', *BIFD* (July 1988), 292. For a critical response see Muten, 'A new international tax order?', *BIFD* (November 1988), 471.

171 Note 146 above; see also Muten, ibid.

172 OECD (1979, note 41 above), at para. 14.

173   Ibid.

174   See: Plasschaert (note 7 above), at paras 10.12–10.14; McDaniel and Ault (note 13 above), at pp. 118–19, on which the following paragraph is based. See further Picciotto (note 2 above), chapter 5.

175   For further information on tax havens see: Spitz, *Tax Havens Encyclopedia* (Butterworths, loose-leaf); M. Grundy (ed.), *Grundy's Tax Havens*, 6th edn (Sweet & Maxwell, 1993); A. Ogley (ed.), *Tolley's Tax Havens* (Tolly Publishing); M. Finney and J. C. Dixon, *Tolley's International Tax Planning* (Tolley Publishing). For a survey of the principal tax havens see: R. A. Johns, *Tax Havens and Offshore Finance* (Frances Pinter, 1983). See further Picciotto (note 2 above), chapter 6.

176   See Adams and Whalley (note 1 above), at pp. 129–32; OECD, *International Tax Avoidance and Evasion: Four Related Studies Issues in International Taxation No. 1* (1987), 'Tax havens: measures to prevent abuse by taxpayers', at paras 6–45, pp. 21–9.

177   See chapter 5.

178   OECD (1987, note 176 above), at para. 30, p. 25.

179   See Plasschaert (note 7 above), para. 10.18.

180   OECD (1987, note 176 above), para. 27, p.25.

181   Ibid., para. 34, p. 26.

182   Ibid., para. 38.

183   Other countries now employing similar anti-avoidance provisions include France, Japan, Germany, Canada and the UK: ibid., para. 62, pp. 32–3. The OECD report contains a comparative analysis of the principal features of these laws at para. 63, p. 33. The US legislation is summarized in annex II to the report. The UK legislation was introduced by the Finance Act 1984, c. 43, ss 82–91. See further Baxter, 'The United Kingdom and tax havens: a comparative comment', 33 Am. Jo. Comp. L. 707 (1985); Picciotto (note 2 above), chapter 7. The French legislation can be found in article 209B of the Code Général des Impôts: see further Pascal Picault, *Fiscalité Française des Investissements a l'Etranger* (Dunod, 1986), pp. 159–85. On the New Zealand law see Prebble, 'The New Zealand controlled foreign company regime', 8 *Asian Pacific Tax and Investment Bulletin* (1990) 186. See also, for a comparative study of six jurisdictions, B. J. Arnold, *The Taxation of Controlled Foreign Corporations: an International Comparison* (Canadian Tax Foundation, 1986). On recent reforms in Japan see Magnin and Rautalahti, 'Japan; tax haven and foreign tax credit rules: 1992 amendments and their impact on Dutch holding companies', *BIFD* (May 1993) 286.

184   See McDaniel and Ault (note 13 above), chapter 7, pp. 109–20; Kaplan (note 13 above), chapter 6.

185   Defined as a US citizen owning at least 10 per cent of the total combined voting power: s. 951(b) IRC.

186   s. 957(a) IRC.

187   Kaplan (note 13 above), at p. 218.

188   Ownership by US shareholders includes stock held directly or indirectly through foreign corporations, partnerships, trusts and estates: ss 957(a), 958(a)(1)(B).

189 *CCA Inc.* v *CIR* 64 TC 137 (US Tax. Ct 1975).
190 *Garlock* v *CIR* 489 F. 2d 197 (1973); *Kraus* v *CIR* 490 F. 2d 898 (2nd Cir. 1974).
191 See *Koehring Company* v *US* 583 F. 2d 313 (7th Cir. 1978).
192 S. 951 (a)(1)(A)(i),(B).
193 S. 952(a)(1) and s. 953.
194 S. 952(a)(2) and s. 954.
195 See s. 954 and Treas. Reg. s. 1.954.
196 See Treas. Reg. s. 1.954-3(a)(2) and s. 1.954-3(a)(4)(i)–(iii); *Dave Fischbein Manufacturing Company* v *CIR* 59 TC 338 (US Tax. Ct 1972).
197 OECD (1987, note 176 above), para. 108, p. 44.
198 S. 956 IRC.
199 Note 13 above at p. 120.
200 See OECD (1987, note 176 above), paras 99–102 at pp. 42–3.
201 See further ibid., paras 105–11 at pp. 43–5.
202 See Bird, Muten (note 170 above); Easson, 'A new international tax order – responding to the challenge', *BIFD* (October 1991), 465.

9

Group Liability and Directors' Duties

This chapter develops the themes of corporate control and liability first mentioned in chapter 3. It examines in more detail the implications for existing principles of company law of integrated group enterprises and transnational contractual network enterprises (TNNs). This is done by reference to the distinct issues that affect the various classes of claimants who may wish to invoke the liability of the enterprise or, indeed, of its directors. The first class of potential claimants are the minority shareholders in the subsidiaries of the MNE. Their principal interest lies in obtaining the full financial value of their investment in the subsidiary. They are dependent on the actions of the directors of the subsidiary for the realization of their gains. The second class are the voluntary creditors who enter into commercial relations with affiliates of the MNE and who depend on the ability of the affiliate to meet its contractual liabilities to them. The third class consist of involuntary creditors who are forced by circumstances not of their choosing into a claim for compensation against the enterprise, usually as victims of corporate negligence.

The specific legal principles that have been developed in the context of each relationship are discussed in turn. The first and second sections of the chapter deal with the general issue of the liability of the parent for the actions of its subsidiaries both in an equity based group and in a transnational network enterprise based on contract. The principles considered in these sections will be of relevance to the claims of both voluntary and involuntary creditors. The approach is to describe the limits of existing law and then to consider various suggestions for reform that have been made in the context of MNE operations.

The third and fourth sections of the chapter go on to deal, respectively, with the more specialized issues surrounding the protection of minority shareholders in subsidiaries and the compensation of creditors on the insolvency of the affiliate with which they are dealing. These matters raise questions that go beyond the general principles of group liability discussed in the first section and, moreover, introduce issues relating to the personal liability of directors. It is important not to limit the discussion to the liability of the corporation alone, but also to consider that of its senior officials, as in many cases such personal liability may ensure more effective compliance with good business practice.

1   The Regulation of MNE Group Liability under Existing Legal Principles

1.1   Equity Based MNE Groups

1.1.1   Direct liability of the parent company   In litigation involving issues of MNE liability, once the question of jurisdiction has been answered in favour of impleading the foreign parent company,[1] the extent of its responsibility for the acts of its local subsidiary will depend on the applicable principles of law concerning corporate group liability.[2] In many cases concepts of contractual or tortious liability will suffice to establish the liability of the parent company, without the need to resort to liability based on control which serves merely to reinforce conclusions arrived at on other grounds. Liability based primarily on control becomes significant in those cases where the direct liability of the parent is doubtful in the light of established legal rules, but where, for reasons of policy, it may be desirable for the parent to be answerable for losses suffered by the plaintiff.

In Anglo-American jurisprudence, the direct liability of the parent company can arise in both contract and tort. First, if the foreign parent company is a party to a contract entered into between its subsidiary and a third party, it can be held liable on that contract. This depends on whether the subsidiary has acted as the agent of the parent for the purposes of the contract, which involves difficult problems of proof. In the absence of an express provision authorizing the subsidiary to act as the agent of the parent and/or establishing the parent as a party to the contract, the issue will turn on the extent to which the parent in fact controlled the acts of the subsidiary in relation to the transaction in question. Under English law, although the parent may exercise a high degree of general managerial control over the subsidiary, this may not be enough to show that, for the purposes of the transaction in issue, the subsidiary acted as the agent of the parent.[3] On the other hand, certain American cases suggest that an inference of 'agency' can arise simply out of the fact of common ownership between the parent and subsidiary, or between affiliates. This inference can be negated in the absence of equity links, despite the existence of contractual relations between two firms where one firm closely controls the activities of the other, as in the case of a franchising agreement.[4] However, the liability of controlling and/or collaborating enterprises in TNNs was not considered relevant in these cases. Consequently, their utility as precedents in such situations may be open to doubt. This matter is considered further in sub-section 1.2.

A further question has arisen as to the liability of the parent company as a guarantor of the subsidiary's obligations under a contract. In this connection, the English courts have held that the use of equivocal language renders the alleged guarantee too uncertain to be enforceable. There must be a clear assumption of the duties of a guarantor by the parent company.[5] A mere statement of intent will not do.[6]

Secondly, in tort, the parent company can be liable if it is shown that, by its acts or omissions, it was a joint tortfeasor with its subsidiary. The decision of the US District Court in the *Amoco Cadiz* case illustrates such an approach.[7] The court was faced with *inter alia* claims of negligence from French plaintiffs against Amoco Transport Co. (Transport), Amoco International Oil Co. (AIOC) and their parent, Standard Oil Co. (Indiana) (now Amoco Corporation), arising out of the oil spillage caused by the grounding of their tanker, Amoco Cadiz, off the coast of Northern France in 1978. Judge Frank McGarr found, on the facts, that the proximate cause of the grounding and spillage was the failure of the ship's steering mechanism. That failure was attributable to negligence in the design, maintenance and repair of the system, and to negligent crew training, which left the latter unprepared to avoid and remedy such a failure.

Judge McGarr then undertook a detailed analysis of the organization and functioning of Standard's shipping operations.[8] He concluded that both the subsidiaries and the parent company were liable.[9] The reasons for holding the parent corporation liable are worthy of citation:

43. As an integrated multinational corporation which is engaged through a system of subsidiaries in the exploitation, production, refining, transportation and sale of petroleum products throughout the world, Standard is responsible for the tortious acts of its wholly owned subsidiaries and instrumentalities AIOC and Transport.

44. Standard exercised such control over its subsidiaries AIOC and Transport that those entities would be considered to be mere instrumentalities of Standard. Furthermore, Standard itself was initially involved in and controlled the design construction operation and management of Amoco Cadiz and treated that vessel as if it were its own.

45. Standard therefore is liable for its own negligence and the negligence of AIOC and Transport with respect to the design, operation, maintenance, repair and crew training of Amoco Cadiz.

46. Standard therefore is liable to the French claimants for damages resulting from the grounding of Amoco Cadiz.[10]

Thus, the parent was liable on two grounds: by its own active involvement in the alleged negligence, and through its close control over the operating subsidiaries.[11] Unfortunately, no authorities were cited or discussed in the case. The finding of direct negligence on the part of the parent is consistent with general Anglo-American doctrines of liability involving joint tortfeasors. The finding of liability against the parent on the basis of integrated management is, however, more difficult to reconcile with authority.[12] It suggests that the simple fact of managerial control is enough to establish a case against the parent. It remains to be seen whether this aspect of the decision will be followed in future cases.

Judge McGarr's judgment can be defended on the ground that, on the facts, decision-making in relation to the global transport policy of the corporation was so centralized that major policies could not have been formulated without the direct involvement of the parent company. However, the case does not offer much guidance on the circumstances under which the court will conclude that the parent company is liable on the basis of integrated management. The business manager is left uncertain as to the legal significance of separate incorporation in a group, making it harder for him or her to be able to plan the allocation of risk among the units of the enterprise. This issue will be considered further below in relation to the effect of the 'enterprise entity' doctrine.

1.1.2 Lifting the corporate veil   In relation to the liability of foreign parent companies, the Anglo-American doctrine of 'lifting the corporate veil' offers a means of justifying group liability in circumstances where the subsidiary has insufficient assets to meet the claims against it, but where the case for compensation of the claimants is hard to resist on moral grounds.[13] It was in this sense that the Indian courts applied the doctrine in the *Bhopal* case, during the course of hearings on interim measures.[14] Of particular importance is the Judgment of Seth J, given in the High Court of Jabalpur, on appeal from the order of the Bhopal District Court.[15]

Judge Seth based his decision on the rule, contained in the English Rules of the Supreme Court,[16] that an interim payment could be made where, if the action proceeded to trial, the plaintiff would obtain judgment for substantial damages against the respondent.[17] The question was, therefore, whether the Union of India could get an award of substantial damages against Union Carbide Corporation (UCC) under the applicable principles of Indian tort law.

This matter turned on the effect of the Indian Supreme Court's decision in *Mehta* v *Union of India*,[18] which concerned a leak of oleum gas from a caustic chlorine plant resulting in some 340 injuries and, possibly, one fatality. In the course of its judgment, the Supreme Court laid down a new principle of absolute liability for enterprises engaged in a hazardous or inherently dangerous industry.[19] The order of the Bhopal District Court was founded upon this new principle. The question for Seth J was whether the new doctrine indeed represented Indian law, and whether it could justify the imposition of liability against UCC.

Having held that the doctrine elaborated in *Mehta* provided the substantive law by which the final decision on the merits would be made, Seth J stated that only two questions remained to be answered before an interim payment could be ordered: first, whether it was permissible to lift the corporate veil between UCC and its Indian subsidiary so as to hold the former liable for the tort; secondly, whether a *prima facie* case could be made out showing that UCC had real control over the Bhopal plant for purposes of liability. Seth J found no difficulty in answering both questions in the affirmative. Not only was this a proper case for lifting the corporate veil in accordance with Indian and English case-law,[20] but UCC did, in fact, exercise real control over the enterprise which was engaged in carrying on the hazardous activities at the Bhopal plant, on the basis that UCC owned the majority of the equity (50.9 per cent) in the Indian subsidiary, controlled the composition of the Board of Directors of the Indian company and also had full control over its management. A perusal of the American corporation's 'corporate policy' document showed that it was a multinational corporation with the avowed purpose of managing and running industries like its own in other countries of the world through local subsidiaries, if necessary, over which it had full and effective control.

It is noteworthy that Seth J felt it necessary to lift the corporate veil in order to decide whether UCC, as the parent company, was the 'enterprise' that 'carried on' the dangerous activity for purposes of liability under the terms of the *Mehta* doctrine.[21] It is unclear from the Judgment of the Indian Supreme Court in *Mehta* whether the concept of 'enterprise' includes the 'economic entity' of the group, and hence involves the liability of the parent, where the dangerous activity is conducted by a subsidiary. Judge Seth's approach suggests that the parent may not be automatically liable, as its liability depends on the extent of control exercised by the parent over the subsidiary. This involves difficult, and often disputable, questions of fact.[22] The disagreement between the US and Indian Courts on the question of whether UCC actually controlled its Indian subsidiary testifies to this.[23] Furthermore, Judge Seth's analysis of UCC's control over the Indian subsidiary can be criticized on the ground that he confuses the overall strategic control of a multinational group by its parent company with the day-to-day running of its subsidiaries. In practice the two are quite distinct. This illustrates the practical difficulties of relating the legal justification for lifting the corporate veil to the evidence of relevant managerial control.

1.2   Liability of Transnational Network Enterprises

The major problems associated with establishing liability in TNNs rest with their unique legal character as enterprises consisting of entities that are linked by contract rather than equity, but which display systems of managerial control and productive cooperation not dissimilar to those found in equity based corporate groups. The responsibility of the controlling entity for the acts of the controlled entity may be avoided by reference to the contract between them, which may include risk-shifting clauses in the form of exemptions of liability for the controlling entity. The question arises whether the 'contractual veil' between the associated contracting parties should be lifted, so that the controlling party could be made liable, along with the controlled party, for acts causing loss to third parties in which both contracting parties have participated by reason of the economic and business relationship underlying the contract between them.[24]

According to Professor Teubner, the correct legal response is the simultaneous assignment of responsibility for the act giving rise to the claim upon 'the network, the centre, and the individual unit'.[25] The governing principle of liability should be that 'where the internal division of labour involves all the members of the system in performance of the contract, then all such members and not only those who happen to have contractual relations with third parties, should come within the ambit of the heightened duties of care.'[26]

Clearly, this represents a desirable principle of justice. It is the 'network' counterpart of lifting the corporate veil in equity based groups. As with that doctrine, the crucial question is to establish the extent to which entities other than the one directly dealing with the claimant are involved in the impugned acts. Again detailed analysis of the economic and business reality of the enterprise is required. Again disputes over facts are likely. The contractual allocation of risk in the enterprise may be undermined in future litigation. Uncertainty will result.

2   New Approaches to MNE Group Liability

2.1   The 'Enterprise Entity' Theory and Its Limitations

The *Mehta* doctrine represents an attempt by the Indian legal system to break out of the limitations of fault based liability in cases involving ultrahazardous industrial activities carried on by national or multinational corporations. However, the doctrine, as applied by Seth J, does not appear to have gone beyond the logic of corporate separation between the parent and subsidiary for the purposes of establishing liability.

In this the judge's reasoning is in line with the general state of national laws in the area of parent company responsibility. Most legal systems admit the direct liability of the parent company for the acts of its subsidiary only in special circumstances. The prevailing principle remains that of preserving the legal separation of parent and subsidiary.[27] Indeed, even the most advanced corporate group law, the German Stock Corporations Act 1965 (*Aktiengesetz*),[28] seeks to preserve the subsidiary as a separate enterprise in that the parent owes duties of compensation to the creditors and minority shareholders of the subsidiary in return for the power of control.[29] In this the German law remains grounded in the logic of the classical theory of the corporation.[30] It has not created a new form of business association, the 'group enterprise', as the object of rights and duties, save perhaps in the exceptional case of the 'integrated group'. This is formed where at least 95 per cent of the shares in the subsidiary are held by the parent and a resolution for integration is approved by at least 75 per cent of the shareholders in the parent company, thereby allowing the parent to manage the subsidiary without consideration as to its legal separation, in return for the assumption of full liability by the parent for the debts and obligations of the subsidiary.[31]

'Enterprise entity' doctrine differs from existing concepts of group liability in that it replaces an approach based on exceptions to the otherwise inviolable corporate separation between parent and subsidiary (whether through the lifting of the corporate veil or through specialized group liability laws) with one that deduces parent company liability from the fact of economic integration between itself and the subsidiary. This recognizes the corporate group as a distinct form of business association, thereby opening the way for the evolution of a specialized legal regime going beyond the paradigm of the single unit limited liability joint stock company.

Apart from the above-mentioned judgment of Judge McGarr in *Amoco Cadiz*, there have been other instances in which the logic of the enterprise entity has been adopted as a justification for the group liability of MNEs. First, as noted in chapter 5, in relation to the issue of jurisdiction, certain legal systems have asserted the right to extend their law extraterritorially on the basis of the economic unity of the MNE group.[32] Thus, in relation to non-EC firms operating through EC subsidiaries, jurisdiction has been asserted by the EC Commission in anti-trust cases on the basis of the parent–subsidiary relationship. Secondly, in relation to substantive liability, throughout the proceedings in the *Bhopal* case, the Indian government and the private plaintiffs argued that UCC should be liable for the acts leading to the accident, regardless of the legal separation between itself and its Indian subsidiary. Before the American courts it was argued that UCC, a 'monolithic multinational, controlled the design, construction and operation of the Bhopal plant through its global network of corporate planning, direction and control',[33] and should therefore be accountable for the acts of the subsidiary. However, it is not entirely clear from the plaintiffs' argument whether they sought to suggest that UCC's liability was strict in view of the economic unity of the enterprise, or whether the US parent was a direct wrongdoer and thus a necessary and proper defendant. Prior to the settlement of the case, the Indian government had maintained, in its submissions to the Indian Supreme Court, that UCC was strictly liable for the accident. It is significant that the Indian government did not see it as necessary to refer to the lifting of the corporate veil as an aspect of the *Mehta* doctrine. In the government's submission liability was not to be determined by way of an exception to the principle of corporate separation, but by reference to the enterprise as a whole and to the *capacity* of the parent to control the subsidiary. Clearly, the government was asserting a principle of liability based on the economic entity of the enterprise.[34]

Despite their persuasive force, these examples do not show a widespread acceptance of the logic of 'enterprise liability' for multinational corporate groups. The advantages of limited liability offered by the doctrine of corporate separation provide strong reasons for the retention of existing approaches to group liability. A radical abandonment of the traditional approach to group liability is unlikely. The major practical problem underlying the evolution of an enterprise entity approach to group liability rests in identifying the existence of such a business association. This requires the use of economic theories of corporate integration so as to develop a clearer concept of the type of firm in which the parent can be said to control its subsidiaries for the purposes of liability.[35] Thus, the outcome of any claim based on the enterprise entity theory depends on an interpretation of evidence that a lawyer may not be best educated to appreciate. Uncertainty is bound to result. In this respect the enterprise entity doctrine of corporate liability does not offer a significant practical advance over the requirements of lifting the corporate veil, although it does represent a conceptual shift away from the legal formalism of the doctrine of corporate personality as applied to corporate groups.

Finally, in the case of TNNs, the enterprise entity doctrine has been criticized by Professor Teubner as an inadequate response to the problems of establishing group liability. In particular, he feels that the approach is too 'hierarchical', in that it concentrates on locating responsibility with the parent, and thereby fails to appreciate the need for more decentralized systems of attributing liability in a more loosely formed 'network' enterprise.[36]

As stated above, it is not clear whether Professor Teubner's alternative will be any easier to apply in practice than the existing exceptions to the doctrines of corporate separation and contractual risk shifting. However, it does have the merit of offering more alternative combinations of liability across the enterprise than the vertical approach of enterprise entity doctrine. Given that a unitary principle of group liability may not always be necessary for the achievement of regulatory goals,[37] the flexibility inherent in Professor Teubner's analysis may be of considerable practical value in the evolution of future regulatory regimes.

2.2   Towards a New Law of MNE Group Liability?

The foregoing analysis has been conditioned by the existence of two competing objectives: first, the need to ensure sufficient certainty in the law to permit the efficient allocation of risk in a corporate group, whether through the creation of subsidiaries or through the contractual allocation of rights and duties; secondly, the need to ensure that the resulting allocation of risk in the group does not result in a failure to compensate third parties for losses caused by the activities of group members. There may be at least three distinct approaches to the reconciliation of these interests.

The first is to retain the limits to liability inherent in the traditional concepts of corporate personality and contractual freedom and stability, and to provide *ad hoc* exceptions thereto, which deal with individual abuses. This has been the broad approach of existing laws. Arguably, little more may be needed.[38]

On the other hand, the manifest failure of traditional legal concepts to deal adequately with cases such as *Bhopal* suggests that some changes in legal policy are required. In response to such cases the second approach is that of developing a unitary concept of the group liability, along the lines of the enterprise entity doctrine. As noted above, the principal weakness of the enterprise entity doctrine is the potential uncertainty that surrounds the identification of the relevant entity on a case-by-case basis. If the law is to offer certainty as to the type of corporate group that will be regarded as a single entity for the purposes of liability, some *a priori* judgment to this effect should be made. This may be achieved in one of two ways.

First, a new type of incorporation for corporate groups, which assumes group liability as one of its consequences, can be adopted. In the case of MNEs this could be provided by some form of supranational incorporation. Indeed, the original proposal for a European Company (SE) contained provisions similar to those of the above-mentioned German *Aktiengesetz*, which would permit for the management of the company as a single economic unit.[39] This approach has since been abandoned in favour of one that leaves the protection of third parties and minorities to the national laws governing public limited companies of the Member States in which the individual units of the SE operate.[40] This new approach envisages that the draft Ninth Directive on groups of companies will be adopted and will thereby harmonize the laws of the EC Member Countries on group liability. However, at present, neither proposal looks likely to be adopted.

Secondly, a presumption of control by the parent over the subsidiary has been put forward as an alternative.[41] The presumption of control gives advance notice to the parent of the risk of liability, and places the onus on the parent to rebut the presumption with conclusive proof of the independence of the subsidiary. In the case of a highly integrated company that presumption may be almost impossible to rebut. However, it may be rebutted where it can be shown that the third party has transacted with the subsidiary in the full knowledge that the parent had expressly excluded its liability. On the other hand, where the third party has reasonably relied on the parent to underwrite the subsidiary's liability, then even the strongest proof of corporate independence should not excuse the parent. Furthermore, in line with the *Mehta* doctrine, where the claimant is the victim of a major industrial accident, and the subsidiary cannot meet the resulting liabilities, the parent company should be strictly liable to make up the outstanding amount of the claim.

A number of objections may be put against this presumption. First, it practically destroys limited liability for corporate groups. That may not be a fatal objection if effective compensation can only be obtained by making the parent liable, as in the case where the subsidiary has insufficient funds to meet the claim. Furthermore, as the Fourth Edition of Gower's *Principles of Modern Company Law* points out, such an inroad into limited liability does not affect the privilege of limited liability for the shareholders of the parent. It merely makes the assets of the parent company available to satisfy claims made against subsidiaries in cases where the parent ought, in principle, to account for the loss to the third party.[42] Indeed, the acceptance of a presumption of liability by the parent may protect the commercial interests of the group, by encouraging business confidence among outsiders dealing with the group.

Secondly, it may be objected that the presumption does not remove the need for a forensic examination of the relationship between the parent and the subsidiary.[43] The existence of a parent–subsidiary relationship, and a causal connection between the control of the subsidiary by the parent and the resulting harm suffered by the claimant, would still need to be shown. Thus the presumption of liability may not, in fact, take us beyond the uncertainties caused by the doctrines of lifting the corporate veil or enterprise entity. On the other hand, given that, in the majority of cases of inward direct investment, it is clear from the outset who the parent company is, it may not be difficult in practice to identify the company upon which the onus of the presumption falls.

It is arguable that a presumption of parent company liability for the acts of its overseas subsidiaries may remove some of the conceptual difficulties inherent in justifying an exercise of extraterritorial jurisdiction by the host or home state. In chapter 5 it was argued that, in relation to the operations of MNEs in host countries, a presumption of liability can serve as notice to the foreign parent that, on setting up a subsidiary within the jurisdiction, it is subject to all the liabilities that a locally incorporated parent company may bear.[44] However, objections from the home country may result, as shown by the New York Supreme Court's refusal to recognise the effect of the Argentine Supreme Court's judgment in the *Deltec* case, where the latter had ruled that, in view of the 'unified socio-economic unity' of the Deltec group, the multinational group as a whole was jointly and severally liable for the debts of its Argentinian subsidiary.[45]

The third approach to reconciling the competing interests of group limitation of liability and adequate compensation of parties dealing with the group is the 'network liability' approach favoured by Professor Teubner. As noted earlier, this approach is specifically geared to the distinct problems of non-equity networks that are more loosely connected than those based on parent–subsidiary relations. Certain problems associated with the operation of this doctrine of liability have already been considered and need not be repeated. The remaining issue is whether such an approach, with its advantage of flexibility, can be extended to equity based groups as well.

In principle, the allocation of responsibility among any relevant combination of affiliates in the group, without necessarily involving the parent – unless appropriate on the facts – is attractive. In most cases, the nature of the claim and the sum involved will not require the resources of the group as a whole to ensure effective compensation. However, when an accident of the magnitude of the *Bhopal* case occurs, effective compensation can only be achieved by involving the assets of the group as a whole.

In such extreme cases the network liability approach could lead to an excessive decentralization of the *locus* of liability. Acting rather like the traditional doctrine of corporate separation, the network approach could subdivide the allocation of risk in the group to the entities actually connected with the harmful acts, while shielding the parent and other affiliates. However, given Professor Teubner's insistence on joint and several liability, this argument may be a misrepresentation of his intentions. Liability may, in fact, be joint and several across the group. If so, it is hard to see how the approach offers a truly radical advance upon enterprise entity doctrine or, indeed, upon traditional notions of joint liability in tort. The required evidence of group liability would be much the same in all these cases.

3 The Protection of Minority Shareholders in the Subsidiary of a MNE

It was seen in chapter 3 that equity-based MNEs will operate and control an international network of subsidiaries on the basis of integrated line management. This means that the directors of the various subsidiaries will in reality be little more than line managers who carry out the group's business plans. This may create special problems in the case of subsidiaries that are jointly owned with local minority shareholders. The risk arises that the directors of the subsidiary will make decisions that are in the group's interests but that may adversely affect the interests of the minority. For example, the parent company may wish to use the assets of the subsidiary to subsidize investment elsewhere in the group. It may raise loans from the subsidiary, thereby reducing the funds available for distribution to shareholders. Equally, the subsidiary may be instructed deliberately to effect transfer pricing manipulations so as to reduce the profits available for distribution to local shareholders and thus increase the value of the group's share thereof. Furthermore, the parent may, with the full knowledge of the subsidiary's directors, divert business opportunities from the subsidiary for the benefit of other entities in the group, thereby reducing the prospects of the subsidiary. In all of these cases the minority shareholders' interests are subordinated to those of the group enterprise. This may have consequences for the liability of the directors of the subsidiary and of the parent under the applicable local law.

Under English law, the fact that a company is owned and controlled as part of a group does not remove the general principle that directors owe a duty to act in the best interest only of the company of which they are directors. Thus directors of a holding company have no duties as such to protect the interests of its subsidiaries where these have independent boards.[46] Similarly, the directors of a subsidiary owe their primary duty to the subsidiary.[47] They owe no fiduciary duties to the holding company as the majority shareholder.[48]

The duties of a director include a duty to have equal regard to the interests of all the present and future members of the company, which requires them to act fairly as between different classes of shareholders. This includes a duty not to make decisions that may adversely affect one group of shareholders to the benefit of another.[49] Thus, where the directors of the UK based subsidiary of a MNE make a decision that is in the interests of the group as a whole, they will be in breach of their duty to act in the interests of the members as a whole unless they can show that the decision reasonably coincides with the interests of the subsidiary as well.[50] For example, on analogy with the facts of the leading English case, *Charterbridge Corporation* v *Lloyds Bank*,[51] if the subsidiary were to forward funds to its parent in an attempt to preserve the latter's solvency, this may be regarded as reasonably within the interests of the subsidiary where the latter depends on the parent for the services and know-how that keep the subsidiary in business. On the other hand, where the directors of the subsidiary are deliberately siphoning funds out of the jurisdiction as part of the group's corporate plan, thereby affecting the value of the subsidiary as a going concern, they would almost certainly be held liable for breach of duty.[52] This argument is borne out by reference to the statutory remedy that minority shareholders have under English law against unfairly prejudicial conduct on the part of the company.

By s. 459 of the UK Companies Act 1985 any member of the company may apply to the court for an order on the ground that the affairs of the company are being or have been conducted in a manner that is unfairly prejudicial to the interests of some part of the members, of whom the petitioner is one. The right of petition extends to any actual or proposed act or omission of the company that is or would be unfairly prejudicial. In *Scottish Co-operative Wholesale Society* v *Meyer*,[53] a case decided under s. 210 of the Companies Act 1948, the predecessor to s. 459, the House of Lords held that the minority shareholders in a subsidiary are entitled to a statutory remedy where the directors of the subsidiary knowingly acquiesce in the parent's policy of running down the subsidiary, as this constitutes a breach of their duties as directors. The acts of the parent are attributable to the subsidiary's directors as the latter's decisions are determined by the policy of the former. Thus, under English law there appears to be some protection for minorities subjected to group policies that are unfavourable to their interests. However, given the complexity of group transactions and the limited disclosure to which they are subjected, it will often be difficult for the minority to prove their case. Furthermore, the cost of bringing an action may act as a deterrent.[54] In any case, s. 459 is designed to act in the context of private companies where there is no ready market for the shares. In the case of a public company a disgruntled minority will normally sell their shares as a less expensive option to litigation.[55] Indeed, if the minority succeeds under s. 459 the usual remedy will be the compulsory purchase of their shares by the majority at their original market value had there been no prejudicial acts.[56]

Turning briefly to other jurisdictions, in the USA the rights of action of the minority are based on the fiduciary duty of the majority to respect their interests.[57] This duty has developed from the fiduciary duty owed by directors to the corporation. It requires fair treatment of the minority by the majority. This duty has been extended to the case of parent–subsidiary relations involving a minority shareholding in the latter.[58] In Germany the 1965 *Aktiengesetz*[59] provides for the protection of minority interests by imposing certain duties upon the controlling undertaking. Thus, where a 'control contract' group is formed,[60] the controlling undertaking must offer to pay a guaranteed dividend to minority shareholders,[61] or to buy out their shares at a fixed price.[62] Where a *de facto* group exists,[63] the controlling undertaking is obliged to compensate the controlled undertaking for any losses suffered by it as a result of the controlling undertaking's influence over its business activities.[64] Failure to compensate will give rise to a claim for compensation from the controlled undertaking and from the shareholders for any damage apart from the damage they have suffered by the controlled undertaking being damaged.[65] Under French and Argentinian law, the rights of minority shareholders may be capable of protection under the principle of abuse of rights (*abus de droit*), whereby the rights to control the company granted to the directors must be exercised in its interests. However, it is not clear whether the interests of the company are commensurate with the interests of the shareholders or are sperate therefrom.[66]

Finally, it should be recalled that certain states may require as a condition of entry that a foreign investor enters into a joint venture with local shareholders. Where this is the case, either the foreign investor or the local shareholder may be in the numerical minority. However, as was shown in chapter 6, this may not necessarily reflect the balance of decision-making power between the parties. The foreign party is more likely to possess the commercial advantages required for the success of the venture. Provided that the local shareholders derive a fair return on the venture no difficulties should arise. On the other hand, where the foreign partner fails to fulfil its side of the bargain, the local authorities may intervene and require the observance of the terms of the joint venture. The law upon which entry was authorized, and the terms of the investment authorization, may allow for administrative intervention in the interests of the local partner.[67]

The preceding discussion has centred on the national laws of states concerning minority protection or the protection of local shareholders. It is not an issue that has given rise to distinct laws for MNEs. Thus the domestic law of each state in which the firm operates must be consulted to gauge the extent of local shareholder protection. However, a problem that is unique to MNEs arises as a result of the foreign nationality of the parent. The directors of a subsidiary may be required by the parent company to make decisions that are in the interests of the parent, in that failure to effect the decision will result in the parent being in breach of home country laws, but that conflict with the interests of the local subsidiary. Here the local law protecting minority interests in the subsidiary might be invoked to prevent the decision from being made. It will be recalled that the French courts used the French law concerning abuse of rights in this way in the case of *Société Fruehauf Corp.* v *Massardy*, discussed in chapter 5.[68] This case shows that the host state is entitled to subject a foreign-owned subsidiary to local company law. This is correct in view of the fact that, by reason of domicil, host state law is the proper law of the subsidiary.[69]

4   Protection of Creditors upon the Insolvency of the Subsidiary of a MNE

The final issue to be considered in this chapter relates to an aspect of creditor protection that was not dealt with in section 1, namely the rights of a creditor against the foreign parent of an insolvent subsidiary with which the creditor has been doing business.

Under English law directors are not in general bound to have regard to the interests of creditors.[70] However, where a director of a company that has gone into liquidation knew or ought to have concluded, some time before the commencement of the winding up of the company, that there was no reasonable prospect that the company would avoid going into insolvent liquidation then he or she may be held liable for wrongful trading under s. 214 of the Insolvency Act 1986. His only defence is that he took every step with a view to minimizing the potential loss to the company's creditors that he ought to have taken, assuming him to have known that there was no reasonable prospect that the company would avoid going into insolvent liquidation.[71]

Thus, if the director of a UK subsidiary of a foreign-owned parent is ordered to run that subsidiary without sufficient assets to meet its liabilities he or she may be exposed to personal liability under s. 214. Furthermore, the parent company may be jointly liable as a 'shadow director',[72] that is as 'a person in accordance with whose directions or instructions the directors of a company are accustomed to act'.[73] The parent will have to contribute to the payment of the subsidiary's creditors if, while exercising control over the latter, it allows the subsidiary to fall into insolvent liquidation.[74] This raises the question of whether the foreign parent could be impleaded before the English courts to answer a case under s. 214. Given that the English courts are reluctant to implead a foreign parent in an action involving the insolvency of a local subsidiary,[75] the creditor or his or her representative may have a difficult task to show that the foreign parent ought to be answerable.[76]

In other jurisdictions similar laws exist. Under French law, where a parent company acts as a *de facto* director of an insolvent subsidiary it may be liable where it has acted in contravention of its fiduciary duties as a director of the subsidiary and there is a causal connection between those acts and the damage caused to the subsidiary. However, this remedy may be limited by the fact that the parent's fiduciary duties will be defined in accordance with the legitimate pursuit of group interests. Consequently successful actions under these rules are rare.[77] Under the German *Aktiengesetz*, the controlling undertaking will take on full liability for the debts and obligations of the controlled undertaking.[78] However, the provisions of the *Aktiengesetz* have not been effective as a means of creditor redress. The German courts have stepped in and have partly remedied this situation by use of the 'qualified concern' doctrine, whereby a controlling undertaking that exerts permanent and extensive involvement in the management of an insolvent subsidiary will be presumed to have failed to show concern for the interests of the controlled undertaking, and will be directly liable to the creditors of the controlled undertaking.[79]

In New Zealand, the Companies Amendment Act 1980 introduced new powers whereby a court can, in its discretion, order any other company in the group to pay to the liquidator of an insolvent company the whole or part of any or all of the debts provable in the winding-up. This is done in the light of evidence as to the extent that another company in the group has involved itself in the management of the insolvent company, its conduct towards creditors of the insolvent company and the extent to which the winding-up of the insolvent company is attributable to the actions of the first company. The courts may also wind up two or more companies in the group and pool their assets in the satisfaction of creditors where this is warranted by the facts.[80] In the USA, creditor actions that seek redress from parent corporations for the unpaid debts of their subsidiaries will involve the piercing of the corporate veil based on arguments concerning the undercapitalization of the subsidiary or its use as a vehicle of fraud. This involves difficult questions of proof, as what constitutes undercapitalization or fraud is often unclear.[81]

The international dimension to insolvency situations in multinational corporate groups has not been adequately resolved. The success of a creditor's claim against the foreign parent will hinge on the initial question of whether the latter is capable of being impleaded before the courts of the host state in insolvency proceedings. Assuming that personal jurisdiction is obtained, the problems of proving parent liability under local law will pose significant obstacles to success. The logic of corporate separation is as hard to defeat in this situation as in others, and, as the requirements of the sample of laws summarized above show, the legal tests imposed on the plaintiff creditor can be very onerous.

However, the present discussion should be kept within a reasonable perspective. Empirical evidence suggests that MNEs are very unlikely to allow their subsidiaries to go bankrupt and will often guarantee their debts.[82] Thus, the situation contemplated in this section can be seen as exceptional, though obviously not unprecedented.[83] In times of global recession the incidence of subsidiary default may increase, giving rise to more claims in insolvency. However, the insolvency of an entire MNE group is very unlikely. Thus, where part of a MNE network defaults, it may be reasonable to expect the surviving parts to compensate the creditors of the insolvent entity as a matter of commercial prudence. Furthermore, where a large MNE is in serious financial trouble, governments are unlikely to allow it to cease operations, as the social and economic costs may be too great when compared to some form of public subsidy. The US government's subsidy to Chrysler in 1979 is a case in point.[84] Therefore, some element of (albeit informal and case based) public insurance against the default of a major MNE may be practised by the home government, assuming it can raise sufficient revenue to effect such action.

5   Concluding Remarks

This chapter has raised a number of basic issues relating to the establishment of group liability for the acts and defaults of individual units of a MNE. In each case the logic of existing law, based as it is on the concept of the single unit enterprise, fails to grasp the realities of interdependence between affiliated enterprises in the national or multinational corporate group. However, legal systems are responding with piecemeal reforms and by adapting existing legal doctrines to modern day phenomena. There is undoubtedly evolution in legal thought and practice in this area. None the less, significant legal and practical obstacles remain for the effective protection of those who make claims against MNEs. Furthermore, the responsibilities of MNEs may be seen as going beyond those owed to creditors (whether voluntary or involuntary) and shareholders, and to encompass other classes of 'stakeholders', such as employees and the general public at large. In all these cases significant issues of accountability emerge. These can be addressed by reforms in the internal governance of MNEs and by effective duties of disclosure. These matters are examined in the next chapter.

Notes

1   On which see chapter 5.

2   See further: Hofstetter 'Parent responsibility for subsidiary corporations: evaluating European trends', 39 ICLQ 576 (1990); 'Multinational enterprise parent liability: efficient legal regimes in a world market environment', 15 N. C. J. Int'l & Com. Reg. 299 (1990). The most comprehensive survey of the principles involved has been undertaken in relation to US law by Professor Philip Blumberg. See: P. Blumberg, *The Law of Corporate Groups: Procedural Problems in the Law of Parent and Subsidiary Corporations* (Little, Brown & Co., 1983, Supp. 1992); *The Law of Corporate Groups: Problems in the Bankruptcy or Reorganization of Parent and Subsidiary Corporations, Including the Law of Corporate Guarantees* (Little Brown & Co., 1985, Supp. 1992); *The Law of Corporate Groups: Tort, Contract and Other Common Law Problems in the Substantive Law of Parent and Subsidiary Corporations* (Little, Brown & Co., 1987, Supp. 1992); *The Law of Corporate Groups: Problems of Parent and Subsidiary Corporations under Statutory Law of General Application* (Little Brown & Co., 1989, Supp. 1992); with Kurt Strasser, *The Law of Corporate Groups: Problems of Parent and Subsidiary Corporations under Statutory Law Specifically Applying Enterprise Principles* (Little, Brown & Co., 1992); *The Multinational Challenge to Corporation Law* (Oxford University Press, 1993). Professor Blumberg's views are conveniently summarized in 'The corporate entity in an era of multinational corporations', 15 Del. J. Corp. L. 285 (1990).

3   See *Adams* v *Cape Industries plc* [1990] Ch 433; [1991] 1 All ER 929 (Scott J and CA) leave to appeal to the House of Lords refused by the Appeal Committee of the House 24 October 1989. See further Fawcett, 'Jurisdiction and subsidiaries' [1985] JBL 16 at p. 20; Paul L. Davies *Gower's, Principles of Company Law*, 6th edn (Stevens, 1998), p. 173.

4   See *Frummer* v *Hilton Hotels International* 19 NY 2d 533, 227 NE 2d 851, 281 NYS 2d 41 cert. denied 389 US 923 (1967); *Delagi* v *Volkswagenwerk AG* 29 NY 2d 426, 278 NE 2d 895, 328 NYS 2d 653 (1972). For analysis see C. D. Wallace, *Legal Control of the Multinational Enterprise* (Martinus Nijhoff, 1983), at pp. 115–16.

5   See *Amalgamated Investment & Property Co.* v *Texas Commercial Bank* [1982] QB 84 (CA) where a bank was estopped from denying that it had agreed to guarantee loans made by its wholly owned subsidiary which was set up specifically to effect the loans in question.

6   See, in this connection, the cases on letters of comfort: *Re Augustus Barnett* [1986] BCLC 170 noted Prentice 103 LQR 11 (1987); *Kleinwort Benson* v *Malaysian Mining Corporation* [1988] 1 All ER 714 QBD reversed [1989] 1 All ER 785 (CA), leave to appeal refused HL 10 May 1989 [1989] 2 All ER xviii.

7   [1984] 2 Lloyds Rep. 304.

8   Ibid., at pp. 308–311; 319–328.

9   For the liability of Amoco International see ibid., at pp. 328–36; for the liability of Amoco Transport see ibid., at pp. 337–8.

10 Ibid., at p. 338.

11 For the facts that were held to show Standard's control over its subsidiaries see ibid., pp. 332–4.

12 There are several cases from various US state jurisdictions suggesting that the existence of the parent–subsidiary relationship, and integrated nature of the corporate group, are insufficient to ground parent company liability of the tortious acts of its subsidiary. See: *Moffat* v *Goodyear Tyre & Rubber Co.* 652 SW 2d 609 (Texas CA 1983); *Liberty Financial Management Corp.* v *Beneficial Data Processing Corp.* 670 SW 2d 40 (Missouri CA 1984); *Brock* v *Alaska International Industries Inc.* 645 P 2d 188 (Alaska Sup. Ct 1982); *Grywczynski* v *Shasta Beverages Inc.* 606 F. Supp. 61 (California, 1984). These cases are discussed more fully in Muchlinski, 'Lifting the corporate veil on the Western multinational corporate group', in M. A. Jakubowski (ed.), *Anglo-Polish Legal Essays Volume 1* (University of Warsaw Faculty of Law and Administration, 1986), at pp. 183–4 (cited hereafter as *Corporate Veil*).

13 Civil law systems have achieved a similar objective through concepts of fraudulent corporate simulation, abuse of corporate personality, *actio Pauliana* (giving creditors powers over debtors who act in a manner prejudicial to the creditors' rights of execution) and '*abus de droit*'. See Dobson "'Lifting the veil" in four countries: the law of Argentina, England, France and the United States', 35 ICLQ 839 (1986).

14 *Union of India* v *Union Carbide Corporation* (Gas Claim Case No. 113 of 1986) Order 17 December 1987, Deo J. Upheld in part: *Union of India* v *Union Carbide* Corporation Civil Revision No. 26 of 1988 4 April 1988,

Seth J (referred to hereafter as Civil Revision 4 April 1988).

15   The District Court had ordered Union Carbide to pay 3,500 million rupees ($270 million) by way of interim relief. That order was upheld by the High Court though the sum awarded was reduced to 250 crores rupees ($190 million).

16   Order 29, rule 11.

17   Civil Revision 4 April 1988, paras 13.01.01–13.01.07.

18   AIR 1987, SC 965, 1086.

19   Ibid., paras 31–33 at pp. 1098–1100. The Supreme Court formulated the applicable principle as follows: 'An enterprise which is engaged in a hazardous or inherently dangerous industry which poses a potential threat to the health and safety of the persons working in the factory and residing in the surrounding areas owes an absolute and non-delegable duty to the community to ensure that no harm results to anyone on account of hazardous or inherently dangerous nature of the activity which it has undertaken. The enterprise must be held to be under an obligation to provide that the hazardous or inherently dangerous activity in which it is engaged must be conducted with the highest standards of safety and if any harm results on account of such activity, the enterprise must be absolutely liable to compensate for such harm and it should be no answer to the enterprise to say that it had taken all reasonable care and that the harm occurred without any negligence on its part' (para. 31 at p. 1099).

20   The Judge cited in support the Indian cases *Tata Engineering and Locomotive Co. Ltd* v *State of Bihar AIR* 1965 SC 40, *and Life Insurance Corporation of India* v *Escorts Ltd* AIR 1986 SC 1370, and the English case *DHN Food Distributors Ltd* v *Tower Hamlets London Borough Council* [1976] 1 WLR 852 (CA). It should be noted that the concept of 'economic entity' used in the DHN case has not been widely followed in English law: see *Woolfson* v *Strathclyde Regional Council* (1978) 38 P & CR 521; *National Dock Labour Board* v *Pinn & Wheeler Ltd* [1989] BCLC 647. For a full discussion see Rixon, 'Lifting the veil between holding and subsidiary companies', 102 LQR 415 (1986). For a contrasting view see Schmitthoff, 'Salomon in the shadow' [1976] JBL 305. See also Gower (note 3 above), at pp. 166–70, discussing *Adams* v *Cape Industries* (note 3 above) on this point.

21   See note 19 above.

22   See Wallace (note 4 above), at pp. 110–20. For a full survey of recent research into MNE control structures see OECD, *Structure and Organization of Multinational Enterprises* (1987).

23   See, for an analysis of the American court's reasoning on this question, in the context of argument over the appropriate forum: *In Re Union Carbide Gas Plant Disaster at Bhopal India Opinion and Order* 12 May 1986: 634 F. Supp. 842 (SDNY 1986), 25 ILM 771 (1986); aff'd as modified 809 F. 2d 195 (USCA 2d Cir), 26 ILM 1008 (1987); cert. den. 108 S. Ct. 199 (1987). For analysis see: Muchlinski, 'The Bhopal case: controlling ultrahazardous industrial activities undertaken by foreign investors', 50 MLR 545 at pp. 556–8 (1987).

24   See further G. Teubner, 'The many-headed Hydra: networks as higher-order collective actors', in J. McCahery, S. Picciotto and C. Scott (eds),

Corporate Control and Accountability (Clarendon Press, 1993), p. 41 (referred to hereafter as Many-headed Hydra); 'Beyond contract and organisation? The external liability of franchising systems in German law', in C. Joerges (ed.), *Franchising and the Law: Theoretical and Comparative Approaches in Europe and the United States* (Nomos, 1992), p. 105 (referred to hereafter as Franchising); '*Unitas multiplex*: corporate governance in group enterprises', in D. Sugarman and G. Teubner (eds), *Regulating Corporate Groups in Europe* (Nomos, 1990), p. 67 (referred to hereafter as *Unitas multiplex*).

25   See Many-headed Hydra, at p. 59.

26   Franchising, note 24 above.

27   See OECD, *The Responsibility of Parent Companies for Their Subsidiaries* (1980), 'Summary of comparative findings', paras 65–70.

28   See articles 17–18, 291–323, reproduced in English in K. Hopt (ed.), *The Legal and Economic Analysis of Multinational Enterprises Vol. II* (De Gruyter, 1982), at pp. 265–95. For analysis see Wiedemann, 'The German experience with the law of affiliated enterprises', in ibid., p. 21; F. Wooldridge, *Groups of Companies: The Law and Practice in Britain, France and Germany* (IALS, 1981); Lutter, 'The liability of the parent company for the debts of its subsidiaries under German law', [1985] JBL 499; Sargent, 'Beyond the legal entity doctrine: parent–subsidiary relations under the West German Konzernrecht', 10 Can. Bus. L. Jo. 327 (1985); Wälde, 'Parent–subsidiary relations in the integrated corporate system: a comparison of American and German law', 9 Jo. Int'l L. & Econ. 455 (1974); Hofstetter (note 2 above), at pp. 579–83; Schiessel, 'The liability of corporations and shareholders for the capitalization and obligations of subsidiaries under German law', 7 NW. J. Int'l L. & Bus. 480 (1986).

29   On which see further pp. 335 and 337.

30   See Lutter, ibid., Wiedemann, ibid., at p. 23.

31   German Stock Corporation Law 1965, articles 319–22.

32   See, for example, article 10 of the Argentinean Draft Code of Private International Law. The full text of the Code can be found in 24 ILM 269 (1985). For background see Goldschmidt (1972), II Hague Recueil 201.

33   See the Indian Government's complaint before the US District Court, *Southern District of New York Union of India* v *Union Carbide Corporation* Complaint 85 CIV 2696, April 8, 1985 at para. 21; Plaintiff's Executive Committee, *Memorandum of Law in Opposition to Union Carbide Corporation's Motion to Dismiss on Grounds of Forum Non Conveniens*, December 6, 1985 at p. 3.

34   See *Submissions of the Union of India in its Appeal before the Supreme Court*, paras 118–21. The author is grateful to Praveen Pavani, Advocate of the Indian Supreme Court, for supplying a copy of this document.

35   The studies of corporate integration made by the US courts in the 'unitary tax' cases illustrate what may be required: see the cases referred to in chapter 8 at note 148.

36   See Teubner, *Unitas multiplex* (note 24 above), at pp. 87–92.

37   See further T. Hadden, 'Regulating corporate groups: an international perspective', in J. McCahery, S. Picciotto and C. Scott (eds), *Corporate Control and Accountability* (Clarendon Press, 1993), p. 343.

38   On which see further Hofstetter, 'Multinational enterprise parent liability' (note 2 above); D. D. Prentice, 'Some comments on the law relating to corporate groups', in McCahery *et al.*, ibid., pp. 371–4.

39   See the Commission Proposal for a Council Regulation on the Statute for a European Company: COM (89) 268 final – SYN 218 at p. 42. These provisions were to be found in articles 223–40 of the 1975 Draft Statute.

40   Ibid., article 114, at p. 127.

41   See Schmitthoff, 'The wholly owned and controlled subsidiary' [1978] JBL 218; Wallace (note 4 above), at p. 115.

42   See L. C. B. Gower, *Principles of Modern Company Law*, 4th end (1979), at p. 124. Subsequent editions have omitted this point.

43   I am grateful to my colleague Judith Freedman for this observation.

44   See chapter 5 at pp. 138–9.

45   See Gordon, 'Argentine jurisprudence: the Parke-Davis and Deltec cases', 6 *Lawyer of the Americas* 320 (1974); *Deltec Banking Corporation* v *Compania Italo-Argentina de Electricidad SA* 171 NYLJ 18 col. 1, April 3, 1974.

46   *Lindgren* v *L & P Estates Ltd* [1968] Ch 572. But see text at notes 53–6 below.

47   *Charterbridge Corporation* v *Lloyds Bank* [1970] 1 Ch. 62 per Pennycuick J at p. 74 E-F: 'Each company in the group is a separate legal entity and the directors of a particular company are not entitled to sacrifice the interest of that company. This becomes apparent when one considers the case where the particular company has separate creditors. The proper test, I think, in the absence of actual separate consideration, must be whether an intelligent and honest man in the position of a director of the company concerned, could, on the whole of the existing circumstances, have reasonably believed that the transactions were for the benefit of the company.'

48   *Bell* v *Lever Bros.* [1932] AC 161 at p. 228 per Lord Atkin: 'It will be noticed that Bell was not a director of Levers and, with respect, I cannot accept the view of Greer LJ that if he was in a fiduciary relationship to the Niger Co he was in a similar fiduciary relationship to the shareholders, or to the particular shareholders (Levers) who held 99% of the shares'.

49   See J. H. Farrar, N. E. Furey and B. M. Hannigan, *Farrar's Company Law*, 4th edn (Butterworths, 1998), at pp. 381–2.

50   See the dictum of Pennycuick J in *Charterbridge Corporation* v *Lloyds Bank* (note 47 above).

51   Note 47 above.

52   See T. Hadden, *The Control of Corporate Groups* (Institute of Advanced Legal Studies, 1983), p. 32.

53   [1959] AC 325 (HL).

54   Hadden (note 52 above). In *Prudential Assurance* v *Newman Industries (No. 2)* [1982] 1 All ER 354 the costs of a minority action at common law were put at £750,000.

55   See D. Prentice, 'Groups of companies: the English experience', in K. Hopt (ed.), *The Legal and Economic Analysis of Multinational Enterprises, Vol. II* (De Gruyter, 1982), at pp. 116–17.

56   This was the remedy offered to the minority in *Scottish Co-operative Whole-sale Society* v *Meyer* (note 53 above). The Companies Act 1985 provides for the purchase of a minority's shares by the majority under contract in

accordance with the terms of s. 425 (see Gower, note 3 above, at pp. 694–9) or by way of a takeover bid in accordance with part XIIIA of the Act (see Gower, at pp. 732–41).

57 See Wälde (note 28 above), at p. 457.

58 See further cases discussed by Wälde, ibid., at pp. 460–5. See also *Zahn* v *Transamerica Corp.* 162 F. 2d 36 (1947); *Sinclair Oil Corp.* v *Levien* 280 A. 2d 717 (Del. Sup. Ct 1971). This doctrine cannot be brought to bear in the case of a wholly owned subsidiary: *Donahue* v *Rodd Electrotype Co.* 328 NE 2d 505 (Mass. 1975).

59 Note 28 above.

60 A 'control contract' group is formed when 75 per cent of the shareholders of the controlled company vote to adopt a control contract which entitles the controlling enterprise to give binding instructions to the management board of the controlled company in exchange for the undertaking of financial responsibilities on behalf of the controlled company: ibid., ss 291–310.

61 Ibid., s. 304(1).

62 Ibid., s. 305(1).

63 A '*de facto*' group comes into existence by operation of the law where a legally independent enterprise (the dependent enterprise) is dominated by another enterprise (the dominant enterprise) which is able to directly or indirectly exercise a dominating influence: ibid., s. 17.

64 Ibid., s. 311.

65 Ibid., s. 317(1).

66 See Dobson (note 13 above), at pp. 854–956.

67 See further chapter 6 at pp. 184–94.

68 *Société Fruehauf* v *Massardy* [1968] D. S. Jur. 147 [1965] JCP II 14, 274 bis (Cour d'Appel, Paris); 5 ILM 476 (1966). For a summary of the case see chapter 5 at pp. 127–8. This case led to legislative amendments protecting the minority shareholders of MNE subsidiaries against decisions that could risk the ruin of the subsidiary: see Law No. 66–537 of 24 July 1966 discussed by Wallace (note 4 above), at p. 102.

69 See P. M. North and J. J. Fawcett, *Cheshire and North's Private International Law*, 12th edn (Butterworths, 1992), p. 897.

70 By s. 309 of the Companies Act 1985: 'The matters to which the directors are to have regard in the performance of their functions include the interests of the company's employees in general as well as the interests of its members.' The interests of creditors are not mentioned. Judicial opinion is divided on the extent to which creditors interests should be considered by directors. In favour of such consideration are: *Lonrho Ltd* v *Shell Petroleum* [1980] 1 WLR 627 at 635 per Lord Diplock; *Walker* v *Wimbourne* (1976) 50 ALJR 446 (Aust HC); *Nicholson* v *Permakraft (NZ)* (1985) NZCLC 96-032. Contra: *Multinational Gas and Petrochemical Co.* v *Multinational Gas and Petrochemical Services* [1983] 2 All ER 563 (CA) at 585g per Dillon LJ.

71 UK Insolvency Act 1986, s. 214(3).

72 Ibid., s. 214(7).

73 Ibid., s. 251.

74 Gower (note 3 above), at p. 114.

75 See, for example, the *Multinational Gas* case (note 70 above).

76 The creditor must show that service on the foreign parent is appropriate under the applicable provisions of Order 11 rule 1(1) of the Rules of the Supreme Court on which see further Cheshire and North (note 69 above), at pp. 191–210.

77 See Hofstetter (note 2 above), at p. 585.

78 *Aktiengesetz* (note 28 above), ss 303, 309, 317(4), 322.

79 See *Autokran* 95 BGHZ 330 (1985), *Tiefbau* BGH ZIP 1989, 440z and NJW 1800 (1989) summarized in Hofstetter (note 2 above), at p. 583; see also Schiessel (note 28 above).

80 Summary taken from the *Report of the Cork Committee on Insolvency Law and Practice* (Cmnd 8558 1982) paras 1947–9.

81 See further Whincup, 'Inequitable incorporation – the abuse of privilege', 2 Co. Law 158 (1981); Landers, 'A unified approach to parent, subsidiary, and affiliate questions in bankruptcy', 42 U. Chi. L. Rev. 589 (1975); Posner, 'The rights of creditors of affiliated corporations', 43 U. Chi. L. Rev. 499 (1976); Easterbrook and Fischel, 'Limited liability and the corporation', 52 U. Chi. L. Rev. 89 (1985).

82 See Stobaugh, 'Financing foreign subsidiaries of US controlled multinational enterprises', 1 J. Int'l Bus. Stud. 43 (1970) who found that of 20 medium-sized and large US MNEs studied, none would let a subsidiary default on its debt, even if it were not formally guaranteed, and of 17 small MNEs studied only one is reported to have been willing to contemplate such an event. See, for similar findings, 'Determining overseas debt/equity ratios', *Business International Money Report*, 27 January 1986, p. 26, cited in A. C. Schapiro, *Multinational Financial Management*, 4th edn (Allyn and Bacon, 1992), at pp. 462–4.

83 See, for example, the English case-law on 'letters of comfort' at note 6 above and see the *Multinational Gas* case cited in note 70 above. Schapiro, ibid., cites two cases where MNEs allowed their affiliates to go bankrupt: Raytheon in Sicily (1968) and Freeport Sulphur in Cuba (1960). He writes, 'the publicity surrounding these events makes it clear how unusual they were'.

84 See N. Hood and S. Young, *Multinationals in Retreat: the Scottish Experience* (1982), at pp. 73–4; A. Altshuler *et al.*, *The Future of the Automobile* (Counterpoint, 1984), at pp. 152–3.

10

Accountability and Disclosure

This chapter deals with the related issues of MNE accountability and disclosure. Both home and host states may require information from a MNE about its worldwide operations for their respective regulatory purposes. In addition, there may be non-governmental stakeholders,[1] most notably investors, creditors, employees and consumers, who need information from the firm about matters of direct concern to their interests. The resulting demand for increased disclosure has given rise to significant developments in national and regional disclosure laws and has stimulated new policy proposals. Furthermore, the same demands have given rise to calls for the enhancement of MNE accountability through changes in the internal structure of the corporation. The second part of the present chapter will focus on this issue. The third part will then consider the problems associated with MNE disclosure. Before that, the principal motives for increased MNE disclosure and accountability will be considered, with particular emphasis on the interests to be furthered.

1 Principal Motives and Interests behind Enhanced MNE Accountability and Disclosure

The concern over MNE accountability and disclosure has many diverse sources. According to Gray et al.,[2] apart from the traditional recipients of corporate information, namely its finance providers (the shareholders, bankers, lenders and creditors), those interested in disclosure and accountability now include employees, trade unions, consumers, governments and the general public. This has resulted in calls for a wider conception of disclosure than that needed by the financiers of the corporation.

Responding to such demands, concerned international organizations have produced recommendations that widen the elements which may have to be included in a firm's annual report and in supplementary statements.[3] The general approach is well illustrated by the OECD Guideline on Disclosure and Information, which deserves quotation in full:

Enterprises should, having regard to their nature and relative size in the econ-omic context of their operations and to requirements of business confidentiality and to cost, publish in a form suited to improve public understanding a sufficient body of factual information on the structure, activities and policies of the enterprise as a whole, as a supplement, in so far as necessary for this purpose, to information to be disclosed under the national law of the individual countries in which they operate. To this end, they should publish, within reasonable time limits, on a regular basis, but at least annually, financial statements and other pertinent information relating to the enterprise as a whole, comprising in particular:

(a) The structure of the enterprise, showing the name and location of the parent company, its main affiliates, its percentage ownership, direct and indirect, in these affiliates, including shareholdings between them;

(b) The geographical areas (*) where operations are carried out and the principal activities carried on therein by the parent company and the main affiliates;

(c) The operating results and sales by geographical area and the sales in the major lines of business for the enterprise as a whole;

(d) Significant new capital investment by geographical area and, as far as practicable, by major lines of business for the enterprise as a whole;

(e) A statement of the sources and uses of funds by the enterprise as a whole;

(f) The average number of employees in each geographical area;

(g) Research and development expenditure for the enterprise as a whole;

(h) The policies followed in respect of intra-group pricing;

(i) The accounting policies, including those on consolidation, observed in compiling the published information.

*For the purposes of the Guideline on Disclosure of Information the term 'geographical area' means groups of countries or individual countries as each enterprise determines is appropriate in its particular circumstances. While no single method of grouping is appropriate for all enterprises for all purposes, the factors to be considered by an enterprise would include the significance of geographic proximity, economic affinity, similarities in business environments and the nature, scale and degree of interrelationship of the enterprises' oper-ations in the various countries.[4]

The Guideline offers a summary of responses to the various concerns underlying MNE disclosure. Thus, investors will need information on the performance of the group as a whole, through consolidated accounts, and segmental information based on geographical areas and lines of business. Governments will require information about the long-term prospects of MNEs operating within, or from, their territory as part of their economic policy making process, while information on intra-group pricing practices will allow for increased intelligence relevant to the control of transfer pricing abuses. Employees and trade unions will be concerned about the long-term stability of the firm and hence about the levels of investment undertaken, the nature of that investment and employment levels relative to other locations. In all the Guideline seeks to encourage greater specialized disclosure by MNEs for public policy purposes, alongside their existing national disclosure requirements, as a means of creating a more informed environment for policy responses to be formulated. In this the Guideline clearly goes beyond disclosure aimed at mere investor protection, the traditional concern of corporate disclosure laws.[5]

However, the OECD Guideline does not go as far as some proposals, notably those put forward by the UN in 1977.[6] This is not surprising given the fact that the OECD Guidelines on Multinational Enterprises are a direct response to the more radical policies on MNEs proposed by the UN in the 1970s.[7] Consequently, the Guideline is a rather general statement of desirable practice, leaving much to the discretion of the firm, whereas the original UN proposals set out a detailed list of financial and non-financial items for disclosure. Moreover, the OECD Guideline shows a sensitivity to the concerns of corporate managers, specifically mentioning confidentiality and cost as factors to be considered when contemplating the form and extent of the recommended disclosure.[8] Finally, it should be noted that the Guideline has only persuasive and not legal force. The ultimate arbiter of disclosure requirements still remains the law of the OECD Member Country in which the MNE operates.

The disclosure of information may be required by law as part of the system of corporate governance to which the corporation must subject itself in return for the privilege of incorporation, the purpose being to ensure good corporate behaviour in relation to the user of the information. However, the mere disclosure of information may not ensure that the user is effectively protected, let alone given all the facts that he requires.[9] Consequently, developments in disclosure requirements must be considered alongside moves to reform the internal organization of publicly held corporations for the sake of greater accountability, whereby the interested party becomes a part of the corporate decision-making process. To this we now turn.

2 Reforming the Internal Structures of MNEs to Ensure Accountability

Traditionally, the publicly held corporation has been perceived as an entity whose purpose is the making of profit for its members. The resulting internal legal structure has generally reflected this fact, in that it aims at the regulation of decision-making in the interests of the shareholders alone. Thus, in Anglo-American law, the corporation typically consists of a unitary board of directors and a general meeting of shareholders. The former undertakes the management of the company while the latter acts as the elector of the board and the general controlling body of the company.[10] In certain European legal systems, most notably that of Germany, an alternative three-tier system is found. In addition to the general meeting and the executive board of directors there is the supervisory board. Its function is to control the executive board, stressed by its distinct membership in that dual membership of both boards is prohibited.[11] Yet here too the aim is the organization of the company in the interests of its principal investors, often represented as members of the policy-making supervisory board.[12]

This classical legal model of the corporation has been found wanting as a means of ensuring shareholder control, given the rise of a professional managerial class distinct from the principal shareholders and the fragmentation of corporate ownership through the rise of mass stock markets.[13] The issue of whether shareholders' interests are effectively protected by corporate structures has given rise to calls for stronger shareholder powers, including the strengthening of the powers of the general meeting and, as seen in chapter 9, more effective remedies for minorities.[14]

In addition, the classical model may not give adequate voice to the interests of stakeholders other than shareholders. Of significance in this respect are developments in the EC aimed at harmonizing the structure of public limited companies and at enhancing workers' access to information and participation in the decision-making structures of companies operating within the Community. Equally, the possibility of outside, non-executive directors sitting on the boards of MNEs is a major policy option that has been used, particularly in the USA. To these matters we now turn.[15]

2.1 The Use of Non-executive Directors on the Managerial Boards of MNEs

The practice of appointing non-executive directors to the boards of major corporations has become well established in the USA.[16] This practice is also used in the UK.[17] The desire has been to ensure that independent outsiders be present at board meetings so as to introduce a dimension to decision-making that would be more sensitive to broader public concerns. They may also form an independent 'audit committee' of the board, charged with overseeing the company's audit.[18]

However, in practice such directors may be unable to alter the decision-making process very much. They may, in fact, be highly dependent on the 'inside' directors, to whom they often owe their initial appointment, and on whom they will rely for information about the company's operations.[19] This factor may become particularly pressing in the case of the parent board of a MNE. The complexity of the firm's worldwide operations may not be well understood by non-executive directors, who may have little time to devote to their duties, and who may lack sufficient expertise of foreign operations to make a meaningful judgment on corporate policy matters. Furthermore, a non-executive director who shares the nationality and background of the executive directors on the parent board may lack the ability and incentive to stand up for the needs of a foreign host state and its people. Even if the outsider does have the relevant expertise, his or her voice may be bypassed in practice by decisions taken at the level of the overseas subsidiary board. Thus, the non-executive director may have little to offer in terms of enhancing the accountability of a MNE, in the absence of a framework of corporate governance that obliges effective disclosure to such a person, and ensures that he or she has effective power inside the corporation to influence policy.[20]

2.2 European Initiatives for the Enhancement of MNE Accountability

The European approach to corporate accountability has gone beyond the limited Anglo-American concerns that have focused on non-executive directors.[21] In particular, the EC has stressed the need for a new organization of corporate structures which can *inter alia* accommodate the interests of workers as a distinct group of stakeholders in the corporation, building on the experience of certain member states, particularly the Netherlands and Germany, in the operation of 'codetermination' laws.[22] This has generated heated debate both within and outside the Community among Member States, European trade unions and EC and non-EC based business interests.

EC policy has evolved along two distinct but complementary lines. The first seeks to ensure employees' access to information and decision-making through changes in internal corporate structures, while the second involves attempts to introduce general rights of information and consultation of employees into the existing structures and operations of complex transnational undertakings.

The first approach is exemplified by the draft Fifth Directive on Company Law.[23] This sees worker participation as part of a broader reform of the internal structures of public limited companies operating in the EC.[24] The draft Directive provides for two approaches to the organization of public companies, the two-tier structure with a management and supervisory organ, and the one-tier system with a single administrative organ. Member States can make provision for one or both of these systems, and in the latter case each company may be permitted to choose one of the two systems.[25] In either case, the worker participation provisions shall apply to any public limited company employing more than 1,000 people in the Community either directly or in subsidiaries. The draft Directive lists four methods of worker participation. First, in the case of a two-tier company, employees can elect between one-third and one-half of the members of the supervisory board;[26] secondly, employee representatives might be co-opted on to the supervisory board, subject to any objections from the general meeting or employee representatives;[27] thirdly, representation may occur through an organ representing company employees;[28] fourthly, participation may occur through a system agreed by collective agreement which provides for employee participation in the supervisory organ in accordance with the foregoing provisions.[29] In the absence of such an agreement one of the alternative options would apply.[30] Should the company be organized around a single-tier board the same options would be available, with worker representatives being elected, or co-opted, to the administrative organ as non-executive members.[31] The employee representatives would be entitled to receive the same information as the other members of the supervisory board or the other non-executive members of a single-tier board.[32] However, a separate right to information and consultation pertaining to the employee representatives, contained in the 1983 draft, has been deleted from the 1988 draft.[33]

The second approach is contained in the various proposals, put forward since 1980, that seek to institute the provision of information and consultation of workers in undertakings operating in more than one Member State. The first attempt was contained in what is commonly called the 'Vredeling Directive'.[34] This proposal was first submitted to the Council in 1980. The 1980 draft required international management in the parent company of a transnational undertaking, every six months, to 'forward relevant information to the management of its subsidiaries in the Community giving a clear picture of the activities of the dominant undertaking and its subsidiaries as a whole'.[35] In addition, the proposal contained duties of information and consultation on any decision which was liable to have substantial effect on the interests of the subsidiary's employees.[36] The 1980 draft produced a strong counter-reaction from both European and non-European MNEs.[37] The result was a watered-down version in 1983. Adoption of the revised proposal required unanimity in the EC Council. This has not been forthcoming due, in particular, to the opposition of the UK Government.[38] As a result, despite efforts to keep the proposal alive, it has been shelved.[39] Discussions were to have resumed in 1989, but no timetable for these was announced.[40]

The Vredeling proposal was superseded by a proposal for the establishment of a European Works Council (EWC) in Community-scale undertakings. This sought to achieve information and consultation of employees by means of a distinct institutional system, which stopped short of worker participation on managing boards, but sought the establishment of a forum, within the firm, for such information and consultation to occur.[41] The original proposal did not achieve the unanimity required for its adoption, due in large measure to the opposition of the UK. The Commission responded by offering a watered down version of the EWC Directive, which allows for more use of voluntary arrangements agreed between workers and employers at company level.[42] The basic object of informing and consulting employees in Community-scale undertakings[43] or groups of undertakings[44] is to be achieved through the establishment, by agreement, in every such undertaking of a EWC or a procedure for informing and consulting employees.[45] The scope, composition, competence and mode of operation of the EWC or procedure is to be determined by means of a written agreement between the central management of the Community-scale undertaking or, in the case of a Community-scale group, the controlling undertaking,[46] and a special negotiating body drawn from and elected by representatives of employees of the undertaking or group.[47] This procedure may be initiated by the central management or upon the written request of at least 100 employees or their representatives in at least two undertakings or establishments in at least two different Member States.[48] The special negotiating body may decide by a two-thirds vote not to open negotiations or to terminate negotiations already opened. A new request may be made for the renewal of negotiations after two years have elapsed since this decision.[49] In the absence of an agreement being concluded, or where the parties so decide, the subsidiary requirements laid down by legislation in the Member State in which the central management is situated shall apply. These subsidiary requirements must conform to the rules contained in the Annex to the Directive.[50] The minimum standards laid down in the Annex relate to the competence, composition and rights to information and consultation to be enjoyed by a EWC.

The EWC Directive is expressly linked to the Community Charter of the Fundamental Social Rights of Workers, in that the preamble of the Directive refers to point 17 of the Charter, which states:

Information, consultation and participation for workers must be developed along appropriate lines, taking account of the practices in force in the various Member States.

This shall apply especially in companies or groups of companies having establishments or companies in two or more Member States of the European Community.

The aim behind the Directive is to ensure that such rights are protected in the process of international business restructuring likely to follow from the completion of the Single European Market. It is put forward in the belief that national procedures for informing and consulting workers are 'often not geared to the transnational structure of the entity which takes the decisions affecting those employees', and that 'this may lead to unequal treatment of employees affected by decisions within one and the same undertaking, or group of undertakings'. Furthermore, the proposal is deemed necessary to ensure proper information and consultation in cases where the employees concerned are affected by a decision taken outside the Member State in which they are employed.[51]

The EWC Directive became binding in all Member States, except the UK, under the social provisions of the Maastricht Treaty on 22 September 1996. Indeed, the UK remained firmly opposed to worker participation and information measures, arguing that they would do no more than undermine economic growth and employment opportunities in the EC.[52] However, the Directive is likely to extend in practice to the UK employees of Community-scale enterprises, given that the EWC must cover all undertakings or group undertakings in the Community. In any case, it would make no managerial sense for such an enterprise to introduce industrial relations complications by excluding the UK workforce. Nor would it accord with the practice, among European-based MNEs, of company-wide international works councils. Furthermore, the Commission estimates that around 100 UK companies operating across the EU will be covered by the Directive.[53] Thus, UK opposition may be meaningless, as Community-scale enterprises with operations in the UK, and UK companies with operations in Europe, can be expected to extend the EWC to their British workers.

3 Disclosure by MNEs in Annual Accounts and Other Statements

Corporate disclosure by MNEs in annual accounts and other financial statements raises special problems not encountered by uninational enterprises. In particular, MNEs will face differing national disclosure requirements in home and host states, all of which have to be met. Furthermore, the creation of useful financial information will be more difficult than for purely national companies. Accounting practices differ considerably between states, resulting in financial information that may be hard to compare.[54] Comparability will be further hindered by the fact that MNEs will earn their profits in different currencies. Thus, the need arises to devise methods of transnational accounting and foreign currency translation, both for the drawing up of accounts within the MNE and for comparing the performance of different MNEs. Furthermore, as corporate groups, MNEs will be required to produce consolidated accounts for their worldwide profits and losses. Given the foregoing factors the difficulties surrounding this exercise are considerable.

New complications are added by growing requirements for segmental reporting, and for social disclosure aimed not at investors, but at other constituencies representing wider social and political interests as described in section 1. Moreover, new reporting devices, such as value-added statements, showing the economic contribution of the MNE to a given host state, and environmental audits, showing the environmental impact of the enterprise's activities, have been proposed.

In response to these problems international organizations have sought to introduce harmonized disclosure requirements for multinational groups. The greatest progress has been made by the EC through the introduction of the Fourth and Seventh Directives on Company Law, which have created, respectively, more uniform disclosure standards for single unit companies and for corporate groups operating within the EC. In addition, the accounting profession, through the International Accounting Standards Committee (IASC), has been active in trying to encourage the harmonization of national accounting standards.[55] Though these standards have no legal standing, several MNEs expressly refer to the fact that their financial statements are prepared and presented in accordance with them.[56] Finally, the UN Intergovernmental Group of Experts on International Standards of Accounting and Reporting has worked, since 1977, on the harmonization of international accounting standards. It published, in 1988, its Conclusions on Accounting and Reporting by Transnational Corporations as a contribution to the harmonization process. This states, in the form of a code of principles, the UN Group's recommendations as to the best standards of accounting practice that should be adopted in the effort to create uniform and informative disclosure requirements for MNEs.[57]

The legal aspects of MNE disclosure will be discussed under four major sub-headings. First, the problem of consolidated accounts will be considered, with particular emphasis on the provisions of the Seventh EC Directive as the foremost attempt at international harmonization. Secondly, the growing demand for segmented disclosure will be discussed, with emphasis on the difficulties that are inherent in the production of disaggregated information on a worldwide basis. Thirdly, the special difficulties of social disclosure will be considered. Finally, the problems of foreign currency translation will be briefly described, although these issues are more fully within the concerns of accountancy than company law.

3.1   Consolidated Financial Statements

Consolidated financial statements emerged with the rise of the holding company as a significant form of business organization.[58] Their aim is to provide information on the financial performance and future prospects of the group as an economic entity. Thus, consolidated statements aggregate the financial information on each legal entity in the group into a single set of data.[59] In relation to MNEs, this process will occur on an international level.

In the present legal and accounting environment, the practice of consolidating MNE accounts is still evolving. Certain national laws require consolidated information on the worldwide activities of MNEs whose parent is based in the country. The UK and USA have led the way, being the first countries to have evolved consolidated disclosure rules.[60] Continental European countries have only recently begun to introduce consolidated accounting rules for groups, spurred on by the initiative of the Seventh EC Company Law Directive.[61] The IASC has contributed through the issuing, in 1976, of International Accounting Standard No. 3 (IAS 3) on consolidated financial statements. This has since been replaced in April 1989 by IAS 27.[62] New standards have also been introduced in the fields of mergers and acquisitions (IAS 22),[63] associated companies (IAS 28)[64] and joint ventures (IAS 31).[65] None the less, considerable national and regional disparities remain. It is not possible to give a comprehensive analysis of all the major national systems in a work of this size.[66] Rather, a sense of the legal problems created by demands for consolidated disclosure by MNEs can be given through a brief examination of the Seventh EC Directive.[67]

The original proposal, introduced in 1976, was explicit in its aims. According to the Commission's explanatory memorandum:

The harmonization of national laws on group accounts would also make a contribution to the work currently in progress at various levels to take better account of the situation relating to multinational companies and, if possible, to provide an appropriate legal framework for them. Following this process of harmonization, multinational companies having their registered offices in the Community will be required to draw up and publish clear and complete information which will ensure that their relationships with other group companies, as well as their activities, will be clearly visible. Such companies will have to publish consolidated accounts covering all their affiliated companies throughout the world and drawn up on the basis of principles and methods of consolidation which are uniformly applicable throughout the Community. These provisions also apply to multinational companies having their registered offices outside the Community as far as their activities through companies established in the Community (sub-groups) are concerned.[68]

Contrary to these initial objectives, complete harmonization has not proved possible. The Seventh Directive allows for certain important matters to be introduced at the option of the Member State in its implementing legislation, as will be seen below. Nor has the Directive achieved maximum information disclosure by MNEs, given the wide-ranging exemptions from the duty to consolidate that it contains. None the less, the Directive represents a significant advance in that it made the hitherto predominantly Anglo-American practice of consolidated disclosure into the Community standard to be adopted by Member States who had not, as yet, imposed legal requirements for consolidation of group accounts.[69]

The Seventh Directive seeks to ensure that the consolidated accounts of EC-based groups 'shall give a true and fair view of the assets, liabilities, financial position and profit or loss of the undertakings included therein taken as a whole'.[70] To achieve this, the Seventh Directive extends the formats of accounts and valuation rules applicable to individual companies under the Fourth Directive[71] to groups of companies.[72] It also introduces prescribed consolidation techniques. These can only be listed here, as they are more appropriately discussed in specialized accounting texts.[73] Full consolidation is required for subsidiary undertakings (articles 18 and 22); the purchase accounting (or acquisition) method is the preferred consolidation technique, but the merger accounting (or pooling of interests) method is an option (articles 19 and 20); the method used must be applied consistently (article 25); debts and claims between undertakings included in a consolidation, income and expenditure relating to transactions between such undertakings and the resulting profits on these transactions must be eliminated (article 26); the consolidated accounts must be drawn up as at the same date as the annual accounts of the parent undertaking (article 27); an extensive range of items must be disclosed in notes to the accounts (article 34) and in the directors' report (article 36); the consolidated accounts must be audited (article 37) and published once approved (article 38).

The foregoing accounting provisions were not controversial, as many had already been agreed in the Fourth Directive. The most controversial provisions relate to company law matters concerning the definition of the undertakings to which the duty to consolidate should apply, and the circumstances in which such a duty can be dispensed with.[74] The text of the Seventh Directive represents a series of compromises on these matters, resulting in a legal regime that has fallen short of original intentions.

The first step in any consolidation regime is to define the group of undertakings to which the duty of consolidation attaches. When this regime is to be supranational in nature, it must take into account differences in national approaches to the definition of a corporate group for disclosure purposes. In this respect the European Commission had a choice between the UK approach, based on the legal control exercised by a parent over its subsidiaries, which concentrates on linkages of majority shareholdings and voting rights in the subsidiary, and the German approach, which concentrates on effective managerial control by means of control contracts or the *de facto* ability to exercise a dominant influence over a subordinate undertaking. Initially, the Commission's proposal favoured the German model.[75] However, after discussions in the Council of Ministers significant concessions were made to the UK approach, with the resulting text taking elements from both national models.

Thus, article 1 of the Directive includes, in its definition of an undertaking required to draw up consolidated accounts, linkages between parent and subsidiary undertakings that rely on the parent undertaking's majority voting rights (article 1(1)(a)), its right to appoint or remove a majority of the members of the administrative, management or supervisory body of the subsidiary undertaking (article 1(1)(b)),[76] and the parent's right to exercise a dominant influence over a subsidiary pursuant either to a control contract or to a provision in its memorandum or articles of association, where the law governing the subsidiary undertaking permits its being subjected to such contracts or provisions (article 1(1)(c)).[77]

In addition to the above, a parent undertaking will be obliged to draw up consolidated accounts where it is a shareholder in or member of a subsidiary undertaking and either the majority of the members of the administrative, management or supervisory bodies of the subsidiary, who have held office in the previous financial year up to the time when consolidated accounts are drawn up, have been appointed solely as a result of the parent's voting rights (article

1(1)(d)), or the parent controls alone, in agreement with other share-holders in or members of the subsidiary, a majority of shareholders' or members' voting rights in the subsidiary (article 1(1)(d)). The Member States must introduce measures for at least the second case and may introduce more detailed measures concerning the form and contents of such agreements.[78]

Article 1(2) of the Directive gives Member States the option to impose a duty to prepare consolidated accounts on a parent under-taking which holds a participating interest in a subsidiary undertaking and actually exercises a 'dominant influence' over the subsidiary, or where the parent and the subsidiary undertaking are managed on a unified basis by the parent. The UK has implemented article 1(2).[79] This was done to avoid the practice of companies using controlled non-subsidiaries as a means of keeping assets or liabilities off the consolidated balance sheet.[80]

The final linkage giving rise to a duty to consolidate accounts is laid down in article 12 of the Seventh Directive. This extends the duty to horizontal groups that are linked not by shareholding but by unified management based on a contract or provision in the memo-randum or articles of association, or in which the management of both companies is substantially the same in the financial year for which accounts are to be drawn up. This covers European transnational groups such as the British and Dutch parent companies of Unilever, which operate under common sets of objectives and identical management boards,[81] and the Dutch group Philips, whose US holdings are controlled by a separate trust in which its Dutch shareholders have an interest.[82]

Having established the principal types of group to which the duty to consolidate attaches, we look at the next question, which concerns the extent, if any, to which exemption from that duty can be granted. In this respect the Seventh Directive has undergone substantial changes in comparison with the initial proposal, reflecting intensive lobbying for particular corporate and national interests. The most important compromise occurred in relation to the issue of sub-consolidation, whereby a duty of consolidation is placed upon every intermediate holding company within a group. The initial version of the Seventh Directive favoured this approach.[83] It has the advantage of giving segmented information about the group's ac-tivities, in particular about the location of profits and losses. It has the disadvantage of increasing the administrative burdens and costs of the group as a whole. In a complex MNE these could be considerable.[84]

In response to such criticisms the original proposal was not fol-lowed in the final text of the Directive. Instead there exist certain compulsory and optional exemptions from subconsolidation, based on the size of the ultimate parent's shareholding in the exempted undertaking and on the applicability to the ultimate parent of consolidated accounting obligations that are in accordance with the requirements of the Seventh Directive.[85] A Member State need not apply these exemptions to companies whose securities have been admitted to official listing on a stock exchange established in a Member State.[86] In addition to the conditions stated in the Seventh Directive, a Member State may make exemption conditional upon disclosure in the consolidated accounts of additional information required of undertakings governed by the national law of that Member State which are obliged to prepare consolidated accounts and are in the same circumstances as the exempted undertaking.[87] A Member State may further require disclosure of all or some of the following information from the exempted parent undertaking regarding the group of which it is the parent: the amount of fixed assets, net turnover, profit and loss for the financial year; the amount of capital and reserves, and the average number of employees in the financial year.[88] None of these compulsory or optional exemptions shall affect the Member State's legislation on the drawing up of consolidated accounts as far as these are required for the information of employees or their representatives or for administrative or judicial purposes.[89]

Finally, an optional exemption is given, by article 11 of the Directive, to EC-based intermediate parent undertakings whose ultimate parent is a non-EC based company. This exemption is conditional upon the consolidation of the exempted undertaking and all of its subsidiaries in the accounts of a larger body of undertakings, those accounts being drawn up in accordance with the Directive, or in an equivalent manner, and upon their being audited by one or more authorized auditors under the national law governing the undertaking which drew them up.[90] The absence of a definition of equivalence in the Directive means that it is for each Member State that adopts the exemption in article 11 to determine whether the consolidated accounts drawn up by the non-EC parent meet the required standards. The Contact Committee set up to consider the harmonized application of both the Fourth and the Seventh Directives may have to clarify this concept in future.[91] The UK has not introduced an exemption under article 11.

In accordance with general practice on consolidation, the parent undertaking is given a measure of discretion under the Seventh Directive when determining which subsidiaries to include in its consolidated accounts. Thus, while a parent undertaking is obliged to include all of its subsidiary undertakings on a worldwide basis, and to include the subsidiaries of its subsidiaries,[92] undertakings whose inclusion would not be material for giving a true and fair view of the assets, liabilities, financial position and profit and loss of the group need not be included.[93] In addition, where severe long-term restrictions hinder the parent undertaking from exercising its rights over the assets or management of a subsidiary undertaking the latter need not be included.[94] Similarly, subsidiaries may be excluded where unified management between parent and subsidiary as defined in article 12(1) of the Directive exists,[95] where the gathering of information needed for consolidation would involve disproportionate expense or undue delay,[96] or where the shares in the subsidiary undertaking are held exclusively with a view to their immediate resale.[97]

The previous provisions are no more than guidelines to management as to the proper exercise of their discretion. On the other hand, a subsidiary undertaking must not be included where its activities are so different that its inclusion would be incompatible with a true and fair view of the group's finances.[98] For this purpose it is not enough of a difference that the subsidiary undertaking may be partly industrial, partly commercial and partly provide services or that it carries on different industrial or commercial activities involving different products or services.[99] The exemption is meant to apply, for example, where a manufacturing group also owns a bank or an insurance company. The assets and liabilities of the different lines of business are so distinct that any attempt to consolidate them may give a distorted view of the group's position.[100] However, much is left to the discretion of the parent company's management in determining what is a different activity.

Further exemptions from the obligation to publish consolidated accounts may be introduced by Member States. First, a Member State may exempt a parent undertaking that is not a limited liability company (article 5(2)).[101] Secondly, exemption may be granted where a parent company is a financial holding company and it has not taken an active part in the running of a subsidiary undertaking, and has made loans only to undertakings in which it has a participatory interest (article 5). This provision was included on the insistence of Luxembourg, which acts as host to a large number of such holding companies.[102] Thirdly, a Member State may exempt a parent undertaking on the basis of the small size of the group. The exemption will apply where the latest annual accounts of the parent and its subsidiaries, if taken together, do not exceed the size threshold laid down in article 27 of the Fourth Directive, as periodically amended, which takes account of the balance sheet total, net turnover and average number of employees in the group.[103] This exemption has been introduced into English law by s. 13(3) of the Companies Act 1989, as a new s. 248 of the Companies Act 1985. This extends the exemption to companies that qualify as a small or medium-sized group[104] and are not an ineligible group.[105]

The Seventh Directive has been extended in its application. In November 1990 a directive was adopted that extends the requirement to produce consolidated accounts under the Seventh Directive to parent undertakings taking the form of partnerships, limited partnerships or unlimited companies if all the unlimited members are themselves public or private limited companies.[106] Furthermore, the Seventh Directive is complemented by specific provisions on the consolidated accounts of credit institutions[107] and of insurance undertakings.[108] The experience of the Seventh Directive highlights the difficulties inherent in developing a harmonized international system of consolidated reporting for MNEs. None the less, it is significant as the only legally binding supranational model for worldwide consolidated reporting, one that is mandatory in a major economic area of the world. In this respect the experience with this Directive may be useful for other areas of the world when they consider the introduction of similar transnational disclosure mechanisms.

3.2   *Segmental Disclosure*

While the worldwide consolidation of MNE accounts is useful when one is seeking to judge the performance of the enterprise as a whole, it may also serve to conceal the details of that performance. In particular, consolidated accounts will not disclose the geographical spread of the enterprise's profits, losses and risks, or the extent to which one line of business is performing better than another. Such disaggregated, or segmented, information may be required for a more accurate analysis of the firm's operations by investors and their advisers.[109] Furthermore, for certain purposes, such as disclosure to the host state or the information of employees, the degree of disaggregation might have to be very high, operating at individual country and plant levels, if useful information is to be obtained. Thus degrees of disaggregation will vary with the purposes for which the information is needed.[110]

As noted above, the OECD Guideline on Disclosure and Information calls for segmental disclosure in several areas, including lines of business and geographical markets.[111] However, the most comprehensive requirements for segmental disclosure were put forward by the UN Group of Experts on International Standards of Accounting and Reporting in 1977. The Group recommended segmentation by geographical area and line of business for the enterprise as a whole and for individual operating companies.[112] According to the UN Group of Experts the enterprise as a whole should segment and disclose geographically the following: sales to unaffiliated customers;

transfers to other geographical areas that have been eliminated in consolidation; operating results, such as profit before general corporate expenses, interest expense, taxes on income and unusual items. To the extent identifiable with a geographical area, the enterprise should also disclose: total assets or net assets or total assets and liabilities; property, plant and equipment gross; accumulated depreciation; other long-term assets; and new investment in property, plant and equipment. Furthermore, the enterprise should describe principal activities in each geographical area or country, disclose the basis of accounting for transfers between areas or countries and disclose exposure to exceptional risks of operating in other countries. The same items should be disclosed by the enterprise for discrete lines of business. In addition, individual companies in the group should disclose similar items relating to their foreign assets and operations and, where applicable, to operations in more than one line of business.

By contrast, the Seventh EC Directive[113] contains few requirements for disaggregated information. Although it was suggested during negotiations that the number of employees inside the EC and the value of sales within the EC should be disclosed, the only disaggregated disclosure requirements are that the notes to the accounts should include, first, the consolidated net turnover broken down by categories of activity and into geographical markets in so far as these differ substantially from one another, and, secondly, the average numbers of employees in a financial year broken down by categories.[114] In this the provisions of the Seventh Directive reproduce the requirements placed on individual companies under the Fourth Directive. As will be seen below, these requirements have had a significant influence on the content of English law in the area of segmental reporting.

At the level of national laws the most comprehensive system of segmental reporting for firms with foreign operations is to be found in the USA. Since 1969 the Securities and Exchange Commission (SEC) has required the disclosure of line of business information in securities registration documents, and in 1970 this requirement was extended to the annual submission required from registered companies under Form 10-K.[115] These requirements now conform to Financial Accounting Standard No. 14 (FAS 14), issued by the US Financial Accounting Standards Board in December 1976. Under FAS 14 the enterprise concerned must provide disaggregated information about line of business and geographical segments, including revenue from unaffiliated customers, sales or transfers between geographical areas and the transfer pricing methods used, and operating profits and losses as long as a consistent measure is used in all geographical areas and in relation to the assets held by segment. Separate information is required for the foreign operations of the enterprise if these contribute 10 per cent or more of consolidated revenues or the assets identifiable with the foreign operations exceed 10 per cent or more of consolidated assets.[116] FAS 14 does not offer much guidance on segment identification. A segment is considered significant if its revenues or identifiable assets are more than 10 per cent of the consolidated figures. The identification of geographical segments is left to the discretion of management.[117] They can report foreign operations as a single segment or as a number of segments based on individual countries or groups of countries defined by reference to their 'physical proximity, economic affinity, the similarities in their business environments and by the nature, scale and degree of the enterprise's operations in the various countries'.[118]

The approach of FAS 14 is closely followed in International Accounting Standard No. 14 (IAS 14), issued in 1981 by the IASC.[119] IAS 14 recommends segmentation on the basis of the materiality of the segment to the business as a whole, using the 10 per cent of consolidated revenue, operating profit or total assets criterion as a guideline, though not as an exclusive guideline.[120] IAS 14 requires reporting of significant industry segments[121] and geographical areas[122] on the basis of consolidated statement information.[123]

In the UK, the first requirements for segmental disclosure were issued in 1965 by the London Stock Exchange in its listing requirements.[124] The official listing of securities is now governed by the Financial Services Act 1986, Part IV. It is a condition of acceptance on to the Official List that a company publish formal details about the issuers, the company's capital, management, recent development and prospects in accordance with the listing particulars issued by the Council of the Stock Exchange.[125] In addition to the information required by the Council of the Stock Exchange, the listing particulars shall contain all such information as investors and their professional advisers would reasonably require, and reasonably expect to find there, for the purpose of making an informed assessment of the assets, liabilities, financial position, profits and losses, and the prospects of the issuer of the securities as well as the rights attaching to those securities.[126] The Act reflects disclosure requirements based on three EC Directives which seek to harmonize *inter alia* the minimum listing requirements of stock exchanges in the Community.[127] These requirements include *inter alia* duties to disclose segmental information on lines of business and geographical activities, information on the average number of employees broken down by category of employment, and information on the geographical distribution of investments.[128]

Segmental information is also required under the Companies Act 1985 in relation to a group's annual accounts.[129] Such accounts must, as far as is practicable, comply with the provisions of Schedule 4 of the Act as if the undertakings included in the consolidation were a single company.[130] These provisions reflect the requirements of the Fourth EC Directive on Company Law.[131] Included in the provisions of Schedule 4 are requirements that the company must disclose, in the notes to accounts, particulars of turnover by line of business and geographical market, where, in the opinion of the directors, there is sufficient difference to justify segmentation.[132] However, where in the opinion of the directors the disclosure of any information required under this provision would be seriously prejudicial to the interests of the company, that information need not be disclosed, but the fact that such non-disclosure has taken place must be stated.[133] Furthermore, the notes must disclose the average number of employees employed within each category of persons employed by the company in any financial year, the categories being selected by the directors having regard to the manner in which the company's activities are organized.[134]

These provisions leave much to the discretion of directors in identifying relevant segments or employment categories. Some guidance can be obtained on the first matter, though not on the issue of employment categorization, from the UK accounting profession's standard SSAP 25, 'Segmental reporting'.[135] According to the explanatory notes in SSAP 25, when identifying reportable segments directors should have regard to the overall purpose of presenting segmental information and the need of the user of financial statements to be informed, where an entity carries on operations in different classes of business or in different geographical areas, that these earn a return on investment out of line with the rest of the business, are subject to different degrees of risk, have experienced different degrees of growth or have different potentials for future development.[136] Directors should also review their definitions of segments annually and redefine them when appropriate, bearing in mind the need for consistency and comparability between years.[137] Finally, SSAP 25 repeats the above-mentioned statutory right of directors not to disclose information that would, in their opinion, be seriously prejudicial to the interests of the company, provided that the fact of non-disclosure is stated.[138]

As with the US and IASC standards, the basic approach to segmental identification in SSAP 25 rests on the significance of the segment to the business entity as a whole. According to paragraph 9, a segment is significant if: '(a) its third party turnover is ten per cent or more of total third party turnover of the entity; or (b) its segment result, whether profit or loss, is ten per cent or more of the combined result of all segments in profit or all segments in loss, whichever combined result is greater; or (c) its net assets are ten per cent or more of total net assets of the entity.'

SSAP 25 goes on to define a separate class of business as 'a distinguishable component of an entity that provides a separate product or service or a separate group of related products or services'.[139] SSAP 25 suggests that directors should take into account *inter alia* the nature of the products or services involved, the nature of the relevant production processes, the markets in which the products or services are sold, their distribution channels, the manner in which the entity's business is organized, and any relevant legislative framework for business organization.[140] However, it concludes that no single set of characteristics is universally applicable; nor is any single characteristic conclusive. Consequently, 'determination of an entity's class of business must depend on the judgment of the directors'.[141]

A geographical segment is defined as 'a geographical area comprising an individual country or group of countries in which the entity operates, or to which it supplies products or services'.[142] However, unlike FAS 14, SSAP 25 does not identify any general method of grouping. Instead, paragraph 15 asserts that a geographical analysis should help the user of the financial statement to asses the extent to which an entity's operations are subject to factors such as expansionist or restrictive economic climates, stable or unstable political regimes, exchange control regulations and exchange rate fluctuations. The purpose is the identification of investment risk in given areas, as well as the provision of financial information on turnover by origin, results and net assets on a geographical basis.[143]

The principal characteristic of the above-mentioned accounting standards is the degree of discretion left to corporate officials in determining the segments to be reported. This is not surprising, given the difficulty involved in segment identification. However, the potential for inadequate reporting resulting from the wrong identification of segments is considerable.[144] Furthermore, as Gray and Roberts point out,[145] the disclosure of segmental information implies that the segments reported are relatively autonomous and independent of each other. In a highly integrated MNE this may not be the case. There may be large transfers between the segments which cannot be understood in isolation from the rest of the company. However, there is no evidence on this issue to indicate the useful limits of segmental information in a highly integrated enterprise.

As regards the practice of firms, it appears that the degree of disaggregation employed differs considerably between countries. For example, US and Japanese firms tend to disclose a smaller number of geographical segments than European firms.[146] Moreover, while compliance with mandatory segmental reporting requirements is generally high, observance of the voluntary disclosure standards recommended by the OECD or UN is low.[147]

Consequently, segmental reporting is far from being a uniform and well understood practice, even in the countries that have pioneered it. Nevertheless, the demand for improved segmental reporting is likely to continue, given its potential as a device for obtaining detailed information on the international operations of MNEs. The major obstacles remain those of the cost to firms of providing such information and their reluctance to have too much detail about their operations available to competitors and regulators.[148] This suggests that future developments will require the sanction of law behind them to be effective.

3.3 Social Disclosure

As noted above, the activities of large corporations attract the attention not only of financial stakeholders but also of other groups and interests. The latter may require information of an order different from that contained in the firm's financial statements. Thus, according to Choi and Mueller, social disclosure or accounting 'refers to the measurement and communication of information about a firm's effects on employee welfare, the local community and the environment. In contrast to traditional reporting methods, social responsibility disclosures embrace *non-financial* as well as financial performance measures.'[149] Social disclosure challenges the notion that a corporation is not responsible to the community at large for its actions. The demand for social disclosure places the corporation in a position more like that of a provider of public services that must explain and account for its actions in the light of broad conceptions of the public interest.

Such demands have given rise to the practical questions, first, as to what information should be given in addition to the usual information available through annual financial statements, and, secondly, as to the instruments and structures through which this information could be intelligibly conveyed to its intended users. These two related matters will be considered in the context of the three main strands of development in this field that are of especial relevance to the operations of MNEs: disclosures to employees, the use of local value-added statements and environmental disclosure.

3.3.1 *Employee disclosure* The organizational aspects of this matter have already been discussed in the context of corporate accountability. The remaining issue in this section is what employee disclosures should contain. Both financial and non-financial information might be of relevance to employees and trade union representatives. Thus, information on matters of employment might include information not only on its structure but also on income from such employment.[150] Furthermore, given the extensive information required by employees, it may be necessary to present special purpose reports that could present the information in an accessible and useful form.[151] The information offered might include, *inter alia*: information about the number of employees broken down by category, line of business, country and establishment, wages and salaries paid to these various groups, working conditions in countries and establishments including health and safety conditions, training and industrial relations matters, and any other information deemed to be of value to employees. The most extensive employee information requirements are to be found in French law, which requires each enterprise to produce an annual social report, the *Bilan Social*, covering matters of the kind mentioned. This is to be distributed to all shareholders and to the firm's works council.[152] By comparison, in the UK, as seen above, the only employee-oriented information that needs to be disclosed relates to average numbers of employees employed in a financial year segmented by category.[153] The practice of firms in the field of employee disclosure varies from country to country. The general level of employee disclosures is low. Japanese companies provide almost no information of this type. However, individual companies are beginning to experiment with this type of disclosure.[154]

3.3.2 Value-added statements   The value-added statement is an accounting device that seeks to show the production contribution made by the company in the course of an accounting period. Value-added statements are common in European firms' annual reports. They are less common in the reports of UK and Commonwealth countries, although in the mid- to late 1970s they were more common among UK companies.[155] The value added by the company is the difference between the market value of the goods or services produced by the firm and the cost of goods, materials and services purchased from other suppliers in the course of the relevant accounting period.[156] According to the UN Intergovernmental Working Group of Experts on International Standards of Accounting and Reporting, value added should normally be derived from: '(a) sales revenue less costs of material and services purchased from outside suppliers, and excise duty; (b) share of profits earned by or received from associated companies; (c) investment income; (d) surplus on realization of investments; (e) extraordinary items; (f) exchange gain or loss.'[157] Furthermore, the Group recommends that information should be provided in respect of the distribution of value added to different contributors, such as employees and providers of capital, and that value added retained in the business as represented by depreciation and retained earnings should be disclosed.[158]

A local value-added statement by the subsidiary of a MNE can show the overall contribution made by it to the economy of the host state. Such a statement will be of use to the economic policy-makers in the host state government. It will also be valuable to employees by showing the worth, to the firm, of the local operation, thereby indicating the firm's likely attitude to long-term investment and employment maintenance. The value-added statement may be of particular use to developing countries where the prime users of information about the operations of MNE subsidiaries are not investors but the government as principal economic planner, and other groups concerned with the impact of MNEs on national development.[159]

3.3.3 *Environmental disclosure*   Concern about the environmental effects of the operations of MNEs has become an increasingly prominent issue. As part of the policy response to such phenomena, increasing attention is being devoted to the creation of information and reporting structures on matters of environmental concern. Thus, both the USA and the EC have introduced laws requiring the disclosure to public authorities of specific information relevant to the control of industrial hazards in the fields of construction and operation of facilities, sale of products, and health and safety at work.[160] By contrast, national legal requirements for environmental accounting by firms are few.[161]

So far, the main initiatives have occurred through the voluntary efforts of firms which have devised internal accounting standards and have undertaken environmental audits of their activities. However, international organizations are now proposing schemes of environmental accounting. In particular, the UN Intergovernmental Group of Experts on International Standards of Accounting and Reporting by Transnational Corporations has begun to study the problems of environmental accounting, and has put forward proposals for improved disclosure in this field. Similarly, the EC has laid down new standards by way of a Regulation on eco-auditing by firms operating in the Community.

The UN initiative has generated new information about the practices of firms in this area, from which recommendations based on 'best practice' can be made.[162] It appears that German and Swiss firms have the most developed practices in reporting capital and current expenditures related to environmental measures.[163] In particular, the German Chemical Industry Association (Verband der Chemischen Industrie eV) has developed recommendations on the definition of environmental measures taken by firms and the appropriate manner in which to cost these. The measures concerned should be categorized according to the intended purpose of the equipment used by the firm, namely the control of air, water, waste and noise pollution. The calculation of expenditure should rest on either a general ledger account specification or, where necessary, statistical approximations. Furthermore, the estimates must be made to reflect the fact that environmental expenditures are not exclusively related to environmental concerns. Thus, where necessary, an apportionment of expenditures must be made.[164]

A particular problem identified by the UN Intergovernmental Group of Experts is the definition of the border between environmental expenditure and the pre-estimation of environmental liabilities. It is very difficult to quantify the latter, and firm practice in this area appears to be based on little more than 'reasonable estimates'. This is a matter closely bound up with the limits of knowable risk and is, therefore, contingent on changes in the understanding of risk and on the specific circumstances of the firm's activities. Furthermore, the estimation involved is of a long-term character, making pre-estimation still harder.[165]

Based on the above-mentioned research, the UN Intergovernmental Group of Experts has laid down certain recommendations in the field of environmental accounting. First, as regards the report of the Board of Directors, the following matters could be included:

(a) The type of environmental issues that are pertinent to the enterprise and its industry; (b) The formal policy and programmes that have been adopted by the enterprise with respect to environmental protection measures (if no formal policy and programmes exist, it should be stated); (c) The improvements in key areas that have been made since the introduction of the policy, or over the past five years, whichever is shorter; (d) The environmental emission targets that the enterprise has set for itself; and how the enterprise is performing relative to those targets; (e) The extent to which environmental protection measures have been undertaken due to governmental legislation and, if so, the extent to which governmental requirements (for example, a timetable for the reduction of emissions) are being achieved; (f) Any material proceedings under environmental laws; management should disclose a known potentially significant environmental problem unless it can objectively conclude that the problem is not likely to occur or, if it does, that the effect is not likely to be material; (g) The financial or operational effect of environmental protection measures on the capital expenditures and earnings of the enterprise for the current period and any specific impact on future periods; (h) When material, the actual amount charged to operations in the current period, together with a description of the environmental measures to which they relate. This amount might be subdivided into the following ledger accounts: (i) liquid effluent treatment; (ii) waste gas and air treatment; (iii) solid waste treatment; (iv) analysis, control and compliance; (v) remediation; (vi) recycling; (vii) Other (for example accidents, safety etc.); (i)

When material, the actual amount capitalized during the current period, the accumulated amount capitalized to date, and the period for amortizing, or writing off, such amounts, together with a description of the environmental measures to which they relate. This amount might be subdivided into the categories listed in (h). (Where it is not possible to segregate the amount that relates to environmental measures, this fact should be stated.)[166]

Secondly, in relation to the notes to financial statements the UN Intergovernmental Group of Experts recommends that these should describe the environmental accounting policies used by the firm when recording liabilities and provisions, the setting up of catastrophe reserves through appropriations of retained earnings, and the disclosure of contingent liabilities. Furthermore, where they are material, current liabilities and contingent liabilities should be disclosed in the notes.[167]

The EC eco-audit Regulation[168] introduces a voluntary scheme for environmental auditing which aims at the establishment, by firms, of effective environmental protection systems, the carrying out of regular evaluations of the performance of such systems and the provision of information about this performance to the public.[169] The evaluation of these systems is to be carried out by means of an environmental audit, defined in the Regulation as 'a management tool comprising a systematic, documented, periodic and objective evaluation of the performance of the organization, management system and equipment designed to protect the environment with the aim of: (i) facilitating management control of practices which may have an impact on the environment; (ii) assessing compliance with company environmental policies.'[170] An environmental audit will be carried out for each site upon which relevant industrial activities take place. The relevant industrial activities are those listed under sections C and D of the EC classification of economic activities[171] where the said activity involves the addition of electricity, gas, steam and hot water production, and the recycling, treatment, destruction or disposal of solid or liquid waste.[172] The issues to be covered by the audit include *inter alia* the assessment, control and prevention of environmental impact of the activity concerned, energy management savings and choice, raw materials management and savings, waste avoidance and recycling systems, selection of industrial processes, product planning, prevention and avoidance of accidents, staff training, external information and public participation.[173] The results of the environmental audit shall form the basis of an environmental statement relating to each site for which an audit has been carried out, which shall be written specifically for public disclosure in a concise and non-technical form.[174] This statement shall be validated by accredited environmental auditors.[175] Each Member State shall ensure, within twenty-one months of the entry into force of this Regulation, that systems for the accreditation of environmental auditors and for the supervision of their activities are put into place.[176] Firms participating in the eco-audit scheme may use a special EC logo on sites owned by them that have received validated environmental statements.[177]

The scheme shall be reviewed five years after its entry into force.[178] It has come about amid criticism from European industry.[179] However, the scheme should be seen as part of a wider movement towards environmental auditing. The International Chamber of Commerce has consistently supported the extension of voluntary environmental auditing by firms, although it has expressed concern that the EC scheme is over-prescriptive and over-intrusive.[180] Furthermore, the British Standards Institute has recently issued a new British Standard on environmental management systems, BS 7750, which is designed to complement the EC eco-audit scheme. The International Standards Organization has been asked by the EC to develop an International Standard based on BS 7750.[181]

3.4   Foreign Currency Translation

The matters covered in this section may be dealt with briefly, as they are primarily the concern of accountants rather than lawyers. However, no legally oriented discussion of the problems of MNE disclosure would be complete without a basic description of the practical problems involved in accounting for profits and losses incurred in different currencies.

According to Flower, 'The special problem of consolidation to be faced by multinational groups is that the component financial statements are denominated in different currencies.'[182] It is not possible to consolidate such statements without selecting a single currency in which the consolidation will appear. Thus the MNE must choose a currency in which its consolidated accounts will be drawn up. Usually, this will be the currency in which the parent operates. Then the individual financial statements of the component companies will be recast, or 'translated', into that currency. The purpose is to give a true and fair view of the MNE's business operations. Consequently, the consolidated statement should 'reflect the financial results and relationships as measured in the foreign currency financial statements prior to translation'.[183]

The major accounting problem in this area arises from the lack of fixed exchange rates. This raises the question of whether translation should be based on the exchange rate in operation at the time the affiliate acquires or disposes of an asset (for balance sheet purposes) or makes a profit or loss on a transaction (for profit and loss account purposes) or whether it should be based on the rate applicable at the time the consolidated accounts are drawn up. The former approach is known as the 'historic rate', while the latter is referred to as the 'closing rate'.

There has been considerable disagreement over which approach should be used.[184] However, the major national and international statements of standard accounting practice now appear to have accepted the closing rate approach as the usual method, with the historic or 'temporal' method being used in cases where the business activities of the foreign affiliate are so closely interlinked with those of the parent that they should be expressed in the currency of the parent using the exchange rate in operation at the time the relevant transactions are carried out, taking account of local levels of inflation where these are high.[185]

4 Concluding Remarks

This chapter has taken account of possible changes to the internal organization of MNEs that are designed to enhance accountability and the principal issues in MNE accounting relevant to ensuring the provision of relevant information to the principal classes of stakeholders. In each case the major legal developments are in a state of evolution, particularly at the EC level. As yet it is not possible to talk of long-settled approaches to MNE accountability and disclosure. However, the main issues in this area are being examined by international organizations and by the accounting profession at both national and international levels. There can be little doubt as to the economic utility of having increasingly harmonized financial information about MNEs that is of use to investors. Developments in this area can be expected to continue. Considerable evolution and change can also be expected in the more politically contentious aspects of MNE accountability, particularly in the topical areas of environmental control and public accountability. The direction and speed of change will be dependent on the degree to which political interest in the regulation of MNEs for public purposes can be aroused, and in the willingness of policy-makers to impose new administrative and expenditure burdens on MNEs. Considerable lobbying on these matters by both interest groups and MNEs can be expected.

Notes
 1 'Stakeholders' may be defined as 'any identifiable groups or individuals who can affect the achievement of the corporation's objectives or who are affected by such achievement': M. Zubaidur Rahman, 'The local value added statement: a reporting requirement of multinationals in developing

host countries', 25 Int. J. Acctg 87 at p. 88 (1990). See further: R. E. Freeman and D. L. Reed, 'Stockholders and stakeholders: a new perspective on corporate governance', *California Management Review* (Spring 1983), 83–106.

2   See: S. J. Gray with L. B. McSweeny and J. C. Shaw, *Information Disclosure and the Multinational Corporation* (Wiley/IRM, 1984), chapter 3.

3   See Gray et al., ibid., at pp. 110–19; UN Group of Experts Report, *International Standards of Accounting and Reporting for Transnational Corporations* (UN Doc E/C. 10/33, 18 October 1977), paras 9–12 at p. 28 and pp. 53–79. See also Draft UN Code of Conduct on Transnational Corporations, text of 24 May 1990 (UN Doc. E/1990/94, 12 June 1990), paras 44–6, at pp. 12–14.

4   OECD, *The OECD Declaration and Decisions on International Investment and Multinational Enterprises 1991 Review* (1992), p. 105 and pp. 44–6. The Disclosure Guideline is periodically clarified on the basis of studies undertaken by the Working Group on Accounting Standards of the OECD Committee on International Investment and Multinational Enterprises. See further OECD, *Multinational Enterprises and Disclosure of Information: Clarification of the OECD Guidelines* (1988).

5   See C. D. Wallace, *Legal Control of the Multinational Enterprise* (Martinus Nijhoff, 1983), at pp. 149–50.

6   See UN, 1977 (note 3 above).

7   On which see further chapter 16.

8   On the concerns of managers in relation to disclosure by MNEs see further Gray (note 2 above), chapter 4.

9   See further T. Hadden, *The Control of Corporate Groups* (IALS, 1983), chapter 6.

10   Paul L. Davies, *Gower's Principles of Modern Company Law*, 6th edn (Sweet & Maxwell, 1998), chapter 7; J. H. Farrar, N. E. Furey and B. M. Hannigan, *Farrar's Company Law*, 4th edn (Butterworths, 1998), chapter 22.

11   Gower, ibid., at p. 62.

12   See the paper by Reich in N. Horn and J. Kocha, *Law and the Formation of Big Enterprises in the Nineteenth and Early Twentieth Centuries* (Göttingen, 1979), at pp. 262–5.

13   See A. Bearle and G. Means, *The Modern Corporation and Private Property* (Macmillan, 1932, rev. edn 1967). See also R. I. Tricker, *Corporate Governance* (Gower, 1984), at pp. 14–15. However, this fact may not have diminished the modern corporate manager's commitment to the maximization of profits as the major corporate goal: see E. S. Herman, *Corporate Control, Corporate Power* (Cambridge University Press, 1981).

14   See Hadden (note 9 above); see also chapter 9 at pp. 333–6.

15   See further Lord Wedderburn of Charlton, 'The legal development of corporate responsibility: for whom will corporate managers be trustees?', in K. Hopt and G. Teubner (eds), *Corporate Governance and Director's Liabilities, Legal Economic and Sociological Analyses on Corporate Social Responsibility* (Walter de Gruyter, 1985), p. 3.

16   See Herman (note 13 above), at pp. 31–8; V. Brudney, 'The independent

director – heavenly city or Potemkin village?', 95 Harv. LR. 597 (1982); Wedderburn, ibid., at pp. 15–17.

17   Farrar (note 10 above), at p. 332. In the UK, the Cadbury Committee on the Financial Aspects of Corporate Governance has recommended increased use of non-executive directors on the boards of English companies. For a critical analysis see Finch, 'Board performance and Cadbury on corporate governance', [1992] JBL 581 at pp. 591–4 and see further Finch, 'Company directors: who cares about skill and care?', 55 MLR 197 (1992).

18   See Tricker (note 13 above), at pp. 193–6.

19   Herman (note 13 above), at p. 47.

20   See further, for a discussion of corporate governance by institutional investors in MNEs, T. Hadden, 'Corporate governance by institutional investors? Some problems from an international perspective', in T. Baums, R. Buxbaum and K. Hopt (eds), *Institutional Investors and Corporate Governance* (De Gruyter, 1994), esp. at pp. 97–100.

21   Wedderburn (note 15 above), at pp. 18–20.

22   See R. Nielsen and E. Szyszczak, *The Social Dimension of the European Community*, 3rd edn (Handelshojskolens Forlag, 1997), chapter 7. On 'co-determination' in Europe see F. Fabricius, 'A theory of co-determination', in C. M. Schmitthoff (ed.), *The Harmonisation of European Company Law* (UKNCCL, 1973), p. 138; S. Simitis, 'Workers' participation in the enterprise – transcending company Law?', 38 MLR 1 (1975); Adomeit, 'Unser Arbeitsrecht – Europaisch Getestet', 42 *Neue Juristische Wochenschrift* 155 (1989).

23   First proposed in 1972: OJ [1972] C 131/49. Greatly revised after consultations following the Commission Green Paper on Employee Participation and Company Structure in the European Communities (EC Bull Supp 8/75): OJ [1983] C 240/2. The latest revision is that of 1988, which is available in a consultative document published by the Department of Trade and Industry in January 1990. See also Second Amendment, OJ [1991] C 7/4; Third Amendment, OJ [1991] C 321/9, both dealing with improved voting rights for shareholders. For analysis and comment see: F. Wooldridge, *Company Law in the United Kingdom and the European Community* (Athlone Press, 1991), pp. 80–90; J. Welch, 'The Fifth Directive: a false dawn', (1983) ELR 83; J. Dine, 'The draft Fifth EEC Directive on Company Law', 10 Co. Law 10 (1989) and 'Implications for the United Kingdom of the EC Fifth Directive', 38 ICLQ 547 (1989).

24   In addition to worker participation, the draft Fifth Directive also seeks to revise directors duties and their enforcement (articles 14–21 and 21u), strengthen the powers of the general meeting, making the executive directors of the company more accountable to the shareholders (articles 22–47), and introduce new provisions relating to the functions and liabilities of auditors (articles 48–63). It also contains certain derogations for corporate groups (article 63b). See further Wooldridge, ibid., at p. 89; DTI Consultative Document 1990, ibid., at paras 13–20.

25   1988 Text (note 23 above), article 2(1).

26   Ibid., article 4b.

27 Ibid., article 4b(3) and article 4c.
28 Ibid., article 4d.
29 Ibid., article 4e.
30 Ibid., article 4h.
31 See ibid., articles 21d, e and f.
32 Ibid., articles 11 and 21r.
33 Ibid., articles 4g and 21h
34 Proposal for a Council Directive on procedure for informing and consult-
    ing employees of undertakings with complex structures, in particular
    transnational undertakings (the so-called 'Vredeling Proposal'), OJ [1980]
    C 297/3, also reproduced in 21 ILM 422 (1982); revised in 1983, see EC
    Bulletin Supplement 2/83, and for revised text see OJ [1983] C 217/3. See
    further: J. Pipkorn, 'The Draft Directive on Procedures for Informing and
    Consulting Employees', 20 CMLR 725 (1983); C. Docksey, 'Employee
    information and consultation rights in the Member States of the European
    Communities', 6 *Comparative Labour Law* 32 (1985) and 'Information and
    consultation of employees: the United Kingdom and the Vredeling Direc-
    tive', 49 MLR 281 (1986); G. Hamilton, *The Vredeling Proposal and Multi-
    national Trade Unionism* (Centre for Multinational Studies, Occasional
    Paper No. 11, September 1983); T. De Vos, *Multinational Corporations in
    Democratic Host Countries: US Multinationals and the Vredeling Proposal*
    (Dartmouth, 1989).
35 Ibid., 1980, Text, article 5(1). For a list of the matters that had to be
    disclosed see article 5(2).
36 Ibid., article 6.
37 For an account of this opposition and the resulting lobbying of the EC
    Commission and Parliament by MNEs see the works by Hamilton and De
    Vos (note 34 above).
38 Nielsen and Szyszczak (note 22 above), at p. 314. See further De Vos (note
    34 above), at pp. 209–12.
39 For detailed analysis see further De Vos (note 34 above), at pp. 217–40.
40 UK Department of Trade and Industry, *The Single Market: Company Law
    Harmonisation* (March 1993), p. 8.
41 Proposal for a Council Directive on the establishment of a European
    Works Council in Community-scale undertakings or groups of undertak-
    ings for the purposes of informing and consulting employees: OJ [1991] C
    39/10 COM(90) 581 final; amended proposal OJ [1991] C 336/11
    COM(91) 345 final. See, for a detailed summary of the terms of the final
    version of the Directive, Nielsen and Szyszczak (note 22 above), at pp.
    315–21. A scheme of employee participation has also been put forward in
    the context of the proposed Statute for a European Company: Proposal for
    a Directive on Employee Participation in the European Company
    COM(89) 268 Final – SYN 219 25 August 1989.
42 Proposal for a Council Directive on the establishment of European com-
    mittees or procedures in Community-scale undertakings and Community-
    scale groups of undertakings for the purposes of informing and consulting
    employees: COM(94) 134 final-94/0113(PRT) OJ [1994] C 135/8. See,
    for background, 'Brussels retreat on works councils', *Financial Times*, 4

February 1994, p. 2; 'Brussels to draft works directive', *Financial Times*, 31 March 1994, p. 3. The proposal was finally adopted as Council Directive 94/451/EC on 22 September 1994: OJ [1994] 254/64. The term 'European Works Council' has been reintroduced into this Directive. All references are to Directive 94/451 EC.

43 Defined as 'any undertaking with at least 1000 employees within the Member States as a whole and at least 150 employees in each of at least two Member States' (ibid., article 2(1)(a)).

44 Defined as 'a group of undertakings with the following characteristics: – at least 1000 employees within the Member States – at least two group undertakings in different Member States, and – at least one group undertaking with at least 150 employees in one Member State and at least one other group undertaking with at least 150 employees in another Member State' (ibid., article 2(1)(c)).

45 Ibid., article 1(2).

46 Defined in article 3(1) as an 'undertaking which can exercise a dominant influence over another undertaking ("the controlled undertaking") by virtue, for example, of ownership, financial participation or the rules which govern it'. Article 3(2) goes on to say that dominant influence will be presumed where an undertaking, directly or indirectly, holds a majority of another undertaking's subscribed capital, or controls a majority of the votes attached to that undertaking's subscribed capital or can appoint more than half of the members of that undertaking's board or supervisory board. In the case where the central management of an undertaking or controlling undertaking is located outside the Community, the responsibility to set up a EWC or information and consultation procedure will lie with its representative agent or with the management of the establishment, or group undertaking, employing the greatest number of employees in a Member State (ibid., article 4(2)).

47 Ibid., article 5. The negotiating body must include at least one employee from each Member State. The resulting agreement shall determine the scope and composition of the EWC, the number of members, the allocation of seats and their term of office; the functions and the procedure for informing and consulting the EWC; the venue, frequency and duration of meetings of the EWC; the financial and material resources to be allocated to the EWC; the duration of the agreement and the procedure for its renegotiation (ibid., article 6).

48 Ibid., article 5(1).

49 Ibid., article 5(5).

50 Ibid., article 7.

51 Ibid., preamble.

52 See The UK Government White Paper, 'Employment for the 1990s', Cm 540 (1988), at paras 2.20–2.21. The UK is excluded from any future deliberations and adopted measures concerning the social provisions of the Maastricht Treaty. However, one of the first acts of the new Labour government was to remove the opt-out from the Social Chapter of the Maastricht Treaty, paving the way for the EWC Directive: *Financial Times*, 6 May 1997, p. 10.

53 Companies already using such councils include Bull, Thomson, Elf-Aquitaine and Volkswagen: see further the interesting background article by Seamus Milne, 'Never mind European unity – what about the unions?', in *The Guardian*, 19 May 1992, p. 13. For a description of Daimler-Benz's practice in this field see the extract from the company's annual report for 1989 in F. D. S. Choi and G. G. Mueller, *International Accounting*, 2nd edn (Prentice-Hall International Editions, 1992), at pp. 348–54. See further Warwick Papers in Industrial Relations (Industrial Relations Research Unit, University of Warwick) Nos 38 (February 1992), 39 (March 1992) and 41 (November 1992). See further chapter 13 at pp. 478–9. See also EC Commission, *The Week in Europe*, WE/24/94, 23 June 1994.

54 For a full discussion of such differences see C. Nobes and R. Parker, *Comparative International Accounting*, 5th edn (Prentice-Hall Europe, 1998) esp. chapters 2, 3, part II, 'Country studies', and chapter 18. See also Choi and Mueller, ibid., chapter 3. See also UNCTC, *International Accounting and Reporting Issues 1991 Review* (UN, 1992, UN Doc. ST/CTC/124), chapter II, for a review of the accounting and reporting laws and practices of 44 states.

55 See further Nobes and Parker, ibid., at pp. 70–81; Choi and Mueller, ibid., at pp. 263–73.

56 For example, Fujitsu Limited (Japan), Olivetti (Italy), Saint-Gobain (France) and Scandinavian Airline Systems. See further Choi and Mueller, ibid., at pp. 271–2.

57 UNCTC, *Conclusions on Accounting and Reporting by Transnational Corporations* (UN, 1988, UN Doc. ST/CTC/92). A new edition of this document has recently been published; see UN Doc. UNCTAD/DTCI/1 (1994).

58 See Nobes and Parker (note 54 above), at pp. 307–8.

59 Grey et al. (note 2 above), at p. 64.

60 Disclosure in the USA is governed by the reporting requirements established by the Securities Exchange Commission under the Securities Act 1933 and the Securities Exchange Act 1934. The major reporting requirements for US firms are to be found in SEC Regulation S-X (17 CFR pt. 210): see A. Gutterman, *Regulatory Aspects of the Initial Public Offering of Securities 60 CPS* (BNA, 1991), esp. pp. A-65 to A-67. The presentation of consolidated and combined financial statements is governed by article 3A of Regulation S-X. This Regulation has been adapted for use by foreign MNEs that issue securities within the USA: see further Choi and Mueller (note 53 above), at pp. 306–12. In the UK consolidated disclosure is covered in ss 227–32 and Schedules 4A and 5 of the Companies Act 1985 as amended by the Companies Act 1989. These amended provisions introduce the requirements of the Seventh EC Directive on Company Law into English Law. For full analysis see N. Furey and D. Parkes, *The Companies Act 1989: a Practitioners' Guide* (Jordans, 1990). A shorter summary can be found in Farrar (note 10 above), at pp. 471–4, Gower (note 10 above), at pp. 515–18, or Wooldridge (note 23 above), at pp. 54–68.

61 See: France, Law No. 85–11 of 3 January 1985, JO 4 January 1985, p. 101; Germany, Bilanzrichtliniengesetz, 19 December 1985, BGBl. 1,

2355; Greece, Presidential Decrees No. 409/86, 8 November 1986, and No. 419/86, 10 December 1986; Luxembourg, Law of 11 July 1988, Memorial JO A No. 45 of 18 August 1988; Spain, Law 19/1989 of 25 July 1989 and Decree Law 1564/89; Belgium, Royal Decree 90/763 of 27 March 1990, Moniteur Belge, 27 March 1990, 5675.

62 See Robert Willott (ed.), *Current Accounting Law and Practice*, 13th edn (Sweet & Maxwell/ICAEW, 1988, loose-leaf periodically updated), Vol. 2, D-572 (all references are to release of 14 June 1993).

63 Ibid., D-048.

64 Ibid., D-087.

65 Ibid., D-634.

66 On which see generally Nobes and Parker, Choi and Mueller and UNCTC, 1992 (note 54 above).

67 83/349/EEC OJ [1983] L 193, 18 July 1983. The text of the Directive is also reproduced in Gray et al. (note 2 above), appendix III, and in Sharon M. McKinnon, *The Seventh Directive: Consolidated Accounts in the EEC* (Kluwer/Arthur Young International, 1984), appendix I. For detailed analysis see McKinnon, ibid., chapters 1–3; M. Petite, 'The conditions for consolidation under the 7th Company Law Directive', 21 CMLRev 81 (1984); T. E. Cooke, 'The Seventh Directive – an accountant's perspective', 9 ELR 143 (1984).

68 See Bull. EC. Supp. 9/76 (1976), at p. 19.

69 For detailed analysis of individual country positions prior to the enactment of the Directive see McKinnon (note 67 above), chapters 4–14; see also Cooke (note 67 above), at pp. 151–60.

70 Seventh Directive (note 67 above), article 16(3).

71 OJ [1978] L 222/11. See further Companies Act 1985, s. 226 and Schedule 4, which implement the requirements of the Fourth Directive into English Law.

72 Seventh Directive (note 67 above), articles 17 and 29.

73 See e.g. McKinnon (note 67 above), chapter 3.

74 For a valuable and detailed discussion of these matters see Petite (note 67 above).

75 See Petite (note 67 above), at pp. 87–8.

76 Where the duty to draw up consolidated accounts is founded on the basis of voting rights, or rights of appointment and removal, any such rights exercised by another subsidiary or by a person acting on behalf of the parent or another subsidiary must be added to those of the parent: Seventh Directive (note 67 above), article 2(1).

77 Despite the absence of control contract arrangements in English law, the UK has accepted the linkages set down in article 1(1)(c). See s. 258 (2)(c) of the Companies Act 1985, inserted by the Companies Act 1989 s. 21(1), which lays down the definition of a parent undertaking for accounting purposes.

78 The UK has provided for the second case in s. 258 (2)(d) of the Companies Act 1985 as inserted by s. 21(1) of the Companies Act 1989.

79 Companies Act 1985 s. 258(4) as inserted by Companies Act 1989 s. 21(1).

80 See Furey and Parkes (note 60 above), at paras 2.11–2.12, pp. 8–9, and para. 2.13 at pp. 10–11.
81 On which company see further chapter 3 at pp. 67–8.
82 See McKinnon (note 67 above), at p. 39.
83 Bull EC. Supp. 9/76 (note 68 above).
84 Unilever argued that the original proposal would have required it to produce over 200 additional sets of consolidated accounts, BP estimated the increased reporting burden at 36 sets: McKinnon (note 67 above), at p. 40.
85 Space prevents a detailed analysis of these provisions. See further Seventh Directive (note 67 above), articles 7 and 8; UK Companies Act 1985 s. 228 inserted by Companies Act 1989 s. 5(3).
86 Ibid., article 7(3). The UK has elected not to apply the exemption in article 7 to this class of companies: Companies Act 1985 s. 228(3) as inserted by s. 5(3) Companies Act 1989.
87 Ibid., article 9(1).
88 Ibid., article 9(2).
89 Ibid., article 10.
90 Ibid., article 11(2).
91 See Fourth Directive, article 52; Seventh Directive, article 47. For fuller discussion of this issue see Petite (note 67 above), at pp. 113–14; McKinnon (note 67 above), at pp. 44–5.
92 Seventh Directive (note 67 above), article 3; Companies Act 1985 s. 229(1) as inserted by Companies Act 1989 s. 5(3).
93 Ibid., article 13(1); ibid., s. 229(2).
94 Ibid., article 13(3)(a)(aa); ibid., s. 229(3)(a).
95 Ibid., article 13(3)(a)(bb); not applied in the UK.
96 Ibid., article 13(3)(b); Companies Act 1985 s. 229(3)(b) as inserted by Companies Act 1989 s. 5(3).
97 Ibid., article 13(3)(c); ibid., s. 229(3)(c), which adds the condition that the subsidiary undertaking has not previously been included in consolidated group accounts prepared by the parent company.
98 Ibid., article 14(1); ibid., s. 229(4).
99 Ibid., article 14(2); ibid.
100 McKinnon (note 67 above), at p. 53; Petite (note 67 above), at pp. 118–19. The UK Accounting Standards Board issued a new Financial Reporting Standard, FRS No. 2, 'Accounting for Subsidiaries', on 29 July 1992, which deals *inter alia* with this head of exemption. Under the new standard banking and insurance subsidiaries should be consolidated whereas previously they could be exempted. FRS No. 2 is reproduced in *Current Accounting Law and Practice* (note 62 above), at D-514 and D-526.
101 For the background to this option see McKinnon, ibid., at pp. 45–6.
102 See further ibid., at pp. 46–8.
103 For a recent revision see Council Directive 84/569 OJ L 314/28, 27 November 1984.
104 The applicable qualifying conditions are met if the group in a year satisfies two or more of the following requirements: to be designated a small group its aggregate turnover must be not more than £2 million net (or £2.4

million gross), its aggregate balance sheet total must be not more than £1 million net (or £1.2 million gross), and the aggregate number of employees must be not more than 50; to be designated a medium-sized group its aggregate turnover must be not more than £8 million net (or £9.6 million gross), its aggregate balance sheet total must be not more than £3.9 million net (or £4.7 million gross), and the aggregate number of employees must be not more than 250 (Companies Act 1985 s. 249(3) inserted by s. 13(3) Companies Act 1989).

105   An ineligible group is defined as existing if any of its members is: '(a) a public company or body corporate which (not being a company) has power under its constitution to offer shares or debentures to the public and may lawfully exercise that power, (b) an authorised institution under the Banking Act 1987, (c) an insurance company to which Part II of the Insurance Companies Act 1982 applies, or (d) an authorised person under the Financial Services Act 1986' (Companies Act 1985 s. 248 (2) as inserted by s. 13(3) Companies Act 1989).

106   Council Directive 90/605/EEC OJ L 317, 16 November 1990. The implementation date is 1 January 1993 but the law need not apply to annual and consolidated accounts until 1995.

107   See Directive of 8 December 1986 on the annual and consolidated accounts of credit institutions 86/635/EEC OJ [1986] L 372, 31 December 1986, implemented into English law by Companies Act 1985 (Bank Accounts) Regulations 1991 SI 1991 No. 2705.

108   Council Directive of 19 December 1991 on the annual accounts and consolidated accounts of insurance undertakings 91/674/EEC OJ [1991] L 374, 31 December 1991.

109   On the possible benefits of segmental reporting for these users see C. Roberts, 'Segmental reporting', in Nobes and Parker (note 54 above), p. 364 at pp. 378–85 and the studies there discussed.

110   Ibid., at p. 369; S. J. Gray et al. (note 2 above), at p. 81.

111   See text at p. 347 above.

112   See note 3 above at pp. 66–7, 75. See further UNCTC, *Towards International Standardisation of Corporate Accounting and Reporting* (UNCTC, 1982), pp. 72–4; Intergovernmental Group of Experts on International Standards of Accounting and Reporting, *Conclusions on Accounting and Reporting by Transnational Corporations* (1988, note 57 above), paras 62–6 at pp. 19–20; ibid. (1994, note 57 above), paras 76–80 at pp. 12–13.

113   Note 67 above.

114   Seventh Directive (note 67 above), article 34(8) and (9).

115   Roberts (note 109 above), at p. 371.

116   FAS No. 14, para. 32. See FAS 131 of 1997: Roberts *ibid.*, pp. 376–7.

117   Ibid., para. 12.

118   Ibid., para. 34. See further S. J. Gray and L. H. Radebaugh, 'International segment disclosures by US and UK multinational enterprises: a descriptive study', 22 *Journal of Accounting Research* 351 at 352–3 (1984).

119   See *Current Accounting Law and Practice* (note 62 above), at D-144.

120   Ibid., para. 14.

121   Defined as 'the distinguishable components of an enterprise each engaged

in providing a different product or service, or a different group of related products or services, primarily to customers outside the enterprise' (ibid., para. 4).

122 Defined as 'the distinguishable components of an enterprise engaged in operations in individual countries or groups of countries within particular geographical areas as may be determined appropriate in an enterprise's particular circumstances' (ibid.).

123 Ibid., paras 20–5. See now revised IAS 14 of 1997: Roberts (note 109 above), p. 377.

124 Roberts (note 109 above), at p. 370. For a comparative analysis of listing requirements on leading international stock exchanges and their effects on corporate decisions regarding listing see: R. H. Tondkar, A. Adhikari and E. N. Coffman, 'The internationalization of equity markets: motivations for foreign corporate listing and filing and listing requirements of five major stock exchanges', 24 Int. J. Acctg 143 (1989); G. C. Biddle and S. M. Saudagaran, 'The effects of financial disclosure levels on firm's choices among alternative foreign stock exchange listings', 1 *Journal of International Financial Management and Accounting* 55 (1989).

125 Financial Services Act 1986, s. 144(2).

126 Ibid., s. 146(1).

127 See: Council Directives, 79/729 of 5 March 1979, OJ [1979] L 66/21; 80/390 of 17 March 1980, OJ [1980] L 100/1 as amended by Dir. 94/18/EC OJ [1994] L 135/1; 82/121 of 15 February 1982, OJ [1982] L 48/26. The requirements of the Directives are met by the above-mentioned provisions of the Financial Services Act and the rules issued by the Council of the Stock Exchange, which in fact exceed the minimum requirements of the Directives. For a summary of the law see Farrar (note 10 above), at pp. 550–2 or Gower (note 10 above), at pp. 406–18. The Stock Exchange requirements are to be found in the Admission of Securities to Listing ('The Yellow Book') published by the Council of the Stock Exchange (loose-leaf).

128 See Directive 80/390, ibid., Schedule A, chapter 4, 'Information concerning the issuer's activities'.

129 Requirements for segmental reporting by holding companies were first introduced by the Companies Act 1967.

130 Companies Act 1985, Schedule 4A, para. 1(1).

131 Note 71 above.

132 Ibid., Schedule 4, para. 55.

133 Ibid., para. 55(5).

134 Ibid., para. 56.

135 See *Current Accounting Law and Practice* (note 62 above), at D-845.

136 Ibid., para. 8.

137 Ibid., para. 10.

138 Ibid., para. 43.

139 Ibid., para. 11.

140 Ibid., para. 12.

141 Ibid., para. 13.

142 Ibid., para. 14.

143 See ibid., para. 34.
144 See Roberts (note 109 above), at pp. 374–6.
145 In Nobes and Parker (note 54 above), at p. 378.
146 See Roberts in Nobes and Parker (note 54 above), at p. 373; Choi and Mueller (note 53 above), at pp. 328–9.
147 See S. J. Gray and C. Roberts, 'Voluntary information disclosure and the British multinationals: corporate perceptions of costs and benefits', in A. G. Hopwood (ed.), *International Pressures for Accounting Change* (Prentice Hall, 1989), p. 116.
148 See further Gray and Roberts, ibid.
149 Choi and Mueller (note 53 above), at p. 330 (emphasis in the original).
150 UN Group of Experts Report 1977 (note 3 above), at para. 52, p. 37.
151 Ibid.
152 Article L. 432–1 C trav; article L. 432–4 al. 5 et 8. C. trav. See further: A. Brunet and M. Germain, 'L'information des actionnaires et du comité d'entreprise dans les sociétés anonymes depuis les lois du 28 octobre 1982, du 1er mars 1984 et du 25 janvier 1985', (1985) *Revue des Sociétés* p. 1.
153 See text at notes 129–134 above.
154 See Choi and Mueller (note 53 above), at p. 333 and 336. See further C. Roberts, *International Trends in Social and Employee Reporting* (Chartered Association of Certified Accountants, 1990).
155 Choi and Mueller (note 53 above), at p. 337; Burchill, Clubb and Hopwood, 'Accounting in its social context: towards a history of value added in the United Kingdom', 10 *Accounting Organizations and Society* 381 (1985).
156 See Zubaidur Rahman (note 1 above), at pp. 89–90; Choi and Mueller (note 53 above), at pp. 333–7.
157 UNCTC (1988, note 57 above), para. 153, at pp. 40–1; UNCTAD (1994, note 57 above), para. 180, pp. 26–7.
158 Ibid., para. 154, at p. 41; UNCTAD 1994, para. 181, p. 27.
159 Zubaidur Rahman (note 1 above), at p. 87.
160 For a detailed analysis see UNCTC, *Transnational Corporations and Industrial Hazards Disclosure* (UN, 1991, Environmental Series No. 1, UN Doc. ST/CTC/111).
161 Choi and Mueller note that only Norway and the USA require any from of environmental reporting (note 53 above), at p. 341. In the Netherlands environmental reporting is being developed through a joint government–industry commission: see Huizing and Dekker, 'The environmental issue on the Dutch political market', 17 *Accounting Organizations and Society* 427 (1992).
162 See Report of the Secretary-General on Accounting For Environmental Protection Measures, UN Doc. E/C. 10/AC. 3/1991/5, 11 February 1991; reproduced in UNCTC, *International Accounting and Reporting Issues 1991 Review* (UN, 1992, UN Doc. ST/CTC/124), chapter IV.
163 Dutch firms have also been at the forefront of such developments. See Huizing and Dekker (note 161 above) and 'Helping to pull our planet out of the red: an environmental report of BSO/Origin', 17 *Accounting Organizations and Society* 449 (1992).

164 See further note 162 above, paras 11–17.

165 Ibid., paras 37–56.

166 Ibid., para. 64.

167 Ibid., paras 66–7.

168 Council Regulation (EEC) No 1836/93: OJ [1993] L 168/1.

169 Ibid., article 1(2).

170 Ibid., article 2(f).

171 See Council Regulation (EEC) No. 3037/90 OJ L No. 293/1, 24 October 1990.

172 Council Regulation (note 168 above), article 2(i).

173 Ibid., annex I(C).

174 Ibid., article 5.

175 Ibid., article 5(3).

176 Ibid., article 6.

177 Ibid., article 10. The logo is reproduced in annex IV of the Regulation.

178 Ibid., article 20.

179 See Paul Hatchwell, 'Eco-auditing – the new EC proposals', *Environment Information Bulletin*, 7 (May 1992), p. 9.

180 See ICC, *Environmental Auditing Publication 468* (ICC Publishing, 1989). See also, on the UK ICC's views on the draft of the EC Regulation, ICC UK Doc 29/91.

181 Hatchwell (note 179 above), at p. 13.

182 J. Flower, 'Foreign currency translation', in Nobes and Parker (note 54 above), at p. 329, on which this account draws heavily. See also Choi and Mueller (note 53 above), chapter 4.

183 ICAEW SSAP No. 20, 'Foreign currency translation' (1983) reproduced in *Current Accounting Law and Practice* (note 62 above), at D-348.

184 On which see further Flower (note 182 above).

185 See: US Financial Accounting Standards Board, *Statement of Financial Accounting Standards No. 52: Foreign Currency Translation* (1981); SSAP No. 20 (note 183 above); International Accounting Standards Committee, *IAS No. 21, Accounting for the Effects of Changes in Foreign Exchange Rates* (1983), reproduced in *Current Accounting Law and Practice* (note 62 above), at D-364.

11

Regulation through Antitrust Law

The primary aim of antitrust laws is to control competition and not to control MNEs.[1] Nevertheless, where a MNE acts in a way that violates such laws it will be subjected to control in the same way as a local enterprise. The main jurisdictional implications of antitrust control have already been considered in chapter 5.[2] This chapter concentrates on the substantive issues of antitrust regulation that arise in the context of MNE operations. As will be shown below, the operations of MNEs in an increasingly global economy create new dimensions to issues that are well known in relation to the promotion of competition in national markets. As already mentioned in chapter 2, these new dimensions centre on the international market power that arises from the development, by MNEs, of international networks of production and distribution in what are often concentrated global markets. Furthermore, the expansion of MNEs creates new questions for regulators who might be intent on using antitrust as a barrier to the entry and establishment of foreign firms on the ground of preserving the national economy from what they may perceive as destructive foreign competition. Finally, the global operations of MNEs, and the global nature of their markets, have given rise to calls for international antitrust regulation. Although the results have so far been limited to attempts, conducted under the auspices of UNCTAD, at the harmonization of the principles by which restrictive business practices should be controlled, the possibility of a future global approach to antitrust regulation cannot be ignored. Each of these issue areas will be considered in turn.

1 The Use of Antitrust Laws in the Regulation of the Anti-competitive Activities of MNEs

1.1 The Nature and Aims of Antitrust Regulation

The basic purpose of antitrust laws is to promote competition through the control of restrictive business practices.[3] It is assumed that competition between firms will enhance the overall efficiency of the economy, first, by encouraging price competition, resulting in lower prices for consumers, and, secondly, by forcing firms to produce more efficiently so as to compete on price with their rivals.[4] Free competition in markets is assumed to be possible, with no single producer or buyer having the power to control supply or demand. Consequently, the market will set prices and firms will act as 'price takers'. However, in practice, markets do not conform to this model of free competition. The distribution of market power will be uneven and anti-competitive practices may result. These must be curtailed through regulation so as to restore competitive conditions in the market.

Anti-competitive practices are generally divided into three main groups. The first consists of agreements or concerted practices between otherwise independent competitors that serve to reduce competition between them.[5] These arrangements may arise between competitors at the same level of the economy, as, for example, between rival producers in the same market. These are termed 'horizontal' arrangements. Alternatively, such arrangements may be concluded between businesses at different levels of the productive process. For example, a producer may enter into a distribution agreement with a reseller. Such arrangements are referred to as 'vertical' arrangements. Some types of anti-competitive arrangements will be absolutely prohibited. In most antitrust systems price fixing cartels between competitors come within such a prohibition. Other arrangements may not be subject to absolute prohibition, but will be prohibited only if their anti-competitive aspects outweigh any consequential benefits to consumers or in the improvement of productive or distributional efficiency. This is often referred to as the 'rule of reason' standard.[6]

The second main group of anti-competitive practices stems from the acquisition of a dominant position in a market by a single enterprise. A dominant producer may emerge that will be able to determine supply because of the extent of its control over output, as compared to its closest rivals. The dominant producer can increase its profits by creating scarcity through lowering output, thereby forcing consumers to pay higher prices for a commodity that they cannot replace with other products. It may also prevent the entry of competitors on to the market. Antitrust law will intervene and control such an abuse of a dominant position, not only to protect consumers from unfair pricing behaviour, but also because the dominant enterprise may become inefficient in that it has no reason to innovate or to reduce costs in the absence of competitive incentives.[7]

Where the dominant producer is the only supplier on a market it will enjoy a pure monopoly in that market. Such pure monopoly is rare. More commonly, a market may be dominated by a small number of major producers (oligopolists) who have little room to compete on price, as the pricing decisions of one firm will be immediately matched by those of its rivals.[8] In such cases the temptation to control the market by way of collusive arrangements may be considerable, though it is not an infallible method of reducing competition between the participants, as the threat of non-compliance with the arrangement is ever-present.[9]

The third class of regulated anti-competitive conduct relates to mergers and acquisitions. A company may expand its operations by voluntarily combining with another company to create a new company, the merged company, or it may acquire a controlling interest in another company, thereby allowing it to control that other company. A merger may be horizontal, as where it takes place between competitors at the same level of the market, or vertical, as where it takes place between a company and its supplier or distributor. Expansion through mergers and acquisitions may be pro-competitive where it results in greater economies of scale and scope, or in the replacement of inefficient management with more efficient successors.[10] On the other hand, a merger or acquisition may result in the creation of a dominant enterprise with the potential to control competitive conditions on the market, without producing any compensating efficiency gains.[11] Where this is the case the merger or acquisition may be prohibited by the antitrust authorities.[12]

1.2 The Incidence of Anti-competitive Conduct on the Part of MNEs and Regulatory Responses

Having outlined the principal types of anti-competitive conduct that antitrust laws seek to control, we now need to analyse the incidence of such conduct in the operations of MNEs, and to examine regulatory responses thereto. As a preliminary matter, it should be recalled that MNEs grow as a result of market failure, which stimulates the internalization of markets in intermediate products.[13] This leads to a concentration of ownership and control over such markets in the integrated MNE. It also leads to a concentration of competing firms in those sectors where MNEs are likely to be prevalent. Thus MNEs tend to operate in oligopolistic or monopolistic markets.[14] The effect of this process is that MNEs display competitive characteristics which are identical to several significant barriers to entry into industries: they engage in high cost advertising, they operate in industries where there are high capital costs to entry and they engage in high cost research and development.[15]

However, it would be wrong to conclude that MNEs are therefore anti-competitive combinations. On the contrary, they may be the most competitive form of business organization available for the market in question. As noted in chapter 1, MNEs may exist in highly competitive environments. That competition will not always be over prices. It may take place in non-price areas such as the production of high quality goods or in after-sales service. Furthermore, certain types of product may be capable of being produced only by highly concentrated firms.[16] These potential benefits have been recognized in law by the fact that most antitrust systems do not prohibit corporate group structures *per se*, and will not treat agreements between a parent and its majority owned and controlled subsidiaries as anti-competitive conspiracies, on the ground that the firms involved constitute a single economic entity in which the subsidiary has no choice but to carry out its parent's plans.[17] However, should the parent not be in actual control of its affiliate, and it acts as an independent party, then a conspiracy between the two entities is in principle possible.[18]

The anti-competitive activities of MNEs will now be considered in turn, beginning with the incidence of anti-competitive agreements or concerted practices operated by MNEs, followed by discussion of abuse of a dominant position by MNEs and concluding with an analysis of international merger and acquisition activities on the part of MNEs.

1.2.1 Anti-competitive agreements and concerted practices
MNEs have been found to have engaged in a number of anti-competitive arrangements with other firms. In particular, concern has centred on horizontal international marketing and price-fixing cartels, vertical international distribution systems established by MNEs for the sale of their products and the use of joint ventures with other firms. MNEs have also encountered antitrust controls in relation to restrictive terms in technology transfer licences. These will be considered in detail in chapter 12, as part of the wider issue of technology transfer regulation.

As noted in chapter 2, prior to the Second World War *international producers' cartels* were commonplace. These sought to coordinate the marketing activities of MNEs by dividing global markets into exclusive spheres of influence, and to dampen price competition through resale price maintenance agreements.[19] However, since 1945 the incidence of such arrangements has decreased. This may be owing to increased antitrust regulation both in the USA and in Europe.[20] Indeed, the destruction of pre-war international cartels was high on the agenda of the US authorities in the early post-war period.[21] This resulted in some of the most controversial cases of extraterritorial action on the part of the USA.[22] Furthermore, Japan, a number of leading European states and the EEC passed new antitrust laws during the late 1940s and 1950s, acting in line with the post-war policy of economic liberalization.[23] A further factor deterring the use of cartels may be the increased incidence of competition between MNEs from the USA, Europe and Japan, and a shift away from primary industries towards those producing differentiated goods in which competition is more likely.[24]

Nevertheless, cases involving international cartels have surfaced from time to time in recent years.[25] The major problem in such cases has been to distinguish genuine concerted action from the kind of parallel behaviour on prices and marketing strategies that is common in oligopolistic markets. According to the European Court of Justice (ECJ) in the recent *Wood Pulp* case,[26] parallel conduct cannot be regarded as furnishing evidence of unlawful concertation unless this is the only explanation of the conduct. If practices such as parallel price increases can be satisfactorily explained by the oligopolistic tendencies of the market then there is no proof of concertation between competitors. A similar approach has been taken in the USA. There must be clear evidence of conspiracy to found a violation of the Sherman Act and this cannot be furnished by 'circumstantial evidence of consciously parallel behaviour'.[27]

MNEs are likely to establish *international distribution networks* for their products either through their subsidiaries or through independent distributors. Usually, such networks will be based on agreements between the multinational producer and its controlled or independent distributor. These may include restrictive conditions. In particular, the distributor may be bound by an exclusive distribution arrangement, whereby it agrees to distribute only the products of the MNE in question and to do so only in a defined sales territory. Where such restrictions extend to an international network of sales subsidiaries or independent distributors, there arises the danger that the network will be used to partition geographical markets and to insulate them from competition originating from distributors, or third parties, operating outside the relevant sales territory.

Where significant price differences exist between the various territories, an incentive is created for distributors or third parties in a low price territory to export the contract products to customers in a high price territory by way of parallel trade. If this is prohibited by the terms of the applicable distribution agreement, consumers in the high price territory will be deprived of cheaper goods as intra-brand competition will have been restricted. On the other hand, the MNE may be unable to build up a significant international market for its products without offering its distributors the prospect of earning a reasonable return in exchange for the obligations they undertake to promote the product. Exclusivity offers such an incentive as it protects against sales by third parties ('free riders') who may benefit from the distributor's promotional efforts. Therefore a degree of territorial protection and partitioning may be acceptable for legitimate commercial reasons.

Antitrust authorities will not normally strike down an exclusive distribution network involving sales subsidiaries on the basis of the economic unity of the multinational group. However, such arrangements may amount to an abuse of a dominant position if the firm forecloses competition through the use of its controlled network, a matter to be considered in sub-section 1.1.2 below. In the case of independent distributors, antitrust authorities have tended to use a case-by-case analysis applying a 'rule of reason' approach.[28] Only if the network is part of a more general pattern of similar networks used by competing firms, and the market is highly concentrated and has high entry barriers, will the arrangement be subject to control.[29] However, if the network is used as a means of maintaining resale prices it will be struck down.[30]

Some systems may control distribution networks for policy reasons that go beyond the sole concern of maintaining competition. Thus, the EC Commission will strike down a distribution network that prevents single market integration by way of restrictive terms in distribution agreements. Such terms may include exclusive licences of industrial property rights which are used by the licensee to prevent parallel imports from outside the contract territory.[31] In Japan, highly restrictive exclusive distribution networks based on *keiretsu* groups[32] have been subjected to the 1991 Guideline on Distribution Systems and Business Practices.[33] This is in part a response to criticism from foreign firms that they have been forced to enter the Japanese domestic market at a competitive disadvantage owing to the need to build up distribution networks from scratch, as existing networks were prohibited from dealing in competing goods. Furthermore, considerations of maintaining good international economic relations with the USA were a significant factor in these reforms, as the issue of the anti-competitive effects of *keiretsu* companies was a major topic in the recent USA–Japan Structural Impediments Talks.[34] However, despite its findings that *keiretsu* groups have had the effect of excluding foreign competitors, the Japanese Fair Trade Commission has not imposed any punitive sanctions against such companies.[35] This inaction should be seen against the background of the US Department of Justice policy statement of 3 April 1992, which asserts that the Department will take antitrust action against conduct occurring overseas that would be contrary to US antitrust laws and that restrains US exports whether or not there is direct harm to US consumers. This is aimed at *keiretsu* practices. However, for practical and diplomatic reasons it may not be possible for the USA to effect the threat of extraterritorial enforcement that is explicit in the statement.[36]

It was seen in chapter 3 that MNEs may use *joint ventures* with other enterprises as a means of developing their international operations. Joint ventures have been used as a means of effecting strategic alliances for the purposes of research and development and/or production and/or distribution of goods or services. Such joint ventures can be horizontal or vertical or combine elements of both. Although not objectionable in principle, joint ventures can be and have been used as a vehicle for anti-competitive concertation between firms. At least three main types of anti-competitive risk have been identified.[37]

First, a joint venture can be used as a vehicle for anti-competitive collusion between participants who may coordinate output decisions and exchange commercially sensitive information which enables them to reduce competition *inter se* and to cartelize the market in which the joint venturers operate.[38] Such collusion has been a feature of raw materials industries where competitors have established upstream joint ventures, thereby creating the possibility of control over output through control over the supply of the raw material in question.[39] Secondly, the joint venture may reduce or eliminate actual or potential competition between the parents. Thus, it is unlikely that the parents will continue to operate as independent competitors in the market covered by the joint venture, should they already be involved in that market. Furthermore, potential competition between the parents and the joint venture is likely to be curtailed as the parents are unlikely to enter into any new market covered by the joint venture. Where such a reduction of competition is expressly agreed it may have a market dividing effect not dissimilar to that of a cartel.[40] The potential competition doctrine assumes that independent entry by the parents into the market covered by the joint venture is possible, and that the non-entry of the parents will significantly reduce the number of competitors in the market. These elements have not always been rigorously analysed in earlier decided cases, leading to criticism that pro-competitive joint ventures have been struck down on the basis of a purely theoretical possibility that the parents could have entered the market independently.[41]

In addition to a dampening of competition in the market in which the joint venture operates, there may be a danger that the cooperation engendered by the joint venture will encourage a dampening of competition in other markets in which the parents are actual or potential competitors. Such 'spill-over' effects will be monitored by antitrust authorities.

Thirdly, a joint venture can be used as a means of excluding or hampering access for third party firms to raw materials or finished goods. This may act as a barrier to entry for new firms, and increase the cost of operations to existing firms. The problem can arise at the upstream end of an industry where the parents set up a joint venture to develop a new raw material supply. Should the joint venture control access to a very high proportion of the total supply of the raw material in question, then third parties will be at its mercy as regards access to that raw material. Similarly, at the downstream end, a joint distribution venture can create a monopolistic market for the goods or services in question, restricting alternative sources of direct supply from the parents and giving the joint venturers control over the market. Such an arrangement can be used as a method of partitioning markets between the parents, especially where there are few, if any, competing suppliers.[42]

Despite the above-mentioned dangers to competition, international joint ventures can be regarded as generally pro-competitive. First, such arrangements can create greater stability for high risk projects that one firm might find too uncertain to undertake. The pooling of technological skills, capital and personnel may be the only way to secure an advance in research and development leading to new products or processes. As seen in chapter 3, MNEs are increasingly using joint ventures to develop and produce high technology goods. Indeed, some goods, for example a 500–800 seat airliner, may be impossible to produce without such cooperation.[43] Secondly, a joint venture may be required to achieve sufficient economies of scale to make production viable without forcing the participants into a permanent union through merger. This may be an important consideration where the partners are firms from different countries, making merger a more difficult option. Thirdly, a joint venture might permit greater specialization in production, allowing the partners to develop their particular competitive advantages more fully.[44] Finally, in a market with appreciable numbers of competitors, joint distribution arrangements between producers may be acceptable where the product lines of each partner are complementary and the joint distribution agreement will increase consumer access to a larger product range.[45] This may be particularly true where a smaller firm allows a larger firm with a more extensive distribution network to market its range across a territory that the smaller firm could not reach by itself. It is a means of permitting international distribution for the products of a firm that could not otherwise afford to go multinational.

In the light of such considerations anti-trust authorities are taking an increasingly lenient approach towards joint ventures. Thus the US Department of Justice stated, in 1988, 'Because joint ventures typically achieve integrative efficiencies, the Department judges the likely competitive effects of joint ventures under a rule of reason.'[46] The US rule of reason analysis involves four steps:

First, the Department determines whether the joint venture would likely have any anticompetitive effect in the market or markets in which the joint venture proposes to operate or in which the integration of the parties' operations occurs (the joint venture markets). Second, the Department determines whether the joint venture or any of its restraints would likely have an anticompetitive effect in any other market or markets ('spill-over markets') in which the joint venture members are actual or potential competitors outside the joint venture. Third, the Department analyzes the likely competitive effects of any nonprice vertical restraints imposed in connection with the joint venture. The Department will not challenge a joint venture if under the first three steps, the Department concludes that the joint venture would not likely have any significant anticompetitive effects. If, however, the Department's analysis under the first three steps reveals significant anticompetitive risks, then, under step 4, the Department considers whether any procompetitive efficiencies that the parties claim would be achieved by the joint venture would outweigh the risk of anticompetitive harm.[47]

The EC Commission also takes a positive view of joint ventures, although this has not always been the case.[48] Since 1985, joint ventures in research and development (R&D) have been exempt from article 85(1) EEC Treaty, provided they conform with the requirements of the block exemption in this field.[49] This exemption has been extended to the joint distribution of the products of such joint R&D, provided that the parties' production of the products in question does not exceed 10 per cent of the market for all such products in the Common Market or a substantial part thereof.[50] This is more restrictive than the market share requirement applicable to R&D joint ventures that do not have joint distribution arrangements. Here, for exemption to be granted, the combined market share of the parents' production of products capable of being improved or replaced by the joint R&D must not exceed 20 per cent of the EC market or a substantial part thereof.[51] Joint distribution in the context of specialization agreements is also subject to a similar exemption.[52] Furthermore, grants of patent and know-how licences by a parent to a joint venture now enjoy block exemption provided that the products concerned and any substitutable products produced by the participating undertakings do not exceed 20 per cent of the EC market where the licence is for production only and 10 per cent where the licence covers both production and distribution.[53] Moreover, the EC Commission has issued a Notice on cooperative joint ventures which sets down a more realistic economic approach to the assessment of joint ventures.[54]

1.2.2 'Abuse of a dominant position' or 'monopolization'   It was seen in the introduction to this section that MNEs tend to be highly concentrated firms operating in concentrated markets. Consequently, they may enjoy a measure of market power in international and national markets that purely national firms cannot match. To some extent this is inevitable and does not, of itself, create antitrust problems. As long as dominant MNEs do not deliberately seek the destruction of smaller competitors, or thwart the entry of new competitors, their operations are unlikely to attract the concern of antitrust authorities. Indeed, the presence of large internationally integrated firms may be beneficial to consumers, offering new products and services at a reasonable cost that is achieved through the greater economies of scale and scope offered by international production.

On the other hand MNEs may be able to use their internalization advantages in ways that abuse competition.[55] For example, the MNE may use transfer pricing manipulations to extract monopolistic profits from the host state. A notable example of such abuse was condemned in the early 1970s in the UK and Germany, when the pharmaceutical company Hoffmann–La Roche was found to have manipulated its transfer prices for librium and valium, resulting in the remittance of excessive profits from the UK and Germany.[56] Arguably, transfer pricing abuses are better seen as issues for tax rather than antitrust authorities. However, antitrust authorities will become involved where the result of such abuses is the overcharging of customers and/or the driving out of existing competition and/or the creation of barriers to entry as a result of the greater market power enjoyed by the MNE through its increased profitability.

Similarly, a MNE can restrict competition through its exclusive ownership of proprietary technology that may be required for the operation of effective competition in the market concerned. Thus, in 1984, IBM was required by the EC Commission to make available to its competitors its System 370 products without which the latter could not upgrade their 'IBM compatible' computer products.[57]

Furthermore, the international integration of the MNE may serve to reduce competition to an unacceptable level. This may happen where the firm has exclusive control over a vital raw material that it alone can extract or produce.[58] Equally, the firm's control over an integrated international production, transport and distribution network may be abused. This is of particular concern where the network is significantly larger than that of its nearest competitor and is therefore insulated from inter-brand competition. Thus, in *United Brands v EC Commission*[59] the ECJ found that United Brands, one of the world's leading vertically integrated producers and distributors of bananas, had abused its dominant position on that market *inter alia* by charging discriminatory prices in each national market, a practice that could not be justified by local commercial conditions, and by limiting intra-brand price competition through bans on parallel trading in unripened bananas between lower and higher price sales areas.

Other marketing practices that have been condemned as abuses of a dominant position enjoyed by a MNE include: refusals to supply;[60] loyalty rebates to customers that tie them into the sales of the dominant firm;[61] target discounts for distributors which force them to purchase their requirements from the dominant firm;[62] tied sales of goods as a condition of access to the dominant firm's products;[63] and predatory price cutting as a means of driving out competitors.[64]

The major legal issues to be determined in a case of alleged unilateral anti-competitive conduct are as follows. First, the dominance of the firm on the market must be established. This involves a two step analysis. At the outset, the relevant market must be defined.[65] This requires an often difficult analysis of the product or products involved on the basis of demand side substitutability. In essence, if the product in question is interchangeable with another then both are within the same market. Then the geographical scope of the market must be determined on the basis of the similarity of costs and other competitive conditions in a particular area of operations. Finally, the temporal scope of the market must be determined to ascertain whether there are seasonal variations in competitive conditions.

When the relevant market has been defined the firm's dominance in that market must be shown. A monopoly of the market would be clear evidence of dominance. Usually, this is a very rare case, although in developing countries a MNE may be the sole operator in a particular market. In most situations the firm will coexist with other firms. Thus the main issue is whether the firm can act independently without regard for its competitors, customers or consumers and be able to prevent competition.[66] In this respect a number of factors are relevant. They include, *inter alia*, the market share of the firm,[67] the technological advantages it possesses, the extent of vertical and/or horizontal integration, economies of scale, access to capital, product differentiation and overall size, strength and performance.[68]

Once the dominant position of the firm has been established, then the legality of the alleged abusive conduct will be considered. Although the kinds of practices described in the introduction to this sub-section will offer strong evidence of an abuse, antitrust authorities will analyse the facts in the light of any objective justifications offered for the conduct.[69] Equally, where alleged abusive conduct would make no economic sense for the dominant enterprise, the theoretical possibility of such conduct might be insufficient to ground a finding to this effect. For example, in *Matsushita Electric Industrial Co. v Zenith Radio Corp.*[70] the US Supreme Court rejected a private suit brought by a group of US corporations that manufactured or sold consumer electronic products, alleging that twenty-one Japanese competitors were engaging in a long-term conspiracy to undercut prices on the US market so as to expand their market share, on the ground that it made no reasonable business sense for the Japanese firms to sustain losses for decades without any foreseeable profits. This case illustrates a feature of US law in this area, namely that the court will consider the reasonableness or otherwise of inferring market power from the evidence before it.[71]

In conclusion, it should be stressed that the mere fact that MNEs may dominate certain markets, and may even be monopolists in certain jurisdictions, does not of itself indicate anti-competitive conduct. Each case should be considered on its facts, and only where the internalization advantages of the MNE are being abused should control occur. However, it should be noted that the mere possibility of anti-competitive effects may prompt certain states to control the entry and establishment of MNEs on the basis of preliminary screening procedures such as those outlined in chapter 6.

1.2.3 Mergers and acquisitions[72]   During the 1980s the incidence of international mergers and acquisitions (M and A) involving MNEs reached unprecedented levels. This was particularly evident in the developed countries of the North.[73] The reasons behind this lay primarily in the need for firms to expand their international operations so as to become international players in the emerging global economy.[74] Further stimulus has come from the deregulation and globalization of securities markets, resulting in an internationalized market for corporate control, with shares being traded in several regional markets and shareholders and creditors being located throughout the world.[75] Since the end of the 1980s the level of M and A activity carried on by MNEs has slowed down, although it is likely to remain a permanent feature of the international economy.[76] International M and A by MNEs confronts directly the national, or regional, orientations of existing regulatory systems with a commercial phenomenon that takes the global market place as its economic basis. This has both jurisdictional and substantive implications.

Regarding jurisdictional concerns, an international merger situation can create at least four alternative cases.[77] First, the subsidiary of a foreign MNE may be acquired by a host state company. This will normally be the concern of the host state antitrust authorities alone, and the foreign character of the acquired company will disappear after the acquisition. Secondly, the acquisition of the foreign subsidiary of a home based parent company may be of interest to home state authorities if the level of concentration in the host state may prevent competitive exports from the home state, or monopolize supplies of imports to the home state. This case involves the exercise of extra-territorial jurisdiction by the home state. Thirdly, two parent companies located in one state may merge and their affiliates in another state may also merge as part of the merger plan. The host state authorities may see this as an unacceptable concentration. They will act on a territorial basis as they are unlikely to seek the dissolution of the parent company merger.[78] The lawfulness of that merger is for the home state authorities to determine. Fourthly, there is the case where a subsidiary of a foreign parent, or the foreign parent itself, acquires a host state corporation. Here the host state authorities may extend their jurisdiction extraterritorially to the foreign parent to control the merger.[79] Equally, the home state authorities may be worried by the increased concentration and international market power that the parent company acquires. They may be tempted to prohibit the parent from carrying out the acquisition.

From the above examples it is clear that multiple review of inter-national M and A is likely. This may result in conflicting decisions. For example, the bid for the UK company Consolidated Gold Fields by Luxembourg based Minorco was approved in the UK by the Monopolies and Mergers Commission (MMC),[80] but was seen as having potentially anti-competitive effects in the USA by the US Federal courts.[81] In the EC, the possibility of conflicting decisions has been recognized for a long time, with both national and EC merger authorities having potential control over a merger situation.[82] In order to avoid this risk – and a costly duplication of effort – the EC Merger Regulation[83] lays down a division of jurisdiction between Member States and the EC Commission's Merger Task Force. The EC authorities have jurisdiction only in respect of a concentration[84] which has a 'Community dimension'.[85] A concentration has a 'Community dimension' where the aggregate worldwide turnover of all the undertakings concerned is more than 5000 million ecu and the aggregate Community-wide turnover of each of at least two under-takings concerned is more than 250 million ecu, unless each of the undertakings concerned achieves more than two-thirds of its aggre-gate Community-wide turnover within one and the same Member State.[86] In the case of credit or other financial institutions one tenth of their total assets must equal or exceed 5 billion ecu. This figure is then multiplied by the ratio between loans and advances to credit institutions and customers in transactions with Community residents and the total sum of those loans and advances. The resulting figure must amount to 250 million ecu or more for each institution, thereby showing that the parties to the concentration do substantial business in the EC. To determine whether more than two-thirds of the Community business is done in one Member State, one-tenth of the total assets is multiplied by the ratio between loans and advances to credit institutions and customers in transactions with residents of that Member State and the total sum of those loans and advances.[87] Where these thresholds are met, review by the EC authorities will be final.[88]

This formula will not always eliminate dual jurisdiction problems. For example, when the Hong Kong and Shanghai Banking Corporation (HKS) bid for the UK based Midland Bank, the Commission took the view that this bid had a Community dimension, but that the it raised no serious anti-competitive effects.[89] At the same time the UK based Lloyds Bank made a competing bid for Midland. This was held to fall outside Community competence as over two-thirds of the EC business of both Lloyds and Midland was carried out in the UK. This bid was referred to the MMC on 22 May 1992, but was set aside when Lloyds withdrew its offer.[90] Had Lloyds maintained its bid, it may have been at a procedural disadvantage, as it would have had to await the outcome of the MMC investigation before proceeding with its bid. Meanwhile, HKS could continue its negotiations with Midland free of any further intervention from the UK or EC merger authorities. Furthermore, given that the principal competitive effects of the Midland takeover would occur in the UK, it would not be unreasonable to allow the UK authorities to review both bids. Thus, the division of competence between the EC and national authorities is not without its difficulties.[91] In 1997 Regulation 1310/97 introduced a new, additional criterion for assessing the 'Community dimension' of concentrations which permits review of cases involving smaller turnovers (2.5 billion ecu worldwide; 100 million ecu in member states) but across three member states.[92]

Turning to substantive issues, the main concern of various national and regional authorities has been to prevent a merger or acquisition that would create or substantially increase market domination on the part of the new concentration and thereby increase the risk of competition being significantly impeded.[93] This requires, first, the delimitation of the relevant product and geographical market in which the concentration occurs. This is done in much the same way as for cases of abuse of a dominant position that have been discussed above. Secondly, an analysis of the degree of concentration created by the merger or acquisition must be undertaken. Under US law, this is assessed according to a mathematical index of market concentration, the Herfindahl–Hirschman Index (HHI).[94] Under EC law, an economic analysis of market shares is undertaken based on the facts of the case. Thirdly, the merger or acquisition will be assessed as to its effect on existing competitors and on customers, and as to the likelihood of new entrants being deterred from the market.[95]

A concentration is likely to be struck down where it enjoys a significant increase in market share coupled with a reduction in the number and market strength of competitors, where it can act independently of its competitors and customers, and where there is little or no likelihood of new entrants on to the market.[96] Equally, where a concentration leads to an increased risk of collusion between the remaining firms on the market it will be struck down.[97] On the other hand, where the concentration serves to improve competitive conditions, as where it contributes to the development of technical and economic progress that is of advantage to customers, then it may be approved.[98] It is not uncommon for the antitrust authority concerned to clear the concentration on the basis of legally binding undertakings being given by the parties. Failure to observe such commitments will result in clearance being withdrawn.

There are numerous problems associated with the substantive regulation of international mergers and acquisitions. First, the relevant authority may be unable to amass and analyse all the relevant information on the likely competitive effects of a new concentration involving a MNE. Professor Caves offers the following illustration:

One national MNE acquires a company selling the same product line in another country. If the two nations' officials detect monopolistic tendencies by watching the concentration of domestic *producers*, the usual practice, neither authority sees anything amiss. That is because producer concentration remains unchanged (at least initially). But the merger leaves one less independent firm in the world market, and so international *seller* concentration results in one or both countries if either of the now-combined firms formerly exported to the other nation. The world's interest in competitive markets is therefore not automatically tended by national authorities, even if they forswear taking monopolistic advantage of each other.[99]

Much therefore depends on what the antitrust authority sees as the relevant market that it has to consider in relation to its activities. Without some form of international cooperation it may be impossible to see the effect on the world market of a given concentration.

However, this is to assume that antitrust authorities act to further international competition. In practice other factors may enter into account. In particular, antitrust authorities may be expected by their political masters to intervene in the competitive process so as to increase the likelihood that the given country or region will be a beneficiary of international competition, even at the expense of other countries or regions. Much depends on the dominant ideological orientation of the political system in question. However, certain common issues arise.

First, there is the question whether international controls over M and A should be linked to the industrial policy of the regulating country or region. The problem has been graphically illustrated by the EC Commission's decision in the case of *Aerospatiale and Alenia/ De Havilland*.[100] Aerospatiale of France and Alenia of Italy set up, in 1982, the joint venture Avions de Transport Regional (ATR), which has since become the world's leading designer and manufacturer of turboprop regional airliners. In May 1991 the ATR partners notified the EC Commission of their proposed acquisition of the Canadian based De Havilland division of Boeing, which specializes in the design and manufacture of regional turboprop aircraft. The Commission blocked the proposed acquisition on the ground that it would unduly concentrate the Community market in regional turboprop aircraft,[101] thereby risking its monopolization by the proposed joint enterprise. This decision was strongly criticized by a dissenting minority of the EC Advisory Committee on Concentrations, at its eighth meeting on 20 September 1991, on the ground that the Commission had overestimated the market shares of the participants and underestimated the strength of competitors and customers in the market. In their opinion, the decision was 'not so much protecting competition but rather protecting the competitors of the parties to this proposed concentration'.[102] The decision was greeted with criticism from the French and Italian transport ministers, who argued that it undermined EC industrial policy. The French minister M. Paul Quiles said at the time, 'It seems to me imperative that the Commission should not content itself with looking at competition [criteria]. It's not enough.'[103]

Thus, the decision was criticized for concentrating too much on competition issues. This might have been a valid point if the European regional aircraft industry was at risk from larger foreign competitors, making the increased concentration of European firms a valuable defensive strategy. However, this was a market in which ATR was the leading firm. Allowing it to take over De Havilland would have increased the risk that other firms would leave the market, notably British Aerospace and Fokker of the Netherlands, with serious social and economic consequences for their home countries.[104] Thus, the Commission's decision may well have served

European interests better than if it had allowed the concentration to proceed. However, this case shows how non-competition issues may be expected to be taken into account in the course of an investigation of a merger or acquisition.

Secondly, competition authorities may be expected to protect 'national champions' against foreign takeover. According to the UNCTC one consequence of international M and A strategy is that:

industries are becoming increasingly concentrated as firms pursue the acquisition of brands which give them a leading rank or share in key markets. Therein lies the root of the major problem which international acquirors are likely to face in the future, and which has already surfaced in numerous countries. . . . Throughout the industrialized world, a political backlash to international takeovers is emerging. Even in nations that have prided themselves on their open door policy to foreign investors, there has been strong political opposition to foreign bidders.[105]

The issues referred to by the UNCTC are well illustrated by the debate in the UK concerning the takeover of Rowntree–Macintosh by Nestlé in 1988. Lord Young, the then Secretary of State for Trade and Industry, refused to refer the proposed bid to the MMC, on the ground that it did not raise any competition issues or wider issues relating to the public interest.[106] This was met with strong criticism from the Labour Opposition and from Conservative MPs with constituencies in Yorkshire, where Rowntree was based.[107] The critics were concerned about the government's willingness to allow British firms to fall into foreign hands at the risk of turning Britain into a 'branch economy'. The government was motivated by its view that British interests were best served by preserving an open economy for foreign investors, given the benefits obtained by British firms from their extensive overseas investments, which might be jeopardized by signs of protectionism in the UK market. This debate illustrates a division between economic 'nationalists' and economic 'internationalists' which is common in many countries. In the UK the 'internationalist' position is at present dominant. This approach was outlined in 1984 by former Secretary of State for Trade and Industry, Norman Tebbit, and has since become known as the 'Tebbit Doctrine'. He stated:

I regard mergers policy as an important part of the Government's general policy of promoting competition within the economy in the interests of the customer and of efficiency and hence of growth and jobs. Accordingly my policy has been and will continue to be to make references primarily on competition grounds. In evaluating the competitive situation in individual cases I shall have regard to the international context: to the extent of competition in the home market from non-United Kingdom sources and to the competitive position of United Kingdom companies in overseas markets.[108]

Thus, UK mergers policy is based primarily on the concerns of economic efficiency and not on wider national sovereignty issues.[109]

The MMC has generally followed this approach when considering whether a merger or acquisition between a UK and non-UK firm is in the public interest under the merger provisions of the Fair Trading Act 1973.[110] Thus in *Elders IXL Ltd/Allied Lyons plc*,[111] the MMC held that the proposed takeover of Allied Lyons by the Australian brewer Elders IXL was in the public interest, despite the highly leveraged nature of the bid, as the Australian company could help improve the UK company's marketing and product innovation skills, and increase exports. The fact that there was a lack of reciprocity between the then restrictive Australian controls over foreign investment and the absence of such restrictions in the UK was not held to act against the public interest.

On the other hand, the statutory powers of the MMC to review a merger in the public interest do not exclude broader socio-economic considerations.[112] Thus, the Commission will consider the employment and balance of payments effects of a foreign takeover of a UK firm.[113] Furthermore, in *Hong Kong and Shanghai Banking Corporation/Royal Bank of Scotland* the MMC laid down a rebuttable presumption that the takeover of a UK based bank by a foreign bank is against the public interest as the 'transfer and ultimate control of a significant part of the clearing bank system outside the United Kingdom would have an adverse effect of opening up possibilities of divergence of interest which would not otherwise arise'.[114] Moreover, in 1990, the Secretary of State for Trade and Industry expressed the view that he would be more likely to make a reference to the MMC where a foreign state-owned company made a bid for a UK company, in that such a company was deemed less likely to operate in an efficient manner, or to compete on even terms with private firms.[115] However, the MMC has not accepted as a principle that the public ownership of the foreign bidder raises a presumption that the bid is against the public interest. In 1991 five references were made by the Secretary of State involving bids by state owned enterprises for UK companies. Only one was found to raise public interest objections.[116] One of the companies affected, Credit Lyonnais (which had two bids referred), complained to the EC Commission that the UK policy was discriminatory. After intervention by the Commission, the UK accepted that state ownership *per se* could not constitute sufficient grounds for the making of a reference.[117]

A third common issue that antitrust authorities may be expected to consider is the protection, against foreign takeover, of national firms operating in sectors vital to national security. It was seen in chapter 6 that many states have passed specialized laws to achieve this aim. These may be laws designed specifically to protect national security, as in the case of the US Exon-Florio amendment, or they may be general foreign investment screening laws which give the screening authority the discretion to consider national security issues. Thus, for example, Japan has used its foreign investment law to investigate foreign bids for Japanese companies on national security grounds.[118] However, where a country does not have a specialized law that can deal with national security issues, antitrust law may be used instead. This has been the case in the UK. Thus the MMC will take strategic considerations into account when judging whether a foreign takeover of a British firm operates against the public interest.

A notable example occurred in the case of *Kuwait/British Petroleum plc*.[119] The case arose out of the acquisition by the Kuwait Investment Office (KIO), the Kuwaiti government's London based investment arm, of some 22 per cent of the stock of British Petroleum (BP) between October 1987 and March 1988. KIO had bought up large amounts of BP stock which had been offered for sale by the British government as part of its privatization programme, but which had fallen in value drastically as a consequence of the stock market crash of 19 October 1987. The Secretary of State for Trade and Industry referred the case to the MMC, concerned that the build up of shares in BP by a government with substantial oil interests raised issues of public interest. The MMC found that the Kuwaiti stake gave it the capacity to control BP's policy in the future. The holding was some twelve times the size of the next largest beneficial holding, that of Prudential Assurance, which was 1.8 per cent, followed by HM Treasury at 1.7 per cent.[120] The Kuwaiti holding was held to constitute a merger situation that was against the public interest because future conflicts of interest between Kuwait, as a member of OPEC, and BP and the British government were foreseeable. Furthermore, Kuwait could block commercial policies of BP that were likely to compete with Kuwaiti oil interests, and BP could be prejudiced in third states, especially the USA, because of its links with Kuwait. The Commission recommended that the Kuwaiti shareholding be reduced to 9.9 per cent.

Security considerations were also present in the findings of the MMC in the case of *GEC plc and Siemens AG/Plessey plc*.[121] The MMC held unanimously that the joint bid of GEC and Siemens for Plessey should be allowed to proceed subject to certain undertakings from GEC and Siemens that would serve to safeguard the public interest. *Inter alia* the Commission was worried that Siemens's participation could raise issues of national security because it was a German company. In order to meet this concern, the Commission proposed that all executive directors and the majority of non-executive directors of Plessey companies owned by Siemens, or jointly owned by GEC and Siemens, should be British nationals. This would be the subject of undertakings to be negotiated with the Secretary of State.[122]

By way of conclusion, the above examples illustrate the need to reconcile national economic and social priorities with the globalization of companies and industries. Protectionism through a restrictive antitrust policy is tempting, especially for regions with underdeveloped or uncompetitive industries. However, the approach currently favoured in most advanced states requires the maintenance of an open market coupled with investment in locational advantages, while at the same time ensuring that international competition is workable and efficient. This last element may require the development of an effective global antitrust system. The EC already points the way with its regional approach but, as certain views expressed in the context of the *Aerospatiale* decision suggest, in different political conditions it could become part of a system dedicated to the protection of European industry against global competition.

2   International Developments in the Regulation of Restrictive Business Practices Undertaken by MNEs

Attempts to create an international machinery for the regulation of restrictive business practices (RBPs) are not new. At the end of the Second World War the USA proposed that the planned International Trade Organization (ITO) should include a Commission on Business Practices which would 'inquire into the activities on the part of private commercial enterprises which have the effect or purpose of restraining international trade, restricting access to international markets, or of fostering monopolistic controls in international trade'.[123] The Havana Charter for the ITO contained a list of prohibited business practices in article V. These included price fixing, exclusion of businesses from markets, discrimination against particular firms, production limits or quotas, preventing the development of technology, illegal extension of industrial property rights and any similar practices that the ITO might declare to be restrictive business practices by a majority of two-thirds of the members present and voting.[124] However, the ITO Charter was never adopted as a result of US opposition to its foreign investment provisions.[125] Thereafter, during the 1950s, the USA tried to secure UN agreement on the drafting of international rules on RBPs, but without success.[126] The USA also pursued a bilateral policy by including a clause on RBPs in its Friendship, Commerce and Navigation treaties.[127] In the 1970s, the OECD set up a Committee of Experts on RBPs which led to a Report on the RBPs of MNEs. The Committee came out against the creation of a different substantive antitrust law for MNEs and national enterprises, or the abandonment of the general exemption from anti-trust control of parent–subsidiary relations.[128] The OECD has not established any international machinery for setting standards or for investigating RBPs carried out by MNEs.

It was not until the advent of the United Nations Conference on Trade and Development (UNCTAD) that new initiatives for the development of an international antitrust regime were introduced.[129] At its Second Session in New Delhi, UNCTAD placed RBPs upon its agenda. In 1972 at the Third Session, the possibility of drawing up guidelines for the control and elimination of RBPs adversely affecting less developed countries was raised. This led to the establishment of an *ad hoc* Group of Experts with a brief to consider the issue. In 1976, at the Forth Session in Nairobi, Resolution 96(IV) was passed. It authorized negotiations leading towards the formulation of a Set of Principles and Rules on RBPs, which covered not only LDCs but international trade in general. A fourth *ad hoc* group was set up in 1978. It made significant progress and, by 1979, a Conference was established to negotiate and finalize a Set of Principles and Rules. The final agreed version of the code, known as the Set of Multilaterally Agreed Equitable Principles and Rules for the Control of Restrictive Business Practices (the Set), was adopted by UNCTAD in April 1980, and by the UN General Assembly in December 1980.[130]

The Set represents an acceptance of the view that the basic norms of antitrust law, which have long been in use in developed states, should extend to the operations of enterprises, including MNEs, in LDCs.[131] Thus, the Objectives section of the Set emphasizes that the interests of developing countries in particular should be taken into account in the elimination of RBPs that may cause prejudice to international trade and development.[132] Furthermore, the Objectives section sees the Set as an international contribution to a wider process of encouraging the adoption and strengthening of laws and policies in this area at the national and regional levels.[133] This objective should be seen alongside UNCTAD's work on the formulation of a Model Law on RBPs. The draft Model Law embodies the principles laid down in the Set and couples these with a scheme for a national antitrust authority. It is aimed at LDCs which do not as yet have a domestic system of antitrust regulation.[134]

Finally, section C(iii)(7) of the Set lays down a principle of preferential treatment for LDCs as an aspect of the equitable application of the principles contained in the Set. Thus states, in particular developed countries, are to take into account in the application of their RBP controls the 'development, financial and trade needs of developing countries, in particular of the least developed countries, for the purposes especially of developing countries in: (a) promoting the establishment or development of domestic industries and the economic development of other sectors of the economy, and (b) encouraging their economic development through regional or global arrangements among developing countries.' Therefore, the Set envisages 'infant industry' and regional economic integration exceptions to the application of antitrust controls to enterprises and other organizations from LDCs. This provision was accepted by the developed states in return for the LDC's acceptance of the principle that 'States, while bearing in mind the need to ensure the comprehensive application of the Set of Principles and Rules, should take due account of the extent to which the conduct of enterprises, whether or not created or controlled by States, is accepted under applicable legislation or regulations'.[135] Thus the Set accepts that states cannot interfere with another state's decision to exempt certain activities from the operation of antitrust laws. However, there is no mention of the issue of extraterritoriality in the Set.[136]

Apart from offering special concessions to LDC interests, the Set also deals specifically with MNEs, which are referred to in the text as transnational corporations (TNCs), in accordance with UN practice.[137] Section B(ii)(4) of the Set states that 'The Set of Principles and Rules applies to restrictive business practices,[138] including those of transnational corporations, adversely affecting international trade, particularly that of developing countries, and the economic development of those countries. It applies irrespective of whether such practices involve enterprises in one or more countries.' Of particular importance to TNCs are the contents of section D, entitled 'Principles and Rules for Enterprises, Including Transnational Corporations'. Section D begins by exhorting enterprises to conform to the RBP laws of states in which they operate,[139] and to consult and cooperate with the competent authorities of countries whose interests are adversely affected by RBPs.[140] The principal provisions of section D are provision 3, which deals with anti-competitive agreements or arrangements between enterprises, and provision 4, which deals with abuse of a dominant position. Both provisions refer to issues arising out of the operation of affiliated enterprises.

Section D(3) introduces the economic entity doctrine as a limitation on the applicability of RBP controls in the case of anti-competitive agreements or arrangements.[141] It states:

Enterprises, except when dealing with each other in the context of an economic entity wherein they are under common control, including through ownership, or otherwise not able to act independently of each other, engaged on the market in rival or potentially rival activities, should refrain from practices such as the following when, through formal, informal, written or unwritten agreements or arrangements they limit access to markets or otherwise unduly restrain competition, having or being likely to have adverse effects on international trade, particularly that of developing countries, and on the economic development of these countries:

(a) Agreements fixing prices, including as to exports and imports;
(b) Collusive tendering;
(c) Market or customer allocation arrangements;
(d) Allocation by quota as to sales and production;
(e) Collective action to enforce arrangements, e.g. by concerted refusals to deal;
(f) Concerted refusal of supplies to potential importers;
(g) Collective denial of access to an arrangement, or association, which is crucial to competition.

The list of RBPs covered is unremarkable, though it has been criticized for being less clear than it appears, involving many fine points of law and policy.[142] What is of considerable interest is the compromise reached over parent–subsidiary issues. The wording suggests that economic unity between parent and subsidiary is an issue of fact in each case.[143] Thus, it has been said that the possibility of 'intra-enterprise conspiracy' is not ruled out.[144]

Section D(4) lists certain abuses of a dominant position committed by affiliated enterprises. It states:

Enterprises should refrain from the following acts or behaviour in a relevant market when through an abuse or acquisition and abuse of a dominant position of market power, they limit access to markets or otherwise unduly restrain competition, having or being likely to have adverse effects on international trade, particularly that of developing countries, and on the economic development of these countries:

(a) Predatory behaviour towards competitors, such as using below-cost pricing to eliminate competitors;
(b) Discriminatory (i.e. unjustifiably differentiated) pricing or terms and conditions in the supply and purchase of goods or services, including by means of the use of pricing policies in transactions between affiliated enterprises which overcharge or undercharge for goods or services purchased or supplied as compared with prices for similar comparable transactions outside the affiliated enterprises;
(c) Mergers, takeovers, joint ventures or other acquisitions of control, whether of a horizontal, vertical or a conglomerate nature;
(d) Fixing the prices at which goods exported can be resold in importing countries;
(e) Restrictions on the importation of goods which have been legitimately marked abroad with a trademark identical with or similar to the trademark protected as to identical or similar goods in the importing country

where the trademarks in question are of the same origin, i.e. belong to the same owner or are used by enterprises between which there is economic, organizational, managerial or legal interdependence and where the purpose of such restrictions is to maintain artificially high prices;

(f) When not ensuring the achievement of legitimate business purposes, such as quality, safety, adequate distribution or service:

    (i) Partial or complete refusals to deal on the enterprise's customary commercial terms;

    (ii) Making the supply of particular goods or services dependent upon the acceptance of restrictions on the distribution or manufacture of competing or other goods;

    (iii) Imposing restrictions concerning where, to whom, or in what form or quantities, goods supplied or other goods may be resold or exported;

    (iv) Making the supply of particular goods or services dependent upon the purchase of other goods or services from the supplier or his designee.

This provision contemplates transfer pricing abuses by affiliated enterprises as a species of abuse of a dominant position. This was opposed in principle by the Western developed countries, which argued that such practices were better seen as taxation issues. However, these states compromised on the basis that the OECD Guidelines on Multinational Enterprises include as an abuse of a dominant position transfer pricing manipulations that adversely affect competition outside the affiliated enterprises.[145] The restrictions on trademark abuses by groups of companies echo similar restrictions in the laws of developed countries.[146] Section D(4) contains a definition of 'abuse' in a footnote that has implications for group enterprises. The footnote states that the determination of whether acts or behaviour are abusive should be examined 'with reference to whether they limit access to markets or otherwise unduly restrain competition' and to whether they are, *inter alia*, 'Appropriate in the light of the organizational, managerial and legal relationship among the enterprises concerned, such as the context of relations within an economic entity and not having restrictive effects outside the related enterprises'. Thus acts engaged in by related enterprises which are inappropriate to their organizational arrangements, and which result in the limitation of access or other restraints of competition outside the related enterprises, are covered where the related enterprises are in a position of market dominance. This suggests that intra-firm practices in general are subject to review under the Set. It is not clear how the line between legitimate and anti-competitive intra-firm practices should be drawn.

The Set provides a rudimentary international system of cooperation between states in the regulation of RBPs. In section C(i)(1) the

Set contemplates mutually reinforcing action at the national, regional and international levels to deal with RBPs, especially those that affect LDCs. The Set further contemplates intergovernmental collaboration at bilateral and multilateral levels, including exchanges of information on RBPs and the holding of multilateral consultations.[147] The Set envisages that states with greater experience in the operation of systems of RBP control should share that experience with, or otherwise render technical assistance to, other states wishing to develop or improve such systems.[148] However, the primacy of national laws is preserved, in that 'The provisions of the Set of principles and Rules should not be construed as justifying conduct by enterprises which is unlawful under applicable national or regional legislation.'[149] Thus the Set lays down a minimum definition of offences, leaving individual states free to expand this at the national level. It does not lay down a maximum system of control that is internationally acceptable.

On the other hand, the Set offers some guidance as to acceptable behaviour on the part of states when controlling RBPs. Thus section E, entitled 'Principles and Rules for States at National, Regional and Subregional Levels', includes requirements that states, 'in their control of restrictive business practices, should ensure treatment of enterprises that is fair, equitable, on the same basis to all enterprises, and in accordance with established procedures of law. The laws and regulations should be publicly and readily available.'[150] Furthermore, states should protect the confidentiality of sensitive business information received from enterprises on the basis of reasonable safeguards normally applicable in this field.[151]

The Set concludes with a section on international measures to be taken under the auspices of UNCTAD for the control of RBPs, and establishes an institutional structure for the development of the Set by means of an Intergovernmental Group of Experts acting as a Committee of UNCTAD. Section F, entitled 'International measures', envisages international collaboration aimed at achieving common approaches in national RBP policies,[152] annual communications to the Secretary General of UNCTAD on national and regional steps taken to implement the principles embodied in the Set,[153] an annual report by UNCTAD on developments in this field,[154] the use of UNCTAD as a forum for interstate consultations over RBP issues,[155] the continuation of work on a Model Law or Laws on RBPs,[156] and the implementation within or facilitation by UNCTAD and other relevant UN organizations of technical assistance, advisory and training programmes on RBPs, particularly for developing countries.[157] This is to be funded from the UN Development Programme and from individual country contributions.[158]

The Intergovernmental Working Group has the functions of: providing a forum for multilateral consultations, discussions and exchanges of views by states on the Set; undertaking studies and research on RBPs; inviting studies by other UN organizations in this field; studying matters arising under the Set and collecting and disseminating information on such matters; making appropriate reports and recommendations to states on matters within its competence, including the application and implementation of the Set; and, finally, submitting an annual report.[159] The Set makes clear, however, that 'neither the Intergovernmental Group nor its subsidiary organs shall act like a tribunal or otherwise pass judgment on the activities or conduct of individual Governments or of individual enterprises in connection with a specific business transaction'.[160] Furthermore, 'The Intergovernmental Group or its subsidiary organs should avoid becoming involved when enterprises to a specific business transaction are in dispute.'[161] Thus, the institutional machinery set up under the auspices of UNCTAD cannot act in an investigative or adjudicatory capacity. In this the Intergovernmental Group is unlike bodies such as the EC Commission's Competition Directorate, which enjoys the above-mentioned powers.

The Set is a voluntary code having the status of a non-binding UN General Assembly resolution. Thus is it hortatory in nature. However, it has considerable moral authority as it was adopted unanimously by the General Assembly.[162] Furthermore, according to UNCTAD, 'the Set has the same status in terms of international law as other resolutions of the General Assembly: in a litigation it can be cited as applicable law, in particular in the absence of domestic legislation dealing with the issues under discussion'.[163] Nevertheless, the subsequent history of the Set shows its limited impact on international action over RBPs. It is characterized by disagreements over the scope and development of the Set and by the limited funding of UNCTAD's activities in this area.

Regarding the first of these difficulties, at the first Review Conference, carried out five years after the adoption of the Set,[164] the participating states were unable to adopt an agreed text of proposals for further improvements and further development of the Set.[165] In particular, the developed free-market economy states and the Group of 77 could not resolve a fundamental disagreement over whether the Set covered RBPs affecting trade that were government inspired, such as export joint ventures or voluntary export restraints. The Group of 77 argued that these were nothing more than government imposed international cartels. The developed countries responded by pointing out that the Set did not extend to governmental or government inspired RBPs, citing section B(9) in support.[166] As a result several proposals for the strengthening of the Set were not adopted.

As regards limited funding, this has retarded the ability of UNCTAD to carry out effectively its task of offering technical assistance to LDCs in RBP regulation. To date a small number of regional seminars have taken place.[167] At the second Review Conference in 1990, the seventy-five participating countries resolved to provide the necessary expertise and resources for technical assistance activities.[168] However, in the context of a global recession it may be doubted whether substantial funding will be forthcoming. In the meantime the Intergovernmental Group of Experts has embarked on several studies and reports in the fields of M and A,[169] the means of state control of RBPs, the relationship between industrialization policies and RBP control, and RBPs in the food industry.[170] It has also continued its work on the compilation of a handbook on RBP laws,[171] and on the formulation of the Model Law.[172] It continues to meet on a regular basis.[173]

In all, the Set offers a rudimentary step towards the creation of a global antitrust authority. It lacks the legal standing and financial resources to grow into anything like an effective agency. Furthermore, its orientation towards the protection of LDC interests makes it incompatible with the dominant international trend towards a liberal international economic order, which would demand a global antitrust authority that concentrated on competition issues rather than on the redistribution of competitive equality. However, as was pointed out at the second Review Conference on the Set, in a world with fewer barriers to international trade and investment LDCs may be placed in a very vulnerable competitive position if some form of antitrust protection for infant industries and against unfairly restrictive technology licensing agreements were not forthcoming. This view was justified by analogy with the fact that the competition laws of many countries allow smaller firms a measure of protection against larger firms.[174] Therefore, an international system of RBP controls which includes special consideration for LDC interests might be defensible.

On a broader level, the limitations of national or regional responses to RBPs that were noted in the previous section of this chapter point to the need for greater internationalization of antitrust controls. Otherwise national regulation may become increasingly ineffective. Arguably, the antitrust problems posed by the globalization of markets could be dealt with through unilateral extraterritorial measures. However, as was seen in chapter 5, this does not represent a path towards effective regulation given the political costs involved. Thus, increasing international antitrust regulation may prove to be inevitable as long as an integrated global economy develops and a pro-competitive consensus prevails among states.[175]

3   Concluding Remarks

This chapter has outlined some of the major antitrust issues arising out of the internationalization of markets through the growth of MNEs and of international markets for corporate control. It has considered national, regional and international responses to those issues. The emphasis has been mainly on the practice of developed countries. These countries have the most experience with the problems of antitrust in international markets for two reasons. First, the developed countries form the core geographical areas in which the global economy is evolving and, secondly, they have the most advanced systems of antitrust regulation. By contrast few LDCs have such regulatory systems and experience the evolution of a global economy differently, being peripheral to the major centres of development. For these countries the principal competition problems revolve around their vulnerability on the international market for commercial technology. It is to these issues that we turn in the next chapter.

Notes

1   C. D. Wallace, *Legal Control of the Multinational Enterprise* (Martinus Nijhoff, 1983), p. 177.

2   However, certain jurisdictional issues arising in the context of the regulation of mergers and acquisitions remain to be considered. See text at notes 77–92 below.

3   For those unfamiliar with antitrust laws and enforcement procedures, useful comparative introductions can be found in the following articles: Grendell, 'The antitrust legislation of the United States, the European Economic Community, Germany and Japan', 29 ICLQ 64 (1980); Boyer, 'Form and substance: a comparison of antitrust regulation by consent decrees in the USA, Reports of the Monopolies and Mergers Commission in the UK, and Grants of Clearance by the European Commission', 32 ICLQ 904 (1983). For an analysis of UK and EC law and practice see R. Whish, *Competition Law*, 3rd edn (Butterworths, 1993); on EC law see D. G. Goyder, *EEC Competition Law*, 3rd edn (Oxford, 1998). On US law see E. Gellhorn and W. E. Kovacic, *Antitrust Law and Economics*, 4th edn (West Publishing Co., 1994) (referred to below as Gellhorn). Also useful are the US Department of Justice Antitrust Division, *Antitrust Enforcement Guidelines for International Operations* (1988). The Guidelines are not a restatement of US antitrust law, and should not be used as such, but they offer a guide to the risks of US enforcement action. Revised draft guidelines were issued jointly by the Department of Justice and the Federal

Trade Commission on 13 October 1994. The draft Guidelines were issued for a 60-day comment period and replace the 1988 Guidelines. See Trade Reg Rep. No. 338, part 2, pp. 37–67 (1994). See also Terry Calvini, 'Long arm of US regulations', *Financial Times*, 25 October 1994, p. 16. On Japanese Law see H. Oda, *Japanese Law* (Butterworths, 1992), chapter 16; M. Matsushita, *International Trade and Competition Law in Japan* (Oxford University Press, 1993). On German law see D. M. Raybould and A. Frith, *Law of Monopolies: Competition law and Practice in the USA, EEC, Germany and the UK* (Graham and Trotman, 1991), pp. 382–429. This chapter concentrates on the laws of developed market economy countries, especially US and EC law. Less developed countries have passed antitrust laws but their experience in this field is as yet limited. See further note 73 below.

4   See further F. M. Scherer and D. Ross, *Industrial Market Structure and Economic Performance*, 3rd edn (Houghton Mifflin, 1990), chapter 2.

5   See US, Sherman Act (26 Stat. 209 (1890) as amended), s. 1; article 85(1) EC Treaty; Japan, Anti-Monopoly Law 1947 (Law No. 54, 1947) article 2(6), article 3; Germany, Act against Restraints of Competition of 27 July 1957 (1957 BGB1, I 1081 as amended 1980) s. 1: Commercial Laws of Europe [1980] 2.85 [German text] 5.1 [English translation].

6   The 'rule of reason' standard is derived from US law. See further: *Continental TV Inc.* v *GTE Sylvania* 433 US 376 (1977); Whish (note 3 above), at pp. 206–11, 227–36. Under EC law the balancing of pro- and anti-competitive effects is done under the terms of article 85(3) EEC Treaty, which lays down criteria for determining whether an agreement or practice caught by article 85(1) can nevertheless be exempted from the legal invalidity that follows from a prohibition under article 85(1).

7   See e.g. article 86 EC Treaty; Sherman Act (note 5 above), s. 2, Clayton Act (38 Stat. 730 (1914); 15 USCA ss 12–27), ss 2–4; Japan, Anti-Monopoly Act 1947 (note 5 above), article 3; Germany, Act against Restraints of Competition (note 5 above), s. 22(1).

8   This is known as 'parallel pricing behaviour'. See further Whish (note 3 above), at pp. 197–201 and *Re Wood Pulp Cartel: A. Ahlstrom OY and Others* v *EC Commission* [1993] 4 CMLR 407 (ECJ).

9   See Gellhorn (note 3 above), at pp. 159–62.

10   See further Whish (note 3 above), at pp. 666–8.

11   Whish, ibid., at pp. 668–71; Scherer and Ross (note 4 above), at pp. 167–74.

12   See: US Clayton Act (note 7 above), s. 7; UK, Fair Trading Act 1973 (1973 Chapter 41) Part V Mergers; EC Commission Regulation 4064/89 OJ [1989] L 395/1 as corrected OJ [1990] L 257/13; Japan, Anti-Monopoly Law 1947 (note 5 above), article 15(1); Germany, Act against Restraints of Competition (note 5 above), ss 23, 24.

13   See chapter 2.

14   See J. H. Dunning, *Multinational Enterprises and the Global Economy* (Addison Wesley, 1992), at pp. 429–30.

15   See R. Caves, *Multinational Enterprise and Economic Analysis* (Cambridge University Press, 2nd edn, 1996), at pp. 83–4.

16 Dunning (note 14 above), at p. 431.

17 See *Copperweld Corporation* v *Independence Tube Corp.* 467 US 752 (1984): US Supreme Court overruled the 'intra-enterprise conspiracy' doctrine and held that a parent and its wholly owned subsidiary cannot be 'conspiring entities' under the Sherman Act. The 'intra-enterprise conspiracy' doctrine has not been adopted by the European Court of Justice. Thus article 85 of the EC Treaty cannot apply to an agreement between a parent and subsidiary: *Béguelin Import* v *GL Import Export* Case 22/71 [1971] ECR 949; [1972] CMLR 81. However, the economic unity between parent and subsidiary will extend the operation of EC competition law to the parent even if it is not present in the EC as a result of the conduct of its subsidiaries in the Community: see chapter 5 at pp. 137–8.

18 See *Corinne Bodson* v *Pompes Funèbres des Régions Libérées* SA [1989] 4 CMLR 984 (ECJ).

19 See chapter 2 at pp. 22–5.

20 Caves (note 15 above), at p. 105. See further J. A. Rahl, 'International cartels and their regulation' in O. Schachter and R. Hellawell (eds), *Competition in International Business: Law and Policy on Restrictive Practices* (Columbia University Press, 1981), p. 240.

21 See Haight, 'The restrictive business practices clause in United States treaties: an antitrust tranquillizer for international trade' 70 Yale LJ 240 at pp. 240–241 (1960).

22 See chapter 5 at pp. 129–31.

23 See note 5 above.

24 Caves (note 15 above), at pp. 106–7.

25 See e.g. the EC cases: *ICI* v *EC Commission* [1972] ECR 619; [1972] CMLR 557; *Suiker Unie* v *EC Commission (Sugar Cartel)* [1975] ECR 1663; [1976] 1 CMLR 295; *Compagnie Royale Asturienne des Mines SA and Rheinzink Gmbh* v *EC Commission* [1984] ECR 1679; [1985] 1 CMLR 688; *Zinc Producer Group* OJ [1984] L 220/27; [1985] 2 CMLR 108; *Re Polypropylene Cartel: SA Hercules NV* v *EC Commission* [1992] 4 CMLR 84 (CFI); *Wood Pulp* OJ [1985] L 85/1; [1985] 3 CMLR 474 overturned on appeal: *Re Wood Pulp Cartel: A. Ahlstrom OY and Others* v *EC Commission* [1993] 4 CMLR 407.

26 Ibid., previous note.

27 *Theatre Enterprises Inc.* v *Paramount Film Distributing Corp.* 346 US 537 (1954); see also Gellhorn (note 3 above), chapter 7.

28 On 'rule of reason' see note 6 above.

29 See US Department of Justice 1988 (note 3 above), at pp. 60–1, *GTE Sylvania* (note 6 above); EC Commission Regulation 1983/83 OJ [1983] L 173/1; EC Commission Regulation 1984/83 OJ [1983] L 173/5; *Stergios Delimitis* v *Henninger Brau AG* [1992] 5 CMLR 210 (ECJ). On EEC law see further: V. Korah and W. Rothnie, *Exclusive Distribution and the EEC Competition Rules*, 2nd edn (Sweet & Maxwell, 1992).

30 See on US law *Dr Miles Medical Co.* v *John D. Park and Sons Co.* 220 US 373 (1911); *GTE Sylvania* (note 6 above), 433 US 51 n. 18. On EC law see Korah and Rothnie, ibid., pp. 270–5.

31   See: *Consten and Grundig* v *EC Commission* [1966] ECR 299; [1966] CMLR 418; *LTM* v *Maschinenbau Ulm* [1966] ECR 235; [1966] CMLR 357; *Centrafarm* v *Sterling* [1974] ECR 1147; [1974] 2 CMLR 480; *Centrafarm* v *Winthrop* [1974] ECR 1183; [1974] 2 CMLR 480; *Nungesser* v *EC Commission (Maize Seeds)* [1982] ECR 2015; [1983] 1 CMLR 278.

32   On which see chapter 3 at pp. 69–70.

33   Executive Office Fair Trading Commission, *The Antimonopoly Act Guidelines Concerning Distribution Systems and Business Practices* (11 July 1991).

34   See Oda (note 3 above), at pp. 359–61. See further *Joint Report of the US–Japan Working Group on the Structural Impediments Initiative* (28 June 1990); P. Sheard *The Economics of Japanese Corporate Organisation and the 'Structural Impediments' Debate: a Critical Review* (Australia–Japan Research Centre, Australian National University, Canberra, Pacific Economic Paper No. 205, March 1992).

35   'Japan's corporate groups are accused of obstruction', *Financial Times*, 30 June 1993, p. 8.

36   See US Department of Justice Press Release 92–117, 3 April 1992. The full text of the policy statement is reproduced in the *Financial Times*, 30 April 1992, p. 18. For a discussion of the legal problems associated with the policy statement see Coppel, 'A question of keiretsu: extending the long arm of US anti-trust', [1992] 5 ECLR 192. The policy of the 1992 statement has been reasserted in the 1994 draft guidelines (note 3 above), s. 3.133, at p. 51.

37   See Brodley, 'Joint ventures and antitrust policy', 95 Harv. LR. 1521 at 1530–1534 (1982).

38   See e.g. *US* v *ICI* 100 F. Supp. 504 (SDNY) mod. 105 F. Supp. 215 (SDNY 1951); *US* v *Minnesota Mining and Manufacturing Co.* 92 F. Supp 947 (D. Mass 1950) mod. 96 F. Supp 356 (D. Mass 1951).

39   See Caves (note 15 above), at pp. 107–8, discussing the oil and aluminium industries. Such anti-competitive effects can be offset by the entry of new firms. However, this may be difficult in industries such as oil where there exist high levels of vertical integration. New entrants may simply be absorbed by allowing them to join existing joint ventures.

40   See e.g. *Yamaha Motor Co.* v *FTC* 657 F. 2d. 971 (8th Cir. 1981) cert. den. 50 USLW 3799 (US April 4, 1982): discussed Brodley (note 37 above), at pp. 1576–8.

41   See e.g. the US case *US* v *Penn Ohlin Chemical Co.* 378 US 158 (1964) criticized by Gellhorn (note 3 above), at pp. 390–1. For criticism of the potential competition theory as applied by the EC Commission see: V. Korah, *An Introductory Guide to EEC Competition Law and Practice*, 6th edn (Hart Publishing, 1997), chapter 11; Pathak, 'The EC Commission's approach to joint ventures: a policy of contradictions', [1991] 5 ECLR 171, discussing the EC Commission cases of *Re Vacuum Interrupters (No. 1)* OJ [1977] L 48/32, [1977] 1 CMLR D67, *Re Vacuum Interrupters (No. 2)* [1981] 2 CMLR 217, *Re Optical Fibres* OJ [1986] L 236/30, *Mitchell Cotts/Sofiltra* OJ [1987] L 41/31, [1988] 4 CMLR 111. See now for a more sympathetic view of the pro-competitive effects of joint ventures: *Re ODIN* [1991] 4 CMLR 832, *Re ECR 900* [1992] 4 CMLR 54, where the EC Commission cleared each joint venture under article 85(1); but see *BBC*

Brown Boveri/NGK [1989] 4 CMLR 610, *Eirepage* OJ [1992] L 306/22, [1993] 4 CMLR 64, where the EC Commission held each joint venture to be caught by article 85(1), but gave individual exemption under article 85(3).

42 See e.g. *Siemens/Fanuc* [1988] 4 CMLR 945 (EC Commission), where a reciprocal exclusive distribution agreement for numerical controls (NCs) between the leading European and Japanese producers was found to have violated article 85(1) EEC on the ground *inter alia* that it divided world markets by denying European customers access to supplies from Japan, where the Japanese partner was selling its NCs at prices some 34 per cent below those charged in Europe by its exclusive distributor. However, this case can be explained by the market dominance of the parties, especially of the Japanese partner, which is the global leader in NC technology. In a less concentrated market such a horizontal joint selling arrangement might have pro-competitive effects: see text at note 45 below.

43 Such an airliner is beyond the economic capabilities of any of the existing manufacturers working alone, but may be feasible should a global joint venture involving a number of the major manufacturers be established. This might create a monopoly at the top end of the airliner market: see 'Airbus hits crosswinds', *Financial Times*, 6 January 1993, p. 13.

44 See e.g. EC Commission Regulation 417/85 OJ [1985] L 53/1 as amended by Commission Regulation 151/93 in [1993] 4 CMLR 155. A joint venture arrangement may be used to effect a restructuring between firms in an industry suffering from overcapacity see: *Re Enichem and ICI* [1989] 4 CMLR 54.

45 See US Department of Justice Guidelines (1988, note 3 above), at pp. 57–9. Detailed discussion of joint ventures is absent from the 1994 draft guidelines.

46 Ibid., at p. 15.

47 Ibid. The analysis is described in detail at pp. 16–22 of the 1988 Guidelines. As noted above, the 1994 draft Guidelines offer no detailed guidance on this issue, which is regrettable as it may cause uncertainty.

48 See references in note 41 above.

49 Commission Regulation 418/85 OJ [1985] L 53/5 as amended by Commission Regulation 151/93 OJ [1993] L 21/8; see text in [1993] 4 CMLR 163.

50 Ibid., articles 2(e), 3(3a) and 4(fa–fc) as amended.

51 Ibid., article 3(2).

52 See Commission Regulation 417/85 as amended (note 44 above).

53 Commission Regulation 2349/84 OJ [1984] L 219/15 as amended by Commission Regulation 151/93 article 5(2), text in [1993] 4 CMLR 177; Commission Regulation 556/89 OJ [1989] L 61/1 as amended by Commission Regulation 151/93 article 5(2), text in [1993] 4 CMLR 195. See also draft Commission Regulation of 30 June 1994 on technology transfer agreements OJ [1994] C 178/3, article 5. The final version of this draft Regulation will replace Regulation 2349/84, and Regulation 556/89 once it is adopted. This occurred in 1996; see Regulation 240/96 OJ [1996] L 31/2.

54 See further EC Commission Notice concerning the assessment of coopera-

tive joint ventures pursuant to article 85 of the EC Treaty: OJ [1993] C 43/ 2. For the background to the EC Commission's thinking see Draft Co-operative Joint Ventures (Antitrust) Guidelines: [1992] 4 CMLR 504 and comment thereon by Fine [1992] 2 ECLR 51.

55 The examples below are taken from EC case-law, which highlights the transnational nature of certain abuses of dominant position. US case-law has tended to concentrate on similar abuses effected by dominant domestic firms: see Gellhorn (note 3 above), chapter 4; US Department of Justice Guidelines (1988, note 3 above), at pp. 9–10.

56 See UK Monopolies and Mergers Commission, *Chlordiazepoxide and Diazepam* (HMSO, 1973) and *Bundeskartellamt G. Beschlussabteilung* 36-432190-T-37/73, both summarized in Greenhill and Herbolzheimer, 'International transfer pricing: the restrictive business practices approach', 14 JWTL 232 (1980). Recently, Brazil has accused pharmaceutical companies of imposing abusive price increases on 150 products. This is blamed on the oligopolistic nature of the market. For example, seven MNEs control 87 per cent of the antibiotics market: 'Brazil's drug companies face anti-trust action', *Financial Times*, 27 January 1993, p. 6.

57 *The Community* v *International Business Machines Corporation* [1984] 3 CMLR 147.

58 See *Commercial Solvents* v *EC Commission* [1974] ECR 223; [1974] 1 CMLR 309.

59 [1978] ECR 207; [1978] 1 CMLR 429.

60 *United Brands*, ibid.

61 *Hoffmann-La Roche & Co. AG* v *EC Commission* [1979] ECR 461; [1979] 3 CMLR 211.

62 *Nederlandsche Banden-Industrie Michelin NV* v *EC Commission* [1983] ECR 3461; [1985] 1 CMLR 282.

63 *Hilti AG* v *EC Commission* [1992] 4 CMLR 16 (CFI); appeal dismissed, Case C-53/92 P, *Hilti* v *Commission*, interveners, Bauco (UK) Ltd and Profix Distribution Ltd (ECJ, 2 March 1994) [1994] 4 CMLR 614.

64 *ECS/AKZO* OJ [1985] L 374/1; [1986] 3 CMLR 273 (EC Commission) C-62/86 *AKZO Chemie BV* v *EC Commission* [1993] 5 CMLR 215 (ECJ).

65 See Whish (note 3 above), at pp. 249–59 for EC approach. For US approach see Gellhorn (note 3 above), at pp. 93–115.

66 See *United Brands* (note 59 above), at para. 38; *Hoffmann-La Roche* (note 61 above), at para. 38.

67 Usually, the larger the share the more likely there is to be dominance. However, even very large shares do not inevitably point to dominance. In *Hoffmann-La Roche* (note 61 above) the ECJ held that a very large share is evidence of a dominant position in the absence of exceptional circumstances and where it is held for some time (at para. 41). In *United Brands* (note 59 above) the ECJ held that a market share of 40–45 per cent was enough to show the firm's dominance in the circumstances of the case. For criticism of this analysis see: Whish (note 3 above), at p. 262; Valgiurata 'Price discrimination under article 86 EEC: the United Brands Case', 31 ICLQ 36 (1982). According to the US Department of Justice Guidelines (1988, note 3 above), the Department will not, in general, be concerned

with unilateral conduct if a firm has a market share of less than 35 per cent (p. 9, n. 52). This statement should be read in the light of section 2 of the 1992 Department of Justice Horizontal Merger Guidelines as applicable to the unilateral effects of mergers: 4 Trade Reg. Rep. (CCH) s. 13,104. See further Leddy, 'The 1992 US Horizontal Merger Guidelines and some comparisons with EC enforcement policy' [1993] 1 ECLR 15 at p. 19; Gellhorn (note 3 above), at pp. 109–12, 394–9.

68 See Whish (note 3 above), at pp. 263–8, on EC approach; Gellhorn (note 3 above), at pp. 113–20, on US approach.

69 See e.g. *Hilti AG* v *EC Commission* (note 63 above), where the defendant company argued, unsuccessfully, that it had prohibited the use of nails manufactured by competing firms in its nail guns to protect health and safety.

70 475 US 574 (1986).

71 See further *Eastman Kodak Co.* v *Image Technical Services Inc.* 112 S. Ct 2072 (1992); 62 ATRR 780 (1992) (US Sup. Ct).

72 See generally J. W. Rowley QC and D. I. Baker, *International Mergers – the Antitrust Process* (Sweet & Maxwell, 2nd edn, 1996), covering the laws of the EC, Germany, UK, France, Spain, Ireland, USA, Canada, Australia, Japan.

73 M and A activity in Southern countries has been more restricted, though some activity did occur during the 1980s in Latin America and Far Eastern Asia. See further UNCTAD Secretariat Report, 'Concentration of market power through mergers, take-overs, joint ventures and other acquisitions of control and its effects on international markets, in particular the markets of developing countries' (UN Doc. TD/B/RBP/80, 22 August 1991). Because of the spread of international M and A activity this section will concentrate on developed countries' laws. However, a number of developing countries from all regions have adopted competition laws which may be applied to M and A activities. The laws of Brazil, India, Pakistan, Gabon, Kenya and Sri Lanka are briefly discussed in the UNCTAD Report at paras 114–20 and Korea's law is discussed in the annex thereto. Brazil's latest competition law (Act No. 8,158 of January 1991 on Provisions for the Protection of Competition and Other Measures) can be found in UNCTAD Doc. TD/B/RBP/82, 14 August 1991. This law was replaced by Law 8, 884/94. UNCTAD is currently compiling a handbook on restrictive business practices legislation which should bring together the main competition laws of the world, including those of LDCs. The 1991 Report was recently revised: see UN Doc. TD/RBP/80, Rev. 2.

74 See UNCTC, *The Process of Transnationalization and Transnational Mergers* (UN Doc. ST/CTC/SER. A/8, 1989), at pp. 24–5. This study contains valuable quantitative information on international merger activity during the 1980s in the USA, Western European countries and Japan. See also M. Bishop and J. Kay, *European Mergers and Merger Policy* (Oxford University Press, 1993).

75 See Pinto, 'The internationalization of the hostile takeover market: its implications for choice of law in corporate and securities law', 16 Brooklyn J. Int'l L. 55 at 61–4 (1990).

76 See further 'International mergers and acquisitions', *Financial Times Survey*, 19 October 1992, p. 27.
77 See Wallace (note 1 above), at pp. 186–201 (and summaries of cases cited therein), on which this paragraph draws heavily. See further OECD, *Merger Cases in the Real World: a Study of Merger Control Procedures* (OECD, 1994).
78 But see US practice in this field: US Antitrust Enforcement Guidelines (1988, note 3 above), at pp. 45–6; a merger between two foreign firms may create reporting requirements under the Hart–Scott–Rodino Antitrust Improvements Act 1976 (15 USC s. 18a) although certain international transactions may be exempt (see 16 CFR ss 801.1(e), 801.1(k), 802.50–802.52). The draft guidelines of 1994 assert jurisdiction over the merger of two foreign companies, neither of which has a subsidiary or productive assets in the USA, but which make sales into the US market: draft guidelines 1994 (note 3 above), s. 3.12 at p. 48. See also, on Hart–Scott–Rodine exemptions, ibid., s. 4.22 at pp. 60–1.
79 See *Continental Can* v *EC Commission* [1973] ECR 215; [1973] CMLR 199.
80 Cm 587 (1989).
81 See *Consolidated Gold Fields plc* v *Minorco* 871 F. 2d 252 (2d Cir.) cert. dismissed. 110 S. Ct 29 (1989).
82 See e.g. *Guest Keen and Nettlefolds Limited, Sachs AG and the Brothers Sachs* v *Bundeskartellamt* [1978] 1 CMLR 66.
83 Council Regulation 4064/89 OJ [1989] L 395/1 as amended OJ [1997] L 180/1. For full analysis see: J. Cook and C. Kerse, *EEC Merger Control Regulation 4064/89* (Sweet & Maxwell, 2nd ed, 1996); C. Jones and E. Gonzalez-Diaz, *The EEC Merger Regulation* (Sweet & Maxwell, 1992); T. Antony Downes and J. Ellison, *The Legal Control of Mergers in the European Communities* (Blackstone Press, 1991).
84 A 'concentration' arises, by article 3(1) of Regulation 4064/89, where: '(a) two or more previously independent undertakings merge or (b) one or more persons already controlling at least one undertaking or – one or more undertakings acquire, whether by purchase of securities or assets, by contract or by any other means, direct or indirect control of the whole or parts of one or more other undertakings.'
85 Ibid., article 1(1).
86 Ibid., article 1(2).
87 Ibid., article 5(3).
88 By article 21 of Regulation 4064/89: '1. Subject to review by the Court of Justice, the Commission shall have sole competence to take decisions provided for in this Regulation. 2. No Member State shall apply its national legislation on competition to any concentration that has a Community dimension'. This provision seeks to establish a 'one stop shop' in the regulation of EC wide mergers. For possible inroads into this principle see Whish (note 3 above), at pp. 724–7, Downes and Ellison (note 83 above), chapter 7 and article 9, Regulation 4064/89, discussed note 91 below.

89   Case No. IV/M. 213 – Hong Kong and Shanghai Bank/Midland: Prior notification of a concentration: OJ [1992] C 113/11; ibid. Non-opposition to a notified concentration: OJ [1992] C 157/8.

90   Whish (note 3 above), at p. 715. 'Lloyds gives up battle to acquire Midland Bank', *Financial Times* Weekend, 6/7 June 1992, p. 1.

91   See, however, article 9 of Regulation 4064/89, which empowers the EC Commission to allow Member State authorities to take action in a case where a notified concentration threatens to create or to strengthen a dominant position on a distinct market in that Member State. So far only one reference has been made under this power: see: Case IV/M. 180 *Steetly plc/Tarmac* 12 February 1992 [1992] 2 ECLR R-54.

92   Regulation 1310/97 OJ [1997] L 180/1 Article 1(1).

93   See Regulation 4064/89 (note 83 above), article 2 and *Continental Can* v *EC Commission* (note 79 above), at para. 26, *BAT & Reynolds* v *EC Commission* [1987] ECR 4487, [1988] 4 CMLR 24 at paras 36–40. US, Merger Guidelines 1992 (note 67 above), s. 0.1; Japan, Anti-Monopoly Law (note 5 above), article 10(1) and article 9 (prohibition on holding companies); Germany, Law against Restraint of Competition (note 5 above), s. 24(2).

94   The Herfindahl–Hirschman Index (HHI) distinguishes between unconcentrated markets (where the HHI is under 1,000), moderately concentrated markets (where it is between 1,000 and 1,800) and highly concentrated markets (HHI above 1,800). In highly concentrated markets an increase of more than 100 raises a presumption that the merger is anti-competitive, and the merger will be declared illegal in the absence of evidence showing that anti-competitive effects are unlikely. In moderately concentrated markets, intervention may occur where the post-merger HHI exceeds 1,800 but this is unlikely if the concentration does not exceed 1,800 by at least 50 points: US Merger Guidelines 1992, s. 1.

95   See US Merger Guidelines 1992 (note 67 above), ss 2, 3.

96   See *Aérospatiale and Alenia/De Havilland* OJ [1991] L 334/42; [1992] 4 CMLR M2. This was the first case in which the EC Commission blocked a proposed merger under article 2(3) of regulation 4064/89. See further text at notes 100–4 below.

97   See US Merger Guidelines (note 67 above), s. 2, 'Co-ordinated interaction'; *Nestlé/Perrier* (EC Commission) OJ [1992] L 356/1; [1993] 4 CMLR M17 on appeal Case T-12/93 *Vittel and others* v *EC Commission*, note in New Cases [1993] 4 CMLR 398.

98   See Regulation 4064/89 (note 83 above), article 2(1)(b). US Merger Guidelines 1992 (note 67 above), s. 4.

99   Caves (note 15 above), at p. 100. Emphasis in original.

100 Note 96 above. See Hawkes, 'The EC Merger Control Regulation: not an industrial policy instrument: the De Havilland decision', [1992] 1 ECLR 34.

101 According to the Commission, the new entity's share of the 40–59 seat aircraft market would be about 64 per cent of the world market and 72 per

cent of the EC market, and in the 60 plus seat market the world share would be 76 per cent and the EC share 74 per cent.

102 [1992] 4 CMLR M2 at M35; OJ [1991] C 314/7.
103 Quoted in 'Brussels merger policy attacked', *Financial Times*, 8 October 1991, p. 22.
104 See 'Competition stirs the EC', *Financial Times*, 8 October 1991, p. 20.
105 UNCTC (note 74 above), at p. 25.
106 'Young sets stage for Suchard counter-bid in battle over Rowntree', *Financial Times*, 26 May 1988, p. 1.
107 'Labour widens the takeover debate', *Financial Times*, 28 May 1988, p. 5.
108 House of Commons written answer by the Secretary of State for Trade and Industry (5 July 1984), reproduced in annex 2 of the Office of Fair Trading guide *Mergers* (HMSO, 1987, current edition 1991, available on request from the OFT). The Secretary of State's statement is not reproduced in the 1991 edition of the OFT guide but is referred to in para. 2.7. See also Department of Trade and Industry *Mergers Policy* (1988).
109 The 'Tebbit doctrine' was reaffirmed by the Secretary of State at the time of writing, Mr Michael Heseltine, in a Written Parliamentary Answer: see *Hansard*, Wednesday 13 May 1992 Col. 146 and 'Heseltine reaffirms mergers policy', *Financial Times*, 14 May 1992, p. 20. The new Labour government has not initiated any significant shift away from this position. However, the forthcoming Competition Act will bring UK law closer to EC principles.
110 For a full analysis of MMC decisions in this area see: Whish (note 3 above), at pp. 692–700; Raybould and Firth (note 3 above), at pp. 493–511. By s. 84 of the Fair Trading Act 1973, in considering whether a merger operates or may operate against the public interest, the Commission shall take into account, 'all matters which appear to them in the particular circumstances to be relevant and, among other things, shall have regard to the desirability – (a) of maintaining and promoting effective competition between persons supplying goods and services in the United Kingdom; (b) of promoting the interests of consumers, purchasers and other users of goods and services in the United Kingdom in respect of the prices charged for them and in respect of their quality and the variety of goods and services supplied; (c) of promoting, through competition, the reduction of costs and the development and use of new techniques and new products, and of facilitating the entry of new competitors into existing markets; (d) of maintaining and promoting the balanced distribution of industry and employment in the United Kingdom; (e) of maintaining and promoting competitive activity in markets outside the United Kingdom on the part of producers of goods, and of suppliers of goods and services, in the United Kingdom.'
111 Cmnd 9892 (1986). See also *Weidmann/Whiteley*, Cmnd 6208 (1975).
112 See s. 84 Fair Trading Act 1973 (note 110 above).
113 See e.g. *Enersch/Davey International*, Cmnd 8360 (1981). In this case the MMC also felt that the lengthening of the chain of management command that would result from the merger was detrimental to

Davey's ability to make quick decisions about competitive overseas project bids.

114   Cmnd 8472 (1982), para. 12.39, at p. 92. See further paras 12.20–12.29. The Commission's thinking appears to have been influenced by the belief that the Royal Bank of Scotland was well managed and did not need more capital. Otherwise it might have concluded that the takeover was consistent with the public interest: see para. 12.40. See also the Note of Dissent by Mr R. G. Smethurst, at pp. 94–7, who disagreed that the transfer of control to the Hong Kong and Shanghai Bank would be detrimental to the public interest in the way outlined by the majority.

115   DTI Press Notice, 26 July 1990; OFT Guide, *Mergers* (1991), para. 3.17.

116   The five references were: *Crédit Lyonnais SA/Woodchester Investments plc* Cm 1404 23 January 1991; *Silgos SA/Signet Ltd*, Cm 1450 26 February 1991 (Silgos is a subsidiary of Crédit Lyonnais); *Société Nationale Elf Aquitaine/Amoco Corporation* Cm 1521 3 May 1991; *British Aerospace plc/Thomson-CSF SA* Cm 1416 30 January 1991; *Kemira Oy/ICI* Cm 1406 23 January 1991. Only the last was objected to by the MMC: *Annual Report of the Director General of Fair Trading, 1991* (HMSO, 1992). A bid by Allied Irish Banks for TSB's Northern Ireland network was also cleared but this is not reported in the Director General's Annual Report: see 'Lilley clears three acquisitions by foreign groups', *Financial Times*, 31 May 1991, p. 7.

117   'UK gives way on foreign takeover bids', *Financial Times*, 31 October 1991, p. 2.

118   The bid by Trafalgar Holdings Ltd for Mineba in 1985 was subjected to review on this ground as Mineba supplied aircraft parts and flight instruments to the Japanese military. See Corcoran, 'Foreign investment and corporate control in Japan: T. Boone Pickens and acquiring control through share ownership', 22 Law & Pol. Int'l Bus. 333 at 348–9 (1991). For Japanese law on foreign investment see chapter 6 above at p. 176.

119   Cm 477 (1988).

120   Ibid., para. 8.9.

121   Cm 676 (1989).

122   Ibid., para. 6.85 and appendix 6.1.

123   *Havana Charter for an International Trade Organisation*, March 24, 1948, US Dept of State Pub. No. 3206, Commercial Policy Series 114 (1948) cited in Haight (note 21 above), at p. 241. See further: Knorr, 'The problem of international cartels and intergovernmental commodity agreements', 55 Yale LJ. 1097 (1946); Lockwood and Schmeisser, 'Restrictive business practices in international trade', 11 *Law and Contemporary Problems* 663 (1946).

124   See J. Davidow, 'The seeking of a world competition code: quixotic quest?', in O. Schachter and R. Hellawell (eds), *Competition in International Business: Law and Policy on Restrictive Practices* (Columbia University Press, 1981), at p. 362.

125   See further chapter 16 at p. 574.

126   See Davidow (note 124 above), at pp. 363–4.

127   See further Haight (note 21 above).

128   OECD, *Restrictive Business Practices of Multinational Enterprises* (1977).
129   See Brusick, 'UN control of restrictive business practices', 17 JWTL 337
      at pp. 340–2 (1983), on which this paragraph is based. See also: Greenhill,
      'UNCTAD: control of restrictive business practices', 12 JWTL 76 (1978);
      Brewer, 'International regulation of restrictive business practices' 16
      JWTL 108 (1982); Davidow (note 124 above), pp. 365ff.
130   UNCTAD Doc. TD/RBP/CONF/10 Annex: 19 ILM 813 (1980); UN
      Doc. A/C 2/35/6 of 23 October 1980 Annex; adopted by UN GA Res. 35/
      63, 5 December 1980.
131   See J. Robinson, *Multinationals and Political Control* (Gower, 1983), p.
      177.
132   Set: section A(1)–(4).
133   Ibid., section A(5).
134   For background references to UNCTAD documents that originally elabo-
      rated this policy see Brewer (note 129 above), at p. 109, n. 7; Thompson,
      'UNCTAD: model law on restrictive business practices', 14 JWTL 444
      (1980). For a recent revised draft of the Model Law with commentary see
      UNCTAD Secretariat, 'Revised draft of possible elements for article of a
      model law or laws and commentaries on the elements' (UNCTAD Doc.
      TD/B/RBP/81, 12 August 1991).
135   Set s. C(ii)(6). See also Davidow (note 124 above), at p. 375.
136   See further Brusick (note 129 above), at pp. 343–4.
137   See chapter 1.
138   The Set defines restrictive business practices in s. B(i)(1) as 'acts or
      behaviour of enterprises which, through an abuse or acquisition and abuse
      of a dominant position of market power, limit access to markets or other-
      wise unduly restrain competition, having or being likely to have adverse
      effects on international trade, particularly that of developing countries,
      and on the economic development of these countries, or which through
      formal, informal, written or unwritten agreements or arrangements among
      enterprises, have the same impact.' According to Davidow (note 124
      above), at pp. 373–4, this provision does not define any offence as
      this is done in other provisions (see below). In his view, the definition
      should be read as stating that an offence exists when a practice abuses a
      dominant position in the ways listed and such a practice has an adverse
      effect on trade or development. It does not, in his opinion, make the
      adverse effect on developing countries the sole test of a RBP. In s. B(ii)(9)
      the Set makes clear that it does not apply to 'intergovernmental agree-
      ments, nor to restrictive business practices directly caused by such agree-
      ments'. Thus intergovernmental commodity cartels like OPEC are not
      covered.
139   Section D(1).
140   Section D(2).
141   On the 'economic entity' doctrine see text at notes 16–18 above.
142   Davidow (note 124 above), at p. 380.
143   See further the *Bodson* case cited in note 18 above.
144   Brusick (note 129 above), at p. 345.
145   See OECD, *The OECD Declaration and Decisions on International Invest-*

ment and Multinational Enterprises 1991 Review (1992), Competition
Guideline 1(e) at p. 106; Davidow (note 124 above), at p. 385.

146 See e.g. *SA CNL-Sucal NV* v *Hag GF AG (Hag No. 2)* [1990] 3 CMLR
571 (ECJ); *Consten* v *Grundig* [1966] ECR 299; [1966] CMLR 418.

147 The Set (note 130 above), s. C(i)(2)–(4).

148 Ibid., s. E(8).

149 Ibid., s. C(i)(5).

150 Ibid., s. E(3).

151 Ibid., s. E(5).

152 Ibid., s. F(1).

153 Ibid., s. F(2).

154 Ibid., s. F(3).

155 Ibid., s. F(4).

156 Ibid., s. F(5) and see text at note 134 above.

157 Ibid., s. F(6).

158 Ibid., s. F(7).

159 Ibid., s. G(ii)(3).

160 Ibid., s. G(ii)(4).

161 Ibid.

162 See Brusick (note 129 above), at p. 342.

163 'Restrictive business practices (RBPS) at the crossroads of the 1990s',
UNCTAD Bulletin, No. 250, February 1989, p. 10 at p. 12.

164 In accordance with the terms of Set s. G(iii)(6). The Review Conference
took place at Geneva from 4 to 15 November 1985.

165 See summary in 'United Nations Review Conference on Restrictive Business Practices fails to reach agreement', UNCTAD Bulletin, No. 217,
December 1985.

166 See note 163 above at pp. 12–13.

167 The first was in Africa in 1986. See 'Technical assistance on restrictive
business practices', UNCTAD Bulletin, No. 226, November 1986, p. 10.
This was followed by an Asian seminar in 1987: UNCTAD Bulletin, No.
236, October 1987, p. 16. Other seminars are reported to have taken place
in Latin America and in French-speaking Africa organised by France, and
one seminar for LDCs was organized by Germany: UNCTAD Bulletin
(note 163 above), at p. 13.

168 See UNCTAD Bulletin, No. 7 January–February 1991, p. 14. The second
Review Conference took place in Geneva between 26 November and 7
December 1990: see further *Report of the Second United Nations Conference
to Review all Aspects of the Multilaterally Agreed Equitable Principles and Rules
for the Control of Restrictive Business Practices* (UNCTAD Doc. TD/RBP/
CONF. 3/9), summary of issues discussed in UNCTAD Bulletin, No. 6,
November–December 1990, p. 7.

169 See note 73 above.

170 UNCTAD Bulletin, No. 238, December 1987, p. 9.

171 See further note 73 above.

172 See note 134 above.

173 See further *Report of the Intergovernmental Group of Experts on Restrictive
Business Practices on Its Eleventh Session* (23–27 November 1992):

UNCTAD Doc. TD/B/RBP/92. The most recent annual review of competition policy was undertaken by the UNCTAD Intergovernmental Group of Experts on RBPs on 18–22 October 1993: Notes, UNCTAD Bulletin, No. 23, November–December 1993, p. 13.

174   See UNCTAD Bulletin, No. 6, November–December 1990, at p. 8.

175   See further, on the issue of MNEs, market structure and national, regional and multilateral competition policy: UNCTAD *World Investment Report 1997* (United Nations, New York and Geneva, 1997) Part Two.

12

Technology Transfer

This chapter aims to describe and analyse the course of the conflict between the regulatory models of the developed and less developed countries (LDCs) that has been taking place over the past two decades in the field of technology transfer. It will begin by describing the nature of technology transfer and how the market for technology shapes the interests of technology-exporting states and technology-importing states. Secondly, it will describe the process of technology transfer as it is conducted by MNEs, and the principal legal issues that this raises. Thirdly, the main models of technology transfer regulation as espoused by the developed technology-exporting and importing states, and the less developed, primarily technology-importing, states will be described and contrasted. Fourthly, the course of negotiations concerning the draft International Code of Conduct for Technology Transfer (the TOT Code) will be considered. The chapter will end with an assessment of the current trends in technology transfer regulation.

1 The Nature of Technology Transfer

1.1 'Technology' and 'Technology Transfer'

'Technology' can be defined in various ways.[1] The present concern is to identify, for legal purposes, a definition that encompasses all forms of commercially usable knowledge, whether patented or unpatented, that can form the subject matter of a transfer transaction. The Draft TOT Code suggests, in its definition of 'technology transfer', that 'technology' should be described as 'systematic knowledge for the manufacture of a product, for the application of a process or for the rendering of a service and does not extend to the transactions involving the mere sale or lease of goods'.[2] This is not particularly enlightening, save for the fact that it clearly excludes goods that are sold or hired from the ambit of 'technology'. Thus it is the knowledge that goes into the creation and provision of the product or service that is of importance.

Such knowledge should be seen as encompassing both the technical knowledge on which the end product is based and the organizational capacity to convert the relevant productive inputs into the finished item or service, as the case may be. Thus, as Santikarn[3] points out, 'technology' includes not only 'knowledge or methods that are necessary to carry on or to improve the existing production and distribution of goods and services', but also 'entrepreneurial expertise and professional know-how'. The latter two elements may often prove to be the essential competitive advantage possessed by the technology owner. As will be shown below, MNEs will be in a particularly advantageous position in this regard.

'Technology transfer' is the process by which commercial technology is disseminated. This will take the form of a technology transfer transaction, which may or may not be a legally binding contract,[4] but which will involve the communication, by the transferor, of the relevant knowledge to the recipient. Among the types of transfer transactions that may be used, the draft TOT Code has listed the following:

(a) The assignment, sale and licensing of all forms of industrial property, except for trade marks, service marks and trade names when they are not part of transfer of technology transactions;

(b) The provision of know-how and technical expertise in the form of feasibility studies, plans, diagrams, models, instructions, guides, formulae, basic or detailed engineering designs, specifications and equipment for training, services involving technical advisory and managerial personnel, and personnel training;

(c) The provision of technological knowledge necessary for the installation, operation and functioning of plant and equipment, and turnkey projects;

(d) The provision of technological knowledge necessary to acquire, install and use machinery, equipment, intermediate goods and/or raw materials which have been acquired by purchase, lease or other means;

(e) The provision of technological contents of industrial and technical co-operation arrangements.[5]

The list excludes non-commercial technology transfers, such as those found in international cooperation agreements between developed and developing states. Such agreements may relate to infrastructure or agricultural development, or to international cooperation in the fields of research, education, employment or transport.[6]

1.2   The Generation and Use of Technology: the Interests of Technology-exporting and Technology-importing States Compared

The respective interests of technology-exporting and technology-importing states are best understood in the context of the international market for commercial technology. Although technology exists in non-proprietary forms that can be generally accessed, as, for example, in publicly available books or journals, the present concern focuses on proprietary technology, that is technology that is capable of generating a profit for its owner.

The first assumption underlying the market for commercial technology is that such technology should be treated as the private property of its owner and not as a public good capable of general use at little or no cost to its user. Commercial technology is usually commoditized through the application of intellectual property rights, which give the owner a legally determined monopoly over the use and disposal of that right, or by way of protected and restrictive contractual transfer as in the case of non-patentable know-how that is secret. This process of commoditization may help to increase the value of the technology to its owner by creating relative scarcity through legally restricted access to it. However, not all types of useful knowledge are so treated. Thus, knowledge in agriculture, health sciences or services is relatively free from private claims based on intellectual property and should be more freely available.[7]

The generation of commercial technology is closely bound up with the technological infrastructure of a country. This includes the public and private organizations which fund the development and adaptation of technology, the public and private research and development (R&D) organizations that conduct work on new and improved technology, the intermediaries who move the technology around the country and across its borders and the users who apply the technology in their business activities or who are the end consumers of products incorporating the technology in question.[8] Consequently, the states that possess the more developed systems for generating, delivering and using technology are likely to be the leading sources of proprietary technology.

MNEs are strongly influential in the operation of national and international technological infrastructures. They can be found operating at each stage of such a system in the most technologically advanced economies of the world. That this should be so stems from the fact, discussed in chapter 2, that one of the main ownership specific advantages of MNEs is their ability to 'produce, acquire, master the understanding of and organise the use of technological assets across national boundaries'.[9] Consequently, MNEs are a major force in shaping international markets for technology, particularly on the supply side. Their influence on the demand side is also significant, given that increasing amounts of international technology transfers occur between related enterprises.[10]

With regard to the supply side, the world's major MNEs will seek to control commercial technology markets for maximum gain, exploiting their dominant position in such markets. However, the degree of control exercised by these firms may vary according to the type of technology involved. A distinction has been drawn between markets for 'conventional' technology, where the technology is sufficiently distributed for many firms from many countries to be able to supply it, and markets for 'high' technology, where the technology can be developed only by a few very large firms with very high R&D spending and where constant innovation is the basis for competitive success.[11] Examples of the former include footwear, textiles, cement, pulp and paper or food processing. Examples of the latter include aerospace, electronics, computers, chemicals and machinery. The supply of technology in 'conventional' industries is said to be relatively competitive, given the stable and generally non-proprietary nature of the technology involved. By contrast, in 'high' technology areas competitive supply is likely to be restricted. Owners will guard the source of their competitive advantage, making their technology available only on restrictive terms favourable to the earning of a monopoly rent. This tendency may be reinforced because of the absence of viable alternative technology suppliers that could offer competition over the terms and conditions of transfer. However, not all 'high' technology markets should be seen as uncompetitive on the supply side. For example, in the newer high technology industries, such as semiconductors or computers, the entry of smaller, innovative firms has stimulated choice in sources of technological supply, making for increased competition in that field, although in the long term concentration can be predicted to occur.[12] Furthermore, as high technology matures into conventional technology, new entrants into the field can be expected. The competitive situation on the supply side of a market for technology is not, therefore, a static phenomenon, and each industrial sector should be analysed on its own terms.

The demand side of the market will also be conditioned by the nature of the technological infrastructure present in the state where the recipient is situated. Thus a distinction can be made between conditions in technologically advanced recipient states and those in technologically less developed states.[13] Conditions in the former are characterized by an ability to absorb technology effectively through advanced production systems, a highly trained workforce, high demand for the technology concerned and the ability to pay for it. Furthermore, technologically advanced recipients will be in a stronger position to bargain over the terms of supply. Alternative local sources of technology that can compete with the technology on offer from outside are more likely to exist. Furthermore, there exists a greater likelihood that the purchaser will itself be in a strong position to condition the market, as where it is another major corporation operating at the same level of the market as the supplier, or where it is in a quasi-monopolistic position, such as the postal and telecommunications authority of a major advanced country.[14] As will be shown in more detail below, in advanced countries the principal concern is that of ensuring the existence of workable competition even in highly concentrated technology markets. Thus competition law plays a significant role in the regulation of technology transfers to such countries.

By comparison, the absorption of proprietary technology in LDCs is more problematic. The absence of a sophisticated technological infrastructure has significant consequences for demand conditions. In particular, a high level of dependency on outside suppliers is created due to the lack of alternative, domestically generated, technology. This creates a weak bargaining position which is exacerbated by the relative lack of information about technology caused by the absence of adequate numbers of skilled specialists who could evaluate the technology on offer. In such cases the technology owner is likely to enjoy a monopolistic position in relation to the recipient market and may be able to exact excessive prices and restrictions on the utilization of the imported technology.[15]

Furthermore, as is elaborated in the next section, it is less likely that the technology owner will be able to introduce the technology by means other than direct investment through a controlled subsidiary. In LDCs, the incidence of firms that can act as licensees of advanced technology is much smaller than in developed countries. Consequently, the conditions of technology transfer will be determined by the needs of the MNE as an integrated enterprise. These may be inimical to the interests of the importing state, to the extent that control over technology within the firm is less likely to result in its dissemination to potential competitors, if any, in that state.

During the 1970s, when the debate on technology transfer to LDCs became a significant pillar of the wider call for a New International Economic Order,[16] one issue in particular stood out as encapsulating the inequitable situation of LDCs in the market for technology. This was the issue of whether MNEs could supply 'appropriate technology' to LDCs. It was argued that LDCs were

disadvantaged in technology markets because the available technology was inappropriate to their real needs. The argument was put
on two levels. First, the type of technology that had been generated
by MNEs from the developed countries was incapable of utilizing the
primary factor endowment of LDCs, namely unskilled labour, as it
was geared to capital-intensive forms of production requiring fewer,
high-skilled personnel. Thus, in LDCs, MNEs tended to set up
production enterprises that had little effect on local skill and employment patterns. Secondly, the types of products made by MNEs were
said to be inappropriate to LDC markets. Either they were high-
technology products with highly specialized uses that few consumers
in LDCs could use, or they were mass consumption items geared
towards the wants of Western consumer markets that distorted consumption patterns in LDCs by persuading consumers to spend what
little disposable income they had on unnecessary products, such as
soft drinks, 'junk foods', cigarettes or cosmetics.[17]

The first argument has been challenged on economic grounds, in
that there may be no necessary correlation between labour-intensive
technologies and welfare in LDCs.[18] In any case, there is considerable evidence showing that much investment by MNEs in LDCs is of
a labour-intensive kind that is geared to take advantage of lower
labour costs in the production of goods for export markets.[19] The true
problem may be that MNEs are uninterested in transferring any but
the more mature and labour-intensive technologies to LDCs, given
the limitations of local markets for advanced technology goods and
processes, and the uneconomic costs of adapting existing proprietary
technology to LDC conditions.[20]

The second argument can be opposed on the ground that it is
based on a subjective opinion as to what is 'appropriate' as a consumer good in a LDC. In a free-market economy, the fact that the
demand exists is more important in economic terms than its social
implications.[21] Thus, MNEs can be expected to generate demand for
their products among those in LDCs who can afford them and/or
who can be persuaded to buy them. None the less, despite the
weaknesses of the 'appropriate technology' argument, it offered an
impetus for the reconsideration of policy in this area.

Thus, concerns over the monopolistic tendencies of suppliers in
LDC technology markets and the 'appropriate technology' argument
provided the main justifications for calls for greater regulation of
international technology transfers in the interests of LDCs. This gave
rise to new kinds of legal regimes, pioneered by the Latin American
states, based on specialized technology transfer laws, and to negotiations for an international code of conduct on technology transfer
under the auspices of UNCTAD. However, before these are

considered in detail, it is necessary to examine, first, the principal techniques of technology transfer used by MNEs and, secondly, the principal legal issues that they create, these being the technical matters that the above-mentioned regulatory structures aim to control.

2 Technology Transfer by MNEs and Its Legal Effects

There are two principal methods of technology transfer open to the MNE. The first is to license the technology at arm's length to an independent licensee or to a joint venture with a local partner. The second is to transfer the technology internally to a subsidiary. This may involve the licensing of intellectual property rights and/or know-how by the parent to the subsidiary in return for royalty payments, although informal, royalty-free, transfers may also take place. The choice of methods will be determined by what will serve to maximize the MNE's income from the technology in question.

The choice is conditioned by a number of factors.[22] Assuming that a suitable licensee, or joint venture partner, exists in the host country, the MNE is more likely to consider licensing the technology, or setting up a joint venture, where the entry barriers, such as the relatively limited size of the market, are too great to make an independent direct investment viable. Indeed, in some cases, a licensing arrangement or a joint venture may be the only legally permissible from of entry. Furthermore, where the firm is a newcomer to international markets and lacks the expertise to undertake direct investment, licensing to a third party or to a joint venture may be preferable. On the other hand, licensing may create too many medium- to long-term costs to be worthwhile. In particular, the MNE must consider whether licensing will increase the risk of deterioration in quality owing to the licensee's misuse of the technology, and whether the licensee will pass on the technology to competitors. Such problems may be diminished by the imposition of restrictive conditions on the licensee in the licensing agreement. However, if the technology concerned is a 'core' technology with a long commercial lifespan, licensing may involve too many risks. In this respect, a joint venture may serve to ensure greater operational control over the use of the technology. However, it may not protect the owner from allowing the other joint venture partner to become familiar with the technology and to use this advantage to set up in competition with the owner. Thus, if the owner has the ability to do so, it may prefer direct investment over licensing, as this permits closer control over the use of the technology and is more likely to preserve its confidential nature.

The transfer of technology by direct investment is more likely in LDCs, given the absence of suitable potential licensees or joint venture partners, and because the MNE can provide the technology as part of a larger 'package' that includes capital, management, back-up services, access to markets and other associated benefits which are locally in short supply. In such cases, the major question is whether the host state will in fact gain any transfer of the technology out of the firm into the wider local economy. Much will depend on the willingness of the MNE to train more personnel than it needs, the surplus employees being free to apply their experience elsewhere in the local economy.[23] However, MNEs do not appear to make the training of local personnel a major priority, and it is questionable whether there will be sufficient outlets for the application of the skills newly learnt by the local employees of MNEs.[24] If there are, then restrictive covenants in contracts of employment may seek to protect the commercial advantage of the MNE by preventing the use of such skills by former employees for the benefit of competitors.

From the above, it can be seen that the legal structure of the recipient of the technology is a significant matter influencing the extent to which the general diffusion of the technology concerned into the wider local economy is likely to occur. Direct investment through a wholly owned subsidiary is most likely to keep the technology under the control of its owner. The terms of transfer to the subsidiary are likely to restrict the use of the technology for the benefit of the MNE alone, and this aim will be enforced by managerial control from the parent. On the other hand, a joint venture or a licensing agreement may allow the local partner or licensee to gain access to the technology and to diffuse it in the wider economy, provided that the terms of the transfer are not too restrictive. Consequently, one legal issue of relevance to the regulator is whether to restrict investments involving technology transfer to legal forms that are more likely to result in technology diffusion. Hence there may be a preference, in host state law, for joint ventures or licensing arrangements over direct investment.

The second major legal issue that arises in all cases of technology transfer, whether between related or between independent entities, concerns the actual terms of the transfer transaction and the degree to which these affect the likelihood that the technology will be made available to those who could benefit from it. The nature and content of such terms form much of the basis for technology transfer regulation, in both technology-rich and technology-poor countries. Therefore, a brief overview of the most common terms in technology transfer transactions is in order.

3   Restrictive Terms in Technology Transfer Transactions[25]

Technology licences, whether between the affiliated undertakings of a MNE or between a MNE and a third party, will contain terms that seek to preserve the competitive advantage of the technology owner against abusive exploitation by the technology recipient. While such terms may be unobjectionable where the legitimate interests of the technology owner are being protected, they may also be used by the owner as a means of obtaining an unfair commercial advantage over the recipient through the exploitation of its generally weaker bargaining position. In developed recipient states, such abusive behaviour by the transferor has been dealt with as a competition issue. However, in LDCs, even if commercially legitimate restraints are placed on the recipient, the effect of these on the ability of the host state to absorb and learn from the imported technology, or to use it as a catalyst for economic development, may be too restrictive. Therefore, controls over restrictive terms based on competition law alone may be ineffective as a means of safeguarding the public interests involved.

Restrictive terms in technology transfer transactions may be conveniently classified into two main categories: those that restrict the recipient's commercial policy in respect of the conduct of business involving the transferred technology and those that seek to preserve the exclusive ownership and use of the technology by the transferor.[26]

3.1   Restrictions on the Commercial Policy of the Technology Recipient

Technology transfer agreements will usually include restrictions on the commercial policy of the recipient that are designed to maximize the profit that the transferor can earn from its inventions and know-how. These will concern *inter alia* restrictions on the purchasing, production and marketing policies of the recipient.

Thus, at the level of purchasing policy, transferors may insist on the recipient buying its requirements for raw materials, plant and machinery and other goods or services from the transferor. Such 'tie-ins' may be legitimate where certain inputs, given their quality and characteristics, can only be obtained from the transferor. However, where suitable substitutes are available more cheaply on the open market, such tie-ins are harder to justify on efficiency grounds. Indeed, they may be a means of extracting monopolistic profits from the recipient that go beyond what may be legitimately expected from the mere ownership of the technology. Such manipulations have been condemned under the competition laws of developed countries, although a tying arrangement will not be upset where there are genuine commercial reasons for its existence.[27] From the perspective of a LDC, tying arrangements may create special problems. First, such an arrangement may conceal the true cost of the technology package, in that although the royalty payments imposed on the recipient may be reasonable, they may be enhanced by the overpricing of tied inputs through transfer pricing manipulations.[28] Secondly, tying arrangements may have the further effect of preventing backward economic integration through the growth of local suppliers. Thus local economic development may be inhibited.

The recipient may be restricted further by clauses requiring the production of minimum quantities of product, which may be linked to a minimum royalty requirement, and by clauses setting the duration of the agreement. Where the agreement is of excessive duration this may force the recipient to acquire obsolete technology and prevent it from obtaining technology from alternative suppliers.[29] The agreement may also contain field-of-use restrictions which limit the application of the technology to particular fields only. This may be reasonable as a means of giving the transferor control over the use of its inventions, but competition authorities will not normally tolerate such a restriction where it acts as a disguised method of dividing markets.[30] For a LDC, field-of-use restrictions may prevent the full exploitation of the technology in all the areas where it may be of value as a stimulus to economic development.

At the marketing level, the recipient may be restricted as to the export markets in which it can sell products incorporating the technology in question. The owner will justify such protection on the basis that it ensures an adequate return on the cost of developing the technology. It is an aspect of the monopoly right that is inherent in patented technology, or in the competitive advantage gained by the development of secret know-how. Reasonable territorial restrictions on the business of technology recipients have been accepted under the competition laws of developed states, on the basis that some restriction of intra-brand competition may be necessary to ensure the widest possible dissemination of products incorporating the proprietary technology. On the other hand, LDCs have argued that such restrictions simply inhibit their ability to earn foreign exchange through exports.[31] There is undoubtedly a danger that an integrated MNE will use technology licences with its subsidiaries to insulate geographical markets. Markets in which high prices prevail may be protected from imports of cheaper products produced in another market by an affiliate, thereby stifling price competition between affiliates. Where the cheaper products originate in a LDC, then some loss to revenue may be predicted as a result of such export restrictions.

A similar restraint on the recipient's commercial freedom may come from price fixing provisions. The transferor may insist that the transferee charges a high price for products incorporating the transferred technology. This may prevent price competition between the transferor and recipient, by protecting the transferor's home market against cheaper imports from the recipient. Where such price controls are imposed on a plant operating in a LDC, the opportunity to earn foreign exchange from exports to higher price areas will be lost.

Although price fixing is generally regarded as a particularly serious anti-competitive practice, in licensing arrangements a degree of price control over the licensee may be justifiable as an aspect of the licensor's monopoly rights that stem from its invention.[32] Given that the licensee is unlikely to license a direct competitor, and that the licensor has an interest in allowing the greatest exploitation of its invention, the licensee may in fact be encouraged to sell at the lowest prices possible.[33] However, in the context of a LDC economy, this argument may not be sufficient to justify restrictions on the earning capacity of the recipient. On the other hand, where the recipient is a wholly owned subsidiary, the ability to control corporate policy may be limited, even under competition principles. It may be necessary to impose export requirements as a condition of entry.

3.2 Restrictions on the Use of Technology on the Part of the Recipient

Restrictions falling under this heading aim at the preservation of the confidential nature of the technology transferred and at the preservation of the owner's competitive advantage stemming from the technology. Thus, it is common to find confidentiality clauses in technology transfer agreements. These are generally unobjectionable, provided they are not of excessive duration, as where the duty continues even though the intellectual property right protecting the technology has run out, or the know-how involved has entered the public domain. Similarly, clauses preventing the recipient from entering into arrangements with competitors of the transferor, from manufacturing competing products or from using competing technology can be justified on the basis of confidentiality. However, in the context of a LDC economy such restraints may inhibit the gaining of experience in the field where the technology is used.[34]

More problematic are clauses that inhibit the acquisition of skill and experience on the part of the recipient as a result of interaction with the technology transferred. This may allow the recipient to compete with the transferor after the expiry of the agreement, a situation that challenges the monopoly of the transferor. To counter this threat, the agreement may prohibit the use of the technology transferred after the expiry of the agreement, or permit use only upon the continued payment of a royalty. This is acceptable where the intellectual property rights involved have not yet expired[35] or the relevant know-how has not entered the public domain.[36] On the other hand, a blanket prohibition on post-term use where such rights have expired,[37] or where the know-how has become public knowledge as a result of the transferor's actions,[38] may be unduly exploitative, as would a requirement to pay further royalties in these circumstances.[39]

In addition the recipient may be prevented from conducting its own research and development work on the transferred technology, or, in the absence of such a prohibition, it may be obliged to transfer any resulting improvements to the transferor on a non-reciprocal basis. Such strong 'grant-back' provisions have been condemned under the competition laws of developed countries.[40] For LDCs such clauses would be especially worrying as they would inhibit the learning process that can result from the use of imported technology, and lessen the likelihood of adaptation to local needs.

Thus, restrictive clauses in technology transfer transactions will have significant effects on the manner in which the technology may be used by the recipient. The extent to which the recipient can benefit in the long term from the use of the technology will depend on the limits of contractual freedom granted to the transferor for the exploitation of its innovation. In this the responses of developed and less developed states have differed, and to these we now turn.

4　The Two Principal Models of Technology Transfer Regulation

From the above it can be seen that the priorities of preserving workable competition in technology markets, as espoused by developed recipient states, may not always answer the priorities of ensuring economic development espoused by less developed recipient states. Thus two distinct models for the regulation of technology transfer have emerged from these two groups of states. The developed recipients follow a model that preserves the essential logic of a legally permitted monopoly right in proprietary technology based on intellectual property law and freedom of contract, tempered in its excesses by competition law. By contrast, LDCs have sought to create a regime of technology transfer laws that go beyond the preservation of workable competition and seek to control technology transfers in the interests of development, thereby qualifying the legal effects of private property in innovation. A comparison of these models will now be made.

4.1 The Developed Country Model

Developed recipient countries accept the private property character of commercial technology through their use of patent and trademark laws as the basis for defining the scope of that property.[41] Such rights have been given reciprocal protection between states under international conventions embodying the principles of national treatment, non-discrimination and priority, thereby guaranteeing the same protection of industrial property rights to nationals and to foreign right holders.[42] This reflects the fact that most advanced states are not only purchasers of foreign technology but also exporters in their own right, thereby giving them an interest in the reciprocal protection of intellectual property rights.

As noted above, the principal concerns in this area are related to the preservation of competition in industries where technology is controlled by relatively few owners. This will involve, first, the control of cooperative arrangements and concentrations between competitors that may have an adverse effect on the availability of essential technology to third parties without any compensating technological progress and/or benefits to consumers. Secondly, as already discussed in the previous section, excessive restrictions on the commercial policy and use of technology by a recipient will be regulated. In both cases the aim is to protect the right of the technology owner to profit from its invention or know-how, while at the same time preventing the creation of monopolistic horizontal structures and/or vertical relationships in the market concerned. This balancing of interests is achieved through the use of a 'rule of reason' approach whereby the anti-competitive effects of the technology owner's actions are weighed against the beneficial effects on the economy of protecting its proprietary rights in the technology.[43]

Furthermore, competition policy will be applied so as not to stifle technological innovation. Thus, for example, in the USA the National Cooperation Research Act 1984 relaxed the application of antitrust laws to joint R&D ventures.[44] Similarly the EC has passed Commission Regulations that exempt from the prohibition of anti-competitive agreements or concerted practices in article 85(1) of the EEC Treaty, patent licences,[45] know-how agreements[46] and joint R&D agreements.[47] To qualify for exemption, the agreement in question must offer improvements to productivity and technical development, be of benefit to consumers, contain restrictions on the commercial freedom of the parties which are no more than necessary for the achievement of the afore-mentioned aims, as defined by the relevant Regulation, and must not create an opportunity to eliminate competition in a substantial part of the relevant market.

However, such policies should be seen against the backdrop of attempts to stimulate competition by the deregulation of high technology industries, as exemplified by the privatization of national telecommunications monopolies in several states, and the reduction of entry barriers for foreign firms in this sector.[48] Furthermore, technologically advanced countries may encourage international cooperation in technological innovation through the approval, under competition law, of technologically innovative strategic alliances between firms from more than one country,[49] and through public sector initiatives, which can act as a source of coordination and funding for the development of new technologies by MNEs from more than one state. For example, the EC has been active in this way, in the hope of stimulating EC based firms to develop technology that can compete with US or Japanese firms.[50]

4.2 The LDC Model

This model is characterized by a reserved attitude to the protection of intellectual property rights coupled with the adoption of specialized technology transfer laws. The model is more complex to explain than that evolved by developed recipient states. This is because it attempts to address issues of economic development against the background of the internationalization of the developed country model of technology transfer regulation, a model that is suitable for the needs of technologically mature and innovative economies, and that places considerably more emphasis on the rights of intellectual property holders than might have been the case when the developed states were themselves undergoing the process of industrialization.[51]

4.2.1 Reserved approach to the protection of intellectual property rights Unlike the technologically advanced countries, LDCs have been less willing to accept uncritically the assumptions behind the international system of intellectual property protection. Since 1961, LDCs have been seeking reform of that system.[52] The process started when, in 1961, Brazil introduced a draft resolution in the Second Committee of UN General Assembly calling for a study of the effects of patents on the transfer of technology. This led, in 1964, to a report by the Secretary-General, entitled 'The role of patents in the transfer of technology to developing countries'.[53] It concluded that reform of the system was unnecessary. Most of the states that replied to the UN questionnaire on which the report was based said that patents provided an aid to their development by promoting technology transfer. Only India, Lebanon and Cuba offered the opposite opinion. However, by the 1970s this approach had changed. In particular,

UNCTAD had taken up the issue of technology transfer.[54] In this connection, it undertook several influential studies, including one on the role of patents in technology transfer[55] and one on the role of trademarks in LDCs.[56] Furthermore, in 1974 negotiations were under way to reform the Paris Convention for the Protection of Industrial Property under the auspices of the body charged with its administration, the World Intellectual Property Organization (WIPO).[57] These developments resulted in the formulation of a comprehensive critique as to the appropriateness of traditional intellectual property laws as instruments for the transfer of technology to LDCs. The basic arguments concerned the problems associated with patents and trademarks and with the principles underlying the international system of protection.

As regards patents, it was argued that the granting of patent rights in LDCs would have adverse consequences on development in that they would be taken out for reasons that had little to do with the traditional uses of patents.[58] Given that most of the world's patents were owned by foreign firms operating in developed country markets, patent protection in a LDC was not aimed at encouraging local innovation. Instead, the principal reason for taking out such a patent was attributed to the desire of the firm to protect its markets and licensing rights in the LDC concerned, thereby preventing rivals from entering in its place. Thus the patent would give the owner an import monopoly over the market concerned. Furthermore, the patent owner would rarely, if ever, work the patent in the LDC concerned. Thus, the grant of the patent would retard technology transfer not only by closing off competition but also by allowing the owner to neutralize the technology concerned through non-use. The latter problem is not unique to LDCs. The industrial property laws of most states provide for compulsory licensing of patents that are not worked. However, according to the UNCTAD study of 1975 most LDCs did not use their compulsory licensing procedures because of the costs and delays involved.[59] Finally, it was argued that the existence of patent rights could encourage the conclusion of unduly restrictive licensing agreements, which, given the absence of antitrust laws in most LDCs, could not be effectively controlled.[60]

Regarding trademarks, it was argued that while such rights served the useful functions of guaranteeing quality and source, they also created adverse effects in LDC economies.[61] In particular, trademarks tended to be owned by the subsidiaries of foreign MNEs and used to enhance market power either through their promotion by intensive advertising or through licensing to local distributors. These activities would result in considerable social costs as consumers with limited incomes would pay high prices for foreign branded products.

Furthermore, local distributors would bear the cost of developing market share without any guarantee of benefiting from the resulting goodwill created towards the marked product. This goodwill would accrue to the foreign trademark owner rather than to the local licensee. In the light of such views certain LDCs adopted laws to control the use of trademarks. Thus Mexico enacted a Law on Inventions and Trademarks in 1976, which required the concurrent use of the local licensee's mark with that of the foreign licensor, in the belief that the goodwill generated by the licensee would be associated not only with the foreign mark but also with the local mark.[62] In 1972, under the Generic Names Drug Act, Pakistan banned the use of trademarks in the pharmaceutical industry. This had disastrous results, leading to sales of ineffective counterfeit drugs bearing the permitted generic name and to a black market in branded drugs. This law was repealed in 1976.[63]

Finally, as regards the international system of protection, the LDCs have sought to reform, in particular, the application of the national treatment standard to their national legal regimes. Thus the 1975 UNCTAD study on patents proposed the introduction of preferential treatment for LDCs.[64] This has been justified on the ground that LDCs and developed countries are in an unequal relationship based on the fact that most of the patent rights that stand to benefit from national treatment are held by MNEs from developed countries, and because the few patents that are issued for the nationals of LDCs involve individual inventors, not MNEs, and create distinctive needs for protection.[65] In addition LDCs sought to reform the principle of priority contained in article 4 of the Paris Convention. By this principle, any person who has filed an application for a patent in one of the contracting states has a right to claim similar protection as a matter of priority in other contracting state for up to twelve months. The LDCs have argued that this period is too long and acts as a disincentive to invention in LDCs.

All the above arguments have been subjected to forceful criticism. The LDC position on patents has been doubted by proponents of the developed country approach, who still assert the original justification for patent protection as lying in the provision of incentives for innovation by enterprises. According to Professor Beier, 'it is only patent protection which gives enterprises the necessary incentive to file their important inventions abroad and converts an invention into an object of international trade that can be transferred without too great a risk'.[66] Such a position lies behind the greater controls over TRIPs in the Uruguay Round Final Act, already discussed in chapter 7.[67]

However, as pointed out in chapter 2,[68] a MNE may not require the possession of patent rights to protect its competitive advantage in technology. More significant are its abilities to conduct costly R&D and to integrate patented technology with non-patentable know-how, without which the patented elements of the technology may be useless. Thus the true problem for LDCs is not so much that patents are taken out by foreign firms, but that the major producers of technology tend to possess considerable market power to which the protection of intellectual property is no more than a subsidiary form of protection.[69] This suggests policy responses in other fields of law, especially competition law.

The arguments relating to trademarks have been criticized on the grounds that, in the absence of assured quality in the products of local firms and of effective consumer protection legislation, foreign trademarks can act as marks of quality. Furthermore, the adverse effects stemming from the link between foreign trademarks and advertising is seen as a purely theoretical argument that cannot support the view that removal of trademark rights will prevent socially inefficient consumption.[70] Furthermore, as Blakeney points out, the commercial functions that trademarks perform may lead to the creation of a marketing infrastructure in LDCs that will facilitate the distribution of goods containing transferred technology.[71]

Finally, the arguments concerning reform of the international system of protection have not led to the hoped for reforms. Given the relatively weak bargaining position of the LDCs this is not surprising. The technologically advanced countries have few incentives to modify a system that suits their needs. However, as described in chapter 7, some recognition of the interests of LDCs appears in the Final Act of the Uruguay Round negotiations, in that such countries can postpone the patent protection contained therein for up to ten years, and developed countries are encouraged to ensure adequate technology transfer to LDCs.

There may be some advantages to be gained by LDCs from adhering to a traditional system of intellectual property law. In particular, it may indicate that the state concerned has a favourable attitude to foreign investors who rely on patented technology.[72] It may also avoid the risk of economic retaliation against the LDC on the ground that it does not respect intellectual property rights as provided, for example, under the US Trade and Competitiveness Act 1988.[73]

On the other hand, a recent study by the UN Transnational Corporations Management Division (the successor to the UNCTC), into the link between intellectual property protection and foreign investment finds that heightened intellectual property protection provides no clear impetus to investment flows. The issue depends on the industry concerned, the types of intellectual property rights granted and the general level of technological and economic development of the host state.[74] Thus, there remains considerable doubt as to the effect of intellectual property laws on the development process.

4.2.2   *Specialized technology transfer laws*   As part of the movement for greater control over the process of technology transfer, numerous LDCs began, in the 1970s, to experiment with specialized technology transfer laws. Space permits only a brief description of the common features of such laws. More detailed accounts can be found elsewhere.[75] The main thrust for these developments came from Latin America, with the adoption in 1969 of the Andean Foreign Investment Code under Decision 24 of the Cartagena Agreement,[76] and the passing of several national laws between 1971 and 1981.[77] Other LDCs from Africa and Asia followed suit,[78] as did a small number of Southern European and formerly socialist Eastern European states.[79] Of developed countries only Japan has used such laws.[80]

The essence of technology transfer laws is the screening of international technology transfer transactions by a national authority with the aim of ensuring that the technology transferred is of use to the national economy and that the terms and conditions of transfer do not amount to an abuse of the transferor's superior bargaining power. Such laws are normally limited to transactions between a foreign transferor and a local recipient. Transactions between related enterprises are not addressed in most statutes,[81] although some laws have contained strict controls over royalty payments for technology transferred between affiliated enterprises, as a means of controlling transfer price manipulations.[82] Indirect transfers between foreign transferors and local recipients effected through a local intermediary, who receives the technology under an approved contract and then transfers it subject to unacceptable terms, may also be covered.[83]

The normal procedure is for the parties to submit either a draft or an executed contract for approval. This may involve a registration of the agreement with the screening authority. The authority will then assess the contract in the light of the legal standards laid down for review. These will concern *inter alia*: an examination of the restrictive clauses imposed on the recipient with a view to identifying prohibited restrictions; the reasonableness of the consideration payable; the costs and benefits of the transaction in relation to the economic and social development of the recipient state; the nature of the technology involved, paying particular attention to its positive effects on local productive capacity and skills development, the ability of the local economy to develop the technology by itself, and the age and effectiveness of the technology; whether the package involves excessive tie-ins and other costs; the extent of any warranties limiting or excluding the transferor's liability for the technology; and the duration of the agreement, which must not be excessive.

Failure to register the agreement for approval may lead to its being nullified.[84] Other sanctions may include fines for the performance of an unapproved transaction, prohibition of payments in favour of the transferor and the denial of fiscal benefits.[85] The approving authority may impose conditions on the parties as the price for approval. This may include amendments to the agreement itself.[86] In particular, the relevant law may require the adoption of local law as the proper law of the agreement, thereby preventing its avoidance through the choice of a foreign law.[87]

Technology transfer laws share many features in common with other areas of law applicable to MNEs. However, they fill a distinct niche in the system of MNE regulation. This can be explained by a comparison of technology transfer laws with related areas of law, in particular with foreign investment screening laws, antitrust laws and foreign exchange and tax laws.

Like foreign investment screening laws, technology transfer laws introduce an administrative review procedure as a condition of entry into the local economy. Indeed, they may complement the foreign investment law of a host state by regulating non-equity forms of entry such as licensing agreements.[88] Secondly, in common with antitrust laws, technology transfer laws regulate restrictive practices in technology transfer agreements. However, unlike antitrust laws, technology transfer laws seek to intervene in the operation of commercial markets in technology and regulate them in favour of the broader national economic interest in economic development. Although the use of antitrust law as an instrument of national or regional industrial policy is often debated, its primary aim is to prevent anti-competitive practices in the market, not to control it.[89] Thirdly, technology transfer laws may be used as an additional means for regulating balance-of-payments issues by controlling the terms on which royalties will be paid for the importation of foreign-owned technology, by regulating tying arrangements involving the importation of inputs from abroad and by controlling the total number of technology transfer transactions that may be permitted at any one time. Similarly, as noted above, such laws may close off a potential conduit for transfer pricing manipulations by MNEs based on royalty remittances.

On the other hand, technology transfer laws pose a clear challenge to the logic of intellectual property laws. First, by regulating the consideration to be paid, they do not accept the legitimacy of allowing the owner of commercial technology to obtain monopoly rents from its application in the recipient state. Secondly, such laws may impose restrictions on the use of the technology by way of performance requirements, and may include limitations on the protection afforded to foreign patents or trademarks. Thirdly, as a consequence of these characteristics, technology transfer laws question the basis of the international system of intellectual property protection in that they reject the principles of national treatment and non-discrimination between foreign and local intellectual property rights, a rejection reinforced by the mandatory requirement of local law as the proper law of the technology transfer transaction. Thus, it is not surprising that such laws have become a target for limitation in the Uruguay Round negotiations, as shown in chapter 7.

5   The Draft UNCTAD Code of Conduct on the Transfer of Technology

In order to acquire international legitimacy for the kinds of technology transfer policies outlined in the previous section, LDCs have sought the adoption of an international code on technology transfer (TOT Code). This has been done under the auspices of UNCTAD, which, as noted above, was active in articulating the LDC perspective on this issue.[90] The participating states have been grouped into three interest groupings for the purpose of negotiating the TOT Code.[91] The LDCs formed the Group of 77. They sought a legally binding code, which would cover all forms of technology transfer transactions and give primacy to the recipient state's laws and dispute settlement procedures. The developed market economy countries formed Group B. They sought a voluntary code that would balance the rights and duties of the technology transferor and recipient, and leave the parties free to decide on dispute settlement procedures. The third group, Group D, comprised the former Eastern Bloc states and Mongolia. These states took broadly the same position as the Group of 77, though they did not take a view on the legal character of the code, or on applicable laws and dispute settlement procedures. They stressed the equality of states and the need for non-discrimination in technology transfer transactions. Subsequently, the People's Republic of China joined the Conference as an independent participant, aiming to learn from the experience and to use this in formulating its own technology transfer policy.

The process began with extensive preliminary negotiations between 1976 and 1978 which led to the formulation of a draft negotiating text.[92] Thereupon the UN General Assembly, by its resolution 32/188 of December 1977, decided to convene a UN Conference, under the auspices of UNCTAD, to negotiate a final draft and to take all the necessary decisions for its adoption. The Conference held six sessions between 1978 and 1985.[93] However, no further sessions have taken place, due to deadlock over several crucial issues. It is not proposed to undertake a detailed analysis of the draft Code. This has been done elsewhere.[94] The present concern rests with the reasons behind the above-mentioned deadlock.

The issues that remain to be settled are those where the developed country and LDC models of technology transfer regulation fail to converge. The first of these concerns the regulation of restrictive business practices in technology transfer agreements, covered by chapter 4 of the draft Code.[95] The Group B countries wish to control such restrictions on the basis of competition law, and emphasize that only those practices which unreasonably restrain trade should be prohibited.[96] The Group of 77, on the other hand, see such practices as being inherently unfair, being a product of superior bargaining power on the part of the transferor. They favour the prohibition of such restrictions altogether.[97] The issues involved have been considered in detail in section 3 above. The disagreement stems from the fear of LDCs that a competition based approach will allow the avoidance of the TOT Code on the part of the supplier, given that it is not likely to be adopted as a legally enforceable instrument.[98] Further disagreement exists under chapter 4 as to whether different standards should apply to transfers of technology between commonly owned enterprises. The Group B states see no reason for different treatment, limiting control only to those cases where the transaction amounts to an anti-competitive abuse of a dominant position. By contrast the Group of 77 wish to introduce a standard that permits such transactions as long as they do not adversely affect the transfer of technology.[99]

The second major area of disagreement concerns the issues of applicable law and settlement of disputes under chapter 9.[100] The LDCs have advocated a restrictive regime on the choice of law governing technology transfer agreements. They wish to see the law of the recipient country as the mandatory proper law of the contract, thereby avoiding the 'delocalization' of technology transfer agreements. On the contrary, the Group B states favour the preservation of the parties' freedom to choose the proper law provided it has a genuine connection with the transaction.[101] As regards the settlement of disputes, the Group of 77 have opposed an absolute right for the parties to settle their disputes by arbitration. In their view, such a right has to be determined in the light of any rules to the contrary in the law of the technology-importing state. By contrast both the Group B and Group D states have favoured free choice of arbitration. It was on this issue that the Conference broke down in 1981.[102] At the

Sixth Session this issue was not discussed and negotiations concentrated exclusively on the choice of law question.[103]

In order to salvage the negotiating process, the Secretary-General of UNCTAD and the President of the Conference have held regular consultations with interested governments. However, significant divergences of opinion have remained on the above-mentioned issues.[104] Indeed, at the eighth session of UNCTAD it was recognized that

> conditions do not currently exist to reach full agreement on all outstanding issues in the draft code of conduct. Should governments indicate, either directly or through the Secretary-General of UNCTAD reporting according to General Assembly resolution 46/214, that there is the convergence of views necessary to reach agreement on all outstanding issues, then the Board should re-engage and continue its work aimed at facilitating agreement on the code.[105]

At the time of writing, the Secretary-General of UNCTAD has been collecting the opinions of governments as to their views on the outstanding issues. However, there appears to be little interest in the matter, given the slow rate of response received by him.[106] Perhaps the position of the USA best summarizes the situation:

> The Government of the United States is of the opinion that there is no basis to believe that there is a 'convergence of views' on the outstanding issues in the draft code of conduct, nor is there likely to be. Therefore, the Government opposes resumption of negotiations on the draft code of conduct on the transfer of technology.[107]

Whether these disagreements can be resolved remains to be seen. The Secretary-General of UNCTAD will continue to gather views on these matters. However, the adoption of a finalized code appears unlikely at the time of writing, for reasons that will be explored in the next and final section of this chapter.

6   Concluding Remarks: the Demise of the LDC Challenge to the International System of Technology Transfer?

It is arguable that, in contemporary economic and political conditions, the challenge of the LDCs to the established international technology transfer system is weakening and may have failed. The reasons for this can be seen both at the level of national laws and in the ascendancy of developed country positions in international organizations.

At the national level, specialized technology transfer laws have not delivered the hoped for improvements in access to modern productive technology. For example, in Nigeria the system of technology transfer regulation set up under the National Office of Industrial Property Act 1979 has been largely ignored by foreign and Nigerian businessmen when entering agreements involving the licensing of technology. Thus contracts often contain restrictive clauses that are prohibited under the law.[108] A failure to obtain modern technology has also been noted in relation to the technology transfer provisions in Nigerian petroleum legislation.[109] Indeed, it is arguable that the existence of controls over technology transfer agreements may simply act as a deterrent to the importation of technology in that the incentive for the technology owner to exploit its competitive advantage in the recipient state is reduced.

As a consequence of the relative ineffectiveness of technology transfer controls, developing host states appear increasingly to be modifying, if not abandoning, such controls. Most notably, the ANCOM countries, which pioneered technology transfer laws, have abandoned their attempt to create a standardized interregional regime for technology transfer. The original ANCOM regime under Decision 24 required member states to screen all contracts on the importation of technology and on patents and trademarks, and prohibited the authorization of agreements containing any of the restrictive clauses listed in article 20 thereof.[110] By contrast Decision 291, the current successor to Decision 24, simply requires the registration of technology transfer agreements under the respective laws of the ANCOM member states, leaving the details of the registration process to the relevant national laws.[111] The only clear prohibition in Decision 291 relates to clauses that prohibit or limit the exportation of products produced on the basis of the technology transferred.[112]

Similarly, India has recently reformed its hitherto extensive administrative procedures for the review of technology imports.[113] In accordance with the Statement on Industrial Policy of 24 July 1991, automatic permission will now be given for foreign technology agreements in high priority industries up to a lump sum payment of Rs1 crore, 5 per cent royalty for domestic sales and 8 per cent for exports, subject to total payments of 8 per cent sales over a ten year period from the date of the agreement or seven years from the commencement of production. In industries other than high priority industries, automatic permission will be given subject to the same guidelines if no free foreign exchange is needed for any payments.[114] Indian companies are now free to negotiate the terms of technology transfer with their foreign counterparts according to their own commercial judgment.[115] The philosophy underlying this change is explained as follows:

There is a great need for promoting an industrial environment where acquisition of technological capability receives priority. In the fast changing world of technology the relationship between suppliers and users of technology must be a continuous one. Such a relationship becomes difficult to achieve when the approval process includes unnecessary governmental interference on a case by case basis involving endemic delays and fostering uncertainty. The Indian entrepreneur has now come of age so that he no longer needs such bureaucratic clearances of his commercial technology relationships with foreign technology suppliers. Indian industry can scarcely be competitive with the rest of the world if it is to operate within such a regulatory environment.[116]

Likewise, Brazil has been liberalizing its technology transfer regime. Of particular note is the ending of the protected status of the informatics industry. As part of Brazil's technology policy, Law No. 7232 of 29 October 1984 established a number of restrictions on foreign investment in informatics goods and on their importation.[117] The aim was to reserve the market in mini- and microcomputers for national firms, until such time as they could compete on international markets. However, between 1990 and 1991, the Brazilian government, following the liberalizing policy of former President Collor, introduced legislation which dismantled this protective regime through the gradual extension of the categories of informatics goods that could be imported. Initially, importation of certain listed goods was made subject to approval by the Science and Technology Office (SCT), while non-listed goods could be freely imported.[118] Subsequently, exemption from the requirement of SCT approval was extended.[119] Then, by Law No. 8238 of 23 October 1991, significant alterations were made to the 1984 Informatics Law.[120] The 1991 law revoked numerous tax incentives offered to Brazilian companies under the 1984 law, and effectively ended the Brazilian Informatics and Automation Council (CONIN). Outside the informatics area, the law has also been liberalized. Thus, in 1991, restrictions on the payment of royalties by subsidiaries for technology or industrial property rights transferred to them by their foreign controlling company were lifted.[121] More recently, in 1993, further liberalization of the rules has occurred. By Ruling 120 of 17 December 1993 of the Institute of Industrial Property (INPI), the examination, by INPI, of contracts concerning trademarks or patent licences, transfer of know-how, cost-sharing and technical and scientific assistance will be limited to formal issues, including the validity of the relevant registration, privileges and the consideration to be paid. In the areas of the transfer of industrial technology and technical and scientific assistance, parties are now free to agree the terms of their contract and INPI will no longer limit the amount of consideration to be paid. However, restrictions on the export of products produced with the technology transferred are still prohibited.[122]

Apart from changes in national regimes, attempts at instituting reforms in the international system of intellectual property protection have not been successful. As noted earlier, the proposed reforms of the Paris Convention have not come about, the negotiations over the TOT Code are stalled and, as noted in chapter 7, a new regime aimed at the strengthening of the international system of intellectual property protection has been put forward as part of the Uruguay Round Final Act. In these circumstances it is hard to envisage the broader development of national or international regimes that place the interests of LDCs in the acquisition of technology above the interests of the owners of commercial technology in protecting its status as private property. At the time of writing, the LDCs themselves appear to be acquiescing to this view.

Notes

1 See further: M. Blakeney, *Legal Aspects of the Transfer of Technology to Developing Countries* (ESC Publishing, 1989), at pp. 1–2; Miagsam Santikarn, *Technology Transfer* (Singapore University Press, 1981), pp. 3–6; C. Ubezonu, 'The law policy and practice of technology transfer to Nigeria (1990), PhD Thesis, University of London, pp. 24–39.

2 UNCTAD, *Draft International Code of Conduct on the Transfer of Technology*, as at the close of the sixth session of Conference on 5 June 1985 (TD/CODE TOT/47 20 June 1985), chapter 1, para. 1.2. This is the last full draft of the Code to have been published. See further below.

3 Santikarn (note 1 above), at p. 4.

4 Blakeney (note 1 above), at p. 136.

5 Draft TOT Code (note 2 above), chapter 1, para. 1.3. During negotiations the Group of 77 countries wished to see these as mere examples of technology transfer transactions, while the major developed capital- and technology-exporting states, Group B, and the then socialist Group D saw them as exhaustive.

6 Blakeney (note 1 above), at p. 3.

7 See G. K. Helleiner, 'International technology issues: Southern needs and Northern responses', in J. Bhagwati (ed.), *The New International Economic Order: the North–South Debate* (MIT Press, 1977), at p. 309.

8 See T. Anyos, 'Mechanisms for technology transfer: the role of the infrastructure', in S. Gee (ed.), *Technology Transfer in Industrialized Countries* (Sijthoff, 1979), pp. 195–212. See further R. Van Tulder and G. Junne, *European Multinationals in Core Technologies* (Wiley/IRM, 1988), esp. chapters 6 and 7.

9 J. H. Dunning, *Multinational Enterprises and the Global Economy* (Addison-Wesley, 1992), at p. 290. Professor Dunning observes that in the late

1980s MNEs were accounting for between 75 and 80 per cent of privately undertaken R&D in the world.

10   See G. K. Helleiner, 'The role of multinational corporations in the less developed countries' trade in Technology', 3 *World Development* 161 (1975).

11   See D. Greer, 'Control of terms and conditions for international transfers of technology to developing countries', in O. Schachter and R. Hellawell (eds), *Competition in International Business* (Columbia University Press, 1981), at p. 48, citing W. Chudson, *The International Transfer of Commercial Technology to Developing Countries* (UNITAR, 1971), p. 18.

12   See Van Tulder and Junne (note 8 above), chapter 2.

13   See further Greer (note 11 above), at pp. 56–60.

14   See e.g. *Re ECR* 900 [1992] 4 CMLR 54. The EC Commission found that the market for new cellular telephony technology in the EC is dominated by a small number of national telecom companies which set the terms of technological innovation and conditions of supply.

15   See, for an economic analysis of this situation, Rodriguez, 'Trade in technological knowledge and the national advantage', 83 Jo. Pol. Econ. 121 (1975).

16   See G. K. Helleiner (note 7 above), p. 295; Hope, 'Basic needs and technology transfer issues in the "New International Economic Order"', 42 Am. J. Econ. & Soc. 393 (1983); Blakeney (note 1 above), at pp. 57–67.

17   See further Helleiner (note 10 above).

18   See Santikarn (note 1 above), at pp. 17–20. Furthermore, it may be argued that this position tends towards the perpetuation of underdevelopment by assuming that the most modern capital-intensive technologies should not be exported to LDCs, thereby depriving them of the source of economic modernity. See further Arghiri Emmanuel, *Appropriate or Underdeveloped Technology?* (Wiley/IRM, 1982).

19   Helleiner (note 10 above), at pp. 170–2. See also chapter 7 at pp. 228–34 on Export Processing Zones.

20   Blakeney (note 1 above), at pp. 64–5.

21   Lall, 'The patent system and the transfer of technology to less developed countries', 10 JWTL 1 at 5–6 (1976).

22   See R. Caves, *Multinational Enterprise and Economic Analysis* (Cambridge University Press, 2nd edn 1996), pp. 68–72. See also chapter 3 at pp. 73–81, where this issue is addressed in the context of MNE growth strategies.

23   Santikarn (note 1 above), at p. 12.

24   See Caves (note 22 above), at p. 228.

25   See Santikarn (note 1 above), at pp. 24–35; Blakeney (note 1 above), at pp. 35–42 and 67–70; R. Whish, *Competition Law*, 3rd edn (Butterworths, 1993), pp. 624–8.

26   Santikarn, ibid.

27   See e.g. *Jefferson Parish Hospital District No. 2* v *Hyde* 466 US 2 (1984); *United States* v *Jerrold Electronics Corp.* 187 F. Supp. 545 (E. D. Pa. 1960)

aff'd 365 US 567 (1961); EC Commission Regulation 2349/84 OJ [1985] 1 113/34 article 3(9) (patent licensing agreements); EC Commission Regulation 556/89 OJ [1989] L 61/1 article 3(3) (know-how licensing agreements). See further draft EC Commission Regulation of 30 June 1994 on technology transfer agreements: OJ [1994] C 178/3, article 2(5). The draft Regulation is to replace Regs 2349/84 and 556/89. See now Commission Regulation 240/96 OJ [1996] 31/2 Article 2(1)(5).

28 Santikarn (note 1 above), at pp. 28–9.

29 Blakeney (note 1 above), at p. 41.

30 See e.g. *Windsurfing International* v *EC Commission* [1986] ECR 611; [1986] 3 CMLR 489; Commission Regulation 2349/84 (note 27 above), article 2(1)(3) and article 3(7); Commission Regulation 556/89 (note 27 above), article 2(1)(8) and article 3(6); Technology Transfer Regulation 240/96 (note 27 above), articles 2(1)(8) and 3(4); *Talking Pictures Corp.* v *Western Electric Co.* 305 US 124 (1938).

31 Blakeney (note 1 above), at p. 39.

32 Ibid.

33 See V. Korah, *Patent Licensing and EEC Competition Rules: Regulation 2349/84* (ESC Publishing, 1985), at p. 76.

34 Blakeney (note 1 above), at p. 39.

35 Commission Regulation 2349/84 (note 27 above), article 2(1)(4); Regulation 240/96 (note 27 above), article 2(1)(3).

36 See e.g. Commission Regulation 556/89 (note 27 above), article 2(1)(3) and (7); Regulation 240/96 (note 27 above), article 2(1)(3).

37 Commission Regulation 2349/84 (note 27 above), article 3(2); Regulation 240/96 (note 27 above), article 2(1)(3).

38 Commission Regulation 556/89 (note 27 above), article 3(1); Regulation 240/96 (note 27 above), article 2(1)(3).

39 Commission Regulation 556/89. See also Commission Regulation 2349/84 (note 27 above), article 3(4); Regulation 240/96 (note 27 above), article 2(1)(7).

40 See e.g. Commission Regulation 556/89 (note 27 above), article 3(2); Commission Regulation 2349/84 (note 27 above), article 3(8); Regulation 240/96 (note 27 above), articles 2(1)(4) and 3(6).

41 See generally W. R. Cornish, *Intellectual Property: Patents, Copyright, Trade Marks and Allied Rights*, 3rd edn (Sweet & Maxwell, 1996).

42 See the Paris Convention for the Protection of Industrial Property 1883 (as amended), articles 2 and 4. For a full list of the major conventions covering patents, trade marks, industrial designs and biotechnology see Blakeney (note 1 above), at pp. 14–21.

43 On the 'rule of reason' in competition law see chapter 11 at p. 385.

44 15 USC ss 4301–6. For analysis see US Department of Justice draft Antitrust Enforcement Guidelines for International Operations (13 October 1994), Trade Reg. Rep. No. 338, part 2, p. 37 at s. 2.5, p. 42.

45 Commission Regulation 2349/84 (note 27 above); Regulation 240/96 (note 27 above).

46 Commission Regulation 556/89 (note 27 above); Regulation 240/96, ibid.

47   Commission Regulation 418/85 OJ [1985] L 53/5. For analysis see: V. Korah, *R and D and the EEC Competition Rules: Regulation 418/85* (ESC Publishing, 1986).
48   See Van Tulder and Junne (note 8 above), at pp. 201–6.
49   See chapter 11 at pp. 391–3.
50   For example, the European ESPRIT Programme in Information Technology and other initiatives, discussed by Van Tulder and Junne (note 8 above), chapter 7. See also, on EC backing for the development of wide-screen television, *Financial Times*, 17 June 1993, 'UK agrees wide-screen TV plan for Europe', p. 1, and 'A viewer's guide to TV – for next four years', p. 2.
51   See further Blakeney (note 1 above), at pp. 49–50.
52   See Jayagovind, 'The international patent system and the developing countries', (1980) Ind. JIL 47 at pp. 56–62, on which the next paragraph is based.
53   UN Doc. E/3681/Rev. 1. 1964.
54   See Blakeney (note 1 above), at pp. 21–4; Ewing, 'UNCTAD and the transfer of technology', 10 JWTL 197 (1976).
55   UNCTAD, *The Role of the Patent System in the Transfer of Technology to Developing Countries* (UN Doc. TD/B/AC 11/19, 1974).
56   UNCTAD, *The Role of Trademarks in Developing Countries* (UN Doc. TD/B/C. 6/AC. 3/3 Rev. 1, 1979). Comment: Wasserman, 14 JWTL 80 (1980).
57   See Vaitsos, 'The revision of the international patent system: legal considerations for a Third World position', 4 *World Development* 85 (1976); Blakeney (note 1 above), at pp. 24–6 and 90–104.
58   See Vaitsos, ibid., at pp. 87–8; Vaitsos, 'Patents revisited: their function in developing countries', 9 *Journal of Development Studies* (1972), at pp. 73–83; Roffe, 'Abuses of patent monopoly: a legal appraisal', 2 *World Development* 15 (1974); Penrose, 'International patenting and the less developed countries', 83 Econ. Jo. 768 (1973). See also the *Official Report of the Revision of the Patents Law* (Government of India, 1959, 'The Aygangar Report'), for a significant early analysis of the issues facing LDCs.
59   See UNCTAD (note 55 above), at para. 339, cited in Roffe, ibid., at p. 26.
60   Roffe, ibid., at pp. 18–20; Mangalo, 'Patent protection and technology transfer in the North–South conflict', 9 IIC 100 at p. 110–11 (1978).
61   See UNCTAD, 1979 (note 56 above); Chudnovsky, 'Foreign trademarks in developing countries', 7 *World Development* 663 (1979); Greer, 'The economic benefits and costs of trademarks: lessons for the developing countries', 7 *World Development* 683 (1979).
62   See Ball, 'Attitudes of developing countries to trademarks', 74 TMR 160 at 164–6 (1984). Other countries to have used such devices in past legislation include Brazil (Normative Act No. 15, 11 September 1975, article 3.5.1) and Yugoslavia (Law for the Protection of Inventions Technical Improvements and Distinctive Signs 1981, article 134).
63   Ball, ibid., at p. 167.
64   Note 55 above at paras 394–412.

65   Vaitsos (note 57 above), at p. 90.

66   Beier, 'The significance of the patent system for technical, economic and social progress', 11 IIC 563 at 584 (1980).

67   See pp. 254–7 above.

68   At pp. 39–40 above.

69   See further Lall (note 21 above).

70   See Ball (note 62 above). See further Cornish and Phillips, 'The economic function of trademarks: an analysis with special reference to developing countries', 13 IIC 41 (1982).

71   Blakeney (note 1 above), at p. 109.

72   Lall (note 21 above), at p. 11.

73   See Public Law 100–418, 23 August 1988, 102 Stat. 1107 s. 1303, which empowers the US Trade Representative to identify countries that deny adequate and effective intellectual property protection and to initiate an investigation which may lead to economic sanctions being taken against the target state. This power was used in 1992 against the People's Republic of China. Thereupon China agreed to improve protection of computer software, sound recordings, pharmaceuticals and agri-chemicals, to increase copyright protection to 50 years and to join the Berne Convention by October 1992 and the Geneva Phonogram Convention by June 1993: 'US and China resolve copyright row', *Financial Times*, 17 January 1992, p. 3. See further revised Patent Law 1993 discussed by Huang Wei, 'New Patent Law Promotes Opening', 35 *Beijing Review* No. 48, 30 November to 6 December 1992, p. 14. India has also been the target of action under this provision in 1993: 'India complains as US threatens retaliation', *Financial Times*, 8/9 May 1993, p. 3.

74   TCMD, *Intellectual Property Rights and Foreign Direct Investment* (1993, UN Doc. ST/CTC/SER. A/24).

75   See further: Blakeney (note 1 above), chapter 7, who provides references to literature for 33 countries that have used such laws at pp. 162–4; G. Cabanellas, *Antitrust and Direct Regulation of International Transfer of Technology Transactions IIC. Studies in Industrial Property and Copyright Law, Vol. 7* (Verlag Chemie, 1984), chapter 2; Correa, 'Transfer of technology in Latin America: a decade of control', 15 JWTL 388 (1981); UNCTAD, *Control of Restrictive Practices in Transfer of Technology Transactions* (UN Doc TD/B/C. 6/72, 1982). The laws described in these works represent policy responses of the 1970s. It should not be assumed that all the laws mentioned in these works have remained in force unamended.

76   See: 11 ILM 126 (1972); as amended see 16 ILM 138 (1977).

77   See Correa (note 75 above), who lists: Argentina, Law 19,231 of 1971, Law 20,794 of 1974, Law 21,617 of 1976 and Law 22,426 of 1981; Brazil, Law 4,131 of 1962. Law 5,772 and Normative Act No. 15 of 11 September 1975; Bolivia, Decree 9,798 of 1971; Colombia, Decree 1,234 of 1972; Equador, S. Decree 974 of 1971; Peru, incorporated Decision 24 in 1971; Venezuela, incorporated Decision 24 in 1973; Mexico, Law of 28 December 1972 on the Registration of Contracts and Agreements Regarding the Transfer of Technology: see now chapter 6 at pp. 195–6 (FDI Law 1993) and chapter 7 at pp. 241–5 (NAFTA).

78   See, for example, Nigeria: National Office of Industrial Property Decree 1979, discussed extensively by Ubezonu (note 1 above). Ghana has recently adopted new technology transfer regulations under s. 30 of the Investment Code 1985: Technology Transfer Regulations 9 September 1992 (L. I. 1547). China: Law on Technology Contracts 23 June 1987, Detailed Rules for the Implementation of the regulations of the PRC on the Administration of Technology Import Contracts of 20 January 1988 (Vol. 2, 3 *China Law and Practice*, 28 March 1988 p. 38). For background to the evolution of China's policy in this areas see Lubman, 'Technology transfer to China: policies, law and practice', in M. J. Moser (ed.), *Foreign Trade, Investment, and the Law in the People's Republic of China*, 2nd edn (Oxford, 1987), chapter 4. China's legislation in this area began with the Interim Regulations on the Transfer of Technology, 24 ILM 292 (1985), and the Regulations Controlling Technology Import Contracts, 24 ILM 801 (1985). India has regulated technology transfer transactions by way of administrative procedures outlined in periodic policy statements: see Industrial Policy Statement of 23 July 1980, Technology Policy Statement, January 1983, in *National Science and Technology Policy*, 3rd edn (Lok Sabha Secretariat, 1989), Statement on Industrial Policy of July 24 1991, in UNCTC, *Foreign Direct Investment and Technology Transfer in India* (UN Doc. ST/CTC/117, 1992), annex VII.

79   Blakeney (note 75 above) cites as examples Bulgaria, the former German Democratic Republic, Greece, Portugal, Spain and the former Yugoslavia.

80   Cabinet Order Concerning Direct Domestic Investments October 11, 1980, chapter III, Conclusion etc. of Agreements for Importation of Technology articles 4–6; Ordinance Concerning Direct Domestic Investment, Order No. 1, 20 November 1980 as amended by Order No. 1, 6 April 1989, article 5, 2(3); Notification No. 3, of 27 November 1980; all in Japan, *Laws, Ordinances and Other Regulations Concerning Foreign Exchange and Foreign Trade* (Chuo Shuppan Kikaku Co., 1990). See further Ohara, 'Japanese regulation of technology imports', 15 JWTL 83 (1981); Ohara, 'Regulations on transfer of technology in Japan', 15 IIC 121 (1984).

81   Blakeney (note 1 above), at p. 167.

82   See Andean Investment Code, Decision 24 (note 76 above), article 21, which prohibited the authorization of royalty payments and their deduction for tax purposes between affiliated enterprises. By Andean Commission Decision 291 of March 21, 1991, article 15, the payment of royalties between affiliated enterprises may now be authorized in the cases previously approved by the competent national authority of the recipient country. Thus this matter is referred back to national law: 30 ILM 1283 at 1293 (1991). See also Argentina Law 22,426 of 1981, articles 2 and 5: Cabanellas (note 75 above), at pp. 26–7.

83   See e.g. Brazil Normative Act No. 15, of 11 September 1975 article 1.3.

84   In some cases it is arguable whether the law allows for nullification. See e.g. the debate over the effect of non-registration under Nigeria's National Office of Industrial Property Decree 1979 ss 4, 5 and 7, Ubezonu (note 1 above), at pp. 366–75; Osunbor, 'Law and policy on the registration of

technology transfer transactions in Nigeria', 21 JWTL 18 (1987);
Fagbemi, 'Registration of technology transactions in Nigeria: another
view', 22 JWTL 95 (1988).

85 Cabanellas (note 75 above), at pp. 20–1.

86 Correa (note 75 above), at pp. 391–2.

87 Cabanellas (note 75 above), at pp. 29–30.

88 Cabanellas, ibid., at p. 45.

89 For a full discussion of this issue see ibid., chapter 3.

90 For the historical background to the TOT Code negotiations see: Blakeney
(note 1 above), at pp. 131–3; Patel, 'Transfer of technology and the third
UNCTAD', 7 JWTL 226 (1973); Roffe, 'UNCTAD: Code of Conduct
on Transfer of Technology: a progress review', 12 JWTL 351 (1978);
Zuijdwijk, 'The UNCTAD Code of Conduct on the Transfer of Tech-
nology', 24 McGill LJ 562 (1978); Thompson, 'The UNCTAD Code on
Transfer of Technology', 16 JWTL 311 (1982); Roffe, 'UNCTAD:
Transfer of Technology Code: Fifth Session of the UN Conference', 18
JWTL 176 (1984); Roffe, 'UNCTAD Code of Conduct on Transfer of
Technology', 19 JWTL 669 (1985).

91 See Thompson, ibid., at pp. 313–14.

92 See *Report of the Intergovernmental Group of Experts on an International Code
of Conduct on the Transfer of Technology to the United Nations Conference on
an International Code of Conduct on the Transfer of Technology* (UNCTAD
Doc. TD/CODE TOT/1, 1978).

93 See Sixth Session of the UN Conference on an International Code of
Conduct on the Transfer of Technology, Background Note (UNCTAD
Secretariat, UN Doc. TD/CODE TOT/49 9 October 1985).

94 The most recent version of the draft TOT Code can be found in UN Doc.
TD/CODE TOT/47, 20 June 1985. For a full analysis see Blakeney (note
1 above), at pp. 133–61.

95 See TD/CODE TOT/47, at pp. 8–11.

96 See TD/CODE TOT/47, appendix D, p. 1.

97 Ibid.

98 See Thompson (note 90 above), at p. 326. On the legal effect of the draft
code see Blakeney (note 1 above), at pp. 134–5.

99 Ibid. For further details of the negotiations on chapter 4 at the Sixth
Session see the *Report of the Chairman of Working Group I* (UN Doc. TD/
CODE TOT/SR. 21), p. 4, paras 5–24.

100 See TD/CODE TOT/47, at p. 21.

101 See TD/CODE TOT/47, appendix A, p. 10, and see the Chinese compromise proposal in ibid., appendix A, p. 9.

102 See Thompson (note 90 above), at pp. 333–4.

103 See further the *Report of the Chairman of Working Group II* (UN Doc. TD/
CODE TOT/SR 21), p. 5, para. 25; TD/CODE TOT/47, appendix A,
pp. 7–8.

104 See further: *Report by the Secretary-General of UNCTAD on Consultations
Held Pursuant to General Assembly Resolution 41/166 of 5 December 1986*
(UN Doc. TD/CODE/TOT/51, 21 October 1987); 'Further con-
sultations on a draft international code of conduct on the transfer of

technology, report by the Secretary-General of UNCTAD' (UN Doc. TD/CODE/TOT/57, 1991); 'Negotiations on an international code of conduct on the transfer of technology: consultations carried out in 1992, report by the Secretary-General of UNCTAD' (UN Doc. TD/CODE/TOT/58, 22 October 1992).

105   UN Doc. TD/CODE/TOT/58, 22 October 1992, para. 6, citing the Cartagena Commitment, para. 173.

106   See ibid., paras 7–8. Only ten responses had been received by the time this document was published.

107   Ibid., at p. 7.

108   See Osunbor (note 84 above), at pp. 21–2; See also Omorogbe, 'The legal framework and policy for technology development in Nigeria', 3 RADIC 156 (1991).

109   See Alegimenlen, 'Petroleum development technology acquisition: a synopsis of the Nigerian experience', 3 RADIC 526 (1991).

110   Note 76 above.

111   Note 82 above, articles 12–15.

112   Ibid., article 14.

113   See references at note 78 above for details of the old regime.

114   See UNCTC, 1992 (note 78 above), at p. 135.

115   Ibid., para. 28, at p. 132.

116   Ibid., para. 27, at p. 131.

117   For the background to this policy see the National Informatics and Automation Plan, reproduced in English in the *Brazilian Informatics Industry Directory 1986/87* (Abicomp, 1986), at pp. 169–76. An English version of Law No. 7232 of 1984 is reproduced in this publication at pp. 147–51. For developments in informatics policy in Latin America see Correa, 'Informatics in Latin America: promises and realities', 23 JWT 81 (1989).

118   See Decree No. 99541 of 21 September 1990, CONIN Resolution No. 20 of 26 October 1990, SCT Ordinance No. 223 of 10 May 1991: *Legal Letters* of 1991 and 1992 in N. Pinherio (ed.), *Doing Business in Brazil* (September 1992, Release No. 25); Schwimmer, 'A brave new world for informatics in Brazil', 7 *Computer Lawyer* 24 (1990).

119   SCT Ordinances Nos 543 and 544 of 5 September 1991.

120   See *Legal Letter* of November 1991 in Pinhero (note 118 above).

121   See Law No. 8383 of 30 December 1991, Central Bank of Brazil circular letter No. 2282 of 2 June 1992 in *Legal Letter*, June 1992, in Pinheiro (note 118 above).

122   INPI Ruling 120 of 17 December 1993 published in *Industrial Property Review* of 21 December 1993, noted in *Tax News Service*, TNS-68 (1994).

13

Labour Relations

The present chapter deals with the development of specialized standards for the conduct of labour relations by MNEs. These are contained in the OECD Guideline on Employment and Industrial Relations (the OECD Guideline),[1] and in the International Labour Organisation's (ILO) Tripartite Declaration of Principles on Multinationals and Social Policy (the ILO Declaration).[2] Both are products of the movement, in the 1970s, for the adoption of international codes of conduct on MNEs. Moreover, both codes are based on a consensus between governments, industry and trade union representatives, and, as such, represent 'corporatist' policy responses.[3] Despite significant changes in political attitudes towards labour issues since that time, both codes remain in effect and offer a good starting point for the study of how international practice in this area has evolved since the 1970s.

The structure of the present chapter follows the principal headings in the ILO Declaration. Thus the issues of employment, training, conditions of work and life and industrial relations are each studied in a separate section. The terms of the ILO Declaration are discussed alongside the corresponding provisions in the OECD Guideline, given that the two codes are complementary. Indeed, as the more elaborate code, the ILO Declaration has been said to be of use in interpreting the OECD Guideline, though this must bear in mind their distinct follow-up procedures.[4] Reference is also made, where appropriate, to EC law and policy. This has made significant advances in areas expressly directed at the employment consequences of MNE operations in the Single European Market. Before that is done, the scene is set by a brief review of the reasons behind the adoption of the two codes, and of the general policies they espouse, especially their relationship to national laws.

1   The Evolution of the ILO and OECD Codes

The ILO has been at the forefront of the movement for the international regulation of minimum labour standards since its inception in 1919 under Part XIII of the Treaty of Versailles. To this end the ILO has adopted numerous International Labour Conventions, laying down the minimum standards for the treatment of labour that are acceptable to the international community.[5] These form the background principles on which the ILO Declaration is based. Indeed, the Declaration refers to the relevant ILO Conventions both in its text and in its Annex.[6] Furthermore, the ILO is a tripartite organization with representatives of governments, business and labour having access to its decision-making organs as members of national delegations.[7] For these reasons, it was natural for the ILO to be used as the vehicle for the development of new principles applicable to MNEs.

The ILO became involved in the formulation of a code of conduct in response to demands from labour representatives and less developed countries that had been made since the 1960s.[8] In the early 1970s the LDCs pressed for an ILO conference which could adopt a binding international code for MNEs. This was resisted by the employers' representatives, who favoured the adoption of a voluntary code. In 1972 the negotiating process started with the first 'Tripartite meeting on the relationship between multinational enterprises and social policy'. The meeting set up a series of research studies that were carried out between 1972 and 1976. These resulted in a recommendation that a non-binding tripartite declaration of principles concerning multinational enterprises and social policy should be drafted. The ILO Declaration was finally adopted on 16 November 1977.

The Declaration did not provide for any follow-up machinery. However, in 1980, such a procedure was adopted. The Governing Body of the ILO established a Committee on Multinational Enterprises (the Committee). This was charged with three tasks.[9] First, states are to make periodic reports on the implementation of the Declaration on the basis of questionnaires sent through governments to unions and business organizations. Secondly, it is to conduct periodic studies on labour issues involving MNEs. Thirdly, it is to interpret the Declaration through a disputes procedure. This was revised in 1986.[10] Requests for interpretation are submitted to the Committee by governments and by national or international organizations of employers or workers. Workers' requests will be received only if they are not able to have these submitted through a national government. Requests are admissible if they do not conflict with or duplicate appropriate procedures at national level, in the case of issues involving national laws, and with the ILO's international procedures under ILO Conventions, in the case of Convention-based issues. If the request is receivable, the International Labour Office will prepare a draft reply which is considered by the Committee. The reply is then submitted for approval by the Governing Body and, if approved, is published in the ILO *Official Bulletin*.[11] This procedure is not judicial in nature. It serves merely to clarify the standards contained in the Declaration. However, the Committee can only do so in the context of an 'actual situation'.[12] Thus the procedure may involve the ascertainment of certain facts but not a resolution of disputes over facts and laws.

The OECD Guideline on Employment and Industrial Relations is part of the more general OECD Guidelines on Multinational Enterprises. It is, therefore, less detailed than the ILO Declaration. The background to the passage of the OECD Guidelines is discussed in chapter 16. For present purposes it is enough to note that the OECD Employment Guideline has been the subject of extensive interpretation by the OECD Committee on International Investment and Multinational Enterprises under its powers of interpretation.[13] As with the ILO Declaration, these powers stop short of pronouncing on the outcome of a dispute. Nevertheless, in the early years of its operation, the OECD Employment Guideline was frequently used by West European trade unions to obtain general interpretations of principles from the OECD Committee, arising out of disputes involving MNE employment and industrial relations practices.[14] However, in more recent years, the Guideline has declined as a means of bringing pressure to bear on a MNE, owing largely to a shift in Western European trade union strategy towards lobbying for the development of EC policies in the labour and social fields.

2   General Policies of the Codes and Their Relationship to National Laws

The principal difference in the general approaches of the codes concerns their respective addressees. The OECD Guideline is jointly addressed by the Member Countries to multinational enterprises operating in their territories.[15] The ILO Declaration is addressed to governments, to the employers' and workers' organizations in both home and host countries and to MNEs themselves.[16] On the other hand, both codes share much in common. First, they are voluntary in nature.[17] Indeed, it is hard to envisage that binding provisions would ever have been accepted on the basis of consensus. Employers' representatives before both bodies were opposed to binding instruments. Secondly, both instruments are addressed to MNEs and national enterprises. They aim to reflect good practice for all, without discrimination as to nationality.[18] Thirdly, both codes envisage the primacy of national law. Thus the ILO Declaration states:

All the parties concerned by this Declaration should respect the sovereign rights of States, obey the national laws and regulations, give due consideration to local practices and respect relevant international standards.[19]

The primacy of national law is reinforced by the requirement that the above-mentioned disputes procedure cannot be used to determine issues arising out of national law. Similarly, the OECD Employment Guideline begins by stating that enterprises should respect the standards it contains, 'within the framework of law, regulations and prevailing labour relations and employment practices, in each of the countries in which they operate'.

The reference to the primacy of national law severely weakens the effectiveness of both codes. The codes preserve the right of each state to determine the nature, scope and effect of its national labour laws. Consequently, despite exhortations to the contrary that will be mentioned below, the codes can do nothing to prevent competition between states over the reduction of labour standards as a means of reducing the cost of investment in their respective territories. Furthermore, the codes do not address the problem of conflicting labour standards that may arise as a result of the international operations of MNEs.[20] For example, where the firm employs a national of the home state in the host state, it may wish that person's employment contract to be governed by the law of the home state. Where home state law sanctions terms and conditions that are contrary to host state law, the contract may be unlawful in the host state. Indeed, many states may have mandatory rules of employment law that cannot be avoided through the choice of a foreign law as the proper law of the contract of employment. The territorial principle of jurisdiction still prevails in the field of labour law, making for considerable differences in the content of laws that will govern employment issues within the MNE. This is a major reason why MNEs tend to treat employment issues on a decentralized basis.

The ILO Declaration contains certain additional provisions of a general nature, not found in the OECD Guideline. Thus, governments which have not yet done so are urged to ratify ILO Conventions Nos 87 on freedom of association, 98 on the right to organize and bargain collectively, 111 on discrimination in employment and 122 on employment policy, and in any event to observe, in their national policy, the principles embodied in Conventions 111, 119 on termination of employment and 122.[21] Furthermore, MNEs are expected to take full account of the general policy objectives of the countries in which they operate, especially the development priorities and social aims and structures of these countries. To this end, consultations should be held between the firm and the government and employers' and workers' organizations in these countries.[22]

Finally, governments of home countries are urged to promote good social practice in accordance with the ILO Declaration, having regard to the social and labour law, regulations and practices in host countries as well as to relevant international standards. Both home and host countries are encouraged to have consultations with each other on these matters.[23] This provision urges home states to ensure that home-based corporations observe good practice in their overseas operations, and at all times observe host states' laws. It therefore reinforces the territorial nature of labour regulation, in that this provision does not envisage the extraterritorial application of superior home country standards to employees in host states. This suggests that bilateral arrangements may offer a way forward in ensuring the observance of higher standards throughout the network of countries in which a MNE operates. Such efforts could be conducted under the auspices of the ILO itself.[24]

More recently, it has been suggested that the new World Trade Organization, established under the Final Act of the Uruguay Round GATT Negotiations, should have its mandate extended to cover workers rights, thereby establishing an international regime of minimum standards of treatment that could avoid distortions of trade and investment flows caused by competition over the lowering of labour standards. Thus, in future, a new multilateral 'floor of rights' may be in place, although this faces stiff opposition from certain newly industrializing states, which see such initiatives as a method of preserving the living standards of workers in developed countries by protecting them against competition from lower labour cost areas.[25]

3 Employment Issues

The ILO Declaration deals with three issues under this heading: employment promotion, equality of opportunity and treatment and security of employment. The OECD Employment Guideline contains standards pertaining to the second and third issues, but does not espouse the broader goal of employment promotion. However, para. 2 of the General Policies Guideline in the OECD code mentions the 'creation of employment opportunities' as a matter to which MNEs should give due consideration.[26]

3.1   Employment Promotion

The ILO Declaration asserts that governments should 'declare and pursue, as a major goal, an active policy designed to promote full, productive and freely chosen employment',[27] and that MNEs, 'particularly when operating in developing countries, should endeavour to increase employment opportunities and standards, taking into account the employment policies and objectives of the governments, as well as security of employment and the long-term development of the enterprise'.[28] To this general objective are added specific duties to consult with host country authorities and national employers' and workers' organizations in order to keep manpower plans in harmony with national social development policies,[29] to give priority to the employment and promotion of host country nationals[30] and, when investing in developing countries, to use technologies which generate employment.[31] Furthermore, supply contracts with local enterprises should be concluded whenever practicable, so as to stimulate the use and the processing of local raw materials.[32]

These aspects of the Declaration now appear rather dated in the light of the abandonment, by many states, of full employment policies, and in the wake of the recessions of the 1980s and early 1990s. Indeed, in 1986 the ILO Committee on Multinational Enterprises found, not surprisingly, that MNEs made little difference in the creation of employment opportunities and that such firms suffered the same employment constraints as other firms operating in the throes of recession. Furthermore, there was generally little adaptation of productive technology to the employment needs of host states.[33] In all, the Declaration appears to have been based on an exaggerated belief in the ability of MNEs to act as agents of economic and social development. Thus, while it contains a sentiment that is no doubt generally accepted, the practical utility of its exhortations may be doubted. Full employment in a global high-technology economy is becoming harder to envisage, as the demand for unskilled and semi-skilled labour decreases and automation reduces the total number of jobs required for profitable operation.[34]

3.2   Equality of Opportunity and Treatment

The ILO Declaration states that 'all governments should pursue policies designed to promote equality of opportunity and treatment in employment, with a view to eliminating any discrimination based on race, colour, sex, religion, political opinion, national extraction or social origin'.[35] MNEs should be guided by the same principles throughout their operations but without prejudice to preferential treatment for host country employees or to governmental policies designed to correct historical patterns of discrimination.[36] Equally, governments should never encourage MNEs to pursue discriminatory policies.[37] The OECD Employment Guideline echoes the ILO Declaration by recommending that enterprises should

Implement their employment policies including hiring, discharge, pay, promotion and training without discrimination unless selectivity in respect of employee characteristics is in furtherance of established governmental policies which specifically promote greater equality of employment opportunity.[38]

Thus, both codes accept positive discrimination, or 'affirmative action', on the basis of governmental policies. The ILO Declaration goes further and accepts the legitimacy of preferential treatment for host state employees. Neither code has raised significant issues of interpretation in this area. Most states accept non-discrimination in employment as a principle, though it is unrealistic to expect that this is always observed in practice.[39] In this respect MNEs are subject to the same requirements and pressures as national enterprises. Much depends on the internal 'management culture' and whether, regardless of legal rules, a moral principle of non-discrimination is observed.

In the context of MNE operations, it is arguable that non-discrimination laws should apply extraterritorially, thereby ensuring the same legal protection to all employees wherever they work. The issue has arisen in relation to the application of US non-discrimination laws to US employees working in the foreign subsidiaries of US corporations. In 1991 the US Supreme Court held that Title VII of the Civil Rights Act 1964, which prohibits discrimination in employment on the basis of race, religion or national origin, did not have extraterritorial reach so as to protect a US citizen working abroad in a US controlled company.[40] This ruling was reversed by the Civil Rights Act of 1991, ensuring that US citizens working abroad in US controlled foreign corporations did not lose the protection of Title VII.[41] Equally, Title VII applies to the US-based subsidiaries of foreign corporations. This is so despite the protection of the right of free management of foreign companies in the USA under US Friendship Commerce and Navigation treaties, which includes the right to hire executive and other specialized employees of the foreign firm's choice.[42]

Furthermore, when MNE employees are sent on a short-term posting to another state it is arguable that they should be entitled to benefit from the protection of host state labour rights even though their contract of employment with the MNE may be governed by the law of another state, for example, the home state. This problem is likely to increase in the EC as the Single European Market develops. In order to ensure that such protection exists the EC Commission has adopted a Directive on the protection of posted workers in the services sector which seeks to ensure that certain employment laws generally applicable in the Member State to which the worker is posted apply to him or her even though the contract of employment is governed by the law of another Member State.[43]

3.3   Security of Employment

The ILO Declaration recommends that governments study the impact of MNEs on employment and develop suitable policies to deal with the employment and labour market impacts of MNE operations.[44] In their turn, MNEs and national enterprises should, through active manpower planning, 'endeavour to provide stable employment for their employees and should observe freely negotiated obligations concerning employment stability and social security'.[45] Furthermore, MNEs, because of the flexibility they are assumed to have, are exhorted to assume a leading role in promoting security of employment, particularly in countries where the discontinuation of operations is likely to accentuate long-term unemployment.[46] The Declaration further states that arbitrary dismissal procedures should be avoided,[47] and that governments, in cooperation with MNEs and national enterprises, should provide some form of income protection for workers whose employment has been terminated.[48]

Both the ILO Declaration and the OECD Employment Guideline accept that MNEs are free to change their operations, even if this results in major employment effects, as in the case of the closure of an entity involving collective lay-offs or dismissals,[49] or in a merger, takeover or transfer of production which results in employment rationalization.[50] In such cases, MNEs should provide reasonable notice of the impending changes to the representatives of their employees[51] and to relevant governmental authorities, and should cooperate in the mitigation, to the greatest possible extent, of any adverse effects.[52] In the *Badger* case, where a US parent closed down its Belgian subsidiary, the OECD Committee on International Investment and Multinational Enterprises stated that this obligation included assistance to the subsidiary so as to enable the payment of termination claims to be made in accordance with the national law of the host state.[53] However, in the *Philips* case the OECD Committee noted that, 'once multinational enterprises have made a decision to terminate branch activities, the Guidelines do not require them to solve or improve resulting regional development problems of host countries'.[54]

In general, for notice to be reasonable, it should be sufficiently timely for the purpose of mitigating action to be prepared and put into effect. Furthermore, management should normally be able to provide notice prior to the final decision being taken.[55] However, what constitutes 'reasonable notice' may be affected by the sensitivity of the business decisions involved, which may make it commercially difficult to give early notice of impending changes. The OECD Committee on Multinational Enterprises has envisaged that such cases would be exceptional, and that early notice could be given in most situations.[56]

Within the EC significant advances have been made in the protection of employment rights that are of direct relevance to the operations of MNEs. Collective redundancies and employees rights on the transfer of undertakings have been the subject of harmonization measures in the form of Directives.[57] The contents of Directives must be incorporated into the national laws of the Member States. Failure to do so may result in an enforceable right to damages against the defaulting Member State.[58] Thus EC law offers a source of developing and effective rules for the protection of employment in situations of change.

As regards collective redundancies, Council Directive 92/56/EEC was passed to ensure that existing workers' rights to information and consultation in cases of collective redundancies could not be undermined where such redundancies were caused by decisions of undertakings, other than the immediate employer, located in another Member State. The Commission saw this as a problem that was likely to increase with the growing concentration of undertakings across national frontiers in the Single European Market.[59] Directive 92/56 requires appropriate information to be given to workers' representatives so that consultation can take place with a view to avoiding collective redundancies, or to reducing the number of workers affected, and mitigating the consequences by recourse to social measures aimed, *inter alia*, at aid for redeploying or retaining workers made redundant.[60] Such consultation must take place in good time and with a view to reaching agreement.[61] The required information must be supplied in good time and must be relevant. It must specify the reasons for the projected redundancies, the numbers and categories of workers to be made redundant, the number of workers and categories normally employed, the period during which the projected redundancies are to be effected, the criteria of selection to be employed, and the method of calculating redundancy payments.[62] These obligations apply whether the decision concerning the redundancies is being taken by the immediate employer or by an undertaking controlling the employer. The immediate employer cannot rely on the failure of the controlling undertaking to furnish it with the relevant information as a defence to non-compliance with the Directive.[63] The group as a whole must ensure conformity with the terms of the Directive. Employers are further obliged to inform the relevant public authorities in writing of any projected redundancies. The document concerned must contain all the relevant information supplied to workers' representatives.[64] The proposed redundancies must not take place less than thirty days after the date of notification. This period may be reduced by Member States.[65]

With regard to EC provisions relating to employees' rights on the transfer of undertakings, Directive 77/187/EEC serves to protect the rights of an employee of an undertaking that is transferred or merged.[66] The Directive applies to 'the transfer of an undertaking, business or part of a business to another employer as a result of a legal transfer or merger'.[67] When this results in a change of employer from the transferor to the transferee, the latter must continue to observe the conditions of employment agreed in a collective agreement on the same terms applicable to the transferor under that agreement.[68] Furthermore, neither the transferor nor the transferee can use the transfer as grounds for dismissal, although this 'shall not stand in the way of dismissals that may take place for economic, technical or organisational reasons entailing changes in the workforce'.[69] The Directive does not apply to a transfer on insolvency, or where an employment relationship does not actually exist at the date of transfer.[70] There are duties of information and consultation concerning the proposed transfer on both the transferor and transferee.[71] The European Court of Justice has recently held that employees can opt out of the provisions of Directive 77/187 and the consequences of so doing are for national law to determine.[72]

4   Training of Workers

On the issue of training, the ILO Declaration encourages governments to develop national policies for vocational training and guidance, closely linked with employment.[73] MNEs are encouraged to ensure that relevant training is provided for all levels of employees in the host country to meet the needs of the enterprise as well as the development policies of the country. This should develop generally useful skills and promote career opportunities.[74] Furthermore, in developing countries, MNEs should participate in special programmes aimed at encouraging skill formation and development.[75] The OECD Employment Guideline provides for much the same approach. It states that MNEs, 'In their operations, to the greatest extent practicable, utilise, train and prepare for upgrading members of the local labour force in co-operation with representatives of their employees and, where appropriate, the relevant governmental authorities.'[76]

National training schemes will apply to MNEs and national enterprises without distinction. However, MNEs may offer special skills based on their international experience.[77] Thus they may be expected to provide greater assistance, particularly in LDCs. This may be reflected in incentive schemes. However, MNEs have been criticized by the ILO Committee on Multinational Enterprises for aiming their main training effort at their own needs rather than those of LDCs.[78] In a world economy characterized by increased industrial restructuring, training issues may acquire an importance far greater than before. Consequently, the ILO and OECD Committees may have to consider these provisions in more detail in the future than they have in the past.

5   Conditions of Work and Life

The ILO Declaration divides the issues under this heading between, on the one hand, wages, benefits and conditions of work and, on the other, safety and health matters. The OECD Employment Guideline says little on the first set of issues, simply asserting that MNEs should observe standards of employment not less favourable than those observed by comparable employers in the host country.[79] The second set of issues is implicit in the OECD Environmental Protection Guideline, which is discussed in chapter 16.[80]

5.1   Wages, Benefits and Conditions of Work

Like the OECD Guideline, the ILO Declaration applies the national treatment standard to these matters. Thus, 'Wages, benefits and conditions of work offered by multinational enterprises should be not less favourable to the workers than those offered by comparable employers in the country concerned.'[81] When operating in LDCs, where comparable employers may not exist, MNEs should provide the 'best possible wages, benefits and conditions of work, within the framework of government policies'.[82] These should be related to the 'economic position of the enterprise, but should be at least adequate to satisfy basic needs of the workers and their families'.[83] Where MNEs provide workers with basic amenities such as housing, medical care or food, these should be of a good standard.[84] Finally, the Declaration exhorts governments, especially in developing countries, to endeavour to adopt suitable measures to ensure that lower income groups and less developed areas benefit as much as possible from the activities of MNEs.[85]

Thus, the Declaration does not prevent MNEs from moving their operations to lower wage areas if they so choose. It preserves the ability of MNEs to scan investment locations for lower cost operating bases. All that is required is that the firm does not fall below the national treatment standard in the host state. In its 1986 review of the Declaration, the ILO Committee on Multinational Enterprises found that MNEs offered wages, benefits and conditions of work equal or comparable to those offered by local employers and, in some cases, generally superior to local terms and conditions. It found that MNEs paid according to what they could afford rather than by reference to the local labour market and local standards of living, while the payment of better than average wages depended on the technology, marketing and competitive skills of the given firm.[86] This conclusion has been confirmed more recently by Professor Dunning, who shows that MNE affiliates may often offer higher wages, particularly for skilled workers, and that most MNEs offer world-standard working practices, which may be better than the local average.[87] However, as Professor Dunning points out, 'it is not normally in the interest of MNEs to provide better working conditions than those necessary to ensure economic success. Consequently, they will usually be fairly close to the norm for the particular country or industry.'[88]

The approach of a MNE to wages, benefits and conditions will depend considerably on its 'management culture'. A firm may wish to act as a 'model employer' and unilaterally monitor, if not raise, standards. This policy is not without its pitfalls. These are well illustrated by the stand of the jeans manufacturer, Levi-Strauss, on workers' rights in the host countries where it seeks to operate.[89] Recently, this company adopted strict ethical guidelines covering the 'terms of engagement' that its overseas sub-contractors have to meet in order to obtain business from the company. The guidelines cover environmental requirements, health and safety standards and employment practices. Levi-Strauss will not allow sub-contractors to employ child or prison labour, working hours must not exceed sixty per week and wages must at least meet local standards. Since the adoption of these standards the company has withdrawn from Burma (Myanmar) and has refused to invest in China. However, the latter decision cannot remain unaltered indefinitely, if Levi-Strauss is not to risk losing its place on this potentially vast future market. Furthermore, in Bangladesh the company has had to compromise on the issue of child labour. It decided not to close down its factories, despite the employment of child labourers, as the children were the sole source of income for their families, and would not find altern-ative employment. Accordingly, the company ensured that sub-contractors would pay full wages to the children if they attended school up to the age of fourteen, whereupon they could then work full-time in the sub-contractors' factories. The company would pay for their tuition, books and uniforms.

5.2   Safety and Health

The ILO Declaration urges governments that have not already done so to ratify ILO Conventions in this field,[90] while MNEs are required to maintain the 'highest standards of safety and health, in conformity with national requirements, bearing in mind their relevant experience within the enterprise as a whole, including any knowledge of special hazards.'[91] Furthermore, MNEs should make available information on safety and health standards relevant to their local operations, which they observe in other countries, to workers' representatives in the enterprise and, upon request, to the competent authorities and to workers' and employers' organizations in the countries in which they operate.[92] In particular, special hazards and related protective meas-ures associated with new products and processes should be made known to those concerned.[93] This part of the Declaration ends with exhortations to MNEs to cooperate with international organizations in the preparation of international safety and health standards,[94] and with national authorities and representatives of workers' organizations and specialist safety and health organizations.[95] Where appropriate, matters relating to safety and health should be in-corporated into agreements with workers' representatives and their organizations.[96]

These provisions of the ILO Declaration relate to a matter of recent concern regarding the operations of MNEs. There is con-siderable evidence that MNEs export hazardous operations to LDCs where more lenient health and safety standards apply.[97] As noted in chapter 7, the problem of attracting investment to a location on the basis of lower labour and environmental standards has been an issue in the negotiations leading to the NAFTA, especially in relation to Mexico.[98] Furthermore, there is evidence suggesting that safety standards at Union Carbide's pesticides plant at Bhopal were very low, and may have been a significant contributing factor to the catastrophe of 1984.[99] On the other hand, in the 1986 review of the Declaration, the ILO Committee stated that in most cases MNEs were found to comply satisfactorily with health and safety standards and in some cases played a leading role in setting standards.[100] What is clear is that practice varies from firm to firm. Thus, in an ILO study of 1984 into the health and safety policies of eight MNEs, it was found that some firms controlled their foreign affiliates very closely while other exercised little or no control at all.[101]

The Declaration suggests that all firms should standardize their health and safety operations to the firm's best practice, through intra-firm exchanges of information. However, it stops short of requiring the establishment of managerial structures that would oversee this policy. In that respect the Declaration may fall short of the practice adopted by the best firms. Furthermore, the Declaration is weak on the responsibility of host state governments in this field. Ultimately, the development of adequate safety and health standards falls on the local authorities. They should not avoid this by passing the problem over to MNEs alone, or by resting on the ratification of ILO Conventions without giving full effect to them in domestic law. LDCs may argue that their limited resources prevent the operation of effective policies in these areas. That should not act as an excuse for inaction, but as a spur for greater international action in this field.

6   Industrial Relations

The ILO Declaration deals with five issues under this heading: freedom of association and the right to organize, collective bargaining, consultation, examination of grievances and the settlement of industrial disputes. Each area is subject to the overriding general principle of national treatment, in that 'multinational enterprises should observe standards of industrial relations not less favourable than those observed by comparable employers in the country concerned'.[102] The OECD Employment Guideline contains the same general principle.[103] National treatment leaves much to the discretion of the host government in the conduct of its industrial relations policy. Although it is recommended to observe the standards in the ILO Declaration, there is no legally binding international sanction should the host state fail to do so.[104] This considerably weakens the standard-setting function of the two codes. It is against this background that the ILO Declaration and OECD Guideline should be examined.

6.1   Freedom of Association and the Right to Organize
In accordance with the most central guiding policy of the ILO, the ILO Declaration recognizes the right of workers to establish and to join organizations of their own choosing without previous authorization, and to enjoy adequate protection against anti-union discrimination in respect of their employment.[105] This right has the status of a fundamental human right. Thus, article 22(1) of the International

Covenant on Civil and Political Rights 1966 states: 'Everyone shall have the right to freedom of association with others, including the right to form and join trade unions for the protection of his interests.'[106] Article 22(2) enumerates certain public interest exceptions to this principle. These must be prescribed by law and be necessary in a democratic society for the protection of those interests. However, article 22(3) stresses,

Nothing in this article shall authorise States Parties to the International Labour Organisation Convention of 1948 concerning Freedom of Association and Protection of the Right to Organize to take legislative measures that would prejudice, or apply the law in such a manner as to prejudice, the guarantees provided for in that Convention.

This right is addressed primarily to states. MNEs are not the object of the right. It is for the government of the host state to ensure that the freedom of association is observed in law and in fact.[107] It is for the MNE to observe the law of the land. However, foreign firms may be in a position to take the lead in the removal of restrictions over the freedom of association, by encouraging trade unions in their plants and by defending their right to exist. Again, the prevalent 'management culture' will be decisive. On the other hand, the incidence of non-unionized MNE plants appears to be growing, as technological change and the growth in service over manufacturing industries continue to erode the traditional base for mass trade unionism.[108] Thus the role of trade unions may itself be changing in ways that the Declaration has not contemplated.

The ILO Declaration goes on to enumerate certain specific policies that governments should and should not follow in the furtherance of the freedom of association. On the positive side, governments are encouraged, first, to ensure that workers in MNEs are not hindered in meeting and consulting with one another.[109] Secondly, they should not restrict the entry of representatives of workers' and employers' organizations from other countries.[110] Thirdly, governments should permit workers' and employers' organizations, which represent, respectively, the workers and the MNEs in which they work, to affiliate with international organizations of workers and employers of their choosing. This may be of importance in relation to the development of international collective bargaining, as it accepts the legitimacy of entering organizational structures that can facilitate this.[111] Indeed, the OECD Employment Guideline includes, among 'other *bona fide* organizations of employees' International Trade Secretariats as a body entitled to represent workers.[112]

International Trade Secretariats represent affiliated national unions in the same, or similar, industries. They can offer coordinating facilities for the exchange of information and, in exceptional cases, they have acted as the organizers of international industrial action. The most notable example has been the campaign organized, since 1948, by the International Transport Workers' Federation (ITF) against the use of 'flag-of-convenience' (FOC) vessels as a means of circumventing labour standards for seamen.[113] Although not involving MNEs as such, the campaign offers a useful insight into the legal environment surrounding international industrial action, as it has resulted in litigation in numerous jurisdictions. The campaign is aimed at the improvement of the terms of employment for crews serving on FOC vessels that do not respect the terms recommended by the ITF. When a FOC vessel suspected of violating ITF terms enters a port, the ITF will request the locally affiliated dockers' union to engage in sympathy action by 'blacking' the vessel. The local union members may refuse to load or unload the vessel, or to allow it to leave port, until the owner agrees to enter into an agreement regarding the crews' terms of employment that conforms to ITF standards.

Many cases have been brought in an attempt to stop such sympathy action. The response of the courts has depended on the attitude of the relevant national law to international sympathy action.[114] Thus, US courts have held that such action did not come within the National Labor Relations Act, even when the foreign ship was berthed in a US port, as the activities of the foreign ship-owner did not affect commerce between states as federal law required. Thus, under US law, the international dimension of the dispute was enough to remove the protection afforded to sympathy action under US law.[115] In the UK, ITF sympathy action has been treated in accordance with the applicable national law relating to such action. No distinction has been made between domestic and international sympathy action. Up to 1980, most kinds of sympathy action were held to be covered by the statutory immunity for industrial action in the Trade Union and Labour Relations Act 1974.[116] In 1980, following the accession of the Conservative government to power, statutory restrictions were placed on secondary action, motivated to a considerable extent by a desire to control the ITF campaign. This has led to court decisions that have restricted the rights of national unions to engage in sympathy action as part of the ITF campaign.[117] Under Dutch law a strike of crew members on a Saudi Arabian ship that was supported by the ITF was held to be unlawful as the crewmen's contracts of employment were governed by Philippine law, which rendered the strike unlawful.[118] Only under Swedish law has the ITF action been treated preferentially.[119] Most national laws will not offer such protection.

From the above examples, it can be seen that international sympathy action can be easily prevented through national laws. The secondary action need only be made unlawful under the law of the place where it occurs, regardless of the legality of the primary action. Apart from such legal obstacles, international trade union action faces serious obstacles in the form of: the relative weakness of International Trade Secretariats as conduits for such action; the often significant differences in policies and objectives among national trade union organizations, which may make agreement on an international strategy in alliance with other national organizations impossible; the differences in real interests between groups of workers in the various national affiliates of MNEs, resulting in competition for jobs between them (most obviously between higher and lower paid employees in different countries or regions); and, finally, the reluctance of MNE management to abandon local level bargaining in favour of international negotiations.[120] Such transnational industrial relations activities as do occur are most likely within relatively homogeneous labour markets and economies. European initiatives in this area may prove to be fruitful. For example, the adoption of the revised European Works Councils Directive, discussed in chapter 10, introduces an organizational structure into MNEs capable of adaptation into a forum for collective bargaining on a MNE-wide basis, although it must be stressed that this is not the avowed aim of the Directive.[121] However, interregional collective bargaining between MNEs and transnational labour unions remains an ideal that has little prospect of turning into reality, unless and until a more homogeneous global economy and society evolves.[122]

On the negative side, governments are urged not to offer any limitation of the workers' freedom of association, or of the right to organize and bargain collectively, as special incentives to attract foreign investment. Thus, the ILO Declaration exhorts governments not to engage in a 'race to the bottom' over trade union rights. However, as noted in the introduction to this section, there is nothing in the Declaration to prevent states from doing just that. Furthermore, MNEs need do no more than follow the policy of the host state. Consequently, a firm may acquiesce to repressive labour laws and standards of treatment if it so wishes. Again, as with the matter of employment conditions, much depends on the firm's 'management culture',[123] and on whether the firm can withstand the possible economic losses that a 'model' industrial relations strategy might entail. Indeed, competitive pressures have often been invoked as the reason why a MNE might disinvest if its plant(s) in a host state were to become unionized. In response, certain governments, especially in LDCs that are dependent on export-oriented foreign investment, have sought to restrict trade union rights by law.[124] This has led to accusations that some states practice 'social dumping' as an economic policy, in that they seek to compete in the international economy by subsidizing international producers to locate on their territory by offering lower wages and working conditions coupled with controls over trade unions.

This accusation has not been confined to LDCs. In Europe, the UK has been accused of this practice by other EC Member States, who point in evidence to the UK's reluctance to support the Social Provisions of the Maastricht Treaty. Some further support for this view can be gathered from the ILO Committee's observations on UK labour law reforms in 1992, when it found that the UK had not observed the terms of ILO Conventions on Freedom of Association.[125] However, according to Professor Dunning, 'throughout the 1970s, the poor industrial relations environment in the UK led some UK- and foreign-based MNEs to eschew new production facilities in the UK. By contrast, in the 1980s and early 1990s, foreign firms have responded to dramatic improvement in this environment by favouring the UK for their EC-based operations.'[126] Thus 'social dumping' appears to have benefited the UK in the short term. On the other hand, in an economic downturn, it will be easier to make UK workers redundant, which might lead to more plant closures than in EC Member States espousing stronger employee protection.[127] Furthermore, the southern Member States and Eastern European states may be able to offer still lower wages and working conditions than the UK.[128] Thus 'social dumping' may backfire on a country espousing this policy. It may also lead to social unrest as workers in economically successful countries that repress labour rights demand a fuller share of the resulting wealth. This has been the case in, for example, Korea and Malaysia in recent years.[129]

A further factor that may discourage 'social dumping' is the possibility of economic retaliation by countries whose business and employment prospects are threatened by it. For example, the USA retains powers to deny to LDCs trading privileges under the Generalized System of Preferences (GSP) if they do not observe the following minimum labour rights: the right of association; the right to organize and bargain collectively; the prohibition against the use of any form of forced or compulsory labour; a minimum age for the employment of children; acceptable conditions of work with respect to minimum wages, hours of work, and occupational safety and health.[130] However, in recent years this power has not been systematically used. This resulted in an unsuccessful lawsuit being brought by US labour unions and human rights groups against former President Bush.[131] It is yet to be seen whether the Clinton administration will change this policy. Further powers for retaliation are available to the US government under s. 301 of the Trade Act 1974 as amended in 1988.[132] This empowers the US Trade Representative (USTR) to take action against a country which is found to pursue policies or practices that 'constitute a persistent pattern of conduct denying internationally recognized worker rights, unless the USTR determines the foreign country has taken or is taking actions that demonstrate a significant and tangible overall advancement in providing those rights and standards throughout the country or such acts, policies, or practices are not inconsistent with the level of economic development of the country.'[133] Again, strong enforcement is unlikely given the wide qualifications attached to these statutory powers. In any case, the USA is currently at the forefront of the movement to include worker's rights on the agenda of the new World Trade Organization (WTO). Should this be successful, the USA may prefer not to use its unilateral powers in this field, but to rely on the WTO instead.

An alternative approach might be to challenge imports from countries that condone unfair labour practices under competition law and/or under human rights law. Such an initiative was attempted by German producers of asbestos products, who sought an injunction against imports of competing products from South Korea, on the ground that they were exposed to unfair competition contrary to s. 1 of the West German Act against Unfair Competition. The plaintiffs argued that the imports had been made by workers subjected to health risks against which German workers had to be protected, in accordance with ILO Convention No. 139 of 1974 on the 'protection against carcinogen materials and related occupational hazards', which had been put into effect by legislation in force in Germany since 1977. Furthermore, the plaintiffs argued that consumers were being misled by not being informed of the true circumstances behind the production of these goods, contrary to s. 3 of the Unfair Competition Act. The German Supreme Court (*Bundesgerichthof*) dismissed the action. The products had not been made in violation of industrial health protection rules as South Korea was not at that time a member of the ILO, nor had it acceded to the relevant Convention. Furthermore, the ILO Convention did not represent common standards of human rights applicable to all humanity. To be effective the Convention had to be incorporated into national law. The Supreme Court further rejected the argument concerning the right of consumers to know of the conditions under which the products were made. Consumers were assumed only to be interested in information concerning the economic value of the product, and not in the employment conditions of those who produced it.[134]

This case well illustrates the weakness of ILO protection through Conventions, as these are not accorded the status of fundamental rights provisions that might be binding *erga omnes* without the need for further legislative intervention by states.[135] However, it is doubtful whether consumers are as uninterested in the treatment of foreign workers as the German Supreme Court has assumed. It may be very damaging for a MNE to be associated in the public mind with the non-observance of good employment standards in its overseas plants or sub-contractors. A more significant objection to legal action such as the above is that it may be motivated by no more than protectionist sentiments, and may in fact serve to retard the growth of gainful employment in LDCs. The balance of interests is not easy to draw in such cases.

6.2   Collective Bargaining and Consultation

Both the ILO Declaration and the OECD Employment Guideline assert that the employees of MNEs should have the right, in accordance with national law and practice, to have representative organizations of their own choosing recognized for the purpose of collective bargaining.[136] What constitutes collective bargaining is a matter for interpretation in the context of different national situations.[137] The ILO Declaration may offer some harmonization in this regard in that it recommends the taking of measures appropriate to national conditions for the encouragement and promotion of negotiations through collective agreements in accordance with ILO Convention No. 98, article 4.[138] The ILO Convention may provide a basis for identifying the common expectations that a system of collective bargaining should fulfil. The ILO Declaration also seeks to encourage the development of systems for consultation between employers and workers and their representatives on matters of mutual concern. However, such consultations should not substitute for collective bargaining.[139]

According to the OECD Committee on Multinational Enterprises, employees' representatives may be entitled to negotiations not only with integrated MNEs but also with strategic alliances of national companies where certain decisions that they take in common were previously taken at national level and were discussed with employees' representatives.[140] On the other hand, where a MNE operates a policy of union non-recognition, the Committee has held that the right of employees to be represented by unions depends on national laws, practices and regulations. However, the Employment Guideline suggests that management should adopt a positive approach to the activities of unions and other *bona fide* organizations of employees and espouse an open approach towards organizational activities within the framework of national rules and practices. In particular, MNEs should recruit personnel regardless of their union membership.[141]

Both codes expect MNEs to provide the facilities necessary for the development of effective collective agreements, and to provide workers' representatives with information required for meaningful negotiations on conditions of employment.[142] This should give a 'true and fair view of the performance of the entity or, where appropriate, of the enterprise as a whole'. The OECD Committee of Multinational Enterprises has interpreted this as requiring the provision of more specific information to employees' representatives than would be available to the general public under the OECD Disclosure Guideline, and in a form suitable for their interests and purposes. In certain cases, as where the MNE is engaged in restructuring activities, this may cover information about the enterprise as a whole, subject to considerations of business confidentiality.[143] Both codes stress that the provision of information must accord with local law and practice. Thus, it would appear that the host state is free to protect against employee disclosure through strict business secrecy laws. Furthermore, according to the OECD Committee on Multinational Enterprises, legal loopholes that allow the MNE to avoid its obligations as to codetermination are not the concern of the Guideline but are for national legislators to deal with.[144] On the other hand, the ILO Declaration urges governments to help workers' representatives by furnishing them, where the law permits, with information about the industry in which the MNE operates. It urges MNEs to observe any requests from governments for relevant information on their operations.[145]

Both codes recognize the implications of the group structure of MNEs for effective collective bargaining. Each code demands that the authorized representatives of employees conduct negotiations with representatives of management who are authorized to take decisions on the matters under negotiation.[146] Under the OECD Guideline this requirement has been interpreted to mean that parent companies may be obliged to take the necessary organizational steps to enable their subsidiaries to observe the Guidelines, *inter alia*, by providing them with sufficient and timely information and ensuring that local managers are duly authorized to take the decisions on matters under negotiation.[147] Alternatively, the parent company may delegate a member of the decision-making centre to the negotiating team of the subsidiary, or engage directly in negotiations, so as to achieve the same result.[148] Furthermore, employees' representatives may be entitled to information about the decision-making structure within the enterprise, but such a right of information is confined to the negotiating situations referred to in the Guideline. There is no general right to be informed about the decision-making structure within the enterprise.[149] Additionally, negotiations should take place in a language understood by both sides. This may necessitate the use of an interpreter where representatives from the parent company do not speak the language of the host state.[150]

Both the matter of furnishing adequate information and the authorization of managers to take decisions can be helped by the institution of specialized structures within MNEs. Many European firms have already taken the first step through transnational works' councils. Although not designed as forums for MNE-wide collective bargaining, such bodies offer a forum for regular enterprise-wide consultations and exchanges of information. For example, in 1985 Thomson–Grand Public established, with the European Metalworkers' Federation, a liaison committee which includes workers representatives from France, Germany. Italy, Spain and the UK. In 1986 BSN–Gervais Danone established, with the International Union of Food Workers, a permanent international consultation mechanism covering plants in Austria, Belgium, France, Germany, Italy, the Netherlands and Spain.[151] Furthermore, national unions representing workers employed by the same MNE in more than one European country are establishing formal links with each other as a method of preparing for Europe-wide negotiations and consultations with the firm concerned. For example, after the share transfer deal between Volvo and Renault in 1990,[152] the metalworking sections of the French confederations FO and CFDT met with their Swedish counterparts under the auspices of the International Metalworkers' Federation and the European Metalworkers' Federation. They decided to form a joint trade union committee involving the various unions represented in the joint operations of the two companies across Europe. The committee's function was to examine issues arising from the agreement between the companies and its consequences for the employment and status of employees.[153] Similarly, unions representing Ford's European workers have combined to make joint representations to the company concerning plans to subcontract parts of the firm's production. However, Ford unions have encountered disagreements in negotiations leading to the establishment of a European works' council in the firm, which caused delays in its inception.[154]

Transnational works' councils may be of considerable significance in taking account of workers' interests in the planning of restructuring policies. Such policies may become more common with the advent of the Single European Market. Indeed, as seen in chapter 10, the EC Directive on European Works Councils is motivated, in part, to meet this problem. However, the creation of such bodies on a global or interregional basis is still far off. For now, this should be seen as a European initiative.

Finally, both codes address the problem of unfair pressure being brought to bear upon negotiations with workers' representatives by MNEs as a result of the international scope of their operations. Thus the ILO Declaration states:

Multinational enterprises, in the context of bona fide negotiations with the workers' representatives on conditions of employment, or while workers are exercising the right to organise, should not threaten to utilise a capacity to transfer the whole or part of an operating unit from the country concerned in order to influence unfairly those negotiations or to hinder the exercise of the right to organise; nor should they transfer workers from affiliates in foreign countries with a view to undermining bona fide negotiations with the workers' representatives or the workers' exercise of their right to organise.

The OECD Employment Guideline contains essentially the same formulation.[155] It adds that 'bona fide negotiations may include labour disputes as part of the process of negotiation. Whether or not labour disputes are so included will be determined by the law and prevailing employment practices of particular countries.'[156] The OECD Committee on Multinational Enterprises has stressed that an important issue arising from this provision is the distinction between the legitimate provision of information and threats designed to influence negotiations unfairly. In its view, a distinction should be drawn between giving employees information to the effect that a particular demand has serious implications for the economic viability of the enterprise, and the making of a threat. Management should be prepared to offer information that could support its claim.[157] Furthermore, the Committee has noted that the Guideline was drafted to consider only operations involving existing plant and equipment. Nevertheless, future investments, such as the replacement of equipment or the introduction of new technology, could be crucial to the survival of the enterprise in the medium to long term and thus might be of interest in this context.[158] So, not only threats of withdrawal from current operations but also threats to run down an operation might be seen as 'unfair', in the absence of information that justifies such a decision.

The requirement not to 'import' strike-breaking employees from affiliates in other countries was absent from the original formulation of the OECD Employment Guideline. However, it was inserted in 1979 as a result of the OECD Committee's interpretation of the Guideline in the light of the *Hertz* case.[159] The OECD Trade Union Advisory Committee (TUAC) brought this case to the attention of the Committee on behalf of the Danish LO union confederation, which had complained that Hertz Rentacar was bringing in employees from other parts of Europe to cover for staff shortages caused by a strike at its Danish affiliate. After the strike was over, Hertz Rentacar (Denmark) took back only half of the original staff because of structural and operational changes, and continued to employ some of the foreign workers. The Committee observed that the transfer of employees from foreign affiliates had unfairly influenced negotiations and was contrary to the general spirit and approach of the Guidelines even if it did not contravene them. Consequently, this gap in the original formulation had to be remedied through the insertion of appropriate words.

6.3   Examination of Grievances and Settlement of Industrial Disputes

These issues are dealt with by the ILO Declaration alone. Regrading workers' grievances the following principle is recommended to MNEs: 'that any worker who, acting individually or jointly with other workers, considers that he has grounds for a grievance should have the right to submit such grievance without suffering any prejudice whatsoever as a result and to have such grievance examined pursuant to an appropriate procedure.'[160] This is seen as particularly important where the MNE operates in a country that does not abide by the principles of ILO Conventions relating to freedom of association, the right to organize and bargain collectively, and forced labour.[161]

The ILO Declaration ends with a recommendation that MNEs should seek to establish, with the representatives and organizations of the workers whom they employ, voluntary conciliation machinery to assist in the prevention and settlement of industrial disputes. This machinery should include equal representation for employers and workers, and it should be appropriate to national conditions. It may include provisions for voluntary arbitration.[162]

7   Concluding Remarks

The ILO Declaration and OECD Employment Guideline offer a statement of desired practice on the part of governments and MNEs in the field of labour relations. They may be criticized as representing weak legal responses, given their non-binding nature. Furthermore, the pressures of international competition may be forcing some states to weaken their existing labour protection standards or to resist improvements. In these circumstances the two codes may be seen as relics of the 'corporatist' 1970s that have little of relevance to offer.

However, they still represent the minimum international labour standards that states have agreed should apply to the operations of MNEs. As such they have at least the status of 'soft law'. Furthermore, not all legal systems are retreating from the principles that the codes espouse. Most notably, the EC is making advances in these areas, although some fears are being expressed that these initiatives are undermining the competitiveness of European industry. Moreover, it remains to be seen whether the WTO will develop new international minimum standards. However, should the future involve a 'race to the bottom' in international labour standards, it would reflect a decline not only in morality but also in reason. The end result may be protectionist responses from states whose businesses and workers are threatened by such competition, and a retardation of economic and social development in LDCs.

Notes

1   OECD, *The OECD Declaration and Decisions on International Investment and Multinational Enterprises 1991 Review* (Paris, 1992), at pp. 106–7.

2   Adopted 16 November 1977: 17 ILM 422 (1978). For comment see Gunter, 'The ILO tripartite declaration of principles concerning multinational enterprises and social policy', *The CTC Reporter* (No. 12, Summer 1982), pp. 27–9.

3   See chapter 4 at pp. 94–5.

4   OECD, 1991 Review (note 1 above), at p. 53.

5   There are now some 172 ILO Conventions. See also the *ILO Declaration on Fundamental Principles and Rights at Work 1998* (International Labour Organization, Geneva 1998). The ILO Conventions are collected in ILO International Labour Conventions and Recommendations (1919–1991) (2 vols, plus supplements). For background on the ILO see Brown and McColgan, 'UK employment law and the International Labour Organisation; the spirit of cooperation?', 21 ILJ 265 (1992). See also S. A. Ivanov, 'The International Labour Organisation: control over application of the conventions and recommendations on labour', in W. E. Butler (ed.), *Control over Compliance with International Law* (Kluwer, 1991), p. 153.

6   The annex was updated by an addendum to the Tripartite Declaration passed by the Governing Body of the International Labour Office at its 238th Session, Geneva, 1987. It covers new ILO Conventions passed since 1977 that are of relevance to provisions in the Declaration. This list is periodically updated and appended to the ILO's current published version of the Declaration.

7   By ILO Constitution, article 3(5), Member States are entitled to send four representatives: two governmental representatives and, by agreement, one each from the most representative employers' and trade union organizations in the country.

8   See G. Hamilton, *The Control of Multinationals: What Future for International Codes of Conduct in the 1980s?* (IRM Multinational Reports No. 2,

IRM/Wiley, 1984), pp. 9–10; J. Robinson, *Multinationals and Political Control* (Gower, 1983), pp. 171–3.

9 See Lemoine, 'The ILO Tripartite Declaration: ten years after', *The CTC Reporter* (No. 25, Spring 1988), p. 22; Robinson, ibid., at pp. 175–6.

10 See Procedure for Examination of Disputes Concerning the Application of the Tripartite Declaration of Principles Concerning Multinational Enterprises and Social Policy by Means of Interpretation of its Provisions, adopted by the Governing Body of the International Labour Office at its 232nd Session, Geneva, March 1986, appended to the ILO Tripartite Declaration.

11 For a summary of the main interpretations see Lemoine (note 9 above).

12 ILO Doc. GB. 232/12/15 February–March 1985, cited in Lemoine, ibid., at p. 26.

13 See Second Revised Decision of the OECD Council on the Guidelines for Multinational Enterprises, as amended, June 1991 in OECD 1991 Review (note 1 above), at pp. 116–17.

14 See further Robinson (note 8 above), chapter 9, and R. Blanpain, *The Badger Case* (Kluwer, 1977), and *The OECD Guidelines for Multinational Enterprises and Labour Relations: Experience and Review* (Kluwer, Vol. I, 1979; Vol. II, 1982; Vol. III, 1985). The Committee's principal interpretations are reproduced in the periodic reviews of the OECD Guidelines. See 1979 Review, or 18 ILM 986 (1979) at paras 59–72; 1986 Review, paras 53–87; 1991 Review (note 1 above), at pp. 43–4, 46–9.

15 OECD Guidelines (note 1 above), introduction, para. 6.

16 ILO Declaration (note 2 above), para. 4.

17 ILO Declaration, para. 7; OECD Guidelines, introduction, para. 6.

18 ILO Declaration, para. 11; OECD Guidelines, introduction, para. 9.

19 ILO Declaration, para. 8.

20 On which see further Morgenstern and Knapp, 'Multinational enterprises and the extraterritorial application of labour law', 27 ICLQ 769 (1978).

21 ILO Declaration (note 2 above), para. 9.

22 Ibid., para. 10.

23 Ibid., para. 12.

24 See Zimmerman, 'International dimension of US fair employment laws: Protection or interference?', 131 Int'l Lab. Rev. 217 (1992).

25 See David Goodhart, 'A bid to push the world to rights', *Financial Times*, 5 April 1994, p. 14; 'Mahatir assails Uruguay Round labour–trade link', *Financial Times*, 6 April 1994, p. 6; 'Agreement on worker's rights removes hurdle to Gatt accord', *Financial Times*, 8 April 1994, p. 18. See further Compa, 'Labor rights and labor standards in international trade', 25 Law & Pol. Int'l Bus. 165 (1993).

26 See 1991 Review (note 1 above), at p. 105.

27 ILO Declaration, para. 13, and Convention No. 122 and Recommendation No. 122 concerning employment policy.

28 Ibid., para. 16.

29 Ibid., para. 17.

30 Ibid., para. 18.

31 Ibid., para. 19.

32 Ibid., para. 20.

33 Lemoine (note 9 above), at p. 24.

34 See further R. Van Tulder and G. Junne, *European Multinationals in Core Technologies* (Wiley/IRM, 1988), chapter 4; UNCTAD, *World Investment Report 1994: Transnational Corporations, Employment and the Workplace* (UN Doc. UNCTAD DTC1/10, 1994) Parts Two and Three.

35 ILO Declaration para. 21, and Convention No. 111 and Recommendation No. 111 concerning discrimination in respect of employment and occupation and Convention No. 156 (165 sic) concerning equal opportunities and equal treatment for men and women workers: workers with family responsibilities, 1981.

36 Ibid., para. 22.

37 Ibid., para. 23.

38 OECD Guideline (note 1 above), para. 7.

39 See e.g. article 119 EEC Treaty guaranteeing that men and women should receive equal pay for equal work. See further R. Nielsen and E. Szyszczak, *The Social Dimension of the European Community*, 3rd edn (Handelshojskolens Forlag, 1997), chapter 4. For a recent account of UK law and practice see I. T. Smith and J. C. Wood, *Industrial Law* (Butterworths, 1993), chapter 5. See also the important case *Equal Opportunities Commission* v *Secretary of State for Employment* [1994] 1 All ER 910 (HL). On the limitations of legal controls over discrimination in employment see B. Hepple and E. Szyszczak (eds), *Discrimination: the Limits of Law* (Mansell, 1992). See also ILO World Labour Report 1992 (Geneva, 1992), pp. 26–30.

40 *EEOC/Boureslan* v *ARAMCO* 113 Sup. Ct 274 (1991).

41 See Zimmerman (note 24 above), at p. 221.

42 See *Sumitomo Shoji America* v *Avagliano* 457 US 176 (US Sup. Ct 1982). For a critical view of this decision see Ishizuka, 'Subsidiary assertion of foreign parent corporation rights under commercial treaties to hire employees "of their choice"', 86 Col. LR 139 (1986).

43 See Directive 96/71/EC OJ [1997] L 18/1. See further House of Lords Select Committee on the European Communities, *Protection of Posted Workers* (HL Paper 16, Session 1992–3, 5th Report, 14 July 1992).

44 ILO Declaration (note 2 above), para. 24.

45 Ibid., para. 25.

46 Ibid.

47 Ibid., para. 27 and Conventions Nos 158 and 166 (both of 1982) and Recommendation No. 119 concerning termination of employment at the initiative of the employer.

48 Ibid., para. 28.

49 In the *Batco* case, the OECD Committee on Multinational Enterprises held that the Employment Guideline cannot be interpreted as prohibiting the closure of even a profitable subsidiary, as this remained a prerogative of management. All that the firm had to do was to follow the requirements of national law regarding the effects of the closure: Blanpain (note 14 above), vol. I, at pp. 150–73.

50   ILO Declaration, para. 26; OECD Guideline, para. 6.
51   The OECD Committee on Multinational Enterprises has stated that, where the affected employees have no trade union or other *bona fide* representation, enterprises must take all practical steps to ensure the observance of the terms of the Guideline within the framework of national laws, regulations and prevailing labour relations practices: 1991 Review (note 1 above), at p. 43.
52   Ibid.
53   Blanpain (note 14 above), vol. I, pp. 125–46; Robinson (note 8 above), at pp. 125–8.
54   Cited by Robinson (note 8 above), at p. 133. See also OECD interpretations in the *Siemens* and *Litton Industries* cases in Robinson, ibid., at pp. 130 and 132; and see *Hyster* case, Blanpain (note 14 above), vol. III, at pp. 139–54.
55   OECD 1991 Review (note 1 above), at p. 49.
56   Ibid., at p. 44.
57   See Nielsen and Szyszczak (note 39 above), chapter 6. Arguably these developments have been more concerned with the effectiveness of market integration than with the protection of workers rights: see P. Davies in W. McCarthy (ed.), *Legal Interventions in Industrial Relations* (Blackwell, 1992), chapter 10.
58   See *Francovich* v *Italian Republic* [1993] 2 CMLR 66; [1992] IRLR 84 (ECJ); comment, Szyszczak, 55 MLR 690 (1992).
59   OJ [1992] L 245/3. The original Directive which harmonized standards in this area was Directive 75/129/EEC OJ [1975] L 48/29, which is amended by the 1992 Directive. For the Commission's background proposal see COM (91) 292 Final 13 November 1991. Directive 75/129 has recently been interpreted as requiring consultation to begin as soon as the employer contemplates redundancies, whereas the implementing provision in English law, s. 188 of the Trade Union and Labour Relations (Consolidation) Act 1992, has been interpreted as applying only once the decision to make a person redundant has been made: *R* v *British Coal Corporation and Secretary of State for Trade and Industry ex parte Vardy and others* [1993] 1 CMLR 721 (DC). The UK has been found to have violated the requirements of Directive 75/129: Cases C-383 and 382/92 *Commission* v *UK* Judgment 8 June 1994 (ECJ).
60   Ibid., article 2(2).
61   Ibid., article 2(1).
62   Ibid., article 2(3).
63   Ibid., article 2(4).
64   Ibid., article 3(1); article 2(3).
65   Ibid., article 4(1).
66   OJ [1977] L 61/26. It is proposed to replace Directive 77/187/EEC with a new consolidating Directive that embodies more recent developments in case-law. See Proposal 94/C 274/08 COM(94) 300 final – 94/0203(CNS) OJ [1994] C 274/10.
67   Ibid., article 1(1). The Directive does not apply merely because a majority of shares in a limited company is acquired by another company. There

must be a change of employer. In the 1994 proposed Directive the words 'as a result of a legal transfer or merger' are replaced by the broader words 'effected by contract or by some other disposition or operation of law, judicial decision or administrative measure'.

68 Ibid., article 3(2). This provision remains unchanged in the 1994 proposed Directive.
69 Ibid., article 4(1). This provision remains unchanged in the 1994 proposed Directive.
70 See further Nielsen and Szyszczak (note 39 above), at pp. 269–77 and cases cited therein. For the application of the Directive in English law see The Transfer of Undertakings (Protection of Employment) Regulations 1981 SI 1981/1794; *Litster and others* v *Forth Dry Dock & Engineering Co. Ltd* [1989] ICR 341; [1989] IRLR 161 (HL); J. McMullen, *Business Transfers and Employee Rights*, 3rd edn (Butterworths, 1998).
71 Ibid., article 6. See also article 6 of the 1994 proposed Directive (note 66 above).
72 *Katsikas* v *Konstantinidis* [1993] 1 CMLR 845 (ECJ).
73 ILO Declaration para. 29, and Convention No. 142 and Recommendation No. 150 concerning vocational guidance and vocational training in the development of human resources.
74 Ibid., para. 30.
75 Ibid., para. 31.
76 OECD Employment Guideline, para. 5.
77 See J. H. Dunning, *Multinational Enterprises and the Global Economy* (Addison Wesley, 1992), at pp. 372–5.
78 See Lemoine (note 9 above), at p. 25. See further ILO, *Technology Choice and Employment Generation by Multinational Enterprises in Developing Countries* (1984).
79 OECD Employment Guideline, para. 4.
80 See chapter 16 at p. 590.
81 ILO Declaration para. 33 and Recommendation No. 116 concerning Reduction of Hours of Work. In the *Warner Lambert* case, the OECD Committee on Multinational Enterprises held that the national treatment standard did not exclude the possibility that, temporarily and under exceptional circumstances, agreement may be reached on wages less favourable than those observed by comparable employers in host countries. The MNE concerned should in good faith aim at restoring wages to the national standard as soon as the specific circumstances which gave rise to such agreement no longer persisted: Blanpain (note 14 above), vol. I, at pp. 217–18; Robinson (note 8 above), at p. 131. However, national law may have the effect of destroying workers' rights if they voluntarily opt out of them: see UK Trade Union Reform and Employment Rights Act 1993, s. 20(4).
82 Ibid., para. 34.
83 Ibid.
84 Ibid., and Convention No. 110 and Recommendation No. 110 concerning conditions of employment of plantation workers; Recommendation No.

115 concerning workers' housing; Recommendation No. 69 concerning medical care; Convention No. 130 and Recommendation No. 134 concerning medical care and sickness.

85 Ibid., para. 35.

86 See Lemoine (note 9 above), at p. 25.

87 See Dunning (note 77 above), at pp. 375–7, 381–2. See also UNCTAD, *World Investment Report 1994* (note 34 above).

88 Ibid., at p. 377.

89 See 'Bold fashion statement', *Financial Times*, 8/9 May 1993, p. 9, on which this paragraph draws heavily.

90 ILO Declaration, para. 36, which specifically refers to Convention No. 119 on guarding of machinery, No. 115 on ionizing radiation, No. 136 on benzine, No. 139 on occupational cancer and, in the 1987 Addendum, Nos 148 and 156 on the protection of workers against occupational hazards in the working environment due to air pollution, noise and vibration (1977), Nos 155 and 164 on occupational safety and health and the working environment (1981), No. 171 concerning occupational health services (1985), No. 172 concerning safety in the use of asbestos (1986).

91 Ibid., para. 37.

92 Ibid.

93 Ibid.

94 Ibid., para. 38.

95 ibid., para. 39.

96 Ibid.

97 See B. I. Castleman, 'Workplace health standards and multinational corporations in developing countries', in C. Pearson (ed.), *Multinational Corporations, Environment and the Third World: Business Matters* (Duke University Press, 1987), p. 149.

98 See chapter 7 at pp. 243–4. See further Zamora, 'The Americanisation of Mexican law: non-trade issues in the North American Free Trade Agreement', 24 Law & Pol. Int'l Bus. 391 (1993).

99 See T. Gladwin, 'A case study of the Bhopal tragedy', in Pearson (note 97 above), at pp. 229–30.

100 Lemoine (note 9 above), at p. 25.

101 ILO, *Safety and Health Practices of Multinational Enterprises* (Geneva, 1984), esp. pp. 28–42 (covering BASF AG, Royal Dutch/Shell, Merck & Co. Inc., Bechtel Companies, BICC Group, Volkswagenwerk AG, Xerox Corp, Brown Boveri & Co.).

102 ILO Declaration (note 2 above), para. 40.

103 OECD Employment Guideline (note 1 above), para. 4.

104 See, for example, the UK's apparent disregard for ILO Convention No. 87 on freedom of association and for the subsequent ILO Committee of Experts' Report of 1992 criticizing the UK on this matter: Brown and McColgan (note 5 above). On the other hand, complaints against Malaysia appear to have had more effect: see A. Wangel, 'The ILO and protection of trade union rights: the electronics industry in Malaysia', in R. Southall (ed.), *Trade Unions and the New Industrialisation of the Third World* (Zed Books, 1988), p. 287.

105   ILO Declaration, para. 41 and Convention No. 87, article 2, Convention
      No. 98, article 1(1). The establishment, functioning and administration of
      such organizations should not be interfered with by other organizations
      whether representing MNEs or workers in their employment: ibid., para.
      42.

106   999 UNTS 171; UKTS 6 (1977) Cmnd 6702; 61 AJIL 870 (1967). See
      also European Convention on Human Rights 1950, article 11.

107   For a recent survey of practice in this area see ILO, *World Labour Report
      1992*, at pp. 10–13. See also *Annual Reports of the ILO Committee of Experts
      on the Application of Conventions and Recommendations* (Report III, part
      4A).

108   See Van Tulder and Junne (note 34 above), at pp. 121–3; ILO, *World
      Labour Report 1993*, at pp. 33–9, which notes a general decline in union
      membership in developed countries.

109   Note 2 above, para. 46.

110   Ibid., para. 47.

111   On international collective bargaining see further: K. W. Wedderburn,
      'Multinational labour law', 1 ILJ 12 (1972); Roberts, 'Multinational col-
      lective bargaining: a European prospect?', 9 Brit. J. Ind. Rel. 1 (1973); H.
      R. Northrup and R. L. Rowan, *Multinational Collective Bargaining Attempts*
      (Industrial Research Unit, Wharton School, 1979). Northrup, Campbell
      and Slowinski, 'Multinational union-management consultation in Europe:
      resurgence in the 1980s?', 127 Int'l Lab. Rev. 525 (1988).

112   OECD Employment Guideline, para. 1, as interpreted in the 1986 *Review
      of the OECD Guidelines* (Paris, 1986), para. 56 at p. 32. See also Blanpain
      (note 14 above), vol. I, at pp. 186–7.

113   See ITF, *Flags of Convenience – the ITF's Campaign* (ITF, periodically
      updated) and issues of the *Seafarer's Bulletin* for more recent news. See
      also Northrup and Rowan (note 111 above), chapter 27.

114   See P. Davies, 'Labour law and multinational groups of companies', in K.
      Hopt (ed.), *Legal and Economic Analysis of Multinational Enterprises, Vol. II*
      (De Gruyter, 1982), at pp. 216–22.

115   See cases cited by Davies, ibid., at p. 216, n. 22.

116   See *Camelia Tanker SA v ITF* [1976] ICR 274 (CA); *NWL v Woods* [1979]
      ICR 867 (HL); Davies, ibid., at p. 219.

117   Employment Act 1980, s. 17, as interpreted in *Merkur Island Shipping v
      Laughton* [1983] 2 All ER 189 (HL): for criticism see Wedderburn 46
      MLR 632 (1983). See now Trade Union and Labour Relations (Consoli-
      dation) Act 1992, s. 224. ITF action has also been caught under the
      common law of economic duress, which will apply to any contract whose
      proper law is English law: *Universe Tankships of Monrovia v ITF 'The
      Universe Sentinel'* [1983] 1 AC 366; [1982] 2 All ER 67 (HL); *Dimskal
      Shipping Co. SA v ITF 'The Evia Luck'* [1991] 4 All ER 871; [1992] 2
      Lloyds Rep. 115 (HL). ITF action has been caught under the Trade
      Union Act 1984 which requires a ballot of the members of a union before
      a lawful strike can be called. See now Trade Union and Labour Relations
      (Consolidation) Act 1992, ss 226–34. The workers engaging directly in
      ITF 'blacking' action have normally been only members of their national

union and not of the ITF. The ITF could not, therefore, hold a lawful ballot of the membership and any action ordered by the ITF would be unlawful: *Shipping Co. Uniform Inc.* v *ITF Allen Ross & Davies 'The Uniform Star'* [1985] 1 Lloyds Rep. 173 (QBD). The ITF has to ensure, by a change to its rules, that members of affiliated national unions are automatically members of the ITF for the purposes of lawful balloting.

118   *The Saudi Independence* (Hoge Raad, 1983), noted in 16 Jo. Mart. L. & Com. 423 (1985).

119   See Davies (note 114 above), at pp. 221–2.

120   See further Northrup and Rowan (note 111 above), chapter 2; Enderwick, 'The labour utilisation practices of multinationals and obstacles to multinational collective bargaining', 26 Jo. Ind. Rel. 345 (1984).

121   See further chapter 10 at pp. 352–3.

122   The ideal of transnational trade unionism was a major feature of writings emanating from trade unionists and their supporters in the early 1970s. See, for example: UK Trades Union Congress, *International Companies* (1970); C. Levinson, *International Trade Unionism* (London, George Allen & Unwin, 1974); K. W. Wedderburn, 'Industrial relations', in H. R. Hahlo, J. Graham Smith and R. W. Wright (eds), *Nationalism and the Multinational Enterprise* (Sijthoff, 1977), p. 244. The OECD Committee on Multinational Enterprises has declined to say that the Employment Guideline sanctions international collective bargaining, given that it is virtually non-existent in practice: *International Metalworkers' Federation* case (Blanpain, note 14 above, vol. I, at pp. 187–91).

123   For example, Japanese firms tend to prefer single-union arrangements (as at the Nissan plant in Sunderland), while many US firms follow a non-union approach (such as IBM or MacDonalds).

124   See Barnard, 'Labor law in Malaysia: a capitalist device to exploit Third World workers', 23 Law & Pol. Int'l Bus. 415 (1991–92).

125   See Brown and McColgan (note 5 above). The Trade Union Reform and Employment Rights Act 1993 has also been held by the ILO to include several provisions that violate ILO Conventions on the freedom of association: 'ILO rebukes Britain over unfair trade union pay rules', *The Guardian*, 25 June 1994, p. 6. See further Simpson, 22 ILJ 181 (1993); S. Auerbach, *Derecognition and Personal Contracts: Fighting Tactics and the Law* (Institute of Employment Rights, 1993).

126   Note 77 above, at p. 352.

127   See David Goodhart, 'Social dumping: hardly an open and shut case', *Financial Times*, 4 February 1993, p. 2.

128   On North–South employment issues in the EC see P. Buckley and P. Artisien, *North–South Direct Investment in the European Communities* (Macmillan, 1987). The ILO hopes that the Tripartite Declaration will help to improve working conditions and trade union activities in Eastern Europe. See R. Morawetz, *Recent Foreign Direct Investment in Eastern Europe: towards a Possible Role for the Tripartite Declaration of Principles Concerning Multinational Enterprises and Social Policy* (ILO, 1991).

129   On Malaysia see Barnard (note 124 above), and on both Malaysia and Korea see ILO, *World Labour Report 1993*, at p. 51.

130   19 USC s. 2462(a) (4) (1988).
131   See *Re International Labour Rights Fund* 752 F. Supp. 495 (DDC 1990) aff'd No. 90-00728 (DC Cir., 31 January 1992), discussed in Barnard (note 124 above), at pp. 434–6.
132   S. 1301 Omnibus Trade and Competitiveness Act 1988 Pub. Law. No. 100–418, 102 Stat. 1107.
133   US Congress, Committee of Ways and Means, *Overview and Compilation of US Trade Statutes* (1989), reproduced in J. Bhagwati and H. T. Patrick (eds), *Aggressive Unilateralism: America's 301 Trade Policy and the World Trading System* (Harvester Wheatsheaf, 1991), at p. 40.
134   BGH, 1 ZR 76/78 Judgment 9 May 1980 summarized in A. H. Hermann, *Conflicts of National Laws with International Business Activity: Issues of Extraterritoriality* (British–North American Committee, 1982), at pp. 71–72.
135   On which see *The Barcelona Traction, Light and Power Company Case* ICJ Reports (1970), p. 3, paras 33–4.
136   ILO Declaration (note 2 above), para. 48; OECD Employment Guideline (note 1 above), para. 1.
137   See OECD, *1986 Review of the Guidelines on Multinational Enterprises* (Paris, 1986), paras 71–3, at pp. 35–6.
138   Ibid., para. 49.
139   ILO Declaration, para. 56. The EC espouses a policy of 'social dialogue' between workers and employers. However, it is unclear whether this includes rights to collective bargaining.
140   *European Airline Groupings* case: Blanpain (note 14 above), vol. I, at pp. 229–35 and vol. II, at pp. 119–35; Robinson (note 8 above), at pp. 135–6. The ITF was held entitled to meaningful negotiations with the groupings of European airlines KSSU (KLM, Swissair, SAS, UTA) and ATLAS (Alitalia, Lufthansa, Air France, Sabena), as these came within the definition of a MNE in para. 8 of the introduction to the Guidelines. In any case, the Guidelines applied to both national and multinational enterprises and represented good practice for all.
141   *Citibank-Citicorp* case (complaint of anti-union policy run by a multinational bank), Blanpain (note 14 above), vol. I, at pp. 174–86 and vol. II, at pp. 107–18 (further complaints concerning anti-union policies in multinational banks brought by the International Federation of Commercial Clerical and Technical Employees); Robinson (note 8 above), at pp. 134–5. See also the *Norsk Hydro* (USA), *Quantas Airlines* (USA), and *NAM* (USA) cases in Blanpain, vol. III, at pp. 75–96.
142   ILO Declaration, paras 51 and 54; OECD Employment Guideline, paras 2 and 3.
143   See OECD, *1986 Review of the Guidelines on Multinational Enterprises*, paras 85–7 at pp. 39–40; reaffirmed in the 1991 Review (note 1 above), at pp. 46–8.
144   *ITT (Germany)* case: Robinson (note 8 above), at pp. 133–4.
145   ILO Declaration (note 2 above), para. 55.
146   ILO Declaration, para. 51; OECD Employment Guideline, para. 9.

147   OECD, *1986 Review of the Guidelines on Multinational Enterprises*, paras 65–6 at p. 34.
148   *Firestone* case: Blanpain (note 14 above), vol. I, at pp. 146–50; Robinson (note 8 above), at pp. 136–7. *British Oxygen* (Sweden) case: Blanpain, vol. II, at pp. 195–220; Robinson, at pp. 137–8. *Phillips* (Finland) and *Ford* (Amsterdam) cases: Blanpain, vol. II, pp. 135–95, vol. III, pp. 154–60 (further review of Ford case).
149   OECD 1986 Review (note 137 above), paras 80–1 at p. 38.
150   *Citibank* (Denmark) case: Blanpain (note 14 above), vol. III, at pp. 97–100.
151   See Northrup *et al.* (note 111 above), at pp. 532–7; ILO, *World Labour Report 1992*, box 3.1 at p. 57. This lists as other examples: Bull's information committee established in 1988 covering 12 countries; Nestlé's first meeting in 1990 with the International Union of Food Workers and national trade union officials in what are expected to become annual meetings; Volkswagen has had a European works council since 1990 with representatives from VW, Audi and Seat (Spain) and will include its East European joint ventures such as Skoda; Elf-Aquitaine established a European information and consultation committee in 1991. See further the discussion of the Directive on European Works Councils in chapter 10 at pp. 352–3 and associated references.
152   See chapter 3 at pp. 68–9.
153   196 EIRR 3 (May 1990).
154   'Ford unions in Europe join forces', *Financial Times*, 13 July 1993, p. 7; 'European works council marks Ford policy shift', *Financial Times*, 1 October 1993, p. 12.
155   OECD Employment Guideline, para. 8: 'Enterprises should, within the framework of law, regulations and prevailing labour relations and employment practices, in each of the countries in which they operate: . . . In the context of bona fide negotiations with representatives of employees on conditions of employment, or while employees are exercising a right to organise, not threaten to utilise a capacity to transfer the whole or part of an operating unit from the country concerned nor transfer employees from the enterprises' component entities in other countries in order to influence unfairly those negotiations or to hinder the exercise of the right to organise.'
156   Ibid., n. 6.
157   1986 Review (note 137 above), para. 63 at p. 33.
158   Ibid., para. 62.
159   See Blanpain (note 14 above), vol. I, at pp. 219–28; Robinson (note 8 above), at p. 129.
160   ILO Declaration, para. 57 and Recommendation No. 130 concerning the examination of grievances within the undertaking with a view to their settlement.
161   Ibid.
162   Ibid., para. 58.

Part III

The Emerging System of
International Regulation

14

Renegotiation and Expropriation

This chapter introduces part III of this work by considering the major issues arising in MNE–host state relations that are regulated primarily by international law. These centre on the revision or termination of an international investment agreement entered into between the host state and a foreign investor,[1] and on the expropriation of assets belonging to the foreign investor. Legal conflict is likely in these situations. Such conflict was most pronounced in the 1970s and early 1980s, in the wake of major renegotiations and nationalizations of foreign owned natural resource operations, particularly in the oil industry.[2] At present the incidence of such events is rare.[3] However, that cannot rule out the possibility of future conflicts over the control and ownership of foreign investments, especially in a future period of increased prosperity, in which the sense of dependence on foreign investors may be reduced and nationalistic sentiments heightened.

Although the internal law of the host state may be the proper law of the investment agreement,[4] and will therefore offer the initial legal framework for determining the legality of a contractual renegotiation or expropriation of foreign owned assets, international law can be – and has been – invoked by foreign investors as the ultimate standard of legality in such cases. How this view is justified in terms of legal doctrine will now be considered, as a general introduction to the more specific legal questions raised by renegotiation and expropriation.

1 The Restriction of State Sovereignty in the Field of Contractual Relations with Foreign Investors

Capital-exporting countries have sought to control host state sovereignty in this field by way of two principal legal techniques: first, by asserting that the proper law governing the international investment agreement is international law;[5] secondly, by the adoption of so-called 'stabilization clauses' in international investment agreements under which 'the government party undertakes neither to annul the agreement nor to modify its terms, either by legislation or by administrative measures'.[6] This invokes the doctrine of 'sanctity of contract' as a justification for limiting the ability of the host state subsequently to alter the terms of the investment agreement by law. Both approaches are controversial as they assert a contractually based restriction upon the sovereignty of the host state over internal economic affairs.

1.1   The 'Internationalization' of International Investment Agreements

The suggestion that international investment agreements are governed by international law as their proper law was discussed in a number of international arbitrations in the late 1970s and early 1980s arising out of expropriations, during the early 1970s, in the Middle Eastern oil industry. Of these, perhaps the most controversial was the *Texaco* arbitration.[7] In that case the arbitrator, Professor Dupuy, held that an oil concession agreement between a US oil company and the Government of Libya was 'internationalized', that is assimilated to international law, on two principal grounds. First, the reference to principles of international law, and to general principles of law,[8] in the choice of law clause in the concession agreement was held to define the extent to which Libyan law could apply.[9] Only if Libyan law was in conformity with international law should it be applied to determine the legality of Libya's expropriation of the US company's assets. Secondly, the fact that the contract was an economic development agreement emphasized the need for internationalization. According to Professor Dupuy, such agreements justified assimilation to international law on the basis of their broad subject matter, their long duration and the magnitude of the investment made by the foreign party. This required a measure of stability by which the investor could be protected against legislative uncertainties and governmental measures that might lead to an abrogation or rescission of the contract. Hence stabilization clauses were inserted which removed all or part of the agreement from the internal law and provided for its correlative submission to *sui generis* rules or to a system which was properly an international law system.[10]

Professor Dupuy's approach was followed in the *Revere Copper* arbitration.[11] However, it was not followed in the subsequent oil arbitrations of the early 1980s. In *Liamco v Libya*[12] the arbitrator, Dr Mahmassani, considered that the mere characterization of the concession as an 'economic development agreement' was, without more, insufficient to assimilate it to international law. However, on the basis of the express terms of the choice of law clause, Dr Mahmassani concluded that the proper law of the concession was Libyan law, excluding any part of that law which was in conflict with principles of international law.[13] In the *Aminoil* arbitration,[14] which involved an expropriation dispute between a US oil production company and Kuwait, the Tribunal took a similar approach to that of Dr Mahmassani in *Liamco*. It held that the law of Kuwait applied subject to established public international law, which was found to be a part of the law of Kuwait, and to general principles of law, which were part of public international law.[15]

From the above it can be concluded that Professor Dupuy's approach, based on internationalization implied from the context of the agreement, does not find uniform support in arbitral awards.[16] The decisive factor appears to be the actual content of the agreement. Of particular importance are the terms of any express choice of law clause used by the parties and, in addition, whether there exists a stabilization clause restricting the host state's sovereign powers.[17] Furthermore, the *Liamco* and *Aminoil* awards are noteworthy for their assimilation of the national law of the host state with international law.[18] In particular, the *Aminoil* award appears to be adopting something akin to a 'transnational law' approach.[19] In that case the concession agreements themselves referred to general principles of law. However, in article III(2) of the arbitration agreement, the parties referred to the transnational character of relations with the concessionaire and to general principles of law. The Tribunal held that the different sources called upon in this article were not in contradiction with one another. Indeed, they formed a blend of sources as international law was a part of the law of Kuwait, and general principles of law correspondingly recognized the rights of the state in its capacity as protector of the general interest.[20]

This approach may serve to avoid choice of law problems by adopting an eclectic attitude to the sources of law governing international economic transactions. Instead of there being a need to make a simple choice between national law or international law supported by general principles of law recognised by civilized nations, all these sources are held to be available for the international tribunal to apply.[21] However, the adoption of this approach appears to have been made conditional upon an express acceptance of it by the parties to the dispute. This raises interesting issues concerning the relative bargaining positions of the parties, and how these may influence the content of the choice of law clause. The transnational law approach may avoid the stultification of dispute resolution procedures which might otherwise have become enmeshed in futile conflicts over the applicable law, with the host state favouring exclusive use of its law and the foreign investor insisting on the internationalization of the dispute. Where both parties are of equal bargaining power the compromise of adopting 'transnational law' may be used. On the other hand, where the power of the host state is superior, its internal law may be chosen to the exclusion of international law. In such a case it is unlikely that the dispute will be heard before an international arbitral tribunal. However, where the foreign investor is dominant, it may be a condition of the investment that it is completely delocalized, with international arbitration and international law as the proper law of the agreement being chosen.

1.2   Sanctity of Contract and Stabilization Clauses

Following on from the 'internationalization' doctrine, the classical legal doctrine of 'sanctity of contract' has been invoked as a limitation on the absolute sovereignty of the host state over its relations with foreign investors. In this context, the legal effect of stabilization clauses in investment contracts has caused controversy. Stabilization clauses can be used to exclude rules of the host state's law from the regulation of the agreement, by making international law or general principles of law the proper law of the agreement. Stabilization clauses may further exclude subsequent amendments of host state law from operating upon the investment contract. Thus the original terms of the investment agreement can be preserved from subsequent legal challenge by virtue of the stabilization clause.

Under the theory of sanctity of contract, the will of the parties must serve as the foundation of their agreement. Consequently a stabilization clause, as an expression of the will of the parties, must be upheld. This view led Professor Dupuy to hold, in the *Texaco* award, that the effect of the stabilization clause was to limit the state's sovereignty in relation to its rights over natural resources for the limited period of the concession.[22] On the other hand, in the *Liamco* award, Dr Mahmassani maintained that the principle *pacta sunt servanda* was qualified by the right of states to nationalize subject to the obligations of compensation.[23] In *BP* v *Libya*[24] the sole arbitrator, Gunnar Lagergren, simply held that the concession involved constituted 'a direct contractual link between the respondent and the claimant'.[25]

In the *Aminoil* arbitration,[26] the Tribunal held that the host state was in no way prevented from granting stability guarantees by contract.[27] However, the Tribunal required an express provision restricting the state's power of nationalization. The contractual limitation of the state's right was 'a particularly serious undertaking which would have to be expressly stipulated for, and be within the regulations governing the conclusion of State contracts'.[28] Furthermore, the

Tribunal did not wish to prohibit the state's power to nationalize in the context of the great changes that had in fact come about in the agreement through a prolonged process of renegotiation.[29] The Tribunal concluded that, owing to the changing nature of the concession, brought about by periodic renegotiation, the stabilization clauses had lost their absolute character. This was not a fundamental change in circumstances involving a departure from the contract, but a change in the nature of the contract itself, brought about by time, and the acquiescence or conduct of the parties.[30] Furthermore, it appears from the Tribunal's reasoning in *Aminoil* that the stabilisation clause, on its terms, could not effectively limit the host state's power.[31] Thus, the case of a fundamental change of circumstances has been recognized in the *Aminoil* award as a justification for renegotiation. Presumably, in such cases, the existence of a stabilization clause cannot serve to justify the continuation of arrangements which were agreed before the full value of the investment was known, and which, if continued, would adversely affect the value of the project to the host state.

Finally, the use of stabilization clauses, just like the question of the proper law of the investment agreement, is a matter to be determined on the basis of the relative bargaining power of the parties. In the oil industry, for example, the practice of submitting oil contracts to the law and jurisdiction of the host state increased during the 1970s as a result of increased host state power.[32] On the other hand, a shift in bargaining power back to the foreign investor may result in the provision of guarantees, akin in their effect to stabilization clauses, under host state law.[33] Thus, while formal use of stabilization clauses in investment agreements has been in decline, the substance of their effect cannot be presumed to have disappeared from the legal regulation of international investment agreements.

2   Renegotiation of International Investment Agreements

Despite the above-mentioned arguments favouring the strict stability of international investment agreements, international practice in this field has increasingly favoured the periodic renegotiation of such agreements.[34] In these circumstances the international legality of renegotiation *per se* can no longer be doubted. In order to avoid the inflexibility that a contract governed by a stabilization clause may create, the view has been put forward that investment agreements should, as a matter of standard form, include renegotiation clauses.[35] The inclusion of such a clause would clearly place renegotiation on a plane of legal acceptability and avoid arguments that taint renegotiation with illegality.[36]

According to Dr Cynthia Wallace, the renegotiation of contracts at the initiation of the host is the result of a gradual shift in bargaining power away from the MNE towards the host state.[37] Whether the government can renegotiate successfully is, however, a matter of fact in each case. Furthermore, despite Dr Wallace's suggestion to the contrary, renegotiation will not always be at the instigation of the host state alone. There may be good reasons for the MNE to seek renegotiation. The MNE may welcome renegotiation initiated by the host state, especially where this might lead to a diffusion of hostility towards the firm's operations and guarantee long-term stability. Thus renegotiation may be a commercially desirable process for both parties.

However, as Dr Wallace points out,[38] if negotiations lead to unreasonable terms being imposed on the MNE, this may amount to unacceptable economic coercion by way of a diminution of corporate assets, or a partial sale thereof at undervalue, resulting from pressure in negotiations. This allows the state to achieve lawfully what it could not achieve lawfully through, say, nationalization without compensation. There may exist a fine line between government coercion and unlawful expropriation. This raises the question of whether there exists a doctrine of unfair coercion at international law that can control abuses of power on the part of the host state in the renegotiating process.[39]

The control of coercion on the part of the foreign corporation may also need to be subjected to such a regime, although this raises difficult questions as to the amenability of corporations to regulation by international law. Consequently, the discussion that follows may be of relevance only to host state behaviour. The behaviour of the foreign corporation will remain to be judged in accordance with the proper law of the investment agreement, usually the law of the host state. Thus an imbalance in the legal regime applicable to each party may exist in this area.

In the absence of established rules of international law on the matter, the control of unreasonable terms imposed on foreign investors by way of contractual renegotiation must be analysed by analogy with general principles of contract law found in modern legal systems.[40] In particular, the issues of duress and discrimination should be considered as vitiating factors in renegotiations between host states and foreign investors. Some instructive dicta on duress were given by the Tribunal in the *Aminoil* award,[41] in the context of renegotiations undertaken in the light of a threat of expropriation against Aminoil. The US corporation argued that certain renegotiations of the concession agreement with Kuwait were tainted by duress in that the undertaking was threatened with 'shutdown' or a total prohibition on exports and that, accordingly, the corporation could not be bound by their outcome.[42] The Tribunal rejected this argument. It made a distinction between strong economic pressure to conform to disagreeable terms and true coercion or duress that would invalidate agreement:

it is necessary to stress that it is not just pressure of any kind that will suffice to bring about a nullification. There must be a constraint invested with particular characteristics, which the legal systems of all countries have been at pains to define in terms either of the absence of any other possible course than that to which the consent was given, or of the illegal nature of the object in view, or of the means employed.... But the illicit character of the threats against AMINOIL has not been fully proved.[43]

The Tribunal went on to say that even if there were illicit threats in the circumstances they could not be said to have vitiated consent. First, Aminoil gave way without even making the qualification that the company was conscious that something illicit was being imposed upon it. It was understandable that it avoided resorting to arbitration because of costs and delays, but it entered neither reservations of position nor protests.[44] Secondly, the Tribunal felt that, in truth, the company had made a choice: 'disagreeable as certain demands might be, it considered that it was better to accede to them because it was still possible to live with them. The whole conduct of the company shows that the pressure it was under was not of a kind as to inhibit its freedom of choice. The absence of protest during the years following upon 1973 confirms the non existence, or else the abandonment of this ground of complaint.'[45]

The Tribunal was thus emphasizing the need for the company persistently to object to the alleged duress for the argument to be credible. On the facts it appeared that the company had acquiesced to the new terms. In taking this stance, the Tribunal shows that it would not readily interfere with the bargaining process between the parties and would not rewrite a contract simply because it contained disagreeable terms that a foreign investor had accepted where, on balance, it was commercially better to accept them rather than to end the operation. This 'laissez-faire' approach is emphasized by the Tribunal's view of the effects of the balance of negotiating power between the parties. The Tribunal noted that the balance of advantage in the Gulf region had tilted in favour of governments and that Aminoil had been subjected to strong pressure to accept the repeated demands of the Kuwaiti government. But all the Tribunal had to decide was whether these constraints were of such a nature as to cause the malfunction of the interim agreement of 1973 or of certain other consents. This had not been shown.[46] Thus the mere fact that the balance of negotiating power lay with the government did not amount to conclusive evidence of coercion.

It is not clear from the award whether the investor must persistently object to the unfair terms in all cases or whether this is unnecessary in cases where clearly it has no choice but to succumb to coercive pressure. It is submitted that the correct view should be that where it is clear that the investor has no choice but to accept (as where the alternative is confiscation) the absence of protest cannot be decisive. Indeed the absence of protest may itself be an effect of the threat. Where, however, there is some element of choice (as where non-acceptance may result in nationalization with full and effective compensation) then acceptance of the new terms without protest would, arguably, vitiate any claim of duress. This is consistent with the view that the successful use of economic pressure by the state is not duress *per se*. There must be, in addition, proof of the unwillingness of the investor to accept the terms.[47]

The award leaves open the question of what evidential weight should be given to the investor's objections. Is the fact of objection, in itself, sufficient to vitiate consent, or must the tribunal consider further the question of whether objection is justifiable on the facts? The latter view ought to prevail. Not every objection is with foundation. Furthermore, to decide the question on evidence of protest alone would be contrary to the view that disagreeable terms obtained as a result of economic pressure are not invalid by that fact alone. Thus the protest must be coupled with proof of some illicit action on the part of the state. Proof of the effects of the renegotiation on the corporate 'state of mind' are too subjective to be clear proof of duress.

This raises a further question: how are we to distinguish between acts of the state that are merely a legitimate exercise of economic power and those that are sufficiently coercive to vitiate consent on the part of the investor to renegotiate terms? No absolute rules can be laid down. Each case must be judged on its own facts. However, certain guidelines can be suggested. First, threats of physical injury to the personnel of the corporation should always vitiate consent. This is a principle well known to most systems of contract law.[48] Secondly, threats of the physical destruction or legal attachment of the firm's property should have a similar effect where there is no legal justification for such interference.[49] On the other hand, threats of nationalization with the payment of full and effective compensation should not be treated as acts of duress *per se*, given the essential legality of such action. However, where the compensation offered is derisory when compared to the value of the foreign investor's assets, this might amount to evidence of duress in the absence of further objective justification. These issues are more fully discussed below.

A further issue to be considered when assessing the legality of renegotiation is whether the foreign investor has been unfairly discriminated against in the renegotiating process. The applicable legal principles are similar to those pertaining to non-discrimination in relation to expropriation, which is considered below.

3   Expropriation of Foreign Corporate Assets

This section of the chapter is divided into four parts. The first considers what constitutes expropriation; the second deals with the legality of expropriation in the law of the host state; the third examines the legality of expropriation in international law; and the fourth deals with the most controversial aspect of the international legality of expropriation, namely the issue of compensation.

3.1   What Constitutes Expropriation?

An act of expropriation involves the compulsory taking of property belonging to another upon payment of compensation for its loss. The taker is usually a public authority or a private entity acting on behalf of a public authority. The expropriated property may be acquired by a third party or be taken into public ownership and control, in which case it is said to have been nationalized. The more general term 'taking of property' may be used to cover both cases.[50]

What constitutes a 'taking of property' is a matter of some debate. It has been argued that not only express policies of nationalisation or expropriation fall to be considered, but also methods that do not involve an overt taking but that effectively neutralize the benefit of the property for the foreign owner. These have been referred to as cases of 'constructive taking' or 'creeping expropriation'.[51] Thus, for example, where a foreign investor is irrevocably deprived of its contractual rights in a joint venture created under an investment agreement, such an interference will give rise to a right of compensation.[52] This view is justified in the light of the theory of property ownership: the incidents of ownership include not only possession but use and free alienation. Any measure that irrevocably interferes with any one of these attributes of ownership deserves to be considered as a mode of expropriation entailing an obligation of compensation for any resulting economic loss suffered by the owner.[53]

It has been suggested that a distinction should be made between a temporary administrative interference with property rights and the permanent deprivation of those rights.[54] Otherwise, the legitimate exercise of a state's regulatory powers could be unduly impeded by reference to international legal standards that go beyond what is generally accepted in the municipal laws of the world.[55] This distinction may raise controversies. For example, the Iran–US Claims Tribunal has had to address the issue in relation to emergency measures taken by Iran to preserve commercial property in the wake of post-revolutionary chaos in 1978–9, which has led to claims of unlawful constructive taking by Iran.[56] Furthermore, it has been suggested that laws requiring the participation of workers in the management of a company could amount to creeping expropriation.[57] It is submitted that this view is unduly restrictive of the host state's right to evolve company law in the light of its chosen policy, and ignores the distinction between the regulation and expropriation of property.

3.2   The Legality of Expropriatory Measures under the Law of the Host State

The legality of a measure of expropriation is at first instance a question for the internal law of the host state. An act of expropriation is generally taken in pursuit of a statutory or other legal authority of the host state.[58] Furthermore, host state law may provide the means by which the titleholder can challenge the taking. Local administrative law may provide for judicial review, or special provisions under the legislation governing the expropriation may set up a disputes procedure. Such measures can serve to control excesses of executive power where they are applied with regard to due process. Moreover, the law of the host state may provide constitutional controls over the passage of laws authorizing expropriation.[59]

In this field, the primacy of internal review and judicial control should be stressed. Indeed, under public international law the foreign investor is obliged to exhaust local remedies, unless they are obviously futile, before it can present a claim under international law.[60] It is likely that most acts of expropriation, if carried out under legal authority and in accordance with the requirements of procedural justice, will raise no questions of conformity with either internal or international law. Consequently, the legality of a nationalization or expropriation of foreign owned property has become a question of international law only in those cases where local law has failed to satisfy the claims of the foreign investor to adequate compensation and to due process. The role of international law in this area is that of an exceptional standard of control to be used only in relation to extraordinary abuses of power by the host state in its treatment of the foreign investor.[61]

3.3   The Legality of Expropriation at International Law [62]

3.3.1   The conflict of norms in this area   The legality of expropriation has been one of the most contentious problems in international law. Due to changes in the international political system over the past century, uncertainty has arisen as to the norms of international law applicable to foreign investors.[63] This broader question will be considered in more detail in chapter 16. For now a brief summary of the differing positions in the expropriation debate will suffice. According to the repeated practice of the major capital-exporting powers, expropriation is lawful only in cases where it is carried out for a clear public purpose, without discrimination and upon payment of 'prompt adequate and effective compensation'.[64] This is often referred to as the international minimum standard for the treatment of property belonging to aliens. On the other hand, the major capital-importing states have periodically doubted the validity of this standard, which they see as having been evolved to serve the interests of capital-exporting states and, therefore, lacking the generality of acceptance required of a norm of customary international law.[65] During the 1970s these states were active in proposing alternative standards through the UN that centred on increased host state control over expropriation and, in particular, over levels of compensation.[66]

However, a number of factors point to the continual dominance of the international minimum standard in the legal analysis of the consequences of expropriation. First, the standard is increasingly accepted by capital-importing countries in bilateral investment treaties.[67] Secondly, it continues to inform the expropriation policies of major capital-exporting states. For example, the French government was concerned to conform with international law when compensation for foreign shareholders was in issue during the nationalizations of 1982. Thus, foreign banks were excluded from nationalization and foreign shareholders in the nationalized companies were promised prompt, adequate and effective compensation. Thirdly, the courts of major capital-exporting countries may not give effect to an expropriatory measure that does not conform to the international minimum standard, at least as regards the requirements of public purpose and non-discrimination.[68] Fourthly, although newer international investment agreements tend to be governed by the law of the host state rather than by international law, the contents of national law will often conform to the international minimum standard.[69] Thus the difference in applicable principles may not be that great where host state law accepts the international standard. Fifthly, the international minimum standard continues to be a major source of legal principle applied by international arbitral tribunals.[70]

None the less, it is important to be aware of the limitations of the above-mentioned factors. In particular, inroads may be made into the philosophy of 'prompt adequate and effective' compensation for practical commercial and political reasons, leading to less than full compensation in negotiated settlements or lump sum agreements. This issue will be considered in more detail in sub-section 3.4 below. Furthermore, investment treaties may incorporate the international minimum standard precisely because its status as customary law is in doubt.[71] Moreover, arbitral jurisprudence has often evolved in the context of factors that may limit its claim to represent an international consensus on applicable standards. These include the non-appearance of Libya in the oil arbitrations of the late 1970s and early 1980s[72] and the persistent lodging of dissenting opinions, critical of the application of the international minimum standard, by the Iranian arbitrators sitting in the Chambers of the Iran–US Claims Tribunal.[73] As these two sets of awards are among the most cited in favour of the acceptance of the international standard, these facts should not go unnoticed. In any case, as will be seen below, there is considerable disagreement among writers as to whether recent international awards do apply the standard of full compensation for expropriatory acts. Notwithstanding these factors, the international minimum standard retains considerable force as an ordering principle for the legal discussion of expropriation and will be so used in the remainder of this chapter.

3.3.2   *The elements of lawful expropriation*   To be lawful, expropriation must be for a public purpose, be non-discriminatory and be accompanied by compensation. There is general agreement between states on the content of this aspect of the law. Expropriation is usually treated as a sovereign power that is exercised for the purposes of the expropriating state's national economic policy. That power cannot, however, be exercised arbitrarily. Thus it is subject to two qualifications: first it must be exercised for a genuine public purpose, and not for a purpose of private gain; secondly, it must conform to basic principles of justice. Hence it must be non-discriminatory and compensation must be provided.

The question of public purpose is a question of fact in each case. It is generally not in issue that a measure of expropriation is undertaken for a public purpose. States enjoy a wide discretion in this respect.[74] However, certain kinds of taking would be beyond the state's lawful discretion. The clearest example arises where members of the government are using expropriation as a means of obtaining private gain, rather than acting for the enrichment of the country. The same legal consequence may attach where the taking is not recognized by law in effect at the time of taking as being for a public purpose.[75]

Furthermore, should the property be seized in the course of committing crimes against humanity, or genocide, or other violations of human rights, the taking would be contrary to public purpose.[76] Equally, where the taking is motivated by political concerns that are not directly relevant to the state's economic policy, and is not justified by exceptional circumstances,[77] it may well be unlawful.[78]

The question of non-discrimination is closely connected to the issue of public purpose in that a discriminatory expropriation cannot be an expropriation for a public purpose.[79] The issue of discrimination involves a comparison, if any exists,[80] with the treatment afforded to domestic competitors, to other foreign investors operating in the same field and to foreign investors in general. The basic principle of equality of treatment is in issue. Thus any difference in treatment must be objectively justifiable.

In this respect, discriminatory treatment which cannot be justified by reference to the host state's economic policy has been presumed to be illegitimate. Thus an expropriation motivated by extraneous political concerns, such as retaliation against the home state of the investor for the conduct of its foreign policy, may not be acceptable.[81] On the other hand, the mere fact that different treatment is being meted out to certain corporations of foreign nationality would appear to be insufficient, in itself, to vitiate an act of expropriation.[82] Unless it is clear that the differentiation is without objective justification, this phenomenon cannot act as a vitiating factor, as it would render policy responses based on distinctions in corporate nationality unlawful *per se.*[83]

Thus, modern international law may give a certain margin of discretion to the host state in this area. However, it is not entirely clear whether this margin should be the same in all cases. Recent arbitral jurisprudence has mainly dealt with differences of treatment between foreign corporations possessing the same or different nationalities.[84] More problematic is the case of differing treatment between a foreign corporation and a domestic competitor which is unfavourable to the foreign entity.[85] Such treatment may violate the 'national treatment' standard, which is present in numerous bilateral investment treaties.[86] However, in the absence of specific treaty protection, it is submitted that such discrimination is subject to the same test of objective justification as cases involving foreign corporations alone.

Should a discriminatory taking be found to have taken place, it might not be open to legal challenge, provided a just measure of compensation has been paid.[87] In this way state sovereignty and corporate interests may be reconciled. However, the issue of compensation has raised controversial questions, to which we now turn.

3.4   The Issue of Compensation

There is general agreement that, to be lawful, an act of expropriation requires compensation. On the other hand there continues to be disagreement as to how that compensation should be measured. This process involves two interrelated stages. First, the expropriated property must be valued to ascertain the actual economic loss sustained by the property owner. Secondly, the extent to which the owner is entitled to be compensated for the economic loss suffered must be determined.[88] Each stage will be considered in turn.

3.4.1   *The valuation of expropriated property*[89]   According to Eli Lauterpacht the value of property is 'an objective concept with an economic content' which should be ascertained by reference to 'objectively relevant factors' before the question of the extent of compensation is addressed.[90] The choice of relevant factors is not easy. As the economists Penrose, Joffe and Stevens point out:

There is not just *one* incontrovertible intrinsic value of any asset, but several possible values, depending not only on the purpose but also on the circumstances and the point of view; buyer or seller, public or private entities, insurance appraiser, economist or accountant. Moreover, calculations of 'value' from any given point of view and using the same methods can diverge widely, depending on the assumptions on which they are based. . . . It is not surprising, therefore, that there has been a considerable variety of approaches to the valuation of nationalised assets for the purpose of compensation to the private owner.[91]

Thus the approach to valuation will itself be conditioned by the purpose behind it.

In cases of expropriation the aim of the foreign investor will be to show a valuation that takes into account what Penrose et al. term the 'private' value of the expropriated assets to it.[92] This may result in the use of a valuation method that will ignore the wider public costs associated with the operation of those assets. In particular, the investor may ignore the costs of externalities associated with the use of those assets, and may incorporate a calculation of expected future profits based on the degree of monopoly power that it exercises in the national and/or international market concerned.

Furthermore, where the expropriated asset is a subsidiary of a foreign parent company, the ascertainment of an appropriate value may be difficult if there is no 'market' for that company, as where it is not quoted on international stock markets. In such cases a valuation will be made by looking at the asset value of the group as a whole and effecting a profit split between the subsidiary and the other affiliates. In addition, the future profitability of the subsidiary will have to be assessed. This is done by discounting an estimated future net cash flow to produce a present value, referred to as the discounted cash flow method (DCF). This is a process fraught with subjective assumptions about the future performance of the business.[93]

By contrast the expropriating state will seek a valuation that emphasizes the public interests involved. Thus, it will advocate a valuation method that reduces the actual cost of compensation by reference to the negative costs of the foreign enterprise to the host economy. This will be done in terms of the above-mentioned externalities and/or monopoly profits earned or expected to be earned. This position may be justified by reference to the 'unjust enrichment' of the foreign enterprise by an allegation that it has earned excess profits.[94] Habitually, host states have argued for the use of the 'net book value' method, which restricts valuation to the current replacement cost or depreciated replacement cost of the expropriated assets, with little or no allowance for estimated future profits. However, this has not been accepted by international tribunals as the appropriate method of valuation.[95]

It appears that a broader approach has been taken by certain international tribunals on the matter of valuation. This seeks to favour neither the foreign investor nor the host state, but, rather, to ensure a valuation that takes reasonable account of both the private and public interests involved. The approach is exemplified by the award in the *Aminoil* arbitration, and by certain awards of the Iran–US Claims Tribunal.

In the *Aminoil* award,[96] the Tribunal began by saying that a distinction had to be made between states that wished to eliminate foreign investors from their territory and that would adopt very restrictive rules as to compensation,[97] and states that welcomed foreign investment and that even engaged in it themselves. Such states could be expected to espouse an attitude towards compensation such as would not render foreign investment economically useless.[98] As Kuwait fell into the latter category there was 'no room for rules of compensation that would make nonsense of foreign investment'.[99] The Tribunal then considered the notion of 'legitimate expectations', which both parties had invoked for the purpose of deciding compensation.[100] The legitimate expectations of the parties were signified by the contract itself. Thus the text should be precise and exhaustive. However, this was not only a question of the original text but also of amendments, interpretations and behaviour manifested along the course of its existence that indicated (often fortuitously) how the legitimate expectations of the parties were to be seen, and sometimes seen as modified according to the circumstances.[101]

In the light of these general pronouncements, the Tribunal went on to consider the competing valuations put forward by Aminoil and

Kuwait, which, respectively, relied on the DCF and 'book value' methods, and then to evaluate the 'legitimate expectations' of Aminoil. First, although they did not prohibit nationalization the stabilization clauses in the concession created a legitimate expectation that measures of a confiscatory character would be prohibited.[102] Secondly, Aminoil expected a 'reasonable rate of return', and not speculative profits, from its investment once production had reached a satisfactory level. It was in the light of this expectation that compensation had to be assessed.[103] The Tribunal went on to hold that a 'reasonable rate of return' in the present case would include a reasonable profit margin that would preserve incentives and allow for risks, whether commercial or technological, and for reinvestment of a proportion of the profits.[104] Having considered the principles upon which compensation would be assessed on a loss of a corporation's assets, the Tribunal calculated the sum of compensation owing at date of nationalization in 1977. After Aminoil's liabilities were deducted the sum owed came to $83,000,000. In order to establish what was due in 1982 account had to be taken of a reasonable rate of interest (7.5 per cent) and of a level of inflation – fixed at 10 per cent. Thus a total annual increase of 27.5 per cent in the amount due over the amount due for the preceding year was applied. This gave a total figure of $179,750,764.

A further indication of a broader approach is given in case-law emanating from the Iran–US Claims Tribunal.[105] The general value of these awards as precedents should be treated with caution. The awards made by individual Chambers of the Tribunal differ in their content, and, as already noted, the Iranian members have habitually dissented. Furthermore, it appears that since the award in *Phelps Dodge*[106] subsequent awards have been made on the basis of the Treaty of Amity between the USA and Iran, rather than by reference to customary international law alone. That treaty contains an obligation of 'prompt payment of just compensation', which shall be in 'an effectively realizable form and shall represent the full equivalent of the property taken'.[107]

None the less, as regards the issue of valuation, certain important developments have occurred. In particular, in *Amoco International*[108] Chamber Three elaborated the 'going concern value' method as the appropriate means of valuation:

Going concern value encompasses not only the physical and financial assets of the undertaking, but also the intangible valuables which contribute to its earning power, such as contractual rights (supply and delivery contracts, patent licences and so on), as well as goodwill and commercial prospects. Although these assets are closely linked to the profitability of the concern, they cannot and must not be confused with the financial capitalization of the revenues which might be generated by such a concern after the transfer of property resulting from the expropriation (*lucrum cessans*).[109]

The reference to the undertaking's commercial prospects may allow for the recovery of profits by way of a 'reasonable rate of return' in all the circumstances. However, it is clear that Chamber Three did not allow for the recovery of all lost profits. Earlier in its opinion the Tribunal stated:

'future prospects' does not equal lost profit (*lucrum cessans*). Those are two different concepts. The first one clearly refers to the fact that the undertaking was a 'going concern' which had demonstrated a certain ability to earn revenues and was, therefore, to be considered as keeping such ability for the future: this is an element of its value at the time of the taking. The second relates to the amount of earnings hypothetically accrued from the date of the taking to the date of the expert opinion, had the enterprise remained in the hands of the former owner.[110]

Thus, according to Chamber Three, loss of future profits *per se* was not recoverable in the case of a lawful expropriation, and full restitution could not be claimed.[111] The 'going concern' approach emphasizes the real commercial prospects of the expropriated undertaking as the basis of calculating compensation. Thus, where these prospects are shown to be poor the amount of compensation awarded under this head will be considerably discounted.[112] However, other awards of the Iran–US Claims Tribunal have simply asserted that the 'full compensation' standard was applicable and that loss of full future profits could be recovered.[113]

Finally, brief reference should be made to awards made under the auspices of the International Centre for the Settlement of Investment Disputes (ICSID).[114] By article 42 of the Convention establishing ICSID[115] the parties are free to determine the law by which the dispute between them is to be determined. In the absence of such agreement, the Tribunal shall apply the law of the contracting state party to the dispute (i.e. the host state) and such rules of international law as may be applicable. In two of the four reported cases in which issues of compensation for expropriation have been considered, no stipulation as to the applicable law was made, which ensured that the law of the host state would be applied in accordance with international law.[116] In the other reported case the parties expressly stipulated that the law of the host state (Congo), supplemented if necessary by any principles of international law, should apply.[117] In the final reported case, the parties agreed that the law of the host state (Egypt) applied but they disagreed over the extent of the role of international law. The Tribunal held that Egyptian law applied, subject to the corrective application of international law where the exclusive application of municipal law violated international law.[118] Thus these awards are of some value as indications of the rules of international law applicable to expropriation cases, although they should be treated with caution given the specialized nature of ICSID awards.[119]

It would appear that the ICSID Tribunal accepts, in principle, the right of a foreign investor to recover compensation for both the lost value of its assets and the loss of non-speculative future profit.[120] In *Amco Asia* the first arbitral tribunal held that the appropriate principle was the loss of a 'going concern', requiring the establishment of the net present value calculated on a DCF basis.[121] The second tribunal award expressly rejected the use of the net book value method which was favoured by Indonesia. Instead, it used two methods of valuation. The first, for the period from 1980 to 1989, looked at the actual loss of contractual benefit suffered by the claimant from the date of the expropriation up to the date of the award. The second, for the period from 1990 to 1999, calculated the loss of contractual benefits from the date of the award to the end of the investment agreement by use of the DCF method.[122] However, in *Southern Pacific Properties (Middle East) Limited* v *Arab Republic of Egypt*,[123] the Tribunal rejected the use of the DCF method because the expropriated construction project had not been in existence for a sufficient period of time to generate the data necessary for a meaningful DCF calculation. It would result in a speculative calculation of loss. Furthermore, the application of the DCF method would have awarded *lucrum cessans* for a period that included a time during which the investment project would have become illegal under international and Egyptian law.[124] The Tribunal went on to reject a confirmation of the DCF valuation by reference to private sales of shares in the project.[125] Instead the Tribunal preferred a method based on the 'fair compensation' of the claimants for the amounts of capital contributions and loans made to the project and the expenditure incurred on marketing, detailed engineering designs and the partial completion of the infrastructure and golf course that was part of the development.[126] The Tribunal also added an element that represented the value of the investment in excess of the claimant's out-of-pocket expenses,[127] and interest that took account of the devaluation of the US dollar in the period since the expropriation.[128]

In *Benvenuti and Bonfant*[129] the Tribunal also held that 'fair compensation' was payable. The amounts were to be determined by the Tribunal *ex aequo et bono* in accordance with the earlier agreement of the parties, pursuant to article 42(3) of the Convention.[130] Thus the case may not be indicative of applicable international law, as it was decided *ex aequo et bono*. None the less, the Tribunal's approach to determining the precise amount of lost profits is worthy of note. The claimant had made an estimation of loss on the basis of a projection over the ninety-nine years of the investment agreement. The Tribunal appointed an independent expert from another company in the same industry as the expropriated company (soft drinks). The expert stated that the projected profit was speculative as the market price for the expropriated interest had never been established, and because the host state retained full authority to fix the prices of the products made by the claimant. He advised that the more objective measure of loss was the value of the recent investment in the expropriated company. This came to a sum higher than that claimed by the company. The claimant declared that it would not insist on this higher sum and limited its petition to the lower sum originally claimed.

From the above cases it is clear that no single method of valuation is preferred over the others. There is a tendency towards a middle way between claimant's and respondent's positions that is centred on concepts such as 'legitimate expectations' or 'going concern value', assuming there is a going concern to value. However, there are some instances of 'full compensation', which includes loss of future profits, being required. Furthermore, the DCF method has been used in some cases where loss of future profit has been held to be recoverable. The net book method appears to have been generally avoided. However, as Dr Amerasinghe notes, tribunals almost never grant the amounts requested by claimants and will take all the facts of the case into account.[131]

3.4.2 The measure of compensation From the above it is clear that the choice of valuation method will have a significant bearing on the actual measure of compensation to be awarded in cases of expropriation. The most striking contrast is between cases in which some detailed attention is paid to the valuation issue and those in which it is simplified by reference to the 'full compensation' standard. Perhaps such an approach is no more than an expression of the tribunal's belief in the illegitimacy of expropriation as a device of national economic policy, notwithstanding its formal legal validity.[132]

Such an approach makes little distinction between lawful and unlawful expropriation. The payment of 'full compensation', if it includes all future lost profits, would have the effect of neutralizing the economic objective behind the expropriation, and so make a lawful policy option untenable in practice.[133] Furthermore, such an approach might encourage host states not to comply with awards of compensation, should the host state feel that an award has taken no account of its legitimate expectations, based on public interest concerns, in determining the measure of compensation. In these circumstances, as the opinion of the Iran–US Claims Tribunal in *Amoco* notes, a clear distinction should be made between the effects of a lawful and an unlawful expropriation.[134] The Tribunal highlighted the fact that *restitutio in integrum* (full restitution) or full, but not punitive, damages in lieu of restitution was the appropriate remedy in cases of unlawful expropriation, while the payment of 'fair compensation' was the appropriate remedy in cases of lawful expropriation.[135]

Full restitution for unlawful expropriation was the remedy awarded against Libya in the *Texaco* arbitration.[136] However, that approach was not followed in *Liamco*, where the arbitrator found Libya's acts to have amounted to lawful expropriation, entitling Liamco to compensation, on essentially similar facts.[137] In *BP* v *Libya* the sole arbitrator, Gunnar Lagergren, held that *restitutio in integrum* had been employed as a vehicle for establishing the amount of damages for breach of an obligation to perform a contractual undertaking,[138] but refused to apply it to the facts. The arbitrators in both the *BP* and *Liamco* cases noted the practical difficulties associated with full restitution, in particular that it amounts to an intolerable interference with the sovereignty of the host state, as it demands the cancellation of the expropriatory measure,[139] and that compliance by the host state would be unlikely.[140]

Thus the actual utility of restitution as a remedy may be doubtful.[141] Indeed, the dispute between Texaco and Libya was eventually settled by an agreement to pay compensation in the form of supplies of crude oil to the value of $152 million, as were the other disputes that led to the oil arbitrations against Libya.[142] It should not be forgotten that arbitration, unlike litigation before courts, concerns the settlement of a dispute rather than the formal vindication of rights. Thus a pragmatic approach to remedies should be adopted if arbitration is not to be disregarded as an avenue of effective redress.

Given the foregoing discussion, debates as to whether international law requires the measure of compensation that reflects the 'prompt adequate and effective' standard, or whether it will accept something less, often described as 'appropriate'[143] or 'equitable' compensation,[144] appear increasingly obsolete and unhelpful.[145] As long as expropriation is regarded as a legitimate exercise of sovereign power, the measure of compensation payable in the case of a lawful expropriation will have to moderate the valuation of private losses in the light of broader public interest concerns. This may lead to the recovery of less than the full loss to the owner, where that is objectively justifiable in the light of the political and economic realities of the case. Thus, even in cases where loss of future profits has apparently not been recovered, it is arguable that adequate and effective compensation has been awarded.[146]

3.4.3   Settlement of claims through lump sum agreements   In cases involving a large number of claims of compensation for expropriation, and/or a host state that refuses to accept international minimum standards and/or international arbitration to resolve the matter, settlement has been achieved in many cases by the use of a lump sum agreement. For example, the former Soviet Union paid sums owed to Sweden in 1941 and 1946 and, in 1986, paid the UK government a lump sum of some £45 million to compensate for the confiscation of British owned property during the Revolution of 1917.[147] In 1973, the government of Hungary agreed with the US government to settle outstanding claims for compensation arising out of measures of nationalization carried out against the property of US nationals.[148] In 1975 Chile agreed to pay compensation to dispossessed US firms.[149] Numerous further examples of such settlements have been documented.[150]

A recent illustration of a lump sum compensation agreement occurred in relation to the dispute between the USA and Ethiopia over the compensation payable for the property of the Kalamazoo Spice Extraction Co. (Kal-Spice) that had been expropriated by the Provisional Military Government of Ethiopia in 1975.[151] Kal-Spice sought to attach accounts payable to Ethiopia in the USA under continuing supply contracts with Kal-Spice. Ethiopia argued that it had jurisdictional immunity. The issue was considered before the US District Court for the Western District of Michigan (Southern Division).[152] The action in this case was discontinued after the USA and Ethiopia signed a compensation agreement on 19 December 1986 in Addis Ababa.[153]

The agreement, which extended to any natural person or corporation that is a national of the USA, as defined in article I, provided for the payment by the Ethiopian government of a sum of US $7 million 'in full settlement and discharge of all claims of nationals of the United States against the Ethiopian government described in this agreement'.[154] The payment was to be effected as follows. An initial down payment of $1.5 million was to be made within thirty days of entry into force of the agreement with the balance of $5.5 million to be paid in ten equal six monthly instalments.[155] The distribution of the compensation amounts to claimants falls within the exclusive competence of the US government.[156] Upon completion of these payments the government of Ethiopia will have fully discharged its obligations and liabilities to the USA in respect of all claims covered by the agreement.[157] This applied to the Kalamazoo counterclaims. Indeed the claims and counterclaims in this case were the subject of an Agreed Minute appended to the Agreement.[158]

The status of such agreements as evidence of contemporary state practice in the field of compensation for expropriation has been doubted in recent arbitral awards, on the basis that the agreed settlements are the product of non-judicial bargaining considerations which negate their value as a source of *opinio juris*.[159] This has led to criticism that a major, if not *the* major, source of state practice in this area has been ignored by international tribunals in the formulation of standards of compensation.[160]

4   Investment Guarantee Schemes

The threat of political risks, such as expropriation, is a factor that will increase the perceived costs of investment in a host state. However, these costs may be reduced if insurance is taken out against political risk. This kind of cover may be available through private insurers, although this has not always been easy to obtain given the difficulties of quantifying the risk involved. Thus, to ensure the availability of political risks cover, the governments of capital-exporting states have sponsored public sector or mixed public/private sector schemes. Such schemes have traditionally focused on developing host states and have been administered as part of the home state's foreign aid programme, although some schemes, such as the UK Export Credit Guarantee Department (ECGD), are directed at foreign trade and investment generally.[161] Therefore, such schemes may be more than merely an insurance service; they may be an instrument of the home state's foreign economic and development policy.

The first national scheme of this kind was introduced by the USA under the Economic Co-operation Act 1948.[162] Its aim was to offer investment guarantees for the reconstruction of post-war Europe. However, it was subsequently amended to cover investment in less developed countries.[163] Under the Foreign Assistance Act of 1961 the scheme was to be run as part of the US foreign aid programme by the Agency for International Development (AID).[164] After a major review of the AID scheme, a new investment guarantee agency was proposed. This was set up in 1969 under the name of the Overseas Private Investment Corporation (OPIC).[165] The operations of OPIC came under close scrutiny in the 1970s as a result of its close involvement with the insurance of US copper and telecommunications investments in Chile at the time of their nationalization by Salvador Allende's government.[166] This resulted in a restriction of OPIC's powers in 1974 followed by further restrictions in 1978.[167] In 1981 most of these restrictions were removed and the scheme was expanded to cover 'civil strife' and insurance of letters of credit.[168]

At present OPIC is empowered to offer investment insurance on a commercial basis backed by the full faith and credit of the US government.[169] Cover is provided only with the agreement of the host state. To this end the USA negotiates investment guarantee agreements with host states.[170] These agreements ensure that the rights of OPIC (or its successors in title or assigns) to subrogation upon payment of a claim are recognized by the host state. They also provide for international arbitration in the case of disputes that cannot be settled by negotiation. Insurance is available against expropriation, war risks, inconvertibility of currency and, as noted above, civil strife and letters of credit. Upon the occurrence of an insured event the investor will present a claim to OPIC, which will then consider whether it comes within the terms of the cover. Should a dispute arise, the investor and OPIC may resort to arbitration.[171] After a claim has been paid, OPIC will pursue its subrogation rights against the host state under the terms of the investment guarantee agreement.

Other countries have adopted similar investment insurance schemes. Thus, the UK offers insurance for overseas investments through the ECGD. By s. 2 of the Export and Investment Guarantees Act 1991,[172] any person carrying on business in the UK, whether in person or through a company controlled directly or indirectly by him or her, is eligible for cover in connection with any investment of resources in enterprises carried on outside the UK, or in connection with guarantees given by that person in respect of investments by other in such enterprises. Cover is given only for new direct investments in overseas enterprises against losses resulting directly or indirectly from war, expropriation, restrictions on remittances and other specific political risks that could have a vital bearing on the viability of an investment.[173] In the Netherlands, Dutch companies are offered political risks cover by NCM, a private agency owned by thirteen banks, ten insurance companies and other corporate shareholders. The Dutch Minister of Finance sits on the board and the government reinsures any political risks taken on for Dutch exporters.[174] In Germany, investment guarantees have been available since 1959,[175] while Japan introduced its scheme in 1956.[176]

A significant recent development has been the entry into force of the World Bank Convention Establishing the Multilateral Investment Guarantee Agency of 1985 (MIGA).[177] This Convention establishes the first multilateral system for investment insurance against stipulated political risks in the host state. In addition the Convention offers a technical advisory and standard setting service to developing countries aimed at improving investment conditions and flows of new investment. This will be considered briefly in chapter 16. The advantages of the MIGA system are claimed to include: a more comprehensive and complete system of cover which would have the benefit of aggregating investments from many countries and would enjoy access to a wider range of reinsurers and coinsurers than national systems; a depoliticized approach to underwriting decisions; consideration of the soundness of the investment and its developmental impact; and a broader role in the creation of a good international investment climate by the offering of additional specialist advisory services.[178] Together, these factors should encourage the flow of investments for productive purposes among member countries.[179]

Regarding the insurance of political risks, the basic scheme of the Convention system is as follows.[180] All member states of the World Bank are eligible to join MIGA on payment of a share subscription in accordance with the number of shares required under Schedule A to the Convention.[181] In return MIGA will offer investment guarantees against loss resulting from one or more of the following types of risk: restrictions on currency transfer outside the host country, expropriation and similar measures, breach of contract and war and civil disturbance.[182]

Regarding expropriation, cover extends to 'any legislative action or administrative action or omission attributable to the host government which has the effect of depriving the holder of a guarantee of his ownership or control of, or a substantial benefit from, his investment, with the exception of non-discriminatory measures of general application which governments normally take for the purpose of regulating economic activity in their territories.'[183] This definition makes clear that cover against 'creeping expropriation' is available. The MIGA Operational Regulations (the Regulations) state that coverage may encompass, but is not limited to, measures of expropriation, nationalization, confiscation, sequestration, seizure, attachment and freezing of assets.[184] Coverage also extends to cases of breach of contract as where, in the case of an equity investment, the right to a dividend or to control and to dispose of shares is interfered with. In the case of a non-equity investment, interference may take the form of claims against the project enterprise for agreed payments, rights to transfer such claims to third parties or rights of participation in management.[185] Cover is excluded where the host government is acting in the public interest for the purpose of regulating economic activity in its territory. The Regulations give, as examples of such activity, 'the *bona fide* imposition of general taxes, tariffs and price controls and other economic regulations as well as environmental and labour legislation and measures for the maintenance of public safety'.[186] However, even such measures may come within the coverage if they are applied in a discriminatory manner and are designed to have a confiscatory effect, such as causing the investor to abandon the investment or to sell at a distressed price.[187]

The contract of guarantee will specify the scope of coverage.[188] The Underwriting Authority (the relevant official of MIGA charged with concluding the guarantee contract) will elect to provide either total or partial loss cover. In a case of expropriation, total loss occurs where the guarantee holder has been unable to exercise a fundamental covered right for a consecutive period of one year, or such period as the contract of guarantee may provide, or the investment project has ceased operations for such a period.[189]

The inclusion of breach of contract as a covered risk protects the investor against abuses of due process. This may occur through denial of access to a judicial or arbitral forum to determine the validity of a claim of breach alleged by the host state, or through inordinate delay in the rendering of such a decision, or where such a decision cannot be enforced.[190] This is an innovative form of cover not normally found in national systems save in relation to breaches of contract associated with expropriations.[191] The coverage for currency transfer risk and for war and civil disturbance need not be commented upon here.[192] Other non-commercial risks not covered by the four categories above can be included by joint application of the investor and host country to the Board, which must approve by a special majority.[193] However, losses arising from acts or omissions of the host government to which the guarantee holder has consented or for which he or she is responsible, or losses arising from acts or omissions occurring before the conclusion of the contract of guarantee, are not covered.[194]

Investments eligible for cover include equity investments and non-equity direct investments.[195] All forms of equity investment are covered regardless of the legal form of the project or of the share held by the applicant for cover.[196] Examples of non-equity direct investments covered include: production sharing contracts, profit sharing contracts, management contracts, franchising agreements, licensing agreements, turnkey contracts, operating leasing agreements, subordinated debentures, other forms that may be recommended by the President and approved by the Board, the remuneration for which substantially depends on the performance of the investment project, and guarantees and loans made by the person making any of the foregoing forms of non-equity investment. In all cases the investment must have terms of at least three years' duration and depend substantially on the production, revenues or profits of the investment project for repayment. In particular, projects of long duration and high developmental potential will be included.[197] Both investments in monetary form and investments in kind will be covered.[198] However, in accordance with article 12(c) of the Convention an investment is eligible for cover only if it is a new investment.[199]

Investors eligible to benefit from MIGA may be either natural or juridical persons. To qualify, a natural person must be a national of a member country other than the host country. A juridical person must be incorporated and have its principal place of business in a member country, or the majority of its capital must be owned by a member or members or nationals thereof, provided that the member in question is not the host country. In addition, the juridical person must operate on a commercial basis, whether it is privately or publicly owned.[200] Eligibility for cover may be extended to a natural person who is a national of the host country, or to a juridical person incorporated in the host country or the majority of whose capital is owned by its nationals, where the assets invested are transferred from outside the host country and the Board, on a joint application from the investor and the host country, approves by a special majority.[201]

To be eligible for cover, the investment concerned must be made in the territory of a developing member country.[202] Such countries are listed in Schedule A to the Convention. No contract of guarantee shall be issued before the host government has approved the issuance of the guarantee by MIGA against the risks designated for cover. In this way the host state retains a measure of sovereign authority over the operation of MIGA cover in relation to investments made in its territory.

The payment of claims is made by the President of MIGA under the direction of the Board, in accordance with the contract of guarantee and the Board's general policies. The investor will have to seek appropriate administrative remedies under the laws of the host state before making a claim.[203] Payment of a claim will subrogate the Agency to the rights or claims of the investor against the host country and other obligors.[204] Any dispute between the Agency and the holder of a guarantee shall be submitted to arbitration in accordance with the terms of the contract of guarantee.[205] The Agency is empowered to enter into arrangements with private insurers and reinsurers to enhance its own operations and to encourage the provision of non-commercial risks coverage by such insurers.[206] This is useful as the Agency is restricted to no more than 150 per cent of its unimpaired capital and reserves in the liabilities that it may undertake.[207]

The advent of MIGA constitutes a further significant involvement of the World Bank in the creation of a multilateral system of investment protection and promotion. It should be seen alongside the World Bank's International Centre for the Settlement of Investment Disputes (ICSID), which will be considered in the next chapter, as part of an emerging international institutional order that is instrumental in moving the development of international regulation away from the UN-centred NIEO policies of the 1970s. In its first two years of operation MIGA issued direct guarantees involving investments in Indonesia and Chile and entered two reinsurance guarantees involving Chile and Hungary. In 1991 it had thirty applications from seventeen different countries under active consideration, out of a pool of some 300 applications received.[208] As of 11 March 1993 MIGA had 102 Member Countries.[209] Thus MIGA appears to have made an immediate impact. However, it is as yet too early to assess its work in the light of extensive experience.

5   *Concluding Remarks*

This chapter has considered the principal areas in which substantive international law has been invoked as a standard for the regulation of relations between foreign investors and host states. Although considerable doctrinal conflict exists over applicable norms, a matter to be considered further in chapter 16, there is an underlying sense of a generally understood and accepted process for dealing with renegotiation and expropriation issues, coupled with the evolution of pragmatic approaches to the problems involved as exemplified through the use of lump sum agreements and investment guarantee systems. None the less, a perspective favourable to the continuation of a global free-market economy underlies the phenomena described above. It forms the backdrop to the more recent institutional initiatives, of which one has already been considered in some detail. In the next chapter the focus of attention will move to the international procedures used for the settlement of investment disputes, giving an opportunity to examine another significant international institution in the field of foreign investment, namely ICSID.

Notes

1   See further Wolfgang Peter, *Arbitration and the Renegotiation of International Investment Agreements* (Kluwer, 2nd edn, 1995), chapters 1 and 2. Peter uses the term 'transnational investment agreement', which he defines as referring to 'legal relationships, whereby a state, generally a Third World country, or a state enterprise enter into an agreement with a foreign investor, usually a *transnational* company . . . , for the purpose of an investment project' (at p. 5, emphasis in the original).

2   See further Korbin, 'Expropriation as an attempt to control foreign firms in LDCs: trends from 1960–1979', 28 *International Studies Quarterly* 329 (1984); A. Akinsanya, *The Expropriation of Multinational Property in the Third World* (Praeger, 1980); P. T. Muchlinski, 'Law and the analysis of the international oil industry', in J. Rees and P. Odell (eds), *The*

International Oil Industry: An Interdisciplinary Perspective (Macmillan Press, 1987), p. 142.

3 See UNCTC, *The New Code Environment*, UNCTC Current Studies Series A No. 16 (UN, 1990), p. 18.

4 See *Serbian and Brazilian Loans Cases*, PCIJ Ser. A. Nos 20/21 (1929) at p. 41: 'any contract which is not a contract between states in their capacity as subjects of international law is based on the municipal law of some country'. See further D. P. O'Connell, *International Law*, 2nd edn (Stevens, 1970), at pp. 978–9.

5 On which see further F. A. Mann, 'The law governing state contracts', 21 BYIL 11 (1944), 'The proper law of contracts concluded by international persons', 35 BYIL 34 (1959). However, Dr Mann recanted on this position in his case-note on the House of Lords decision in *Amin Rasheed Shipping Corporation* v *Kuwait Insurance* Company [1983] 2 All ER 884 see: 33 ICLQ 193 at 196–197 (1984). See also Jennings, 'State contracts in international law', 37 BYIL 156 (1961); Brown, "Choice of law provisions in concession and related contracts', 39 MLR 6 (1976); Peter (note 1 above), chapter 3. For a critique of the 'internationalization' theory see Tang An, 'The law applicable to a transnational economic development contract', 21 JWTL 95 (1987); Sornarajah, 'The myth of international contract law' 15 JWTL 187 (1981); Bowett, 'State contracts with aliens: contemporary developments on compensation for termination or breach', 59 BYIL 49 at pp. 51–2 (1988); M. Sornarajah, *The International Law on Foreign Investment* (Grotius Publications, 1994), at pp. 338–55.

6 I. Brownlie, *Principles of Public International Law*, 5th edn (Oxford, 1998), p. 554; Sornarajah, *International Law . . .* , at pp. 325–38.

7 *Texaco* v *Libya* 17 ILM 1 (1978). For comment see: Bowett, 37 CLJ 5 (1978); Fatouros, 74 AJIL 134 (1980); Von Mehren and Kourides, 75 AJIL 476 (1981); White, 30 ICLQ 1 (1981); Greenwood, 53 BYIL 27 (1982).

8 General principles of law recognized by civilized nations have been included in numerous international investment agreements as the governing law. They form part of the sources of public international law as defined in article 38(c) of the Statute of the International Court of Justice. See further the following awards upon which Prof. Dupuy relied as indicating that a reference to general principles was sufficient to show that the agreement was internationalized: *The Lena Goldfields Arbitration, Cornell Law Quarterly*, 1950, p. 42; *Annual Digest*, 5 (1929–30), pp. 3, 426; *Sheikh of Abu Dhabi* v *Petroleum Development (Trucial Coast) Ltd* 1 ICLQ 247 (1952); 18 ILR 144 (1951); *Sapphire International Petroleum Ltd* v *National Iranian Oil Company* 35 ILR 136 (1963); *Aramco Case* 27 ILR 117 (1963). See further McNair, 'The general principles of law recognised by civilised nations', 33 BYIL 1 (1957).

9 By Clause 28 of the Deeds of Concession: 'This concession shall be governed by and interpreted in accordance with the principles of the law of Libya in common to the principles of international law and in the absence of such common principles then by and in accordance with

general principles of law, including such of those principles as may have been applied by international tribunals.'

10 Note 7 above, at para 45, ILM, pp. 16–17.

11 17 ILM 1321 (1978) or 56 ILR 258.

12 20 ILM 1 (1981) or 62 ILR 140. For comment see Greenwood (note 7 above).

13 Award, pp. 66–7 ILM, pp. 34–5.

14 21 ILM 976 (1982); 66 ILR 519. For comment see: Fernando Teson, 24 Va. J. Int'l L. 323 (1984); Mann, 54 BYIL 213 (1983); Redfern, 55 BYIL 65 (1984); Gann, 23 Col. J. Transnt'l L. 615 (1985).

15 Ibid., para. 6.

16 See also the ICSID award in *Klöckner v Cameroon* extracted in Paulsson, 'The ICSID Klöckner v Cameroon award: the duties of partners in North–South economic development agreements', 1 Jo. Int'l Arb. 145 at p. 157 (1984): 'We do not intend to apply new or exceptional legal principles to turn-key operations only because they concern projects affecting the economic and social development of a given country'. See further Pogany, 'Economic development agreements', 7 ICSID Rev-FILJ 1 (1992).

17 See Greenwood (note 7 above), at p. 53.

18 See further chapter 15 at pp. 549–51 on the choice of law in ICSID arbitrations, where such assimilation also appears to have been accepted.

19 On which see further P. Jessup, *Transnational Law* (New Haven, 1956); E. Langen, *Transnational Commercial Law* (Sijthoff, 1973); Lalive, 'Contracts between a state or a state agency and a foreign company', 13 ICLQ 987 (1964). For a critical view of this concept see Mann, 33 ICLQ 193 (1984); Delaume, 'The proper law of state contracts and the *lex mercatoria*: a reappraisal', 3 ICSID Rev-FILJ No. 1 (1988).

20 Ibid., para. 10.

21 It is noteworthy that a decision of an arbitrator to decide the case before him on the basis of 'internationally accepted principles of law governing contractual relations' was endorsed by the English Court of Appeal, which refused to hold that the resulting award was unenforceable as being uncertain or as contravening public policy: *Deutsche Schachtbau-und-Tiefbohrgesellschaft GmbH v R'As Al Khaimah National Oil Company* [1987] 2 All ER 769 (CA) reversed on other grounds: [1988] 2 All ER 833 (HL).

22 See *Texaco v Libya* (note 7 above), at paras 71–7.

23 See *Liamco v Libya* (note 12 above), at pp. 89–113 of the award at ILM, pp. 46–56 and award p. 120 at ILM, p. 61 for summary.

24 53 ILR 297 (1974).

25 Ibid., at p. 327.

26 At note 14 above.

27 Ibid., at para 90.

28 Ibid., at para 95, ILM, p. 1023.

29 Ibid., paras 97–8.

30 Ibid., paras 100–1, at ILM, p. 1024.

31 According to Professor Rosalyn Higgins QC, the Tribunal's award is, in this respect, based on unpersuasive and contradictory reasoning: see Higgins 'The taking of property by the state: recent developments in

international law', 176 Hague Recueil (1982 III) 259 at pp. 303–5. See
also the Separate Opinion of Sir Gerald Fitzmaurice in *Aminoil*, who felt
that the nationalization of Aminoil's undertaking was irreconcilable with
the stabilization clauses in the concession, although he agreed with the
operative part (dispositif) of the award and did not dissent: note 14 above
at ILM, pp. 1043–53.

32   See J. Kuusi, *The Host State and the Transnational Corporation* (Saxon
House, 1979), pp. 140–5.

33   See Muchlinski (note 2 above). For more recent analyses of regulatory
trends and contractual regimes in the international oil industry, see B.
Taverne, *An Introduction to the Regulation of the Petroleum Industry* (Graham
and Trotman, 1994); Z. Gao, *International Petroleum Contracts* (Graham
and Trotman, 1994).

34   See Asante, 'Stability of contractual relations in the transnational investment process', 28 ICLQ 401 (1979) and 'Restructuring transnational
mineral agreements', 73 AJIL 335 (1979); Brown 'The relationship between the state and the multinational corporation in the exploitation of
resources', 33 ICLQ 218 (1984) and 'Contract stability in international
petroleum operations', *The CTC Reporter* No. 29 (Spring 1990), p. 56;
Wälde, 'Revision of transnational investment agreements: contractual
flexibility in natural resources development', 10 Law. Am. 265 (1978) and
'Third World mineral investment policies in the late 1980s: from restriction back to business', 3 *Mineral Processing and Extractive Metallurgy Review* 121, esp. pp. 161–74 (1988); Peter (note 1 above), esp. chapter 2; M.
Sornarajah, 'Supremacy of the renegotiation clause in international contracts', 5 J. Int'l Arb. 97 (1988).

35   See references cited in previous note.

36   See M. Sornarajah, *International Commercial Arbitration: the Problem of State
Contracts* (Longman, 1990), pp. 248–62.

37   C. D. Wallace, *Legal Control of the Multinational Enterprise* (Martinus
Nijhoff, 1983), at p. 236. See generally pp. 236–47.

38   Ibid., at p. 243.

39   See further Vagts, 'Coercion and foreign investment rearrangements', 72
AJIL 17 (1978).

40   See further ibid.

41   Note 14 above.

42   Ibid., para. 40 at ILM, p. 1007.

43   Ibid., para. 43, ILM, p. 1007; para. 45, ILM, p. 1008. On the English law
of 'economic duress' see: *Pao On v Lau Yiu Long* [1980] AC 614 (PC);
North Ocean Shipping Co. Ltd v Hyundai Construction Co. Ltd [1979] QB
705. On US law see: Dawson, 'Economic duress – an essay in perspective',
45 Mich. L. Rev. 253 (1947).

44   Ibid., para. 44, ILM, p. 1008.

45   Ibid.

46   Ibid., para. 45, ILM, p. 1008.

47   See in this connection *North Ocean Shipping Co. Ltd v Hyundai Construction
Co. Ltd* (note 43 above), where consent to a variation of contract obtained

by economic duress was held to have affirmed the validity of the varied agreement.

48   See e.g. *Barton* v *Armstrong* [1975] 2 WLR 1050 (PC); *Bernstein* v *van Heyghen Frères SA* 163 F. 2d 246 (2d Cir 1947) cert. denied 332 US 772 (1948); *Bernstein* v *NV Nederlandsche-Amerikaansche Stoomvart Maatschappij* 173 F. 2d 71 (2d Cir. 1949); 210 F. 2d 375 (2d Cir. 1954); *Zwack* v *Kraus Bros & Co.* 237 F. 2d 255 (2d Cir. 1956). See also *American Bell International Inc.* v *Iran* 6 Iran-US CTR 74 (1984), which involved threats of 'serious personal consequences' for company representatives.

49   See e.g. the English case on 'duress of goods', *Maskell* v *Horner* [1915] 3 KB 106. See further Beatson, 'Duress as a vitiating factor in contract' [1974] CLJ 97.

50   See Domke 55 AJIL 585 at 588 (1961). See further Sornarajah (note 5 above), chapter 7.

51   See Wallace (note 37 above), chapter 12.

52   See *Southern Pacific Properties (Middle East) Limited* v *Arab Republic of Egypt Award on the Merits 20 May 1992*: 32 ILM 933 paras 160–73 at pp. 967–71 (1993).

53   See further Higgins (note 31 above) esp. at pp. 267–78 and 322–54.

54   See generally Christie, 'What constitutes a taking of property under international law', 38 BYIL 307 (1962).

55   Indeed, the European Court of Human Rights has accepted the distinction between a legitimate administrative interference with property rights and expropriation: *Case of Sporrong and Lonnroth* (European Court of Human Rights) Judgment of 23 September 1982, Series A, No. 52. But see Higgins (note 31 above), at pp. 343–7 and 367–8 for a strong critique of the Court's approach.

56   See *Sea-Land Services Inc.* v *Ports and Shipping Organisation of the Islamic Republic of Iran* 6 Iran–US CTR 149 (1984); *Starrett Housing Corp.* v *Iran* (Interlocutory Award) 4 Iran–US CTR 122 (1984); 23 ILM 1090 (1984); *Otis Elevator Co.* v *Iran and Bank Mellat* 14 Iran–US CTR 283 (1987). For analysis see: R. Khan, *The Iran–United States Claims Tribunal: Controversies, Cases and Contribution* (Martinus Nijhoff, 1990), pp. 171–202.

57   See Wallace (note 37 above), at pp. 268–76.

58   But see cases before the Iran–US Claims Tribunal, raising issues concerning the responsibility of the host state for the acts of Revolutionary Guards or Committees that interfered with property belonging to US nationals: *William Pereira Associates, Iran* v *Iran* 5 Iran–US CTR 198 (1984); *Sola Tiles Inc.* v *Iran* 14 Iran–US CTR 223 (1987). Where Revolutionary Guards acted as instrumentalities of the state in the absence of a confiscatory decree, Iran was held responsible for resulting losses of property belonging to foreign claimants.

59   See, for example, the background to the French nationalizations of 1981: Alison Doyle, 'The French nationalisations: Mitterand challenges the multinationals', in B. S. Fisher and J. Turner (eds), *Regulating the Multinational Enterprise: National and International Challenges* (1983), p.

67; L. Favoreu, *Nationalisations et Constitution* (Economica, 1982); Linotte, 'Les nationalisations de 1982' (1982) *Revue de Droit Publique* 435; Juillard, 'Les nationalisations Françaises' (1982) AFDI 767.

60   See further chapter 15 at p. 535.

61   This view appears has been reinforced by the refusal of the European Court of Human Rights to examine cases involving a taking by a state of the property of its own nationals by reference to international law under the European Convention on Human Rights. See *The Case of Lithgow and Others* ECtHR Judgment of 8 July 1986 paras. 111–119. Confirmed by the European Commission on Human Rights in the *Case of Scotts' of Greenock (Est'd 1711) Ltd and Lithgows Limited* (Strasbourg, 1989) Commission Report of 17 December 1987 at para. 81.

62   Among the extensive literature on this subject the following are recommended as valuable overviews containing extensive further references: I. Brownlie (note 6 above), chapter 24; D. J. Harris, *Cases and Materials on International Law*, 5th edn (Sweet & Maxwell, 1998), at pp. 548–85; Higgins (note 31 above); American Law Institute, *Third Restatement on the Foreign Relations Law of the US* (St Paul, 1987), s. 712, at pp. 196–216.

63   See generally C. Lipson, *Standing Guard: Protecting Foreign Capital in the Nineteenth and Twentieth Centuries* (University of California Press, 1985), part I.

64   This term is attributed to the US Secretary of State Cordell Hull, who used words to this effect in a note to Mexican government of 21 July 1938 concerning the latter's expropriation of US agrarian interests in 1938. See 32 AJIL Supplement pp. 181–207 (1938) or 3 *Hackworth Digest of International Law* 655–61 (1942). For background see Kunz, 'The Mexican expropriations', 17 NYULQR 327 (1940).

65   See further Lipson (note 63 above); Dolzer 'New foundations of the law of expropriation of alien property', 75 AJIL 553 (1981); Schachter, 'Compensation for expropriation', 78 AJIL 121 (1984); Jimenez de Arechaga, 'State responsibility for the nationalisation of foreign owned property', 11 NYUJ Int'l L. & Pol. 179 (1978); A. Akinsanya, 'Host government's responses to foreign economic control: the experiences of selected African countries', 30 ICLQ 769 (1981), and *The Expropriation of Multinational Property in the Third World* (Praeger, 1980); Sornarajah, 'Compensation for expropriation: the emergence of new standards', 13 JWTL 108 (1979); Sornarajah (note 5 above), chapter 9.

66   According to the Charter of Economic Rights and Duties of States (UNGA Resolution 3281 (XXIX) 12 December 1974) 14 ILM 251 (1975), article 2 (2)(c): 'Each State has the right . . . to nationalize, expropriate or transfer ownership of foreign property in which case appropriate compensation should be paid by the State adopting such measures, taking into account its relevant laws and regulations and all the circumstances that the State considers pertinent. In any case where the question of compensation gives rise to a controversy, it shall be settled under the domestic law of the nationalising State and by its tribunals, unless it is freely and mutually agreed by all States concerned that other peaceful means be sought on the basis of the sovereign equality of States and in

accordance with the principle of free choice of means'. See also UNGA Resolution 3171 (XXVIII) GAOR 28th Sess. Supp. 30 p. 52 (1973), 68 AJIL 381 (1974); Declaration on the Establishment of a New International Economic Order, para. (4)(e), UNGA Resolution 3201 (S-VI) 13 ILM 715 (1974).

67 See further chapter 17.

68 See further M. Sornarajah, *The Pursuit of Nationalized Property* (Martinus Nijhoff, 1986). On US law see: Foreign Sovereign Immunity Act 1976, s. 1605(3); *Kalamazoo Spice Extraction Co. v The Provisional Military Government of Socialist Ethiopia* 24 ILM 1277 (1985); *First National City Bank v Banco Para El Commercia Exterior de Cuba* 462 US 611 (1983); 22 ILM 840 (1983); US Third Restatement (note 62 above), para. 444, comment d at p. 385 and para. 455(3) and comment c at pp. 412–13; *Banco Nacional de Cuba v Sabbatino* 376 US 398 (1964); *Banco Nacional de Cuba v Farr* 383 F. 2d 166 (2d Cir. 1967) cert. den. 390 US 956 (1968); *First National City Bank v Banco Nacional de Cuba* 406 US 759 (1972); *Banco Nacional de Cuba v Chase Manhattan Bank* 658 F. 2d 875 (2d Cir. 1981). On English law see: *Williams and Humbert Ltd v W and H Trade Marks (Jersey) Ltd* [1986] AC 368; [1985] 2 All ER 208 (Nourse J); [1985] 2 All ER 619 (CA); [1986] 1 ALL ER 129 (HL); *Settebello Ltd v Banco Totta e Acores* [1985] 2 All ER 1025; [1985] 1 WLR 1050 (CA); *Luther v Sagor* [1921] 3 KB 532; *Anglo-Iranian Oil Co. v Jaffrate: The Rose Mary* [1953] 1 WLR 246; P. M. North and J. J. Fawcett, *Cheshire and North's Private International Law*, 12th edn (Butterworths, 1992), at pp. 122–8.

69 In the *Aminoil* award (note 14 above), the law of Kuwait was characterized as consistent with the international standard. See also *Letco v Liberia* (ICSID Tribunal) 26 ILM 657 (1987), where the law of Liberia was found to be in conformity with international law. However, this is not to say that national laws reflect a general acceptance of the principle that full compensation is always payable for a taking of property: see further Amerasinghe, 'Issues of compensation for the taking of alien property in the light of recent cases and practice', 41 ICLQ 22 at pp. 25–7 and 30–1 (1992).

70 See further Norton, 'A law of the future or a law of the past? Modern tribunals and the international law of expropriation', 85 AJIL 474 (1991); Amerasinghe, ibid. Note that Amerasinghe sees the international minimum standard as being subject to exceptions in which less than full compensation may be payable for an expropriatory measure, and views the case-law of international tribunals as contributing to this development of the law.

71 This argument is elaborated in chapter 17.

72 Cited at notes 7, 12 and 24 above.

73 See Norton (note 70 above), at p. 486; Khan (note 56 above), at p. 251.

74 See *Amoco International Finance Corporation v Iran* 15 Iran–US CTR 189 (1987) at para. 145.

75 Harvard Research Draft Convention on the International Responsibility of States for Injuries to Aliens, article 10(1)(a): 55 AJIL 548 (1961).

76 See *Oppenheimer v Cattermole* [1976] AC 249 (HL).

77 For example, the existence of a state of war between the home and host state of the foreign investor.

78 See *BP* v *Libya* 53 ILR 297 (1974).

79 As stated above the principles discussed in the following paragraphs may equally apply to discrimination in cases of renegotiation.

80 This may be so where the foreign investor is the only enterprise engaged in a particular line of business or industry, and there is no domestic or foreign competitor.

81 See *BP* v *Libya* (note 78 above). In that case the sole arbitrator held that the taking of BP's property by Libya had been discriminatory. It had been motivated by the Libyan government's opposition to the British government's refusal to oppose Iran's occupation of the Tunb Islands in the Persian Gulf on 29 and 30 November 1972. Libya had argued that Britain was obliged to protect the islands under treaties of protection between Britain and the Trucial States (now the United Arab Emirates), which were due to end on 30 November.

82 See *The Oscar Chinn Case* PCIJ Series A/B No. 63 (1934). In this case the Belgian government, in response to the prevailing economic recession, had reduced the tariffs to be charged by a river transportation company, operating under its control in the Congo Basin, in return for a promise of compensation. This had the result that other transportation companies could no longer compete on price with the state controlled company. The United Kingdom government brought a claim alleging that Belgium had infringed the Treaty of St-Germain, 1919, which obliged Belgium *inter alia* to maintain commercial freedom and equality, and freedom of river navigation, in the Congo Basin. The PCIJ rejected the UK contention on the ground *inter alia* that the discrimination covered by the treaty related to Belgian and non-Belgian companies, and did not extend to companies under the control of the Belgian government. This case has been criticized as having failed to deal with the necessity of the measures adopted. See W. McKean, *Equality and Discrimination under International Law* (Clarendon Press, 1983), pp. 194–5; but see, for the view that the PCIJ was not insensitive to the implications of greater state involvement in economic regulation, H. Lauterpacht, *The Development of International Law by the International Court* (Stevens, 1958), at pp. 262–5.

83 See *Amoco International Finance Corp.* v *Iran* 15 Iran–US CTR 189 (1987), at paras 139–142. The Tribunal held that the expropriation of Amoco's interests in petrochemical joint ventures with the Iranian company NPC was not discriminatory merely because the Japanese share of a similar consortium had not been expropriated: '142. The Tribunal finds it difficult, in the absence of any other evidence, to draw the conclusion that the expropriation of a concern was discriminatory only from the fact that another concern in the same economic branch was not expropriated. Reasons specific to the non-expropriated enterprise, or to the expropriated one, or to both, may justify such a difference of treatment. Furthermore, as observed by the arbitral tribunal in Kuwait v American Independent Oil Company (AMINOIL) . . . a coherent policy of nationalization can reasonably be operated gradually in successive stages.' See *Kuwait* v *Aminoil*

(note 14 above), at paras 84–7. Differences in treatment between Aminoil and the other remaining American concessionaire, which was not national-ized, were held to be explicable on the ground that the other conces-sionaire worked on offshore operations jointly run by Kuwait and Saudi Arabia, and it possessed expertise needed by Kuwait.

84   See the cases referred to in the previous note.

85   According to McKean (note 82 above), at p. 197: 'It is . . . generally accepted that nationalization measures are invalid under international law if they make distinctions between nationals and aliens to the detriment of the latter.'

86   See further chapter 17 at pp. 626–7.

87   See Third Restatement on the Foreign Relations Law of the US (note 62 above), para. 712, comment f, at p. 200.

88   See E. Lauterpacht, 'Issues of compensation and nationality in the taking of energy investments', 8 *Journal of Energy and Natural Resources Law* 241 at 249–50 (1990).

89   See further R. Lillich (ed.), *The Valuation of Nationalized Property in International Law*, 4 vols (Virginia, 1972, 1973, 1975, 1987).

90   Note 88 above at p. 249.

91   Penrose, Joffe and Stevens, 'Nationalisation of foreign-owned property for a public purpose: an economic perspective on appropriate compensation', 55 MLR 351 at 359 (1992). The following paragraphs rely heavily on the valuable economic analysis developed by Penrose et al.

92   Ibid., at p. 357.

93   Ibid., at pp. 361–4.

94   Such an approach was initially used by the Chilean government in relation to the expropriation of US copper companies in 1971: see 10 ILM 1067 (1971). See further R. B. Lillich, 'The valuation of copper companies in the Chilean nationalization', 66 ASIL Proc. 213 (1972); for a critical analysis see Orego-Vicuna, 'Some international law problems posed by the nationalization of the copper industry in Chile' 67 AJIL 711 (1973); for argument in support see Sornarajah, 13 JWTL 108 (1979) (note 65 above), at pp. 123–6. However, compensation was eventually set in ac-cordance with the net book value approach: see 13 ILM 1190 (1974), 14 ILM 131 (1975).

95   See e.g. *Kuwait* v *Aminoil* (note 14 above), at paras 155–7, where the Tribunal rejected Kuwait's claim that the consistent use of the net book method by OPEC countries in their nationalizations of oil concessions in the years 1971–7 had created a legal precedent requiring its use. See also *Amoco International Finance Corp.* v *Iran* (note 74 above), where Iran's valuation based on the net book method was also rejected. However, the net book value of the expropriated business was awarded by the US Court of Appeals for the Second Circuit in *Banco Nacional de Cuba* v *Chase Manhattan Bank* 658 F. 2d 875 (2nd Cir. 1981) and see comment thereon in Amerasinghe (note 69 above), at pp. 46–7. Net book value compen-sation was also awarded in the Chilean nationalization case mentioned in note 94 above.

96   Note 14 above at paras 137–78.

97   Ibid., para. 145.

98   Ibid., para. 146.

99   Ibid., para. 146.

100   Ibid., para. 148.

101   Ibid., para. 149.

102   Ibid., para. 159.

103   Ibid., para. 160.

104   Ibid., para. 163.

105   For a fuller analysis than is possible here see: Khan (note 56 above), chapter 10; Westberg, 'Compensation in cases of expropriation and nationalization: awards of the Iran–United States Claims Tribunal', 5 ICSID Rev-FILJ 256 (1990); Norton (note 70 above), at pp. 482–6; Amerasinghe (note 69 above), at pp. 41–6 and 53–9.

106   10 Iran–US CTR 121 (1986 I); 25 ILM 619 (1986).

107   Article IV(2) of the US–Iran Treaty of Amity, Economic Relations and Consular Rights, August 15, 1955, 284 UNTS 93.

108   15 Iran–US CTR 189 (1987 II); 27 ILM 1314 (1988). See also *American International Group* v *Iran* 4 Iran–US CTR 96 (1983).

109   Ibid., para. 264 (emphasis in original).

110   Ibid., para. 203 (emphasis in original).

111   This led to a concurring opinion that disagreed with the Tribunal's reasons by the US member Judge Brower, who felt that loss of future profits was wrongly excluded from the available compensation: ibid., p. 290, at pp. 300–5.

112   See, for example, *Phelps Dodge* (note 106 above). See also *Sola Tiles* v *Iran* 14 Iran–US CTR 223 (1987); *Thomas Earle Payne* v *Iran* 12 Iran–US CTR 3 (1986); *CBS Inc.* v *Iran* Award No. 486–197–2 28 June 1990 (held: the effects of the revolution upon the business caused it to have a negative worth at the time of expropriation and therefore no compensation was payable).

113   See, for example, *Sedco Inc.* v *National Iranian Oil Co. and Iran* 10 Iran–US CTR 180 (1986); 25 ILM 629 (1986).

114   See further chapter 15.

115   The Washington Convention on the Settlement of Investment Disputes 1965: 4 ILM 524 (1965).

116   *Benvenuti and Bonfant* v *People's Republic of the Congo* 21 ILM 740 at paras 4.1–4.4 (1982); *Amco Asia Corp.* v *Republic of Indonesia* ruling of first arbitration panel: 24 ILM 1022 at para. 148. (1985); vacated on grounds of improper application of Indonesian law: 25 ILM 1441 (1986); ruling of second arbitration panel: 89 ILR 580, para. 40 at p. 594 (1992). A further award of an *ad hoc* Committee concerning the annulment of the second award was made on 17 December 1992, but is as yet unpublished: *News from ICSID* (Vol. 10, No. 1, Winter 1993), p. 2.

117   *AGIP Company* v *Popular Republic of Congo* 21 ILM 726 at para. 18 (1982).

118   *Southern Pacific Properties (Middle East) Limited* v *Arab Republic of Egypt* Award on the Merits 20 May 1992: 32 ILM 933 para. 84, at p. 952 (1993).

119   See Amerasinghe (note 69 above), at p. 38.

120 See *AGIP* (note 117 above), at paras 95–109 (applying article 1149 of the French Civil Code incorporated into Congolese Law); *Amco Asia* (note 116 above), at paras 266–8 (referring to Indonesian Civil Code Art 1246, French and English law and international law); in *Benvenuti and Bonfant* there was no extensive discussion of the applicable rules but a detailed analysis was made both of the loss of assets and of the alleged loss of future profits put forward by the claimant, on which see text for discussion.

121 First award (note 116 above), at paras 271–3.

122 Second Tribunal award (note 116 above), at paras 188–200, ILR pp. 633–6.

123 Note 118 above.

124 Ibid., paras 188–91 at pp. 973–4.

125 Ibid., paras 192–7 at p. 974.

126 Ibid., para. 198 at p. 975. For the detailed application of this approach to the facts see ibid., paras 199–211, pp. 975–7.

127 Ibid., paras 212–18 at pp. 978–9. This was based on a calculation of the balance between the claimant's share of the revenues from existing sales of properties completed as part of the project as against expenses incurred.

128 Ibid., paras. 219–44 at pp. 979–83.

129 Note 116 above, paras 4.73–4.79.

130 Ibid., paras 4.4 and 4.63–4.65.

131 See Amerasinghe (note 69 above), at pp. 59–61, 63.

132 Some weight for this view can be gathered from the Separate Opinion of Judge Brower in the *Sedco* case, regarding the remedies that should be available in the case of lawful and unlawful expropriation: note 113 above, ILM, p. 636 at pp. 641–7.

133 Note that in *INA Corp.* v *Iran* 8 Iran–US CTR 373 (1985) Judge Lagergren, the Chairman, said that 'an application of current principles of international law, as encapsulated in the 'appropriate compensation' formula, would in the case of lawful large-scale nationalizations in a state undergoing a process of radical economic restructuring normally require the 'fair market value' standard to be discounted in taking account of 'all circumstances'. However, such discounting, may, of course, never be such as to bring compensation below a point which would lead to 'unjust enrichment' of the expropriating state. It might also be added that the discounting often will be greater in a situation where the investor has enjoyed the profits of his capital outlay over a long period of time, but less, or none, in the case of a recent investor, such as INA' (at p. 390). See *contra* Judge Holtzman, at p. 401.

134 On this see further Bowett (note 5 above), at pp. 59–74.

135 Ibid., paras 191–7. Note that the Second Tribunal in *Amco Asia* v *Indonesia* (note 116 above) held that, where there was an unlawful taking of contract rights, lost profits were in principle recoverable, but it reserved its position on the situation in a lawful taking, the taking in this case being found to have been unlawful: para. 178, ILR, p. 631.

136 Note 7 above at paras 92–112.

137 Note 12 above.

138 Note 24 above at p. 347.

139   *Liamco* (note 12 above), at ILM pp. 63–4.

140   *BP* (note 24 above), at pp. 351, 353.

141   See Bowett (note 5 above), at p. 60; Higgins (note 31 above), at pp. 314–21 who sees restitution as promoting values important to the international community but finds 'very little evidence that restitution is perceived as a required remedy or that it is anticipated as being likely to be granted'.

142   For details see Von Mehren and Kourides (note 7 above), at pp. 545–8.

143   See UNGA Resolution 1803, 14 December 1962, 17 UN GAOR Supp (No. 17) at 15, where the term 'appropriate compensation' is first used.

144   See *Liamco v Libya* (note 12 above), at ILM, pp. 76–7.

145   Indeed, even the US Third Restatement (note 62 above) has conceded the need to move away from this issue by adopting the term 'just compensation' in s. 712, and by acknowledging that, while the USA has consistently used the Hull Formula, other states have resisted it: comment c at p. 198 and reporter's note 2 at p. 206. As to the effect of this terminological change see the debate between Robinson, 'Expropriation in the restatement revised', 78 AJIL 176 (1984) and Schachter, 'Compensation for expropriation', ibid., 121.

146   See e.g. Gann, 'Compensation standard for expropriation', 23 Col. J. Transnat. L. 615 (1985), who argues that the 'going concern' value incorporates an element for loss of future profits. Gann argues that in *Aminoil* an element for lost future profits was included in the going concern valuation, and, possibly, in an unusually high interest and inflation figure: see pp. 638–9. Amerasinghe also feels that the compensation awarded included an element for lost profits: note 69 above at pp. 62–3. However, F. A. Mann feels that the failure to award full loss of profits as expected at date of concession amounted to a failure to compensate adequately for what was, in his opinion, an unlawful taking: 'The Aminoil arbitration', 54 BYIL 213 (1983).

147   'Windfall from imperial Russia', *Financial Times*, 16 July 1986, p. 1.

148   13 ILM, pp. 407–12 (1973).

149   14 ILM, pp. 131–7 (1975).

150   See: G. Schwarzenberger, *Foreign Investment in International Law* (Stevens, 1969), pp. 40–7; Lillich and Burns (eds), *International Claims: Their Settlement by Lump Sum Agreement*, 3 vols (1975–6); Dawson and Weston, 'Prompt adequate and effective: a universal standard of compensation?', 30 Fordham L. Rev. 727 at pp. 740–57 (1962).

151   For the main facts see the judgment of the US District Court for the Western District of Michigan (Southern Division) in *Kalamazoo Spice Extraction Co. v The Provisional Military Government of Socialist Ethiopia*, reproduced in 24 ILM 1277 (1985).

152   Ibid.

153   25 ILM 56 (1986).

154   Ibid., article III(1).

155   Ibid., article III(2)(a) and (b).

156   Ibid., article IV.

157   Ibid., article V(1).

158 Ibid., at pp. 61–2.
159 See e.g. *Sedco* v *National Iranian Oil Co.* (note 113 above), at p. 8, ILM, p. 633; *Aminoil* (note 14 above), at paras 156–7; *Barcelona Traction Case* ICJ Reports (1970) p. 3 at p. 40.
160 See Bowett (note 5 above), at pp. 65–6; Lillich and Weston, 'Lump-sum agreements: their continuing contribution to the law of international claims', 82 AJIL 69 (1988).
161 See UK Export and Investment Guarantees Act 1991, ss 1 and 2 (1991), chapter 67.
162 62 Stat. 144 (1948).
163 Mutual Security Act of 1954 s. 413, 68 Stat. 846 (1954) as amended 22 USC s. 1933 (Supp. III, 1962).
164 75 Stat. 424 (1961).
165 Foreign Assistance Act of 1969, 22 USC s. 2191 (1970). For background see: US International Private Investment Advisory Council, *The Case for a US Overseas Private Enterprise Development Corporation* (1968). See further, on the history of US investment guarantee policy: C. Lipson (note 63 above), chapter 7; Brewer, 'The proposal for investment guarantees by an international agency', 58 AJIL 62 at pp. 67–70 (1964); Clubb and Vance, 'Incentives to private US investment abroad under the Foreign Assistance Program', 72 Yale LJ 475 (1963).
166 See Lipson (note 63 above), at pp. 245–8.
167 See OPIC Amendments Act 1974 (PL 93-390); OPIC Amendments Act 1978 (PL 95-268), comment Meron, 'OPIC investment is alive and well', 73 AJIL 104 (1979).
168 OPIC Amendment Act 1981: 95 Stat. 1021 (1981); Smapliner, 'The 1981 OPIC amendments and Reagan's 'Newer Directions' in Third World development policy', 14 Law & Pol. Int'l Bus. 181 (1982); Zylberglait, 'OPIC'S investment insurance: the platypus of governmental programs and its jurisprudence', 25 Law & Pol. Int'l Bus. 359 (1993).
169 See: 22 USC ss 2191–2200a.
170 See e.g. US–Equador Investment Guaranty Agreement, 28 November 1984: 24 ILM 566 (1985); US–Poland Investment Guarantee Agreement: 28 ILM 1393 (1989).
171 22 USC s. 2197(i). See e.g. the arbitration in *ITT, Sud America* v *OPIC* 13 ILM 1307 (1974).
172 Note 161 above.
173 See C. M. Schmitthoff, *Export Trade*, 9th edn (Stevens, 1990), at p. 483; ECGD, *Overseas Investment Insurance: a Brief Guide* (H130 O11 UDI January 1993).
174 *The Guardian*, 11 January 1991, p. 26. NCM recently took over the short-term export credit insurance functions of the ECGD in the UK. This was achieved by the sale of the Insurance Services Group, a part of the ECGD, to NCM under the terms of the Export and Investment Guarantees Act 1991. See also Export and Investment Guarantees Act (Commencement Order): SI 1991/2430.
175 See Budget Law of 1959, article 18 (1959).
176 Export Insurance Law 1950 as amended in April 1956 and May 1957.

177   See 24 ILM 1598 (1985). For the historical background to and analysis of
the Convention see further: I. F. I. Shihata, *MIGA and Foreign Investment:
Origins, Operations, Policies and Basic Documents of the Multilateral Investment Guarantee Agency* (Martinus Nijhoff, 1988); Voss, 'The Multilateral
Investment Guarantee Agency: status, mandate, concept, features, implications', 21 JWTL 5 (1987); Rowat, 'Multilateral approaches to improving the investment climate of developing countries: the cases of ICSID and
MIGA', 33 Harv. ILJ. 103, esp. pp. 119–34 (1992). This article contains
a useful tabular comparison of the MIGA Convention system with the US,
Japanese and German systems at pp. 139–44. The MIGA Convention has
been incorporated into English law by the Multilateral Investment
Guarantee Agency Act 1988 (c 8, 1988) Commencement Order: SI 1988/
715.

178   See Shihata, ibid., at pp. 17–21.

179   MIGA Convention (note 177 above), article 2.

180   For a full discussion see Shihata (note 177 above), chapters 3 and 4. See
also MIGA Operational Regulations of 22 June 1988: 27 ILM 1227
(1988) (cited hereafter as MIGA Regs).

181   MIGA Convention (note 177 above), articles 4–10.

182   Ibid., article 11(a)(i)–(iv).

183   Ibid., article 11(a)(ii).

184   MIGA Regs, para. 1.29.

185   Ibid., para. 1.30.

186   Ibid., para. 1.36. Emphasis in original.

187   Ibid.

188   The contract will follow the standard form agreement drawn up by MIGA:
MIGA Standard Contract of Guarantee and General Conditions of
Guarantee for Equity Investments of 25 January 1989: 28 ILM 1233
(1989).

189   See, for the full analysis of scope of coverage: MIGA Regs, paras 1.39–
1.41. See also MIGA Standard Contract of Guarantee, ibid., article 8, at
ILM, pp. 1249–52.

190   MIGA Convention (note 177 above), article 11(a)(iii).

191   Shihata (note 177 above), at p. 131.

192   See ibid., at pp. 123–4, 134–8, MIGA Regs, paras 1.23–1.28; 1.46–1.52.

193   MIGA Convention (note 177 above), article 11(b).

194   Ibid., article 11(c).

195   Ibid., article 12(a).

196   MIGA Regs, at para. 1.04.

197   MIGA Regs, paras 1.05–1.06.

198   Ibid., paras 1.09–1.10.

199   Ibid., para. 1.11.

200   MIGA Convention (note 177 above), article 13(a).

201   Ibid., article 13(c).

202   Ibid., article 14.

203   Ibid., article 17.

204   Ibid., article 18.

205   Ibid., article 58.

206   Ibid., article 21.
207   Ibid., article 22.
208   MIGA *Annual Report* 1991, at 4, cited in Rowat (note 177 above), at pp. 132–4.
209   See List of Member Countries, 11 March 1993, available from MIGA. This includes 17 industrialized countries and 85 developing countries. Two industrialized and 29 developing countries are in the process of fulfilling membership requirements.

15

The Settlement of International Investment Disputes

The present chapter concentrates on the problems associated with international dispute settlement as a method of resolving the kinds of differences between MNEs and host states that were analysed in chapter 14. This chapter is primarily concerned with the system for the settlement of international investment disputes set up by the World Bank under the Washington Convention on the Settlement of Investment Disputes between States and Nationals of Other States 1965 (the Washington Convention), which established the International Centre for the Settlement of Investment Disputes (ICSID).[1] However, this system of dispute settlement cannot be fully appreciated without a preliminary introduction to the weaknesses of traditional methods of international dispute settlement when applied to MNE–host state relations. Accordingly, the chapter begins with a brief overview of those weaknesses.

1 The Limitations of Traditional International Dispute Settlement Mechanisms in MNE–Host State Relations

Under the classical theory of public international law only states have the capacity to bring international claims as they are the only subjects of that law.[2] A private person, natural or legal, lacks the legal personality at international law to pursue a claim in its own right.[3] Consequently, MNEs are not regarded as subjects of international law. 'In principle, corporations of municipal law do not have international legal personality.'[4]

However, leading jurists in the field of international law have argued for the treatment of corporations as subjects of international law to the extent that they enter into agreements with foreign governments.[5] There is some authority in international arbitral jurisprudence for the view that an investment agreement between a state and a foreign corporation is an international contract subject to international law.[6] This has been read as acknowledging at least a qualified international legal personality for the foreign corporation. However, all that can be said with certainty is that the parties to a state contract retain the right to choose the governing law of the contract.[7] This is insufficient to show that the corporate party acts like a full subject of international law.

Given the absence of international personality for the MNE, the only means open, under international law, for the bringing of a claim against the respondent state is through the intervention of the state entitled to exercise diplomatic protection on behalf of the MNE. This is the state of which the MNE is a national.[8] However, the possibility of diplomatic protection by the national state of the MNE is a remedy so replete with pitfalls that it is unlikely to be of much practical value as a means of settling an investment dispute with the host state. These difficulties stem from the discretionary nature of the remedy and from several restrictions as to its availability which are exacerbated in the case of a MNE claimant.

If the state takes up the claim of its subject, according to the case-law of the Permanent Court of International Justice, the claim becomes in effect the claim of the state.[9] This may be regarded as a legal fiction, given that the primary right giving rise to the claim is a right of the individual protected by international law.[10] However, behind this legal fiction lies the fact that international law endows the national state with a discretion.[11] That state has no obligation to pursue the claim or to vindicate the rights of its subject. At all times the claim will be subject to considerations of interstate relations and may be subordinated, in certain cases, to other, more important, political goals pursued by the protecting state.[12] Furthermore, the protecting state need not even pay over to the claimant any reparations received from the respondent state, although there may be a strong moral duty to do so.[13] Consequently, there is no guarantee that, once started, an international claim brought by the protecting power of the individual will act as an effective remedy for the claimant.

Secondly, before any right to diplomatic protection can arise, the claimant must exhaust all effective local remedies within the national legal system of the respondent state. Only where such remedies are ineffective will the claimant be excused from this requirement.[14] This rule emphasizes the contingent nature of diplomatic protection, and the supplementary role that international law in fact plays in the regulation of disputes between individuals, including foreign corporations, and host states.

A further difficulty associated with reliance on diplomatic protection concerns the establishment of a link of nationality between the claimant and the protecting power. In the absence of such a link the protecting power has no right in international law to intervene on behalf of the claimant. This causes particular difficulties where the claimant is a MNE, given that it will be linked to more than one country by reason of the international character of its operations and given the differing nationalities of the parent company and its overseas subsidiaries. These difficulties have been increased by the decision of the International Court of Justice (ICJ) in the *Barcelona Traction* case.[15] The ICJ held that, for the purposes of diplomatic protection, the nationality of a company should be established by reference to its place of incorporation and its principal seat of management, and not by reference to the nationality of the controlling shareholders through a lifting of the corporate veil. Thus, the Court was unwilling to accept that the corporate veil should be lifted between a local subsidiary and its foreign parent. Only where the local subsidiary had ceased to exist as a legal entity could this course of action be permitted. The result is that where a MNE takes the very common course of organizing its investment in the host state as a locally incorporated company, possessing the nationality of the host state, there is no guarantee of diplomatic protection.

The effect of the *Barcelona Traction* case is, therefore, to deny the existence of any general rule of international law or of equity which confers a right of diplomatic protection on the national state of shareholders in a foreign company where that company is injured by the acts of a third state. The protection of shareholders demands recourse to treaty stipulations or to special agreements directly concluded between the foreign investor and the state in which the investment is placed.[16]

Arguably, the very idea of extending diplomatic protection to the MNE might be inappropriate, given that its interests may not be precisely identifiable with any particular state.[17] Furthermore, it amounts to a rather limited and anachronistic method for the resolution of investment disputes. Invoking the protection of the national (i.e. the home) state of the MNE in its dealings with the host state is reminiscent of 'gunboat diplomacy'. Moreover, it may make little business sense, particularly where the corporation and the host state intend to continue their economic relationship with one another, but have encountered difficulties requiring the use of some means of dispute settlement. In the overwhelming majority of cases a method other than diplomatic protection will be used to settle investment disputes. These will involve the MNE and host state directly without the intervention of the home state. The most important alternatives are negotiation and, should negotiation fail, conciliation and/or arbitration. To these we now turn.

2   Alternatives to Diplomatic Protection: International Dispute Settlement Mechanisms Involving the MNE and Host State Inter Se

The present section deals with disputes between the MNE and the host state *inter se*. Such disputes will normally arise under the terms of an international investment agreement, as described in chapter 14.[18] Disputes between the MNE and a private entity within the host state – for example, a partner under a management cooperation agreement or a licensee under a technology transfer contract – will not normally be subject to international methods of dispute settlement. In such a case the MNE must usually rely on the law of the host state for the protection of its rights.

As regards investment disputes between the MNE and the host state, from the corporation's perspective the major problem is to find a means of dispute settlement which will act as a reliable method for protecting the corporation's commercial interests. This may require the avoidance of subjection to the host state's legal system, should that system be perceived as an inadequate means of protection. In such cases the corporation may prefer the use of a 'delocalized' dispute settlement mechanism that has limited connections with the host state's legal system. A system based on international law may be preferred, given that system's traditional support for the protection of foreign investors' rights in their relations with host states.[19]

From the host state's perspective, the major problem is to retain control over the dispute. Ideally, this would entail the complete exclusion of international methods of dispute settlement and the restriction of the foreign investor to local remedies alone.[20] However, the desire for foreign direct investment may prompt the host state to accept international methods of dispute settlement as a means of displaying concern for the rights of the foreign investor, thereby helping to create a 'good investment climate'. Consequently, in practice many host states have accepted international methods for the settlement of disputes with foreign investors within their jurisdiction.

Assuming that the host state and the MNE agree to the use of international methods of dispute settlement, the following choices are open. At the most basic level lies negotiation. Indeed, many dispute settlement clauses in investment agreements specify this as the first step in the settlement process. Beyond negotiation lie methods of dispute settlement involving third party intervention, in the form of conciliation[21] or arbitration.[22] Conciliation and/or arbitration procedures may be instituted on an *ad hoc* basis by the agreement of the parties themselves. Alternatively, they may choose to avail themselves of one of the institutional systems of conciliation and/or arbitration. Furthermore, the United Nations Commission on International Trade Law (UNCITRAL) has sought to improve *ad hoc* arbitration through its efforts at establishing internationally acceptable rules, and through the evolution of internationally agreed standards for national arbitration laws. Each approach will be considered in turn, with emphasis on its utility in investment disputes.

2.1   Ad Hoc *Arbitration and Conciliation*

Ad hoc arbitration or conciliation depend upon the initiative of the parties for their success. The parties must make their own arrangements regarding the procedure, the selection of arbitrators or conciliators, as the case may be, and the administrative support.[23] The principal advantage of *ad hoc* dispute settlement is that the procedure can be shaped to suit the parties.[24] However, there are numerous problems associated with *ad hoc* arbitration. First, the process is governed by the arbitration agreement between the parties. Its content will depend on the relative bargaining power of the parties. The stronger party may therefore obtain an arrangement advantageous to its interests. Secondly, it may be impossible to agree on the exact nature of the dispute, or on the applicable law. Thirdly, there may be difficulties in selecting acceptable arbitrators who can be relied on to act impartially and not as 'advocates' for the side that had selected them. Fourthly, the proceedings may be stultified by inordinate delay on the part of one side or both, or through the non-appearance of a party.[25] Finally, there may be a problem in enforcing any award before municipal courts should they decide that the award is tainted with irregularity, or should the state party to the proceedings enjoy immunity from execution under the laws of the forum state.[26] These difficulties have led to the use of institutional systems of arbitration or conciliation.

2.2   *Institutional Systems for International Dispute Settlement*

An institutional system of arbitration or conciliation may prove to be a more reliable means of resolving a dispute than an *ad hoc* approach. Once the parties have consented to its use they have to abide by the system's procedures. These are designed with a view to ensuring that, while the parties retain a large measure of control over the arbitration or conciliation, they are constrained against any attempt to undermine the proceedings. Furthermore, an award made under the auspices of an institutional system is more likely to be consistent with principles of procedural fairness and so is more likely to be enforceable before municipal courts. Indeed, recognition may be no more than a formality. Two systems in particular appear suitable for use in investment disputes between the host state and the foreign investor: the conciliation and arbitration procedures available under the auspices of International Centre for the Settlement of Investment Disputes (ICSID) and the International Chamber of Commerce Court of Arbitration(ICC).[27]

The next section of the chapter concentrates on arbitration and conciliation under the ICSID system. The ICSID system is the only institutional system of international conciliation or arbitration specially designed to deal with investment disputes, and deserves closer scrutiny.

Apart from ICSID, ICC arbitration clauses have been used in international investment agreements, resulting in ICC arbitration in the event of a dispute.[28] However, one of the criticisms lodged against the ICC Court of Arbitration as a forum for the resolution of foreign investment disputes is that, being primarily a centre for the resolution of commercial disputes between private traders, it has relatively little experience in the complexities of long-term investment agreements involving a state as a party.[29] This may account for the observation that ICC arbitration clauses appear to be used relatively infrequently in international economic development agreements.[30] However, the evidence of the actual use of the ICC Court of Arbitration in disputes involving governments or state owned enterprises is by no means negligible.[31] Therefore this criticism of the ICC should not be overstated.

2.3   The Contribution of UNCITRAL

Although they are not institutional systems for international dispute settlement, the UNCITRAL Arbitration Rules 1976, the UNCITRAL Conciliation Rules 1980 and the UNCITRAL Model Law on International Commercial Arbitration 1985 should be considered as possible improvements to *ad hoc* international arbitration or conciliation.[32] The UNCITRAL Rules on Conciliation and Arbitration and the Model Law on Arbitration may be of value in disputes between foreign investors and host states. The Arbitration Rules were adopted as a set 'of rules for *ad hoc* arbitration that are acceptable in countries with different legal, social and economic systems' and that, 'would significantly contribute to the development of harmonious economic relations'.[33] Thus their primary aim is to harmonize the rules used in commercial arbitration by providing an optional and generally acceptable system of procedural norms for the conduct of such arbitrations.[34] In relation to foreign investment disputes, although the UNCITRAL Rules do not provide for the institutional back-up available under the ICC and ICSID systems, they can remove some of the difficulties associated with *ad hoc* arbitration by basing it on internationally acceptable procedures. However, the success of the resulting award still depends to a great degree on the parties' acceptance of their obligation to observe it. There is no legal basis for the automatic recognition or enforcement of the award. Furthermore, the award is subject to the possibility of pleas of sovereign immunity by the state party, should the award be unfavourable to it.

The importance of the UNCITRAL Rules in international commercial arbitration cannot be doubted. They have been adopted by several countries and international arbitration agencies.[35] However, it is fair to say that their primary importance lies in the field of international trade disputes between private parties rather than in the field of foreign investment disputes between the private investor and the host state.

The UNCITRAL Model Law on International Commercial Arbitration was adopted on 21 June 1985 at the close of the Commission's eighteenth annual session.[36] Its purpose is not to set up an institutional system of international commercial arbitration. Rather, the Model Law seeks to promote the harmonization of national laws relating to arbitral procedures. It does so by providing accepted international standards of arbitral procedure that can be adopted by a national legal system, thereby converting them into binding rules of law. This process may be of particular value in the context of investment disputes. Should the host state adopt the Model Law into its legal system, it would offer internationally acceptable standards of arbitral procedure within its domestic arbitration system. This should go some considerable way towards alleviating any fears that the foreign investor might have as to the adequacy of the host state's arbitration laws. At the same time it would allow the host state to retain legal control over any disputes that might arise out of the investment. This approach could obviate the need for 'delocalized' international arbitration, which might serve only to embarrass the host state and which runs the risk that any award unfavourable to the host state would not be recognized or enforced under its legal system.

3   The International Centre for the Settlement of Investment Disputes[37]

Despite the existence of the above-mentioned alternatives, a comparison of these systems with ICSID shows that the latter offers the best institutional framework for the settlement of investment disputes.[38] Above all, the procedures for conciliation and arbitration offered by ICSID are specifically designed for the settlement of disputes between foreign investors and host states, whereas the ICC and UNCITRAL are mainly concerned with traditional commercial disputes. It is not proposed to deal with conciliation in any detail.[39] The focus will be on arbitration as the most significant function of the Centre. The Centre also offers an Additional Facility for conciliation and arbitration, where one of the parties to the dispute is not a Contracting Party or a national of a Contracting Party under the Washington Convention, and/or where the dispute does not relate to investment, and for fact-finding which is not provided for under the Washington Convention. The Additional Facility procedure will not be studied here.[40]

3.1 The Aims of ICSID

The Washington Convention on the Settlement of Investment Disputes between States and Nationals of Other States was adopted by resolution of the Executive Directors of the World Bank on 18 March 1965. It entered into force on 14 October 1966.[41] As of 30 September 1994 it had 130 signatories and 114 ratifications.[42] There is a regular, if not growing, case-load submitted to ICSID, established by the Convention as the principal organ for the Convention's system of dispute settlement.[43]

The Washington Convention developed out of proposals made by the World Bank's General Counsel following the Bank's previous experiences in the provision of good offices for the solution of investment disputes.[44] In their report on the Convention, the Executive Directors of the Bank stated that the Convention would offer an international method of settlement which was designed to take account of the special characteristics of investment disputes and of the parties to whom it would apply. It would provide facilities for conciliation and arbitration by specially qualified persons of independent judgment carried out according to rules known and accepted in advance by the parties. In particular, once the parties to the dispute had given their consent to arbitration or conciliation under the auspices of ICSID, such consent could not be unilaterally withdrawn. A most important feature of the Convention is its 'delocalized' system of dispute settlement operating independently and exclusively of domestic legal systems.[45] The role of domestic courts is limited to that of judicial assistance in the recognition of ICSID awards.[46]

The Executive Directors believed that adherence to the Convention by a country would provide an additional inducement for, and stimulate a larger flow of, private international investment into its territory. This was, in their opinion, the primary purpose of the Convention.[47] Thus the Convention should not be seen merely as a machinery for dispute settlement. It is also 'an instrument of international policy for the promotion of economic development'.[48]

The response was the creation of a system which seeks to ensure authoritative, final and effective dispute resolution in the context of a permanent international institution. In this the Convention can be placed firmly within the 'investor protection' approach to foreign investment. By acceding to the Washington Convention the host state accepts that its sovereign power to regulate disputes with foreign investors is to be subjected to review in accordance with the international procedures set out under the Convention and the Rules promulgated under its authority. Against this background we shall now turn to consider how far the dispute settlement system thereby created is likely to impact upon Contracting States' power to control investment disputes.

3.2   The Washington Convention and Its Effect on State Sovereignty over Investment Disputes

This section will consider: first, the extent of the personal jurisdiction of the Centre, and the extent of the Contracting State's ability to control such jurisdiction; secondly, the Centre's subject matter jurisdiction; thirdly, the precise means by which the Convention seeks to 'delocalize' the resolution of investment disputes brought before it; fourthly, the extent to which a party to a dispute can challenge an award made against it; fifthly, how far other Contracting States will recognize and enforce ICSID awards made against the respondent Contracting State; finally, the procedures for bringing a case before the Centre and the costs thereof.

3.2.1   The Contracting State's ability to control jurisdiction[49]   The cornerstone of the jurisdiction of ICSID is article 25(1) of the Convention:

The jurisdiction of the Centre shall extend to any legal dispute arising directly out of an investment between a Contracting State (or any constituent subdivision or agency of a Contracting State designated to the Centre by that state) and a national of another Contracting State, which the parties to the dispute consent in writing to submit to the Centre. When the parties have given their consent, no party may withdraw its consent unilaterally.

Article 25(1) makes consent in writing of both parties the basis of ICSID jurisdiction. This will usually be given in an ICSID arbitration clause contained in an investment agreement.[50] However, it is possible for the Contracting State to make a unilateral offer of ICSID arbitration in its foreign investment law, which will amount to consent for the purposes of article 25 if the foreign investor accepts the offer in writing.[51] Alternatively, consent may be deduced from a series of agreements of which only some mention ICSID arbitration. This is an issue to be decided on the facts in each case.[52] Furthermore, consent has been held to exist where the host state accepts an investment application containing a clause obliging the host state and the investor to put disputes before ICSID.[53]

In all these instances the consent of the host state is voluntarily and freely given. There is no warrant for interpreting strictly the requirement of consent on the part of the state party to the dispute simply because such consent may amount to a restriction on state sovereignty.[54] Should the host state be concerned about the extent of its consent to ICSID arbitration, article 25(4) of the Convention empowers any contracting state to 'notify the Centre of the class or classes of disputes which it would or would not consider submitting to the jurisdiction of the Centre'. This can be done at the time of acceptance or approval of the Convention or at any time thereafter, although any subsequent change in the Contracting State's initial consent to ICSID jurisdiction has only prospective, and not retroactive, effect. Consequently a Contracting State is unable to use the article 25(4) procedure to remove from the jurisdiction of ICSID proceedings to which it has already consented.[55] Nevertheless, article 25(4) affords to the Contracting State a wide discretion to exclude such classes of investment dispute as it sees fit from its consent to ICSID jurisdiction. However, if the article 25(4) notification is ambiguous it would fall to the ICSID Tribunal to determine its meaning and scope.[56] Thus the Contracting State must ensure that its notification is clear if it wishes to preserve its sovereign rights in particular areas of inward foreign investment.

In addition to consent, a further requirement of jurisdiction is that the parties to the dispute are proper parties to appear before ICSID. As regards the state party to the dispute, only a state that has become a Contracting State to the Washington Convention can be a party to ICSID proceedings. A Contracting State is one which has confirmed its signature of the Convention at least thirty days prior to the bringing of the dispute by depositing an instrument of ratification, accession or approval with the World Bank.[57] The state party to the dispute need not be a Contracting Party at the time a clause consenting to ICSID arbitration is concluded. However, such consent is insufficient to ensure the jurisdiction of ICSID. The state must become a Contracting State by the date that a request is submitted to the Secretary-General of ICSID if such contingent consent is to become binding upon the state party to the dispute.[58]

The reference in article 25(1) of the Convention to the 'constituent sub-division' of a Contracting State may be interpreted to cover a range of sub-divisions including federal states, semi-autonomous dependencies and municipalities.[59] The reference to an 'agency' of a Contracting State creates greater problems of interpretation. It seeks to include within the jurisdiction of the Convention a wide range of bodies operating as state agencies, including not only departments of government but perhaps even government-owned or government-controlled corporations. It may, however, exclude entities in which the government merely owns shares.[60] Such definitional problems may be considerably reduced given the requirement, in article 25(1) of the Convention, that constituent sub-divisions or agencies must be 'designated' to the Centre by the Contracting State. Such designation would raise a strong presumption in favour of granting the sub-division or agency *locus standi* before the Centre.[61] Furthermore, article 25(3) of the Convention demands that consent by a constituent sub-division or agency of a Contracting State requires approval by the Contracting State unless that State notifies the Centre that such approval is not required.[62]

The other party to the dispute must be the national of a contracting state other than the host state. This party may be a natural or a juridical person.[63] A natural person must possess the nationality of a Contracting State upon the date on which the parties consent to submit the dispute to the Centre and on the date that the request is registered by the Secretary-General of ICSID. This does not include any person who on either date also has the nationality of the Contracting State party to the dispute.[64]

As regards a juridical person, the nationality requirements are not as strict. By article 25(2)(b) the term 'national of another contracting state' means, for the purposes of article 25(1),

any juridical person which had the nationality of a Contracting State other than the State party to the dispute on the date on which the parties consented to submit such dispute to conciliation or arbitration and any juridical person which had the nationality of the Contracting State party to the dispute on that date and which, because of foreign control, the parties have agreed should be treated as a national of another contracting state for the purposes of this Convention.

This provision covers two cases. The first is that of a juridical person possessing the nationality of a Contracting State other than that of the Contracting State party to the dispute. Unlike the case of natural persons, there is no requirement for such nationality to continue at the date of registration of the request with the Secretary-General of ICSID. A particular problem has arisen in the context of a MNE group. Where the foreign parent assigns its rights under an investment agreement to another foreign-incorporated subsidiary, does the latter inherit the right to make a claim before ICSID? In such a case, it has been held that the host state may not be permitted to circumvent the jurisdiction of ICSID by denying the recognition of the assignee as an investor under its investment laws, where such recognition may be a condition for the host state's consent to ICSID jurisdiction, and where, on the facts, the host state knew of the proposed assignment and acquiesced in it.[65]

The second case is that of a juridical person possessing the nationality of the Contracting State party to the dispute at the date on which the parties consented to ICSID arbitration. The purpose of this part of article 25(2)(b) is to ensure that foreign investments carried out by means of a locally incorporated subsidiary or joint venture are not excluded from the Convention. If that were so, then a major category of investments would fall outside the scope of the Convention, causing it to lose much of its utility. To that extent the Convention goes beyond the limitations laid down in the *Barcelona Traction* case concerning the protection of foreign shareholders in a locally incorporated company.[66] However, the host Contracting State is given discretion over whether to extend ICSID arbitration to locally incorporated entities. The extent of this discretion has been clarified to a certain extent in the reasoned awards of ICSID Tribunals.

First, the agreement to treat the locally incorporated entity as the national of another contracting state should normally be express and explicit. However, implied agreement can be found if the circumstances of the case would exclude any other interpretation of the intention of the parties.[67] Such circumstances do not arise in the case where the local entity is created after the investment agreement containing the ICSID arbitration clause has been concluded, and where the creation of that entity was not contemplated at the time of conclusion by the foreign parent company and the host state.[68] By contrast, where it is at all times contemplated by both the foreign investor and the host state that the investment will take the form of a locally incorporated entity, and the host state acknowledges the foreign ownership of that entity in the course of approving the investment application, there is no need for a separate agreement on the nationality of the entity for the purposes of ICSID jurisdiction.[69] Furthermore, where a host state enters into an investment agreement containing an ICSID arbitration clause with a foreign controlled juridical person possessing the same nationality as the host state, it may be presumed, in the absence of cogent evidence to the contrary, that the host state has agreed to treat that entity as a 'national of another contracting state'.[70] It is clear from these principles that ICSID Tribunals have taken a broad view of the circumstances in which the consent of the host Contracting State exists to treating a locally incorporated entity as the 'national of another contracting state' for the purposes of ICSID arbitration. Thus if a host state wishes to restrict ICSID arbitration only to disputes between the parent company and itself this should be made explicit.

A final matter relating to the host state's control over the availability of ICSID arbitration arises out of the willingness of the Tribunal in *Amco Asia* v *Republic of Indonesia*[71] to imply ICSID arbitration rights to the parent company of a locally incorporated subsidiary in circumstances where the host state wishes to deal exclusively with the local subsidiary. Such implied jurisdiction *ratione personae* can serve to frustrate the host state's desire to regulate the investment by dealing only with the local subsidiary, in that the foreign parent can invoke ICSID arbitration against the state while the state cannot exercise regulatory control over the parent.[72] There may be legitimate reasons for implying ICSID arbitration rights, as where, for example, the parent company acts as guarantor of its subsidiary or where the host government wishes to deal with the entire group of foreign companies, as, for example, in the *Holiday Inns* case.[73] But in the absence of such facts the approach of the *Amco Asia* Tribunal shows a considerable restriction on the host Contracting State's ability to choose the limits of ICSID arbitration.

To summarize, the host Contracting State has control over ICSID jurisdiction by means of its power to withhold consent to such jurisdiction. It also retains an important power of refusing to treat a locally incorporated entity as the national of a foreign contracting state under article 25(2)(b). However, ICSID Tribunals will be swift to find either type of consent without deference to the host Contracting State's sovereignty in cases where consent is ambiguous.[74] The Tribunals have the task of applying the Convention in accordance with its meaning and intent. This has resulted in an approach that will not readily accept objections to the jurisdiction of the Centre. Indeed, if a restrictive approach were taken the credibility of ICSID as an effective forum could suffer. However, such an approach could lead to a cavalier attitude to jurisdictional issues if it were taken too far.[75] That, too, cannot be good for the reputation of ICSID.

3.2.2 Subject matter jurisdiction Article 25(1) of the Convention imposes two subject matter requirements on the jurisdiction of ICSID: first, that the dispute must arise directly out of an 'investment' and, secondly, that the dispute must be a 'legal' dispute.

Turning first to the notion of 'investment', this is not defined in the Convention. According to George Delaume, this deliberate lack of definition has enabled the Convention to accommodate both traditional types of investment, in the form of capital contributions, and new types of investment, including service contracts and transfers of technology.[76] In proceedings before the ICSID Tribunal the parties have only once raised objections as to jurisdiction on the basis of a definition of an 'investment'. This may be because of a view held by the parties that the term should be broadly defined. It would appear that as long as the arrangement between the parties involves a long-term outlay of capital on the part of at least one party, there will be no doubt that this constitutes an 'investment'.[77] However, it is ultimately for the ICSID Tribunal to decide the issue for itself. The parties' characterization of a dispute as an 'investment dispute' is not decisive.[78] Nevertheless, a clear description of the salient features of the transaction should be included by the parties in their instrument of consent to ICSID arbitration, so as to avoid the risk of the request for ICSID arbitration being turned down for lack of subject matter jurisdiction.[79] Should a state wish to exclude certain classes of investment from ICSID jurisdiction then, as noted above, under article 25(4) of the Convention, it may notify the Centre of the class or classes of disputes which it would or would not consider submitting to the jurisdiction of the Centre.

As regards the requirement that the dispute be a 'legal' dispute, in the drafting stages of the Convention an attempt was made to define a 'legal dispute' for the purposes of the Convention. This proved to be impossible and the definition was left open. The Executive Directors of the World Bank explained, in their report on the Convention, that while conflicts of rights were within the jurisdiction of the Centre, mere conflicts of interest were not. The dispute had to concern either the existence or scope of a legal right or obligation, or the nature or extent of the reparation to be made for breach of a legal obligation.[80]

3.2.3 The delocalized character of ICSID arbitration The delocalized character of ICSID arbitration is emphasized by the principles contained in articles 26 and 27 of the Convention. By article 26, 'consent of the parties to arbitration under this Convention shall, unless otherwise stated, be deemed consent to such arbitration to the exclusion of any other remedy'. By article 27 (1) of the Convention:

No Contracting State shall give diplomatic protection, or bring an international claim in respect of a dispute which one of its nationals and another Contracting State shall have consented to submit or shall have submitted to arbitration under this Convention, unless such other Contracting State shall have failed to abide by and comply with the award rendered in such a dispute.

Thus article 26 excludes other national remedies, while article 27 excludes other international remedies, for the duration of ICSID proceedings. Once those proceedings are concluded, if they end in an award against the respondent Contracting State, then the courts of that state and of the other Contracting States must give effect to any 'pecuniary obligations' thereby imposed on the respondent. Only if the respondent state fails to honour such obligations do the international remedies of the foreign investors' national state revive.

However, there are certain limits placed upon the principle of delocalization. The first is under article 26 itself. It continues: 'A Contracting State may require the exhaustion of local administrative or judicial remedies as a condition of its consent to arbitration under this Convention.' Thus the host Contracting State retains some control over the point at which ICSID arbitration becomes available. However, once made available, the consent of the parties to ICSID arbitration brings the principle of exclusivity into operation. Notwithstanding this fact, the effectiveness of article 26 depends on the willingness of the national courts of the Contracting States to refrain from adjudicating in disputes that have been taken to ICSID by consent of the parties. The response from national courts has, in this respect, been uneven.

Thus, in the case of *MINE* v *Republic of Guinea*,[81] when faced with the question of whether an American arbitration award could be enforced under US law while proceedings were pending before ICSID, the US courts answered, at first instance, that it could,[82] but on appeal that it could not, on the grounds that the Republic of Guinea had not waived its right to sovereign immunity before the US courts.[83] At neither instance was the exclusivity of ICSID proceedings accepted as a reason for not recognizing the American arbitral award.[84] By contrast, the Belgian courts did recognize the primacy of ICSID proceedings in the *MINE* case when they were called upon to recognize the American award,[85] as did the Swiss courts.[86]

In another case involving ICSID proceedings, this time between the Republic of Guinea and Atlantic Triton, the French courts had the opportunity to consider the effect of article 26. The Court of Appeal at Rennes upheld the exclusivity of ICSID proceedings in the course of an appeal challenging measures of attachment taken by Atlantic Triton against Guinean ships present within French jurisdiction. In the Court's opinion, such exclusivity pertained not only to consideration of the merits of the dispute, but also to all provisional measures. If local tribunals were able to impose provisional measures while ICSID proceedings were pending, the task of ICSID arbitrators would be unduly complicated and the effectiveness of any eventual award could be prejudiced.[87] This decision was overturned by the Court of Cassation, which took the position that the exclusive character of ICSID arbitration set forth in article 26 did not prevent a party to an ICSID proceeding from seeking provisional measures of attachment before the French courts. The Court of Cassation felt unable to pronounce upon the effect of the ICSID Convention, which was a matter for the French government. Furthermore, the power of national courts to order pre-emptive measures could only be excluded by express consent of the parties or by implied convention resulting from the adoption of arbitral rules calling for such waiver.[88] Clearly, therefore, the Court of Cassation was not satisfied that the jurisdiction of national courts could be ousted by article 26 without any clearer indication to this effect that was accepted by the French government.

In response to the uncertainty surrounding the question of provisional measures before national courts, a new paragraph was added to the revised Arbitration Rule 39 which came into force on 26 September 1984. The new paragraph states:

Nothing in this Rule shall prevent the parties, provided they have so stipulated in the agreement recording their consent, from requesting any judicial or other authority to order provisional measures, prior to the institution of the proceeding, or during the proceeding, for the preservation of their respective rights and interests.[89]

However, in the absence of such express agreement, the Convention prevents parties from seeking provisional measures other than those that may be recommended by the Tribunal under article 47 of the Convention and Arbitration Rule 39.[90] This would have serious consequences in the French legal system given the above-mentioned decision to the contrary by the Court of Cassation.

A second limit on delocalization concerns the law applicable to the merits of the dispute as laid down in article 42 of the Convention. By article 42(1) of the Convention:

The Tribunal shall decide a dispute in accordance with such rules of law as may be agreed by the parties. In the absence of such agreement, the Tribunal shall apply the law of the Contracting State party to the dispute (including its rules of the Conflict of Laws) and such rules of international law as may be applicable.

This provision lays down a hierarchy of applicable laws with the law chosen by the parties being the most important, followed by the law of the Contracting State party to the dispute (or the law of some other state if that applies as a result of the Contracting State's rules on conflict of laws) and then rules of international law.

If the host Contracting State is concerned to ensure that investment disputes are decided by reference to its domestic law then it can hold out for an agreement to this effect from the investor. This, in turn, poses the question of the suitability of an ICSID Tribunal as a body charged with the interpretation and application of the host state's law. It is unlikely that an ICSID Tribunal would possess the same expertise in the law of the host Contracting State as the national arbitral or judicial tribunals of that state. Consequently, having an ICSID arbitration determined by reference to host country law may not be a very significant concession to host state interests. Indeed, it could be counterproductive, as where the Tribunal manifestly fails to apply the law of the host state to the disadvantage of either party. If this is the case, a finding of nullity on the grounds of manifest excess of powers by failure to apply article 42 (1) of the Convention is possible.[91] This may serve only to delay the resolution of a dispute. Thus, making the law of the host Contracting State the law governing the dispute seems not to offer many advantages over purely domestic dispute settlement (assuming, of course, that the domestic legal system of the host Contracting State is itself reliable and impartial).

A further question that arises is whether the ICSID Tribunal must apply the host Contracting State's law even where this is inconsistent with the rules of international law. In *LETCO* v *Liberia*[92] the concession agreement in question expressly made Liberian law the law of the agreement. The Tribunal considered whether, in view of the wording of article 42(1), Liberian law could be considered on its own or in conjunction with applicable principles of international law. The Tribunal noted that, although the law of the Contracting State was paramount within its own territory, it was subject to control by international law. However, no such problem arose in the present case as the applicable rules of Liberian law were in conformity with international law.[93] It appears, therefore, that even in cases where the law of the host Contracting State is the law agreed by the parties to govern the dispute, an ICSID Tribunal will review its conformity with international law. Furthermore, it is open to the parties to the dispute to chose international treaty standards as the governing law. Thus, in *Asian Agricultural Products Ltd* v *Republic of Sri Lanka*[94] the Tribunal found that both parties had acted in a manner that demonstrated their mutual agreement to consider the provisions of the Sri Lanka–UK Bilateral Investment Treaty as being the primary source of the applicable legal rules.[95]

Similarly, where no agreement is made on the choice of law, the host Contracting State's law applies subject to any applicable rules of international law. In the *Amco Asia* case the first *ad hoc* Committee held that the role of international law was restricted only to the filling of '*lacunae* in the applicable domestic law' and to ensuring 'precedence to international law norms where the rules of the applicable law are in collision with such norms'. The role of international law was thus 'supplemental and corrective' under article 42(1).[96] However, the Tribunal in the resubmitted case of *Amco Asia* v *Indonesia*[97] rejected this narrow approach and affirmed that

Article 42(1) refers to the application of host state law and international law. If there are no relevant host state laws on a particular matter, a search must be made for the relevant international laws. And, where there are applicable host state laws, they must be checked against international laws, which will prevail in case of conflict. Thus international law is fully applicable and to classify its role as 'only' 'supplemental and corrective' seems a distinction without a difference.[98]

This formulation may overstate the role of international law to the detriment of the reference to host state law in article 42(1). Nevertheless, international law clearly provides a guarantee to the foreign investor against the unfair operation of national law.[99]

This relationship between national and international law is in keeping with the scheme of the Convention, which envisages recognition and enforcement of awards in all Contracting States under article 54(1) and restricts the national state of the investor from invoking its right of diplomatic protection under article 27. Only an award that does not violate applicable principles and rules of international law is consistent with these provisions.[100] Therefore it is clear that even when the parties agree to use host state law the dispute will be effectively internationalized in that the ultimate standard of decision will be provided by international law. The host state's apparent control over the applicable law under article 42(1) is thus quite substantially curtailed.[101] That this is so should come as no surprise. An international tribunal cannot accept a plea from the respondent state that provisions of its own law or deficiencies in that law are an answer to a claim against it for an alleged breach of international law.[102] This principle was affirmed by the Tribunal in *Southern Pacific Properties (Middle East) Limited* v *Arab Republic of Egypt*,[103] where a determination that certain acts of the Egyptian authorities, which resulted in the expropriation of the claimant's investment, were null and void under Egyptian law was held not to exclude the operation of international law as the standard by which the responsibility of Egypt for the unauthorized acts of its officials would be ascertained, even though Egyptian law was held to be the applicable law under article 42(1).

3.2.4   The extent to which an unfavourable decision of an ICSID tribunal can be challenged by the losing party   By article 52(1) of the Convention either party may request annulment of the award by an application in writing addressed to the Secretary-General on one or more of the following grounds:

(a)   that the Tribunal was not properly constituted;
(b)   that the Tribunal has manifestly exceeded its powers;
(c)   that there was corruption on the part of a member of the Tribunal;
(d)   that there has been a serious departure from a fundamental rule of procedure;
(e)   that the award has failed to state the reasons on which it is based.

This power has been used to annul the awards in *Klöckner* v *Cameroon*,[104] *Amco Asia Corporation* v *Indonesia*[105] and *MINE* v *Guinea*.[106] In the *Klöckner* case the *ad hoc* Committee annulled the decision of the Tribunal, first, on the grounds that it had failed to apply the law of Cameroon, the law governing the dispute, constituting a manifest excess of powers under article 52(1)(b), and, secondly, on the grounds that the Tribunal had 'failed to state reasons' by failing to deal with every question put to it. In the *Amco Asia* case the decision of the Tribunal was annulled by the first *ad hoc* Committee on the grounds of manifest excess of powers in that the Tribunal had failed to calculate correctly the amount of Amco's foreign investment in the project. The *ad hoc* Committee held that, by failing to apply the relevant provisions of Indonesian law, the Tribunal had greatly overestimated Amco's contribution.[107] This decision led to the setting up of a second Tribunal in 1987, which rendered its Decision on Jurisdiction on 10 May 1988. This Decision gave rise to lengthy proceedings on the question of what the *ad hoc* Committee had actually annulled in the award of the first Tribunal, and what it had upheld, such matters being *res judicata* between the parties.[108] The second Tribunal gave its Decision on Merits on 31 May 1990. This was rectified on 10 October 1990.[109] On 18 October 1990, the parties applied for an annulment of the Award of 31 May 1990. An *ad hoc* Committee was constituted on 30 January 1991.[110] The *ad hoc* Committee rendered its Decision on 17 December 1992.[111] In *MINE* v *Guinea* the *ad hoc* Committee annulled an award of US$12.3 million against Guinea but upheld the finding of breach of the investment contract. The parties requested the resubmission of the dispute to a new tribunal, but agreed a settlement on 20 November 1990.[112]

The annulment awards in *Klöckner* and *Amco Asia* have been heavily criticized both on their reasoning and on their broader implications for the ICSID system.[113] In each case the *ad hoc* Committee had acted as a *de facto* court of appeal on matters of fact and law, which goes beyond the limited grounds of annulment available under article 52(1). Furthermore, the requirement laid down in the *Klöckner* case, that the Tribunal must deal with every matter put before it, would expose most ICSID awards to the risk of annulment. The procedure of submitting 'memorials' and 'counter-memorials' to the Tribunal, though useful in giving the factual background to the dispute, does not define the issues as precisely as a set of pleadings before a court. Thus there is always a risk of an issue not being dealt with by a Tribunal.[114]

These proceedings have put into question the extent to which ICSID awards are truly final. Indeed, it appears that the *ad hoc* Committee's approaches to both cases are not warranted on the basis of the negotiating history of the Convention, which clearly shows that article 52 was never intended to permit the *ad hoc* Committee to review the application of the law, or the sufficiency of reasoning, of the first Tribunal. Such review was intended to ensure only that the Tribunal did not address matters beyond its competence and that the essentials of national justice had been complied with.[115] These concerns have prompted the Secretary-General of ICSID to propose an amendment to the Arbitration Rules clarifying the exceptional nature of the annulment procedure.[116] In the absence of such clarification it appears that annulment can be used at least as a delaying tactic against the imposition of liability on a respondent state. This may seriously undermine the effectiveness of ICSID arbitration.

3.2.5   Enforcement of ICSID awards   By article 54 of the Washington Convention, 'Each Contracting State shall recognize an award rendered pursuant to this Convention as binding and enforce the pecuniary obligations imposed by that award within its territories as if it were a final judgment of a court in that state'. The party seeking recognition or enforcement need only present a copy of the award certified by the Secretary-General of ICSID.[117] The execution of the award should be governed by the laws concerning the execution of judgments in force in the state where execution is sought.[118] This includes the applicable law relating to a foreign state's immunity from execution.[119] Thus the respondent state still enjoys the protection of the law of sovereign immunity as applied in the enforcing state.[120] In practical terms, therefore, the enforceability of an ICSID award is subject to the overriding principle of protecting the property belonging to a foreign sovereign that is used for sovereign rather than commercial purposes against execution, this being the most commonly applicable rule found in national laws.

3.2.6   Procedure and costs   The ICSID conciliation and arbitration procedures both begin with a request to the Secretary-General of ICSID.[121] The party wishing to institute proceedings sends a request in writing to the Secretary-General, who shall send a copy of the request to the other party. The request must contain information concerning the matters in dispute, the identity of the parties and their consent to arbitration or conciliation in accordance with the rules of procedure for the institution of conciliation and arbitration proceedings.

The Secretary-General thereupon undertakes a preliminary investigation of the jurisdictional admissibility of the request. He may refuse the request if it appears to him, on the basis of the information contained in the request, that the Centre is not competent to admit the dispute. If the dispute appears to be within the jurisdiction of the Centre the Secretary-General registers the request in either the conciliation or arbitration register, notifying the parties of the registration on the same day. The proceedings are deemed to have commenced from the day of registration. The Secretary-General's powers in this respect are not final. The ICSID Tribunal is the ultimate judge of admissibility.[122] The registration of a dispute does not, therefore, prevent the Tribunal from rejecting it for lack of competence. Should a request for registration be refused, the claimant may submit a second request but must ensure that the dispute falls *prima facie* within the jurisdiction of the Centre. The conciliation commission or arbitral tribunal shall be constituted as soon as possible after the registration of the request.[123] Each body shall consist of a sole member or any uneven number of members appointed as the parties shall agree. In the absence of the agreement of the parties the conciliation commission or arbitral tribunal shall consist of three members.[124] Should no appointment be made within ninety days of registration, or such time as the parties agree, the chairman of the body in question shall appoint the conciliators or arbitrators, as the case may be.[125] At this point the conciliation and arbitration procedures diverge.

As to the conciliation procedures, conciliators may be appointed from outside the Panel of Conciliators, provided they possess the qualities required of a member of the Panel.[126] The Conciliation Commission, being satisfied that it has the competence to proceed,[127] has the duty to clarify the issues between the parties and to endeavour to bring about agreement between them on mutually agreeable terms. It may recommend terms of settlement to the parties at any time during the proceedings.[128] If the parties reach agreement, the Conciliation Commission must draw up a report noting the issues in dispute and recording that the parties have reached agreement. If the parties fail to agree the Commission must draw up a report recording the failure of the proceedings.[129] Failure by one party to appear terminates the proceedings and a report to this effect must be drawn up by the Commission.[130] After the conciliation proceedings have ended each party is bound by a duty of confidentiality regarding the matters discussed and offers of settlement made during the course of those proceedings.[131]

As regards the proceedings of the arbitral tribunal, the majority of the arbitrators must be nationals of states other than the state party to the dispute and the state whose national is a party to the dispute, unless the parties agree jointly to the appointment of a sole arbitrator or to each member of a larger Tribunal.[132] The Arbitral Tribunal will consider whether it has jurisdiction over the dispute in accordance with the standards laid down in article 25 of the Convention, and in the light of the applicable law determined in accordance with article 42 of the Convention, as discussed above. Unlike conciliation proceedings, arbitration proceedings will not become invalidated by the non-appearance of a party. The Tribunal may continue at the request of the other party and render an award.[133] In doing so the Tribunal must follow the procedures laid down in the Arbitration Rules regarding the notification of the defaulting party and the granting of a period of grace before continuing with the arbitration.[134]

The Tribunal shall render its award in accordance with the requirements contained in the Convention as to form and content.[135] The award is then subject to the annulment and enforcement provisions discussed above.

The costs of ICSID proceedings are determined by reference to regulations adopted from time to time by the Administrative Council.[136] Each Conciliation Commission and each Arbitral Tribunal shall determine the fees and expenses of its members within the limits established from time to time by the Administrative Council and after consultation with the Secretary-General.[137] However, the parties may agree in advance with the Commission or Tribunal concerned upon the fees and expenses of its members.[138] In the case of conciliation proceedings the costs shall be borne equally by the parties.[139] In the case of arbitration proceedings the Tribunal shall decide, unless the parties otherwise agree, the amount of expenses incurred by the parties and how and by whom those expenses, the fees and expenses of the members of the Tribunal and the charges for the use of the facilities of the Centre shall be paid.[140] Generally, the costs of ICSID proceedings are lower than those conducted under ICC procedures.[141] Administrative charges are assessed on the basis of the Centre's actual expenses,[142] and arbitrators' fees are on a reasonable *per diem* basis.[143]

3.3   The Use of the Convention

3.3.1   The membership   The Contracting States to the Washington Convention may be said to fall into two main groups: first, states that are major exporters of capital; secondly, states that are dependent on private foreign direct investment for their economic well-being and that are highly conscious of the need to adopt incentives for investors. What is notable is the absence of some of the middle-ranking capital-importing states, such as Canada, Brazil, Mexico or India. Similarly,

Australia, though a signatory of the Convention in 1975, only ratified it in 1991.[144] These states may not need to use ICSID procedures as an incentive to attract foreign investors. The business opportunities in these countries are sufficiently attractive in themselves to ensure the inflow of required capital. It is submitted that only where a host country has a reputation for high investment risk, because of internal political and/or economic conditions, will it need to reassure investors by acceding to the Washington Convention. This may lie behind the policy of the People's Republic of China, which ratified the Convention and has made provision for this eventuality in its most recent bilateral investment agreements.[145] However, China has limited the jurisdiction of ICSID under article 25(4) to 'disputes over compensation resulting from expropriation and nationalization'.[146] Similarly, several post-socialist states from Eastern Europe and the former USSR, including the Russian Federation, have signed the Convention.[147] Equally, certain Latin American states have signed the Convention, including, most recently, Argentina in 1991 and Uruguay in 1992. Chile ratified the Convention in 1991. These are significant changes in attitude given the Latin American states' traditional hostility to international dispute settlement techniques in the field of foreign investment.[148] However, it is arguable that the ICSID system is in fact compatible with these concerns.[149]

3.3.2 The caseload   The caseload of ICSID has steadily, if somewhat slowly, increased over the years. Between 1966 and 1981 only nine disputes had been submitted to ICSID arbitration. From 1981 to 1986 thirteen new proceedings were instituted, ten relating to arbitration, two to conciliation and one to annulment of an award.[150] Between 1987 and 1989 six new disputes were submitted to the Centre, bringing the total number of disputes submitted to the Centre since its inception to twenty-six.[151] By 1991, fourteen cases had been settled as compared to nine that have given rise to awards, although two of these have been annulments.[152] In 1992, two new disputes were submitted to the Centre, as were one each in 1993 and 1994.[153] The high proportion of settlements is, in the words of the ICSID Secretary General, 'further encouraging evidence of the ability of the ICSID system to facilitate the resolution of disputes on terms agreed by the parties'.[154] These remarks are, however, tainted with the caution expressed by the Secretary-General regarding the recent incidence of annulment proceedings in two cases.[155]

Two observations may be made. First, if settlement of disputes by negotiation is the main objective of ICSID, and the major means of achieving this is the threat of an award being rendered in the absence of settlement, then the main justification for ICSID lies in what O'Keefe has called an '*in terrorem*' argument.[156] The effectiveness of

ICSID rests, therefore, in large measure upon the ability of the Centre to impose a final, authoritative and effective award on recalcitrant parties. Secondly, the effectiveness of ICSID in achieving this can be questioned given the recent incidence of annulment proceedings and the relatively low number of submissions of disputes to the Centre – even if there has been an increase since 1981. There is insufficient use made of ICSID to suggest its universal acceptance as a channel of dispute settlement, even among the Contracting States. A possible response to this observation is that ICSID should not be judged by the extent of its caseload, or by the number of accessions to the Convention, but by the incidence of references to ICSID arbitration in investment agreements and national laws.

3.3.3 The use of references to ICSID arbitration in investment agreements and national laws   In his annual report for 1989 the Secretary-General of ICSID notes:

The confidence that parties have in ICSID as a neutral and effective dispute-settlement mechanism was demonstrated in various ways during the year. The already widespread use of ICSID clauses in investment contracts continued to expand, with the Centre responding to numerous requests for assistance in drafting such clauses. In addition a further national investment law referring to ICSID was enacted in 1988/89 while the number of bilateral investment treaties with similar references increased to well over 150.[157]

Regarding the use of ICSID arbitration clauses in investment agreements, no systematic study is known to the present writer and it is highly unlikely that anything more than the impressions of the ICSID Secretariat are possible as a guide. Indeed, George Delaume noted in 1986 that there appear to be more ICSID arbitration clauses in existence than even ICSID is aware of, and that the majority of ICSID proceedings have been based on a consent clause of which the Secretariat was unaware before the institution of proceedings.[158] Much depends on the awareness of ICSID procedures among governments and investors. In 1976 an American study found that a substantial proportion of major US companies had never heard of ICSID and that others, though aware of ICSID, had not considered using its facilities.[159] In 1984 the Secretary-General of ICSID wrote:

Some 18 years have passed since the creation of ICSID as an international organisation concerned with the settlement of investment disputes between States and foreign investors. Still, little seems to be known to date in governmental and business circles alike, let alone the public at large, about ICSID's mandate and activities. This lack of information has kept resort to ICSID at a modest level in spite of its wide membership.[160]

A more significant matter is whether the host contracting state refers to ICSID arbitration in its investment laws. The Centre itself has classified such laws into two broad categories, based on the nature of the reference to ICSID. The first includes laws containing a unilateral and express consent to refer investment disputes to ICSID.[161] This type of provision amounts to a unilateral offer by the host state which needs to be accepted by the investor in an investment agreement, a statement contained in an investment application, a simple statement by the investor that he agrees to refer a particular investment dispute to ICSID or a request for arbitration submitted to ICSID after a dispute has arisen.[162] The second category includes laws that refer to the possibility of ICSID arbitration as one of several means of settling investment disputes.[163] In such a case the host government and the investor would have to accept ICSID jurisdiction by subsequent agreement. In the absence of such agreement the law cannot, by itself, make ICSID jurisdiction applicable. Thus references to ICSID arbitration in national investment laws should be treated with caution. Each law must be interpreted to see whether it constitutes an unconditional offer by the state to use ICSID arbitration, which becomes binding on acceptance by the investor, or whether the law simply regards ICSID as an optional procedure, leaving the question of its use to bargaining between the parties. Furthermore, the precise jurisdictional scope of the law must be taken into account so as to ascertain the limits of any unilateral consent, if such exists, on the part of the host state.[164]

Finally, regarding references to ICSID arbitration in bilateral investment agreements, these too should be approached with caution. Such references occur in an agreement between states. At most there may be a commitment, on the part of the states party to the investment agreement, to accept ICSID arbitration as the principal means of dispute settlement with investors from the other state party, should the investor so request.[165] Here the bilateral investment treaty achieves no more than the first category of national investment laws mentioned above. Again the text of the investment agreement must be interpreted to see whether such an offer is in fact made, or whether ICSID arbitration is simply an option available to the state party to the investment agreement in its relations with foreign investors.[166] Ultimately the availability of ICSID arbitration is still conditional upon agreement between the host state and foreign investor, although the reference to ICSID in the bilateral investment agreement may be taken as an indication of the host state's willingness to use ICSID procedures.

3.4 Conclusion

In adopting the aims and methods outlined above, the Washington Convention attempts to remedy a number of problems that were identified at the time of its conclusion as hindering the effective resolution of disputes between foreign investors and host states. In particular these were: the risk of bias in national arbitral and judicial tribunals of, particularly, the host state; the ineffectiveness of diplomatic protection as a means of vindicating the rights of the foreign investor; the problems associated with *ad hoc* international arbitration, in particular the risk of non-recognition before national tribunals and the possibility that the arbitral agreement would favour the party with greater bargaining power, both matters rendering the authority and finality of the award less certain.[167]

From the foregoing discussion, a number of conclusions may be drawn. First, the Washington Convention is an international dispute settlement body whose philosophy is firmly rooted in the desirability of delocalized conciliation and arbitration. This is seen as a means of encouraging foreign investment by guaranteeing its legal security. Consequently the membership of ICSID is centred on the USA and the major European capital-exporting states on the one hand, and the poorer developing states of Africa and Asia on the other. The more independent capital-importing states are as yet under-represented. Secondly, the caseload of ICSID is perhaps less than would be expected of a major centre for dispute settlement, despite a recent increase. Furthermore, if the Centre is to develop its role as a major forum for the settlement of investment disputes it must assure the finality and authority of its awards. This is open to doubt given recent developments in the use of nullity proceedings, especially in the *Amco Asia* case where two rounds of Tribunal *ad hoc* Committees have now sat. Thirdly, the reference to ICSID in national foreign investment laws and in bilateral investment treaties must be treated with caution. Such reference is not conclusive evidence of the consent to ICSID jurisdiction required under the Convention. Fourthly, the emerging case-law under the Convention shows that ICSID Tribunals are ready to extend the jurisdiction of ICSID and to control the application of the host Contracting States' law by reference to international law. In this the control of the host Contracting State over foreign investors is to an extent curtailed. However, it is not impossible for the Contracting State to restrict the operation of the Convention if it withholds its consent to the system's jurisdiction, and limits the range of disputes that can be submitted to ICSID. In such a case it may be legitimate to ask why the state should bother with the Convention at all. On balance, therefore, the ICSID system should not be regarded as a radical advance on more traditional techniques of dispute settlement between states and foreign investors. None the less, it does represent the only concerted international attempt to address specifically the special problems associated with this field, and this gives it a unique place in the international regime relating to foreign investment.

Notes

1   The Washington Convention on Settlement of Investment Disputes Between States and Nationals of Other States 1965: 4 ILM 524 (1965); 575 UNTS 159.

2   See D. P. O'Connell, *International Law*, 2nd edn (1970), vol. 1, pp. 106–7.

3   See, in relation to the status of natural persons under human rights treaties: Muchlinski, 'The status of the individual under the European Convention on Human Rights and contemporary international law', 34 ICLQ 376 (1985). For a discussion of the need to extend international personality to individuals as the scope of international law expands see Higgins, 'Conceptual thinking about the individual in international law', 4 Brit. J. Int. Stud. 1 (1978). On the artificiality of excluding the individual from international personality, see O'Connell, ibid., vol. I, pp. 107–8.

4   I. Brownlie, *Principles of Public International Law*, 5th edn (1998), p. 66.

5   See W. Friedmann, *The Changing Structure of International Law* (1964), pp. 221–31; 127 Hague Recueil (1969, II) p. 121–4; W. Jenks, 'Multinational entities and the law of nations' in W. Friedmann (ed.), *Transnational Law in a Changing Society* (1972), p. 70; D. A. Ijalaye, *The Extension of Corporate Personality in International Law* (Oceana, 1978), pp. 221–46.

6   See the *Texaco Arbitration* 17 ILM 1 (1978).

7   See *Liamco* v *Libya* 20 ILM (1981) p. 1, at pp. 34–5; *Aminoil* v *Kuwait* 21 ILM (1982) p. 976, paras 6–10 at pp. 1000–1.

8   See for the legal background to this issue M. Diez de Velasco, 'La protection diplomatique des sociétés et des actionnaires', 141 Hague Recueil (1974 I) 87–186; P. de Visscher, 'La protection diplomatique des personnes morales', 102 Hague Recueil (1961 I), 427–62; Feliciano, 'Legal problems of private international business enterprises', 118 Hague Recueil (1966 II), 284–95; Staker, 'Diplomatic protection of private business companies: determining corporate personality for international law purposes', 61 BYIL 155 (1990).

9   See *Mavromatis Palestine Concessions Case (Jurisdiction) Greece* v *United Kingdom* (1924) P. C. I. J. Reports, Series A, No. 2, at p. 12. See, to the same effect, the *Panevezys-Saldutiskis Case Estonia* v *Lithuania* (1939) P. C. I. J. Reports, Series A/B, No. 76, at p. 4.

10   As Brownlie puts it, 'The subject-matter of the claim is the individual and his property: the claim is that of the state' (note 4 above, at p. 482).

11   See O'Connell (note 2 above), at p. 109.

12   See Vernon, 'The multinationals: no strings attached', 33 *Foreign Policy* 121 at 126–7 (1978–9).

13 O'Connell (note 2 above), at p. 111.
14 For analysis of the local remedies rule see Brownlie (note 4 above), pp. 496–506; O'Connell (note 2 above), at pp. 1053–9. An exhaustive analysis of the applicable principles can be found in Cancado Trindade,*The Application of the Rule of Exhaustion of Local Remedies in International Law* (Cambridge University Press, 1983).
15 *Case Concerning The Barcelona Traction, Light and Power Company, Limited (New Application: 1962) (Belgium v Spain) Second Phase*, Judgment of 5 February 1970, I. C. J. Reports (1970), p. 3. For critical comment see Mann, 'The protection of shareholders' interests in the light of the Barcelona Traction Case', 67 AJIL p. 259 (1973); Higgins, 'Aspects of the case concerning the Barcelona Traction, Light and Power Company, Ltd.', 11 Virg. JIL p. 327 (1971); Lillich, 'The rigidity of Barcelona', 65 AJIL p. 522 (1971); Metzger 'Nationality of corporate investment under investment guaranty schemes – the relevance of Barcelona Traction', 65 AJIL p. 532 (1971). But see, for a defence of the Court's approach, Briggs, 'Barcelona Traction: the *jus standi* of Belgium', 65 AJIL 327 (1971); Abi-Saab, 'The international law of multinational corporations: a critique of American legal doctrines', 2 *Annals of International Studies* p. 97. (1971). For earlier international arbitral case-law and state practice on the nationality of corporations for the purposes of diplomatic protection see Kronstein, 'The nationality of international enterprises', 52 Col. L. R. p. 983 (1952); Ginther, 'Nationality of corporations', 16 *Osterreichische Zeitschrift für öffentliches Recht* 27 at 29 (1966); Jones, 'Claims on behalf of nationals who are shareholders in foreign companies', 26 BYIL 225 (1949); Harris, 'The protection of companies in international law in the light of the Nottebohm Case' 18 ICLQ 275 (1969). For more recent UK practice see Foreign and Commonwealth Office, *Rules Applying to International Claims* (latest revision March 1990). This revision is unchanged from earlier revisions. For an earlier published revision from 1985 see 37 ICLQ 1006–8 (1988), reproduced in D. J. Harris, *Cases and Materials on International Law*, 5th edn (Sweet & Maxwell, 1998), pp. 595, 622–3. On US practice see The American Law Institute's *Third Restatement of the Foreign Relations Law of the United States* (American Law Institute Publishers, 1987), vol. 2, s. 713, comment e, p. 219.
16 *Barcelona Traction*, p. 47, para. 90; Briggs, ibid., at p. 327.
17 See A. A. Fatouros, 'Transnational enterprise in the law of state responsibility', in R. Lillich (ed.), *State Responsibility for Injuries to Aliens* (University Press of Virginia, 1983), p. 361.
18 See further Wolfgang Peter, *Arbitration and the Renegotiation of International Investment Agreements* (Martinus Nijhoff, 1986).
19 On which see further chapter 16.
20 Latin American states espousing the Calvo Doctrine have sought to do so. By this doctrine a foreign investor is required to agree not to claim diplomatic protection as a means of settling an investment dispute with the host state but to rely on local remedies. See D. Shea, *The Calvo Clause* (University of Minnesota Press, 1955); Freeman, 'Recent aspects of the Calvo Doctrine and the challenge to international law', 40 AJIL 121

(1946). The original statement of the doctrine can be found in the work of its creator: C. Calvo, *Le droit international théorétique et pratique*, 5th edn (6 vols, 1896).

21 Conciliation is defined as 'a method for the settlement of international disputes of any nature according to which a Commission set up by the Parties, either on a permanent basis or an ad hoc basis to deal with a dispute, proceeds to the impartial examination of the dispute and attempts to define the terms of a settlement susceptible of being accepted by them, or of affording the Parties, with a view to its settlement, such aid as they may have requested': article 1 of the Regulations on the Procedure of International Conciliation adopted by the Institute of International Law in 1961, quoted in J. G. Merrills, *International Dispute Settlement*, 2nd edn (Grotius Publications, 1991), p. 59.

22 See generally A. Redfern and M. Hunter, *Law and Practice of International Commercial Arbitration*, 2nd edn (Sweet & Maxwell, 1991).

23 Markham Ball, 'Structuring the arbitration in advance – the arbitration clause in an international development agreement', in J. Lew (ed.), *Contemporary Problems in International Arbitration* (Queen Mary College Centre for Commercial Law Studies, 1986), p. 297 at p. 300.

24 Redfern and Hunter (note 22 above), at p. 56.

25 The non-appearance of the respondent state party to the arbitration is not infrequent. See, for example, the Libyan Oil Arbitrations: *BP* v *Libya* 53 ILR 297; *Texaco* v *Libya* 17 ILM 1 (1978); *Liamco* v *Libya* 20 ILM 1 (1981).

26 On which see chapters 28–33 in Lew (note 23 above), pp. 313–73. While immunity from execution may still be enjoyed by the foreign sovereign, there is a growing national case-law which holds that submission to international arbitration with a foreign corporation constitutes an implicit waiver of immunity from suit at the time of recognition proceedings following the making of an award against the state: *Société Européenne d'Etudes et d'Entreprises* v *Yugoslavia* (Cour de Cassation 18 November 1986) 26 ILM 377 (1987); see also, for other cases in France, the Netherlands and the United States, G. Delaume, *Transnational Contracts*, chapter XIV, para. 14:10 (booklet 16, release 90–2, May 1990).

27 The ICC Court of Arbitration has handled some 7,000 cases, including disputes between investors and host states, since it was founded in 1923. Its procedures are governed by the ICC Arbitration Rules. The ICC also offers Rules of Optional Conciliation. For the current version of the Rules see ICC Publication No. 447, 2nd edn (June 1990). For a full discussion of the history and workings of the ICC Court of Arbitration see W. Lawrence Craig, Williams F. Park and Jan Paulsson, *International Chamber of Commerce Arbitration* (ICC Publication No. 414/2, 1990, co-publication with Oceana); also published in two loose-leaf volumes as part of K. Simmonds and C. Schmitthoff (eds), *International Commercial Arbitration*. See also de Hancock, 'The ICC Court of Arbitration: the Institution and its procedures', 1 J. Int'l Arb. 21 (1984).

28 See, for example, *Southern Pacific Properties Limited v The Arab Republic of Egypt and the Egyptian General Company for Tourism and Hotels* 22 ILM 752

(1983); *Westland Helicopters Limited* v *Arab Organisation for Industrialisation, and United Arab Emirates, and Kingdom of Saudi Arabia, and State of Quatar, and Arab Republic of Egypt, and Arab British Helicopter Company* 23 ILM 1071 (1984). See also *Klöckner* v *Cameroon* extract from Award of 21 October 1983 cited in Paulsson 'The ICSID Klöckner v Cameroon award: the duties of partners in North–South development agreements', 1 J. Int. Arb. 145 at 149 (1984), where an ICC arbitration clause was held capable of ousting ICSID jurisdiction in relation to disputes arising exclusively from the contract containing the ICC clause.

29   See Sutherland, 'The World Bank Convention on the Settlement of Investment Disputes', 29 ICLQ 367 at 371 (1979).

30   Markham Ball (note 23 above), at p. 302.

31   See Craig, Park and Paulsson (note 27 above), para. 1.04, p. 8. A 1976 survey put the figure as high as one-third of all ICC arbitrations: Oppetit, 'Elements pour une sociologie de l'arbitrage', 27 *L'Année Sociologique* 179 at 189 (1976). A more recent study has put the figure of ICC arbitrations involving governmental or para-statal entities at one-sixth of the ICC arbitrations filed in 1986: Bond, 'ICC arbitration theory and practice', XXVI *Rassegna dell'Arbitrato* 141 at 143 (1986).

32   For a detailed analysis of the UNCITRAL Arbitration and Conciliation Rules, and of the Model Law on International Commercial Arbitration, see Isaak I. Dore, *Arbitration and Conciliation under the UNCITRAL Rules: a Textual Analysis* (Martinus Nijhoff, 1986). The United Nations Commission on International Trade Law (UNCITRAL) does not provide an institutional system of conciliation or arbitration. However, it has made major contributions to the development of unified rules of conciliation and arbitration. Thus UNCITRAL has been concerned with international commercial arbitration since its opening session in 1968. At its eleventh session, in June 1978, it included international conciliation in its work programme. These initiatives have resulted in the adoption of the UNCITRAL Arbitration Rules in 1976: UN GA Resolution 31/98 of 15 December 1976; for the text of the Rules see UN publication Sales No. E. 77. V. 6; Dore, ibid., appendix 2. The Conciliation Rules were adopted in 1980: see UNCITRAL, Report of 13th Session 35 UN GAOR Supp. (No. 17), UN Doc. A/35/17 (1980), pp. 32–8; Dore, ibid., appendix 1. In 1985 these Rules were supplemented by the UNCITRAL Model Law on International Commercial Arbitration: UN GA Resolution 40/72 of 11 December 1985; for the text of the Model Law see annex I to the Report of the UNCITRAL 18th Session GAOR, 40th Session Supp. No. 17. UN Doc. A/40/17; 'UNCITRAL – the United Nations Commission on International Trade Law' (UN publication Sales No. E. 86, V. 8) p. 157; Dore, ibid., appendix 4.

33   UNGA Res 31/98 of 15 December 1976, preamble.

34   For example, the Iran–United States Claims Tribunal uses a modified version of the UNCITRAL Rules as its procedural law: Markam Ball (note 23 above), at p. 304.

35   22 *UNCITRAL Yearbook* 441 (1991). For a full discussion see Dore (note 32 above), chapter 5. See also A. Asouzu, 'An introduction to the legal

framework for commercial arbitration and conciliation in Nigeria', 9 ICSID Rev-FILJ 214 (1994).

36   For references to the Model Law see note 32 above. See also the UNCITRAL Secretariat's Information Note on the Model Law UN Doc. A/CN, 9/309, 25 March 1988 (hereafter referred to as 'Note'). For a full commentary on the Model Law and its drafting history see Howard M. Holtzmann and Joseph E. Neuhaus, *A Guide to the UNCITRAL Model Law on International Commercial Arbitration Legislative History and Commentary* (T. M. Asser Instituut and Kluwer, 1989); A. Broches, *Commentary on the UNCITRAL Model Law on International Arbitration* (Kluwer, 1990).

37   The remainder of this chapter is an expanded and updated version of an earlier paper entitled 'Dispute settlement under the Washington Convention on the Settlement of Investment Disputes', presented at the Anglo-Soviet Symposium on International Law in May 1990 and published in W. E. Butler (ed.), *Control over Compliance with International Law* (Martinus Nijhoff, 1991), p. 175. For further references to the ICSID Convention see ICSID, *ICSID Bibliography* (Doc. ICSID/13/Rev. 2, March 1, 1992, and subsequent revisions). For a definitive list of cases brought before ICSID see ICSID, *ICSID Cases* (Doc. ICSID/16/Rev. 2, November 15, 1991 and subsequent revisions). ICSID awards are not published unless the parties give their consent. However, extracts from awards are often published in ICSID Rev-FILJ. ICSID also publishes a newsletter entitled *News From ICSID* twice yearly, and the Secretary-General submits an Annual Report. ICSID should be considered alongside MIGA as part of the World Bank's system of institutions dealing with foreign investment: see I. F. I. Shihata, 'Towards a greater depoliticisation of investment disputes: the roles of ICSID and MIGA', 1 ICSID Rev-FILJ 1 (1986), updated version published by ICSID in 1992; Rowat, 'Multilateral approaches to improving the investment climate of developing countries: the cases of ICSID and MIGA', 33 Harv. ILJ 103 (1992).

38   See further Branson and Tupman, 'Selecting an arbitral forum: a guide to cost-effective international arbitration', 24 Va. J. Int'l L. 917 (1984).

39   On which see the Washington Convention on Settlement of Investment Disputes Between States and Nationals of Other States 1965, articles 28–35: 4 ILM 524 at pp. 536–8. (1965). See further ICSID, *Basic Documents* (ICSID/15, January 1985).

40   See further ICSID, *Additional Facility for the Administration of Conciliation, Arbitration and Fact-finding Proceedings* (ICSID/11, June 1979).

41   Note 1 above.

42   See *List of Contracting States and Signatories of the Convention* in News from ICSID, Vol. 11, No. 2 (Summer 1994), p. 6.

43   The principal organs of ICSID are as follows. (a) The Administrative Council, the governing body of ICSID, comprised of one representative from each contracting state, and chaired *ex officio* by the president of the World Bank. Its principal functions, outlined by article 6 of the Convention, are to adopt financial and administrative regulations, rules of procedure for the institution of conciliation and arbitration proceedings and rules of procedure for the conduct of conciliation and arbitration proceed-

ings. (b) The Secretariat, the principal administrative organ consisting of the Secretary-General, one or more deputy Secretaries-General and their staff. The Secretary-General is charged with the initial review of applications for conciliation or arbitration. He acts as registrar in conciliation and arbitration proceedings. (c) The Panels of Conciliators and Arbitrators, which are separate panels of experts in the fields of law, commerce, industry or finance who are charged to act in ICSID proceedings in the exercise of independent judgment (see article 14 of the Convention). Each Contracting State designates four members to a Panel. They need not be nationals of the appointing state. The Chairman of the Administrative Council may designate ten persons to each Panel, each of whom must be of a different nationality and who must represent the major legal systems and major forms of industrial and commercial activity.

44　See Sutherland (note 29 above), at pp. 374–8. For example, the Bank acted in a conciliatory role between shareholders and the Egyptian government following the latter's nationalization of the Suez Canal Company in 1956.

45　See articles 26 and 53 of the Convention.

46　By article 54 of the Convention each Contracting State is required to enforce the 'pecuniary obligations' imposed by an ICSID award within its territory as if the award were 'a final judgment of a court in that state'. See further below.

47　4 ILM 524 (1965) at 525, paras 11–12.

48　Delaume, 'ICSID arbitration', in J. D. M. Lew (ed.), *Contemporary Problems in International Arbitration* (Queen Mary College, Centre for Commercial Law Studies, 1986), chapter 4, p. 23.

49　It is not intended to review every issue pertaining to the jurisdiction of ICSID here. See further the articles on ICSID jurisdiction by Amerasinghe in 5 J. Mart. L. & Comm 211 (1974); 47 BYIL 227 (1974–5); 19 Indian J. Int'l L. 166 (1979); Tupman, 'Case studies in the jurisdiction of the International Centre for Settlement of Investment Disputes', 35 ICLQ 813 (1986); Lamn, 'Jurisdiction of the International Centre for the Settlement of Investment Disputes', 6 ICSID Rev-FILJ 462 (1991).

50　ICSID has devised model clauses by which consent can be unambiguously given in a manner that fulfils the jurisdictional requirements of the Convention: see ICSID, *Model Clauses* (Doc ICSID/5/Rev. 2 1992), reproduced in 8 ICSID Rev-FILJ 134 (1993). For analysis see Amerasinghe, 'How to use the International Centre for the Settlement of Investment Disputes by Reference to its Model Clauses', 13 Ind JIL 530 (1973), and 'Model clauses for settlement of foreign investment disputes', 28 Arb. J. 232 (1973).

51　This was accepted in the Report of the Executive Directors on the Washington Convention, para. 24: see 4 ILM 524 (1965) at p. 527.

52　*Holiday Inns v Morocco* (Settlement 17 October 1978), discussed by Pierre Lalive in 'The first World Bank arbitration (Holiday Inns v Morocco) – some legal problems', 51 BYIL 123 (1980) at 159–60.

53　*Amco-Asia v Republic of Indonesia* (Award on Jurisdiction September 25, 1983) 23 ILM 351 (1984); 89 ILR 379 (1992).

54   Ibid., para. 14 at p. 359.

55   *Alcoa Minerals of Jamaica* v *The Government of Jamaica* (Decision of July 5–6, 1975) summarized by Schmidt in 17 Harv. ILJ 90, 96 ff (1976); 4 YB Com. Arb. 206 (1979) (excerpts).

56   See Delaume (note 48 above), at p. 796.

57   Washington Convention articles 68, 70, 73. See further IBRD, 'Memorandum on signature and ratification, acceptance or approval of the Convention on the Settlement of Investment Disputes between States and Nationals of Other States' (reprinted May 1991).

58   Amerasinghe, 'Jurisdiction *ratione personae* under the Convention on the Settlement of Investment Disputes Between States and Nationals of Other States', 48 BYIL 227 at 232 (1974). See also *Holiday Inns and Occidental Petroleum Corp* v *Morocco* in Lalive, 'The First "World Bank" arbitration (Holiday Inns v Morocco) – some legal problems', 51 BYIL 123 at 142–6, 'No. 20. The Tribunal is of the opinion that the Convention allows parties to subordinate the entry into force of an arbitration clause to the subsequent fulfilment of certain conditions, such as the adherence of the states concerned to the Convention, or the incorporation of the company envisaged by the agreement.'

59   Amerasinghe, ibid., p. 233.

60   Ibid., p. 234.

61   Ibid., p. 234.

62   On what constitutes approval of consent for the purposes of article 25(3) see ibid., pp. 236–8.

63   Sutherland (note 29 above), p. 383.

64   Washington Convention, article 25(2)(a). For detailed analysis see Amerasinghe (note 58 above), pp. 246–53.

65   See *Southern Pacific Properties (Middle East) Limited* v *Arab Republic of Egypt Award* on the Merits 20 May 1992: 32 ILM 933 at paras 133–44, pp. 962–4 (1993).

66   Note 15 above.

67   *Holiday Inns* v *Morocco* (Decision of 1 July 1973), para. 33, cited in Lalive (note 52 above), at p. 141.

68   Ibid.

69   *Amco Asia* v *Republic of Indonesia* (note 53 above) paras 14–15, at ILM, p. 359–63; ILR, pp. 382–8.

70   *LETCO* v *Liberia* (Decision of 31 March 1986) 26 ILM 647 at 652–4. However, in the absence of clear evidence of actual foreign control, the mere fact of agreement to treat the claimant as a foreign national is insufficient to establish jurisdiction. See *Vacuum Salt Products Limited* v *Ghana* (Case No. ARB/92/1) 9 ICSID Rev-FILJ 71 (1994).

71   Note 53 above.

72   See Tupman, 'Case studies in the jurisdiction of the International Centre for Settlement of Investment Disputes', 35 ICLQ 813 at 837–8 (1986).

73   Note 52 above.

74   See e.g. *Company X* v *State A* in *News from ICSID*, Vol. 2, No. 2, Summer 1985, pp. 3–6. State A objected to ICSID jurisdiction based on the fact that, notwithstanding its apparent consent to jurisdiction under article 25(2)(b), the immediate controller of the local subsidiary, Company X,

had the nationality of a state not party to the Convention and so the requirements of article 25(2)(b) were not met. The Tribunal rejected this argument on the ground that since the immediate controller was itself controlled by nationals of a Contracting State, Company X was entitled to bring ICSID proceedings, it having the nationality of those foreign controllers for the purpose of article 25(2)(b).

75 According to Thompson, the *ad hoc* committee set up to review the award of the Tribunal in *Klöckner* v *Cameroon* may have gone too far in refusing to overturn the decision of the Tribunal, having found that the Tribunal's reasons for giving itself jurisdiction were 'incorrect'. The *ad hoc* Committee held that this did not amount to a 'manifest excess of powers' within article 52(1)(b) of the Convention and, therefore, did not constitute a ground for the annulment of the award: see 3 Jo. Int'L. Arb. 93 (1986); 1 ICSID Rev-FILJ 89 (1986).

76 Note 48 above at p. 26; Delaume, 'ICSID arbitration and the courts', 77 AJIL 784 at 795 (1983) and 'Le Centre International pour le Reglement des Differends Relatifs aux Investissements (CIDRI)', 109 JDI 775 at 800–8 (1982).

77 See *Liberian Eastern Timber Corp. (LETCO)* v *Government of Liberia* 26 ILM 647 (1987); *FEDAX N.V.* v *Venezuela* 37 ILM 1378 (1998).

78 *Alcoa* v *Jamaica* (note 55 above).

79 See Delaume, 77 AJIL 784 at 795 (1983).

80 4 ILM 524 at p. 528. (1965).

81 See 20 ILM 666 (1981).

82 Ibid., at 669 or 505 F Supp. 141–4 (1981).

83 (USCA DC Cir.) 21 ILM 1355 (1982) and 22 ILM 86 (1983) or 693 F. 2d 1094 (1982).

84 See Delaume's criticism of the US Court of Appeals decision (note 76 above), 77 AJIL 784 at pp. 789–92.

85 *Republic of Guinea* v *MINE* 24 ILM 1639 (1985) (Court of First Instance, Antwerp, 27 September 1985).

86 *Guinea* v *MINE* 26 ILM 382 (1987) (Swiss Surveillance Authority 7 October 1986).

87 *SOGUIPECHE* v *Atlantic Triton Co.* 24 ILM 340 (1985) (Court of Appeal, Rennes, 26 October 1984).

88 *SOGUIPECHE* v *Atlantic Triton Co.* 26 ILM 373 (1987) (Cour de Cassation 18 November 1986). For a view supporting this decision on the ground that the ICSID convention was never intended to prevent national courts from imposing provisional measures of attachment while ICSID proceedings were pending see: Gaillard, 114 JDI 125 (1987).

89 ICSID, *Arbitration Rules*, Rule 39(5).

90 *News from ICSID*, Vol. 2, No. 1, Winter 1985, p. 6. See also Gaillard (note 88 above).

91 See the Decision of the *ad hoc* Committee on Annulment of the award of the Tribunal in *Klöckner* v *Cameroon* 1 ICSID Rev-FILJ 89 at pp. 110–13 (1986), where the Committee held that the Tribunal had not applied 'the law of the Contracting State', by reason of its assumption that the principle of good faith was a principle of Cameroonian law without referring to the rules and conditions under which it was implemented or to the limits of its

operation. However, the first *ad hoc* Committee in *Amco Asia* v *Indonesia* 89 ILR (1992) at pp. 521–2 held that the mere misconstruction of the applicable law was insufficient to warrant annulment.

92   26 ILM 657 (1987).

93   Ibid., at p. 658.

94   30 ILM 577 (1991). See too *AMT v Zaire* 36 ILM 1531 (1997).

95   Ibid., para. 20. The Tribunal noted that by article 157 of the Sri Lanka Constitution the Treaty had become part of Sri Lankan law. It went on to hold that the Treaty applied as a *lex specialis* which was part of a wider source of rules, from both international and domestic sources, which helped to define the applicable Treaty norms: ibid., paras 21–4. See, however, the Dissenting Opinion of S. K. B. Asante, ibid., at pp. 630–2 for a strong critique of the majority opinion.

96   *Amco Asia Corp.* v *Indonesia* (Decision of *Ad Hoc* Committee May 16, 1986) 25 ILM 1439 (1986) paras 19–22 at ILM p. 1445–6, 89 ILR (1992) at pp. 519–20; see also *Klöckner* v *Cameroon* (Decision of *Ad Hoc* Committee May 3, 1985), note 75 above.

97   89 ILR 580 at pp. 593–4 (1992).

98   Ibid., para. 40, at p. 594.

99   Redfern, 'ICSID – losing its appeal?', 3 Arb. Int'l 98 at 106 (1987).

100   *Amco Asia Corp.* v *Indonesia* (note 96 above), first *ad hoc* Committee para. 21, ILM, p. 1446; ILR, p. 521.

101   Compare Prof. Dupuy's theory of the 'internationalization' of economic development agreements in *Texaco* v *Libya* 17 ILM 1 (1978), esp. at para. 45.

102   Brownlie (note 4 above), at pp. 34–6. By article 27 Vienna Convention on the Law of Treaties 1969: 'A party may not invoke the provisions of its internal law as justification for its failure to perform a treaty'. Similarly, by article 13 of the Draft Declaration on the Rights and Duties of States 1949, (YBILC 1949, pp. 286–8): 'Every state has the duty to carry out in good faith its obligations arising from treaties and other sources of international law, and it may not invoke provisions in its constitution or its laws as an excuse for failure to perform this duty.'

103   Award on the Merits 20 May 1992: 32 ILM 933 (1993).

104   Note 75 above.

105   Note 96 above.

106   *Ad hoc* Committee Decision of December 22, 1989: 5 ICSID Rev-FILJ 95 (1990).

107   See note 96 above, paras 95–8. The *ad hoc* Committee explained this error on the basis that the Tribunal had failed to distinguish loan capital from equity capital as it should have done in view of article 2 of the Indonesian Foreign Investment Law, which limits qualified foreign investment to equity capital.

108   *Amco* v *Republic of Indonesia* (Resubmitted case) (Res Judicata Effect of Previous Award and Decision), 27 ILM 1281 (1988); 89 ILR (1992) p. 55. For comment see Curtis, 83 AJIL 106 (1989).

109   See 89 ILR (1992) p. 580 (Merits); p. 568 (Rectification).

110   89 ILR (1992) p. 661.

111   It rejects the parties' applications for annulment of the Award of the Second Tribunal and annuls the Decision on Supplemental Decisions and Rectification of October 1990: *News From ICSID*, Vol. 10, No. 1 (Winter 1993), p. 2.

112   ICSID, *ICSID Cases* (note 37 above), at p. 17.

113   See Redfern, 'ICSID – losing its appeal', 3 Arb Int'l 98 (1987); Feldman, 'The annulment proceedings and finality of ICSID arbitral awards', 2 ICSID Rev-FILJ 85 (1987); Schatz, 'The effect of the annulment decisions in Amco v Indonesia and Klöckner v Cameroon: the future of the International Centre for Settlement of Investment Disputes', 3 Am. U. J. Int'l L. & Pol. 481 (1988); Reisman, 'The breakdown of the control mechanism in ICSID arbitration', (1989: 4) Duke LJ 739.

114   Redfern, ibid., at p. 109.

115   See Feldman (note 113 above).

116   Report of the Secretary-General to the Administrative Council ICSID Doc No. AC/86/4, October 2, 1986, annex A at 3; ICSID, *Annual Report 1988*, p. 4. See also K. Jacob, 'Reinvigorating ICSID with a new mission and with renewed respect for party autonomy', 33 Va. J. Int'l L 123 (1993).

117   Article 54 (2) of the Washington Convention.

118   Ibid., article 54(3)

119   Ibid., article 55.

120   See, for example, the US case *LETCO* v *Government of Liberia* 650 F. Supp. 73 (SDNY 1986), 26 ILM 695 (1987) aff'd memo No. 86–9047 (2d Cir., May 19,1987). See also Georges Delaume 'Sovereign immunity and transnational arbitration', in Lew (note 23 above), chapter 28, p. 313. More recently the French courts have had occasion to consider this issue: see *SOABI (SEUTIN)* v *Senegal* (Cour de Cassation, 11 June, 1991) 30 ILM 1167 (1991). The Cour de Cassation held that a foreign state that has consented to ICSID arbitration has thereby agreed that the award may be granted recognition (*exequatur*), which, as such, does not constitute a measure of execution that might raise issues pertaining to the immunity from execution of the state concerned. The ICSID Convention provided an autonomous and simple system of recognition which excluded domestic rules concerning recognition of foreign awards. The Award in *SOABI* v *Senegal* is reproduced in 6 ICSID Rev-FILJ 125 (1991).

121   For conciliation see article 28 of the Convention; for arbitration see article 36 of the Convention.

122   See article 41 of the Washington Convention.

123   Ibid., article 29(1)(conciliation); article 37(1)(arbitration).

124   Ibid., article 29(2); article 37(2).

125   Ibid., article 30(conciliation); article 38(arbitration).

126   Ibid., article 31.

127   Ibid., article 32.

128   Ibid., article 34(1).

129   Ibid., article 34(2).

130   Ibid.

131   Ibid., article 35.

132　Ibid., article 39.

133　Ibid., article 45.

134　See *Liberian Eastern Tree Corp. (LETCO)* v *Government of Liberia* 26 ILM 647 at pp. 654–7 (1987). See ICSID, *Arbitration Rules*, Rule 42 in ICSID, *Basic Documents* (note 39 above).

135　See Washington Convention articles 48–9.

136　Ibid., article 59.

137　Ibid., article 60(1).

138　Ibid., article 60(2).

139　Ibid., article 61(1).

140　Ibid., article 61(2).

141　Markham Ball (note 23 above), at p. 303.

142　ICSID, *Administrative and Financial Regulations*, Reg. 14(3), ICSID, *Basic Documents* (note 39 above), at p. 33.

143　Ibid., Reg. 14(1).

144　See ICSID, *Annual Report 1992*, annex 1, p, 12.

145　*News from ICSID*, Vol. 10, No. 1 (Winter 1993), p. 1. See for examples of such provisions in recent bilateral investment treaties: Australia–China Agreement, July 11, 1988, article XII(4): 28 ILM 121 (1989) at p. 134; China–Japan, August 27, 1988, article 11 (arbitration board to be fashioned after ICSID and procedure shall be determined with reference to ICSID procedures): 28 ILM 575 (1989) at p. 587. In the agreements with France of May 30, 1984, and UK of May 15, 1986, the Parties agree by way of an Exchange of Notes, that should China become a party to the Washington Convention, the Parties will conclude an additional agreement concerning categories of dispute to be submitted to ICSID: see France–China Agreement, 234 ILM 537 (1985) at 565; Denza, 'Investment protection treaties: United Kingdom experience', 36 (1987) ICLQ 908 at 921.

146　Ibid.

147　See chapter 6, notes 180–1 and see note 42 above.

148　See further references at note 20 above.

149　News from ICSID, Vol. 1, No. 2 (Summer 1984), pp. 2–3, 'ICSID and Latin America'.

150　See Delaume (note 48 above), pp. 24–5 and ICSID, *Annual Report 1986*, p. 4. See also for analysis up to 1987 *News from ICSID*, Vol. 4, No. 1 (Winter 1987), pp. 6–7.

151　See ICSID, *ICSID Cases* (note 37 above).

152　See ICSID, *Annual Reports 1987–91*, 'Introduction by the Secretary General'.

153　*News From ICSID*, Vol. 10, No. 1 (Winter 1993), p. 2. The cases submitted in 1992 are: *Vacuum Salt Products Ltd* v *Ghana* (Case ARB/92/1); *Scimitar Exploration Limited* v *Bangladesh and Bangladesh Oil, Gas and Mineral Corp.* (Case ARB/92/2). The case submitted in 1993 is *American Manufacturing & Trading Corp.* v *Zaire* (Case ARB/93/1). The case submitted in 1994 is *Philippe Gruslin* v *Government of Malaysia* (Case No. ARB/94/1).

154　ICSID, *Annual Report 1989*, p. 4.

155 Ibid.
156 O'Keefe, 'The International Centre for the Settlement of Investment Disputes', (1980) *Yearbook of World Affairs* p. 4.
157 Note 154 above.
158 Delaume (note 48 above), p. 25.
159 Ryans and Baker, 'The International Centre for the Settlement of Investment Disputes', 10 JWTL 65 (1976).
160 *News from ICSID*, Vol. 1, No. 1 (Winter 1984), p. 1.
161 See e.g. article 4 of Law No. 85–03 of January 29, 1985, of the Republic of Togo, 'Tout different qui pourrait surgir entre le Gouvernement Togolais et l'investisseur au sujet de l'une ou plusieurs clauses de la présente loi est réglé a l'amiable. En cas de désaccord persistant, le conflit est soumis a l'arbitrage du Centre International pour le Règlement des Differents Relatifs aux Investissements (CIRDI) pour règlement definitif', reproduced in *News From ICSID*, Vol. 3, No. 2 (Summer 1986), p. 8.
162 *News from ICSID*, Vol. 3, No. 2 (Summer 1986), p. 8.
163 For example, articles 30 and 31 of Law No. 85–001 of June 18 1985 of the Democratic Republic of Madagascar. This offers three alternative means of settling disputes between Madagascar and foreign investors: (i) under the provisions of the Malagasy law itself; (ii) the ICSID Convention; or (iii) the Additional Facility administered by ICSID. See, for a similar provision, Tanzania: National Investment (Promotion and Protection) Act 1990 (Act No. 10 of 1990) s. 29(2) (dispute may be submitted to ICSID as one of three alternative methods of arbitration). See also Uganda Investment Code 1991 (Statute No. 1, 1991), s. 30 (2)(a) (ICSID may be mutually agreed by the parties); Zambia Investment Act 1991 (No. 19 of 1991), s. 40(6)(c) (dispute may be referred to ICSID).
164 Such an issue arose at the Hearings on Jurisdiction in *Southern Pacific Properties (Middle East) Limited* v *Arab Republic of Egypt* Decision on Jurisdiction of 27 November 1985, 16 YB Com. Arb. 19 (1991)(excerpts); Decision on Jurisdiction of 14 April 1988, 16 YB. Com. Arb. 28 (1991) (excerpts). See also Award on Merits of 20 May 1992, 32 ILM 933 at paras 8–24, pp. 938–40 (1993); note Dissenting Opinion of Arbitrator El Mahdi, ibid., at pp. 1026–9.
165 See 'ICSID and bilateral investment treaties' in *News from ICSID*, Vol. 2, No. 1 (Winter 1985), p. 12 at pp. 13–14 for examples of clauses containing such a binding commitment: article 11 of the Netherlands–Indonesia Treaty of 7 July 1968; article VIII of the Egypt–Yugoslavia Treaty of 3 June 1977; article 8(1) of the UK–Bangladesh Treaty of 19 June 1980; article 6 of the France–Senegal Treaty of 8 September 1975; article VII of the US–Senegal Treaty of 6 December 1983. On treaties entered into by Nigeria with the UK and the Netherlands see Asouzu (note 35 above).
166 For examples of bilateral treaties which show a willingness, but not a duty, to consent to ICSID arbitration upon request of the investor see ibid., p. 14, article 5, Treaty between France and Malaysia of 24 April 1975; article 6, Treaty between Sweden and Malaysia of 3 March 1979. Other treaties merely note that the host state shall give 'sympathetic consideration' to the possibility of consent to ICSID arbitration: see ibid., p. 14, article XI

Netherlands–Kenya Treaty of 11 September 1970. Some treaties simply list ICSID arbitration as one option should the parties fail to settle their dispute amicably: see ibid., p. 16, UK–St Lucia Treaty of 18 January 1983.

167   Sutherland (note 29 above), at pp. 370–3.

The Codification of International Standards for the Treatment of Foreign Investors

The aim of this chapter is to consider attempts at the codification of agreed international standards by which relations between MNEs and host states can be regulated. Such attempts have been made in the context of conflicts between states over the content and legal validity of international minimum standards for the treatment of aliens and their property, already briefly discussed in chapter 14.[1] The result of these conflicts has been uncertainty as to the content of customary international law in the field of foreign investment. Indeed, in the *Barcelona Traction* case, the ICJ maintained that there was no single accepted body of international law that laid down universally accepted standards for the treatment of foreign investors by host states.[2] The Court saw the reason for this as lying in a period of 'an intense conflict of systems and interests' between states, from which no generally accepted rules of international law in the field could emerge on the basis of an *opinio juris* among states. Such standards as applied were the product of bilateral agreements between states and, therefore, could not bind other states.

Against this background numerous attempts have been made over time to develop an agreed international code for the regulation of foreign investor–host state relations. Initially, attempts at codification sought the conclusion of a multilateral convention under the auspices of an international organization. Such attempts were made periodically between the 1920s and the early 1960s.[3] Thus, in 1929, the League of Nations held a diplomatic conference for the purpose of concluding an international convention on the treatment of foreigners and foreign enterprises.[4] This was followed in 1930 by the Hague Conference on the Codification of International Law, which included the subject of the responsibility of states for damage caused in their territory to the person or property of foreigners.[5] Neither initiative met with success, owing to the refusal of Latin American, East European and ex-colonial states to accept the traditional international minimum standards of treatment insisted upon by the capital-exporting states.[6]

After the Second World War attempts at a general multilateral treaty that included a code on the protection of foreign investment were revived.[7] The major attempt was the Charter of the International Trade Organization signed at Havana, Cuba, on 24 March 1948. The Charter contained a number of provisions relevant to the regulation of foreign investment by corporations, including proposals for the control of restrictive business practices,[8] provisions protecting the security of foreign investments[9] and an assertion of the right of capital importing states to control the conditions of entry and establishment for inward investment.[10] The inclusion of this right, and the absence of any unequivocal provision for compensation in the case of expropriation, caused widespread opposition to the Havana Charter among business interests and led, ultimately, to its demise when the United States and other signatory states did not ratify it.[11]

Thereafter, attempts at stimulating interest in a multilateral convention on foreign investment were made mainly by private sector bodies, including the ICC and various pressure groups.[12] In particular, in 1957, the German Society to Advance the Protection of Foreign Investments published a draft code, entitled 'International Convention for the Mutual Protection of Private Property Rights in Foreign Countries'.[13] In early 1958, another privately inspired draft convention on foreign investments came from a group of European international lawyers headed by Sir Hartley Shawcross.[14] These two initiatives were combined into a single draft convention in 1959.[15] This convention was taken up by the then OEEC (now OECD) for consideration. It led to the OECD Draft Convention on the Protection of Foreign Property.[16] However, this draft convention failed to achieve sufficient support to be opened for signature, owing to the reluctance of the less developed members of the organization (such as Greece, Portugal and Turkey) to bind themselves to some of the proposed provisions, in view of their heavy leaning towards the interests of capital exporters.[17] Instead, the Council of the OECD, by a resolution adopted on 12 October 1967, commended the draft convention to Member States as a model for investment protection treaties and as a basis for ensuring the observance of the principles of international law which it contained.[18] Thus the OECD draft, while failing to contribute to a general codification of the international law relating to foreign investments, has provided 'important guidelines for some of the more fundamental provisions on the treatment and protection of investments included in bilateral investment treaties'.[19]

Although they were not aimed at the regulation of MNEs as such, these earlier attempts at codification are significant as examples of the problems involved in achieving consensus on the rules that govern the relationship between foreign investors (including MNEs) and host states. They are also significant in their emphasis on investor protection, a theme that has been a consistent factor both in moves towards the conclusion of codes of conduct on MNEs and in relation to the content of recent bilateral investment treaties (BITs). The latter are of such significance that they will be studied separately in the next chapter.

Since the early 1970s concern about the activities of MNEs has prompted the negotiation and/or adoption of codes of conduct on the subject by various international organizations. Given the constraints of space it is intended to focus only on those aspects of selected major codes which offer insights into the role of traditional international standards of treatment in the regulation of MNEs, and which illustrate the evolution and decline of the 'codification movement' as a means of regulating host state–MNE relations. Discussion will centre on the ANCOM Code, as the sole example of a supranational approach to MNE regulation undertaken by a group of developing countries, on the OECD Guidelines on Multinational Enterprises and on the now shelved draft UN Code of Conduct for Transnational Corporations. The most recent code of conduct, the World Bank Guidelines on the Treatment of Foreign Investment of 1992, and the standard setting provisions of the Multilateral Investment Guarantee Agency Convention (MIGA) will also be briefly considered.

1 The Andean Common Market (ANCOM)

The ANCOM states[20] were the first to promulgate an interstate code on the regulation of foreign investment when they adopted the Andean Foreign Investment Code, contained in Decision 24 of the Commission of the Cartagena Accord of 21 December 1970.[21] This was repealed and superseded by a revised Code contained in Commission Decision 220 of 11 May 1987,[22] which has in turn been repealed and replaced by Decision 291 of 21 March 1991.[23] The effects of the original and revised Codes on the evolution of international standards for the regulation of MNE–host state relations are instructive, as the changes in the Andean Code are a microcosm of the changing attitude of capital-importing states towards the treatment of foreign investors over the past two decades.

The Andean Code, in its 1970s version, introduced a restrictive regime for the regulation of foreign investments in the sub-region. This was characterized by, *inter alia*: the classification of enterprises according to their degree of foreign ownership;[24] restrictions on the entry of new foreign investments,[25] the repatriation of capital,[26] reinvestment of profits without prior authorization by the relevant national authority[27] and the use of foreign credit;[28] comprehensive controls over the importation of technology by means of technology transfer contracts, including prohibitions against restrictive clauses favourable to the interests of the foreign owner of the technology;[29] provisions for the 'indigenization' of 'foreign' enterprises, by their conversion into 'mixed' or 'national' enterprises as defined in the Code, in return for access to the benefits of the free trade area set up by the ANCOM states;[30] and special regulations concerning specific sectors of industry.[31]

The original Andean Code was ambiguous on the applicability of international minimum standards concerning the treatment of foreign investors. Although its provisions could not be said to violate any such standards, Decision 24 may have excluded the international minimum standard of treatment through the terms of article 50, which accorded no more than national treatment to foreign investors, and article 51, which limited dispute settlement procedures to those of the host state.[32] Furthermore, the Code was silent on the question of expropriation. Thus it would be difficult not to see the original Andean Code as standing in opposition to traditional international standards for the treatment of foreign investors.

The consensus upon which the original Code was based proved to be fragile and short lived. The first dissenter was Chile after 1973.[33] Gradually, the other ANCOM states also distanced themselves from the terms of Decision 24, forced by changed circumstances in the global economy and, in particular, by the consequences of the 'debt crisis' to seek new investment capital by way of foreign equity rather than loans. Peru was the first to do so in 1980.[34] Peru was followed in 1983 by Equador and Colombia, both of which unilaterally enacted regulations favourable to foreign investment in direct violation of the norms of Decision 24.[35] In 1986 Venezuela passed new foreign investment and technology transfer regulations in Decree 1200 of 16 July 1986, which reversed that country's previously strict attitude towards foreign investment.[36]

Clearly, in the circumstances, Decision 24 was becoming a dead letter. It had to be fundamentally revised. The result was Commission Decision 220.[37] This Decision substantially liberalized the terms of Decision 24. Although it retained the broad structure of Decision 24, Decision 220 shifted the emphasis away from mandatory restrictions on foreign investment to be applied uniformly by all ANCOM states, towards greater freedom for investors and increased state autonomy in policy development and application. However, as regards general standards of treatment, Decision 220 retained the principle that Member Countries should not grant foreign investors more favourable treatment than that granted to national investors.[38] On the other hand, in the field of dispute settlement, Member Countries were free to adopt international minimum standards under their local law, if they so chose.[39]

Decision 220 was replaced by Decision 291 in 1991.[40] This has effectively abandoned any common policy on foreign investment. As regards standards of treatment, by article 2 of Decision 291, 'foreign investors shall have the same rights and obligations as pertain to national investors, except as otherwise provided in the legislation of each Member Country'. Thus, the Member Countries are left entirely free, if they wish, to adopt national laws and policies that protect international minimum standards of treatment. Furthermore, as regards dispute settlement, by article 10 of Decision 291, 'Member Countries shall apply that provided in their domestic legislation with respect to the solution of controversies or conflicts deriving from direct foreign investment or subregional investment or the transfer of foreign technology'. Therefore, the answer to the question of whether international minimum standards apply to the treatment of a foreign investment in an ANCOM Member State lies with the content of each respective national law.

The significance of these developments as regards the affirmation of international standards for the treatment of foreign investors is debatable. The change in approach of the ANCOM states is no more than a shift in economic policy. It is uncertain that it represents an endorsement of the international legal standards espoused by the capital-exporting states. Indeed, a recent study of the national foreign investment laws of the ANCOM Member Countries concludes that, although major steps have been taken in liberalizing the conditions of entry and establishment for foreign investors, and to ensure the free repatriation of capital, little has changed in the restrictive approach taken to international minimum standards of treatment. All Member Countries, save for Peru, deny foreign investors the right to diplomatic protection, all guarantee equal treatment but no better than that accorded to national investors, all have exclusive jurisdiction over investment disputes and none accepts the 'Hull formula' on compensation for expropriation.[41] However, this approach may change over time and international minimum standards may be recognized in national laws. Much depends on internal policy developments.

2   The OECD Guidelines on Multinational Enterprises[42]

The origins of the Guidelines lie in the response of the major industrialized countries to the economic and political changes of the early 1970s.[43] This was a time when the less developed countries (LDCs) were demanding a change in the balance of world economic power, through the adoption of a New International Economic Order under the auspices of the UN. Within this process the 'MNE issue' was placed on the international political agenda, resulting in the decision of the UN Economic and Social Committee, in 1974, to set up a Commission on Transnational Corporations charged with the goal of formulating a binding Code of Conduct for Transnational Corporations (TNCs).[44] This was followed in 1976 by the decisions of UNCTAD IV to start negotiations on Codes of Conduct in the areas of Transfer of Technology and Restrictive Business Practices, and of the ILO to draft a set of principles on MNE behaviour in the field of social policy.[45] The threat of increased LDC control over the activities of MNEs was further accentuated by the waves of nationalizations in the 1960s and early 1970s, and by the oil crisis precipitated by the activities of OPEC in 1973. To counter these developments the OECD ministers, urged on by the US government, decided to adopt their own policy on MNEs, which it was hoped would influence the UN's attempts at 'codification' to move away from a highly regulatory position of 'MNE control'.[46]

A second reason for the move towards the adoption of OECD Guidelines on MNEs was to meet demands from within the OECD countries for greater control over MNEs. Canada, the Netherlands and the Scandinavian states supported such controls.[47] Furthermore, demands for controls over MNEs were articulated by the trade unions through the Trades Union Advisory Committee (TUAC) of the OECD. The above-mentioned Member Countries and the unions wanted a legally binding code. This was counterbalanced by calls from the representatives of the business community, articulated through the Business and Industry Advisory Committee to the OECD (BIAC), for greater emphasis on the removal of obstacles to foreign direct investment. Thus the Guidelines can be seen as a 'corporatist' initiative.[48]

To achieve its objectives the OECD set up, in January 1975, the 'Committee on International Investment and Multinational Enterprises'.[49] After eighteen months of negotiations the Guidelines were adopted as an Annex to the 'OECD Declaration on International

Investment and Multinational Enterprises' passed by the governments of the Member Countries on 21 June 1976, with the exception of Turkey, which abstained. In addition to the Guidelines, three further Council Decisions were passed on the same day concerning, respectively, the principle of 'national treatment', 'international investment incentives and disincentives' and 'inter-governmental consultation procedures on the guidelines for multinational enterprises'. Together, these form a comprehensive system for the development of standards on the regulation of MNE–host state relations. The principal provisions will be considered in turn.

2.1   The Policy of the Guidelines

OECD policy on MNEs proceeds with the assumption that such corporations ought to be encouraged to make a positive contribution to the economies of the Member Countries.[50] However, the Guidelines recognize that the organization of MNEs beyond the national framework 'may lead to abuse of concentrations of economic power and to conflicts with national policy objectives. In addition, the complexity of these multinational enterprises and the difficulty of perceiving their diverse structures, operations and policies sometimes give rise to concern.'[51] Accordingly, the Guidelines set out to achieve the common aim of encouraging 'the positive contributions which multinational enterprises can make to economic and social progress and to minimise and resolve the difficulties to which their various operations may give rise' and, thereby, contribute to 'improving the foreign investment climate'.[52]

The Guidelines seek to extend this general approach to all states. They recommend that the Member Countries should 'give their full support to efforts undertaken in co-operation with non-member countries, and in particular with developing countries, with a view to improving the welfare and living standards of all people both by encouraging the positive contributions which multinational enterprises can make and by minimising and resolving the problems which may arise in connection with their activities.'[53] This is a significant objective, given that the headquarters of most MNEs are located in OECD countries.[54] It suggests that the Member Countries may have a moral duty to ensure that the activities of their MNEs in host states do not contribute to the detriment of those states' economies, particularly if they are less developed. This represents an apparent departure from the OECD's earlier policy of preoccupation with the protection of foreign investments, without considering the interests of the host state, and, in particular, those of the less developed host state.[55]

2.2   The Legal Nature of the Guidelines

By para. 6 of the Introduction to the Guidelines:

The Guidelines set out below are recommendations jointly addressed by Member countries to multinational enterprises operating in their territories. These Guidelines, which take into account the problems which can arise because of the international structure of these enterprises, lay down standards for the activities of these enterprises in the different Member countries. Observance of the Guidelines is voluntary and not legally enforceable. However, they should help to ensure that the operations of these enterprises are in harmony with national policies of the countries where they operate and to strengthen the basis of mutual confidence between enterprises and States.

According to the 1979 Review Report on the Guidelines, para. 6 is central to understanding the purpose and nature of the Guidelines. Though not legally enforceable, the Guidelines carry the weight of a joint recommendation by the OECD governments addressed to MNEs which represents their 'firm expectation for multinational enterprise behaviour'.[56] As such, the Guidelines are an example of so-called 'soft law', that is, 'politically agreed guidelines for behaviour which cannot be directly legally enforced but cannot either be legitimately infringed'.[57] It has been argued that the Guidelines could 'harden' into rules of positive international law if they are generally accepted and frequently applied by governments in their dealings with MNEs.[58] That is unlikely to happen as long as OECD governments wish to retain a liberal attitude to foreign investment by MNEs. Indeed, among OECD ministers, the preference appears to be for an extension of investor protection standards, in the form of a binding instrument based on the principles of 'standstill, non-discrimination, transparency and rollback of existing measures constituting exceptions to National Treatment',[59] rather than for a strengthening of the more restrictive provisions contained in the 1976 Guidelines.

2.3   The Role of International Minimum Standards

By para. 7 of the introduction to the Guidelines:

Every State has the right to prescribe the conditions under which multinational enterprises operate within its national jurisdiction, subject to international law and to the international agreements to which it has subscribed. The entities of a multinational enterprise located in various countries are subject to the laws of these countries.

This is an unequivocal acceptance of the controlling role played by international minimum standards over the extent of a Member

Country's sovereign power to regulate the operations of a MNE, once it has been admitted into the jurisdiction. Indeed, in the context of the question of whether a host state can control by law the circumstances in which a MNE decides to disinvest, the requirements of para. 7 demand that any such law must be subject to international law and international agreements, and must respect contractual obligations to which the country has subscribed. Furthermore, such laws and policies must be carried out consistently with the Member Country's responsibilities to treat enterprises equitably.[60]

Paragraph 7 shows that the Guidelines are not intended to act as a substitute for national laws. They do no more than introduce supplementary standards of behaviour of a non-legal character with respect to the international operations of MNEs.[61] Thus the OECD Guidelines cannot be seen as a measure aimed at the harmonization of national legal controls over MNEs. However, the OECD supports the removal of conflicting requirements imposed on MNEs by the governments of home and host states, which might result in conflicts over the exercise of extraterritorial jurisdiction. In its 1984 Review of the Guidelines, the Committee on International Investment and Multinational Enterprises put forward a practical approach to the reduction of conflicting requirements, involving the drafting of new legislation by Member States in a manner that avoids conflicts of standards and hence of jurisdiction, and increased bilateral and multilateral cooperation between Member States over notification and consultation about conflicting requirements.[62]

2.4 The Scope of Application

The Guidelines are applicable primarily to MNEs. Such enterprises are broadly defined in para. 8 of the introduction to the Guidelines as being usually comprised of 'companies or other entities whose ownership is private, state or mixed, established in different countries and so linked that one or more of them may be able to exercise a significant influence over the activities of others and, in particular, to share knowledge and resources with the others.' Para. 8 continues by noting that the degree of autonomy of each entity in relation to the others varies widely from one MNE to another, depending on the nature of the links between such entities and the fields of activity that they are involved with. Consequently, the Guidelines are addressed to the various entities within the MNE, whether parent company or local entities, according to the distribution of responsibilities between them. Each entity is expected to cooperate with the others to ensure observance of the Guidelines.

The broad approach of para. 8 ensures that a wide range of multinational activities and arrangements come within the Guidelines. First, the Guidelines do not distinguish between private and public sector MNEs. The crucial element is not whether the enterprise is privately or publicly owned, but whether it displays the linkages that lead to the ability of one entity within the enterprise to influence the activities of other entities within it. Secondly, not only equity based arrangements but also other methods of achieving the required linkage between entities operating in different countries (e.g. international consortia, contractual joint ventures or licensing arrangements) can be regarded as 'multinational enterprises' for the purposes of the Guidelines.[63] However, the mere sharing of knowledge and resources among companies or other entities would not in itself be a sufficient indication that such companies or entities constitute a MNE. Some further evidence of linkage would be required in such a case.[64] Unfortunately the periodic reviews of the Guidelines offer no examples as to where the line should be drawn. As a matter of speculation, it would appear, for example, that an isolated purchase of technology by one company from another would not be a sufficient linkage to define those companies as a MNE within the meaning of the Guidelines. On the other hand, should such a purchase be accompanied by restrictions on the use of the technology, and by periodic inspection of the buyer company by the seller company, a determination as to the non-applicability of the Guidelines is less certain. The line may have to be drawn at the point where the contractual powers assumed by the seller company would turn the purchaser into a managerially controlled entity. That may be a difficult determination to make.[65]

The Guidelines do not lay down a new legal framework of parent company responsibility for the acts of its subsidiaries.[66] In keeping with their supplementary and non-binding nature, the Guidelines do no more than suggest that parent company responsibility for the financial liabilities of a subsidiary is a matter of good management practice.[67] On the other hand, the assumption of parent company responsibility for the effects of changes in the operations of a subsidiary on employment and industrial relations is considered to be of considerable relevance.[68] This may have implications for the nature of enterprise disclosure under item 1 of the Disclosure Guideline: the Committee recommends that the composition of the enterprise as a whole should be described and it should provide an overview of the linkages between its various entities.[69]

In addition to MNEs, the Guidelines are applicable to domestic enterprises, where relevant, for, according to para. 9 of the introduction to the Guidelines, they 'reflect good practice for all'. The Guidelines are based on the principle of non-discrimination and are not intended to introduce differences of treatment between MNEs and domestic enterprises.[70] Thus, in applying the Guidelines, it may not be necessary in every case to determine whether or not the contractual links of a non-equity character between separate entities lead to the conclusion that such entities, viewed collectively, constitute a MNE within the meaning of the Guidelines.[71] This suggests that as long as the activities involved are covered by the Guidelines, the absence of managerial control of one entity over another may be irrelevant given the general applicability of the standards in the Guidelines. If so then why did not the OECD simply restrict itself to the passing of a general 'Code of Good Conduct in International and Domestic Business', rather than concentrate on a code for MNEs? The requirements of para. 9 appear to be at odds with those of para. 8. Either the Guidelines do introduce different requirements for MNEs – that is, for international businesses characterized by linkages of managerial control across borders, as defined in para. 8 – or they do not. If the Guidelines do not, in fact, distinguish between MNEs and other types of international businesses, they appear to lose much of their apparent purpose, a purpose based on an acceptance that MNEs are a distinct type of business enterprise, creating specific problems of economic and social regulation for states, and requiring specialized policy responses. In their present form the Guidelines leave the precise scope of their applicability *ratione personae* rather obscure.

2.5   National Treatment

Whatever the true position may be on the extension of the Guidelines to domestic businesses, it is clear that the equality of treatment between domestic and multinational enterprises is a basic feature of the OECD 'code system'. This is emphasized by the inclusion of the principle of 'national treatment' in the Declaration of 21 June 1976.[72] According to the Declaration:

Member countries should, consistent with their needs to maintain public order, to protect their essential security interests and to fulfil commitments relating to international peace and security, accord to enterprises operating in their territories and owned or controlled directly or indirectly by nationals of another Member country (hereinafter referred to as 'Foreign-Controlled Enterprises') treatment under their laws, regulations and administrative practices, consistent with international law and no less favourable than that accorded in like situations to domestic enterprises (hereinafter referred to as 'National Treatment').

The Declaration goes on to add that Member Countries will consider applying 'national treatment' in respect of non-member countries, and will ensure that their territorial sub-divisions apply 'national treatment'. Finally, the Declaration stresses that it does not deal with the right of Member Countries to regulate the entry of foreign investment or the conditions of establishment of foreign enterprises, which remains within their exclusive control.

The meaning and effect of 'national treatment' has been regularly reviewed by the Committee on International Investment and Multinational Enterprises under powers granted to it by article 4(a) of the Third Revised Council Decision on National Treatment.[73] This has resulted in the Committee issuing clarifications of the terms used in the Declaration to describe the principle.[74] Furthermore, so as to achieve greater understanding of this principle, the Committee has undertaken periodic surveys of Member Country measures that constitute exceptions to the 'national treatment' principle, based upon its clarifications of the 1976 Declaration.[75] In order to assist the Committee in its work, the Third Revised Council Decision on National Treatment introduced a new requirement that Member Countries should notify to the Committee all measures constituting exceptions to the principle of 'national treatment'.[76] Thereupon the Committee is empowered to examine the notification.[77] Furthermore, a Member Country may refer another Member Country to the Committee where the former considers itself to have been prejudiced by the introduction of measures by the latter.[78] The Committee is also available as a forum for consultations, on the invitation of a Member Country, on any matter related to the implementation of the Declaration.[79] This institutional structure emerged out of the 1991 review. The Decision on national treatment was to have been reviewed in 1990.[80] However, this review was postponed to May–June 1991, owing to disagreements over a proposed strengthening of the national treatment instrument by means of a legally binding provision.[81] Consequently, the current system of notifications may be seen as a compromise measure.

Turning to the substantive content of 'national treatment', the Committee's periodic reports on 'national treatment' remain the most authoritative interpretation to date of this principle.[82] According to the Committee's reports, the key phrase in the Declaration, 'treatment no less favourable than that accorded to domestic enterprises', has the following implications.[83] First, an exception to national treatment is not created by the existence of a public monopoly which results in discriminatory measures against foreign-controlled enterprises. Secondly, if a foreign-controlled enterprise already established in a Member Country receives less favourable treatment, this can constitute an exception to national treatment if it also falls within the other criteria for determining such an exception; on the other hand, if the enterprise under foreign control receives treatment at least as favourable as that given to domestic enterprises, there can be no case of an exception to national treatment. Thirdly, in cases where domestic enterprises do not all receive the same treatment, where a foreign-controlled enterprise already established in a Member Country is treated less favourably than the least well treated domestic enterprise, this can constitute an exception to national treatment; if it receives treatment equivalent to that given to the best treated domestic enterprise there can be no question of an exception to national treatment. In cases where the foreign-controlled enterprise receives treatment at least as favourable as the least well treated domestic enterprise but less favourable than the best treated enterprise, it is not certain that this constitutes an exception to national treatment. Each such case should be reviewed on its facts, taking account of individual national characteristics and the degree to which the foreign and domestic enterprises are placed in comparable circumstances.

According to the Committee's reports, the expression 'in like situations' requires that comparisons between the treatment of domestic firms and foreign-controlled firms already established in the Member Country have to take place within the same industrial sector. National policy objectives in various fields should also be taken into account. A crucial factor in determining whether the measure applied to the foreign-controlled enterprise constitutes an exception to national treatment is whether the discrimination implied by the measure is motivated, at least in part, by the foreign control over the enterprise.

The Committee's reports have considered the role of reciprocity between states as a criterion in determining whether a Member Country should extend the principle of national treatment to foreign-controlled enterprises. The Committee has concluded that where the provision of equal treatment for a foreign-controlled enterprise by a host country is conditional on similar treatment being extended to enterprises from the host country in the home country, that constitutes an exception to national treatment if it results in the foreign-controlled enterprise being treated less favourably than similar domestic enterprises.

The preconditions for the application of national treatment discussed in the Committee's reports are: first, that the foreign-controlled enterprise must be operating within the territory of a Member Country through a local subsidiary, branch, sales office or representative office;[84] and, secondly, that the enterprise must be foreign-controlled, the criteria for determining control being varied among Member Countries but including equity ownership, voting rights and power to appoint directors or otherwise influence the affairs of an enterprise.[85] In each case it appears that the determination will be made in accordance with the law of the host state.

As para. 4 of the 1976 Declaration notes, national treatment does not extend to the regulation of the Member Countries' right to control the entry of foreign investment or the conditions of establishment of foreign enterprises. Initial foreign investments are covered by the OECD Code on Liberalization of Capital Movements.[86] Taken together the Code and the National Treatment instrument cover fully the area of investment controls.[87] In order to avoid conflicting requirements both the Committee on Capital Movements and Invisible Transactions, the body responsible for the Code, and the Committee on International Investment and Multinational Enterprises will cooperate over the relationship between the two instruments. According to the 1991 review, measures affecting investment by 'direct branches' (branches whose parent company is a non-resident) are covered by the Capital Movements Code, while those of 'indirect branches' (branches whose parent company is an established subsidiary of a non-resident) continue to be covered by the National Treatment Instrument.[88]

Finally, the Declaration permits distinctions of treatment for foreign-controlled enterprises where this is consistent with the need to maintain public order, the protection of essential security interests and the fulfilment of commitments to maintain international peace and security. The interpretation of these exceptions is left to the member countries, although the Committee's reports express the need to apply them with caution, bearing in mind the objectives of the national treatment instrument; they should not be used as a general escape clause from the commitments under these instruments.[89]

In the light of the above-mentioned considerations, the Committee on International Investment and Multinational Enterprises has considered the application of national treatment in five main areas: official aids and subsidies, tax obligations, government purchasing and public contracts, investment by established foreign-controlled enterprises and access to local bank credits and the capital market. These are the principal areas in which the OECD Member Countries have passed laws and regulations discriminating against foreign-controlled enterprises. The Committee has also considered the area of nationality requirements, as, for example, the requirement that a certain number of members of the board of a company must possess host state nationality.[90] Under the 1991 review, the application of national treatment to the privatization of enterprises previously under public ownership was considered. Access to the areas newly opened up by such a policy should be on a non-discriminatory basis between private domestic and foreign-controlled enterprises already established in the country in question. Any restrictions applying to foreign-controlled enterprises should be reported as exceptions to national treatment.[91]

2.6 Dispute Settlement

In the matter of dispute settlement between enterprises and Member Countries, the Guidelines recommend the use of appropriate international dispute settlement mechanisms, including arbitration'.[92] This suggests a preference for delocalized means of dispute settlement, given the absence of mention of dispute settlement procedures within the host state. That would be consistent with the concerns of capital-exporting states to limit the influence of local courts and local laws in the settlement of investment disputes. However, the provision is rather short and, perhaps, too much should not be read into it.

As regards issues arising in respect of the Guidelines themselves, the relevant procedures can be found in the Second Revised Council Decision on the Guidelines for Multinational Enterprises.[93] By this Decision the Committee on International Investment and Multinational Enterprises shall periodically, or at the request of a Member Country, 'hold an exchange of views on matters related to the Guidelines and the experience gained in their application'.[94] The Committee shall be responsible for clarification of the Guidelines and such clarification shall be provided as required. The Committee shall report periodically to the Council of the OECD on these matters.[95] In the course of its work on the Guidelines, the Committee shall periodically invite the Business and Industry Advisory Committee (BIAC) and the Trade Union Advisory Committee (TUAC) to express their views on matters related to the Guidelines. The Committee shall take account of their views when reporting to the Council.[96]

If it so wishes, an individual enterprise will be given the opportunity to express its views, either orally or in writing, on issues concerning the Guidelines involving its interests.[97] The presentation of these views is a matter of free choice for the enterprise. It cannot be compelled to do so. The enterprise concerned can present its views through the BIAC or a government delegation, or directly to the Committee itself.[98] Finally, the Council Decision mentions the obligation on member countries to set up so-called 'national contact points' for the purpose of 'undertaking promotional activities, handling enquiries and for discussions with the parties concerned on all matters relating to the Guidelines so that they can contribute to the solution of problems which may arise in this connection'. The business community, employee organizations and other interested parties shall be informed of the availability of such facilities.[99] However, while national contact points can provide explanations and express their views on aspects of the Guidelines, they cannot issue clarifications. That is the sole prerogative of the Committee, to whose clarifications the national contact points should refer.[100] If there is any doubt or divergency as to the interpretation given by a national contact point in the light of OECD clarifications, the matter should be brought before the Committee before the contact point provides a final answer. In that way uniformity of interpretation will be ensured.[101] The experience of national contact points in the various OECD Member Countries has been varied,[102] although the 1991 review expresses satisfaction with their performance.[103]

2.7   Substantive Provisions

With regard to the substance of the Guidelines, they are divided into seven headings, commencing with a statement of general policies followed by sections on disclosure of information, competition, financing, taxation, employment and industrial relations, environmental protection, and science and technology. It is not proposed to analyse each heading here. The more detailed sections of the Guidelines have already been considered in the relevant chapters of part II of this book. The present purpose is to restate the contents of the Guidelines with a view to ascertaining their overall approach to MNE–host state relations.

Under the heading 'General policies', the Guidelines list nine propositions which contain four principal duties that a MNE should observe in the course of its operations. The first is the duty to take into consideration the host state's economic interests by taking into account the general policy objectives of that state and, in particular, its aims and priorities with regard to economic and social progress, 'including industrial and regional development, the protection of the environment[104] and consumer interests,[105] the creation of employment opportunities, the promotion of innovation and the transfer of technology'.[106] Furthermore, the enterprise should supply such supplementary information as requested by the authorities of the host state subject to the legitimate requirements of business confidentiality, favour close cooperation with the local community and business interests, and allow component entities the freedom to evolve their own business strategy consistent with the need for specialization and sound commercial practice.[107] The second general duty is that of not discriminating on the grounds of nationality when filling responsible posts in each country of operation, subject to particular national requirements in this respect.[108] The third duty is that of acting honestly, by refraining from giving bribes or other improper direct or indirect benefits to public servants or public office holders.[109] The fourth duty is to refrain from illegitimate political activity, by not making contributions to candidates for public office or to political parties or other political organizations, unless legally permissible, and to abstain from improper involvement in local political activities.[110]

Under the heading 'Disclosure of information' the Guidelines set out the OECD standard for transparency in MNE operations. This section of the Guidelines has been analysed in detail in chapter 10.[111] For present purposes it is enough to note that the disclosure requirements go beyond actual practice in most Member Countries, which in some cases has presented difficulties and costs in adjusting to these standards.[112] Furthermore, adherence to the OECD standards of disclosure has been uneven. While the largest MNEs appear to adhere to the disclosure standards of the Guidelines, many smaller and medium-sized MNEs do not.[113]

The next heading, 'Competition', adapts the traditional norms of anti-trust law to the special case of the MNE. Thus *inter alia* the Guideline on competition specifically mentions a duty to refrain from discriminatory pricing and transfer price manipulations as a means of unfair competition, and a duty to refrain from the creation of international cartels. In practice the Guidelines have been referred to by Member Country governments when dealing with the restrictive business practices of MNEs.[114] However, the Guidelines are not seen as an alternative to national or intergovernmental initiatives, or as an alternative to other international codes on restrictive business practices.[115]

The next heading, 'Financing', states that 'Enterprises should, in managing the financial and commercial operations of their activities, and especially their liquid foreign assets and liabilities, take into consideration the established objectives of the countries in which they operate regarding balance of payments and credit policies.' The Committee has studied this issue but does not appear to be engaged in any further work in this area. No particular issues arising from this provision of the Guidelines have been raised before the Committee.[116] Similarly, no particular issues of interpretation have arisen out of the next Guideline, on 'Taxation'. Under this heading enterprises should provide the information necessary for the determination of their tax liability to the taxation authorities of the countries in which they operate, including relevant information on their activities in other countries, and refrain from using methods such as transfer pricing, which does not conform to the arm's length standard, as a means of reducing their liability to tax. The most significant work of the OECD on taxation and MNEs has taken place under the auspices of the organization's Committee on Fiscal Affairs rather than under the Guidelines.[117]

On the other hand, the most significant work of the OECD under the Guidelines has occurred in relation to the next heading, namely 'Employment and industrial relations'. The greatest number of complaints under the Guidelines have been brought to the attention of the Committee under this heading. This has resulted in a growing 'case-law' interpreting its provisions. The Employment and Industrial Relations Guideline and the substance of its development through deliberations before the Committee have been studied in chapter 13.

The 1991 Review has introduced a new chapter on 'Environmental protection' into the Guidelines.[118] It recommends that enterprises should take due account of the need to protect the environment and avoid creating environmentally related health problems within the framework of laws, regulations and administrative practices in the countries in which they operate. The Guideline goes on to specify particular duties to be observed by enterprises in relation to the consideration of environmental risks in decision-making, cooperation with the relevant authorities through the provision of information on the environmental impact and health aspects of their operations, and the taking of measures that minimize the risk of accidents and damage to health and the environment. The new Guideline does not single out MNEs for special attention. It is addressed to both multinational and domestic enterprises. The health and safety aspects of the Guideline can be read in the light of the more elaborate standards laid down in the ILO Tripartite Declaration of Principles Concerning Multinational Enterprises and Social Policy, which the Committee regards as running parallel to the Guidelines and not being in conflict with them.[119]

The Guidelines end with a heading on 'Science and technology'. Under this Guideline enterprises should: ensure that their activities fit with the science and technology aims of the countries in which they operate; adopt, to the fullest extent possible, working practices that allow for the rapid diffusion of technologies with due regard to the protection of industrial and intellectual property rights; when granting licences for the use of industrial property rights, or otherwise transferring technology, do so on reasonable terms. This represents the position of the OECD countries on the issue of technology transfer. This position has been more fully articulated during negotiations on the draft UNCTAD Code of Conduct on Transfer of Technology.[120] The principal concern voiced before the Committee in respect of this Guideline has been over the distribution of research and development (R&D) facilities outside the parent company of the group, and over the vulnerability to shutdown of such facilities, located in the overseas subsidiaries of the enterprise, in times of economic difficulty. The Committee's response has been to encourage MNEs to consider seriously the steps they could take to develop R&D facilities outside the home country and to consider ways in which changes in operations could be effected without depriving subsidiaries abroad of the means for technological development in their manufacturing and marketing operations.[121]

2.8   International Investment Incentives and Disincentives

The final element in the OECD 'code system' left to be considered is the area of international investment incentives and disincentives. Under the 1976 Declaration on International Investment and Multinational Enterprises[122] the Member countries of the OECD declared that they recognized the need to strengthen their cooperation in the field of international direct investment. To this end they recognized 'the need to give due weight to the interests of Member countries affected by specific laws, regulations and administrative practices in this field (hereinafter called "measures") providing official incentives and disincentives to international direct investment.' In the 1979 Review of the Guidelines, incentive and disincentive measures were described as measures 'used by member governments to influence the nature, location and size of direct investment for a variety of policy purposes such as industrial, regional, technology, employment and trade policies'.[123] The concern was with incentives and disincentives specifically linked to inward and outward direct investment. Measures of a general or purely domestic nature were not covered.[124] The economic purpose behind these provisions was to avoid damaging competition between Member Countries for investment by use of incentive and disincentive measures, by a kind of 'open door' protectionism, which only the stronger economies could sustain, thereby distorting the economic conditions for direct investment within the OECD area.

The 1976 Declaration urged greater transparency on the part of Member Countries in relation to investment incentives and disincentives. This was to be achieved by means of the consultation procedures put in place under the Council Decision on International Investment Incentives and Disincentives.[125] In 1979 the Council Decision was modified to include periodic consultation with the BIAC and the TUAC on matters relating to investment incentives and disincentives.[126] These provisions appear to have had little impact. In the 1979 Review of the Guidelines, the Committee noted that no member country had as yet availed itself of the consultation mechanism.[127] Two reasons have been put forward for this. First, Member Countries appeared to prefer bilateral government-to-government consultations. Secondly, in its original form the Council

Decision restricted consultations to measures 'specifically designed to provide incentives and disincentives for international direct investment'. Most measures in this area fell outside the scope of the OECD Declaration as they applied equally to foreign and domestic investors. This prompted the Committee to undertake more detailed studies in this area, so as to become better acquainted with the true situation.[128] On the basis of the results so obtained the Committee recommended in 1984 that the Council Decision on Investment Incentives and Disincentives should be amended so as to cover any measure that had the effect of providing 'significant official incentives and disincentives to international direct investment', without the limitation that the measure had to be specifically designed for this purpose. That formulation appeared in the Second Revised Council Decision.[129] Consequently a measure of general application to both domestic and foreign investors, which has the effect of providing significant incentives and/or disincentives to foreign direct investment, can now be subjected to the OECD consultation procedure.[130]

2.9   Concluding Remarks

The OECD Guidelines and associated Decisions provide the most comprehensive 'code system' on MNEs. The Guidelines represent a balance between the aims of controlling the activities of MNEs and reducing obstacles to their operations. That is the inevitable result of the 'corporatism' underlying the OECD's approach to policy-making, involving, as it does, Member Countries, the BIAC and the TUAC. Given their origins as a response to the calls of developing countries for a New International Economic Order, the Guidelines represent a 'Western' consensus on the acceptable features of any such regime. In this respect, it is clear that the Guidelines do not yield on the question of international minimum standards for the treatment of foreign investors. Thus, while states remain free to control the entry and establishment of MNEs on their territory, they must accord to established foreign-controlled enterprises treatment equivalent to that given to similar domestic firms which is at the same time *consistent with international law*. The influence that this assertion of Western legal values has had on the evolution of the other major international code on MNEs, the draft UN Code of Conduct, will now be considered.

3   The Draft UN Code of Conduct on Transnational Corporations[131]

As already noted, the origins of the draft UN Code of Conduct lie in the claim of the newly independent and less developed Member

States of the UN, formed together as the 'Group of 77', for a New International Economic Order.[132] This would include *inter alia* the legal recognition of the right of a state to control the activities of TNCs operating within its borders. In 1972 the Economic and Social Council of the UN requested the Secretary-General of the UN to establish a group of eminent persons to study the impact of MNEs on world development and international relations. That group recommended the setting up of a UN Commission on Transnational Corporations. It further recommended that the Commission should set about the task of formulating a Code of Conduct for TNCs. This was made a priority objective of the Commission at its first session in March 1975.[133] At its second session, the Commission decided to establish an Intergovernmental Working Group which would prepare a draft text of the Code on the basis of proposals or views put to it by states.[134]

From the outset, it was clear that major disagreements existed as to the nature and contents of the draft Code. The capital-exporting states were concerned to use the Code primarily as a means of protecting TNCs against discriminatory treatment contrary to the international minimum standards accepted by these states.[135] The countries belonging to the Group of 77, supported by the former socialist countries, were concerned to use the Code as a means of subjecting the activities of TNCs to greater regulation, in line with the contents of the UN Charter of Economic Rights and Duties of States,[136] so as to avoid the adverse effects of TNC activities on national economic objectives and political independence.[137] In addition, the Latin American states that were members of the Group of 77 submitted that the Code should contain provisions requiring extensive controls over TNCs.[138]

The Intergovernmental Working Group began work on a draft text of the Code in January 1977. An early disagreement occurred over whether the Code should be addressed only to TNCs, as desired by the Group of 77, or whether it should also extend to the treatment of TNCs by host governments, as desired by the major capital-exporting countries.[139] Ultimately the capital-exporting countries succeeded. Thus the Economic and Social Council, by Resolution 1980/60 of 24 July 1980, affirmed in paragraph 6(g) that the Code should 'include provisions relating to the treatment of transnational corporations, jurisdiction and other related matters'.[140] Thereafter the draft Code would consist of two main parts: the first on the activities of TNCs, the second on the treatment of TNCs.

The Intergovernmental Working Group presented its report to the Commission at its eighth session in 1982.[141] Although the report had annexed to it a draft Code, this was still a rather incomplete document. No drafting had been done on the 'preamble and objectives', and major differences existed between states in the drafting of the substantive provisions, especially those dealing with the treatment of TNCs. Accordingly, on the recommendation of the Commission, the Economic and Social Council, in its resolution 1982/68 of 27 October 1982, decided that the Commission on Transnational Corporations should hold a special session, open to all states, early in 1983 for the purpose of concluding the Code.[142]

Since 1983, meetings of the special session were held on numerous occasions,[143] supplemented throughout the period by informal consultations. These meetings resulted in a number of revised drafts of the Code, culminating in the proposed text of 31 May 1990, submitted by the Chairman of the reconvened special session of the Commission to the Economic and Social Council.[144] This represents the last version of the draft Code. Despite continued efforts at revisions of the draft Code, negotiations were in effective deadlock for many years, reflecting deep-rooted disagreements between the developed capital-exporting states and capital-importing members of the Group of 77 over fundamental issues as to the content, legal status and relationship with general international law of the Code. Finally, in July 1992, negotiations over the Code were suspended.[145] The period of negotiations was marked by a shift away from a strongly regulatory approach towards TNCs and its gradual replacement in successive drafts of the Code with formulations closer to those favoured by the capital-exporting countries.[146]

It was generally agreed that states had the right to control the entry and establishment of TNCs within their territory, including the determination of the role that such corporations could play in economic and social development and the prohibition or limitation of their presence in specific sectors.[147] Equally, there was considerable agreement over the contents of the section entitled 'Activities of transnational corporations', which laid down the duties of TNCs towards host states.[148] The major disagreements arose in relation to the treatment of TNCs after they had been admitted into a host country.

The most basic disagreement concerned the question of a reference to international law in the Code. The capital-exporting countries wished to see a reference to international law included in the Code, so that the international minimum standards of treatment favoured by them would be incorporated into the Code, on the ground that they represented customary international law binding on all states. The Group of 77, and the socialist countries, questioned the validity of these standards on the ground that they were established by the practice of the major capital-exporting states at a time when most developing countries were under colonial rule and that, therefore, they did not command the consent of the majority of the contemporary international community.[149] These countries favoured a compromise proposal referring to 'international obligations' rather than to 'international law' as this restricted the relevant standards to obligations derived from treaties, conventions, agreements and other instruments based on the express consent of states, and excluded the traditional norms of customary international law evolved by the past practice of the capital-exporting states.[150] The May 1990 draft provision, contained in para. 47, left the matter unresolved. It states: 'In all matters relating to the Code, States shall fulfil, in good faith, their obligations under international law.' This would appear to leave each state free to determine the extent of its obligations in accordance with its view on the limits of applicable international law.

The next area of serious disagreement concerned the inclusion of standards of treatment for TNCs. International instruments in the investment field usually have recourse to one or more of three principal standards: the standard of national treatment, that of most-favoured-nation treatment and that of fair and equitable treatment.[151] The 1990 draft Code referred to two of these. By para. 49 of the draft Code, 'Transnational corporations shall receive fair and equitable treatment in the countries in which they operate.'[152] Paragraph 49 found general agreement among states. By contrast, para. 50, the provision relating to national treatment, proved to be more controversial.[153] There was general agreement that the standard should be subject to exceptions based on public order and national security considerations, consistent with the requirements of national constitutions and laws, and that it should operate without prejudice to measures specified in legislation relating to the declared development objectives of the developing countries.[154] However, there was disagreement over whether a reference to preferential treatment for TNCs should be included. The capital-exporting countries argued that the provision should be flexible enough to permit such treatment where the host country deemed it appropriate. The Group of 77 argued, in response, that the preferential treatment of TNCs was within the sovereign discretion of individual countries and should not be made a general international standard.[155] It should be noted that the 1990 draft Code had dropped the last sentence of the previous draft of 1988, which referred to the preferential treatment of TNCs.[156]

The draft Code then went on to consider the issue of expropriation. The formulation of an agreed provision on nationalization and compensation proved to be one of the most contentious issues in the drafting history of the Code. There was general agreement that states had the right to nationalize or expropriate the assets of TNCs operating within their territories and that they had a corresponding duty to pay compensation for such a taking. However, the capital-exporting countries maintained their support for a right of national-ization subject to the requirements of international law, including those relating to the payment of 'prompt, adequate and effective' compensation. The capital-importing countries, for their part, dis-puted the existence of any generally accepted principles of inter-national law in this area, rejecting, in particular, the capital-exporting countries' position on lawful compensation.[157] In the earlier stages of negotiations each group had put forward formulations embodying their respective positions.[158] Since then the question of whether the standard of compensation should be specified in the Code became part of the wider question of whether the Code should refer to international law or international obligations. The 1990 draft text shows an interesting change from the position taken in 1988. The 1988 draft states:

It is acknowledged that States have the right to nationalize or expropriate the assets of a transnational corporation operating in their territory, and that appro-priate compensation is to be paid by the State concerned, in accordance with the applicable legal rules and principles.[159]

The 1990 draft is identical except that the word 'appropriate' is replaced by the word 'adequate'.[160] Hitherto, the word 'appropriate' was considered to be an acceptable compromise by all delegations.[161] Does the adoption of the word 'adequate' signify a move towards the capital-exporting countries' position, given its connotation of the 'prompt, adequate and effective compensation' formula? On its face the new formulation does not rule out such an interpretation.

The history of the draft Code represents a growing compromise by those states advocating TNC control of their original objectives. The economic and political conditions which gave rise to the initial calls for a universal code laying down obligations for TNCs have changed.[162] Developing countries are now faced with an acute short-fall of investment by comparison to the days of the early 1970s. While investment by TNCs in developed countries has increased, it has stagnated in developing countries.[163] According to the UN Centre on Transnational Corporations, this has raised new policy questions, leading to what it has called a 'New Code Environment'. No longer is the control of the potentially negative impacts of TNCs the major issue; rather it is how best to reintegrate developing countries into the global economy in a manner that ensures inflows of new investment capital. Given that TNCs are a primary vehicle for such integration, any future Code should be geared to the realization of this goal.[164]

Furthermore, certain fundamental disagreements are becoming increasingly irrelevant given the logic of the 'New Code Environment'. Thus the debates over nationalization and a reference to international law or obligations assume equity ownership structures that are now less frequently used, being increasingly replaced by reduced equity and non-equity forms of investment structures by firms.[165] Moreover, local ownership as evidence of control has also diminished as an objective for host states. They 'may aim instead at capturing a larger share of the economic benefits that derive from a transnational corporation's non-equity competitive advantages'.[166] This phraseology displays an acceptance, on the part of the UN itself, of the dependency of the developing countries on TNCs and their economic power, and of the futility of using international instruments as a means of mitigating international economic inequalities between them.

Such a position begs the question of whether the conclusion and adoption of a Code of Conduct by the UN should ever be revived. A host state can pass laws encouraging inward investment without the need for international resolutions that reaffirm its right to do so, or that constrain its freedom of action to control as it sees fit the activities of TNCs within its territory. Furthermore, the rise of bilateral investment treaties suggests that governments are losing interest in the multilateral approach of the codification movement.[167] As long as the capital-exporting countries are content to protect traditional international minimum standards of treatment on a bilateral basis, the capital-importing countries in fact preserve their freedom to accept or to question those standards, in that they remain free to deny their validity outside the bilateral relationship. Should the capital-importing states agree to a universal Code which has moved towards the capital-exporting countries' position, and which, if adopted, would be persuasive evidence of the prevailing consensus on the content of international standards, they would lose their ability to question those standards when it suited them. Consequently, the idea of a general UN Code, as an instrument for the preservation of LDC economic sovereignty, may be an approach that has had its day.

4 The Contribution of the World Bank: the 1992 Guidelines on the Treatment of Foreign Direct Investment and Standard Setting by MIGA

The development of international standards for the treatment of foreign investors has become part of the agenda of the World Bank

Group (the International Bank for Reconstruction and Development, the International Finance Corporation and the Multilateral Investment Guarantee Agency (MIGA)). In particular, the 1992 World Bank Guidelines on the Treatment of Foreign Direct Investment (the 1992 Guidelines) and the standard-setting provisions of the MIGA Convention are worthy of study.

4.1   The 1992 World Bank Guidelines [168]

The 1992 Guidelines were prepared at the initiative of the Development Committee, a Joint Ministerial Committee of the Boards of Governors of the International Monetary Fund (IMF) and of the World Bank. In April 1991, the Development Committee, working on a proposal from France, requested that MIGA prepare a 'legal framework' to promote foreign direct investment. A working group, consisting of lawyers from each of the World Bank Group institutions, was set up to prepare a report. This was submitted to the Development Committee in April 1992. The report pointed out that the World Bank Group could not issue binding rules that could govern the conduct of states. It noted that a multilateral convention could be drawn up by the Group and opened for signature, but, given the reluctance of states to commit themselves to such an instrument in the field of foreign investment, this was not the approach to be taken. Instead, the working group recommended that a set of non-binding Guidelines be drawn up on the basis of the general trends identified in the surveys of existing legal instruments undertaken by the working group, and on the basis of policies that the World Bank Group institutions had been advocating in recent years. The resulting Guidelines were approved by the Development Committee in September 1992 for circulation among the member states of the World Bank Group. [169]

Given their nature and origins, the Guidelines are not intended, therefore, to codify existing international law. Their aim is to set down emerging rather than settled standards, and, in the process, to emphasize what the World Bank Group sees as desirable practice in the field of direct foreign investment. Furthermore, the Guidelines are addressed to host states alone, covering only their activities and policies towards foreign investors. There are no provisions concerning the behaviour of foreign investors towards host states. Thus the coverage of the 1992 Guidelines is narrower than that of the OECD Guidelines or the draft UN Code of Conduct. The 1992 Guidelines are divided into five headings: I, scope of application; II, admission; III, treatment; IV, expropriation and unilateral alteration or termination of contracts; V, settlement of disputes (referred to as Guideline

I, II etc.). Their form is either normative or that of a policy recommendation, depending on the degree to which the standard concerned is reconcilable with general principles of contemporary
international law.[170]

Guideline I commences by stating that the application of the
Guidelines is complementary to existing bilateral and multilateral
treaties and binding instruments, which take precedence in cases of
conflict between the two. The Guidelines are envisaged as a source of
standards on which national laws may draw. However, it is made
clear that the Guidelines do not suggest that foreign investors should
receive privileged treatment that is denied to national investors in
similar circumstances.[171] Guideline II then sets down the preferred
policy of the World Bank Group as regards entry and establishment
of foreign investors. It urges each state to encourage nationals of
other states to invest capital, technology and managerial skill in its
territory and, to that end, to adopt a policy of open admission, with
full information concerning applicable laws, regulations and procedures.[172] This open approach may be subject to restrictions in
certain areas of investment, but that is preferred to a policy of
imposing performance requirements as a condition of entry.[173] However, Guideline II affirms that each state maintains the right to make
regulations to govern the admission of foreign investments.[174]
Furthermore, states may, exceptionally, refuse entry on the grounds
of national security, or because a sector is reserved to a state's
nationals on account of the state's economic development objectives
or the strict exigencies of its national interest.[175] Restrictions
applicable to national investment on account of public policy, public
health and environmental protection will equally apply to foreign
investment.[176]

Guideline III, on the treatment of foreign investors, affirms the
World Bank Group's commitment to the standards of treatment
commonly found in bilateral investment treaties (BITs). Thus, it
contains provisions recommending fair and equitable treatment,[177]
national treatment and non-discrimination,[178] and the free transfer of
salaries, net revenues, sums for the settlement of debts, net proceeds
of a liquidation or sale of assets,[179] or of compensation for loss due to
war, armed conflict, revolution or insurrection.[180] Guideline III also
recommends the prompt issuing of licences and permits, the authorization of the employment of foreign personnel where the investor so
wishes,[181] permission for investors to reinvest their profits,[182] the
control of corrupt business practices, the promotion of accountability and transparency in dealings with foreign investors,[183] and the
avoidance of competition between states in providing investment

incentives, especially in the area of tax exemptions.[184] Finally, developed states are urged to encourage outward direct investment into developing states through the use of appropriate incentives.[185]

Guideline IV deals with the ever problematic issue of expropriation and unilateral renegotiation or termination of investment contracts. Again, the World Bank Group favours the position taken by states in BITs. Thus expropriation is deemed to be legal provided that it is done 'in accordance with applicable legal procedures, in pursuance in good faith of a public purpose, without discrimination on the basis of nationality and against the payment of appropriate compensation'.[186] 'Appropriate' compensation is then defined as 'adequate, effective and prompt'.[187] 'Adequate' compensation is based on the fair market value of the asset taken immediately before the time at which the taking occurred or the decision to take the asset became publicly known.[188] The fair market value of the asset is to be determined by reference to a method agreed between the foreign investor and the host state or, in the absence of agreement, by the state according to reasonable criteria related to the market value of the investment.[189] The Guideline lists, on a non-exclusive basis, the following standards of valuation as being reasonable:

(i)   for a going concern with a proven record of profitability, on the basis of discounted cash flow value;

(ii)   for an enterprise which, not being a proven going concern, demonstrates lack of profitability, on the basis of the liquidation value;

(iii)   for other assets, on the basis of (a) the replacement value or (b) the book value in case such value has been recently assessed or has been determined as of the date of the taking and can therefore be deemed to represent a reasonable replacement value.[190]

Compensation will be deemed 'effective' if it is paid in the currency bought in by the investor where it remains convertible, in another currency designated as freely usable by the IMF or in any other currency accepted by the investor.[191] Compensation will be prompt if paid in normal circumstances without delay.[192] Guideline IV continues with the recognition of two special cases in which less than full compensation may be legitimately paid. The first case arises where the investor has violated the host state's laws in force prior to the taking, such violation is determined by a court of law and the investment is taken as a sanction for this violation. Here compensation may not be due at all, or will be reduced. Disputes in such cases should be determined in accordance with Guideline V. The second special case arises out of non-discriminatory nationalizations effected in the context of large-scale social reforms under exceptional circumstances of revolution, war and similar exigencies. Here compensation may be determined through negotiations between the home and host states, or through international arbitration.[193] The Guideline ends by extending the standards of compensation it contains to cases of unilateral termination, amendment or other disclaimer of liability by the host state in a contract with an investor for other than commercial reasons. Liability for repudiation for commercial reasons will be determined by reference to the applicable law of contract.[194]

The 1992 Guidelines end with Guideline V on the settlement of disputes. Disputes between foreign investors and the host state will normally be settled through negotiations, and failing this, through national courts or other agreed mechanisms including conciliation and binding independent arbitration.[195] Independent arbitration includes *ad hoc* or institutional arbitration agreed upon in writing by the state and the investor or between the home and host states where the majority of arbitrators are not solely appointed by one party to the dispute.[196] Finally, where independent arbitration is chosen each state is encouraged to use ICSID arbitration if it is a party to the ICSID Convention, or the ICSID Additional Facility if it is not a party to the ICSID Convention.[197]

The 1992 Guidelines offer a clear statement on the policy preferences of the World Bank Group in the field of foreign investment. As such they are in line with the aims of the major capital-exporting states for the creation of a 'New International Order for Trade and Investment' as exemplified by the increased use of BITs, the liberalization of trade and investment through regional agreements, the contents of the OECD Guidelines and the negotiating aims behind the investment related issues of the Uruguay Round. However, the report attached to the Guidelines is at pains to stress the limits of their purpose and effects:

To the extent that the practice of States conforms to these recommended guidelines in a constant manner and reflects a general conviction of their binding character, the guidelines may then positively influence the development of customary international law in so far as they do not already reflect its rules. While the guidelines could serve these important purposes, they are clearly not intended to constitute part of World Bank loan conditionality or to assume for the Bank a legislative role which it does not have.[198]

Therefore, departure from the standards contained in the Guidelines will not have any financial implications for states seeking a loan from the World Bank. This may serve to allay fears that the Guidelines will be used as a means of intervening in the domestic policies of countries in need of such assistance. However, the pressure on states to conform to the policies advocated in the Guidelines should be seen in the context of the standard-setting conditions which may be attached to investment guarantees issued by MIGA. To this we now turn.

4.2   The Standard Setting Provisions of MIGA

By article 12(d) of the MIGA Convention, in guaranteeing an invest-ment, MIGA (the Agency) shall satisfy itself as to *inter alia* the 'investment conditions in the host country, including the availability of fair and equitable treatment and legal protection for the invest-ment'.[199] Article 12(d) makes the provision of adequate standards of investment protection a condition precedent to the issuance of a MIGA investment guarantee, as this helps to reduce the investment risk. The Agency itself must assess whether the host country's legal system meets the standard in article 12(d). Guidance is offered in the MIGA Operational Regulations.[200] By para. 3.16 thereof:

An investment will be regarded as having adequate legal protection if it is protected under the terms of a bilateral investment treaty between the host country and the home country of the investor. When there is no such treaty, adequate legal protection should be ascertained by the Agency in the light of the consistency of the law and practice of the host country with international law. Such assessment shall be conducted in strict confidentiality and its outcome shall be shared only with the government concerned with a view to enabling it to improve the investment conditions in its territory.

The emphasis on BITs coincides with the Agency's general duty to 'promote and facilitate the conclusion of agreements, among its members, on the promotion and protection of investments'.[201] In most cases this requirement should be met, as the majority of MIGA's developing member states have concluded BITs with capi-tal-exporting member states.[202] However, in the absence of a BIT, the Agency must compare the law and practice of the host state with international law. As the leading commentator on MIGA points out, given the absence of well-defined international law in this area, the Agency is in fact mandated to develop standards of this law for the purposes of its operations. This would be relevant to the general development of customary international law, but could not substitute for the will of states in the matter.[203] Indeed, MIGA is placed in a difficult position as an arbiter of the content of international law, given the prevailing disagreement as to its content. It is against this background that the initiative which led to the adoption of the 1992 World Bank Guidelines should be seen.[204] They offer a non-binding statement of policy in a field where general agreement on binding international standards would be impossible. As such they can be seen as the starting point for negotiations between MIGA and a host country over the legal standards that the latter should offer to investors if it is to benefit from MIGA guarantees.

The result of such negotiations may be the conclusion of an investment guarantee agreement between the Agency and the host country as a precondition for a MIGA guarantee.[205] The authority to conclude such agreements is given by article 23(b)(ii) of the MIGA Convention, which states that the Agency shall

endeavour to conclude agreements with developing member countries, and in particular with prospective host countries, which will assure that the Agency, with respect to investment guaranteed by it, has treatment at least as favourable as that agreed by the member concerned for the most favoured investment guarantee agency or State in an agreement relating to investment, such agreements to be approved by special majority of the Board.

Thus MIGA has a role in the development of international standards through the conclusion of specific agreements, whose content will undoubtedly be influenced by the terms of the 1992 Guidelines.

On a more general level, the Agency can be expected to take an active part in developing international standards through its research, information, technical advice and assistance and consultation programmes.[206] These are all aimed at the improvement of the environment for foreign investment flows to developing member countries. In performing these activities the MIGA Convention specifies that the Agency shall be guided by relevant investment agreements among member countries; it shall seek to remove impediments, in both developed and developing member countries, to the flow of investment to developing member countries and coordinate with other agencies concerned with the promotion of foreign investment, and in particular with the International Finance Corporation.[207] These considerations point to the possibility of further work in the area of standard-setting. Furthermore, the Operational Regulations make clear that 'The Agency's technical programs shall support its guarantee operations by strengthening assurance of fair and stable treatment of guaranteed investments in individual host countries'. Clearly, the development of investor protection standards would fall within this broad mandate.

In conclusion, although the work of the Agency in the area of standard-setting will be, like the 1992 Guidelines, only of a persuasive nature, the Agency's view of those standards is likely to influence state practice. Host states run the risk of having their access to its guarantee facilities restricted if they do not adhere to the Agency's preferred standards of treatment. In this respect the future contribution of MIGA to standard-setting may be of some importance.

5   Concluding Remarks

The codification movement of the 1970s had a clear political and legal purpose. This was most vividly displayed in the original model for the now suspended UN Code of Conduct. With the demise of the UN Code, the aim of reforming international law so as to reduce the relative weakness of capital-importing countries in their relations with MNEs has not been achieved. Nor has a new 'international law of multinational enterprises' resulted. At most the proposed Code mobilized the capital-exporting countries into reasserting their adherence to the traditional norms of investor protection. These have been modernized, in the context of investment by MNEs, by the OECD Guidelines and, more recently, by the World Bank Guidelines. At present these represent the strongest code on MNEs in existence. To that extent the views of the capital-exporting countries have gained ascendancy. However, neither set of Guidelines carries the force of binding international law. Indeed, the OECD Code is no more than a joint recommendation of the Member Countries addressed to MNEs. The World Bank Guidelines carry even less weight, being intended as no more than a statement of policy and good practice. However, in the hands of MIGA, they may have some legally significant effects. Thus, the conflict of norms in international law remains.[208] On the other hand, a significant alternative to the elusive search for generally agreed international legal standards for the governance of foreign investor–host state relations comes in the form of BITs. These form the subject matter of the next chapter.

Notes

1   See above at pp. 503–4. See further C. Lipson, *Standing Guard: Protecting Foreign Capital in the Nineteenth and Twentieth Centuries* (University of California Press, 1985).

2   *Case Concerning The Barcelona Traction, Light and Power Company, Limited (New Application: 1962) (Belgium v Spain) Second Phase,* Judgment of 5 February 1970, ICJ Reports (1970), p. 3, at pp. 46–7. paras 89–90.

3   See generally: Fatouros, 'An international code to protect private investment – proposals and perspectives', 14 U of Toronto LJ 77 (1961); Miller, 'Protection of private foreign investment by multilateral convention', 53 AJIL 371 (1959); Snyder, 'Protection of private foreign investment: examination and appraisal', 10 ICLQ 469 [1961]; Boyle, 'Some proposals for a World Investment Convention' [1961] JBL 18,155.

4   See: Cutler, 'The treatment of foreigners in relation to the Draft Convention and Conference of 1929' 27 AJIL 225 (1933); Kuhn, 'The International Conference on the Treatment of Foreigners' 24 AJIL 570 (1930); Potter, 'International legislation on the treatment of foreigners', 24 AJIL 748 (1930). For the proceedings of the conference see League of Nations

Doc. C.97.M.23, 1930 II; for the text of the draft convention under discussion see League of Nations Doc. C.174.M.53, 1928 II.

5   See Hackworth, 'Responsibility of states for damages caused in their territory to the person or property of foreigners', 24 AJIL 500 (1930).

6   See Lipson (note 1 above), pp. 75–6.

7   See Fatouros (note 3 above), at pp. 79–81.

8   Havana Charter, article V. See further chapter 11 at p. 403. Lockwood, 'Proposed international legislation with respect to business practices', XLI AJIL 616 (1947).

9   Havana Charter, article 11(1)(b): 'no member shall take unreasonable or unjustified action within its territories injurious to the rights and interests of nationals of other Members in the enterprise, skills, capital, arts or technology which they have supplied'. Ibid., article 12(2)(a)(i), provision of reasonable security for existing and future investments; article 12(2)(a)(ii), the giving of due regard to the desirability of avoiding discrimination as between foreign investments; article 12(2)(b), entry into consultation or negotiations with other governments to conclude bilateral or multilateral agreements relating to foreign investments.

10 Havana Charter article 12(1)(c): 'without prejudice to existing international agreements to which members are parties, a Member has the right (i) to take any appropriate safeguards necessary to ensure that foreign investment is not used as a basis for interference in its internal affairs or national policies; (ii) to determine whether and to what extent and upon what terms it will allow future foreign investment; (iii) to prescribe and give effect on just terms to requirements as to the ownership of existing or future investments; (iv) to prescribe and give effect to other reasonable requirements as to the ownership of existing or future investments'. For a critical comment on this provision see Woolsey, 'The problem of foreign investment', XLII AJIL 121 at pp. 126–8 (1948).

11 Fatouros (note 3 above), at p. 80; Lipson (note 1 above), at pp. 86–7.

12 Apart from these initiatives certain states also made proposals to international organizations for the adoption of a multilateral convention for the protection of foreign investments. Thus at the 14th Session of the UN Economic Commission for Asia and the Far East (ECAFE) in March 1958, the Prime Minister of Malaya suggested the conclusion of an international investment charter; also in 1958 both the German and Swiss governments submitted draft investment conventions to the OEEC. In 1957 discussions took place under the auspices of the Council of Europe for an investment convention between the Member States of the Council and certain African states.

13 For an analysis of this code see Miller (note 3 above).

14 See Brandon, 'An international investment code: current plans', [1959] JBL 7 at pp. 12–15.

15 The text of this draft can be found in 9 J. Pub. L. 116–18 (1960). See further Shawcross, 'The problems of foreign investment in international law', 102 Hague Recueil 334 (1961).

16 See OECD Publication No. 1563[6]7/Dec. 1962 reproduced in 1–2 ILM 241 (1962–3). The last revision of the draft Convention can be found in

OECD Publication No. 232081/Nov. 1967 reproduced in 7 ILM 117 (1968).

17   See Snyder, 'Foreign investment protection: a reasoned approach', 61 Mich. LR 1087 at pp. 1112–13. (1963); UNCTC, *Bilateral Investment Treaties* (1988, UN Sales No. E. 88. II. A. I), para. 20, p. 7.

18   UNCTC, ibid.; Denza and Brooks, 'Investment protection treaties: United Kingdom experience', 36 ICLQ 908, at p. 910 (1987).

19   UNCTC, ibid.

20   Bolivia, Colombia, Chile, Equador and Peru. Venezuela joined the organization in 1973.

21   The full title of the Code is 'The Common Regime of Treatment of Foreign Capital and of Trademarks, Patents, Licences, and Royalties'. An English translation appears in 11 ILM 126 (1972). The final amended version of Decision 24, as of 30 November 1976, appears in 16 ILM 138 (1977). All references to the Code in the text are to the 1976 amended version.

22   English version in 27 ILM 974 (1988).

23   Andean Commission: Decision 291 – Common Code for the Treatment of Foreign Capital and on Trademarks, Patents, Licenses and Royalties: 30 ILM 1283 (1991).

24   Article 1. The classification distinguished between the following types of enterprises: national (more than 80 per cent of capital belonging to national investors), mixed (51 to 80 per cent owned by national investors) and foreign (50 per cent or more in the hands of foreign investors). In each case not merely ownership but effective management of the enterprise was the relevant criterion, so as to prevent foreign minority control by arrangements with a national majority.

25   See articles 2–6.

26   Article 7.

27   Articles 12–13.

28   Articles 14–16.

29   Articles 18–26. See further chapter 12.

30   Articles 27–37.

31   Articles 38–44.

32   See Oliver, 'The Andean Foreign Investment Code: a new phase in the quest for normative order as to direct foreign investment', 66 AJIL 763 (1972). By article 50: 'Member Countries shall not grant to foreign investors any treatment more favourable than that granted to national investors.' By article 51: 'In no instrument relating to investments or the transfer of technology shall there be clauses that remove possible conflicts or controversies from the national jurisdiction and competence of the recipient country or allow subrogation by States to the rights and actions of their national investors.'

33   See Horton, 'Peru and ANCOM: a study in the disintegration of a common market', 17 Texas Int'l LJ 39 at pp. 45–7 (1982); comment: 'Chile's rejection of the Andean Common Market regulation of foreign investment', 16 Col. J. Transnat. L. 138 (1977).

34   Horton, ibid., at pp. 56–7.

35   See 'Introductory note' to the Venezuelan Foreign Investment and Licensing Regulations and Related Documents of 1986–7 by John R. Pate, 26 ILM 760 (1987).
36   See ibid.
37   Note 22 above. For analysis see: Preziosi, 'The Andean Pact's Foreign Investment Code Decision 220: an agreement to disagree', 20 U. Miami Inter-Am. L. Rev. 649 (1989); Esquirol, 'Foreign investment: revision of the Andean Foreign Investment Code', 29 Harv. Int'l LJ 171 (1988).
38   Article 33.
39   Article 34.
40   Note 23 above.
41   See E. Wiesner, 'ANCOM: a new attitude toward foreign investment?', 24 U. Miami Inter-Am. L. Rev. 435 (1993).
42   The original version of the Guidelines, and the accompanying Communique and Council Decisions on Inter-governmental Consultation Procedures on the Guidelines, National Treatment and International Investment Incentives and Disincentives, are reproduced in 15 ILM 961–80 (1976). For comment see Schwamm 12 JWTL 342 (1978). The Guidelines and accompanying Council Decisions are periodically reviewed by the OECD Committee on International Investment and Multinational Enterprises. Reviews of the Guidelines took place in 1979, 1982, 1984 and 1986. All the relevant extracts from these reviews can be found in the *OECD Guidelines for Multinational Enterprises* (1986) (cited hereafter as the 1986 Review). The Guidelines and the 1991 Review can be found in OECD, *The OECD Declaration and Decisions on International Investment and Multinational Enterprises* (1992) (hereafter referred to as the 1991 Review). The Guidelines were reprinted in 1994 and 1997. The latest review process commenced in 1998.
43   See J. Robinson, *Multinationals and Political Control* (Gower, 1983), pp. 113–20.
44   On which see the next section of this chapter.
45   See further chapters 11, 12 and 13.
46   Robinson (note 43 above), at p. 117.
47   See G. Hamilton, *The Control of Multinationals: What Future for International Codes of Conduct in the 1980s?*, (John Wiley & Sons, IRM Multinational Reports No. 2, October-December 1984), p. 6. See further P. Levy, 'The OECD Declaration on International Investment and Multinational Enterprises', in S. Rubin and G. C. Hufbauer (eds), *Emerging Standards of International Trade and Investment* (Rowman & Allanhead, 1983).
48   See Robinson (note 43 above), at pp. 118–19.
49   See Council Resolution C(74)247 Final of 21 January 1975.
50   See para. 6 of the Communique of the Council of the OECD of 22 June 1976 accompanying the Guidelines: 15 ILM 961–6 at p. 962 (1976).
51   Ibid.
52   Ibid., para. 2.
53   Ibid., para. 3.
54   Ibid., para. 2.
55   See above text at notes 15–19.

56   OECD *Review of the 1976 Declaration and Decisions on International Invest-ment and Multinational Enterprises* (OECD Doc. C(79) 102 (Final) of 5 June 1979) reproduced in 18 ILM 986 (1979). See para. 37 at p. 999 (hereafter referred to as the 1979 Review); or see the 1986 Review (note 42 above), para. 3, pp. 17–18.

57   Robinson (note 43 above), at p. 111. On the nature of 'soft law' see further Baxter 'International law in her infinite variety', 20 ICLQ 549 (1980). For a fuller discussion of the legal nature and effects of international codes of conduct on MNEs see: C. D. Wallace, *Legal Control of the Multinational Enterprise* (Martinus Nijhoff, 1983), chapter 13; R. Waldman, *Regulating International Business* (1980); Baade, 'The legal effects of codes of conduct for multinational enterprises', in N. Horn (ed.), *Legal Problems of Codes of Conduct for Multinational Enterprises* (Kluwer, 1980), pp. 3–38.

58   Submission of the Trade Union Advisory committee and the Belgian Government to the Investment and Multinational Enterprise Committee in the *Badger* case, OECD IME internal document, 8 June 1977, p. 5, cited in Robinson, ibid., at p. 128: 'in the course of time, sections of the Guidelines, although voluntary in their origin and not being sanctioned by law, may pass, by virtue of their general acceptance and frequent applica-tion, into the general corpus of customary international law, even for those international enterprises that have never explicitly accepted them.'

59   See OECD Communique (PRESS/A(90)32 Paris, 31 May 1990) para. 19, p. 7.

60   1979 Review, para. 44; reproduced in 1986 Review (note 42 above), para. 11, at p. 20.

61   1979 Review (note 56 above), para. 38; 1986 Review (note 42 above), para. 4.

62   See the extract from the 1984 Review reproduced as annex II of the 1986 Review at pp. 75–6, especially paras 5–8 thereof. This approach has now been appended to the 1976 Declaration as a result of the 1991 review exercise: see 1991 Review (note 42 above), chapter IV and 1976 Declara-tion on International Investment and Multinational Enterprises, annex 2, ibid., at p. 109. A consultation process has been set up in this field by a decision of the Council of June 1991, ibid., at p. 119.

63   1979 Review (note 56 above), para. 39; 1986 Review (note 42 above), para. 5, at p. 18.

64   1986 Review, para. 9, at p. 19. This view was reaffirmed in the 1991 Review (note 42 above), at p. 48.

65   See further Wilkins 'Defining a firm: history and theory', in Peter Hertner and Geoffrey Jones (eds), *Multinationals: Theory and History* (Gower, 1986), p. 80, especially at pp. 88–91, and see chapter 3 above.

66   1979 Review (note 56 above), para. 42; 1986 Review (note 42 above), para. 8, at p. 19.

67   Ibid.

68   Ibid.

69   1991 Review (note 42 above), p. 51.

70   1991 Review, at p. 37.

71   1979 Review (note 56 above), para. 40; 1986 Review (note 42 above), para. 6, at p. 18.

72   See at note 42 above, 15 ILM at p. 968 (1976); or 1986 Review, at pp. 9–
     10; or OECD publication *National Treatment for Foreign-controlled Enter-
     prises* (1985), at p. 9. The National Treatment instrument was reviewed
     again in the 1991 Review, chapter II. See too the 1993 report note 82
     below.

73   Council Decision C(76) 118 passed on 21 June 1976: see 15 ILM 978
     (1976). Council Decision C(76) 118 was replaced by Revised Council
     Decision C(79) 144 on 13 June 1979 after the 1979 Review of the
     Guidelines: see 18 ILM 1173 (1979). Revised Council Decision C(79)
     144 was in turn replaced by the *Second Revised Decision of the Council on
     National Treatment*: see 1986 Review, at pp. 72–3, or OECD, *National
     Treatment for Foreign-controlled Enterprises* (1985), at pp. 10–11 (hereafter
     cited as National Treatment). The *Second Revised Council Decision* was
     replaced by the *Third Revised Council Decision* of December 1991: see 1991
     Review, at pp. 113–15. All references are to the *Third Revised Decision*. The
     Third Revised Decision is due to be reviewed after three years in 1994.

74   See National Treatment (note 72 above), chapters III and IV. In making
     its reports on 'national treatment' the Committee may request the views of
     the Business and Industry Advisory committee to the OECD (BIAC) and
     the Trade Union Advisory Committee (TUAC): Third Revised Council
     Decision on National Treatment, ibid., article 5(b).

75   The first survey was published by the OECD in 1978 under the title
     *National Treatment for Foreign-controlled Enterprises Established in OECD
     Countries*. The second survey was published in 1985: see National Treat-
     ment (note 72 above), chapter V. A third survey was undertaken in 1994.

76   See *Third Revised Council Decision on National Treatment* (note 73 above),
     article 1.

77   Ibid., article 2.

78   Ibid., article 3.

79   Ibid., article 5. (a)(iv).

80   The *Second Revised Council Decision on National Treatment* was passed in
     1984. By para. 8 thereof it was to be reviewed at the latest in six years, i.e.
     in 1990.

81   In particular, it appears that the United States, after having called for a
     strengthening of the National Treatment instrument, was holding up the
     process, as it would not agree to make the instrument binding at state
     level. This was because of increased concern over the effects of inward
     direct investment among state administrations within the USA. Canada
     also expressed reservations over the applicability of such an instrument to
     its federal provinces. See 'OECD presses for more liberal rules on invest-
     ment', *Financial Times*, 31 January 1991, p. 6.

82   Note 72 above. See too *National Treatment for Foreign-Controlled Enterprises*
     (1993).

83   See ibid., at pp. 16–19; 1993 Report at pp. 14–17.

84   See National Treatment, para. 3.3, at p. 16 and para. 4.5(c), at
     pp. 27–8; 1993 Report at pp. 21–2.

85   Ibid., para. 3.4, at p. 16.

86   See chapter 7 at pp. 248–50.

87   National Treatment, para. 3.7, at p. 19; 1993 Report at p. 23.

88   1991 Review (note 42 above), at p. 34; 1993 Report at p. 23.
89   National Treatment, para. 3.2(b), at p. 16; 1993 Report at pp. 16, 27–8.
90   National Treatment, para. 4.1, at p. 20. For a full analysis of the Committee's view on these areas of law see 1993 Report pp. 24–47.
91   1991 Review, at p. 27.
92   Introduction to the Guidelines, para. 10.
93   The original Council Decision was C(76)117 of 21 June 1976; see 15 ILM 977 (1976). This was replaced by Council Decision C(79)143 of 20 July 1979; see 18 ILM 1171 (1979). This was in turn replaced by the *Second Revised Council Decision on the Guidelines for Multinational Enterprises* in 1984: see 1986 Review (note 42 above), at pp. 71–2. This was amended in 1991: see 1991 Review (note 42 above), at pp. 116–17. All references are to the 1991 amended version.
94   Ibid., para. 3.
95   Ibid.
96   Ibid., para. 4.
97   Ibid., para. 5. This was introduced by the 1979 Revised Council Decision.
98   1979 Review (note 56 above), paras 84–5 at p. 1010; or 1986 Review (note 42 above), paras 130–1, at p. 51.
99   Second Revised Council Decision (note 93 above), para. 1.
100   1986 Review (note 42 above), para. 139, at p. 53.
101   Ibid., para. 151, at p. 56.
102   See further 1986 Review at paras 122–57 at pp. 49–58. See also Robinson (note 43 above), at pp. 144–6.
103   1991 Review, at pp. 41–2.
104   In 1985 the OECD Council decided to add a new chapter on the environment to the Guidelines: see 1986 Review, paras 18–28, at pp. 22–4. The new chapter is discussed in detail below.
105   The reference to consumer interests was added in 1984: 1986 Review, para. 15, at p. 21.
106   Guidelines, 'General policies', para. 2.
107   This last requirement seeks to deal with the situation where the MNE may choose to close down a profitable subsidiary. It suggests that, while the MNE remains free to develop its global commercial strategy as it sees fit, should this involve the closure of a profitable local subsidiary, the firm should consider this decision in the context of the host state's economy. See 1986 Review, para. 12, at p. 20.
108   Guidelines, 'General Policies', para. 6.
109   Ibid., para. 7.
110   Ibid., paras 8 and 9.
111   See pp. 347–8.
112   1986 Review, para. 33, at p. 25.
113   Ibid., para. 30, at p. 24. Unilever draws up its accounts in accordance with the OECD Guidelines: Unilever *Annual Accounts 1992*, p. 2.
114   1986 Review, para. 42, at p. 28, Robinson notes that both the USA and Sweden have referred to the Guidelines on competition policy. See Robinson (note 43 above), at p. 154.
115   See further 1986 Review, 43–8, at pp. 28–29. See also chapter 11 at

pp. 404–11, for discussion of the UNCTAD Set of Multilaterally Agreed Equitable Principles and Rules on Restrictive Business Practices.

116 1986 Review, para. 49, at p. 30. The 1991 Review does not discuss this heading.

117 See further chapter 8.

118 1991 Review, at pp. 107–8; discussed in ibid., at pp. 52–4.

119 1991 Review, at p. 53.

120 See further chapter 12.

121 1986 Review, paras 88–91, at pp. 40–1.

122 Note 42 above.

123 1979 Review, para. 121, at p. 1019. See also 1991 Review, chapter V and OECD, *Investment Incentives and Disincentives and Their Effects on International Direct Investment* (1989).

124 Ibid.

125 Council Decision C(76)119 of 21 June 1976; see 15 ILM 980 (1976). This Decision was replaced by Revised Council Decision C(79)145 of 20 July 1979; see 18 ILM 1175 (1979). This was in turn replaced by the *Second Revised Council Decision* of 1984, reproduced in the 1986 Review, at p. 74, and in the 1991 Review, at p. 118.

126 See ibid., para. 3.

127 1979 Review, para. 126, at p. 1020.

128 See *International Investment and Multinational Enterprises: Investment Incentives and Disincentives and the International Investment Process* (OECD, March 1983, Sales No. 21 83 01 1). The findings of the Committee's work in this area are summarized in the *Mid-term Report on the 1976 Declaration and Decisions* (OECD, 1982), chapter III, and in the *1984 Review of the 1976 Declaration and Decisions* (Doc. OEEC 1198/7), chapter IV.

129 Note 125 above.

130 See 1984 Review, paras 110–12, at pp. 52–3.

131 The term 'transnational corporation' (TNC) will be used in this section in conformity with UN practice. No distinction is intended from the term 'multinational enterprise' used elsewhere in the book.

132 See further: Robinson (note 43 above), at pp. 163–6; Nixson, 'Controlling the transnationals? Political economy and the United Nations Code of Conduct', 11 Int'l Jo. Soc. L. 83 (1983); W. J. Field, *Multinational Corporations and UN Politics: the Quest for Codes of Conduct* (Pergamon, 1982).

133 See Commission on Transnational Corporations, *Report on the First Session 17–28 March 1975* (E/5655; E/C. 10/6 Economic and Social Council Official Records 59th Session Supplement No. 12), para. 9, at p. 2.

134 See Commission on Transnational Corporations, *Report on the Second Session 1–12 March 1976* (Economic and Social Council Official Records 61st Session Supplement No. 5, May 1976), paras 10–17 and 47–51; reproduced in 15 ILM 779 at pp. 782–3 and 790 (1976).

135 Ibid., annex II, 'Areas of concern which relate to relations between transnational corporations and governments': note submitted by the delegations of France, Federal Republic of Germany, Italy, the United King-

dom of Great Britain and Northern Ireland and the United States of America. See at ILM pp. 799–802.

136 See GA Resolution 3281 (XXIX) 14 ILM 251 (1975), especially chapter II, article 2, which states: '1. Every State has and shall freely exercise full permanent sovereignty, including possession, use and disposal, over all its wealth, natural resources and economic activities. 2. Each State has the right: (a) To regulate and exercise authority over foreign investment within its national jurisdiction in accordance with its laws and regulations and in conformity with its national objectives and priorities. No State shall be compelled to grant preferential treatment to foreign investment; (b) To regulate and supervise the activities of transnational corporations within its national jurisdiction and take measures to ensure that such activities comply with its laws, rules and regulations and conform with its economic and social policies. Transnational corporations shall not intervene in the internal affairs of a host State. Every State should, with full regard for its sovereign rights, co-operate with other States in the exercise of the right set forth in this subparagraph; (c) To nationalize, expropriate or transfer ownership of foreign property, in which case appropriate compensation should be paid by the State adopting such measures, taking into account its relevant laws and regulations and all circumstances that the State considers pertinent. In any case where the question of compensation gives rise to a controversy, it shall be settled under the domestic law of the nationalizing State and by its tribunals, unless it is freely and mutually agreed by all States concerned that other peaceful means be sought on the basis of the sovereign equality of States and in accordance with the principle of free choice of means.'

137 Note 134 above, annex I, 'List of areas of concern regarding the operations and activities of transnational corporations': note submitted by the Group of 77. See at ILM pp. 798–9. Annex, III, 'Issues requiring the attention of the Commission and the Information and Research Centre on Transnational Corporations': note submitted by the People's Republic of Bulgaria, the German Democratic Republic, the Ukrainian Soviet Socialist Republic and the Union of Soviet Socialist Republics. See at ILM p. 802.

138 Commission on Transnational Corporations (note 134 above), Annex IV, 'Areas of concern which could be used as a basis for preliminary work for a code of conduct to be observed by transnational corporations': paper submitted by the delegations of Argentina, Barbados, Brazil, Colombia, Equador, Jamaica, Mexico, Peru, Trinidad and Tobago and Venezuela. See at ILM pp. 802–809. (Also published as UN Doc E/C. 10/1.2.)

139 See Asante, 'United Nations: international regulation of transnational corporations', 13 JWTL 55 at 57–8 (1979). This article contains a useful summary of the issues surrounding the draft Code at its inception.

140 See UN Commission on Transnational Corporations, *Information Paper on the Negotiations to Complete the Code of Conduct on Transnational Corporations* (UN Doc. E/C. 10/1983/S/2 of 4 January 1983), para. 13: reproduced 22 ILM 177 at p. 181 (1983).

141 See UN Doc E/C. 10/1982/6 of 5 June 1982.

142 See UN Commission on Transnational Corporations (note 140 above), para. 15 at ILM p. 182.

143 Meetings of the special session have been held on 7–18 March 1983, 9–21 May 1983, 11–29 June 1984, 9–13 November 1984, 17–21 June 1985, 20–31 January 1986, 14 April 1986, 6 April 1987 and 24 May 1990.

144 The 1990 proposed text can be found in UN Doc. E/1990/94 of 12 June 1990 or in annex IV of the UNCTC publication, *Transnational Corporations, Services and the Uruguay Round* (1990, UN Doc. ST/CTC/103). This text supersedes the 1988 text which can be found in UN Doc. E/1988/39/Add. 1 of 1 February 1988. The text of the Code as it stood in the summer of 1986 can be found in annex I to UNCTC publication, *The United Nations Code of Conduct on Transnational Corporations* (September 1986, UNCTC Current Studies Series A, No. 4, UN Doc. ST/CTC/SER. A/4). Earlier formulations of the draft Code can be found in UN Doc. E/C. 10/1984/S/5 of 29 May 1984, reproduced in 23 ILM 602 at pp. 626–40, and UN Doc. E/C. 10/1983/S/2 of 4 January 1983, reproduced in 22 ILM 177 at pp. 192–206. This reproduces the first draft Code submitted by the Intergovernmental Working Group in 1982, referred to in note 141 above. For detailed discussion of the 1990 Draft see M. Sornarajah, *The International Law on Foreign Investment* (Grotius Publications, 1994), at pp. 194–211.

145 International Chamber of Commerce, *Annual Report 1992*, p. 24.

146 See, for example, the preamble to the draft Code and UNCTC, *The United Nations Code of Conduct on Transnational Corporations* (September 1986, UNCTC Current Studies Series A, No. 4, UN Doc ST/CTC/SER. A/4), pp. 2–3. (Cited hereafter as UNCTC Series A, No. 4).

147 1990 Draft Code, para. 48; UNCTC, 1990 (note 144 above), at p. 180.

148 Note 144 above. This section is divided into three parts. The first deals with general obligations of TNCs (paras 7–20). The second part deals with economic, financial and social obligations of TNCs (paras 21–46). The third deals with disclosure (paras 47–58).

149 For a full statement of the developing country position see Patrick Robinson, *The Question of a Reference to International Law in the United Nations Code of Conduct on Transnational Corporations* (July 1986, UNCTC Current Studies, Series A, No. 1, UN Doc. ST/CTC/SER. A/1).

150 UNCTC, 1990 (note 144 above), at p. 180–1. For an attempt to reconcile these conflicting positions see Detlev Vagts, *The Question of a Reference to International Obligations in the United Nations Code of Conduct on Transnational Corporations: a Different View* (September 1986, UNCTC Current Studies, Series A No. 2, UN Doc. ST/CTC/SER. A/2).

151 UNCTC, *Key Concepts in International Investment Arrangements and Their Relevance to Negotiations on International Transactions in Series* (February 1990, UNCTC Current Studies Series A, No. 13, UN Doc ST/CTC/SER. A/13), at p. 11.

152 See further UNCTC, Series A, No. 13, ibid., at pp. 11–12.

153 By paragraph 50 of the draft Code: 'Subject to national requirements for maintaining public order and protecting national security and consistent with national constitutions and basic laws, and without prejudice

to measures specified in legislation relating to the declared development objectives of the developing countries, entities of transnational
corporations should be entitled to treatment no less favourable than that
accorded to domestic enterprises in similar circumstances.'

154 This last qualification appears to meet the concerns expressed by the
capital-exporting states, that development objectives should not be used as
a means of undermining the basic principle of national treatment, in that
it requires specific reference to measures specified in legislation that de-
clares the host state's development objectives. The phraseology used
comes from the compromise formulation put forward by the Chairman of
the special session in 1983: see UN Doc E/C. 10/1984/S/5 of 29 May
1984, paras 27–30, reproduced in 23 ILM 602 at pp. 610–11.

155 UNCTC, 1990 (note 144 above), at p. 181.

156 It read: 'Nothing in this paragraph should be construed as excluding the
right of the host country to grant such special incentives and facilities to
transnational corporations as may be considered necessary in its national
interest.'

157 See further chapter 14.

158 See UN Doc E/C. 10/1983/S/2 of 4 January 1983, para. 49, and UN Doc
E/C. 10/1982/6 of 5 June 1982, annex 1982, draft Code para. 54 (alternative formulations). Both references are reproduced in 22 ILM 177 at p.
190 and p. 203 respectively.

159 UN Doc E/1988/39/Add. 1, at p. 15.

160 See UNCTC, 1990 (note 144 above), annex IV, at p. 241, para. 55.

161 Ibid., at p. 182.

162 See UNCTC, *The New Code Environment* (1990); summarized in UN Doc
E/C. 10/1990/5 of 29 January 1990. See also Report of the Secretary-
General, 'Transnational corporations in the new world economy: issues
and policy implications' (UN Doc. E/C. 10/1992/5, 5 February 1992);
Report of the Secretary-General, 'International arrangements and agreements relating to transnational corporations' (UN Doc. E/C. 10/1992/8,
18 February 1992).

163 E/C. 10/1990/5, paras 16–20, at p. 8.

164 Ibid., paras 39–41.

165 Ibid., para. 45.

166 Ibid., para. 47.

167 Hamilton (note 47 above), at p. 25.

168 World Bank Report to the Development Committee and Guidelines on
the Treatment of Foreign Direct Investment 21 September 1992, published as *Legal Framework for the Treatment of Foreign Direct Investment*
(Volume II, Guidelines) (World Bank, 1992), reproduced 31 ILM 1363
(1992). See also, for the background surveys and reports on which the
Guidelines are based: *Legal Framework for the Treatment of Foreign Direct
Investment* (Volume I) (World Bank, 1992). Both volumes are reproduced
with updated surveys in the Fall 1992 issue of ICSID Rev-FILJ. The
Guidelines, their detailed drafting history, the Report to the Development
Committee and all the above-mentioned supporting documentation are
brought together in I. F. I. Shihata, *Legal Treatment of Foreign Investment:
the World Bank Guidelines* (Martinus Nijhoff, 1993).

169 See I. Shihata, 'Introductory note' to the Guidelines of 25 September 1992, ILM p. 1367 and 'The World Bank Group's new "Guidelines on the Treatment of Foreign Direct Investment" ', *News from ICSID*, Vol. 10, No. 1 (Winter 1993), p. 4.

170 Shihata, *News from ICSID*, previous note at p. 5. For a full analysis of the Guidelines see 'The Report to the Development Committee', in *Legal Framework for the Treatment of Foreign Investment* (Volume II) (note 168 above), reproduced at ILM pp. 1368–79.

171 1992 Guidelines I(3).

172 Ibid., II(3) and (6).

173 Ibid., II(3).

174 Ibid.

175 Ibid., II(4)(i) and (ii).

176 Ibid., II(5).

177 Ibid., III(2).

178 Ibid., III(3)(a) and (b).

179 Ibid., III(6)(1).

180 Ibid., III(4).

181 Ibid., III(5).

182 Ibid., III(7).

183 Ibid., III(8).

184 Ibid., III(9).

185 Ibid., III(10).

186 Ibid., IV(1).

187 Ibid., IV(2).

188 Ibid., IV(3).

189 Ibid., IV(4) and (5).

190 Ibid., IV(6).

191 Ibid., IV(7).

192 Ibid., IV(8).

193 Ibid., IV(9) and (10).

194 Ibid., IV(11).

195 Ibid., V(1).

196 Ibid., V(2).

197 Ibid., V(3).

198 Note 168 above, para. 6, at ILM p. 1369.

199 MIGA Convention 1985, article 12(d)(iv). The Convention is reproduced in 24 ILM 1598 (1985). For detailed analysis of the standard-setting aspects of the MIGA Convention see I. F. I. Shihata, *MIGA and Foreign Investment* (Martinus Nijhoff, 1988), chapter 6.

200 27 ILM 1227 (1988).

201 MIGA Convention (note 199 above), article 23(b)(iii).

202 Shihata (note 199 above), at p. 233.

203 Shihata, ibid.

204 See also Shihata, ibid., who floats the idea of non-binding guidelines at pp. 244–7. Mr Shihata was instrumental in the adoption of the 1992 Guidelines, being General-Counsel of the World Bank, Secretary-General of ICSID and the chairman of the World Bank working group that drew up the Guidelines.

205   By para. 3.17 of the Operational Regulations (note 200 above): 'If the Underwriting Authority is not satisfied as to the availability of fair and equitable treatment and legal protection for the investment, it shall only issue coverage after the Agency has concluded an agreement with the host country under Article 23(b)(ii) of the Convention and Paragraph 3.33(i) below.' Para. 3.33(i) states: 'With a view to enhancing its ability to issue guarantees, the Agency may agree with the host country on: (i) the treatment of guaranteed investment in accordance with Article 23(b)(ii) of the Convention'.

206   See MIGA Convention (note 199 above), article 23(a) and (c).

207   Ibid., article 23(a)(i)–(iii).

208   This has been recently reinforced by the failure of negotiations, under the auspices of the OECD, for a new Multilateral Agreement on Investment (MAI): 'Retreat over OECD pact on investment', *Financial Times*, 21 October 1998, p. 4. The final draft of the MAI negotiating text and commentary (as of 24 April 1998) can be obtained from the OECD MAI website at http://www.oecd.org/daf/cmis/mai. For background see: OECD *Towards Multilateral Investment Rules* (Paris, OECD, 1996); Fatouros, 'Towards an International Agreement on Foreign Direct Investment?', 10 ICSID-FILJ 181 (1995); Engering, 'The Multilateral Investment Agreement', 5, *Transnational Corporations*, 147 (1996); S. Picciotto and R. Mayne (eds) *Regulating International Business: Beyond Liberalization* (Macmillan, 1999).

Bilateral Investment Treaties

A bilateral treaty for the promotion and protection of foreign investments (BIT)[1] can be defined as a legally binding international agreement between two states, whereby each state promises, on a
reciprocal basis, to observe the standards of treatment laid down by
the treaty in its dealings with investors from the other contracting
state. Those standards are designed to protect the proprietary and
other commercial interests of the investor against arbitrary and prejudicial action on the part of the host contracting state, thereby ensuring the maintenance of secure and stable investment conditions
within that state. In this respect the BIT acts as a means of promoting
investment between the contracting states, in that the stability it seeks
to achieve can contribute towards a good investment climate in both
states.

The nature and effects of such treaties will be studied as follows:
first, the origins of BITs will be considered; secondly, the principal
terms found in the majority of BITs will be analysed; thirdly, the legal
effects of such treaties within the national legal systems of the contracting states will be considered; fourthly, the use of such treaties
will be assessed; finally, their effect on the content of customary
international law will be considered.

1 The Origins of BITs

Bilateral commercial treaties have been a long-standing feature of
international relations.[2] The first bilateral agreements to deal with the
protection of foreign direct investments were the friendship, commerce and navigation (FCN) treaties concluded during the period
following the Second World War up to the late 1960s. These were
concluded primarily by the United States with its advanced trading
partners, though other advanced countries also concluded such
treaties.[3] They included provisions on the protection of corporate

investments, based on the national treatment standard.[4] This standard is central to BITs, and is considered below.

FCN treaties are no longer being negotiated, although such treaties remain in force for a number of countries.[5] The principal reason for their demise is that such treaties contain a breadth of provisions dealing not only with commercial matters but also with the protection of the rights of individuals and with general good relations between the signatory states. They do not have a specific business orientation. Nor do they deal in adequate detail with the most pressing problems likely to be faced by foreign investors, such as funds transfers, unfair treatment or dispute settlement.[6] Furthermore, FCN treaties were concluded primarily between the economically advanced states. Their purpose was to further good relations between them. Such treaties were not, therefore, suited to the task assigned to BITs, namely the control of less developed, capital-importing states in their treatment of foreign investors.

The first specialized BIT was concluded in 1959 between the Federal Republic of Germany and Pakistan. Germany has concluded over sixty BITs, making it the leading capital-exporting country to use such treaties.[7] Switzerland concluded its first BIT in 1961 with Tunisia. It now has some twenty such treaties in addition to some seventeen commercial agreements other than BITs which contain extensive investment protection clauses.[8] However, the majority of BITs were not concluded until the 1970s and 1980s. Following the German and Swiss examples, other capital-exporting countries began at this time to conclude BITs with developing, capital-importing countries. This was a deliberate policy response to what the capital-exporting countries perceived as a threat to traditional international standards for the treatment of foreign investors arising from UN resolutions calling for a New International Economic Order, and from demands for binding international codes of conduct on MNEs. Thus France signed its first BIT with Tunisia in 1972 and now has over twenty agreements in force; the United Kingdom signed its first BIT with Egypt in 1975 and has now signed about twenty-eight such treaties; Japan began signing such treaties in 1977 and the United States embarked on such a policy in 1983 with the drafting of a model BIT.[9] It now has some twenty-three agreements, fourteen of which are in force.[10]

In addition to national model treaties certain supranational bodies and organizations have put forward model BITs. Most notably, the Asian African Legal Consultative Committee (AALCC) has prepared three model BITs for use among the Afro-Asian States themselves.[11] These are significant in that they present three alternative models, reflecting differing conceptions of political economy and the divergent nature of commitments already made in bilateral treaties with capital-exporting states. Thus 'Model A' represents a liberal standard of investment protection and follows the pattern adopted in BITs entered into by some Afro-Asian countries subject to certain changes and improvements in relation to the promotion of investments. 'Model B' contains more restrictive provisions in the matter of protection of investments and contemplates a greater degree of flexibility in regard to the reception and protection of investments on the part of the host state – it is, in this respect, closer to the ideals behind the original conception of the UN Code of Conduct for TNCs. Finally, 'Model C' incorporates the terms of 'Model A' but is applicable only to specific classes of investment as may be determined by the host state. It conforms to the practice of certain African states.[12]

Thus, in the past twenty years or so a comprehensive network of bilateral investment treaties has sprung up. Furthermore, the ASEAN Member States have concluded *inter se* a multilateral Agreement on the Promotion and Protection of Investments, modelled closely on the BITs used by the capital-exporting countries, in an effort to stimulate intraregional investment.[13] It has been argued that such treaties have reinforced the legal authority of traditional international minimum standards for the treatment of aliens and their property.[14] This claim will be examined after the substantive content of BITs has been considered.

2   The Principal Provisions Common to BITs

It is beyond the present work to offer a comprehensive and detailed analysis of the principal provisions of BITs. This has been done elsewhere.[15] However, a general analysis of the principal trends in BIT practice is essential for an understanding of their role in the regulation of MNE–host state relations. The major provisions of BITs are broadly similar, although there are some significant national variations. Most BITs follow the pattern used in the text below.

2.1   Preamble
The preambles to BITs set down the general objects and purposes of such treaties. These emphasize the desirability of greater economic integration between the contracting parties through improved conditions of investment as laid down in the treaty. There is little variation between the formulations used. A significant variation is

where the contracting states use the preamble to define specific sectors in which investment is to be protected or promoted. For example, BITs concluded by Switzerland with Sudan and Egypt highlight investment promotion in the fields of 'production, commerce, tourism and technology'.[16]

2.2   Provisions Defining the Scope of Application of the Treaty

BITs contain provisions that define the scope of application of the treaty *ratione materiae, ratione personae, ratione territoriae* and *ratione temporis*. It is in the negotiation of these provisions that the host state can influence the effect of the treaty upon its economy, for example by restricting it to specific sectors.[17]

2.2.1   *Application* ratione materiae   BITs usually commence with a provision that defines the 'investments' of the contracting parties which are covered by the treaty. The capital-exporting states tend to favour broad definitions that include not only physical assets, equity and choses in action but also intellectual property rights and concessions.[18] The aim is to ensure sufficient flexibility to encompass not only equity but also non-equity investments, and to allow for the evolution of new forms of investment between the parties. Furthermore, the notion of direct investment is not taken as the starting point.[19] However, certain treaties concluded by Germany contain a clause which makes clear that all the general categories of investment mentioned in the standard definition clause are to be linked to a direct investment.[20]

The US Model Treaty contains an additional clause in its definition of 'investments' to the effect that 'Any alteration in the form in which the assets are invested or reinvested shall not affect their character as investments.'[21] Such clauses are also found in the majority of treaties concluded by Germany.[22] However, they do not feature in the Swiss, Dutch, British or AALCC models.

It has already been noted that under general international law states have the unlimited right to exclude foreign nationals and companies from entering their territory. There is no international standard requiring states to adopt an 'open door' to inward direct investment.[23] Most BITs reserve the right of the host state to regulate the *entry of foreign investments* into its territory. Therefore, the application of the treaty to an investment is made conditional on its being approved in accordance with the laws and regulations of the host state.[24] On the other hand, states are free to set the limits of permissible entry in their national laws as they see fit. Furthermore, states are free to agree to provisions in BITs securing access to their territory by investors from the other contracting party, along the lines of a FCN treaty. Thus the US Model BIT states, in article II(1):

> Each Party shall permit and treat investment, and activities associated therewith, on a basis no less favourable than that accorded in like situations to investment or associated activities of its own nationals or companies, or of nationals or companies of any third country, whichever is the most favourable, subject to the right of each party to make or maintain exceptions falling within one of the sectors or matters listed in the annex to this Treaty.[25]

This provision makes entry to the host state subject to the MFN principle, and, to that extent, represents a restriction on the host state's sovereign power to regulate the entry of foreign investors. However, the MFN principle is subject to the right of the host state to exclude certain sectors from foreign investment, a principle accepted under US law.[26] Therefore, the US Model accepts restrictions on entry, provided they are applied in a manner that does not discriminate against US investors.[27] Recently, under the Russian Federation–USA BIT, the Contracting States agreed that, for a period of five years, the Russian Federation would be able to require permission for large-scale investments that exceed the threshold amount in the Russian Federation Law on Foreign Investments of 4 July 1991, provided that this power is not used to limit competition or to discourage investment by US companies and nationals.[28]

British practice is broadly similar to US practice, in so far as it extends the MFN standard to the treatment of investors from the UK.[29] However, the UK has agreed to clauses which subject the entry of the UK investor to the requirements of host state laws, including approval procedures.[30] Thus the UK position on this matter appears to be flexible.

It is common to find provisions in BITs which exclude their application from industrial and commercial sectors that are prohibited to foreign investors by the host state. This can be done by implication from a reference, in the admission of investments clause, to the national laws of the host country where such restrictions are to be found, or expressly, by means of a clause enumerating the sectors to which the treaty applies, thereby excluding the sectors not mentioned, or by way of an agreed list of excluded sectors. This latter approach is taken by the USA. Its BITs contain an annex listing the sectors that each party seeks to be excluded from the operation of the treaty.[31] The purpose is to preserve the exclusive control of the US authorities over certain designated sectors of the US economy. That in turn requires the granting of a similar right to the other contracting party.

Most BITs extend their protection to investments already made by nationals of the contracting parties prior to the conclusion of the treaty. However, not all host countries accept such a clause. Thus some treaties extend to prior investments only on condition that the host state approves a special request to that effect in each case, while others only apply to investments made at a specified date prior to the conclusion of the treaty. Some treaties contain a blanket exclusion of investments made prior to the entry into force of the treaty.[32]

2.2.2 Application ratione personae   The protection offered by BITs is limited to investors who invest in the territory of the host contracting state and who possess a link of nationality with the home contracting state. Consequently, the BIT must define both the persons and the corporations that are to be treated as nationals of the other contracting party for the purposes of the treaty.

The attribution of nationality to natural persons is not generally a problem. Most BITs simply refer to the country's citizenship laws as governing the matter.[33] However, further criteria might be introduced, such as a combined requirement of citizenship and residence.[34] In British practice, the right of residence has been used as an alternative to British citizenship in defining British nationals for the purpose of a BIT.[35]

By contrast, the definition of nationality in the case of corporations is more complex. The nationality of a company may be determined by reference to one or more of the following criteria: the place of incorporation, the location of the registered office or seat of the company or the nationality of the controlling interest in the company. All these criteria have been used, alone or in combination, in BITs.[36] Furthermore, the term 'companies' has not been restricted to legally incorporated entities alone; often it includes references to partnerships and other forms of business association.

The most significant issue in the context of the present study is the extent to which BITs cover the case of an investment made by a parent company from the home contracting state through a subsidiary company incorporated under the laws of the host contracting state. This raises matters that have already been encountered in the context of the jurisdiction *ratione personae* of ICSID under article 25(2)(b) of the Washington Convention. Can the BIT extend its protection to the local subsidiary of the foreign parent company notwithstanding its possession of host state nationality? The provisions of BITs have approached this problem in a number of ways.[37] First, some treaties are silent on the matter. This is the case with the majority of BITs concluded by France and Belgium, although some more recent French agreements now include a 'control' criterion.[38]

Similarly, UK practice has been not to use a test of control in determining the nationality of a locally incorporated subsidiary.[39] The legal effect of such an approach is to remove the protection of the treaty from the locally incorporated subsidiary.

However, the provision defining the nationality of the corporation should be read alongside the definition of investments covered by the treaty. This may be broad enough to cover investments carried out through foreign-owned local companies. Thus the US model treaty defines a 'company of a party' as 'any kind of corporation, company, association, or other organization, legally constituted under the laws and regulations of a Party or a political subdivision thereof whether or not organized for pecuniary gain, or privately or governmentally owned'.[40] Without more it would be unclear from this definition whether locally incorporated foreign-owned subsidiaries were within the scope of the treaty. However, the term 'investment' is defined as 'every kind of investment in the territory of one Party owned or controlled, directly or indirectly by nationals or companies of the other party, such as equity, debt, service and investment contracts'.[41] This is sufficient to protect the investment of a national or company of the home contracting state which takes the form of a company established under the law of the host contracting state. In such a case the application of the treaty is not based on the nationality of the subsidiary, but on the nationality of its controlling interest.

A second approach to this issue is for the treaty to contain a definition of corporate nationality that includes a test based on controlling interests as an exclusive or an alternative test. Thus Swiss BITs contain a reference to legal persons or companies with or without legal personality in which nationals of one or other contracting party have a substantial interest (*intérêt prépondérant*).[42] This ensures that locally incorporated foreign-owned subsidiaries are covered by the treaty. However, the control test is exceptional. It makes more of the links with the home country, based on capital, than of the legal links of the subsidiary company with the host country, by reason of its incorporation there. In this the test does not represent the existing state of international law.[43]

A third approach is to infer the nationality of the home country to the subsidiary incorporated in the host country by means of an agreement between the subsidiary and the host country.[44] It is reminiscent of the approach taken under article 25(2)(b) of the Washington Convention in relation to the jurisdiction of ICSID over disputes between the host Contracting State and a local subsidiary owned by investors possessing the nationality of another Contracting State.

The fourth approach is one of specifically extending the protection of the BIT to subsidiaries owned by or under the effective control of nationals or companies from the other contracting state. For example, the German model treaty extends the national treatment and MFN standards to 'investments in [the territory of a Contracting Party] owned or controlled by nationals or companies of the other Contracting Party'.[45] According to Laviec, in such a case the protection of the treaty is extended to the local subsidiary without undermining the test of corporate nationality as established under international law. The link with home country nationals is established on the basis of their economic interests in the subsidiary, without the need to designate the subsidiary as possessing home country nationality in opposition to its nationality of incorporation.[46]

Finally, some BITs provide limited protection for shareholders from the home contracting state in companies incorporated in the host contracting state, even though they do not extend their protection to locally incorporated foreign owned companies. Thus in the UK–Philippines BIT,[47] article V(2) extends the protection against unlawful expropriation to cases where the assets of a company incorporated under the law of the expropriating state are taken, and in which nationals or companies of the other contracting state own shares. Furthermore, by article X(2) companies incorporated under the law of one contracting party, in which a majority of the shares are owned by nationals or companies of the other contracting party, shall be treated, for the purposes of disputes under the Washington Convention, as companies of the other contracting party, in accordance with article 25(2)(b) of that Convention. These provisions represent departures from the law on the diplomatic protection of shareholders, as laid down in the *Barcelona Traction* case.[48] Consequently, these provisions represent specific treaty-based standards of treatment and not general principles of international law.

2.2.3 Application ratione territoriae   It is unnecessary to go into detail on these provisions. The territorial scope of the treaty will be defined by its terms. Usually, the treaty will apply throughout the territory of both contracting states. However, it may contain territorial extension or restriction clauses. A particular problem that has been encountered concerns the applicability of the treaty to maritime exclusive economic zones. This may be particularly important in relation to the treatment of offshore natural resources concessions.[49]

2.2.4 Application ratione temporis   The entry into force of a treaty occurs on the date designated by the parties for this purpose. The usual practice is that the BIT enters force upon the exchange of instruments of approval or ratification, or upon reciprocal notification that the relevant constitutional requirements of each contracting state have been fulfilled, or at a set date after such notification has been given, usually after one month.[50] The termination of the treaty is usually provided for in that the treaty is designated to last for a period of years. The usual period is ten years, although shorter terms of five years and longer terms of up to twenty years have been agreed. Some treaties are open-ended, providing for termination after the giving of the required period of notice.[51] Additionally, there may be clauses that extend the operation of the protection granted by the treaty beyond the date of termination in cases where individual investments, entered into while the treaty was in force, continue after the date of termination.[52]

2.3 Standards of Treatment

The core provisions of BITs concern the standards of treatment to be applied to investments made by nationals and companies of one contracting party in the territory of the other. The applicable standards can be classified into general standards, encompassing both international minimum standards of treatment and standards evolved in earlier FCN treaties, and specific standards applicable to particular incidents of investment activity, such as the transfer of funds and taxation.

2.3.1 *General standards of treatment*   General standards of treatment have been divided into those recognized by general international law and those that have evolved out of commercial treaty practice.[53] The principal general standards of treatment referred to in BITs are those of fair and equitable treatment, national treatment and the MFN standard. Many treaties also contain clauses protecting the observance of obligations entered into between the investor and the host state.

The concept of fair and equitable treatment is not precisely defined. It offers a general point of departure in formulating an argument that the foreign investor has not been well treated by reason of discriminatory or other unfair measures being taken against its interests. It is, therefore, a concept that depends on the interpretation of specific facts for its content. At most it can be said that the concept connotes the principle of non-discrimination and proportionality in the treatment of foreign investors.[54]

It has been suggested that fair and equitable treatment represents a classical international law standard which embodies international minimum standards of treatment.[55] Indeed, the US model BIT contains, in article II(2) thereof, a provision which mentions fair and equitable treatment alongside international minimum standards.[56] According to Laviec, a reference to fair and equitable treatment should not be read as a reference to international minimum standards. If the intention is to assimilate the two concepts, this should be made explicit in the text.[57] Otherwise, the fair and equitable treatment standard should stand on its own.[58]

The practice of capital-importing countries concerning consent to the fair and equitable treatment standard is uneven. It is not included in the AALCC model treaties.[59] Nor has it been accepted by certain Asian and African states in their negotiations.[60] On the other hand, it does appear in some agreements with Central and South American states.[61] Furthermore, China has accepted the standard in some, but not all, of the agreements entered into by it.[62] The standard is accepted in the ASEAN multilateral investment treaty.[63]

As was seen in the context of codes of conduct in the previous chapter, the standard of national treatment requires that foreign investors should receive treatment no less favourable than that accorded to nationals of the host state engaged in similar business activity.[64] In this it represents less than the minimum protection accepted under international law, which demands treatment of foreigners better than that given to nationals where the treatment of nationals falls below international minimum standards. On the other hand, national treatment represents the maximum protection for economic rights accorded to foreign investors under host state law. Thus there is a paradoxical element in this standard.[65]

Though it aims at the elimination of discrimination between foreign and domestic investors, in the practice of capital-exporting states national treatment does not prevent preferential treatment for foreign investors by reference to international minimum standards. In this it differs considerably from the concept of national treatment implicit in the 'Calvo Doctrine' espoused by the Latin American states and other developing countries, which accepts the principle that foreign investors are to be accorded treatment no better than that given to domestic investors, regardless of whether such treatment falls below international minimum standards.

The national treatment standard is a treaty-made standard.[66] It is not a part of the corpus of customary international law. Consequently, its content cannot be derived from international law. Rather, it is a standard defined by reference to the national law applicable to the field of economic activities covered by the treaty. As such the standard has always recognized certain exceptions based on the public interest of the host state. Thus restrictions required by the needs of national security and public order have often been included in BITs.[67] Some treaties contain derogations based on the development objectives of the host state. Accordingly, preferential treatment in relation to investment incentives for nationals of the host state may be protected by the treaty where this is required for the economic development of the host state. Often, such derogations will be subject to the condition that they do not substantially impair competition and/or investment by nationals and companies of the other contracting state.[68]

The Most-Favoured-Nation (MFN) standard has been widely recognized in treaties by which states grant to each other reciprocal freedom of commerce. However, it is not recognized as a principle of customary international law.[69] Thus its content depends on the treaty in which it is included. The inclusion of a MFN clause in a BIT has the effect of extending, to the home contacting state, more favourable terms of investment granted to a third state by the host contracting state. Thereby, discriminatory terms of investment, operating against investors from the home contracting state, are prevented, and the equal treatment of all foreign investors by the host state is ensured.

The scope of MFN treatment is unconditional in the absence of express limitation.[70] However, the standard only operates in relation to the subject matter of the BIT; it cannot be extended by implication to matters covered by other treaties, such as conventions on the protection of intellectual property.[71] The same restriction *ratione materiae* appears to lie behind commonly found exceptions relating to privileges or benefits accorded to nationals and/or companies of third states by reason of the host contracting party's membership of any customs union, common market, free trade area or regional economic organization, or by reason of any international tax agreement entered into by the host contracting party.[72] It is uncertain whether the MFN standard demands that more favourable treatment accorded by a host contracting party to nationals of a home contracting state under one BIT must extend to nationals of the home contracting state under another BIT. Such an argument was put forward by the claimant in the ICSID arbitration *Asian Agricultural Products Ltd v Republic of Sri Lanka*.[73] It was rejected on the ground that the claimant had failed to show that the other BIT did in fact offer more favourable treatment. However, the Tribunal did not rule out such an argument in principle, and it would appear to be consistent with the aims of the MFN standard. However, the MFN standard can be specifically excluded in relation to certain third countries.[74]

In BITs it is common to combine the MFN standard with the national treatment standard in the same paragraph. This has the effect of ensuring that investors can avail themselves of the MFN standard where this is more favourable than the national treatment standard, as where investors from a third state are offered treatment better than national treatment.[75] In other treaties the beneficiary country will be given the choice between the MFN and national treatment standards.[76]

BITs usually contain provisions that ensure the observance of laws and regulations which provide for more favourable treatment of investors than the standards contained in the treaty, and of obligations entered into under investment agreements or authorizations.[77] The former preserves any benefits owed to investors under host state laws, regulations or other international agreements that go beyond the standards of treatment provided for in the treaty, thereby avoiding the use of the BIT as a statement of the maximum possible protection that the investor can enjoy. The latter ensures that the observance of any obligations entered into by the host state towards the foreign investor, either under a state contract or within the terms of an authorization for the admission of the investment, becomes an obligation under the treaty.[78] Such a provision, known as an 'umbrella clause', ensures an additional measure of contractual stability by making the observance of obligations owed to the investor a treaty standard, thereby reinforcing the existing contractual duties owed to the investor.

Contractual stability may also be ensured by the inclusion of a 'stabilization clause' in a BIT. Such a clause provides that if the host state changes its legislation, the law as it stood at the time the investment was made and/or agreed will continue to apply to that investment.[79] Stabilization clauses are rare in BITs. They are more commonly found in investment agreements between the host state and the foreign investor. However, should a BIT contain an 'umbrella clause', the host state would appear bound to observe the obligation contained in the stabilization clause of an investment agreement as part of the more general obligation of contractual observance created by the 'umbrella clause'.

2.3.2 Specific standards of treatment BITs contain standards on specific aspects of the treatment of a foreign investment by the host state. In particular, the following matters have been commonly dealt with by provisions in BITs: the free transfer of payments relating to the investment out of the host country; compensation for losses due to expropriation, armed conflict or internal disorder; the promotion of investments; the rights of entry and sojourn of individuals in connection with the investment; and performance requirements. Taxation is not dealt with under BITs. Some treaties contain provisions expressly excluding this area from their scope.[80]

Provisions on the free transfer of currency are among the most important ones in BITs.[81] They seek to ensure that the investor can transfer the income from its investment out of the jurisdiction of the host state and repatriate its capital on the termination of the investment. At the same time, such provisions may include limits on the free transfer of currency in the interests of the balance-of-payments position of the host country. Thus a balance is generally struck between the interests of the investor and of the host state.

The right to transfer currency is usually subject to the requirements that it shall be made without delay, in convertible currency and at the official rate of exchange at the date of transfer.[82] Some treaties go on to specify the types of transfers protected, often by way of a non-exhaustive list,[83] while others simply refer to transfers 'in respect of investments'.[84]

Most BITs contain restrictions on free transfer based on the interests of the host state. Thus the UK–Philippines BIT states, in article VII(1):

Each Contracting Party shall in respect of investments permit nationals or companies of the other Contracting Party the free transfer of their capital and of the earnings from it, subject to the right of the former Contracting Party to impose equitably and in good faith such measures as may be necessary to safeguard the integrity and independence of its currency, its external financial position and balance of payments, consistent with its rights and obligations as a member of the International Monetary Fund.[85]

The reference to the rights and obligations of the host state as a member of the IMF introduces by implication the standards of the IMF Articles of Agreement into the BIT regime.[86] These aim at the progressive elimination of restrictions on the free transfer of funds arising from current transactions, while accepting the right of states to impose restrictions on the free movement of capital where this is necessary in the interests of that state.[87] However, should the BIT provide for a greater freedom of transfer for the investor than the IMF Articles of Agreement, it is arguable that the terms of the BIT should prevail, as these represent a specialized regime of investor protection that is more elaborate than the IMF regime on the transfer of funds and capital.[88] Where the BIT does not mention the IMF regime, the presumption is that it is ousted by the regime of the bilateral treaty.

Many BITs provide for the progressive phasing out of the repatriation of capital where this is warranted by the host state's foreign exchange situation. Thus, under the German model treaty, in the event of exceptional balance-of-payments difficulties repatriation may be spread out over five years with annual instalments of 20 per cent of the capital to be transferred.[89] Similarly, the UK–Hungary BIT provides that while each contracting party has the right, in exceptional balance-of-payments difficulties and for a limited period, to exercise equitably and in good faith powers conferred by its laws. 'Such powers shall not however be used to impede the transfer of profit, interest, dividends, royalties or fees; as regards investments and any other form of return, transfer of a minimum of 20 per cent a year is guaranteed.'[90] The AALCC Models also introduce restrictions on the free transfer of capital and returns. 'Model A' contains provisions similar to the UK provisions cited above, permitting 'reasonable restrictions' and allowing for a 20 per cent guaranteed minimum right of transfer in any year period where exceptional financial or economic conditions are experienced.[91] 'Model B' leaves the repatriation of capital and returns subject to the terms set out by the host state at the time of the reception of the investment. These shall be set out in the letter of authorization issued by the host state on the approval of the investment and will remain unchanged throughout the period of the investment unless the investor and the host state agree to any alterations.[92]

Most BITs contain clauses providing for the compensation of the investor for losses due to armed conflict or internal disorder. These do not establish an absolute right to compensation. Rather, they lay down that the investor will be treated in accordance with the national treatment and/or MFN standard in the matter of compensation.[93] Some treaties, for example the German model treaty, deal with such compensation in a single provision which also deals with compensation for expropriation.[94] Others deal with these two types of compensation in separate provisions.[95] This may be preferable as compensation for expropriation is not measured by reference to national treatment or MFN standards, but by reference to the standard of 'prompt, adequate and effective compensation'.[96] Most BITs guarantee the free transfer of compensation to the investor's home country.[97]

One of the most contentious disputes between capital-exporting and capital-importing states over international minimum standards of treatment has been that relating to compensation for expropriation. This has already been covered in earlier chapters.[98] The capital-exporting states have embodied their understanding of the applicable rules of international law into the expropriation provisions of BITs.[99] Thus, practically all BITs contain a provision that permits expropriation or nationalization of assets owned by the investor from the other contacting state only where this is done for a public purpose, under due process of law, without discrimination and upon the payment of 'prompt, adequate and effective', 'adequate' or 'just' compensation in accordance with the fair market value of the assets immediately before expropriation.[100]

However, variations from this model do exist. For example, while the AALCC 'Model A' BIT accepts this formulation,[101] 'Model B' refers to 'principles for the determination of appropriate compensation'.[102] Furthermore, the UK–People's Republic of China BIT specifies a standard of 'reasonable compensation' which is defined as the real value of the expropriated investment immediately before the expropriation became public knowledge.[103] This amounts to a derogation from the usual British practice, which specifies the market value of the assets expropriated, or, in the absence of a determinable market value, the actual loss sustained, on or immediately before the date of expropriation.[104] It was necessitated by the refusal of China to accept a reference to 'market' in the treaty in view of her command economy.[105] China has adopted a similar stance in treaties with other capital-exporting countries. Thus the treaty with the Belgium–Luxembourg Union speaks of compensation amounting to 'the value of the property and assets invested on the date immediately preceding the date of expropriation, or on the date on which the expropriation was made public'.[106] In the BIT with France the amount of compensation payable 'shall reflect the true value of the investments in question'.[107] In the BIT with Japan the standard of compensation is different again. Here the compensation payable 'shall be such as to place the nationals and companies in the same financial position as that in which the nationals and companies would have been if the expropriation, nationalization or any other measures the effects of which would be similar to expropriation or nationalization . . . had not been taken.'[108] Thus a restitutionary standard is adopted. It can hardly be said that China has taken a uniform attitude to this question. However, she does not accept the traditional formula of 'prompt, adequate and effective' compensation.[109]

Concerning the modalities of payment, most BITs provide for the payment of interest and for payment without delay in fully realizable and transferable form. Furthermore, many treaties provide for judicial review, before the courts and tribunals of the host state, of the legality of the expropriation and of the amount of compensation being offered.[110] Finally, the majority of BITs cover not only direct expropriation but also indirect measures that have the effect of neutralizing the value of the investors' assets, while leaving their formal ownership intact. This is often referred to as 'creeping expropriation', though this term is not used in the treaty formulations.[111]

Other, less common, specific standards to be found in BITs include: general statements committing the home and/or host state to providing investment promotion incentives;[112] provisions protecting the right of entry and sojourn of individuals in connection with the investment, subject to the laws of the host state;[113] and restrictions on the imposition of performance requirements on investors by the host state.[114]

Restrictions on performance requirements are characteristic of US BITs.[115] By article II(5) of the 1984 revision of the US model BIT:

Neither Party shall impose performance requirements as a condition of establishment, expansion or maintenance of investments, which require or enforce commitments to export goods produced, or which specify that goods or services must be purchased locally, or which impose any other similar requirements.

This bilateral approach has been adopted as the most realistic method of controlling the imposition of performance requirements. Efforts by the USA to raise this issue before GATT have failed over the years,[116] and unilateral measures taken by the USA could prove self-defeating in the long term, as they would lead to a reduction of outward investment and could produce retaliatory reactions.[117]

However, even in the bilateral arena the USA has compromised its stand on performance requirements, where this was necessary to reach overall agreement. Thus the Egypt–USA BIT of 1982 contains the following clause: 'In the context of its national economic policies and objectives, each Party shall seek to avoid the imposition of performance requirements on their investments by nationals and companies of the other Party.'[118] This clearly falls short of the language of the model treaty. On the other hand the treaty between the USA and Panama of 27 October 1982 contains a performance requirements provision closer to that found in the model treaty. Yet even this provision does not cover performance requirements as a condition for expansion or maintenance of existing foreign investments.[119]

2.4 Dispute Settlement Clauses

Dispute settlement clauses in BITs can be divided between those dealing with disputes between the contracting states as to the observance and interpretation of the treaty, and those dealing with disputes between the investor and the host state.

2.4.1 *Disputes between the contracting parties*   Two settlement procedures are used in all BITs, namely negotiation and *ad hoc* arbitration.[120] The usual procedure is for a dispute to be settled by negotiation between the contracting states, or if this is not possible to go to arbitration. The arbitration procedure most commonly followed is that of a three member tribunal, each contracting party appointing one member, with the Chairman being appointed by these two from among nationals of third states.[121] There is usually a time limit specified within which such choices must be made. If they are not then recourse may be had to the President of the ICJ, to the Secretary-General of the UN or to some other specified international figure to make the necessary appointments. The decision of the tribunal is reached by majority vote and is binding on the parties. The tribunal fixes its own rules of procedure although the US model treaty specifies the use of the International Law Commission's Model Rules on Arbitral Procedure in the absence of agreement between the parties.[122] As to the applicable law, few BITs contain specific clauses on this matter. Those that do tend to refer to 'international law' or to 'general principles of law'.[123] Some treaties require the exhaustion of local remedies before any dispute is submitted to an arbitral tribunal. These would only be relevant to the extent that there is a connection between the interstate dispute and a dispute between the investor and the host state.[124]

A particular provision found in virtually all BITs, which can give rise to disputes between the contracting states, concerns the subrogation of the investor's claims against the host state to the home state, after that investor has been compensated for its losses out of 'political risks' insurance taken out with the investment insurance agency of the home state. In such a case, the home state is entitled to benefit from any compensation that the host state is liable to pay to the investor, up to the amount that has been paid out to the investor under the insurance cover.[125] The normal formulation excludes any acceptance of liability on the part of the host state merely by virtue of its recognition of the home state's rights of subrogation, a right that arises from the insurance contract between the home state and the investor, and not from any delictual conduct on the part of the host state.[126]

2.4.2 Disputes between the host state and the foreign investor
Early BITs did not cover the issue of disputes between the host state and the investor. However, the conclusion of the Washington Convention of 1965, setting up ICSID, prompted the inclusion of ICSID jurisdiction clauses in BITs.[127] All the model agreements in their current versions include an ICSID clause.[128] Some treaties refer to ICSID as the only system of dispute settlement to be used between investors and host states,[129] while others offer a choice between ICSID and other systems of international arbitration.[130] By contrast, BITs concluded with China have had a side letter appended to them providing for the conclusion of an Additional Protocol on the categories of disputes submissible to conciliation or arbitration before ICSID, should China become a party to the Washington Convention.[131]

Where a BIT refers to ICSID arbitration the precise wording of the clause is important. If the wording shows complete and unconditional consent on the part of the contracting state to the use of ICSID arbitration, this can amount to a unilateral offer of such arbitration to investors from the other contracting state, which can be turned into a binding consent to ICSID jurisdiction where the investor requests such arbitration in writing.[132] On the other hand, where the clause is conditional on further agreement to submit the dispute to ICSID it will be ineffective, on its own, to found the jurisdiction of the Centre. The host state will then retain the choice whether or not to consent to ICSID jurisdiction. In order to avoid disputes over the effect of clauses purporting to establish ICSID jurisdiction, ICSID has drawn up model clauses for BITs.[133]

3   The Effect of BITs within the National Legal Systems of the Contracting States

The effect of a BIT within the legal systems of the contracting states depends on the applicable rules of national law concerning the domestic effect of treaties. Under English law the conclusion and ratification of a treaty is seen as an act within the prerogative of the Crown. Consequently, if a treaty were to be directly effective within the English legal system, without the need for further legislative enactment, the Crown could bypass the sovereignty of Parliament as the supreme legislature. To avoid such a consequence a treaty can only become a part of English law if an enabling Act of Parliament has been passed.[134] Therefore, a BIT can create no directly effective legal rights within the English legal system without such transforming legislation. As it has not been the practice to pass such legislation, the legal authority of BITs concluded by the United Kingdom remains solely within the international legal system, unless the law of the other contracting state accords the status of municipal law to the treaty. Should the law of the other contracting state accord such status to the BIT, it is at least arguable that its provisions can be invoked before an English court as part of the law governing the investment, given that the governing law will be the law of the other contracting state as the *situs* of the investment. Furthermore, it may be possible to accord some domestic legal force to the BIT by incorporating its terms into a contract governed by English law. The English court may be willing to apply the terms of the treaty as a matter incidental to the construction of the intent of the parties.[135]

Unlike the United Kingdom, a number of countries adhere to the principle that treaties made in accordance with the constitution bind the courts without any specific act of incorporation.[136] However, each system must be carefully examined to see whether it imposes additional conditions before the treaty can be invoked as a source of rights under municipal law. Thus, for example, under French law the treaty must be ratified and duly published before it has the force of law.[137] By article 157 of the Sri Lankan Constitution BITs are given the force of law in Sri Lanka, and no executive or administrative action can be taken in contravention of the treaty, save in the interests of national security.[138] Under US law the issue turns on the question of whether the treaty is 'self-executing', that is whether it is intended to be effective as domestic law without the need of implementing legislation. If it is, then by article VI of the US Constitution, it has the force of law, subject to modification or repeal by subsequent Act of Congress.[139]

The effect of BITs before national courts can, to some extent, be gauged by reference to recent US case-law concerning the question of US jurisdiction in pursuit litigation arising out of a foreign expropriation that has occurred without payment of full compensation. As a general rule, the US courts, in common with other jurisdictions, will not entertain a claim arising out of an expropriatory measure taken by a foreign state, on the ground that such action constitutes an act of state which cannot be subjected to review before the US courts.[140] However, this doctrine recognizes an exception based on the terms of 'a treaty or other unambiguous agreement regarding controlling legal principles'.[141]

This exception to the act of state doctrine has been considered in the context of FCN treaties by the US Court of Appeals for the Sixth Circuit in *Kalamazoo Spice Extraction Co.* v *The Provisional Military Government of Socialist Ethiopia*.[142] In that case the plaintiff corporation sought damages from the defendant government for the expropriation of its share in an Ethiopian joint venture company. The question for the US court was whether it had jurisdiction to hear the claim. The answer depended on whether the terms relating to expropriation in the USA–Ethiopia Treaty of Amity and Economic Relations of 1953 came within the 'treaty exception' to the act of state doctrine, as setting down the 'controlling legal principles'. The plaintiff company argued that article VIII(2) of the said Treaty set down the applicable standards of treatment by which the legality of the Ethiopian government's actions should be judged. It states:

Property of nationals and companies of either High Contracting Party, including interests in property, shall receive the most constant protection and security within the territories of the other High Contracting Party. Such property shall not be taken except for a public purpose, nor shall it be taken without prompt payment of just and effective compensation.

At first instance the US District Court rejected the plaintiff's argument on the ground that the standard of compensation laid down in this provision was too ambiguous to provide a controlling legal standard. The Court of Appeals reversed that finding. It held that the formula for compensation in article VIII(2) of the Treaty was a 'controlling standard in the area of international law'.

The Court of Appeals noted that a similar formulation had been used in many treaties where the United States and other nations were parties. The widespread use of this compensation standard in treaties was evidence that it was an agreed upon principle of international law. Furthermore, a similar formulation in the 1957 Treaty of Amity between the United States and Iran was held to have come within the 'treaty exception', and to have grounded jurisdiction in the case of *American International Group Inc.* v *Islamic Republic of Iran*.[143] The District Court had erred in not following this precedent. The Court also laid stress on the fact that the US Departments of State, Treasury and Justice had filed a joint *amicus* brief urging that the 1953 Treaty of Amity made the act of state doctrine inapplicable. Thus the possibility of judicial interference with foreign policy activity by the Executive branch was not a consideration in this case. Finally, the Court referred to article VI of the US Constitution. Having noted that this provision made treaties concluded under the authority of the United States the supreme law of the land, the Court held that the failure to recognize a properly executed treaty would be 'an egregious error because of the position that treaties occupy in our body of laws'.[144]

In the light of the *Kalamazoo* case, it is arguable that BITs can also come within the 'treaty exception' to the act of state doctrine, given that they contain a similar standard of compensation for expropriation to that found in US FCN treaties. However, this begs the question of whether the US Court of Appeals was right to hold that this standard in fact represents international law. Its reasoning appears to accept that any standard which is used repeatedly in treaties concluded by the United States acquires the status of a 'controlling legal principle'. Such an approach may not be conducive to international comity, or be consistent with the spirit of the US act of state doctrine. It gives weight to the view that BITs are unequal treaties that strengthen the hand of the legal system of the home contracting party to intervene directly in the dispute between the host contracting party and the investor.[145] Furthermore, it remains uncertain whether all the provisions in a BIT are sufficiently clear to act as 'controlling legal principles' within the exception. As noted above, the concepts of 'national treatment' and 'fair and equitable treatment' are rather open-ended. Consequently, the *Kalamazoo* case leaves much room for argument over the legal effects of BITs within the US legal system.

However, there exist more fundamental objections to the use of BITs as a basis for establishing jurisdiction before the courts of the home contracting state in relation to a dispute between the investor and the host contracting state. First, the aim behind BITs has been to reinforce international standards of treatment for foreign investors, which have been put under increased doubt over the past four decades, and not to create new remedies for investors. As Sornarajah points out, a breach of the treaty creates an international obligation between the contracting states and no benefits of rights flow directly to the individual or company involved.[146] Secondly, these treaties display a clear preference for the 'delocalization' of investment disputes, not only by their reference to ICSID or other types of international arbitration,[147] but also by the general absence of provisions requiring the prior exhaustion of local remedies by the investor before a breach of the treaty can arise. In this BITs create a regime distinct from diplomatic protection, and replace it with direct recourse to multilateral international arbitral bodies by the investor and the host state. Thirdly, if BITs were to create new rights that were directly effective before the courts of the contracting states, this could have been done by means of a specific provision in the treaty obliging the contracting states to transform the treaty into their domestic law. In particular, recourse to the courts of the home contracting state could have been permitted, in default of a satisfactory hearing before the courts of the host contracting state, under the provisions guaranteeing due process in cases of expropriation. However, such clauses have not been included. They would probably have been unacceptable to host contracting states, as they would have amounted to a subjection to the extraterritorial application of home contracting states' laws. Given these arguments, it may be questioned whether BITs are in fact 'self-executing' treaties within the meaning of US law, as appears to have been assumed in the *Kalamazoo* case.

4   The Use of BITs

The use of BITs may offer certain political advantages to capital-importing countries concerned with securing foreign direct investment. First, while a capital-importing country might be hesitant in agreeing to traditional international standards of treatment as general rules of international law enshrined in a multilateral code, it may be willing to accept such standards in the context of a bilateral treaty relationship. Such standards would only be binding in relation to the other contracting state. This would leave the capital-importing state free not to apply similar standards in its dealings with other states. Furthermore, such standards could be adapted to suit the particular concerns of the contracting states, a flexibility absent from general statements in multilateral instruments.[148]

Secondly, the utility of investment from a particular capital-exporting country may be vital to the development of the particular capital-importing country. If a condition of assured investment is agreement to international minimum standards of treatment, this may be calculated as a price worth paying for the long-term benefits of that investment. In particular, a major reason why capital-importing countries have entered into BITs is that investors from capital-exporting countries may be denied political risk insurance by their home states unless the host state offers adequate legal guarantees for the protection of their investments. In the absence of a BIT national legal guarantees may be considered inadequate. Sustained inflows of investment could then be put at risk.[149] This justification for the conclusion of BITs has been reinforced by the standard-setting provisions of MIGA, discussed in the previous chapter.[150]

Thirdly, the conclusion of a BIT may be a valuable symbol of the capital-importing country's attitude to foreign investors, particularly where it has a record of past hostility towards private foreign investment. This is no doubt an important reason for the increased conclusion, in recent years, of BITs by socialist and post-socialist states.[151]

Given these considerations, BITs have been concluded primarily between the capital-exporting countries of the OECD area and the capital-importing countries of Africa and South East Asia.[152] Some treaties have also been concluded with the smaller and economically weaker Central and Latin American states. However, even certain advanced developing countries, for example Argentina and Nigeria, have recently entered into such treaties.[153] Equally, the two industrializing countries that were until recently the most hostile opponents of BITs, Brazil and India, have since 1994 concluded BITs, although, in the case of Brazil, these have yet to enter force.[154]

5   Concluding Remarks: the Effect of BITs on the Content of International Law

As mentioned above, some international legal publicists have argued that the BIT system has reinforced the normative significance of traditional international legal standards for protection of aliens and their property, and has undermined the call for increased national sovereignty over foreign investors contained in UN declarations establishing a New International Economic Order.[155] Though compelling, this view has itself been subjected to strong criticism, not least because such treaties are the outcome of individual bargaining relationships which cannot act as a source of general legal obligation.[156]

Given the uncertainty surrounding the content of international standards in this field, the elevation of certain treaty-based standards of treatment to norms of customary international law appears to be mistaken. BITs constitute a special juridical regime designed to restate, in treaty form, international minimum standards of treatment of foreign investors as accepted by the capital-exporting states, and to merge these with established, treaty-based standards of commercial conduct that do not possess the character of customary international law, despite their widespread usage over many centuries. The result is an integrated system of norms for the delocalized regulation of a bilateral investment relationship between a developed capital-exporting state and a less developed capital-importing state, in a manner conducive to efficient capital accumulation by investors from the capital-exporting state. Thus BITs represent a particular legal instrument seeking to solve a specific problem of international economic relations, and creating an effective *lex specialis* between the parties. They are not the equivalent of a codifying convention.

Notes

1   In American terminology this type of treaty is known as a 'bilateral investment treaty' (BIT); the British terminology is 'investment promotion and protection agreement' (IPPA). The American term is used in this work as it is also used in UN practice.

2   For example, the first treaty of amity and commerce signed by the United States was a treaty of 6 February 1778 with France: see Wilson, 'Postwar commercial treaties of the United States', 43 AJIL 262 at p. 277 (1949).

3   On the United States experience of such treaties see: Wilson, ibid.; Walker, 'Treaties for the encouragement and protection of foreign investment: present United States practice', 5 Am. J. Comp. Law 229 (1956); 'Provisions on companies in United States commercial treaties' 50 AJIL 373 (1956); 'The post-war commercial treaty program of the United States', 73 Pol. Sci. Q. 57 (1958).

4   See e.g. article III (2) of the US–Italy FCN Treaty of 2 February 1948; article III(3) of the US–China FCN of 4 November 1946; see Wilson (note 2 above), at p. 265. Article III(2) of the US–Italy Treaty was the subject of recent international litigation before the ICJ in the *Case Concerning Elettronica Sicula S. p. A. (ELSI)* (United States v Italy) Judgment 20 July 1989 ICJ Reports (1989) p. 15.

5   UNCTC, *Bilateral Investment Treaties* (1988, UN Doc ST/CTC/65) para. 9, p. 4 (cited hereafter as UNCTC 1988). See too note 154 below.

6   See Pattison, 'The United States–Egypt bilateral investment treaty: a prototype for future negotiation', 16 Cornell Int'l L. J. 305 at 308–9 (1983).

7   UNCTC, 1988 (note 5 above), para. 19, at p. 7. The FRG–St Lucia BIT of 16 March 1985 is reproduced as an example of the German model BIT in ibid., annex II, at pp. 102–10. On German practice concerning BITs see: Justus Alenfeld, *Die Investitionsforderungsvertrage der Bundesrepublik Deutschland* (Antenaum Verlag, 1970); Heinrich Klebes, *Encouragement et protection des investissements privés dans les pays en développement – les traités bilatéraux de la République Fédéralle Allemagne dans leur contexte* (Thesis, Strasbourg 1983).

8   UNCTC, 1988 (note 5 above), para. 19, at p. 7.

9   The US model, in its 1984 revision, is reproduced in UNCTC 1988 (note 5 above), annex V, at pp. 123–31.

10   The treaties in force are with Argentina, Bangladesh, Cameroon, the Czech Republic, Egypt, Grenada, Morocco, Panama, Senegal, Slovakia, Sri Lanka, Tunisia, Turkey and Zaire: 31 ILM 796 (1992); 33 ILM 836 (1994). Those awaiting ratification are with Armenia, Bulgaria, Congo, Poland, Kazakhstan, Kirghizia, Moldova, Romania and Russia: 33 ILM 836 (1994).

11   See 23 ILM 237–268 (1984) or UNCTC, 1988 (note 5 above), annex VI, pp. 132–155.

12   Ibid., at ILM p. 239.

13   See 27 ILM 612 (1988). See too Framework Agreement on ASEAN Investment Area 1998. http://www.asean.or.id/economic/aem/30/frm_aia.htm

14   See e.g. F. A. Mann, 'British treaties for the promotion and protection of investment', 52 BYIL 241 (1981); Juillard, 'Les conventions bilatérales d'investissement conclués par la France', 2 JDI 274 (1979) and 'Les conventions bilatérales d'investissement conclués par la France avec les pays n'appartenant pas à la zone Franc', AFDI (1982) 760.

15   See, most notably, J. P. Laviec, *Protection et promotion des investissements: étude de droit international économique* (PUF, 1985). See also UNCTC, 1988 (note 5 above), Part Two, 'The provisions of bilateral investment treaties', on which this section relies considerably; M. Sornarajah, *The International Law on Foreign investment* (Grotius Publishers, 1994), chapter 6. See further Akinsanya, 'International protection of foreign investment in the Third World', 36 ICLQ 58 (1987); Salacuse, 'BIT by BIT: the growth of bilateral investment treaties and their impact on foreign investment in developing countries', 24 Int. Law 655 (1990). The texts of BITs are published by ICSID in its periodically updated seven-volume collection *Investment Treaties*. For British practice in this field see: Mann, ibid.; Denza and Brooks, 'Investment protection treaties: United Kingdom practice', 36 ICLQ 908 (1987); for French practice see Juillard, ibid.; for German Practice see references in note 7 above; for US practice see Pattison (note 6 above), Kunzer 'Developing a model bilateral investment treaty', 15 Law & Pol. Int'l Bus. 273 (1983), Bergman, 'Bilateral investment protection treaties: an examination of the evolution and significance of the US prototype treaty' 16 NYUJ Int'l Law and Pol. 1 (1983), Cody 'United States bilateral investment treaties: Egypt and Panama' (1983)

Ga. JIL 491, Coughlin 'The US bilateral investment treaty: an answer to performance requirements', in B. S. Fisher and J. Turner (eds), *Regulating the Multinational Enterprise: National and International Challenges* (Praeger, 1983), chapter 7, pp. 129–42, K. J. Vandevelde, *United States Investment Treaties Policy and Practice* (1992). See also the bibliography in 7 ICSID Rev-FILJ 231 (1992).

16   UNCTC, 1988 (note 5 above), paras 41–6.

17   UNCTC, 1988 (para. 47), at p. 16.

18   See, for example, United Kingdom–Philippines BIT provided by article I(5). This treaty is annexed to the article by Dr F. A. Mann referred to in note 14 above. The definitions used in earlier treaties tended to be of narrower scope. See e.g. Germany–Pakistan BIT 1959, article 8, in UNCTC, 1988, para. 49; France–Sri Lanka BIT 1963, Senegal 1965 and Rwanda 1967: 'the term "capital investment" comprises all categories of assets, including all categories of rights and interests'.

19   Laviec (note 15 above), at p. 31.

20   See e.g. Germany–Israel BIT 1976, where the general clause is preceded by a clause stating that the term investment means: '(i) investment in an enterprise involving active participation therein and the acquisition of assets ancillary thereto, or (ii) the enterprise or assets acquired as a result of such an investment' (quoted in UNCTC, 1988 (note 5 above), para. 51, at p. 17).

21   1984 Revised Text, article I(3).

22   See e.g. Germany–St Lucia BIT 1985 (note 7 above), article 1.

23   Laviec (note 15 above), at p. 77; and chapters 6 and 7 above.

24   See examples cited in UNCTC, 1988, paras 58–63, at pp. 18–19. See also AALCC Model BIT 'Model A' article 3, which states *inter alia* that 'Each Contracting Party shall determine the mode and manner in which investments are to be received in its territory': see note 11 above at ILM p. 245. 'Model B' is more restrictive of investor's rights of entry in that its article 3 makes the screening of investment proposals by the host country a mandatory treaty requirement. See ibid. at ILM p. 258.

25   1984 Revised Version. See UNCTC, 1988 (note 5 above), annex V, at p. 124.

26   See chapter 6 at pp. 175–6.

27   See Pattison's discussion of the US–Egypt BIT in this respect: note 6 above, at pp. 318–19. Pattison is critical of the broad exclusion of industries from the treaty, which, in his opinion, created a substantial void in the protection offered.

28   US–Russian Federation BIT, 17 June 1992 Protocol, para. 4(a), 31 ILM 794 at 810 (1992). On the 1991 Law see chapter 6 at pp. 192–3.

29   See e.g. the UK–Philippines BIT (note 18 above), article IV(1); UK–Burundi BIT, 13 September 1990, article 2, UKTS No. 11 (1991).

30   See UK–Indonesia BIT, 27 April 1976, which extends the treaty only to investments approved under Indonesia's foreign investment legislation; UK–Malaysia BIT, 21 May 1981, which requires that the investment be classified as an 'approved project' by the appropriate Ministry.

31   See e.g. US–Egypt BIT 1986, consolidated text reproduced in UNCTC,

1988 (note 5 above), para. 67, at p. 20.

32   See UNCTC, 1988, ibid., paras 70–4 at pp. 21–2 for examples of each type of provision.

33   For example, the US Model BIT 1984 revision article I(1)(c): ' "National" of a Party means a natural person who is a national of a Party under its applicable law.' See also Netherlands Model BIT 1987, revision article 1(b)(i) in UNCTC, 1988 (note 5 above), annex IV, at p. 117.

34   For example, the Germany–Israel BIT speaks of 'Israeli nationals being residents of the State of Israel': UNCTC, 1988 (note 5 above), para. 79, at p. 22.

35   See UK–Philippines BIT (note 18 above), article I(3)(b).

36   For examples see UNCTC, 1988 (note 5 above), paras 83–93.

37   See Laviec (note 15 above), at pp. 43–8, on which the following paragraphs are based.

38   See e.g. France–Nepal BIT 1984, article I, quoted in UNCTC, 1988 (note 5 above), para. 89, at p. 25.

39   See e.g. UK–Philippines BIT (note 18 above), article I(4): 'The term "company" of a Contracting Party shall mean a corporation, partnership or other association, incorporated or constituted and actually doing business under the laws in force in any part of the territory of that Contracting Party wherein a place of effective management is situated.' According to Dr Mann, under this definition 'A Philippine company cannot claim the protection of the Agreement even if all the shares are owned by a British national': ibid., at p. 242. But see further text at notes 47 and 48 below.

40   US Model BIT 1984, revision article I(1)(a).

41   Ibid., article I(1)(b).

42   UNCTC, 1988 (note 5 above), para. 84, at p. 23; Laviec (note 15 above), at p. 45.

43   Laviec, ibid. See the *Barcelona Traction Case* discussed in chapter 15, at pp. 535–6.

44   See e.g. Netherlands–Kenya Agreement on Economic Co-operation, 11 June 1979, Tractatenblad 1970, No. 166, article XIV: 'For the purpose of the present Agreement: . . . (b) a legal person which is lawfully established in the territory of a Contracting Party shall be a national of that Contracting Party in conformity with its legislation; except where any such legal person, established in the territory of a Contracting Party is controlled by a national or nationals of the other Contracting Party and it has been agreed between the legal person, and the first mentioned Contracting Party that it should be treated for the purposes of this Agreement as a national of the other Contracting Party.'

45   Germany–St Lucia BIT 1985, article 3(1), in UNCTC, 1988 (note 5 above), annex II, at p. 103.

46   Laviec (note 15 above), at pp. 46–7.

47   Note 18 above.

48   ICJ Reports (1970), p. 3. See chapter 15, at pp. 535–6.

49   See further UNCTC, 1988 (note 5 above), paras 95–8, at p. 26.

50   Ibid., para. 100, at p. 27.

51   Ibid., para. 102, at p. 27.

52   Ibid., paras 103–8, at pp. 28–9.

53   See generally Laviec (note 15 above), chapter III.

54   Laviec (note 15 above), at p. 95.

55   See UNCTC, 1988 (note 5 above), paras 113–18, at p. 31.

56   Note 9 above.

57   For example, Agreements concluded by France with Sri Lanka, Nepal, Pakistan and Israel relate fair and equitable treatment to the general principles of international law and require that the right this states must not be impaired *de jure* or *de facto* (article 3) Agreements concluded by Belgium–Luxembourg also normally specify that fair and equitable treatment 'may in no case be less favourable than that recognized by international law'. See article 3. Belgium–Luxembourg Economic Union–Malaysia BIT, 8 February 1982, *Moniteur Belge*, 30 March 1982. Referred to in UNCTC, 1988 (note 5 above), para. 126, at p. 32.

58   Laviec (note 15 above), at p. 94.

59   Note 11 above.

60   For example, Rwanda, Pakistan, Singapore and Saudi Arabia. At the same time fair and equitable treatment has been accepted in the Netherlands–Singapore and Netherlands–Pakistan BITs: UNCTC, 1988 (note 5 above), para. 127, at p. 32 and note 34, at p. 81.

61   Ibid.

62   See Belgium–Luxembourg Economic Union–People's Republic of China (PRC) BIT, 4 June 1984, article 3(1), which accords 'equitable treatment' to direct or indirect investments: 24 ILM 537 at p. 540. This is supplemented by a reference to treatment not less favourable than that provided for in the 'generally recognised principles and rules of international law adopted by the Contracting Parties': ibid., Protocol article 7, at ILM p. 549. France–PRC BIT, 30 May 1984, article 3(1) accords 'fair and equitable treatment to the investments made by investors of the other party': ibid., ILM p. 552. See also Australia–PRC BIT, 11 July 1988, article 3(a): 28 ILM 121 at 127 (1989). Not all BITs concluded by China contain the equitable treatment standard. Thus the Japan–PRC BIT of 27 August 1988 contains only the national treatment and MFN standards: 28 ILM 575 (1989).

63   Note 13 above, article III(2).

64   See especially the OECD Guidelines at pp. 583–7 above.

65   Laviec (note 15 above), at p. 96.

66   UNCTC, *Key Concepts in International Investment Agreements and Their Relevance to Negotiations on International Transactions in Services* (February 1990, UNCTC Current Studies Series A, No. 13, UN Doc. ST/CTC/SER. A/13), p. 15.

67   UNCTC, 1988 (note 5 above), para. 133, at p. 34.

68   Ibid., paras 153–6 (mentioning the Protocol to the Papua New Guinea–Germany and Papua New Guinea–UK BITs of 1980 and 1981; Protocol to Belgium–Indonesia BIT 1970; Switzerland–Indonesia BIT 1974, Protocol No. 2; Germany–Zaire BIT 1969, article 3(3)).

69   G. Schwarzenberger, *International Law and Order* (Stevens, 1971) pp. 137–8. On the MFN standard see: Schwarzenberger, ibid., chapter 8, and 'The

Most-Favoured-Nation standard in British state practice', 22 BYIL 96 (1945); Report of the International Law Commission, *ILC Yearbook* (1978 II), pp. 10–83; Snyder, *The Most Favoured Nation Clause* (Kings Crown Press, Columbia University, 1948); Sauvignon, *La clause de la nation la plus favorisée* (Grenoble University Press, 1972). See also *Asian Agricultural Products Ltd v Republic of Sri Lanka* (ICSID Tribunal, Final Award, 21 June 1990), 30 ILM 577 (1991) at p. 645 (Dissenting Opinion of S. K. B. Asante).

70 Laviec (note 15 above), at p. 99.

71 Ibid.

72 See, for example, UK–Philippines BIT article IV(3)(a) and (b) (notes 18 and 14 above), at pp. 251–2.

73 Note 69 above.

74 For example, Germany–Philippines BIT 1964, Protocol (3)(a): 'Nothing in Article 2 shall be construed to entitle nationals or companies of the Federal Republic of Germany to the special rights and privileges accorded by the Republic of the Philippines to nationals and companies of the United States of America by virtue of existing agreements.' Quoted in Laviec (note 15 above), at p. 102, n. 119.

75 UNCTC, 1988 (note 5 above), para. 141, at p. 35.

76 For example, UK–Thailand BIT 1979, article 10(2): 'Wherever this Agreement makes alternative provisions for the grant of national treatment or of treatment not less favourable than that accorded to the nationals or companies of any third State in respect of any matter, the option as between these alternatives shall rest with the Contracting Party beneficiary in each particular case.' Quoted in Laviec (note 15 above), at p. 101, n. 116; see No. 99 (1979) Cmnd 7732.

77 See UNCTC, 1988 (note 5 above), paras 164–70, at pp. 39–40; US Model BIT 1984, revision (note 9 above), article IX.

78 Ibid., para. 164, at p. 39.

79 On stabilization clauses see further chapter 14 at pp. 496–7.

80 UNCTC, 1988 (note 5 above), para. 174, at p. 41.

81 UNCTC, 1988, para. 175, at p. 41.

82 For example, US Model BIT 1984, revision (note 9 above), article IV; Germany–St Lucia BIT 1985 (note 7 above), article 7.

83 The US Model BIT 1984, revision, ibid., article IV(1), lists: returns, compensation for expropriation of property, payments arising out of an investment dispute, payments under a contract, including amortization of principal and accrued interest payments made pursuant to a loan agreement, proceeds from the sale or liquidation of all or any part of an investment, and additional contributions to capital for the maintenance or development of an investment.

84 For example, UK–Philippines BIT (note 18 above), article VII(1): 'Each Contracting Party shall in respect of investments permit nationals or companies of the other Contracting Party the free transfer of their capital and of the earnings from it'.

85 Note 18 above.

86 Laviec (note 15 above), at p. 142.

87 Ibid., at pp. 138–42.

88 Ibid., at p. 143.

89 UNCTC, 1988 (note 5 above), annex II, article 5(2).

90 UK–Hungary BIT, Treaty Series No. 3 (1988), Cm 281, article 7(1).

91 Note 11 above, article 6.

92 Ibid., article 6.

93 UNCTC, 1988 (note 5 above), para. 197, at p. 46. See also *Asian Agricultural Products Ltd* v *Republic of Sri Lanka* (note 69 above). In this ICSID arbitration the terms of the UK–Sri Lanka BIT of 13 February 1980 relating to the destruction of the claimant's property were considered. The Tribunal rejected the claimant's argument that the Treaty established a 'strict liability' standard for such damage, preferring an approach based on customary international law, whereby the liability of the host state should be determined by reference to a 'due diligence' standard. However, the Tribunal established that the Respondent state was liable to pay some compensation on the basis of article 4(1) of the Treaty, which applied the national treatment and MFN standards to compensation for losses owing to war or other armed conflict, in that the Respondent was obliged under general international law to compensate for such loss where a failure to meet the due diligence standard was involved. This decision was met with a strong dissenting opinion from Dr S. K. B. Asante, who felt that the majority had misunderstood article 4(1), that they could not apply its terms in the absence of consideration as to whether the Respondent had in fact paid compensation to its nationals or to nationals of third states under its laws, and that, in any case, the facts did not justify a holding that the Respondent had failed to act with due diligence.

94 Note 7 above, article 4.

95 For example, UK–Philippines BIT (note 18 above), article V (compensation for expropriation), article VI (compensation for loss due to war, other armed conflicts, revolution, national emergency, revolt, insurrection or riot).

96 See *Asian Agricultural Products Ltd* v *Republic of Sri Lanka* (note 69 above), at p. 653–4 (dissenting opinion of Dr S. K. B. Asante).

97 UNCTC, 1988 (note 5 above), para. 201 at p. 47.

98 See chapter 14 and chapter 16 at pp. 595–6, 600–1.

99 For a full analysis see: UNCTC, 1988 (note 5 above), paras 208–67, at pp. 49–60; Laviec (note 15 above), chapter V.

100 See, for example, US Model BIT (note 9 above), article III(1).

101 Note 11 above, article 7.

102 Ibid., article 7, alternative 1. Note that alternative 2 refers to the 'prompt, adequate and effective' formula.

103 Article 5. See Denza and Brooks (note 15 above), at p. 919.

104 For example, UK–Philippines BIT (note 18 above), article V(1).

105 Denza and Brooks (note 103 above).

106 Protocol to the Belgium Luxembourg–PRC BIT, 4 June 1984, article 2: 24 ILM 537 at 546 (1985).

107 France–PRC BIT, annex, para. 2, ibid., at p. 561.

108 Note 62 above, article 5(3).

109 According to Sornarajah the fact that the 'prompt, adequate and effective' formula is not used consistently in treaty practice weakens the argument that it represents the applicable international standard of compensation: 'State responsibility and bilateral investment treaties', 20 JWTL 79 at 91–2 (1986).

110 For example, UK–Philippines BIT (note 18 above), article V(1); Japan–PRC BIT (note 62 above), article 5(4).

111 For examples of the formulations used see UNCTC, 1988 (note 5 above), paras 262–7, at pp. 59–60.

112 UNCTC, 1988, ibid., paras 202–3, at p. 47.

113 Ibid., paras 204–5.

114 Ibid., paras 206–7, at p. 48.

115 See Coughlin (note 15 above).

116 However, the Final Act of the Uruguay Round of GATT Negotiations has resulted in the adoption of an Agreement on TRIMs: See chapter 7 at pp. 257–60.

117 Coughlin (note 15 above), pp. 134–6.

118 Article II(7), quoted by Coughlin, ibid., at p. 132. The full text of the treaty can be found in 21 ILM 1227 (1982). See now the 1986 consolidated text established following the signature of the supplementary protocol (Senate Treaty, doc. 99–24).

119 Article II(4), quoted in UNCTC, 1988 (note 5 above), para. 207, at p. 48.

120 UNCTC, ibid., paras 271–82, at pp. 61–3, on which the following account is based.

121 See, for example, UK–Philippines BIT (note 18 above), article XI; Japan–PRC BIT (note 62 above), article 13.

122 US Model BIT 1984,revision (note 9 above), article VII.

123 UNCTC, 1988 (note 5 above), paras 283–6, at pp. 63–4.

124 Ibid., para. 285, at p. 64.

125 Ibid., paras 291–4, at p. 65.

126 For example, UK–Philippines BIT (note 18 above), article VIII(1): 'If either Contracting Party makes payment under an insurance or guarantee agreement with its own nationals or companies in respect of an investment or any part thereof in the territory of the other Contracting Party, the latter Contracting Party shall recognise the assignment of any right or claim arising from the indemnity paid, by the party indemnified to the former Contracting Party, and that the former Contracting Party is entitled by virtue of subrogation to exercise the rights and assert the claims of such nationals or companies. This does not necessarily imply, however, a recognition on the part of the latter Contracting Party of the merits of any case or the amount of any claim arising therefrom.'

127 See further chapter 15 at p. 558.

128 UNCTC, 1988 (note 5 above), paras 296 and 305, at pp. 66–7.

129 This is true in UK practice: Denza and Brooks (note 15 above), at p. 920; and see UK–Philippines BIT (note 18 above), article X.

130 For example, AALCC Model 'A' (note 11 above), article 10 (iii)–(v), which offers ICSID as the first choice for the parties to the dispute, with the UNCITRAL Arbitration Rules 1976 applying where ICSID proce-

dures are inapplicable. See also the ASEAN Multilateral Investment Treaty, 15 December 1987 (note 13 above), article X(2), which offers a choice of ICSID, UNCITRAL, the Regional Centre for Arbitration at Kuala Lumpur or any other regional centre for arbitration in ASEAN.

131 See, for example, France–PRC BIT (note 62 above), at ILM p. 565; Denza and Brooks (note 15 above), at p. 921. In the Japan–PRC BIT (note 62 above), article 11(2) provides for the setting up of an arbitration or conciliation board to hear disputes between an investor and the host state which is to be established with reference to the Washington Convention. Presumably, this means that the board will devise a procedure similar to that undertaken by ICSID. China ratified the ICSID Convention on 7 January 1993, entry into force being on 6 February 1993. Under article 25(4) of the Convention China has reserved the jurisdiction of ICSID only to disputes over compensation resulting from expropriation and nationalization: ICSID News Release, 7 January 1993.

132 Thus by article X(1) of the UK–Philippines BIT (note 18 above), 'The Contracting Party in the territory of which a national or company of the other Contracting Party makes or intends to make an investment shall assent to any request on the part of such national or company to submit, for conciliation or arbitration, to the Centre established by the Convention on the Settlement of Investment Disputes between States and Nationals of Other States opened for signature at Washington on 18 March 1965 any dispute that may arise in connection with the investment.' By article X(2) access to ICSID arbitration is extended to 'A company which is incorporated or constituted under the law in force in the territory of one Contracting Party and in which before such a dispute arises the majority of shares are owned by nationals or companies of the other Contracting Party', provided that the requirements of article 25(2)(b) of the Washington Convention are complied with. See also UK–Sri Lanka BIT, 13 February 1980, article 8(1),which formed the legal basis for the ICSID arbitration in *Asian Agricultural Products* v *Republic of Sri Lanka* (note 69 above). On the requirements of article 25(2)(b) see chapter 15 above at pp. 544–6.

133 See ICSID/6 (1969).

134 I. Brownlie, *Principles of Public International Law*, 5th edn (1998), pp. 46–7. See: *The Parlement Belge* [1880] 5 PD 197; *A–G for Canada* v *A–G for Ontario* [1937] AC 326 at 347 per Lord Atkin. See further F. A. Mann, 'The enforcement of treaties by English courts', 44 *Transactions of the Grotius Society* (1958–9) 29, reproduced in F. A. Mann, *Studies in International Law* (Oxford, 1973), chapter VIII; F. A. Mann, *Foreign Affairs in English Courts* (Oxford, 1986), chapter 5.

135 See, for example, *Philippson* v *Imperial Airways* [1939] AC 332; *Lively Ltd* v *City of Munich* [1976] 1 WLR 1004.

136 Brownlie (note 134 above), p. 50. These include Argentina, Austria, France, Luxembourg, Belgium, Greece, Germany, Japan, Netherlands, Switzerland, United States, Mexico and the USSR. See further D. P. O'Connell, *International Law*, 2nd edn (Stevens, 1970), pp. 61–79.

137 Constitution of the Fifth Republic 1958, article 55.

138   See *Asian Agricultural Products Ltd* v *Republic of Sri Lanka* (note 69 above), at p. 632.

139   Head Money Cases: *Edye* v *Robertson* 112 US 580 (1884) US Supreme Court; *Sei Fujii* v *California* 242 P. 2d 617 (1952).

140   This principle was affirmed by the US Supreme Court in *Banco Nacional De Cuba* v *Sabbatino* 376 US 398 (1964).

141   376 US at 428 per Harlan J.

142   729 F. 2d 422 (1984); 23 ILM 393 (1984).

143   493 F. Supp. 522 (DDC 1980)

144   23 ILM at p. 399.

145   See Sornarajah (note 109 above), at pp. 93–4.

146   Ibid.

147   As pointed out again by Sornarajah, ibid.

148   See Voss, 'The protection and promotion of European private investment in developing countries – an approach towards a concept for a European policy on foreign investment, a German contribution', 18 CMLR 363 at p. 373 (1981).

149   UNCTC, 1988 (note 5 above), para. 10, at p. 4.

150   See chapter 16, at pp. 602–3.

151   See, for example, the US–Russian Federation Treaty (note 28 above), the UK–Hungary BIT (note 90 above) and the BITs concluded by the PRC cited in note 62 above. See further, on US practice in relation to the post-socialist states of Eastern Europe, Lewis, 'The United States Poland treaty concerning business and economic relations: new themes and variations in the US bilateral investment treaty program' 22 Law & Pol. Int'l Bus. 527 (1991).

152   See UNCTC, 1988 (note 5 above) for a list of BITs concluded up to mid-1987 in annex I. See also the list of 380 BITs in 30 ILM 252 (1991) as supplemented by further treaties in 31 ILM 491 (1992), 32 ILM 929 (1993) and 33 ILM 833 (1994), where the total of BITs in existence is stated to be 714, of which 488 are known to be in force; in addition there are seven multilateral investment treaties. See further International Chamber of Commerce, *Bilateral Investment Treaties 1959–1991* (1992); M. I. Khalil, 'Treatment of foreign investment in bilateral investment treaties', in I. F. I. Shihata (ed.), *Legal Treatment of Foreign Investment: the World Bank Guidelines* (Martinus Nijhoff, 1993), p. 221, or, for an earlier version, ICSID Rev-FILJ (Fall 1992). See too note 154 below.

153   For more recent treaties entered into by Argentina and Nigeria see 31 ILM 491 (1992) and 32 ILM 929 (1993).

154   See UNCTAD *Bilateral Investment Treaties in the Mid-1990s* (United Nations, New York and Geneva, 1998), Annex 1, pp. 164–5, 182. This publication updates the UNCTC publication of 1988 cited at note 5 above and contains a full list of BITs up to the end of 1996.

155   See references in note 14 above.

156   See Sornarajah (note 109 above).

Index

Note: The following abbreviations are used. DFI, direct foreign investment; GATT, General Agreement on Tariffs and Trade; LDCs, less developed countries; MNE, multinational enterprises; OECD, Organization for Economic Cooperation and Development; RBPs, restrictive business practices

abuse of rights (*abus de droit*) 127,
  335–6, 340 n.13
  see also power
accountability 64, 599
  in alliances 74–5
  and disclosure 81–2, 95, 346–72
  European initiatives 350–3
  and liability 329
  motives for concern 346–8
  and non-executive directors 349–
   50
  and public ownership 76
accounting
  and consolidated financial
   statements 347, 355–61
  environmental 368–71
  and foreign currency
   translation 371–2
  harmonization of standards 354–5
  and segmented disclosure 261–6,
   347–8
  social 366–71
  transnational 354
  and value-added statements 367–8
acquisitions *see* merger; takeovers
advantage
  firm-specific (ownership) 33, 36–7,
   38–42, 46
  and growth of MNEs 33–4, 35, 39,
   41, 93
  location-specific 34, 38, 42–5,
   230–1, 304
  technological 41, 43

advertising
  and competition 386, 439, 441
  effect on local cultures 97, 100
agency, and liability 323–4
Agfa Gevaert, and transnational
  mergers 67
Agricultural Foreign Investment
  Disclosure Act (USA 1978)
  225
Airbus Industrie, as consortium 64–5,
  74, 75
Albania, and joint ventures 186–7
Allende, Salvador 6, 99, 105, 514
alliances
  and collective bargaining 476
  strategic 59, 62, 73–5, 81, 105, 390,
   438
Amerasinghe, C. F. 511, 525 n.70, 530
  n.146
Andean Common Market (ANCOM)
  13, 78, 117
  n.38, 447
  and codification of investment
   protection 575–7
Andean Foreign Investment Code 442,
  575–6
Andean Multinational Enterprise 78–9
Anti-Monopoly Law (Japan 1947)
  69–70
arbitration
  ad hoc 537–8, 540, 601, 632–3
  and expropriation 494–7, 499,
   503–5, 507–14, 601, 637

for free trade areas 240, 241, 243
and investment guarantee 515, 518
for joint venture disputes 190, 193
and technology transfer 445
see also International Centre for the
    Settlement of Investment
    Disputes; International Chamber
    of Commerce, Court of
    Arbitration; UN Commission on
    International Trade Law
Argentina
    and bilateral investment treaties 638,
        640 n.10, 647 n.136
    and dispute settlement 556
    Draft Code of Private International
        Law 138–9, 342 n.32
    and group liability 332
    and Group of Ten 273 n.216
    investment in 28
    and minority shareholders 335
    and UN Draft Code 612 n.138
arms industry, and corruption 7
Asante, S. K. B. 645 n.93
ASEAN, Agreement on the Promotion
    and Protection of Investments
    619, 626, 646 n.130
Asian African Legal Consultative
    Committee (AALCC) 618–19,
    620, 626, 630–1, 646 n.130
association, freedom of 470–6
Atkin, Lord 343 n.48
audit, environmental 370–1
Ault, H. 291, 307, 314 n.87
Australia
    and conflict avoidance 171 n.189
    and dispute settlement 556
    screening laws 197
    and transfer pricing 316 n.126
Austria, and bilateral investment
    treaties 647 n.136
Avions de Transport Regional 399

balance of payments 91–2, 181, 248,
    253, 260, 443, 629–30
    and repatriation of profits 31
Balladur, Edouard 183
Bangladesh
    and bilateral investment treaties 640
        n.10
    and labour relations 468–9
Bankers Books Evidence Act (US
    1879) 150
Banking Act (UK 1987) 151

banks
    and disclosure 150–2, 304
    and Single European Market 247
Barbados, and UN Draft Code 612
    n.138
bargaining
    collective 46, 471, 473, 476–80
    host state/MNE 102, 104–7, 111,
        180
Beier, F. K. 440
Belgium
    and bilateral investment treaties 622,
        631, 643 nn.57, 62, 647 n.136
    and codification of MNE treatment
        608 n.58
    and dispute settlement 548
    and expropriation 526 n.82
    and taxation 280
Bennett, D. L. 118 n.47
Berne Convention 256, 453 n.73
Bhopal disaster 100, 110, 142–3, 325–
    7, 328–30, 333, 469
Blakeney, M. 441
Bowater, as pyramid group 66
BP
    and cartels 24
    and restrictions on foreign ownership
        182, 402
Brazil
    and competition law 417 n.73
    and dispute settlement 555
    and Group of Ten 251
    and investment control 177
    investment in 28, 31
    and technology transfer 438, 448–9
    and transfer pricing 311 n.57
    and UN Draft Code 612 n.138
Brech, M. 92
Breton, Albert 97–8
Brewer, A. 96
British Aerospace, and restriction of
    foreign ownership 181–2
British Airways, and restriction of
    foreign ownership 181–2
British Petroleum 402
British Standards Institute, and
    environmental auditing 371
Brodley, J. F. 87 n.70
Brower, Judge 528 n.111, 529 n.132
Brownlie, I. 124, 158 n.14
Brussels Convention on Jurisdiction
    and Enforcement of Judgments
    (1968) 143–4, 157, 162 n.71

BSN–Gervais Danone, and labour
    relations 478
Buckley, Peter 36–7, 46
Bulgaria
    and joint ventures 186
    and UN Draft Code 612 n.137
Burke–Hartke Bill (USA 1972) 5, 281
Burma (Myanmar), and labour
    relations 468
Bush, George 474

Cadbury Committee on the Financial
    Aspects of Corporate
    Governance 374 n.17
California, and transfer pricing 299,
    301–2
Calvo Doctrine 561 n.20, 626
Cameroon
    and bilateral investment treaties 640
        n.10
    and dispute settlement 552, 567
        n.91
Canada
    and codification of MNE treatment
        578, 609 n.81
    and dispute settlement 555
    and MNE evolution 30, 32
    and patent law 39–40
    screening laws 197–202, 203
    and tax avoidance 320 n.183
    taxation 279
    and Uruguay Round 259
    US investment in 22, 25, 40
    see also North American Free Trade
        Area
capital
    financial/industrial 96
    mobility 34, 228
capitalism
    and ideology 8, 95–7
    monopoly 95–6
Cartagena Agreement 442, 575
cartels 23–5, 41
    and antitrust regulation 385, 387–8,
        589
    and USA 24, 27, 129–30, 387–8
Casson, Mark 36–7, 46
Caves, R. 398, 414 n.39
centralization of control 7, 60–1, 71,
    325
Chandler, A. D. 57
Channon, D. 66
Charter of the International Trade

Organization (Havana
    Charter) 112, 403, 574
Chile
    copper industry 6, 99, 105, 106,
        514, 527 n.94
    and dispute settlement 556
    and expropriation 513, 514, 527
        n.94
    and investment guarantee 519
    and investment protection 576
    and US subversion 6–7, 105
China
    and bilateral investment treaties 626,
        631, 633, 643 n.62, 647 n.131
    and dispute settlement 556
    and economic nationalism 174–5
    and joint ventures 186, 187, 188–92,
        194, 235–6
    and labour relations 468
    liberalization 31–2, 175, 188
    special economic zones 234–8
    and technology transfer 444, 453
        n.73
    and transfer pricing 311 n.57
Chirac, Jacques 183
Choi, F. D. S. 366, 382 n.161
Civil Jurisdiction and Judgments Act
    (UK 1982) 143, 162 n.71
Civil Rights Act
    USA 1964 463
    USA 1991 463
Clayton Act (US) 163 n.76
Clinton, Bill 244, 302, 474–5
Coase, Ronald 35
Coca Cola, in India 56 n.151, 180
coercion, unfair 498–501
Collins, L. 155, 170 n.185
Collor, President 448
Colombia
    and investment protection 576
    and UN Draft Code 612 n.138
Colt, Samuel 49 n.23
combines
    domestic 23–4
    international lii
comity analysis 132–3, 134, 144, 155,
    636
common markets 111
communications
    internal 58–9
    international 27
Companies Act UK
    1948 334

1985 135, 334, 343 n.56, 344 n.70, 360, 364, 378 nn.77–9, 379 n.86
1989 360–1, 378 nn.77–9, 379 n.86
Companies Amendment Act (New Zealand 1980) 337–8
company, joint stock limited liability 40
compensation 241, 242, 325, 328, 330–3, 335, 338, 574, 577
  and bilateral investment treaties 628, 630, 633, 635–6
  for expropriation 187, 193, 240, 503–4, 506–14, 556, 574, 577, 629–30, 635–6
  lump sum 513–14
  measure 240–1, 511–12
  and nationalization 10, 192–3, 496, 500–1, 503–4, 506–14, 556
  and UN Draft Code 596
  and World Bank Guidelines 600–1
  see also valuation
competence, jurisdictional 127–34
competition 11, 28–33
  and antitrust law 384–403, 410, 589
  between firms 107, 112
  EC law 137–8
  for inward investment 10, 108, 228, 281, 307, 599–600
  and labour relations 480–1
  local effects 92, 101–2
  monopolistic 33–4, 259
  perfect 34, 259, 285
  price 385–6, 435
  restriction 23–5
  and technology 428–9, 433–8, 445
concern, qualified 337
concern over MNEs 3–15
  and abuses of power 3, 6–7, 9, 102
  attitudes of countries and regions 3–6
  contemporary views 9–11
  and economic theory of MNE 7–8, 11
  and ideology 8, 9, 92–102
  and problems of definition 12–15
conciliation 537–8, 541, 553–5, 601
confidentiality
  and antitrust regulations 408
  and disclosure 108–9, 148–52, 304, 348, 477
  and dispute settlement 554
  and tax havens 304
  and technology transfer 435

and treatment of MNEs 588
Congo
  and expropriation 509
  and joint ventures 640 n.10
Conservative Party (UK), and inward investment 223–4
consortium, international 64–5, 73
conspiracy, intra-enterprise 387, 406
consumer
  in LDCs 439
  protection 140–1
  and workers' rights 475–6
consumerism, global 93, 100–1, 102
content, local 258
contract 62–5, 80–2
  and alliances 74
  contractual stability 628
  control contracts 71, 335, 357
  and distribution agreements 63
  and group liability 323–4, 327, 330
  and international consortium 64–5
  and production agreements 63–4
  renegotiation 497–501
  sanctity of 494, 496–7
  and technology transfer 447
  see also law, contract
control, corporate
  joint management committees 67
  and legal structures 61–80, 90
  and liability 323–7, 331, 336
  and transnational business organizations 57–61
  see also centralization; decentralization
cooperation, bilateral 151–2
copyright, protection 254–6
core–periphery model 96–7, 99
corporation
  controlled foreign 305–7
  public international 79–80
corporatism 94, 95, 101, 457, 480, 578, 592
corruption, and arms industry 7
cost-sharing, and transfer pricing 292, 294
Council for Mutual Economic Assistance (CMEA) 175, 186
Cowling, K. 46
creditors 336–8
  voluntary/involuntary 322
cross-invoicing 304, 306
Cuba
  and Group of Ten 273 n.216

and joint ventures 186
and technology transfer 438
culture, global 100
culture, corporate 68, 463, 468, 471, 473
culture industry, and free trade 241
currency
  and accounting 371–2
  and compensation 600
  free transfer 187, 629–30
Czech Republic, and bilateral investment treaties 640 n.10
Czechoslovakia, and joint ventures 186, 188

Davidow, J. 422 n.138
Davies, D. R. 280, 309 n.31
debt crisis 10, 31, 576
decentralization 59–61, 71
  of liability 333
decision-making
  and accountability 349–53
  centralized 60–1, 71, 325
  decentralized 59–61, 71
  in joint ventures 336
  and labour relations 477–8
  and legal structure 74, 81–2
Defense Production Act Extension Amendments Public Law (US 1991) 206 n.18
Delaume, George 546, 557
dependency, economic 8–9, 33, 98, 197, 234
dependency theory 98–9, 104–7
  and exclusion of foreign investment 174
Derelict Land Act (UK 1982) 227
diplomacy, and dispute settlement 534–6, 559, 577, 637
directors
  in holding companies 334
  and nationality 242
  non-executive 349–50
  shadow 337
  in subsidiaries 333–6
disclosure
  and accountability 81–2, 95, 346–72
  and balancing test 149–51, 153, 157
  and compulsion 138
  and conflict reduction 151, 156–7
  in consolidated financial statements 355–61
  employee 348, 350–2, 361, 366–7,
  477
  and environment 100, 354, 366–7, 590
  and foreign currency translation 354, 371–2
  and foreign secrecy laws 148–52
  improved 74–5, 95
  and intercorporate alliances 74
  and international law 112
  and minority shareholders 335
  and national law 44, 108–10, 145–53
  and OECD Guidelines 589
  in public statements 354–72
  segmented 354, 361–6
  social 354, 366–71
  and tax havens 304
  and transfer pricing 296–7
  and US law 146–8, 224–5
  in value-added statements 354, 367–8
  see also confidentiality; subsidiaries
discounted cash flow 507
discrimination, in employment 462–3
dispute settlement 534–60, 576–7
  ad hoc 538
  and bilateral investment treaties 632–4
  delocalized 113, 537, 541, 547–51, 559, 587, 637
  institutional systems 80, 193, 538–9, 587–8
  MNE-host state 445, 537–40
  traditional mechanisms 534–6
  and UNCITRAL 539–40
  and World Bank Guidelines 601
  see also arbitration; International Centre for the Settlement of Investment Disputes
distribution
  agreements 63, 385
  franchise 63
  international networks 388–90
  joint 77, 392
  and personal jurisdiction 140
dividend rights 67–8
divisionalization, global 58, 67, 284
dumping, social 474
Dunning, J. H. liv n.1, 59, 61, 449 n.9, 468, 474
  and evolution of MNEs 24, 28
  and theories of MNE growth 33, 37–8

Dupuy, Prof. 494–5, 496, 568 n.101

Eastern bloc
  and codification of treatment of
    investors 573–4
  and critique of MNEs 9
  and dispute settlement 556
  and economic nationalism 101,
    174–5
  and joint ventures 72, 186–8, 194
  and liberalization 9, 10, 26, 31–2,
    175
  and public ownership of MNEs 88
    n.86
EC
  and accountability 350–1
  Advisory Committee on
    Concentrations 399
  and antitrust law 137, 153, 329
  Charter of Fundamental Social
    Rights of Workers 353
  and collective bargaining 489 n.139
  and disclosure 349, 351–3, 368
  and environmental audit 370–1
  Fifth Directive on Company Law
    351
  Fourth Directive on Company Law
    354, 356–7, 359–60, 362, 364
  and group liability 329, 331
  and investment incentives 228, 258
  and labour relations 457, 464, 465–
    6, 4481
  and Merger Regulation 396–8, 403
  and North American Free Trade
    Area 245
  and personal jurisdiction 137–8, 157
  Seventh Directive on Company Law
    354, 355–61, 362
  Single European Market 31, 32, 69,
    238, 245–7, 261, 353, 457, 464,
    478–9
  and supranational structures 77–8
  and taxation 307
  and transfer pricing 298
  and transnational mergers 68–9
  and Uruguay Round 251
  and US investment 4, 27
  Vredeling Directive 351–2
EC Commission
  Competition Directorate 409
  and distribution networks 389
  and extraterritoriality 128–9, 137–8,
    329

and joint ventures 392–3
and labour relations 464
Merger Task Force 396–7, 399–401
and restrictions on foreign ownership
  182, 183
and technology transfer 437–8, 450
  n.14
Economic Co-operation Act (US 1948)
  514
economics
  and growth of MNEs 33–8
  Marxist 92, 95–7, 99, 101
  nationalist 92, 97–9, 101
  neo-classical 8, 9, 10, 92, 93, 97,
    101, 112, 259
  orthodox post-war 92, 101, 103–5
effects doctrine 129–33
Egypt
  and bilateral investment treaties 618,
    620, 632, 640 n.10
  and dispute settlement 551
  and export processing zones 230,
    232–3
  and expropriation 509–10
  and Group of Ten 273 n.216
Electrolux, and heterarchy 59–60
employees, and need for information
  348, 350–2, 361, 366–7
employment
  and collective bargaining 471, 473,
    476–80
  effects of MNE 27, 32–3, 91, 103
  equality of opportunity and treatment
    462–4
  and export processing zones 229,
    231, 233–4
  and free trade areas 243–4
  and health and safety 469–70, 475
  and OECD Guidelines 590
  promotion 462, 599
  rights 231, 237–8, 244, 461, 465–6,
    476
  security 4, 8, 101, 464–6
  and Single European Market 457
  and technology transfer 92, 430
  and training 466–7
  and wages and conditions 467–9,
    473–4, 477
  see also labour relations
enemy, trading with 108, 127–8
enforcement jurisdiction 144–5
enterprise, domestic
  exporting of factor inputs 15

exporting of output 14–15
multilocation 14, 35, 80
enterprise entity
  and antitrust regulation 405–6
  and group liability 145, 326, 328–31
  and personal jurisdiction 137, 138
enterprise zones, UK 224, 227
environmentalism
  and disclosure 368–71, 590
  and free trade agreements 242–4
  and local effects of MNEs 92–3,
    99–100, 102, 197
  and OECD Guidelines 590
Equador
  and investment protection 576
  and UN Draft Code 612 n.138
equity-based groups 65–71, 81, 516–
    17
  and European transnational mergers
    66–9
  and Japanese *keiretsu* 69–70
  and organizational changes 71
  and pyramid group 65–6, 70
Ethiopia
  and compensation 513, 635–6
  and joint ventures 186
Eurofima 79–80
Europe
  and first phase of MNE evolution 21,
    22
  Japanese investment in 29
  and second phase of MNE
    evolution 23–4
  and third phase of MNE evolution
    26, 27–8, 30–1
  transnational mergers 66–9, 74
  and US MNEs 4, 8, 23, 27
European Company 331
European Court of Human Rights, and
    expropriation 523 n.55, 524
    n.61
European Court of Justice
  and antitrust regulation 388, 394
  and extraterritoriality 137
  and intra-enterprise conspiracy 413
    n.17
  and labour relations 466
  and right of establishment 246
European Economic Interest Grouping
    (EEIG) 77–8
European Works Councils 352–3, 473,
    478–9
Eurotunnel, and transnational

mergers 67
Evidence (Proceedings in Other
    Jurisdictions) Act (UK 1975)
    154
evolution of MNEs 19–47
  and competitive advantage 33–4
  eclectic approach 37–8, 47
  and firm-specific advantage 36–7,
    38–42
  first phase 20–2, 40–1
  internalization thesis 35–7, 38
  legal factors 19, 33, 38–47, 90
  second phase 1914–39 22–5, 42
  theories of growth 33–8
  third phase 1945–present 25–33
Exchange Control Act (UK 1947) 223
exchange controls 103, 181, 223–4
exclusion of foreign investment
  sectoral 175–7
  total 174–5
Exon-Florio Amendment 175, 224,
    402
Export and Investment Guarantees Act
    (UK 1991) 515
export processing zones (EPZs)
  evolution 228–30
  legal and administrative features
    230–3
  performance 233–4
exports
  credit guarantee 514
  and locational advantages 42–4
  restriction 126–7, 128–9
  and special economic zones 234–8
expropriation 501–14
  and bilateral treaties 242, 503–5,
    624, 628, 630–1, 635–6
  and compensation 187, 193, 240,
    503–4, 506–14, 556, 574, 577
  creeping 501–2, 516, 631
  definition 501–2
  and host state law 502
  and international law 503–5
  and investment insurance 514–17
  and UN Draft Code 595–6
  and World Bank Guidelines 600
  see also arbitration; nationalization
extraterritoriality 111, 123
  and antitrust regulations 405, 410
  and disclosure 145–51
  and effects doctrine 129–33, 138
  and enforcement 144–5
  and group liability 329, 332

and labour relations 463
legal bases 123–6
limitation of conflicts 133, 156–7
and mergers 396
and nationality 45, 108–10, 124,
    127–9, 131
and objective territorial jurisdiction
    125–6
and personal jurisdiction 134–44,
    338
and prescription 126–34
and protective jurisdiction 124–5
and shared values approach 157
and transfer pricing 297

Fair Trading Act (UK 1973) 223, 401
Fieldhouse, D. K. 7
Financial Services Act (UK 1986) 363
Finance Act (UK 1985) 301, 302
firm
    classical theory 33–4
    size 39, 40–1
Fitzmaurice, Sir Gerald 521 n.31
Flower, J. 371
Ford
    and collective bargaining 478
    as pyramid group 65
Foreign Assistance Act (US 1961) 514
Foreign Capital Enterprises Law
    (China 1986) 189, 191, 236
Foreign Corrupt Practices Act (US
    1976–7) 7, 127
Foreign Exchange Regulation Act
    (India 1973) 179–80
Foreign Investment Act (Poland 1991)
    187
Foreign Investment Acts (Mexico 1973,
    1993) 195–6
Foreign Investment Law
    (Czechoslovakia 1990) 188
Foreign Investment Law (Russia 1991)
    234, 620
Foreign Investment Review Act (FIRA)
    (Canada 1973) 198–9, 201–2,
    203, 259
Foreign Trade Antitrust Improvements
    Act (US 1982) 132
forum non conveniens doctrine 141–4,
    147
forum shopping 142–4
France
    and bilateral investment treaties 618,
        622, 631, 635, 643 n.57, 647

n.131, 647 n.136
and dispute settlement 548–9, 569
    n.120
and employee disclosure 367
and insolvency 337
and mergers 397, 399
and minority shareholders 335, 336
and MNE evolution 4, 8, 27
and nationalization 75, 76, 503
and privatization 183–4
screening laws 197
and taxation 280
and tax avoidance 320 n.183
and UN Draft Code 611 n.135
and World Bank Guidelines 598
franchise
    distribution 63
    and liability 324
    production 63–4
Franko, Lawrence 20, 24
free ports 224, 229
free trade areas 111
    regional effects 243
    USA–Canada 201, 239–40, 244
    see also EC, Single European Market;
        export processing zones; North
        American Free Trade Area
Frei, Eduardo 99

Gabon, and competition law 417 n.73
Gann, P. B. 530 n.146
GATT
    and Canada 199
    and North American Free Trade
        Area 244–5
    Uruguay Round 11, 103, 105, 172,
        247–61, 601
    Final Act 112, 181, 203, 251,
        255–6, 260, 441, 449
    General Agreement on Trade in
        Services (GATS) 113, 203,
        252–4, 256, 261
    Punta del Este Declaration 250–1,
        252, 255, 257
    and technology transfer 444
    Trade Related Intellectual Property
        Measures (TRIPS) 113, 203,
        251, 254–7, 261, 440
    Trade Related Investment
        Measures (TRIMs) 113, 203,
        251, 257–60, 261
    World Trading Organization
        (WTO) 113–14, 256, 260, 461,

475, 481
and US investment 26, 632
Generic Names Drugs Act (Pakistan
1972) 440
Geneva Phonogram Convention 453
n.73
German Democratic Republic
and joint ventures 186
and UN Draft Code 612 n.137
Germany
antitrust law 161 n.57
and bilateral investment treaties 520,
618, 624, 629–30, 644 n.74,
647 n.136
and codetermination laws 350
and codification of treatment of
investors 574
and disclosure 357, 368–9
and fascist economics 23
and first phase of MNE evolution 21,
40–1
and group liability 328, 331
and insolvency 337
and investment guarantee 515
and limited liability company 40
and management 349
and mergers 397
and minority shareholders 335
and second phase of MNE evolution
23–5
and tax avoidance 320 n.183
and third phase of MNE evolution
26–8, 31
and UN Draft Code 611 n.135
and workers' rights 475–6
Ghana, and screening laws 195, 196–7
Gilpin, Robert 4
Goergen, 317 n.141
Goff, Lord 165 n.110
governance, corporate 94–5, 350
Gower, L. C. B. 331
Gray Report (Canada) 198
Gray, S. J. 346, 365
Greece
and bilateral investment treaties 647
n.136
and codification of MNE treatment
574
Grenada, and bilateral investment
treaties 640 n.10
Group of 77 5, 95, 409, 444–5, 449
n.5, 593–5
Group B states 444–5

Group D states 444
Group of Ten 251
groupement d'interêt économique (GIE)
64–5, 74, 77
Guinea, and dispute settlement 548–9,
552

Hadden, T. 66, 81, 84 n.32
Hague Conference on the Codification
of International Law 573
Hague Conventions
on Service Abroad of Judicial and
Extrajudicial Documents (1965)
135, 154
on the Taking of Evidence Abroad
(1970) 151, 153–6
Haiti, and joint ventures 640 n.10
Hannah, Leslie 40
Hart–Scott–Rodino Antitrust
Improvements Act (US 1976)
418 n.78
Harvard University, Comparative
Multinational Enterprise Project
7–8
Haskins, 58
Havana Charter (1948) 112, 403, 574
head office 59, 60–1
health and safety issues 469–70, 475,
590
Herfindahl–Hirschman Index 398
Heseltine, Michael 420 n.109
heterarchy 59–60
Hewlett Packard, and heterarchy 59
Higgins, Rosalyn 521 n.31
Hilferding, R. 96
history of MNEs 7–8, 19–20
Hoffman-La Roche, and transfer
pricing 287–8, 393
Hoffmann, US Judge 150–1, 171
n.187
holding company
intermediate 65–6
twin 67
Holland see Netherlands
home state
and antitrust regulation 396
and disclosure 348, 354
and dispute settlement 535–6
and labour relations 460–1, 464
and taxation 277–9, 280, 285, 287,
297–8, 303–5, 307
and technology transfer 427–31
Hong Kong, Japanese investment in 28

Hood, N. 42, 46, 93, 108
host state
　and antitrust regulation 396
　bargaining power 102, 105–6, 111,
　　180
　benefits of investment 91
　control of investment 9, 172–204,
　　336, 493–7, 597
　equity joint ventures 177, 184–94
　and exclusion techniques 174–7
　and liberalization 203–4, 261
　restriction of foreign shareholding
　　177–84
　scope of discretion 172–3
　and screening laws 176, 194–203,
　　402, 443
　and disclosure 348, 354, 361, 368
　and dispute settlement
　　international 537–60, 576, 587
　　traditional 534–6
　　see also International Centre for the
　　　Settlement of Investment
　　　Disputes
　domestic tariff area 230–3
　and double taxation 277–9
　in EC 245–6
　and export processing zone 228–38
　interaction with MNE 90–102
　and investment agreements 493–
　　501, 503
　and investment guarantee schemes
　　515–18, 602–3
　and investment promotion 44, 222–
　　38, 280, 599, 628, 631
　and investment protection 573–604
　and labour relations 460–4, 466–8,
　　470, 471, 473, 477–8
　and non-executive directors 350
　power of MNE 105–7, 111, 180,
　　579
　and regulation 10, 11, 103–4
　subversion 6–7
　and taxation 285, 287, 297–9, 303–
　　4
　and technology transfer 427–31,
　　432, 433–49
　see also expropriation; nationalization;
　　sovereignty
Hull, Cordell 524 n.64, 530 n.145,
　577
Hungary
　and bilateral investment treaties 630,
　　648 n.151

and compensation 513
and investment guarantee 519
and joint ventures 186, 188
Hymer, Stephen 33–4, 96

IBM
　in India 56 n.151, 180
　and heterarchy 59
　and proprietary technology 393
　as pyramid group 65–6
identity, cultural 97
ideology 8, 9, 92–102
　and control of inward investment
　　174
　and environmental analysis 92–3
　and global consumerism 93
　and Marxist analysis 92, 235
　and nationalist analysis 92
　and neo-classical analysis 92, 93
　and orthodox post-war analysis 92
　as pyramid group 65–6
imperialism, economic 5, 95–7
imports
　control 5, 180
　for export processing zones 230
Income and Corporation Taxes Act
　(UK 1988) 289, 297
incorporation, supranational 331
India
　and bilateral investment treaties
　　638
　and competition law 417 n.73
　and dispute settlement 555
　and export processing zones 230,
　　232, 265 n.54
　and Group of Ten 251
　and indigenization 56 n.151, 177,
　　179–81, 184
　and technology transfer 438, 447–8,
　　453 n.73
　and Uruguay Round 259
　see also Bhopal disaster
indigenization 177–81, 204, 576
Indonesia
　and dispute settlement 551, 552
　and equity joint ventures 185–6
　and expropriation 510
　and investment guarantee 519
Industrial Development Board
　(Northern Ireland) 227
Industry Act (UK 1975) 182–3, 223
infant industry, and inward investment
　5, 176–7, 260, 410

information *see* disclosure

injury, personal, and extraterritoriality 110, 140, 142–3, 154–6

Inner Urban Areas Act (UK 1978) 227

insider dealing 151–3

Insider Trading and Securities Fraud Enforcement Act (US 1988) 153

insolvency, subsidiary 109, 336–8

Insolvency Act (UK 1986) 337

insurance
  investment guarantee 514–19
  political risk 633, 638

integration, business
  contractual 62–5
  and liability 329

interest, national
  and expropriation 504
  and extraterritoriality 124–5, 133, 146, 149, 153, 156–7
  and inward investment 174–7, 223, 599
  and transfer of currency 629
  and treatment of MNEs 588

internalization
  and competition 4, 386, 393, 395, 400
  and dispute settlement 551
  of international investment agreements 494–6
  legal aspects 45–7
  and public ownership 76
  theory 35–7, 38, 60
  and transfer pricing 282

International Accounting Standards Committee (IASC) 354, 355, 363

International Centre for the Settlement of Investment Disputes (ICSID) 243, 509–10, 518, 539, 601, 645 n.93
  Additional Facility 541, 601
  aims 541–2
  caseload 556–7, 559
  and challenging decisions 551–3
  and contracting state control 542–6, 622–4
  costs 555
  and delocalization 113, 541, 547–51, 559, 637
  enforcement of decisions 553
  and investment agreement 190–1, 557–8

membership 190–1, 193, 555–6, 559

procedure 553–5

and subject matter jurisdiction 546–7

and Washington Convention 190, 534, 541, 542–58, 633–4

International Chamber of Commerce
  Commission on Taxation 295
  Court of Arbitration 539, 541, 555
  and environmental auditing 371
  and multilateral convention 574

International Court of Justice (ICJ)
  and expropriation 520 n.8
  and extraterritoriality 126, 128
  and nationality 536
  and public international corporations 80
  and standard treatment of investors 573

International Covenant on Civil and Political Rights 470–1

International Finance Corporation 603

International Investment and Trade in Services Survey Act (USA 1976) 225

International Labour Conventions 458–9, 474, 476

International Labour Organization
  Committee on Multinational Enterprises 458–9, 462, 468
  Tripartite Declaration of Principles on Multinationals and Social Policy 457, 458–80, 578, 590

International Law Commission 633

International Monetary Fund, and inward investment 26, 180, 598, 629

international relations theory, and non-state actors 90–1

International Standards Organization 371

International Trade Organization 112
  Commission on Business Practices 403

International Trade Secretariats 471–3

International Transport Workers' Federation (ITF) 472

internationalization, economic 11, 63, 99

Investment Canada Act (1985) 199–202, 240–1

Investment Codes (Ghana) 196–7

investment, foreign direct
bilateral/multilateral measures 238–
60
competition for 9, 10
control 10, 11, 76, 172–204
and exclusion techniques 174–7
and liberalization 203–4
regulation of equity joint ventures
184–94
restriction of foreign shareholding
177–84
scope of discretion 172–3
and 'screening laws' 176, 194–
203, 204, 225, 271 n.179, 402,
443
cross investment 70, 110
definition liv n.1, 249
and definition of MNE 12, 14
and developing countries 29–31, 32–
3, 37, 112–14, 596
dispute resolution *see* arbitration;
compensation
diversification 41
in Eastern bloc 31–2
in Europe 4, 22, 26–7, 32
European 25, 27, 28
growth 24–5
guarantee schemes 514–19, 602–3
host state benefits 91
and 'infant industry' approach 176–7
international agreements 493–6, 503
and dispute settlement 537, 539,
542, 545–6, 556, 557–9
renegotiation 497–501
stabilization clauses 494–5, 496–7,
508, 628
and international regulation 112–13,
172–3
in Japan 4, 176
by Japan 27, 28–30, 258
location-specific 34, 35, 280–1, 403
in manufacturing 28, 29–30
multilateral convention 573–4
and 'open door' policies 93, 98–9
in primary products 22, 28, 29, 31,
42
promotion 46, 101, 222–38, 628,
631
and China 234–8
and Export Processing Zones 228–
34
incentives 44, 108, 222, 225–8,
257–8, 261, 591–2, 599–600

multilateral arrangements 247–60
regional arrangements 238–47
protection 573–604, 618
in services 29–31
and trade theory 34–5
in UK 223–4, 226–8
by UK 19–20, 24–5, 27, 28, 30–1
in USA 29, 30–1, 156, 175–6, 205
n.15, 223, 224, 259
by USA 5, 24–5, 26, 28, 30, 40,
197–201, 203, 230, 239–45,
250, 259
in USSR 23, 31–2, 186–7, 192–3,
194
see also sovereignty; taxation; treaties
investor, and need for information 347–
8
Iran, and expropriation 502, 504, 507–
9, 511–12, 526 n.83, 527 n.95,
636
Ireland
export processing zone 229, 233
and investment incentives 225–6,
228
Israel
and bilateral investment treaties 643
n.57
and tax incentives 262 n.21
Italy
and mergers 399
and MNE evolution 23, 28
and UN Draft Code 611 n.135
ITT, and overthrow of Allende 6

Jalland, M. 66
Jamaica, and UN Draft Code 612
n.138
Japan
and antitrust laws 388
and bilateral investment treaties 618,
631, 647 n.131, 647 n.136
and disclosure 149, 365–6, 367
and expropriation 526 n.83
Guideline on Distribution Systems
and Business Practices 389
and investment guarantee 515
investment in 4, 176
keiretsu 69–70, 389–90
and MNE evolution 25, 27, 28–30
and national security 402
and regulation of US MNEs 4, 8
screening laws 197
and tax avoidance 320 n.183

taxation 279
and technology transfer 442
and trade unions 488 n.123
Jenkin, Patrick 224
Joffe, G. 506
Johnson, H. G. 98
Joint Enterprise Law (USSR 1987) 192
Joint Venture Laws (China)
  1979 189, 190
  1988 189–91
joint ventures 64, 66, 70, 71, 72–3, 74,
  79
  and anti-competitive agreements
    390–3, 437
  and expropriation 501
  and foreign investment 44, 184–94
  and minority shareholders 335–6
  and personal jurisdiction 136–7
  and socialism 72, 102, 175, 177,
    185, 186–94, 204, 235–6
  and technology transfer 431–2
jurisdiction see extraterritoriality; law;
  regulation

Kahn, P. 79
Kazakhstan, and joint ventures 640
  n.10
Keenan, US Judge 143
keiretsu 69–70, 389–90
Kenya
  and bilateral investment treaties 642
    n.44
  and competition law 417 n.73
  and Group of Ten 273 n.216
Kindleberger, Charles 34, 53 n.110
knowledge
  and distribution agreements 63
  export 15, 92
  and internalization theory 36–7
  and neo-economic theory 93
  and production agreements 64
  see also property, intellectual;
    technology transfer
Kumar, R. 233–4
Kuwait, and expropriation 495, 499–
  500, 507–8, 525 n.69, 526 n.83,
  527 n.95
Kuwait Investment Office 182, 402

labour
  child 468–9, 474
  costs 29, 32, 46, 230, 231, 233–4,
    430, 460–1, 467–8

international division 93, 97, 173,
  184, 192, 204, 235
  and investment control 177
  and law 46–7
  mobility 34
  skilled 32–3, 37
labour relations 46, 457–81
  and collective bargaining 476–80
  employment issues 461–6
  in export processing zones 231
  and freedom of association 470–6
  grievance and dispute settlement
    479, 480
  and national law 459–61
  OECD and ILO Codes 457, 458–9,
    590
  and safety and health 469–70, 475
  in special economic zones 231, 237–
    8
  and training of workers 466–7
  and wages and conditions 467–9,
    473–4, 477
Lagergren, Gunnar 496, 512, 529
  n.133
Laker Airways 146–8, 156–7
Lall, Sanjaya 286, 310 n.48
Latin America
  and codification of MNE treatment
    573–4, 593
  and debt crisis 31
  and dispute settlement 556, 561
    n.20, 626
  investment in 22, 25, 28, 31
  and technology transfer 430–1, 442
  see also Andean Common Market
Lauterpacht, Eli 506
Laviec, J. P. 624, 626
law
  antitrust 44, 45, 82, 112, 184, 384–
    411, 443
  and abuse of power 385–6, 393–5
  and anti-competitive agreements
    387–93
  and anti-competitive conduct 386–
    403
  and EC 137, 153, 329
  enforcement 144, 146–8, 153
  and international developments
    403–11
  and mergers and acquisitions 41,
    386, 395–403
  nature and aims 384–6
  and OECD Guidelines 589

US 24, 27, 109–10, 126, 129–33, 144, 146–8, 153, 389–90, 392, 437
and blocking statutes 144, 146, 149
codetermination 350
competition 101–2, 137–8
consumer protection 140–1
contract 39, 499, 500
and disclosure 348–9
and enforcement 144–5, 153
and evolution of MNEs 19, 33, 38–47, 90
extra-territorial application 108–10, 111, 123–57
and firm-specific advantages 39–42
indigenization 177–81, 204
and internalization 45–7
international 45, 112–13, 123–7, 144, 409, 493–519, 573, 594–5
and jurisdictional competence 127
and labour relations 46–7, 460
and legal structures 57, 61–80, 135
and location-specific advantages 42–5
national 408, 460, 472–3, 475, 502, 634–7
and personal jurisdiction 134–44, 155–6, 338
and prescription 126–34
screening 176, 194–203, 204, 225, 402, 443
   in advanced countries 197–202, 271 n.179
   in LDCs 195–7
secrecy 146, 148–52, 477
securities 109, 112, 126, 151–3
soft 580
and technology transfer 442–9
and theory of control 57–82
transnational 495–6
waiver by conduct 152–3
see also patent; tort
LDCs
and antitrust regulations 404–10, 439
bargaining power 104–5, 433
and codification of MNE treatment 578, 579, 593, 595–7
and core–periphery model 96–7
and dispute settlement 559
and effects of MNEs 5, 8–9, 96–7, 112–13
and employee training 466–7
and export processing zones 229–34

and extraterritorial application of law 110
and GATT 254–6, 257–8, 260
and Group of Ten 251
and health and safety issues 469–70, 475–6
investment in 29–31, 35, 37, 112–14, 174, 596–7, 600
and labour relations 458, 473–4
MNEs 31
and privatization 10
and public ownership of MNEs 75
and screening laws 195–7
and technology transfer 6, 425, 428–30, 432, 433–6, 438–49
and trade unions 473–4
and Uruguay Round 251
see also dependency theory; New International Economic Order
League of Nations, and standardization of treatment 573
Lebanon, and technology transfer 438
Leninism, and critique of capitalism 8
letters of comfort 340 n.6, 345 n.83
letters of request 153–5
Levi-Strauss 468
liability, corporate 44, 112, 322–39
and enterprise entity theory 328–31
in equity based groups 323–7
and extraterritoriality 329, 332
limited 40, 71, 74, 189, 331–2, 360
network 332–3
new trends 330–3
personal 40, 127, 323, 337
and personal jurisdiction 134–44
in transnational network enterprises 327
unlimited 65, 78
liberalism, and managerialism 8
Liberia
and dispute settlement 550
and international investment agreements 525 n.69
Libya, and expropriation 494–5, 504, 512, 526 n.81
licensee, foreign 15, 43–4
and contract law 39
production 63–4
and technology 92, 429, 431–2, 433–5, 443
Lilienthal, David E. 12
liquidation
and creditors 336–8

regulation 191, 193
loans, intra-firm 35, 285–6
Local Government and Housing Act
    (UK 1989) 226
Lorenz, Christopher 60
Luxembourg
    and bilateral investment treaties 631,
        643 nn.57, 62, 647 n.136
    and holding companies 360

Maastricht Treaty 353, 474
McDaniel, P. 291, 307, 314 n.87
McGarr, Judge Frank 324–5, 328
McKean, W. 527 n.85
Madagascar, Democratic Republic, and
    dispute settlement 571 n.161
Mahmassani, Dr 494–5, 496
Malaysia
    and export processing zones 230
    and industrial relations 474
management
    and disclosure 349
    integrated 324–5
    see also control, corporate
managerialism 8, 94
Mann, F. A. 520 n.5, 530 n.146, 642
    n.39
manufacturing
    and export processing zone 228–34
    and host state bargaining power
        105–6
Manufacturing Industries Act (Ghana
    1971) 197
markets
    global 112
    in neo-classical theory 8, 9, 10, 92,
        93, 112
    in orthodox post-war theory 93–4
    socialist 194, 234–8
    and spheres of influence 22, 25
    see also internalization
Marshall Aid, and US investment 26
Marxism
    and critique of capitalism 8
    and regulation 95–7, 99, 101
    see also China; Russia; socialism;
        Soviet Union
Mauritius, and export processing zones
    230
media, and foreign control 100
merger
    and antitrust law 41, 395–403
    control 223

European transnational 31, 66–9, 74
    and law 40
Merkin, R. 137
Mexico
    and bilateral investment treaties 647
        n.136
    and dispute settlement 555
    and export processing zones 230,
        232
    investment in 1, 22, 28, 32
    and screening laws 195–6
    and technology transfer 440
    and transfer pricing 311 n.57
    and UN Draft Code 612 n.138
    see also North American Free Trade
        Area
Minta, I. K. 255
MNE
    concerns over 3–15
    control in 10, 11, 57–82, 172–204
    definitions 12–15, 62, 582–3
    economic theory 7–8, 9
    evolution 19–47
    legal forms 61–80
    transnational 13, 57–61
    uninational/multinational 12–15
    see also investment, foreign direct;
        regulation; structure, legal
monopoly, and antitrust regulation 386,
    391, 393–5
Moran, Theodore 104
Morocco, and bilateral investment
    treaties 640 n.10
Moser, M. J. 189
Mueller, G. G. 366, 382 n.161
Mulroney, Brian 199
Multilateral Investment Guarantee
    Agency (MIGA) 193, 515–19,
    602–3, 604, 638
Myanmar (Burma), and labour
    relations 468

National Cooperation Research Act
    (US 1984) 437
National Labor Relations Act (USA)
    472
National Office of Industrial Property
    Act (Nigeria 1979) 447
nationalism
    economic 23–4, 97–9, 181, 400
    and exclusion of foreign investment
        20, 174
    and Marxism 97, 101

nationality
  and bilateral investment treaties 622–
    4
  and dispute settlement 544–6
  and expropriation 505
  and extraterritoriality 124, 127–9,
    131
  and free trade areas 242
  and joint ventures 185, 336
  and treatment of MNEs 80, 586,
    588
nationalization
  and coercion 498–501
  and compensation 10, 192–3, 496,
    500–1, 503–4, 506–14, 556
  in developed countries 75, 97
  and expropriation 501
  and host state law 502
  impact on investment 31, 493
  and indigenization 178
  and international law 503–5
  and LDCs 6, 105, 106, 578
  and oil industry 46, 493–5
  and UN Draft Code 595–7
  and World Bank Guidelines 600–1
  see also arbitration
Neale, A. 126, 163 n.92, 170 n.186
negligence, corporate 109, 322, 324–5
Nepal, and bilateral investment treaties
    643 n.57
Nestlé, and baby milk sales 17 n.19
Netherlands
  and bilateral investment treaties 620,
    642 n.44, 643 n.60, 647 n.136
  and codetermination laws 350
  and codification of MNE treatment
    578
  and environmental disclosure 382
    n.163
  industrial relations 472
  and investment guarantee 515
  and MNE evolution 21, 30
  and taxation 280
network, transnational 60–1, 63, 80,
    384
  international distribution 388–90
  liability 82, 322, 324, 327, 330
New International Economic Order
    (NIEO) 5, 8–9, 10–11, 112–14,
    429, 519, 578, 592–3, 618, 639
New International Order for Trade and
    Investment 113, 601

New Zealand
  and insolvency 337–8
  screening laws 197
Nicaragua, and Group of Ten 273
    n.216
Nigerian Enterprises Promotion Acts
    177, 178–9, 180–1, 184
Nigeria
  and bilateral investment treaties 638
  and export processing zones 264
    n.45
  and Group of Ten 273 n.216
  and technology transfer 447
North American Free Trade Agreement
    196
North American Free Trade Area 32,
    238–45, 261, 469
North Korea, and joint ventures 186

objective territorial jurisdiction 125–6
OECD
  and antitrust law 153
  Business and Industry Advisory
    Committee 95, 578, 587, 591–2
  and centralized control 60
  Code on the Liberalization of Capital
    Movements 103, 176, 203, 247,
    248–50, 586
  Code on the Liberalization of
    Current Invisible Operations
    103, 247, 248–50
  Committee on Capital Movements
    and Invisible Transactions 249,
    586
  Committee of experts on RBPs 404
  Committee on Fiscal Affairs 294,
    589
  Committee on International
    Investment and Multinational
    Enterprises 95, 250, 373 n.4,
    459, 465, 476–7, 479–80, 485
    n.81, 578–9, 581, 584, 587–8,
    607 n.42
  Declaration on International
    Investment and Multinational
    Enterprises 578–9, 583–5, 587,
    591–2
  and definition of MNEs 13–14, 62
  and DFI in Japan 4
  Draft Convention on the Protection
    of Foreign Property 574
  Environmental Protection

Guideline 467
and foreign investment 112, 176, 223
Guideline on Disclosure and Information 347–8, 361, 477, 582
Guideline on Employment and Industrial Relations 457, 459–80, 590
Guidelines on Multinational Enterprises 348, 459, 578–92, 601, 604
and corporatism 95, 578, 592
and dispute settlement 587–8
and international minimum standards 113, 580–1
and investment incentives 591–2
legal nature 580
and national treatment 250, 583–7
policy 579
scope of application 581–3
substantive provisions 588–91
and transfer pricing 407
Model Double Taxation Convention 280, 288, 297–8
National Treatment Instrument 250
Report on Multinationals and Transfer Pricing 289, 303
and tax havens 304, 307
Trade Union Advisory Committee (TUAC) 95, 479–80, 578, 587, 591–2, 608 n.58
oil industry
and codification 578
and firm-specific advantage 42
and MNEs 31, 494
and nationalization 31, 46, 493, 497, 504, 507–8
O'Keefe, P. J. 556
oligopoly, and antitrust regulation 386, 388
Olivetti, and heterarchy 59
Omnibus Trade and Competitiveness Act (US 1988) 206 n.18, 223, 274 n.240
open door policies 46, 93, 98–9, 101, 222–38, 591, 620
and China 191–2, 235
and Egypt 230
opportunity, equality of 462–4
organization
international 94–5, 102, 112

size 39, 40–1
transnational business 57–61
see also structure, legal
Overseas Private Investment Corporation (OPIC) 514–15
ownership, public 75–6, 82
and public international corporation 79–80

Pakistan
and bilateral investment treaties 618, 643 n.57, 643 n.60
and competition law 417 n.73
and technology transfer 440
and transfer pricing 311 n.57
Panama, and bilateral investment treaties 632, 640 n.10
Paris Convention for the Protection of Industrial Property 439, 440, 449
patents
protection 39–40, 255–6, 392
and technology transfer 437, 438–41, 444
Paterson, R. K. 202
Pattison, J. E. 641 n.27
Pennycuick, Judge 343 n.47
Penrose, E. 506
performance requirements 46, 92, 104, 195, 222, 444, 599
and bilateral investment treaties 628, 632
and free trade areas 239–42, 259
and Uruguay Round 250, 257, 259
Permanent Court of International Justice (PCIJ) 125, 535
personality, legal 64, 73, 78, 189, 330
and bilateral investment treaties 623
and dispute settlement 534–5, 544–5
and insurance guarantees 518
and Single European Market 246
of subsidiary 108–9, 135
and tax havens 304
Peru
and Group of Ten 273 n.216
and investment protection 576, 577
and UN Draft Code 612 n.138
Peter, Wolfgang 519 n.1
Philippines
and bilateral investment treaties 624, 629, 644 nn.74,

84, 645 n.95, 646 n.126,
647 n.132
and export processing zones 230,
233, 265 n.54
planning, regional 226–7
Plasschaert, S. 287
Poland, and joint ventures 186, 187,
188
policy enclaves
and Chinese special economic zones
234–8
and export processing zones 228–34
politics
MNE involvement in 588–9
and subversion of host state 6–7
Portugal, and codification of investor
treatment 574
power
abuse by MNEs 3, 6–7, 9, 97, 102,
393–5, 405–7
host state/MNE balance 90, 105–7,
111, 180, 433, 441, 442, 495–
500, 538
price
below-cost 406
competition 385–6, 435
resale price maintenance 387, 389
and technology transfer 435
see also transfer price; valuation
privatization 204
in Eastern Europe 188
and 'golden share' 181–2, 183–4,
223
in LDCs 10, 178–9
and national treatment 586–7
and restrictions on foreign ownership
181–4
in Russia 193
and service industries 106
Privatization Law (France 1986) 183
product cycle thesis 35
production
costs 282, 284
and export processing zone 228–38
and value-added statements 368–9
production agreements 63–5
franchise 63–4
profits
comparable profit interval 283
distribution 189–90
and double taxation 277–9, 303–4
and expropriation 507–10
profit centres 283–5

reinvestment 193, 226, 236, 303,
576, 599
repatriation 26, 79, 103, 187–8,
191, 193, 236, 287, 629–30
property, intellectual 39, 250
and distribution agreements 63
and technology 427, 431, 435–44,
448–9, 590
and transfer pricing 291–2, 294, 295
and Uruguay Round 254–6
protection
and antitrust laws 130–1, 403, 410
codification 573–604
and extraterritoriality 124–5
and free trade areas 244
and growth of MNEs 23–4
and inward investment 204
and liberalization 26
and locational advantage 44
and national regulation 108
and regional regulation 112
by USA 30
see also indigenization; investment,
foreign direct, control; regulation
Protection of Trading Interests Act
(UK 1980) 146, 147
Puerto Rico, and export processing
zones 230
pyramid groups 65–6, 70

Quiles, Paul 399

R&D
and competition 386
and heterarchy 59
and internalization thesis 36–7
and joint ventures 77, 392, 437
and taxation 281
and technology 427–8, 441, 590–1
Rank Organization, as pyramid group
66
RBPs 385
international regulation 258, 384–5,
403–11, 445, 574, 589
see also law, antitrust
Reagan, Ronald 129, 199
reason, rule of 385, 437
reciprocity 103, 110–11, 243
in EC 247
in intellectual property protection
437
in OECD Codes 248, 585
and taxation 278

Reckitt and Colman, as pyramid group 66
redundancy, collective 465–6
Reed–Elsevier, as transnational merger 68
regions, national, and investment promotion 226–7, 228–38
regulation
   codification 573–604
   conflicts 282–3
   and effects doctrine 129–33
   and environmentalism 99–100, 102
   and global consumerism 100–1, 102
   harmonization 45, 111, 112, 157, 238, 465, 581
   home/host state priorities 103–4
   and host state-MNE interaction 90–102
   and jurisdictional levels 102–14
   and legal structure 62
   and liability 323–7
   and Marxism 95–7, 99, 101
   multilateral 112–14
   national 45, 104–11, 123–57, 410
   and nationalism 97–9, 101
   and neo-classical theory 8, 9, 10, 92, 93, 98, 101
   and orthodox post-war economic theory 92, 93–5, 101
   problems of diversity 110–11
   regional 111–12
   relaxation 9
   theory 90–115
   and transfer pricing 288–99
   and UN 6, 8–9
   see also arbitration; compensation; expropriation; extraterritoriality; law
Renault, and transnational merger 68–9, 75, 478
renegotiation, in international law 497–501
Restatement on Foreign Relations Law (US) 133, 145–6, 148–50, 156, 158 n.16
Rhodesia, oil embargo 17 n.19
right of establishment
   and EC 245–7
   and GATT 252–3
   and OECD 249–50
risk
   allocation 81, 325, 327, 330, 333
   and dispute settlement 556

insurance 514–19, 602–3
political 633, 638
Roberts, C. 365
Rolls-Royce, and restriction of foreign ownership 181–2
Romania
   and bilateral investment treaties 640 n.10
   and joint ventures 186
Rome Treaty
   and investment incentives 228
   and movement of workers 246
   and personal jurisdiction 137
   and restrictions on private ownership 182, 183
   and right of establishment 245–7
Royal Dutch Shell, and transnational mergers 12, 21, 67
Rugman, A. 198
Russia
   and bilateral investment treaties 621, 640 n.10, 647 n.136, 648 n.151
   and dispute settlement 556
   and export processing zone 234
   Free Economic Zones 193
   and joint ventures 72, 186–7, 192–3, 194
   relaxation of restrictions 31–2, 192
   see also Soviet Union
Rwanda, and bilateral investment treaties 643 n.60

Safarian, A. E. 204 n.5
Santikarn, Miagsam 426
Saudi Arabia, and bilateral investment treaties 643 n.60
Savary, J. 49 n.20
Scandinavia, and codification of MNE treatment 578
Scandinavian Airline Systems (SAS), and joint ventures 73, 74, 75, 79
Schapiro, A. C. 345 n.83
Schmitthoff, C. M. 64, 66–7
Second International Steel cartel 24
secrecy laws, and disclosure 146, 148–52, 477
security, national
   and inward investment 5, 175–6, 184, 195, 204, 599, 635
   and mergers 401–3
Seidman 205 n.7
Sells 58

Senegal, and bilateral investment
     treaties 640 n.10
Servan-Schreiber, Jean 3–4
services
  DFI 29–31
  and free trade areas 245, 246–50
  and host state bargaining power 106
  and transfer pricing 286
  and Uruguay Round 113, 203, 251–
     7, 259
Seth, Judge 325–7, 328
Seveso disaster 100
shareholding
  and cross-shareholding 68–9, 70
  and disclosure 349
  dividend rights 67–8
  and indigenization laws 177–81
  and joint ventures 184–94
  minority 286, 322, 333–6, 349
  and privatized companies 181–4
  in subsidiaries 322, 328, 333–6
Sharp, M. 92
Sharpe, K. E. 118 n.47
Shawcross, Sir Hartley 574
sheltering
  primary 304–5
  secondary 305
Sherman Act (US) 129–30, 132, 133,
     163 n.76, 248, 388, 413 n.17
Shihata, I. F. I. 615 n.204
Shipping Contracts and Commercial
     Documents Act (UK 1964) 167
     n.137
Singapore
  and bilateral investment treaties 643
     n.60
  and investment incentives 226, 228
  Japanese investment in 28
Singer Sewing Machine Company 22
Siqueiros, J. L. 111
skills transfer, local effects 92, 430,
     432, 435–6
Sklair, Leslie 100
Slovakia, and joint ventures 640 n.10
smuggling, and export processing
     zones 232, 237
socialism
  and capitalism 8
  and joint ventures 72, 102, 175,
     177, 185, 186–94, 204, 235–6
  see also China; Marxism
Sornarajah, M. 637, 646 n.109

South Korea
  and competition law 417 n.73
  and export processing zones 230,
     233
  investment in 31
  and joint ventures 211 n.82
  and transfer pricing 311 n.57
  and workers' rights 474, 475
sovereignty, national 4, 6–7, 11
  and bilateral investment treaties 621,
     638–9
  and codification of MNE treatment
     581, 597
  and control of inward investment
     173, 189, 195, 222
  and disclosure 151, 155
  and dispute settlement 542–58
  and expropriation 493–7, 504–5,
     512, 518
  and extraterritoriality 109, 123, 125,
     132, 157
  and industrial relations 460
  and locational advantages 42–5
  and raw materials 42
  and regulation 91–2, 99, 493–7, 542
  and stabilization clauses 494–5,
     496–7, 508
  and transnational organizations 112,
     114
Soviet Federated Socialist Republic
     Law (Russia 1991) 192–3
Soviet Union
  and compensation 513
  and DFI 23, 31–2
  and economic nationalism 174–5
  and UN Draft Code 612 n.137
Spain, screening laws 197
Sri Lanka
  and bilateral investment treaties 635,
     640 n.10, 643 n.57, 645 n.93
  and competition law 417 n.73
  and dispute settlement 550
stakeholders
  definition 372 n.1
  and disclosure 346, 349, 350
Standard Oil Co. (Indiana) 324–5
state see ownership, public; regulation;
     sovereignty
Stephens, M. 126, 170 n.186
Stevens, P. 506
Stobaugh, R. B. 345 n.82
Stock Corporations Act (Germany

1965) 328
Stock Exchange, London, and
    disclosure 363
Stopford, J. 106–7
Strange, S. 106–7
structure, legal 61–80, 90
    contractual forms 62–5, 74, 80–2
    and disclosure 349–53
    equity-based 65–71, 81
    informal alliances 73–5
    joint ventures 64, 66, 70, 71, 72–3,
        74, 79
    and personal jurisdiction 135
    publicly owned 75–6, 82
    and regulation 104
    supranational forms 76–80
    and technology transfer 431–2
subcontracting, transnational 97
subrogation rights 633
subsidiaries
    and antitrust regulation 387, 406
    and bilateral investment treaties 622–
        4
    and centralization 60–1
    in China 191
    and codification of MNE treatment
        582, 585, 590–1, 610 n.107
    and corporate veil 81, 109, 136–8,
        145, 300, 325–7, 329, 332, 338
    and creditors 336–8
    and disclosure 66, 108–9, 145, 148,
        149, 151–2, 368, 582
    and dispute settlement 536, 544–6
    and divisionalization 58
    in Eastern bloc 175, 187
    in EC 247
    expropriation 506–7
    and extraterritoriality 108–10, 124,
        127–8, 134–9, 145
    and financial statements 357–60
    and group liability 136, 323–7, 328–
        9, 330–2, 333–6
    and intra-firm conspiracy 387, 406
    and joint venture 72
    and labour relations 464, 477–8
    and legal personality 108–9, 135
    local control 95
    and mergers 396
    and minority shareholders 322,
        333–6
    national treatment 224
    and parent nationality 108

and personal jurisdiction 135–40,
    142–3
production 15, 44, 64, 70
in pyramid groups 65–6
sales 15, 63, 70, 388–9
service 70
and taxation 277–9, 280–1, 282
and tax havens 303–7
and technology transfer 43, 431–2,
    434–5, 439, 448, 590–1
and transfer pricing 125, 285–7,
    290, 297–302, 333
see also profits, repatriation
subversion 6–7
Sudan, and bilateral investment treaties
    620
Sugden, R. 46
Svedberg, P. 16 n.9
Sweden
    and compensation 513
    industrial relations 472
    and MNE evolution 21, 23–4
Switzerland
    and bilateral investment treaties 618,
        620, 623, 647 n.136
    and disclosure 368
    and dispute settlement 548
    and MNE evolution 23–4, 28
    and secrecy laws 151–3
    and taxation 280

Taiwan
    and export processing zones 230,
        233
    Japanese investment in 28
takeovers, restriction 175–7, 182–3,
    201, 223
Tanzania, and Group of Ten 273
    n.216
tax credits 26, 103, 280, 287
    and double taxation 278–9, 281,
        298–9
Tax Reform Act (US 1986) 291
taxation
    avoidance 125, 280, 281, 282–307
    bilateral relief 278
    corporation tax 279, 282, 285
    deferral 287, 303–4, 307
    double 79, 110, 277–80, 281, 294,
        297–8, 300–1, 303, 304
    exemption 279–80, 287, 304–5,
        600

and export processing areas 230
foreign tax deduction system 280–1
and free trade areas 240, 246
impact on investment 44, 187–8,
    191, 193
and incentives 26–7, 225–7, 257,
    280–1, 448
and international regulation 112
and location of investment 280–1
neutrality 278–9
and OECD Guidelines 589
and special economic zones 236
and tax havens 68, 226, 279, 281,
    286, 287, 303–7
and transfer pricing 36, 125, 282–
    303
and transnational mergers 68
unilateral relief 278
withholding tax 279, 285
Tebbit, Norman 400
technology
    access to 6, 10, 410
    'appropriate' 429–30
    and bargaining power 105–6
    in China 189–90, 192
    commoditization 427
    definition 425–6
    and investment in LDCs 32–3, 37
    and monopolization 393
    and OECD Guidelines 590–1
    protection 254–5
    and US MNEs 4
technology transfer 9, 250, 425–49,
    590
    and definition of technology 425–6
    developed country model 437–8
    and draft UNCTAD TOT Code
        425–6, 444–6, 590
    and export processing zones 231,
        233
    and free trade areas 241–2, 576
    importing/exporting states 427–31
    and law 39, 44, 46, 79
    and LDC challenge 446–9
    LDC model 438–44
    legal effects 431–2
    and local economy 64, 92, 104
    and production agreements 63–4
    restrictions on recipient commercial
        policy 433–5
    restrictions on recipient use 435–6
    and Uruguay Round 256–8
Teubner, G. 63, 82, 327, 330, 332–3

Thailand
    and bilateral investment treaties 644
        n.76
    Japanese investment in 28
Thompson, D. 567 n.75
Thomson-Grand Public, and labour
    relations 478
Togo, and group dispute settlement
    571 n.161
tort, and liability 323–6, 333
Trade Act (US 1974) 475
Trade and Competitiveness Act (US
    1988) 441
trade embargoes 124, 127–9, 175
trade, international, theory 34–5
Trade and Tariff Act (USA 1984) 259,
    274 n.240
Trade Union and Labour Relations Act
    (UK 1974) 472
Trade Union Reform and Employment
    Rights Act (UK 1993) 488
    n.125
trade unions
    and codification of MNE treatment
        578
    and collective bargaining 476–80
    and corporatism 95
    in export processing zones 231
    and free trade areas 244
    in LDCs 473–4
    and need for information 348, 367
    and OECD 459
    recognition 46–7
    right to join 46–7, 470–6
trademark
    as intellectual property 63, 437,
        439–41, 444
    protection 39, 406–7
trading companies, colonial, as
    predecessors of MNEs 19–20
training, and Codes of practice 466–7
transaction costs
    and direct sales 43
    internalization 35–6
    and legal structure 8, 61
transfer price 36, 71, 125, 226, 282–
    303, 333, 348
    and antitrust regulations 406–7, 589
    arm's length approach 283, 285–6,
        288–93, 294–6, 298–303
    and comparable profit interval 293–9
    formula apportionment 283, 299–
        303

incentives/disincentives for 286–8
in MNE networks 283–6
and monopolization 393
and tax havens 304–5
and technology transfer 434, 442,
    443
treaties
    bilateral investment 11, 110–11,
        193, 617–37
        and arbitration 190, 550, 558–9,
            632–4
        and disclosure 152–3
        and dispute settlement 632–4, 637
        and expropriation 503–5, 624,
            628, 630–1, 635–6
        and international codification 597,
            599–602
        and international law 638–9
        and national law 173, 621, 634–7
        origins 617–19
        principal provisions 619–34
        scope of application 620–5
        stabilization clause 628
        and standards of treatment 223,
            625–32
        use 637–8
    bilateral tax 278, 280, 281, 297–8,
        305
    FCN 224, 238, 403, 463, 617–18,
        621, 625, 635–6
treatment 573–604
    fair and equitable 462–4, 595, 599,
        625–6, 636
    Most Favoured Nation 241–2, 253–
        4, 256, 595, 621, 624–5, 627–8,
        630
    national
        and arbitration 78, 505
        in bilateral treaties 223, 618, 624,
            625–32, 636
        and EC 247
        and FCN treaties 224, 618
        and GATT 253, 260
        and ILO Declaration 467–8, 470–
            80
        and NAFTA 239, 241–2
        and OECD 103, 250, 470–80,
            583–7
        in Russia 192, 193
        and taxation 79
        and technology transfer 253, 256,
            440, 444
        and World Bank Guidelines 599

in UN Draft Code 103, 593–5
and World Bank Guidelines 113,
    597–602
Tricker, R. I. 74, 81
Trinidad and Tobago, and UN Draft
    Code 612 n.138
Trudeau, Pierre 198
Tugendhat, C. 16 n.1
Tunisia, and bilateral investment
    treaties 618, 640 n.10
Turkey
    and bilateral investment treaties 640
        n.10
    and codification of MNE treatment
        574, 579

UK
    assisted areas 227
    and bilateral investment treaties 618,
        620, 621–4, 629–31, 634, 644
        nn.76, 84, 645 nn.93, 95, 646
        n.126, 647 n.132
    and directors 334–5, 336–7, 349
    and disclosure 145, 146–8, 150–1,
        154, 297, 352–3
        consolidated financial statements
            355, 357–61
        segmented 363–5
        social 367
    and dispute settlement 550
    and enforcing jurisdiction 145, 146–
        8
    Export Credit Guarantee
        Department 514, 515
    and expropriation 513, 526 n.82
    and first phase of MNE evolution
        20–1
    and industrial relations 472, 474,
        486 n.104
    and investment promotion 22–8,
        223–4
    and liability 323–4
    and limited liability company 40
    and mergers 400–3
    Monopolies and Mergers
        Commission (MMC) 287–8,
        396–7, 401–3
    and neo-classical economics 10
    non-executive directors 350
    and personal jurisdiction 136–7,
        139–40, 143–4
    and privatization 181–3, 184
    and pyramid groups 65–6

and second phase of MNE evolution 23–4
and taxation 279, 320 n.183
and third phase of MNE evolution 26
and transfer pricing 287–8, 289, 296–7, 300, 302
and UN Draft Code 611 n.135
see also investment, foreign direct
Ukraine, and UN Draft Code 612 n.137
UN
    Charter of Economic Rights and Duties of States 524 n.66, 593
    Code of Conduct on Transfer of Technology 257
    Code of Conduct on Transnational Corporations 10, 11, 14, 103, 113–14, 400, 578, 592–7, 604, 619
    Conference on Trade and Development see UNCTAD
    Development Programme 408
    and disclosure 348
    Economic and Social Committee 578, 593–4
    Group of Eminent Persons 5–6, 10, 13, 593
    Intergovernmental Group of Experts on International Standards of Accounting and Reporting 354–5, 361–2, 367–70
    International Trade Organization 114
    and multinational/transnational corporations 13, 405, 592–7
    and newly independent states 5, 8–9
    and technology transfer 438–9
    see also Group of 77
UN Centre on Transnational Corporations (UNCTC) 6, 114, 441, 596
UN Commission on International Trade Law (UNCITRAL) 538, 539–40, 541, 646 n.130
UN Commission on Transnational Corporations 6, 114, 578, 593–4
UN Economic and Social Commission for Asia and the Pacific 234
UN Transnational Corporations Management Division (TCMD) 6, 114, 441–2

UNCTAD
    Draft TOT Code 425–6, 444–6, 449
    Intergovernmental Group of Experts 408–10, 593
    Model Law 404, 408, 410
    the Set of Regulations 404–10
    and technology transfer 439–40, 578, 590
underdevelopment, core and periphery model 96, 99
Unfair Competition Act (Germany 1977) 475
Unilever, as transnational merger 12, 21, 67–8, 358
Union Carbide Corporation (UCC), and Bhopal disaster 100, 110, 142–3, 325–6, 329
Urban Development Corporations (UK) 227
Uruguay, and dispute settlement 556, 561
US MNEs
    and centralization 61
    and Europe 4, 8, 22, 25, 27
    and first phase of MNE evolution 20, 21–2
    and Japan 4, 8, 29–30, 389
    and political subversion 6–7
    and product cycle thesis 35
    as pyramid groups 65–6
    and renegotiation 498–9
    in research 11
    and second phase of MNE evolution 24–5
    spread 3–4
    and third phase of MNE evolution 25–8, 30, 32
    and trade embargoes 124, 127–9
    US fears of 4–5, 8
US Senate, Sub-Committee on Multinationals 6–7
USA
    Agency for International Development (AID) 514
    antitrust law 24, 27, 109–10, 126, 129–33, 144, 146–8, 389–90, 392, 395, 403, 437
    and bilateral investment treaties 618, 620–1, 623, 625, 632–3, 635–7, 644 n.83, 647 n.136
    and codification of MNE treatment